THE
CIVIL WAR
IN
LOUISIANA

THE
CIVIL WAR
IN
LOUISIANA

by John D. Winters

LOUISIANA STATE UNIVERSITY
PRESS

FOR FRANCES

FOREWORD

IN THESE years of the Centennial of the Civil War many people wonder at the enthusiasm and the energy of those men and women from all walks and stations who are devoted to this observance. They wonder particularly at the writers, those industrious individuals who are always producing books about the war and who keep insisting that still more are needed. Are there not already too many books about this war? the skeptics ask. What more can there be to write about in this particular four-year span of the history of a nation?

The questions are in part justified. There have been too many books about the Civil War—too many poorly researched and written and too many on minor aspects—and there will be more of both in the future. The writers apparently are not going to stop until they have worried this bone to the last bite. But it may be surprising to people outside the field of Civil War history—as it often is to those in it—to learn that many important areas of the conflict have not been surveyed adequately and some not at all. One of these slighted areas is the Trans-Mississippi Department, the Confederate military term for the states of Arkansas, Texas, and Louisiana west of the Mississippi River. No single work treats comprehensively the events in this theater. Nor has there been a completely satisfactory and scholarly history of the war in any of these three states. Here, indeed, is one of the neglected facets of America's most tragic experience.

That writers have overlooked the Trans-Mississippi is regrettable but understandable. The explanation is simple. The military operations in this theater were not as large nor as spectacular as those east of the great river. Historians have fastened their eyes on the battles that seemed to decide the fate of two nations—on the hills of Gettysburg and the heights of Chattanooga and the bluffs of Vicksburg. All this is as it should be, but in the process some pretty important episodes beyond the river have slipped into oblivion. Nobody in his right senses would contend that the war was decided in the Trans-Mississippi. But it is perfectly possible to demonstrate that some fairly decisive operations occurred here and especially in Louisiana. The Federal capture of New Orleans in 1862 was a shining triumph for the North and a sickening disaster for the South. At one stroke the Confederacy lost the tremendous economic resources of its only urban center. The sustained Federal attempt to seize Port Hudson against prolonged Confederate resistance in 1863 was one of the memorable siege operations of the war. Although Port Hudson was only a phase of the Vicksburg campaign, it is obvious that if the Louisiana stronghold had fallen earlier, Vicksburg would have had to yield sooner than it did. And as far as Vicksburg itself is concerned, the most important part of Grant's campaign against the city was conducted on the Louisiana side of the river. The Red River expedition of 1864—the Federal thrust up the tawny stream toward Texas—had unforeseen and important effects on the outcome of the war. Not only was the Federal army halted and repelled at Mansfield, it was so badly used up that it could not take its place in the great Union offensives of 1864. If this army had been able to advance as planned from New Orleans to Montgomery, while Grant was grinding south in Virginia and Sherman was slashing south in Georgia, the Northern timetable of victory would have been immeasurably speeded up.

These and other aspects of the war in Louisiana have received some attention in history. The war is better recorded in Louisiana, in fact, than in the other states of the Trans-Mississippi Department. We have Charles L. Dufour's vivid description of the fall of New Orleans, *The Night the War Was Lost;* Ludwell H. Johnson's solid *Red River Campaign;* Charles P. Roland's scholarly *Louisiana Sugar Plantations During the American Civil War;* and good biographies of some of the state's civil and military leaders. We have too a general study of the state during the war, Jefferson Davis Bragg's *Louisiana in the Confederacy,* published by the Louisiana State University Press in 1941. Professor Bragg's book was recognized as a valuable study when it appeared, and it is still useful. It had, however, some limitations in scope. Notably, it tended to emphasize political and economic developments at the expense of military events, because in the era in which Professor Bragg wrote, it was not fashionable to stress battles. In our own age we know that whatever else war is, it is an exercise in violence.

It is this need for a wider book, a martial book, that Professor John Winters has tried to meet. Surely any reader of these pages will affirm that the author has come up to his mark. Professor Winters has researched widely and deeply, in scattered and sometimes fugitive sources, and he has produced a fuller story of Louisiana in the Civil War than has ever before been told. He spreads out a full story but not a mere accumulation of facts. He has written his narrative with sympathy and humor and interest and always with objective restraint. It is a work that should stand for many years as authoritative in its field.

The Louisiana Civil War Centennial Commission has had a part in bringing this book into print. The Commission has underwritten a portion of the publishing expense. It has done this gladly because it believes that the most enduring heritage of the Centennial will be books, good books that will be read and pondered long after the more ephemeral aspects of the commemoration have been forgotten. This book should be a worthy addition to that heritage.

T. HARRY WILLIAMS

Boyd Professor of History,
Louisiana State University

Vice Chairman, Louisiana Civil War
Centennial Commission

PREFACE

THE CONTRIBUTIONS of Louisiana to the Confederacy during the Civil War were many. From a total white population of 350,000, Louisiana raised nearly 1,000 military companies. Some 56,000 troops served in the Confederate army, and there were nearly 10,000 additional boys and over-age men in home-guard units. Between five and six hundred battles and raids took place within the state during the four years of war. Although most of these were minor skirmishes, some of them were battles and campaigns of major importance.

This work attempts to give the most complete and comprehensive picture of the military action possible without losing focus of the other elements involved: politics, economics, and social interaction. It presents a picture of the whole people of Louisiana—leader and follower, patrician and plebian, free Negro and slave—during the traumatic experiences of secession and civil war. Every effort has been made to maintain a dispassionate balance in this report.

In the research, writing, and publication of a book of such length and scope, the author is indebted to many persons who have given generously of their time, labor, and advice.

Without Dr. T. Harry Williams and my wife, Frances Locke Winters, who guided me, encouraged me, helped me, comforted me, and goaded me all along the way, this book would never have been published. Their many contributions can never be adequately acknowledged.

The writer is most grateful to Dr. F. Jay Taylor, President of Louisiana Polytechnic Institute and an able historian, who read the entire rough manuscript and offered many criticisms and suggestions for improving this work.

To Fred G. Benton, Jr., for his aid in securing illustrations, and to Robert W. Arnold and Thomas J. Waxham, who carefully prepared the maps, I am deeply indebted.

I wish to thank the following for their aid and encouragement: the co-operative staff of the Louisiana State University Library, especially Lucy B. Foote and Evangeline Lynch; E. J. Scheerer, Librarian, Louisiana Polytechnic Institute, and his able staff, particularly Caroline Paddock, who proofread the manuscript and gave other valuable assistance, Marjorie Leigh, Mrs. Thesta Hogan, Mrs. Portia Stokes, and William H. O. Scott; Vergil L. Bedsole and Marcelle Schertz of the Louisiana State University Department of Archives; Edith Atkinson of the Louisiana State Library; my colleagues, Dr. G. W. McGinty, Dr. William Y. Thompson, Lorimer E. Storey, Edward H. Moseley, and Dr. Robert W. Mondy; Virginia Moseley; Dr. Frances Fletcher; Wilma Baugh; and a succession of very able student assistants, Mrs. Janet Mahaffey Morgan, Hilda Taylor, Judy Dodds, and Billie Vic Bozeman.

Last, but by no means least, I wish to acknowledge my gratitude to the Louisiana Civil War Centennial Commission and the Louisiana State University Press for financial assistance in the publication of this book.

JOHN D. WINTERS

CONTENTS

ILLUSTRATIONS

Between pages 208–209

Mortar boat used in bombardments along the Mississippi River

Major General Mansfield Lovell

Lieutenant General Edmund Kirby Smith

Major General Benjamin F. Butler

Major General Nathaniel P. Banks

Union gun emplacement at Port Hudson

Gunboat *Signal*

The destruction of the ram *Arkansas*

Banks's army advances on Shreveport

The battle of Pleasant Hill

The Union flag is raised over Baton Rouge

The monitor *Osage* before Alexandria

MAPS

PART ONE

PRELUDE: 1861

I

THE HOUSE DIVIDES

FOR MORE than a year Louisiana had poised at the water's edge, waiting to see which way the political tides would flow. Real and imagined threats against the continuation of slavery; fear of economic ruin and loss of national political prestige; the election of a "Black Republican" president—these were the rip tides of fear and discontent. In the minds of the political leaders the course was clear. Drastic thinking must be translated into drastic action. There must be no more waiting.

On January 26, 1861, the fateful, irrevocable decision was made. On that day, Saturday, in the drafty halls of the ornate state house at Baton Rouge, the secession convention severed Louisiana's connections with the United States. Voices had been raised in protest; delaying tactics had been introduced; compromises and plans had been offered to keep Louisiana a part of the Union; but in the face of overwhelming prosecessionist power, one by one the opposition had been won over, discouraged, overridden, or ignored. By a vote of 113 to 17 the delegates of the convention declared Louisiana to be a "free" and "independent power."

Outside the Gothic capitol, a large group of citizens had begun to assemble around noon. They seemed unaware of the raw, gray chill of the January day. The prosecession majority waited quietly and hopefully for the final vote. The Unionists waited, too, dreading the inevitable.

Inside, in the House chamber, amid wild applause and lusty cheering, Alexander Mouton, president of the convention, proclaimed the dissolution of the union with the United States. Outside, the citizens picked up the cheers and echoed them throughout the town. Crowds surged into the House, packing the rotunda and giving full voice to their sentiments. A spontaneous procession formed, headed by Governor Thomas Overton Moore and his two military aides, Colonel Braxton Bragg and Captain Henry Watkins Allen. Carrying a white Pelican flag with one red star, they wove their way through the press of cheering celebrants and moved slowly out to a flagpole in front of the building. The excited crowd sent up new waves of cheers as the flag of "freedom" was raised. Meanwhile, telegraph wires were carrying the news to the rest of the waiting state and to the country, and other secessionists began to celebrate.[1]

All over New Orleans bells rang and cannons boomed when the news arrived. The Pelican flag was hoisted on every pole. Large groups of people congregated on the main streets, shouting, laughing, thrilled with the clamor and military display heralding secession. The renowned Washington Artillery, attired in full military dress, paraded through the streets. From fortifications along the levee, soldiers deafened the populace with a hundred-gun salute to independence. Business houses closed. Hotels and theaters with all lights blazing were alive with excited people. In the secessionists' jubilant holiday mood, few foresaw the hunger, desolation, and ultimate defeat in store for them. Those who opposed secession remained silent.[2]

Secession had not come to Louisiana unexpectedly. As in other Southern states, the social, economic, and political crisis of 1860 had finally produced a feeling of hopeless defeat and ruin for the slave-owning aristocracy of the state.

The "Year of Decision," 1860, had been a politically active and exciting year in Louisiana. A new, aggressive governor, Thomas Overton Moore, was installed on January 23, 1860. His inaugural address keynoted the sentiment that was to color the political thinking and action of the entire state. Moore informed the legislature and the visitors that a powerful party in the North threatened the existence of the slaveholding states. In solemn tones he stated: "So bitter is this hostility felt toward slavery which these fifteen states regard as a great social and political blessing that it exhibits itself in legislation for the avowed purpose of destroying the rights of slaveholders guaranteed by the Constitution and protected by Acts of Congress." Governor Moore concluded by saying: ". . . at the north, a wide-spread sympathy with felons has deepened the distrust in the permanent Federal Government, and awakened sentiments favorable to a separation of the states." [3]

National political fever ran high throughout 1860. On March 5 the

Louisiana Democrats held a meeting at Baton Rouge to elect delegates to the national convention at Charleston. The proceedings were not without conflict, for the new-liners, led by Pierre Soulé, supporting Stephen A. Douglas and his "popular sovereignty" policy, clashed with the John Slidell faction, the old-liners, or "Southern rights" group. Senator Slidell's group carried the day.

The twelve delegates chosen at this meeting came from the ranks of the wealthy property owners of the state. They represented cotton, sugar, and slaves. One New Orleans newspaper, referring to the group as a "Mongrel Assembly," stated: "The members of the body as much represent the people or public opinion of Louisiana as the officeholders and their thug allies in this parish. . . ." The people who did not own slaves and who hated the institution of slavery could expect nothing from this partisan group.

The Charleston convention met on April 21, but by April 30 Louisiana had withdrawn from the convention, along with Mississippi, Texas, Arkansas, Florida, and South Carolina. The withdrawing delegates, comprising the anti-Douglas faction, refused to accept the idea of popular sovereignty, since the Dred Scott decision had already provided for congressional protection of territorial slavery. Amid heated words the schism of the Democratic Party became a reality.

In New Orleans, opinions were mixed concerning the withdrawal of the Louisiana delegation. The Douglas supporters accused the delegates of trying to destroy the Union, whereas another group, composed of many of the political and business leaders of the city, unanimously endorsed the policy of the seceding delegation.

While the new-liners and old-liners squabbled, a new party, the National Constitutional Union, met in Richmond and nominated John Bell of Tennessee. A large number of conservatives, led by Christian Roselius and Randall Hunt, held a meeting on May 30 in Odd Fellows Hall in New Orleans, to approve Bell's nomination.

The Democrats who had remained at the Charleston convention had been unable to agree on a candidate, and the meeting had been adjourned, to be resumed in Baltimore. Here the Soulé faction supported Stephen A. Douglas, while the Slidell faction, attending a separate Southern Democratic convention in Baltimore, helped to nominate John C. Breckinridge.

In the months prior to the November election Louisiana enjoyed a heated political campaign. In New Orleans, Bell and Douglas appeared to be the favorites, but Breckinridge was not without his supporters. The New Orleans *Daily True Delta* was full of notices announcing political rallies of the Douglas supporters. The *True Delta* of November 3 invited voters to attend meetings of the "Douglas and Johnson Empire Club," the "Douglas and Johnson Club," "Little Giant Club," and "Young Douglas Guards" being held throughout the city. Fireworks, torchlight parades, bands, slogans, and standards lured people to political rallies. Other New Orleans newspapers carried announcements of the "Breckinridge Guards" and various Douglas and Bell clubs. The voters of the Crescent City seemed to favor Bell and had Douglas as a second choice, a circumstance which might indicate a desire to travel the more cautious and conservative path.

Elsewhere in the state, each presidential candidate was supported by clubs, newspapers, and special functions. In Baton Rouge the Bell supporters tried to win votes with a torchlight parade and colorful transparencies. On October 12 the "Breckinridge Club" baited the citizens of the capital city by presenting the fire-eating Southern orator William L. Yancey as speaker. The Baton Rouge *Daily Advocate* of September 3 came out strongly in support of Breckinridge. Far up the Mississippi in the rich cotton parish of Tensas, where planters owned many slaves, a strong Breckinridge club was established on September 20. Catahoula Parish, a poorer neighbor to Tensas, showed strong activity for Breckinridge, but there was also organized support for Bell. In Concordia, another wealthy riparian parish in the heart of the cotton belt, Breckinridge had a following.

Catering to man's stomach seems to have been one of the most popular forms of winning political favor. Supporters of all three candidates killed the fatted calf and plied the people with delectable viands and political verbosity in a series of barbecues throughout Louisiana.[4]

As the election neared, the pulse of political activity quickened. September, October, and early November saw all-out drives to woo votes for the favorite candidates. Night parades lighted by hundreds of pine torches, screaming rockets and resplendent fireworks displays, groaning festive boards under cool arbors, music from bands and glee clubs, dances and grand balls, and, above all, golden oratory from prominent favorite sons made this Louisiana's most exciting and colorful national political campaign.[5]

On November 6 the people went to the polls and cast their votes and compromise and unionist groups were defeated. Breckinridge, the guardian of Southern rights, received the majority of votes cast (22,681), carrying thirty-six out of forty-eight parishes. Bell, a close second with 20,204 votes, had won only nine parishes, his large vote coming from the more populous Orleans, East Baton Rouge, Ouachita, Tensas, and five other parishes. Only three parishes, representing 7,625 votes, supported Stephen A. Douglas. Lincoln's name, representing the most radical and dread political faction, was not carried on Louisiana's ballot.[6]

When word reached Louisiana that the candidate who had been left off its ballots had won the election nationally, there was great consternation in certain quarters. In others it was hoped that a compromise with the victors might be possible. On November 10, four days after the election, a large crowd of citizens packed the Armory Hall to organize the Minute Men of New Orleans, a military organization; to pledge allegiance to Louisiana; and to agree to help protect the right of any Southern state to secede from the Union. On the same night a meeting was held at Odd Fellows Hall in the Crescent City. The Breckinridge, Bell, and Douglas men were now sitting as brothers in one common cause—protection of Southern rights. Hopes for remaining in the Union had begun to wane.[7]

Other military preparations had already begun. Even before the election of Lincoln, leading citizens in New Orleans and in the parishes had foreseen trouble and had petitioned Governor Moore through his adjutant general, Maurice Grivot, for arms and equipment for companies then forming. Having no state funds, Grivot was powerless to act, but some parishes took independent action and formed military groups to protect their homes, families, and property from aggression.

The November election returns increased state-wide apprehension. Planters and influential merchants of several parishes called mass meetings between mid-November and early December to consider the "political position" and to discuss "Southern Rights." These meetings usually ended with the organization of more parish military companies, often referred to as "Minute Men."[8]

E. J. Ellis, a young medical student at the University of Louisiana in New Orleans, wrote to his mother on November 12, "Politics, (though the election is over) are quite lively here. Many men are wearing the 'blue cockade' in token of sectional feeling." The little cockade, a pelican button with two small streamers attached, became the distinguishing mark of secessionists, and a veritable epidemic of blue cockades raged in New Orleans during the winter of 1860–61 and spread to other areas of the state.[9]

When Governor Moore heard that Lincoln and Hannibal Hamlin had been elected, he was undecided as to the proper action. In answer to numerous petitions and appeals, however, he called the legislature into a special session, to convene early in December.

Meanwhile, tension mounted. "Southern Rights Associations" were increasingly active. From the pulpits noted divines echoed the sentiments of the people. The Reverend Dr. Benjamin M. Palmer and Dr. W. T. Leacock were the golden orators of Southern Rights. Both ministers defended the institution of slavery and upheld the right of a state to resist the "Black Republican" North, to sever connections with a Union that intimidated and hampered the economic well-being of that state. Compromise was impossible. The road ahead was clearly marked; Louisiana must secede.[10]

When word reached New Orleans that South Carolina had seceded, jubilant demonstrations took place. At high noon on December 1, hundreds of guns were fired in salute, and the Pelican flag was proudly displayed, while a band played the Marseillaise and other martial airs.

In Governor Moore's opening address to the extraordinary session of the legislature on December 10, he gave official voice to the growing clamor for secession. The planter-governor, himself the owner of numerous slaves, told the lawmakers that a convention should be called before Lincoln took office, to decide what course Louisiana should follow: "I do not think it comports with the honor and self respect of Louisiana, as a slaveholding state to live under the government of a Black Republican President. I maintain the right of each state to secede from the Union, and, . . . if any attempt should be made by the Federal Government to coerce a sovereign state to compel her to submission to an authority which she has ceased to recognize, I should unhesitatingly recommend that Louisiana assist her sister states with . . . alacrity and courage. . . ."

Moore listed a series of grievances against the United States and proposed means of defending the state if she should secede. He asked for the creation of a special military board to purchase arms and distribute them to the growing list of volunteers.[11]

In three short days the legislature completed its work, satisfactorily answering all the governor's urgent requests. He was authorized to hold an election of delegates to a convention to decide Louisiana's future. Secession was accepted as inevitable—the only question was whether the state should act independently or in concert with all the other Southern states. The legislators approved the establishment of a military board headed by the governor and appropriated half a million dollars to arm and equip the companies that had already formed or were being organized. Each parish was authorized to have at least one company, either infantry or cavalry, consisting of a minimum of thirty-two men.[12]

Election of delegates to the Louisiana convention stirred up more political activity than had the late presidential campaign. The question in choosing delegates was how and when they felt secession should be effected. "Secessionists" stood for immediate, separate state action, whereas most "co-operationists" either advocated waiting for collective Southern action or questioned the wisdom of leaving the Union so suddenly and with so little real cause.[13]

Public halls were crowded during December and January. In New Orleans on January 2, at the Orleans Theatre, a distinguished group of patriots, including the influential editor J. D. B. DeBow and Lieutenant Governor H. M. Hyams, helped to fan the flames for immediate secession. Some of the speeches were delivered in French for the Creole members of the audience. On January 4, the New Orleans *Daily Crescent* noted that more than a dozen "secession" or "states rights" meetings were scheduled.

Voters went to the polls on January 7, 1861, to choose their delegates. Eighty "secessionists," forty-four "co-operationists," and six "doubtfuls" were elected. Some 12,766 fewer votes were cast in this election than in the presidential election.[14]

Before the convention could assemble, however, Governor Moore seized the initiative. Two days after the election, the governor issued an order predicated on secession. On that day troops in New Orleans were ordered aboard the steamboat *National* to proceed to Baton Rouge. After the troops had embarked, early on the morning of January 10, they were told the purpose of their mission—the seizure of the United States Arsenal at Baton Rouge.

Meanwhile, Colonel Braxton Bragg of the governor's staff had assembled three military companies from Baton Rouge, joined by companies from Grosse Tete, West Baton Rouge, and Pointe Coupee, who bivouacked on the neutral ground of North Boulevard, near the capitol and about a mile south of the Arsenal. This group of poorly trained, citizen-soldiers demanded the immediate surrender of the Arsenal.

Major Joseph A. Haskin, in command of the skeleton United States force, a hero of the Mexican War, flatly refused the demand. The Federal garrison thereupon sighted a cannon down Third Street, the route of approach for the local state troops.

Without testing the validity of Major Haskin's threat, the local troops sulked in their tents. Insult was added to injury when they learned of the arrival of the New Orleans companies. The Creole Guards and the Pelican Rifles in high dudgeon marched to the governor's mansion, stacked arms, and resigned. Half of the remaining companies marched out of town and away from danger without benefit of formal resignation. Only the Delta Rifles and the Baton Rouge Fencibles remained in bivouac.

After breakfast, the New Orleans companies, attired in an array of colorful uniforms, marched ashore and joined the remaining "country" companies. Consolidating ranks, the local soldiers, lacking uniforms, marched with their more martial-appearing brothers down Third Street toward the Arsenal.

In the white, Doric-columned, pentagon barracks between Third Street and the river, Major Haskin and about sixty artillerymen waited, prepared to resist attack. Twenty men of the ordnance corps under Lieutenant J. W. Todd occupied the Federal Arsenal, east of Third Street. The attacking force, vastly superior in numbers if not in armament, convinced the brave major that further resistance would result in needless bloodshed. At 5 P.M. on January 10, he agreed to surrender the Federal installations and equipment to Governor Moore. The state troops were enriched by fifty thousand stands of small arms, four howitzers, twenty pieces of heavy ordnance, one battery of 6-pounders, one of 12-pounders, three hundred barrels of powder, and a quantity of ammunition. The Federal troops were to vacate in thirty-six hours by upriver transportation for points outside the state of Louisiana.[15] A portion of the confiscated Federal military stores was shipped to the Louisiana State Seminary at Pineville, where Governor Moore intended to build up a strong state arsenal.[16]

Also on January 10, a detachment of Louisiana militia under command of Major Paul E. Théard was sent down-river from New Orleans by steamboat to demand the surrender of Forts Jackson and St. Philip, some seventy miles below New Orleans. The small Federal garrisons under command of Orderly Sergeant H. Smith had no other recourse but to surrender the forts. Fort Pike, a less important fortification guarding the Rigolets, was surrendered a short time later. Explaining his actions to the legislature on January 22, Governor Moore stated:

> She [Louisiana] has a long exposed frontier, on which the Federal Government possesses forts capable of being used for the subjugation of the country and to annul the declared will of the people. Near this capital, where the delegates of the sovereign people are about to assemble, was a military depot, capable, in unscrupulous hands, of being overawing and restraining the deliberations of a free people. . . . I decided to take possession of the military posts and munitions of war within the state . . . in order to prevent a collision between Federal troops and the people of the state. . . .

Governor John J. Pettus, of the neighboring state of Mississippi, fearing an attack from the North, applied to Governor Moore for assistance. Out of courtesy and from the intimate association of the two states in a common cause, Louisiana responded generously with arms and munitions. Governor Moore assured the legislature and later the convention that this was done without harm to Louisiana's needed military supplies.[17]

Major William Tecumseh Sherman, superintendent of the Louisiana Seminary, was shocked to hear of Governor Moore's seizures of Federal fortifications and denounced these actions: "It amounted to a Declaration of War." Sherman had already notified state authorities that he would quit his post if Louisiana seceded from the Union. Late in January both Governor Moore and his aide, Colonel Braxton Bragg, expressed appreciation for Sherman's excellent work and regretted his decision. Bragg was pessimistic about the future. He informed Sherman that "bloodshed" and armed conflict would probably come between the North and the South.[18]

Like their governor, civic leaders in the parishes also anticipated the convention and pushed forward the organization of military companies in January to join with the Home Guards, Defenders of Southern Rights, and Minute Men established in November and December of 1860. New Orleans, especially, became a center of activity. Policemen deserted their posts and enlisted in the army. Even the firemen turned soldiers; twenty-four engine companies organized the Fire Brigade and prepared to fight with rifle as well as hose. In Plaquemine, between New Orleans and Baton Rouge, the Home Sentinels were forming on January 12. About the same time far up the Red River the Caddo Greys made their first public appearance in a parade at Shreveport, while nearby in Bossier Parish the Red River Volunteers, boasting a total strength of sixty-one men, were readying to aid Randolph's Mounted Riflemen and the Minute Men of Bossier Parish, to protect their home front. On January 14 citizens of Alexandria raised a company of cavalry, and in Morehouse Parish in northeastern Louisiana a company of Minute Men was formed.[19]

When finally the convention met in the capitol at Baton Rouge, on January 23, militant public opinion and the press had wrought a change in the opinions of some of the delegates. There was little evidence of opposition to immediate secession from some 123 members present.[20]

Governor Moore outlined the actions he had taken, deeming them necessary and proper to protect the convention and the sovereignty of Louisiana. Moore felt that compromise with the North had been and ever would be impossible. Louisiana must not submit to "coercion into submission, by force of arms."[21]

The governor was not alone with his bid to win and hold the convention for immediate secession. Two former governors of sympathetic Southern states made dramatic appeals before the delegates on January 25. John L. Manning from South Carolina presented his state's Ordinance of Secession as a possible guide to the Louisiana convention. He endorsed immediate secession by the individual states and urged the formation of a confederation of states for common protection of Southern rights. Alabama sent John A. Winston, who gave additional arguments for prompt action in forming a Southern confederation.[22]

Equally as forceful was a joint letter sent from Washington by Senators Judah P. Benjamin and John Slidell and two of Louisiana's congressmen, T. G. Davidson and John M. Landrum. The communiqué warned of "a plan . . . for subjugation of the seceding states," and recommended immediate secession and a joint effort by the states to create a provisional confederacy to guard against General Winfield Scott's plan to intimidate the South.

On the same busy day (January 25) the Committee of Fifteen made its report on the Ordinance of Secession. Minor challenges were hurled against the Ordinance. Joseph A. Rozier, a "Unionist" and "co-operationist" from New Orleans, made an impassioned but futile plea for a revival of the Nashville convention, the amendment of the Federal Constitution in favor of the South, and the preservation of the Union. He prophesied that Europe would refuse to recognize a Southern government and that secession would mean economic ruin. A second New Orleans co-operationist, Charles Bienvenu, asked the convention to submit the secession ordinance to the vote of the people, but this resolution also went down in defeat.[23]

Among the challengers, delegate James G. Taliaferro from the small farming parish of Catahoula made the most withering denunciation of secession. He denied the constitutional right of Louisiana to leave the Union. He painted a gloomy picture of economic chaos, blighted prosperity, staggering taxation, and "fatal prostration of Louisiana's interests under a Southern Confederation," and he could see no way ahead to prevent final anarchy and war. So "radical" were the ideas of Taliaferro that the convention refused to print his protest in the pages of the *Journal*.[24]

Whatever the opposition could say or do was to no avail. The stronger voice of the political majority had already deafened the ears of most of the delegates to suggestions of compromise. There was no time for reconsideration; there was no turning back. On January 26, 1861, by an overwhelming vote, Louisiana left the Union.[25]

AN OUNCE OF PREVENTION

T HE WORK of the convention was not yet finished. As the regular session of the legislature had convened in Baton Rouge late in January, the convention had to vacate and seek other quarters. By January 29 a move to New Orleans had been made, and the delegates resumed their duties at City Hall. Almost immediately six delegates were chosen by the convention to attend a meeting at Montgomery, Alabama, on February 4, along with delegates from other seceding states. Later in the month the convention seized the United States Mint in New Orleans with nearly $500,000.00 in gold and silver and transferred the Custom House funds of $147,519.66 to the newly created Confederate government. The election of Jefferson Davis as president of the new Confederacy was endorsed, and a state flag was adopted.

Before adjourning on February 12 the convention passed an ordinance declaring that all persons residing in Louisiana for twelve months would become citizens of the state, upon taking an oath of allegiance. Citizens of Louisiana at the time of secession were automatically declared citizens of the independent state. A temporary civil and criminal court system was set up. All former United States court systems and laws, as far as practicable, were retained.[1]

Official copies of the Ordinance of Secession dispatched to Washington were read to the Senate upon the request of Senators Benjamin and Slidell. Shortly afterwards the two Louisianians made dramatic farewell addresses to the Senate and started home, followed by the Louisiana members of the House. John Slidell, fired by patriotism, threatened that all Northern manufactures would be boycotted and that Southern ships would soon ply the oceans. Foreign countries would prevent the North from blockading Southern ports. "This will be war, . . . and we shall meet it with . . . efficient weapons," he warned the Senate.[2]

Despite the increased tempo of military preparedness, there were many people who still thought a peaceful solution could be found. Many believed the Yankee incapable of learning to use a gun or of mustering enough courage to fight; the emergency would soon dissipate.[3]

Governor Moore and his aides were not among the rank optimists. Hurrying to complete the seizure of Federal military installations and properties and thus to strengthen Louisiana's defenses, on January 14, 1861, the United States barracks near New Orleans had been taken over by state officials. Fourteen days later the First Regiment Louisiana Infantry occupied Fort Macomb, guarding one of the eastern water approaches to New Orleans. This same day, January 28, all public property in custody of Federal army officers, including quartermaster and commissary stores, with valuable medical supplies, was appropriated by state authorities.[4]

An ordinance had been approved on February 5 by the convention to set up a regular state military force possessing the same rules, regulations, and pay as the United States army. There was to be at least one regiment each of infantry and artillery, directed by a major general. If this force were no longer needed by the state, it could be disbanded by either the governor or the legislature, or it could be transferred to a confederated Southern government if Louisiana joined such. The legislature was empowered to amend or abolish any part of the ordinance.[5]

Throughout Louisiana in January and February military companies continued to be formed, some with the aid of the Military Board and others with the help of private philanthropy. Early in February a new company, called the Chasseurs à Pied, was formed in Baton Rouge. Later in the same month another company across the river in West Baton Rouge had formed the Tirrailleurs to rival the Delta Rifles of the capital city. In New Orleans eight or nine new military companies were busy drilling each night. Upstate at Trinity, a small shipping center in Catahoula Parish, a large cotton planter, Major St. John R. Liddell, received carbines, sabers, cartridges, and other materials sufficient to equip a small company. These ordnance stores were a part of those seized at the Federal arsenal in Baton Rouge. Joining the increasing number of military units being formed were the Thibodaux

Rifles, Terrebonne Guards, Caddo Rifles, Carroll Guards, Montgomery Guards, Assumption Guards, Clinton Guards, and many others.[6]

By the middle of February the Military Board had furnished arms to twenty-eight volunteer companies with a total enrollment of 1,765 men. The size of the twenty-eight companies varied widely from the standard of 64 privates and 8 officers. The largest was the Lake Providence Cadets with an enrollment of 120 men, and the smallest was the Madison Dragoons with only 30 men, the minimum set by the board for a company entitled to state aid.[7]

The lack of standardization and uniformity caused great confusion and cost the state double the amount it should have. Each company wanted to remain distinctive, and each adopted a uniform that would guarantee individuality. Two early organizations outstripped all others in color and singularity, the Garibaldi Legion and the Louisiana Zouaves. The uniform of the Legion was similar to that of the famous Italian "Expedition of the Thousand" of 1860 but was far more grand and elaborate.

The Louisiana Zouaves were hardly less distinctive in their red, tasseled Zouave caps, tight-fitting red jackets, and full blue pantaloons. This organization, composed mostly of Frenchmen and Italians, was made up of veterans of the Crimean, Italian, and African wars. Many of the men were thieves and murderers recruited in the jails of New Orleans. With their gaudy, dirty uniforms and their terrifying scars, these desperate characters were unforgettable.

Flashy uniforms as well as patriotism had much to do with early enlistments. The Home Sentinels of Plaquemine adopted Zouave-type uniforms with close-fitting jackets, bulging red-striped pantaloons, and small caps, and the New Orleans firemen who formed the Fire Brigade wore bright blue flannel Zouave uniforms.

The Zouave craze was greatly stimulated by a group of itinerant actors who claimed to have served in most of the European and African campaigns of the last decade. Appearing in a New Orleans theater early in 1861, these "heroes" attracted large crowds and inspired embryo military groups. The military thespians gladly visited several New Orleans companies, instructed the men in a new manual of arms, and imparted "invaluable" military information.

After several months of triumph in New Orleans, the "Zouave" company toured many of the river towns of Louisiana. The actors played to an overflow audience at Plaquemine and thrilled the citizens of Alexandria with a "bloody drama of the Crimean War." After the triumphant tour they returned to New Orleans to even greater popularity and prosperity. Some nine months after arriving in Louisiana, the Zouaves finally departed for Mexico.

In the wake of the Zouaves' popularity, the impressionable foreign element in New Orleans adopted their outlandish uniforms. Three regiments, the Louisiana Zouaves, the Avegno Zouaves, and the Tigers, sometimes called "Bob Wheat's Zouaves," were originally outfitted in bright-colored kepis, short coats, and flaring pantaloons. When the battles began, however, the colorful uniforms, so popular on parade grounds, lost their romantic appeal. Riflemen found the brilliant colors an easy target. Sober, subdued, and more practical clothing was then adopted.[8]

The Crescent City had from colonial days been one of the gayest cities in America. Even with war clouds hanging heavy overhead, she did not lose her happy, carefree air. After a fall and winter of continuous balls, theater and opera parties, and sumptuous dinners and banquets, the social season reached its zenith on Shrove Tuesday.

Mardi Gras, February, 1861, found Louisiana a free and sovereign state. Undaunted by threats of war, New Orleans proceeded with her yearly Mardi Gras celebration. Many masked revelers in amusing and often grotesque costumes were seen on the crowded streets.

That night the Mistick Krewe of Comus presented its annual parade. Preceded by musicians and Negroes carrying lighted torches, the members of Comus paraded in costumes representing "Scenes from Life"—Childhood, Youth, Manhood, Old Age, and lastly Death, a shrouded skeleton. Economies in costuming and staging of the parade perhaps reflected a slight apprehension about the future.

According to custom, the Krewe of Comus presented a tableau and ball at the Varieties Theatre. At Odd Fellows Hall, the Young Men's Society Ball was crowded with gay maskers. The fashionably dressed Creole population made merry in the Orleans Theatre. At Armory Hall and at the St. Charles Theatre, happy throngs danced the night through, and the Bakers Society ushered in Ash Wednesday with a lively ball at the Third District Exchange. Many other parties and balls took place in other parts of the city.[9]

The holiday mood was not shared by everyone. Among those who took a more sober view of the times was Major P. G. T. Beauregard, the late superintendent of the United States Military Academy at West Point. Returning home to Louisiana soon after secession, Beauregard resigned his army commission and joined the Orleans Guards, composed of elite Creole gentlemen of New Orleans, as a private.

Shortly after his return, the legislature passed a law creating the Louisiana State Forces. Braxton Bragg of the Military Board was appointed brigadier general, and Beauregard was offered the command of engineers and artillery, with the rank of colonel. Beauregard smarted from the insult of being offered a secondary position and refused all military rank in the state forces; however, he promised Governor Moore that as a private citizen he would co-operate freely with General Bragg in strengthening the defenses of Louisiana.

In answer to requests for assistance from the Military Board, Beauregard stated that the Mississippi River, especially from the Gulf end, was Louisiana's most vulnerable point: ". . . in the present condition of Forts Jackson and Saint Philip any steamer can pass them in broad daylight, and . . . even when in a proper condition for defence, they could not prevent the passage of one or more steamers during a dark or stormy night. . . ." He advised the board to move the land-side guns in Fort Jackson to the river front. Guns then at Baton Rouge, at Forts Pike and Wood, at Battery Bienvenue, and at other points of lesser importance should be transferred to Jackson and St. Philip. "The trees along the river masking the fire of those two forts ought to be cut down at once. . . ."

To delay the passage of hostile steamers and to give the forts time to destroy these vessels with a deadly crossfire, obstructions or booms should be constructed between, or just below, the two forts. Plans for two booms to be used together or separately were submitted by Beauregard. One plan called for a floating barrier of long twelve-inch timbers bound together in sections of four timbers, with heavy iron chains connecting each section. One half of the boom was to be firmly anchored from Fort Jackson and extend halfway across the river, there to be joined by a similar boom from Fort St. Philip. A strong wire rope operated from Fort Jackson could open a channel to allow passage of friendly ships and to relieve the pressure of driftwood. The second plan called for a boom made of five barges, connected from fort to fort with huge chains or heavy wire rope. Well-protected Drummond lights were to illuminate the booms, and patrol boats were to give added safety to the booms.

For months this defensive plan to protect the lower Mississippi was neglected, and when finally a system of obstructions was attempted, the plan was only partially carried out. By this time Beauregard had long since departed for Confederate service and his engineering skill was no longer available.[10]

February found Louisiana delegates in Montgomery occupied with the problems of setting up a confederated government for the Southern states. To protect the new confederation "an act to establish the Navy Department" was approved on February 21, and on February 28 an act was passed creating a provisional army. Soldiers were to volunteer for not less than twelve months' service.[11]

The five-man Louisiana Military Board encountered more work and headaches than it could handle. Monetary matters alone were so complicated that little else could be accomplished. By the end of January, 1861, over $32,500 had been expended, and in February the purchase of five thousand rifles called for additional money not then available. The board thereupon asked the legislature to create a special military bureau to take over the financing of the state troops. In its three months' existence the board had tried to promote uniformity in size of units and in a manual of drill, as well as to effect more economical organization. They had not met with complete success. Appointment of officers, too, had brought harsh criticism of the board. These appointments were rich sources of patronage, and at the expense of military efficiency politicians had forced members of the board to carry out their will. To correct the inadequacies, to throttle the spoils system, and to promote greater efficiency the legislature abolished the Military Board on March 7, 1861, and appointed Governor Moore and his adjutant general to direct future military problems.[12]

On March 4, the convention, which had taken a brief adjournment, resumed session in New Orleans. Important problems still to be solved were then settled. The delegates declared all the public lands within the state to be the property of Louisiana. Richard Taylor, a wealthy planter and the son of former President Zachary Taylor, brought pressure upon the convention to establish an official Louisiana army. As a result of his efforts, one of the last things the convention accomplished was the creation of the state army headed by Braxton Bragg.

On March 21, 1861, the convention ratified the permanent Constitution of the Confederacy by a vote of 101 to 7. The new Confederate government was empowered to use any fortifications, customs, and other former possessions of the United States that had been seized by the state. Having fully cast Louisiana's lot with the Confederacy, the convention repealed or amended all the ordinances concerning her "independence." Their work completed, both the convention and the legislature adjourned on March 26.[13]

The first call for troops from Louisiana to serve in the Confederate army came on March 9, 1861. Secretary of War Leroy P. Walker asked for 1,700 men to be used with other Southern troops to garrison various forts within the Confederacy. Louisiana responded at once to the urgent requests for men and for military supplies. Governor Moore was allowed by the legislature to transfer state troops to the Confederate army and to permit Louisiana citizens to volunteer for Confederate service.[14]

During March Louisiana sent the Confederacy most of the guns, ammunition, and other equipment from the United States Arsenal and the Federal fortifications, leaving herself unprepared and vulnerable to Federal attack. Governor Moore, therefore, issued an order that no more arms could be spared from the state. Major Waldemar Hyllested and four companies of Zouaves were the first to leave Louisiana for service in the Confederacy. On March 29 they departed from New Orleans for Pensacola. At the end of March, Captain Johnson K. Duncan of the artillery was assigned command of Forts Jackson and St. Philip in an effort to strengthen these two fortifications guarding the river.

President Davis on April 8 asked all the seceded states for troops. Louisiana was requested to furnish 3,000 in addition to the 1,700 already solicited. Lincoln had turned down attempts of the Confederate Peace Commission to compromise a settlement of difficulties, and Davis felt that the South must be ready to protect herself from Northern aggression.

New Orleans became "much disturbed" over the pending departure of more of her troops, but despite all protests, four companies were readied for immediate departure for Florida. Governor Moore, in co-operation with Davis' request, called for volunteers to serve twelve months in the Confederate army.

Troop movements from New Orleans to Pensacola continued on April 11, 19, and 20. On the eleventh, the Orleans Cadets and the First Louisiana Regulars, commanded by Colonel A. H. Gladden, embarked. They were followed later in April by the Caddo Greys, Crescent Rifles, Louisiana Guards, and Grivot Guards, comprising the Louisiana Battalion, also called the Dreux Battalion. These troops were convinced that they would meet the enemy at once and easily vanquish him. They would "teach the Yankee a lesson and . . . settle matters inside sixty days." [15]

The bombardment of Fort Sumter in Charleston harbor, April 12 through 14, led by Louisiana's General P. G. T. Beauregard, now in Confederate service, set off a mounting fury in the North that could be resolved only by a shooting war. On April 15, the day after Major Robert J. Anderson surrendered Fort Sumter, President Lincoln called for 75,000 volunteers. President Davis met the challenge on the sixteenth by requesting that the Confederate states furnish 32,000 men. Louisiana was asked to ready 5,000 troops for immediate use as her quota.[16]

The news of Fort Sumter caused "feverish excitement" in New Orleans. Talk of war and militant politics occupied the entire population. Business was brought to a standstill.[17]

Companies already organized waited impatiently for the call to active service. On April 21 Governor Moore asked for five thousand volunteers for twelve months' service, to be received into Confederate service by companies, battalions, or regiments. Each company was to have at least sixty-four privates, eight noncommissioned officers, and three commissioned officers. Until called to New Orleans these outfits were to remain at home perfecting their organization and drill.

From the time of Lincoln's election citizen patrols and home guards had sprung up all over the state. Hunting clubs, political clubs, veterans of former wars, firemen, planters, old men, foreigners, and various groups were organized for the protection of their homes, parishes, and state. These irregular companies, usually armed with their own rifles, were "amateurishly and light-heartedly trained." After the fall of Fort Sumter, these units began to drill in earnest. In some areas drillmasters were employed to turn the raw recruits into competent soldiers. When attempts were made to muster existing state and local troops into Confederate service outside Louisiana, some of the men refused to leave the state and resigned from their outfits. Those who resigned were usually enrolled in the state militia.[18]

To take care of the rapid influx of soldiers awaiting muster into regular Confederate service, the old Metairie Race Course at New Orleans was converted into a military camp, and by early May around three thousand troops were stationed there. At Camp Walker the new civilian-soldier found conditions vastly different from the holiday soldiering he had enjoyed at home. Independence and individuality suffered under the new burden of compulsory drill, guard duty, and rigid military discipline.

The Metairie Race Course, which had ended a successful spring racing season on April 9, was hardly an ideal camping area for troops. It was surrounded by swamps choked with rank vegetation through which deep open ditches sluggishly carried the sewage and drainage of New Orleans. The area was infested by swarms of mosquitoes. Inside the enclosure the soft, marshy soil was turned into a quagmire as wagon teams hauled in supplies during heavy rains. Tents were pitched in the ooze, and the men were drilled in the "soft, tenacious black mud."

Brigadier General Elisha L. Tracy, a veteran of the Mexican War, was in command of Camp Walker. This little man of unheroic proportions had every reason to be as cross looking as he was. His patience and abilities were sorely tried by rain, supply and sanitation problems, undisciplined troops, and inadequate facilities. Troops from all over Louisiana continued to come, and space had to be made for them. Temporary relief was secured in the latter part of April when Camp Lewis near Carrollton, several miles from the city, was prepared for occupation.

Eventually, the shortage of good drinking water and the unhealthy site made Camp Walker intolerable. General Tracy was ordered by Governor Moore to begin on May 13 to transfer most of his men by rail to a new camp near Tangipahoa. The Third Regiment Louisiana Volunteers was to remain at Camp Walker under the command of Colonel Louis Hébert.

Camp Moore was a paradise in comparison with the "scorching and waterless" camp at Metairie Race Course. The camp was located seventy-eight miles north of New Orleans in the piney-woods upland of St. Helena Parish. The troops should have been pleased with the change. There was enough well-drained space for tents to accommodate every soldier Louisiana could muster, and fresh, pure drinking water from Beaver Creek and Tangipahoa River was abundant. There were practically no mosquitoes. To build morale, at night regimental bands filled the camp with martial music.[19]

Some of the men were satisfied. In September a young soldier wrote his sister from Camp Moore, "We have better meat hear then you have in St. James . . . we have Ice Water & Coffee three times a day." [20] Later in the same month another enlisted man wrote, "The health is tolerable good here at this time. With the exception of Diearheer the boys in our company is all up at this time. There's about 4,000 men here." [21]

But some of the men were not satisfied. They found little in the nearby village to compensate them for their distance from the pleasures of New Orleans. There were two hotels of mediocre caliber and six small stores; ". . . at four of them whiskey is sold—and not a piece of letter paper to be had in town." [22] A young medical student fresh from the University of Louisiana complained to his mother of the long hours of training. "I get up at 4 in the morning and retire at 9. Drill about 5 hours a day besides dress parade and general review." [23]

General Tracy, who continued in command at Camp Moore, had even more reason to be discontented. Many of his officers were new to military duties and the enlisted men were raw and undisciplined. Some of the young college-bred officers, who thought they knew all about military tactics and company evolutions, were hard to reason with, and the enlisted men had no respect for them. The fractious Tenth Louisiana was especially hard to handle, and the old general breathed a sigh of relief when the regiment left for Virginia. Drunken and riotous men, excessive rain, sickness, and numerous deaths made the labor of preparing, organizing, and disciplining the state troops for service with the Confederate army a most trying ordeal.

Whisky was a problem. Wines and liquors were sold at the sutler's to an officer in any quantity and to an enlisted man if he could present a written order signed by one of his company officers. There was plenty of liquor to be had, and wise, thirsty troops found ways to get it. To save time and to avoid the risk of refusal, they forged the name of a company officer. Sutlers were always ready to accept their money and did not examine the permits carefully.[24] If all else failed, there was liquor, plenty of it, waiting nearby in the village of Tangipahoa.

On the eve of departure for an active theater of war, many troops tried to drink the camp and town dry. An officer wrote his wife late in August,

On the day before we left Camp Moore I was on duty at Tangipahoa and had a great deal of trouble with drunken soldiers; I put about a dozen in my guard house, and they kept on getting drunk, coming with orders from their captains to purchase whiskey, until finally I called out my guard and shut up every store in the place, and then it was as much as I could do to keep them from breaking open the houses.

That night the Dillons (Guards Co. A., 11th La. Inft.) commenced burning up their floors to their tents, their benches &c. Col. Marks had

no more control. . . . Finally . . . twenty-five from each company of
Rosale Guards, Continentals, and Catahoula Greys, with loaded guns,
were called out and soon the disturbance ceased.

The next morning one half of the Dillons, Home's Light, and Cannon
Guards had to be carried aboard the cars. On the way two dropped off
(one killed and one seriously wounded). Lieut. Favrot shot one of his
men whilst attempting to bayonet another. Two Dillons cut one another
very badly. . . .

In August excessive rain "rendered Camp Moore a very disagreeable
place. Most of the boys have colds and complain of pains and aches
innumerable." On August 27 the same officer complained to his wife:
"Rain, rain, rain the same old wet miserable weather. . . ." August
also brought an epidemic of measles to the camp. The hospital was
filled, and there were many fatalities.[25] In September a soldier wrote,
"Without regret, we bade farewell to the old camp in the pines, with
its six or seven hundred graves, containing the remains of Louisianians
who had yielded up their patriotic young lives without having once
faced the enemies of their beloved South. To measles may be largely
charged the loss of life at Camp Moore. . . ."[26]

First at Camp Walker, then at Camp Lewis, and finally at Camp
Moore single companies, battalions, and other groups of varying sizes
were mustered into Confederate service in 1861. Before leaving one
of these camps, the companies were assigned to regiments for drill
and discipline and for final transfer by regiments to the Confederate
army. When lower echelon units reported to camp, they brought with
them their own officers elected by the men of their outfit. When a
skeleton company reported, company ranks were filled and company
elections for noncommissioned and commissioned officers were held.
In the "ready" camp elections for regimental officers were held as
regiments were formed. After elections, the men were not always
pleased with the results. One officer reported, "The officers and whole
Regiment have fallen out with our Major and have asked him to
resign, and [he] will not listen to it. . . ."[27]

Occasionally enlisted men at Camp Moore were harshly dealt with
because of infractions of military discipline. One private who attempted to strike a superior was court-martialed and "was sentenced
to wear a ball and chain for six weeks. During the first week he stood
at evening parade on a post in public view; the next week he was to
promenade with a barrel over his head."[28]

Supplying adequate and decent food and supplies to large concentrations of troops in the training camps and in the field was always a difficult task for Louisiana. The quartermaster's department furnished the army with camp equipage, arms, ammunition, clothing, food, accouterments, and transportation, when units needed them. Supplies were often obtained from contractors, the quality of the goods was often shocking, and the corruption of some of the contractors was flagrant. When brought to task, contractors usually pleaded that anywhere in the South first-class materials were hard, if not impossible, to procure.

Even more disgraceful was the unprincipled conduct of some of the commissary officers. The commissary drew ration allotments from the quartermaster's service and distributed them to the various troops of the command. It has been estimated that corrupt commissary officers appropriated nearly one third of every ration requisition, sold it, and pocketed the proceeds. Few men who served as commissary officers for a regiment remained completely free of this organized graft. Many of the best stores were labeled "condemned" and sold to agents for a fraction of their value. In the South, after the first year of hostilities there were fewer stores to swindle, and outside markets were even more scarce.[29]

At Camp Moore in October young E. J. Ellis, now a lieutenant of the St. Helena Rebels, reported that "the Quarter Master of this Post has been engaged in a huge swindle and there have [been many?] complaints from the different companies of want of provisions. This continued for two or three days when things begun to look [black?] and finally 6 or 8 companies were in open mutiny . . . the butcher and Quarter Master saved themselves by running off. The excitement was intense but the prompt action of [regimental officers] quieted things and procured a good supply of beef."

Camp Chalmette, eight miles below New Orleans, was activated late in 1861 to guard the lower river approach to New Orleans and to give additional training to the troops. The campgrounds were low and level but well drained. Near the river was an earthworks with ten 32-pound guns commanding the river. Between the works and the levee was a ditch thirty feet wide and eight feet deep. "Woe be to the Yankee that ever attempts to invade the Crescent City," boasted Lieutenant Ellis in December, 1861.[30]

All was not work at the camp. Many of the men spent their leisure time playing poker.[31] Securing a pass to visit New Orleans was easy but often ended in performing a heavy penance. "Some of the men go to the city and get drunk and come back and when the officers go to take them to the guard house they will curse them and then they get bucked and a bayonet tied in their mouth and stay double the length of time. . . ." [32]

A two-and-a-half-hour march from Chalmette led to Camp Benjamin, named in honor of one of Louisiana's most distinguished citizens, then serving in the Confederate cabinet. Camp Benjamin, often called Camp Jerusalem, was far less desirable than Chalmette. "This camp is the D——nist hole on earth mud up to ones knees when it rains. . . ." [33] Another soldier at Camp Benjamin complained: "It rains day and night. Inactivity is the bane of camp life! enervates the men, fills the hospitals. Here are 5,000 men . . . restless, and uneasy, find fault and grumble, are tired of the monotony of camp life & there is no prospect of ever meeting the enemy. Why they are kept here I can't see. . . ." [34]

To guard the upper river approach to New Orleans, Camp Roman was established near Carrollton. Earthworks, gun emplacements, and ditches were constructed for additional protection. The early arrivals in this camp were treated royally by the citizens of the small village. On September 1, Private James D. Durnin wrote his sister, "On Thursday last we had a big barbacue and a nice Ball at night we danced all night   in fact we had a ball two and three times a week since we came down here. . . . the Volunteers are treated splendid. . . ." [35]

Camp Lovell, established in the fall of 1861, was created for a dual purpose. It was to serve as an advanced training center and to man Fort Berwick, which guarded the inlet from Berwick Bay into the Atchafalaya River. From various accounts life at this camp must have been leisurely and comfortable. The camp was surrounded by beautiful sugar plantations. Private Silas White, writing to his father, stated: "The people are generally very hospitable to us. They have sent us at different times all kinds of vegetables potatoes and one or two bbles of molasses since we have been here." [36] Life for a few was not too monotonous. Some of the men found time to play billiards, euchre, and whist, and fishing and reading were very popular. [37]

A private in the Delta Rifles, son of a wealthy planter, writing in December from Camp Lovell, seems to have never heard of the blockade and the acute shortage of food in certain areas of the state: "On Christmas our mess had a grand camp dinner. The table weighed down under the weight of good things. Chicken Roasted & Stewed Ham fried with eggs—lobsters, cabbage & preserved pears—for desert we had pumpkin & apple pies & plenty of wine and coffee. That night Steve . . . gave a supper in my mess room . . . the St. Charles Hotel couldn't boast of better. It was a cold supper from the best restaurant in New Orleans & the turkey & chickens with current jelly were delicious. . . . Coffee was strong & with Irish whiskey punches & song we ended our feast." A few days after Christmas he reported: "On Tuesday evening I gave an egg-nogg treat to our mess & a few invited friends. . . . After this treat we gathered together & serenade all our favorit officers, and I retired toward morning." [38]

Social life in the urban centers, especially New Orleans, was greatly colored by military activities. Attending drill, watching parades, visiting camp, seeing the soldiers off, and promoting military benefits helped to enliven the social scene.

Camp Walker was a very popular and gay resort for visitors. Lady guests of officers and enlisted men ate army rations and viewed with awe the doings of the military. When Camp Walker was vacated for Camp Moore, women occasionally made excursions on the New Orleans, Jackson and Great Northern Railroad to visit their "brave soldiers" in their new home. On July 4 ten thousand visitors swarmed out to Camp Lewis on the Carrollton Railroad and were treated to a "grand review" and a holiday feast by the soldiers.

When the Shreveport Grays departed by steamer for the New Orleans staging area on April 16, the levee was lined with proud citizens. As the boat pulled out into the river, a band struck up a tune, "The Girl I Left Behind Me," and a cannon salute was fired in honor of the brave defenders. "There was waving of handkerchiefs by ladies, tears tracing down smiling faces." [39]

To celebrate the departure of the Washington Artillery for Virginia in May, all business houses along Canal Street in New Orleans closed their doors. Ladies thronged the balconies, waving their handkerchiefs to bid their heroes good-by. At City Hall the Reverend Dr. Palmer delivered a stirring farewell address. Despite the terrible heat, cheering crowds lined the streets, and all of the city troops acted as an honor escort to the station. Amid salvos from the artillery and martial strains from several brass bands, the troop train pulled away from the New Orleans station.[40] One of the departing soldiers reported that aboard the train "There was too much excitement for the first half of the night to allow for much sleep. The men laughed, and danced and sung as if possessed by hysteria. The sardine boxes which we had brought along to be eaten when rations run short, were opened before we reached the first station, and the various flasks much sooner." [41]

Equally colorful was the send-off given the men of the Thirteenth Louisiana as they passed New Orleans en route from Camp Chalmette to Tennessee. As the large transport steamed by, "Nine hundred soldiers, five or six hundred of whom wore brilliant red caps and baggy trousers," clung to "the forecastle, the main upper deck and every spot available." Thunderous applause from the shore greeted the steamer, "as the gold lace and red and blue colors of the uniforms flashed in the evening sunlight." Cannons roared from the levee, bells tolled, steam whistles shrieked shrilly. Aboard the ship, all eyes were turned cityward, hoping to get a last glimpse of home and friends.[42]

Troops departing from Camp Moore for active service missed the fanfare of a New Orleans send-off. There were few civilians at Tangipahoa station, and troop arrivals and departures became commonplace.[43]

On May 27 all of Louisiana, along with the southern portions of Mississippi and Alabama, was designated as Department No. 1 under Major General David E. Twiggs with headquarters in New Orleans. On May 31, 1861, General Twiggs, the ranking general of the South at that time, assumed command.[44] Twiggs was in his seventy-first year, too old a man for the job. His once powerful and robust frame was now weak and infirm. Department No. 1 suffered from neglect, for the elderly general was often unable to leave his quarters.[45]

In spite of the ineffective General, however, by mid-1861 Louisiana was contributing more than her quota of men to the defenses of the Confederate service, having armed and placed in active service nearly 8,000 men. She had sent 2,100 to Pensacola, 2,300 to Virginia, and 1,000 to Arkansas, and had furnished 1,950 men for seacoast and harbor defenses. Four thousand men were still at Camp Moore, organizing and training for Confederate service in the near future. Five thousand men were in New Orleans to provide home protection. Over 16,000 men were already under arms, and out in the state new companies were still organizing.[46]

III

THE ARMED CAMP

FROM JUNE to the end of 1861 there was a general heightening of military activity throughout the state. New Orleans and Camp Moore remained the clearinghouses for most of the newly activated units awaiting muster into Confederate service.

Building an army with volunteers was not altogether satisfactory. Some of the parishes oversubscribed their quotas, and others fell far short. Even as late as February, 1862, seven parishes in South Louisiana had not formed a single company, and three other well-populated southern parishes could claim only one company. Areas made up of rich bottom-land farms and large plantations, such as Bossier, Madison, Ouachita, and St. Landry, which had already sent many men to the front, dug deeper and strained to meet the new needs. The poorer, swampy or pine-barren parishes generally were slower in their response.[1]

Louisiana troops in Virginia did not have long to wait before their mettle was tested in battle. Led by General Beauregard, Louisiana's favorite son, Louisiana outfits, including the famed Washington Artillery and the Sixth, Seventh, and Eighth Louisiana regiments, played an important role in the rout of the Federal troops at Bull Run in July.

When word first arrived in New Orleans of the Confederate victory, the city went wild with joy. It was a gala day. A cannon was shot, and many toasts were drunk to a quick victory. More important to the Confederate war effort, this victory set off a new chain of volunteering throughout the state.

Already the Secretary of War had requisitioned Louisiana for three thousand additional volunteers, and on July 15 Governor Moore had ordered this number of men to proceed to Camp Moore and to another camp in the interior to await shipping orders.[2] President Davis, foreseeing the possibility of a quicker victory if his forces were large enough, issued a call to the Confederate states on August 8 for four hundred thousand men to serve not less than a year nor more than three years.[3]

In August the Third Louisiana Regiment participated in the Confederate victory at Oak Hill, Missouri,[4] and the Eleventh Louisiana fought in the battle of Belmont, in Kentucky. News of both battles stimulated enlistments at home.[5]

Boys too young for the army joined "home protection" units. Many of these local units went with adolescent enthusiasm into active duty, for under-age companies and individual volunteers were readily accepted into state and Confederate service, especially during and after 1862. In New Orleans several boys' high schools closed down for lack of students and teachers. Some of the boys volunteered, and others accepted jobs as clerks to fill vacancies created by the war. Companies of cadets—boys' companies—were organized in several cities. Monroe, a small North Louisiana town, was proud of its two companies, the Monroe Zouaves and the Monroe Cadets. This group, collectively called the Ouachita Fencibles, was made up of boys from twelve to sixteen. They were furnished colorful uniforms and armed with double-barreled shotguns. In New Orleans four different groups of boys, all called the Orleans Cadets, organized, drilled, and went into the army. Several units of Beauregard Cadets, meant only for home duty, were organized in New Orleans.[6]

The effect of war was much more disruptive on higher education than on the lower level because of the departure of college students and professors for military service. Enrollment at the University of Louisiana fell from 404 in 1861 to 94 early in 1862 and in March, 1862, the school closed. The New Orleans Normal School had already closed its doors. David Merrick, a seventeen-year-old student at Centenary College in 1861, reported that most of his fellow students were leaving to join the army; he begged permission to enlist too.[7] Frank L. Richardson, another Centenary student, wrote to his uncle that "there is great excitement" among the students and that they were joining local companies. Frank wanted to join his uncle's cavalry company "provided it is going to war right away."[8]

In November another college, the New Orleans School of Medicine, became a casualty of war. Most of the instructors volunteered to serve as doctors with the Confederate army. Already most of the students had resigned and were by then away at camp or fighting in an active theater.[9]

At the beautiful Louisiana State Seminary of Learning and Military Academy near Alexandria, William Tecumseh Sherman as superintendent had opened the second session on November 1, 1860. Sherman was to be the first war casualty at the school; because of secession he resigned and departed for his home in Ohio in February.

On May 5, 1861, Captain B. Jarreau wrote Sherman: "The seminary is breaking up very fast." Out of 98 cadets there were only 55 left and others were getting ready to leave. On June 30, 1861, the school closed and did not reopen until April, 1862. The Seminary probably contributed more young men, instructors, and equipment to the Confederacy than any other college. Cadets were sought as drillmasters in camps from Louisiana to Virginia.[10]

While regular army units were being raised, men too old for duty, young boys, indispensable men, foreign subjects, and free Negroes organized themselves into local-protection companies. In the early months of the war it was not always easy to distinguish a local-guard unit from an army unit, but after the state militia was reactivated in the fall of 1861, the cleavage between the two became more pronounced.

On September 28, 1861, Governor Moore decreed that all citizens between the ages of eighteen and forty-five were subject to militia duty, and most of the independent home-guard companies were absorbed into the state militia. Only those home-protection units that were composed of foreign subjects or of men over forty-five could continue to exist.[11]

Citizen patrols were revived everywhere. Called by various names, "Home Defenders," "Vigilance Committee," "Home Guards," these special local-protection units policed the slaves and tried to prevent jayhawker raids. They stood ready to fight the enemy from within as well as without.

From the beginning numerous foreigners had rallied to the call to arms. Many of the companies leaving Louisiana in 1861 were composed largely of foreign-born troops. The French and Creole elements set the pace in volunteering for service. Other foreign groups followed, but with far less noise and ostentation. Irish and Germans outnumbered all others, but lacking funds, they attracted little attention to their service. However unheralded, the lowly Irishman and German contributed far more to the cause of the South than most of the richly attired French and Spanish troops who made a fine display on the parade ground but often absented themselves under fire.

One regiment of the Sixth Louisiana, the Irish Brigade, some eight hundred strong, was made up almost entirely of Irish laborers. In New Orleans patriotism was rarely the motive inducing these men to enlist. Out of work and fearing for the welfare of their families, they joined the Confederate ranks.[12] The same was true of a company from northeast Louisiana, the Madison Tips. Many of these Irishmen from the County Tipperary were employed on the levee, and in May, 1861, when a shortage of levee funds threatened them with unemployment, they enlisted. In Shreveport the Landrum Guards was organized in September, 1861, composed largely of Irish railroad laborers imported to build a railroad to Marshall, Texas, and left stranded by the bankruptcy of the contractor.

Another company, the Sons of Erin, citizens of Ireland living in Donaldsonville, volunteered for service in June, 1861. In Vicksburg, an Irish company, the Jeff Davis Guards, drew some of its enlisted men and officers from adjacent areas across the river in Louisiana.

During November, 1861, a new attempt to raise another Irish brigade in New Orleans resulted in the enlistment of six companies, each with an Irish officer. This group existed for local protection only.[13]

Like the Irish, the numerous German nationals helped to color many of the Louisiana regiments and companies. In April, the Protection Guards, composed of German volunteers, organized to help defend New Orleans. Another German company, the Blucher Guards, was formed for the same purpose. Shortly after the fall of Fort Sumter, a group of German gymnasts and athletes organized a military company eighty men strong. The National Guard, a German volunteer company from Baton Rouge, came to New Orleans to await muster into Confederate service. In September, the Florence Guards, made up of German merchants, brokers, and clerks of New Orleans, were in training to strengthen local protection. The German citizens of Shreveport began in July to raise a military company, the Shreveport Rebels.

Because German loyalty was generally distrusted, no purely German regiment was admitted into Confederate service from Louisiana. The Twentieth Louisiana, with its six German and four Irish companies, most nearly answered as a German regiment. Other regiments having strong German representation included the Tenth Louisiana, the so-called Polish Brigade, and the Avegno Zouaves of the Thirteenth Regiment.[14]

New Orleans, where most of Louisiana's foreign born resided, furnished most of the foreign companies for the Confederate service and for local defense. In addition to the Irish and Germans almost every nationality made its contribution. As early as January the Italians of the Second District enrolled over 270 men in the Garibaldi Legion. Italians, too, made up a large segment of the Zouave-uniformed Thirteenth Louisiana Regiment, along with other foreign nationals. Other regiments, such as the Louisiana Zouaves, contained many battle-scarred veterans of the Italian wars. The Tenth Louisiana, which also saw active Confederate service, carried a number of Italian men on its rolls.[15]

It was the French, however, who made the greatest show of their patriotism. By early June the French Legion had already raised five companies. Later, internal strife and social discriminations caused some of the companies to withdraw from the Legion and to establish separate units for local defense. French nationals joined with their brother Creoles in the Louisiana Zouaves, the Polish Brigade, the Spanish Cazadores, and the Tenth and Thirteenth Louisiana regiments.[16]

Less numerous foreign groups also contributed to the defenses of Louisiana. The citizens of Greece formed a company in New Orleans in May. Wearing the national Albanian uniform—Zouave jackets and long, tight underpants with short flared skirts—this group added color to the military parades of the city. As early as April the Spanish joined the growing list of foreigners who were organizing troops. By fall a company of Cubans joined with the Spaniards and formed the Spanish Legion. To the list of foreign companies serving Louisiana in 1861 was added the Scandinavian Guard, the Scotch Rifle Guard, the Belgian Guard, and two companies of Slavonian Rifles.[17]

Although there were only eighty-seven male citizens of Poland residing in New Orleans,[18] in May Major G. Tochman came to the city from Richmond and asked for volunteers for the Polish Brigade. The two regiments of the Polish Brigade, when they left for Virginia in August, were made up primarily of Irish, French, Germans, and a few Americans.[19]

The British were divided in their loyalties, and only one local-protection company, the British Guards, was raised in 1861. Some of the stronger pro-Southern British citizens joined other national companies and fought for the Confederacy, but others were forced to enlist in active companies against their will. The English correspondent William H. Russell visiting in New Orleans reported in the London *Times:* "British subjects have been seized, knocked down, carried off from their labor at the wharf and forced . . . to serve" as volunteers. The British consul, William M. Mure, stated that over sixty impressed British subjects had asked him for assistance. After bitter protests from the consul, Governor Moore discharged all British citizens and publicly condemned impressment of foreigners, proclaiming that any company formed in this way would not be allowed to serve.[20]

In Baton Rouge, Captain H. B. Favrot began a muster of free colored men, and by April 25, 1861, he had enlisted some thirty Negro recruits. A group of free Negroes of Pointe Coupee Parish formed a military company for service with the state or the Confederacy. In April, 1861, the free Negroes of New Orleans began to organize colored military companies and battalions, sanctioned by the state government. These troops soon were taking part in military reviews in the city. By early 1862 there were more than 3,000 members of colored military organizations. This is a surprisingly large number, as the entire free colored population of the state in 1860 was only 18,547, nearly 11,000 of whom lived in New Orleans.[21]

In the Crescent City free Negroes were granted more privileges than elsewhere in the South. They held many of the best jobs in the skilled trades. They were carpenters, metalworkers, stonemasons, tailors, and caterers. White laborers were jealous of the prestige and ability of these Negroes and often refused to work with them. Other free Negroes were physicians, merchants, planters, and barbers. Some of the wealthier free Negroes owned slaves. A city newspaper reported that these Negroes "have no sympathy for abolitionism, no love for the North. . . ."

The free Negro had his reasons for offering his services to his state. He felt a strong local patriotism, and he wanted to hold on to what he already possessed—his property, in some cases wealth and slaves, his job, and his measure of freedom. Perhaps as a token of appreciation, no further restrictive legislation was passed on a state-wide basis against the free Negro.[22]

Secession and war hysteria had their effects in New Orleans, however, where controls were tightened over the free colored population. Many free Negroes were arrested and accused of spreading "incendiary sentiments" among the slaves. Colored churches attended by Negroes, both free and slave, held services under the supervision of a white slaveowner and a policeman. Later this guard was increased.

Despite the fear that the free Negro might incite a slave insurrection, Governor Moore legally enrolled the "Native Guard" as part of the state militia. However, as had been true from the beginning, Negro troops were considered fit only to serve in the enlisted ranks; they must be officered by white men. Social delicacy alone foredoomed the commissioning of Negro officers.

Inasmuch as the nature of the Confederate government prohibited the enlistment of Negroes into regular service, the free Negro gave of his time, effort, and money to Louisiana. Most of the Negro companies provided their own uniforms, rifles, and equipment, sparing the state this burden. Their benevolence, their neat uniforms, and their well-drilled ranks were applauded by New Orleans citizens.[23]

Occasionally one or two Negro slaves accompanied their owner to camp and to the battlefront. Kate Stone reported that in May her two brothers departed from Madison Parish carrying the houseboy, Wesley, to wait on them in the army. The Bossier Volunteers, from the parish of rich plantations, joined the Ninth Louisiana Infantry in July carrying nine slaves with them into the service.[24]

To persuade more men to volunteer, small bounties were often given. In April, 1861, five dollars was offered any man joining a Louisiana regiment, plus two dollars for each friend he induced to enlist. The Marine Corps offered ten dollars, and the army had to raise her payments to the same amount. As the war wore on and volunteers became less plentiful, bounty payments rose higher because of wealthy planters who wanted to raise a company, or a parish police jury that was anxious to fill or exceed its quota. More affluent parishes competed with each other for recruits. To fill vacancies from death, disease, and discharge and thus keep under-strength units intact, recruiting officers visited their home state offering handsome inducements. As money became more scarce and the financial burden too great, many police juries had to abandon the bounty system.

Fraudulent enlistment and bounty jumping were not uncommon. Men joined military companies under aliases and collected multiple bounties. One German who tried this trick was highly successful for a time, but after collecting bounties from several companies he was caught, stripped of his clothing, smeared with tar, covered with cotton, and then released.

It was not until December, 1861, that the Confederate government stepped forward with a bounty plan of its own. A sum of $50 was to be paid all men who had enlisted for three years and all who would volunteer for three years. Few men wished to commit themselves for such a long period, so the response was disappointing. Early the next year the Confederate Congress reduced the time to twelve months for all re-enlistments.[25]

Financially the state of Louisiana was in no position to support the ever-increasing numbers of military companies then forming. The sum of $500,000 that the state legislature had transferred to the military from its levee fund [26] was far from adequate.

Beginning in March and April, 1861, private citizens, city councils, parish police juries, and organized clubs and aid societies came forward with liberal contributions to make up the deficit. To ready the Washington Artillery for Confederate service the citizens of New Orleans and several large business houses contributed $7,000. Up in the small town of Clinton, the people generously subscribed $12,000 to support volunteers' families. The board of trustees of Shreveport met on April 17 and approved the issue of $4,500 in bonds for unusual expenses of the Caddo Rifles. In August, 1861, the city council of New Orleans presented General Twiggs with $100,000 with which to build up the defenses of New Orleans.

On the whole, contributions from business firms in New Orleans and other places were small. Most New Orleans merchants gave money for local protection but were loath to contribute much for troops destined for service outside the state. A happy exception in New Orleans was J. M. Allen and Company, which gave $2,000 to various military units of the city and gave several male employees leave with pay to serve in the army. One lucky company, the Glenn Guards, was sponsored and supported by the firm of L. W. Lyons and Company. A dry-goods house, C. Yale and Company, fully equipped the Crescent Blues for the field. Haggerty and Brothers offered to equip any young man for service if he could not afford to do so himself. Occasionally business houses acted as solicitors and business managers for new companies trying to get outfitted. Brown, Fleming and Company took over this task for the Planters Life Guard, accepting money, molasses, sugar, and marketable produce to finance the company.[27]

The local police juries rendered great assistance to the early war effort. In April the Concordia police jury appropriated $10,000 "for the purpose of arming and equipping such military corps as may be raised in this parish" and agreed to help needy families of volunteers. In October the jury voted over $4,000 to aid the Concordia Rifles, $600 to the

Concordia Star Guards, $3,000 to the Concordia Cavalry, and additional funds to aid womenfolk left destitute by "their men going to war." In October $2,000 was set aside to raise another company. By March, 1862, needy families had been provided with $40,000.[28]

To furnish more funds for Avoyelles Parish volunteers, the police jury began to issue script in denominations of $10 to $50, for a total of $5,000. Two companies raised in the parish were fully equipped with the money thus provided. New taxes brought an additional $10,000 for

LOUISIANA
1861-1865

new companies. From this, $40 was to be furnished each infantry soldier and $75 to each cavalry volunteer. Any soldier's wife or mother who was in need would be given $5 per month. To the Creole Chargers, $2,500 raised through the sale of bonds was presented in October, 1861. The jury also appointed a committee to distribute to the parish poor the corn and rice being sent by Governor Moore to parishes throughout the state.[29]

Parishes in northwest Louisiana did not lag far behind. The Bossier

Parish police jury in July, 1861, voted $35,000 for the benefit of her volunteers and their families. A month before, De Soto Parish gave $2,000 to the De Soto Blues to buy uniforms and munitions. A company of "highlanders" raised in Keatchie moved the parish jury to donate $1,500 to their cause. Their unusual dress, kilts and plaids, purchased with this funds attracted much attention. Sabine, a poor piney-hill parish, met earlier obligations to her men by voting funds to the Sabine Rifles, Sabine Rebels, Sabine Volunteers, and Jordan's Company, and sent $500 to another company already departed for the front. Caddo, a rich "bottom land" parish, could well afford the $2,500 appropriated by the police jury in June to each volunteer company.

After the attack upon Fort Sumter, parish police juries in lower Louisiana increased their aid. Lafayette Parish in June gave her volunteers $6,000. Plaquemines Parish approved a gift of $10 to $15 per month for needy volunteer families. A sugar planter from Assumption Parish reported in July that the police jury had appropriated $1,000 to clothe parish volunteers. Another sum was provided to pay a company raised in April. By July, Carroll Parish, in the northeast, rich in cotton, had raised and equipped five companies, and her police jury had agreed to support each man's family in his absence. Tensas, one of the richest cotton parishes, gave $16,000 to aid the state military organizations, agreed to assume the support of her needy, and presented each soldier with $20 per month. Police juries of many other parishes appropriated from $6,000 to $50,000 for equipping volunteers and for the relief of needy families of soldiers.[30]

Private citizens often helped organize, equip, support, and transport military companies. Planters, especially, were the first and largest contributors. Their reward sometimes was to have a company bear their names or to be elected captains. A. C. Watson, a cotton planter of Tensas Parish, provided one company of artillery with over $40,000. At his own expense another planter, M. D. H. Marks, raised and supplied the eighty-two men of the Twiggs Rifles, giving each a bounty or bonus of $10 before they left New Orleans. Two wealthy planters from the Lafourche region, Robert A. Pugh and J. M. Davidson, financed an entire company. Scott's Cavalry, composed of men from several parishes, was one of the most heavily endowed regiments, receiving some $500,000 largely from planters. Many planters rich in land and slaves were poor in liquid assets. For these patriotic would-be donors mortgages were easily arranged. Not all of the planters were benevolent.

In areas all over the state a certain few gave little or nothing to further the war effort.

Other individuals who were not plantation owners aided the cause with donations or service. Thomy Lafon, a free Negro real estate agent of New Orleans, contributed $500 to aid the Confederate army. Two steamboat captains operating on the Red and Mississippi rivers between New Orleans and Shreveport furnished the Shreveport Grays and the Caddo Rifles with free transportation to New Orleans. Paul Tulane, who had been born in New Jersey but had amassed his fortune in the South, gave more than any other single individual. Many families of Confederate soldiers received liberal donations, and he left no appeal from Confederate prisoners unanswered.[31]

Organized private philanthropy, usually under the direction of patriotic women's groups, greatly assisted in providing for a better equipped army. Sewing societies, fairs, bazaars, auctions, balls, picnics, and concerts raised funds or provided clothing and equipment for soldiers and for their needy families.

The women of New Orleans were determined to do their share in promoting an early victory. They organized sewing societies and worked diligently carding lint, making bandages, and sewing for soldiers. Women who were unable to work away from home were allowed to take cloth and unfinished clothing home with them.

A bazaar organized by the elite of New Orleans opened in April, 1861, at the St. Louis Hotel. Sèvres china, fine furniture, jewelry, groceries, and other offerings were donated. More than $60,000 was collected and was used to purchase sewing supplies. The ladies cut out garments for the soldiers and hired hundreds of poor women to do the sewing.

In May of the same year, a Ladies Military Fair was held in Odd Fellows Hall of New Orleans. Citizens thronged the place and bid eagerly for sewing machines, food, piecework, ponies, and grand pianos. This charitable enterprise cleared $12,000, which went to outfit a military company.

On July 4, 1861, a picnic to raise funds for the soldiers was held in City Park. Large crowds, including several military companies, attended the festivities, and the affair continued for three days.[32]

The German Society, or *Gesellschaft,* originally organized to assist German immigrants but now dedicated to the war effort and war relief, began a monthly subscription system to aid needy families of soldiers. The society sponsored theater performances and fairs, and its

annual May festival, the *Volksfest,* was dedicated to raising money
for the needy. Germans drank beer, listened to speeches, danced,
watched buggy races, ate good food, and enjoyed athletic exercises.[33]

Sewing societies remained popular in the city. Of these, "The Society
of Ladies in Aid of the Confederate Army" worked hard each day at
the YMCA, turning out uniforms. Forty patriotic women gave of
their time and effort to help clothe city volunteers.

A committee called "Aid to Volunteers' Families" solicited funds
throughout the city of New Orleans. By mid-July this group had collected $7,469.30, used to give a dole of $10 per month to needy working-
class families.

The initial relief system maintained by volunteers was soon to break
down. On August 1 funds were exhausted, hungry women milled
around the relief office on Gravier Street, and a mob of three hundred
women marched on city hall. Mayor John T. Monroe promised that
the city would take immediate action. Plans to open a free food market
were pushed, and $10,000 was provided. By August 16 a relief center
was opened in the waterworks building at the foot of Canal Street
near the river.

Every effort was exerted to make the free market a success. Grocers,
bakers, butchers, and planters added their products to the money collected from the many charitable organizations, and volunteers from
New Orleans' finest families helped to distribute them. Steamboats
brought fresh food and vegetables from the outlying farms. About
twice a week over 1,800 poor families were issued rations, including
loaves of bread, molasses, beef, salt mackerel and codfish, rice, and
corn meal. Many of the ladies and gentlemen came to work as early
as two-thirty in the morning, and by eight o'clock most of the people
had been served.

To keep the free market going, fund drives were continuous. The
patriotic German Society in October donated $1,000. A "Free Gift
Lottery Association" was established, and this group boasted of a clear
profit of nearly $60,000 by February, 1862. Lower Louisiana parishes
were visited, and nine of them donated food. The free market continued to operate until May 1, 1862, when Federal forces occupied
the city.

To render direct aid to soldiers already in the service, an association of twenty-five gentlemen opened a dispensary at 58 Gravier Street
to collect and distribute supplies for wounded Confederate soldiers. A

group of Crescent City ladies formed a Soldiers Aid Society to send articles of clothing and delicacies to the men in camp.[34]

Organized aid to soldiers and their families was by no means confined to New Orleans. All over the state patriotic citizens pooled their efforts and resources for this worthy cause. In May the Ladies Society of Baton Rouge asked all of the women of the parish to help make clothes for the volunteers. A rival patriotic group in the same city, the Campaign Sewing Society, also made soldiers' uniforms, using cloth from a factory inside the state prison. In late August, the ladies of West Baton Rouge, across the river, formed a sewing society to make clothing for volunteers.

Following the precedent established by the ladies of New Orleans, the Campaign Sewing Society of Baton Rouge sponsored a bazaar or fair, called a "Tombola." The ladies filled a large hall, a warehouse, and a stable with items ranging from pencils to pianos. Tickets selling for one dollar each entitled the holder to one prize. Over six thousand dollars' profit was realized, but before the money could be used, Union forces had occupied Baton Rouge.

Baton Rouge also opened a free market. A concert by local talent held on July 4 in the rotunda room of the state capitol swelled the relief funds. In December the ladies of the city gave a tableau to raise additional money for volunteers.[35]

The women of Shreveport and vicinity labored long hours over their sewing machines to provide their men with adequate underclothing and uniforms. After the excitement of Fort Sumter, there was a great rush to get the volunteer companies ready and off for New Orleans. On April 16, when the steamboat *Louis D'Or* carrying the Shreveport Grays left the city, all the uniforms were not complete. Ten patriotic ladies came aboard and continued to sew en route to New Orleans. At Alexandria, the governor's wife, Mrs. Moore, joined the ladies and won the admiration of all by her industry and charm.

Forming a Military Aid Society, the ladies of Shreveport requested donations of wool and cotton yarn for knitting socks. Joined by others, the Society collected blankets for the wounded and gave concerts and tableaux to raise funds. Tickets were sold for a diamond ring given by the mercantile house of Hyams and Brothers. In the small town of Bellevue, in the adjacent parish of Bossier, the Ladies Military Aid Society adopted the same functions as the society in Shreveport.

To celebrate the Fourth a "Series of Interesting Tableaux" was presented at the Gaiety Theatre in Shreveport to benefit the Shreveport Grays. In October the Shreveport Rebels at Columbus, Kentucky, were sent supplies bought with money raised by another tableau.[36]

At Oakwood Plantation, near Shreveport, Mrs. Alfred Flournoy, already busy running the plantation, looking after her children, and guarding the Negroes, found time to join with the ladies of Greenwood to sew "drawers for the soldiers." She wrote her husband, serving with the Second Louisiana Regiment, on August 4: "I have several of the women [slaves] drying peaches. A great many of our ladies are drying peaches for the soldiers. They will want something besides pork and beans." [37]

In other areas of northwest Louisiana the women worked equally hard. Early in December a concert of piano and vocal numbers was held at the St. Denis Ball Room in Natchitoches. The dollar admittance was to benefit the sick and wounded of the Third Louisiana. In the same month talented students of the Female College in Mansfield raised ninety-five dollars by presenting "Tableaux Vivants," followed by vocal and instrumental music. The money was to go to sick and wounded Louisiana men in Kentucky.[38]

Citizens of the central and southern parts of the state did what they could to bring an early victory. A planter in Assumption Parish on Bayou Lafourche wrote in his diary on July 9, 1861: "The Ladies held a meeting this afternoon to . . . plan. . . . The gentlemen provide the material and the ladies are to take charge of the clothing in making it up." The plan must have been successful, because Alexander F. Pugh reported on August 30: "I staid home today to attend to preparing the soldiers' clothes for packing." On September 2 he was still "packing the volunteer clothing."

Concerts by local talent in the late summer of 1861 proved popular with the people of Napoleonville. On August 28 a musical was given "to raise funds to provide shirts (woolen) for volunteers." On September 27 Mr. Pugh wrote, "We all attended the concert last night for the soldiers at Napoleonville. There was quite a jam, supposed to be about 200 persons." [39]

North Louisiana, in addition to sewing societies, also adopted the concert idea. In the summer of 1861 some of the concert and supper benefits held in Monroe brought in several hundred dollars.[40]

In Madison Parish on the Mississippi young Kate Stone wrote in her diary on August 24: "The ladies have organized a sewing society to meet at Goodrich's [Landing] . . . ," but cloth was so scarce that the society soon began knitting gloves for the soldiers. On September 10 Kate wrote, "We are leaving the ends of the fingers open so that they can handle their guns well." [41]

Sick and wounded soldiers were not forgotten. Benefits were held for them, and urgent requests were circulated for food, medicine, clothing, blankets, bedclothes, sugar, coffee, tea, rice, cordials, liquors, and wine. In August Governor Moore issued an appeal for blankets for disabled soldiers, and the response was enthusiastic. One zealous lady reported: "We have sent all ours except two thin ones." [42]

BLOCKADE AND
NAVAL PREPARATIONS

As A POSTSCRIPT to the Ordinance of Secession the convention stated: "We, the people of Louisiana, recognize the right of free navigation of the Mississippi River and tributaries by all friendly States bordering thereon; we also recognize the right of the ingress and egress of the mouths of the Mississippi by all friendly States and Powers. . . ." In February, 1861, the Confederate Congress passed an act embodying the same stipulations. Louisiana took over the collection of customs and in March turned over $147,519.66 to the Confederate government, the amount collected between January 31 and March 1, 1861.

The United States revenue cutter *Lewis Cass,* lying at New Orleans awaiting repairs, was seized by order of Governor Moore. A second Federal revenue vessel, *Robert McClelland,* was ordered from the lower Mississippi to the city and was turned over to state officials by the U.S. customs collector, Frank H. Hatch. This was the feeble beginning of a state naval force for the protection of Louisiana.

As the new Confederacy had no navy at all, Congress passed "the act to establish the Navy Department" on February 21, 1861. Naval stations for coaling, repairs, shipyards, and dry docks were a pressing need. In March, a commission was sent by the Confederate Navy Department to New Orleans to purchase or let contracts to build new gunboats. One member of the commission, Commander Laurence Rousseau, was appointed head of the New Orleans naval station. Rousseau spent his time planning how to convert river boats into gunboats, and searching for materials suitable for this purpose.[1]

President Lincoln, after the surrender of Fort Sumter, proclaimed that "an act of insurrection against the Government of the United

States has broken out . . . , and the laws of the United States for the collection of the revenue cannot be effectively executed therein. . . . Now, therefore, I, Abraham Lincoln, . . . deem it advisable to set on foot a blockade of the ports within the states aforesaid. . . . For this purpose a competent force will be posted so as to prevent entrance and exit of vessels from the ports aforesaid." This blockade embraced all of the seceded Southern states from South Carolina to Texas and later was extended to include North Carolina and Virginia.[2]

Lincoln was on the offensive. Every inlet through which Southern cotton and other products could be sent must be bottled up. No materials of war, no manufactured goods from abroad would be allowed to enter. Movement up the Mississippi from the Gulf, accompanied by a simultaneous expedition from above, would be made. Controlling the sea and the Mississippi would result in a quick suppression of the insurrection.

On May 8 the United States took the first step in putting a portion of the plan into action. The head of customs at Louisville, Kentucky, was ordered to prevent shipment of arms, ammunition, and provisions to the seceded states through Louisville. Thus, it was the United States that was first to interrupt the free navigation of the Mississippi River.[3]

The Confederate Congress approved a bill on May 10 to sever all trade with the United States. Northern factories were to be ruined for want of Southern cotton. Countries of Europe, especially England and France, who heretofore had bought most of their cotton through Northern brokers, would be vitally affected. In order to defeat the United States the South wanted to force England and France to support the Confederate cause. On May 20 an act was passed prohibiting the exportation of Southern products, especially "King Cotton," from any but Southern or Mexican seaports. The quasi embargo was to harm the South far more than those against whom it was aimed.

In July and August, 1861, cotton factors in New Orleans asked their customers not to ship any cotton to New Orleans until the blockade was removed, and early in the fall Governor Moore ordered that no cotton could enter the city after October 10. The cotton embargo was respected, and quantities of cotton already in New Orleans were even moved back to the plantations. But the "King Cotton" theory failed, for the 1860 crop had been unusually large, and both England and France had an oversupply of the commodity on hand.

In retaliation against Lincoln's proclamation, President Jefferson Davis asked privateers to prey upon all Northern shipping and drive it from the seas. Immediately, in New Orleans, stock companies with several hundred thousand dollars' capital were organized for this purpose. One privateer steamer, the *Calhoun,* staffed with a crew of a hundred and carrying several guns, left New Orleans on May 14 to cruise the Gulf area. The bark *Ocean Eagle,* out of Portland, Maine, was captured with its cargo of over 3,000 casks of lime valued at $24,000. A prize crew was put aboard and took the vessel to New Orleans. Continuing the hunt, the *Calhoun* shortly intercepted two other enemy merchant ships in the Gulf, taking 1,500 bags of salt and a cargo of fruit. Later the *Calhoun* was used as a blockade runner between Havana and New Orleans.

Three other privateers operating out of New Orleans were the *William H. Webb, V. H. Ivy,* and the *Music.* The *Webb,* a steamer turned gunboat, in May stalked and captured three Massachusetts whalers ninety miles off the passes. The *Music* and the *Ivy* were even more successful. Between May and August they seized five large, valuable merchant ships in the Gulf.[4]

New Orleans was destined to become one of the main targets of the Federal blockade. In the decade prior to the war, New Orleans was one of the world's busiest ports, second only to New York in volume of commerce. The season 1860–61 was a banner one. The river trade had reached its peak by 1860, at which time there were at least thirty-three different steamship lines to the city. River commerce amounted to $289,565,000, and ocean trade brought in $183,725,000, a total of nearly $500,000,000 for one year. Once the blockade was instituted, the total receipts shrank to $51,510,990.[5]

Commander Charles H. Poor, aboard the U.S. steam sloop *Brooklyn,* arrived off Pass à l'Outre on May 26 and immediately announced the establishment of a rigid blockade, allowing neutrals fifteen days to depart "with or without cargo." As there was insufficient water to take his vessel across the bar and no tug to pilot him through the unfamiliar pass, Poor kept the privateers at bay in the river.

To maintain a legal and effective blockade of the Mississippi River passes at least four vessels were needed. The *Brooklyn* could guard only one, the Pass à l'Outre, and the *Brooklyn* itself was so short of enlisted personnel and officers that its own efficiency was impaired. Commander Poor begged for reinforcements.[6]

Lieutenant David Dixon Porter, commanding the *Powhatan,* was sent from Mobile to the Mississippi by Captain W. W. McKean, and on May 30 the *Powhatan* took up station at Southwest Pass. Like Poor,

Porter complained of the shortage of men. Never a stickler for going through channels, Porter wrote directly to Gideon Welles, Secretary of the Navy, pointing out that "the present allowance of crews . . . is for peace establishment and is not suited at all to times of war." On another occasion Porter wrote that coal for his own vessel was badly needed and, further, that small steamers of shallow draft were needed to make the blockade effective. From Mobile to the Mississippi there were numerous inlets that small craft could slip through and elude the larger Federal vessels. Westward from Southwest Pass as far as Berwick Bay blockade runners could easily bring their cargoes into Louisiana. A railroad from Berwick transported supplies and munitions of war from Southern ships to New Orleans. With the *Brooklyn* at Pass à l'Outre and the *Powhatan* at Southwest Pass, thirty-five miles apart, two small passes open to light vessels were left unguarded. Two steamers should be stationed at each mouth, suggested Porter.

State and Confederate authorities were not yet unduly alarmed by the partial blockade of the passes. However, another matter brought down the wrath of Major General Twiggs, commander at New Orleans. Union sympathizers daily were furnishing the "Black Republican blockading vessels" with fresh fruit, vegetables, fish, and meat, as well as late city newspapers. Twiggs therefore ordered that all boats passing down-river by Fort Jackson and the passes and Fort Pike, guarding the Rigolets entrance to Mississippi Sound, were to be stopped and searched. Newspapers were to be thrown overboard, and excess food was to be confiscated. Any person detected in communicating with the Union vessels was to be arrested and prosecuted.

Some forty commercial vessels, including several American merchant ships, were trapped in the mud, and the Confederate government gave permission to river tugs to haul them out and to tow them through the passes to the sea. By June 15 most of the vessels were over the bar, and the tugs scurried up the river out of sight.

"My Blockade duties now commenced in earnest," Porter wrote in his journal, and the deadly monotony of those duties soon wore upon his nerves. West of him, he could see the smoke of Confederate vessels in the vicinity of Barataria Bay, which meant that active trade from Texas to New Orleans was in progress. Lacking a second vessel to guard the pass, he could not move out to attack them nor to give chase to the Confederate privateers that occasionally dashed into the Gulf through one of the shallow passes and captured a Union merchant ship. Nor could he attack by moving into the river. The heavy draft of his ship kept him from crossing the bar to pursue Confederate vessels that tantalizingly appeared almost within his reach each day. Without coal and without assistance, the *Powhatan* remained at anchor, swaying limply to and fro with the tide. The *Brooklyn,* at Pass à l'Outre, was similarly handicapped.

Living conditions became more and more unbearable. Late afternoon winds blew swarms of voracious mosquitoes from the marshy delta toward the ships. Life was a stinging hell for the blockaders, made more miserable by the hot, humid climate. Thick fog often swirled in, blotting out all else. Occasional rain squalls, accompanied by awesome thunderstorms, temporarily relieved the enervating sultriness.

Near the end of June Captain Poor left his station to chase a small sailing vessel headed for one of the secondary passes some miles to the west. In his absence, a Confederate ship, the *Sumter,* appeared at the Head of the Passes. This was a former fruiter called the *Habana,* which had been converted into a Confederate raider at the shipyard in Algiers. Her commander, Captain Raphael Semmes, formerly of the United States Navy, took the *Sumter* easily through the dangerous waters of Pass à l'Outre and into the open sea. Sighting the escaping raider, the *Brooklyn* abandoned her lesser quarry, turned, and started after the *Sumter.* For over three hours the unwieldy blockader pursued the black Confederate ship, but the head start and superior speed kept the *Sumter* out of reach. Then as luck would have it, a sail appeared on the horizon and seemed headed for the *Brooklyn's* rightful station. Realizing that he had neglected his duty, Poor gave up the chase.

Lieutenant Porter condemned Commander Poor for his actions. Porter in his journal revealed a weakness he was to display many times: he belittled a superior officer. He often heaped undue praise upon a subordinate, but rarely could he find much to admire in a superior. Now he wrote, "Commander Poor was by no means a staunch loyalist, and actions since the escape of the 'Sumpter' have given no proof of energy or zeal in the cause of the Union. He has never, to my knowledge, been under fire nor has he sought in any instance, to place himself where he could do the government the least service."

On June 8, Flag Officer William Mervine arrived at Pensacola to take command of the Gulf Blockading Squadron, and a few days later Lieutenant Porter's frequent requests were answered. Mervine sent the *Massachusetts* to strengthen the river blockade. Porter now had a little more margin for action.

For seventy-six days the *Powhatan* lay off Southwest Pass. To break the monotony of blockade duty Porter had his men engage in gun practice.

Eventually Porter was relieved by Captain William W. McKean. With permission from his superiors, Porter set out on a long, fruitless chase of the *Sumter*.[7]

The Confederate naval command at New Orleans had not been idle during this time. Although he was hampered by lack of funds, Commander Rousseau had done everything possible to build up a naval fleet in the lower Mississippi. On July 31 he was replaced by Captain George N. Hollins, who was already popular in New Orleans. While cruising in the Gulf in his United States sloop of war, he had learned of secession and had brought his vessel to New Orleans, surrendering her to the Confederacy. He then offered his services to the South. Hollins energetically began to construct fire rafts and to place impediments in the river and other smaller adjacent streams. At the same time he undertook to convert river boats into ironclad rams and floating batteries.

At the shipyard three steamboats were rapidly turned into men-of-war to augment the pitiful naval fleet at New Orleans. The workmen stripped away the luxurious cabins and girdled the boilers with iron rails to protect them from enemy shot. Mounting four guns, three forward and one aft, these small ships were hardly the deadly weapons that were so badly needed. The *Livingston*, a queer, circular-shaped oddity, mounting six guns (three each, front and rear), was being designed and built exclusively for the navy. Its superior fire power, however, would be offset by its lack of speed. Along with the *McRae*, the *Ivy*, and the tug *Tuscarora*, these additional boats constituted the entire Confederate fleet in the lower Mississippi.

A seagoing tug, the *Enoch Train*, financed as a private venture, had been converted into a turtle-ram and rechristened the *Manassas* in honor of the first great Confederate victory. Her decks had been removed to the water line, and oak timbers covered with iron rails humped like a turtle's back made the *Manassas* a most singular vessel. Vulnerable twin smokestacks poked up near the center of the shell. A single stationary 32-pound gun pointed outward from a forward trap door, and the vessel was equipped with a strong underwater ram.

In September the Federal blockade gained a solid asset. Ship Island, off Biloxi, had to be abandoned by the Confederates because they were unable to keep it adequately garrisoned. General Twiggs sent Colonel

J. K. Duncan from Fort Jackson to effect the evacuation, which was completed on September 16.[8] Immediately the *Massachusetts* proceeded to the island, and a portion of her crew occupied the fort. This island proved to be a valuable base from which to break up the traffic of the small Confederate vessels plying between Mobile and New Orleans through Mississippi Sound.[9]

October was to be both a fruitful and disheartening month for the Federal blockaders. On the fourth, Flag Officer William W. McKean, who had recently replaced Captain William Mervine as commander of the Gulf Blockading Squadron, received a message from the U.S.S. *South Carolina* off Southwest Pass that two more Confederate schooners had been added to the Federal prize list. Both carried an English registry, but both were operated by Confederate personnel.

To tighten the blockade of New Orleans, the small Union boat *Water Witch* steamed over the bar and went up Pass à l'Outre to the Head of the Passes to reconnoiter. Equipment in a Confederate telegraph station was detached and removed, and the cable over the river was cut. Captain Hollins watched this maneuver but failed to drive the *Water Witch* out of the river. Early in October, four Northern vessels steamed up the river to establish the planned battery at the head of the Southwest and South passes. This Federal complement mounted a total of forty-seven guns. In the deep two-mile-wide bay formed by the river at the Head of the Passes, the Federal fleet could easily maneuver. Captain Hollins determined that he must strike before it was too late. The river must be cleared; the Union fleet must be driven from the Gulf if possible. The blockade must be lifted to allow scarce supplies to enter New Orleans.

Early on the morning of October 12 Captain Hollins was ready. Weighing anchor before Fort Jackson the Confederate squadron proceeded as quietly as possible down-river through the darkness. In the lead was the ram *Manassas,* followed by three tugs drawing fire rafts, the flagship *McRae,* and the armed tugs *Ivy* and *Tuscarora.* Following far behind were three more towboats, the *Calhoun,* with a vulnerable walking-beam engine, the *Jackson,* a noisy high-pressure paddlewheeler, and the unarmed *Watson.*

At the Head of the Passes, the Union flagship *Richmond* lay at anchor with a coal schooner tied up to her port side. A coal detail was busy transferring fuel to the *Richmond.* To the west the sailing vessel *Vincennes* rode at anchor, and to the east in haphazard fashion were the *Preble,* the *Water Witch,* and the schooner *Frolic.* Strangely enough, no picket boat patrolled the area, and in violation of security, lights burned aboard several of the vessels. No attack was expected, and no real precautions had been taken by Captain John Pope, commander of the expedition.

Passing the *Preble,* Lieutenant A. F. Warley headed the *Manassas,* under a full head of steam, directly for the *Richmond.* A few minutes later a grinding crunch echoed across the dark waters. Warley was handicapped by the poor visibility, so the point of impact fell partially against the coal vessel, which buffered the ram's blow. The schooner, cut from her moorings, floated free.

Bedlam now broke out. Aboard the *Preble* a beat to quarters was sounded, and sleepy-eyed men rushed to their stations. Immediately the crew of the *Richmond* answered the alarm and watched a signal rocket briefly illuminate the black river. Confused gun crews began to fire their pieces as rapidly as possible, and broadside after broadside blazed aimlessly in the night. A deafening roar filled the air.

Although the force of the *Manassas* had staved in the side of the *Richmond,* her own machinery was dealt a serious injury. Warley, with only one of his ship's engines operating, began to work his way toward the shore, while shot and shell fell thick around the *Manassas.* Suddenly a flare burst in the air above the turtle-ram. This delayed signal informed the rest of the Confederate flotilla that contact with the enemy had been made. From upriver small bright lights were seen approaching the Union fleet. The fire rafts which had been set afire were drifting rapidly downstream. Captain Pope now lost his head. To escape what appeared to be sure destruction, he issued orders to up-anchor and get under way.

The dread fire rafts loaded with pine knots blazed higher and higher, casting eerie, confusing shadows and lighting up the ships' sides. In the commotion the *Manassas* disappeared. The *Vincennes* and *Preble* fled down Southwest Pass. The *Richmond,* due to inept handling, fell broadside of the swift current and drifted helplessly down the pass. By some miracle the fire rafts missed her entirely. The *Water Witch,* refusing to run, easily eluded the blazing rafts and maneuvered in and out of the area for several hours. The rafts lodged against the western bank and soon burned out.

Dawn brought an amazing sight. The *Water Witch* was alone. The two fleets were running away from each other. The wounded *Manassas,* her twin smokestacks sheared away by the hawsers of the collier, had limped and drifted into the marsh, where she was gripped helplessly in

the muck among the willows. The fire-raft tug, *Tuscarora,* was fast
aground higher up. Without aid, the *Water Witch* feared to remain
any longer and followed the retreating Federal fleet down Southwest
Pass. Panic prevailed, and full retreat still held. The lead ship in the
exodus, the *Preble,* easily crossed the bar into the open Gulf. The
Vincennes, with her deeper draft, stuck on the bar, her stern pointing
up the pass. The helpless *Richmond* drifted onto the bar and stuck fast,
her broadside upriver. The other two vessels, the *Water Witch* and the
Frolic, easily cleared the bar and escaped.

Curiosity seized Captain Hollins. He arrested the flight of the Confederate fleet and turned down-river to investigate. Finding the Head
of the Passes free of enemy vessels, Hollins seized the coal schooner,
captured a free cutter containing small arms, and ashore burned a pile
of lumber that was to have been used in the construction of the Union
fort. Next he freed the *Tuscarora* from her mud prison. When the
McRae, the *Tuscarora,* and the little *Ivy* sighted the *Richmond* and
Vincennes floundering on the bar, they timidly moved part way down-
river and opened a long-range fire upon the grounded vessels.

Lieutenant Joseph Fry, commander of the armed tug *Ivy,* moved
in closer to the stern-grounded *Vincennes* and threw 32-pound shells
toward her cabin windows. Although his own ship's fire power
greatly exceeded that of the *Ivy,* Captain Robert Handy momentarily
lost his reason and ordered his men to abandon ship. Aboard the *Richmond,* the surprised gun crews hastily covered the *Vincennes'* boats as
they pulled away from the abandoned ship. Shells from the *Richmond*
engulfed the little *Ivy* with heavy spray, and she retreated to greater
safety.

Before his cowardly withdrawal, Captain Handy had lighted a slow
fuse leading to the magazine, but in his haste, her commander had
botched this task too, and the explosion never came. Captain Handy
was ordered to return to the *Vincennes* to defend her and get her
afloat if possible.

Captain Hollins realized that if the *Richmond* could free herself,
his entire small fleet would be no match for that vessel alone. About 10
A.M., after two hours of firing, he withdrew his ships from action and
proceeded upriver to the protection of the forts, where he dropped
anchor.

The Federal flotilla, free of danger, now rationally proceeded to
float its grounded vessels. Captain Pope lightened the *Vincennes* by
dumping most of her guns and munitions overboard. With the aid of

the *South Carolina,* ordered from Barataria Bay, both the *Vincennes* and the *Richmond* were extricated from the mudbank and hauled into the open waters of the Gulf.[10]

Morale reached a new low aboard the Union vessels. The United States navy, mounting some forty-seven guns, had been put to rout by a very inferior Confederate force. Captain Pope and Captain Handy were removed from command in disgrace. With the Confederates, morale soared to new heights. News of the victory at the Passes caused great jubilation in New Orleans. Citizens of the city expected the Federal blockaders to withdraw immediately.

The accolade enjoyed by Captain Hollins soon lost some of its luster when newspaper editors began to inquire why the Confederate commander had failed to follow the Union vessels into the Gulf, destroy them, or bring them to New Orleans as prizes.[11] Hollins, who had labored wearily in the face of countless obstacles to build up a fleet for the protection of the lower Mississippi and who had gallantly driven the superior Union flotilla from the river, was not to remain in New Orleans. A telegram from Secretary of the Navy Stephen R. Mallory summoned him to Richmond to serve on a court-martial. Louisiana and the river defenses thus lost one of their bravest and most resourceful officers.

The Federal fleet had suffered little physical injury and immediately set up a tighter blockade, keeping constant guard at the mouth of each of the passes. The alerted Gulf squadron was able to report three new captures of blockade runners in late November.

Despite the blockade, New Orleans had carried on some trade with Mobile and Havana via the lake, the Mississippi Sound, and other protected waters. In a ten-month period, more than three hundred vessels ran the blockade.[12]

In comparison with what had been, this was a lean showing, and the Crescent City suffered. One of the best accounts of this period can be found in the diary of Clara Solomon, a young Jewish girl residing in New Orleans. According to Miss Solomon, specie became scarce, and paper money flooded the market. Prices rose higher and higher. Ready-made dresses, cloth, and dry goods were very scarce. A cold snap in September, 1861, found New Orleans with a shortage of coal, and prices for this commodity, even when available, became exorbitant. Shoes for ladies were difficult to procure. In November, 1861, soap was selling for $1.00 a bar. The price of coffee rose to $1.25 a pound, and more people began to drink cocoa. Various coffee substitutes were tried, including dried, ground-up sweet potato, but they did not satisfy the caffeine addict.

Food became increasingly scarce. Clara Solomon's diet during June and July, 1861, included frequent meals of okra, soup, figs, and blackberries. Chickens were still available at a discount, but meat was scarcer. Fish and shrimp were still found in the markets. By September she was complaining of having only bread and molasses for supper. Bread was hard to find in the market, and flour prices soared. Fats, soap, starch, and candles were priced almost out of reach. Thousands of laborers, out of work because of the near-paralysis of trade, faced starvation. Enlistment in the army and food from the free market provided some relief for the poor. But everyone, rich and poor, was to feel the pinch of hunger before the year was out.

While New Orleans suffered, other areas of the state knew shortages too but not of food. North Louisiana had an oversupply of cheap corn and bacon that she wanted to sell in New Orleans. Inadequate transportation and faulty distribution were blamed for shortages in one area and an overstock in another.[13]

On December 7, the West Baton Rouge *Sugar Planter* suspended publication because of paper shortage but resumed it twenty days later, having foraged paper from various towns. Shortages of paper caused other newspapers to cut the number of pages, to reduce the frequency of appearance, or to cancel publication altogether. By early July the *Semi-Weekly Gazette and Sentinel* of Plaquemine was forced to go back to weekly publication, and in November the Shreveport *Daily News* became a semiweekly.[14]

Although prices were advancing in other parts of the state, they were not as high as in southern Louisiana. Shreveport, the gateway for supplies from Texas and Mexico, in November still could enjoy coffee at 40¢ a pound, whisky at $1.00 per gallon, flour at $3.00 per hundred, corn at 55¢ a bushel, sugar at 8¢ per pound, and salt at $4.50 a sack. Community commodities such as fruits, bacon, corn, and vegetables were especially plentiful and cheap. Cheap flour was brought in from recently established Texas mills.[15]

Banking in Louisiana, and especially in New Orleans, was founded on strong principles, using elastic, but well protected, currency. When secession came, there were no banks in America stronger than those of New Orleans.

After secession the banks restricted loans and made every attempt to increase their specie reserve. Practically all outstanding notes were recalled. Late in March the Louisiana convention passed an ordinance to safeguard and strengthen the banks of the state. According to this act notes must not at any time exceed three fourths of the total capital, and notes for less than ten dollars could not be issued. One third of all cash liabilities must be in specie and the rest in paper, payable in ninety days.

In the months that followed, coin money became scarce in New Orleans. People who owned specie refused to part with it, and "it was impossible to get change."

Governor Moore, in September, upon request from the Confederate Secretary of the Treasury C. G. Memminger, asked the banks of New Orleans to suspend specie payment as soon as possible. He urged that all banks issue Confederate treasury notes just as they would currency. By December, most of the banks had complied with this request.

Gold and silver disappeared, and Confederate paper money became the currency. Adding to the confusion and promoting the depreciation of money, the state, New Orleans, and several other towns had their own paper issue. The New Orleans city council allowed business firms to issue checks and certificates, or "shinplasters," a practice that led to inflation. Many merchants refused to accept shinplaster until the council forced them to do so. Butchers and drinking-house keepers led in the issuing of shinplaster. Car tickets, printed tokens, and other printed scraps served as five-cent pieces and other small change.[16]

In the field of industry, the war-imposed blockade worked in two directions. On one hand, it sapped the flow of many raw materials and finished products into the state; on the other, it encouraged the development of new industries. Had the blockade been less effective and had New Orleans been able to withstand capture, manufacturing might have developed even more.[17]

Captain David Porter, who had gone off on the wild-goose chase of the *Sumter,* returned to Pensacola shortly after the engagement at the mouth of the Mississippi. Important news awaited Porter; his long-desired promotion to commander had arrived. His ship, the *Powhatan,* now in poor condition, was dispatched under Porter to New York for necessary repairs. While awaiting his ship, Commander Porter visited Washington and laid his plans for the capture of New Orleans before the proper authorities.

The arguments presented by Porter were favorably received by President Lincoln, General George B. McClellan, and Secretary of the Navy Gideon Welles. Gustavus V. Fox, Assistant Secretary, was assigned the task of providing the necessary ships for the New Orleans expedition.

When Captain David G. Farragut was suggested to lead the expedition, doubts as to his loyalty were voiced. After all, he was a Southerner by birth, residence, and marriage. Could he be trusted? Porter argued in his favor, and since Porter was to play a conspicuous part in the scheme, Farragut was accepted.[18]

V

THE PACE QUICKENS

FROM SEPTEMBER to the end of 1861 troops continued to pour into Louisiana's mustering areas and to depart for the theater of war. Feelings of "uneasiness and apprehension" over a possible Federal attack were felt throughout the state. A. B. Roman, writing to Jefferson Davis on September 15 from New Orleans, stated:

It is generally admitted that we are not now prepared to offer . . . an efficient resistance. Our militia, with the exception of a few volunteer corps, are not disciplined. They can hardly be considered as organized. As we have no muskets to give them they will have to use such shotguns as they can procure, and could scarcely get at the present time powder enough to fire a few rounds. If you except the two forts above the entrance of the Mississippi, there is not a single fortification on our coast which can withstand a coup de main. Preparations for their defense are now undertaken which ought to have been completed long ago.[1]

In a letter to the President, dated September 20, Governor Moore also revealed fears of an imminent invasion. "I am now endeavoring to organize the militia of my state in order that we may be in some state of preparation for an attack." The governor then requested that young, vigorous, and able officers should be sent to aid in these preparations.

Writing to acting Secretary of War Judah P. Benjamin on September 22, Moore again requested able officers, and he begged to keep more of his troops at home to help protect the state. "I am anxious for saltpeter. I am alarmed to death for want of powder. . . . we could fight but a short time with present supply." Benjamin answered a part of the request on September 25. He ordered ten tons of saltpeter from Augusta and one hundred barrels of cannon powder from Nashville to be sent to New Orleans. Earlier General Twiggs had acknowledged receipt of ninety-five guns sent by the War Department from Norfolk. He expected thirty-two more to arrive.

The worried governor resumed his protests against the weakening of state defense in a letter to Benjamin on September 29: "I have about 3,500 men in camp . . . and have not arms for them all. I am now sorry that I ever sent off so many, as they, with the volunteers who took them off, are so occupied I fear I shall not get them back when needed." Governor Moore then complained that General Twiggs was too old to command his post, being unable to visit and inspect the various fortifications and works. The letter continued: "Is the Government doing anything to clothe and shoe our troops? I do not learn that it is. I have sent a suit of clothes and underclothes, blankets, and shoes to our regiment in Missouri, and blankets for our entire force in Virginia, and clothing for the First and Second Regiments, with shoes also for the whole force, but provisions ought to be made for another pair of shoes. . . ."

When Moore saw that the Confederate government would not, or could not, send aid to Louisiana, he set to work to reorganize and strengthen the state militia. On September 28, an order was issued to the militia commanders to proceed immediately with the organization of an effective militia. A census was to be taken of all men between the ages of eighteen and forty-five subject to militia duty. To prevent Confederate recruiting officers from raising men without proper authority there would be no recognition of volunteer companies not authorized by Governor Moore. Only subjects of a foreign government and men over forty-five could form companies for service limited to a parish, town, or city. In the First Division, located at New Orleans, daily company drills were to be held after 3 P.M., and strict order and military discipline would be maintained. Battalion or regimental drills were ordered at least once a week. The other four divisions of the militia were to conduct company drills at least twice a week and battalion or regimental drills at least three times a month. Men who shirked their militia duty would be subject to a fine.[2]

The governor's militia order was rapidly carried out. Local units sprang up overnight. Those Creoles and "Cajuns" who heretofore had displayed no degree of patriotism were now forced into militia service.[3] Previously organized home-protection units increased their drill calls and improved their entire training schedules. Absenteeism was far less than before. So great was the response that as of November 22 the adjutant general reported that 31,251 men were enrolled in the state militia.[4]

Although fewer volunteers were entering Confederate service, there was by no means an end to those seeking immediate service in active theaters. Among the new companies either organized or mustered into the army was Benjamin's Cavalry Regiment. An entire battalion made up of men from Baton Rouge and its vicinity was in training early in November. Two companies, the Natchitoches Guards and the Chasseurs à Pied, had become so expert late in the same month that they were out on parade. Earlier, the Claiborne Grays, organized in Claiborne Parish, had brought eighty men to Camp Moore, where they were joined by thirty men from other parishes and entered Confederate service as a part of the Nineteenth Louisiana Regiment, which was made up primarily of men from Caddo and De Soto parishes.[5]

The response to the call for troops had been truly amazing. According to figures published in one newspaper, by November Louisiana had already supplied 280 companies for Confederate service. Of these 29,000 men, over 20,000 had been enlisted in New Orleans. Some 18,000 Louisianians were now serving on scattered battle fronts throughout the South. Figures released by the adjutant general on November 22 do not tally with the newspaper. According to this report, 20,202 troops had been organized by the state and another 3,375 had independently volunteered for Confederate service, making a total of 23,577. These figures do not include the 1,000 men volunteering for naval service.[6]

Outfitting so many troops and compensating for the lack of imports gave great impetus to the development of local industry. Many old industries began to expand, and new ones arose. Mass production was introduced in the manufacture of civilian and military clothing, including shoes. Iron foundries extended their facilities and began to manufacture cannon, cannon carriages, small arms, and other weapons of war. Other groups showing marked increases in plants, employees, and production in 1861 were the breweries, the sugar refineries, the ship builders, the carriage and wagon manufacturers, confectionary and chocolate shops, sailmakers, brass foundries, and rum distillers.

Several industries showed marked decreases. The shortage of flour forced many bakeries to suspend operations, and soapmakers were driven out of business by lack of grease. Millers deprived of their wheat supply turned to grinding corn meal and grits or closed shop.[7]

In response to military demands a number of the older shops expanded their facilities, and several new and larger clothing establishments were organized. One concern in New Orleans, which had formerly made rough cotton and wool plantation clothing was by June, 1861, employing 130 people and had already furnished the army with three thousand uniforms and an equal number of knapsacks. Another, on St. Charles Street, which made clothes for male civilians, boasted that it could manufacture enough uniforms in one day to clothe an entire military company. The Confederate States Clothing Manufactory, in addition to manufacturing clothing for citizens and slaves, made uniforms to order in any desired lots. Those who wished to make their own tailoring arrangements could buy quantities of blue and gray cloth and wool yarn. Shops that had once been entirely devoted to the manufacture of civilian wearing apparel were flooded with military orders.[8]

Another change in the field of manufacturing of men's clothing was that increasingly more women were employed to replace male workers now in military service. Many women who entered the factories were indigent and anxious to work. Several companies hired scores of females to manufacture drawers for the soldiers. They were paid $1.25 for each dozen pairs they made.[9]

To supply the thread and cloth to feed the clothing industry Louisiana had two cotton mills with 6,725 spindles and 150 looms, valued at over a million dollars. In 1860 these two factories were producing nearly two-and-a-half-million yards of cotton cloth each year, making Louisiana the sixth largest producer in the South. Louisiana had but one woolen mill, which turned out around fifty thousand yards of woolen cloth per year.

Louisiana led the South in the production of shoes. Virginia, the second highest state, produced only about half as many. Shoemaking establishments were very small, employing from one to three workers each. An exception was the Southern Shoe Factory, established in New Orleans in January, 1861, in a three-story brick building. This factory, operated by steam, was an experiment in mass production. The superintendent and all the key workers were from the North. The Yankees demanded high salaries, from $60 to $300 a month, and the officials hoped to replace them with cheaper Southern labor as rapidly as local workers could be trained. Early in March, the factory employed 47 men and was turning out more than 250 pairs of brogans daily. One month later this concern had expanded so much that it occupied a second building located on St. Charles Street, and the quality of the shoes had been considerably improved. Because of the desperate need for army shoes, another shoe factory was established in New Orleans and was soon swamped with army orders, only a small part of which could be filled.

The manufacturers of machinery stood third in the order of industrial prominence. Two of the leading manufacturers of iron machinery were Leeds and Company and John Armstrong's Foundry and Boiler Manufactory. Until the very eve of secession, the fabrication of machinery was the only industry that approached the dimensions of even a small New England factory.

In 1861, the foundries manufacturing agricultural and industrial equipment began to divert many of their resources to the manufacture of war materials. The Leeds foundry reported on May 31, 1861, that it had already turned out several cannon and that its Saunders' rifled cannon, made from brass, was now in production. Another of the large iron manufactories to reconvert for war materials was the Shakespeare Iron Works. By June, still another foundry, Cook and Brother, had supplied arms to several of the outfits serving on the war front. Working in close conjunction with the foundries was the firm of Mulliken and Luster, which was awarded a contract to manufacture cannon carriages of white oak, "and other war appliances." [10]

Many obstacles stood in the way of casting heavy guns. Earth pits for casting proved impractical because any excavation in low-lying New Orleans soon filled with water. Expensive casings had to be placed in the pits to pump out the water. Another hindrance was the lack of suitable furnaces. Before the fall of New Orleans these problems had been largely solved, and several companies were ready to begin full production of heavy guns. Two 8-inch columbiads and two 10-inch mortars were completed, and a mold was ready for the casting of 10-inch columbiads.

Leeds and Company, the largest and best equipped establishment for the manufacture of guns, "was steadily employed for the Confederate States and the State of Louisiana from within a short time after the war began." The owners refused all civilian orders. Leeds devoted most of its time to making light guns and to manufacturing shot and shell. Before Federal occupation, the company succeeded in turning out a few heavy guns for the navy and at least one for the army. A number of obsolete smoothbore 32- and 42-pounders were rifled for the army. Two other New Orleans foundries, Bennett and Surges and S. Wolfe and Company, signed contracts for the erection

of reverberating furnaces and prepared to make 8- and 10-inch columbiads and 10-inch seacoast mortars.

Although the Confederate government did much to stimulate the
manufacture of arms in other sections, it paid little attention to Louisiana until General Mansfield Lovell took charge of the area in October.
Lovell stated:

Obtaining sulphur and saltpeter wherever it could be found, I pressed
to completion a large powder-mill . . . and soon commenced the manufacture of powder. Having arrangements made with foundries of New
Orleans for casting shot and shell, I proceeded . . . to convert one-half
of the new Marine Hospital into an arsenal, where I had a steam-engine
put up for driving the machinery, small-arms prepared and various implements, equipments, and munitions made for the service of heavy guns. A
cartridge manufactory was established, . . . which not only supplied my
department, but enabled me to send more than 1,000,000 rounds to the Army
in Tennessee.

On October 31, General Lovell wrote President Davis: "I have now
one mill in operation which will turn out 1,200 pounds per day, another which can make 1,500, and in two weeks hope to have a third in
full blast which will make 3,000 to 3,500 pounds per day." Two of the
powder mills were privately owned, and one belonged to the city. "We
will want all the saltpeter that can be had," begged Lovell. Powder
for a stockpile was still needed from the Confederacy.

The request for additional powder was answered by the War Department. Three steamers slipped through the blockade and brought
"a considerable quantity of powder," but it was all unfit for use; every
pound had to be remilled in the powder plants of New Orleans. Lovell
gave the navy 25,000 pounds, shipped 17,000 pounds to other departments, and sent 12,000 pounds to Richmond, "besides furnishing ammunition to all the troops sent to Gen. A. S. Johnston in Tennessee,
and giving the river-defense fleet what they required." [11]

On the night of December 28 the powder mill located in the Marine
Hospital, operated by Hobart and Foster, exploded. Eight thousand
pounds of powder was lost. The drying room and the powder cylinders
were a total wreck. At this time the mill was manufacturing over
4,000 pounds of powder a day. The owners planned to start rebuilding
immediately. The new powder mill that Lovell had purchased and
imported from Mississippi was being set up as rapidly as possible.

Shortly after the war began the shipyards switched from the construction of pleasure and commercial crafts to the building of ships for

military purposes.[12] Shipbuilders, hard pressed for time and proper materials, resorted to sundry improvisations. Using iron rails, chains, and hard oak they converted available merchant vessels into ships of war. Several new ships were planned. One of the new vessels was the *Louisiana,* begun in October, 1861. With her powerful engines and her size this ironclad was to have been the pride of the New Orleans fleet when completed.[13]

Jackson and Company, often known as the Patterson Foundry, was well equipped with the necessary tools, lathes, steam hammers, and foundry for the manufacture of marine engines. In September, Thomas Kirk, contractor for the firm, signed contracts for the manufacture of the machinery for a new, giant gunboat, the *Mississippi,* to be built in New Orleans. The designers and agents building the ironclad *Mississippi,* Asa and Nelson Tift, were faced by a formidable task. They had to enlarge a shipyard to accommodate such a large vessel; lumber had to be brought from a distance; and the foundries and metal shops had to make extensive changes to meet the need for ironwork for the new ship. Kirk's own mechanical knowledge was limited, and he had only seventy-five employees. Many delays occurred during construction. Lack of materials and the occasional calling of the workmen for drill with the militia made it impossible to complete the vessel.[14]

Although New Orleans contained most of the large industries in the state in 1860–61, she by no means had a monopoly on small industry. Many of the parishes had shoemaking establishments that could take care of a portion of the local needs. Throughout the state there were nine flour and corn mills, and this number would be greatly increased as war necessity dictated. Shreveport had two firearms shops that expanded later in the war. A woolen mill in Baton Rouge employed 60 hands. Jefferson Parish contained one cotton mill employing 40 workers, and Baton Rouge had one cotton mill, located in the state penitentiary, using an average of 200 male hands per year.[15] In 1861 a tannery and shoe factory was established at Shreveport to mass-produce needed shoes. In the summer of 1861 the Confederate government rented a large building in Baton Rouge, hired 150 mechanics, and prepared to manufacture cannon, tents, and hardware.

Salt, destined to become one of the most scarce items in the Confederacy, was fairly plentiful in Louisiana. At Price's Salt Works, near Dugdemona bottoms in North Louisiana, brine was pumped out by horsepower and boiled in sugar kettles over a large furnace. The residual was then dried and sold. The larger saltworks at Lake Bistineau in Bossier Parish were opened in November, 1861. Brine was taken from shallow wells and evaporated by the sun.[16]

On the military scene, Major General David Twiggs, as Governor Moore had previously stated, had long since proved ineffectual as the head of Department No. 1. The "Old Tiger" was tired. His once-proud figure was now racked with the infirmities of the aged. Confined to his office and to his quarters, his health would not permit active field duty. On October 5 he begged to be relieved of his command. Four days later Judah P. Benjamin accepted General Twiggs's request and stated that Major General Mansfield Lovell would be sent to take over command as soon as possible.

When the people of New Orleans learned that General Twiggs was to be replaced by Lovell, they expressed great dissatisfaction. Most of them wanted either Beauregard or Bragg to receive this appointment.[17] Braxton Bragg, in command of the Confederate forces at Pensacola, felt hurt that the authorities had passed over him. In a letter to Governor Moore on October 31, he complained: "The command at New Orleans was rightly mine. I feel myself degraded by the action of the government and shall take care they know my sentiments."

Bragg followed with another letter to Moore on November 14, in which he attacked the character of the commander of New Orleans. "Gen. Lovell is very competent, and but for his inordinate vanity would be a fine soldier. Still we could do as well without him and he can't make me believe he was not bought." [18]

Lovell arrived in New Orleans and assumed command of the department on October 18. The thirty-nine-year-old leader, a graduate of West Point and a decorated veteran of service with Taylor and Scott in the Mexican War, was well qualified for his position. In 1854 he had resigned from the army to join the abortive Cuban expedition led by General John A. Quitman. Just prior to coming South in 1861 he was serving as deputy street commissioner of New York City and as an instructor of artillery to the Old City Guard of New York.[19]

During a two-week tour of the department the new commander discovered how very little had been done to protect Louisiana. Beginning at once, Lovell requested a few competent officers to help him strengthen the defenses of the department. The request went unanswered. Appeals for mortars and columbiads to Colonel Josiah Gorgas, Chief of Ordnance, and to General Bragg at Pensacola received practically the same answer—"not a gun to spare." It was then that General Lovell contracted with local New Orleans foundries and mills for the manufacture of guns and ammunition. The one hundred obsolete navy guns General Twiggs had received a short time before from the Norfolk navy yard were so worn and old that they had to be reworked before being used. Lovell had carriages and chassis made, mounted the guns, and provided implements for their maintenance.

General Twiggs had planned and had begun a line of entrenchments around New Orleans, but he had not mounted a single gun, laid one platform, nor built a single magazine. The new commander pushed this work, and when completed, the line stretched some eight miles. It was thought that the city was impregnable to any land attack. The interior earthwork line mounted some sixty guns and was fronted by wide, deep ditches filled with water. Manning the line were 3,500 troops, and there were 6,000 well-armed and -drilled local defense troops who could be called in case of an attack. With enough provisions and adequate powder Lovell felt confident of holding New Orleans indefinitely.

The exterior line and the river defenses had been largely neglected too. To guard the many water approaches, existing forts were strengthened and additional forts were hastily built. Sixteen small forts were to mount some 240 guns of various calibers. In December there were 4,500 troops defending the outer lines.

Seventy-five miles below New Orleans and twenty-five miles above the Head of the Passes were two main forts, Jackson and St. Philip, guarding the lower river. Fort Jackson, on the west side, was a bastioned pentagon with a combined front of about 110 yards. The scarps built of brick were 22 feet high and surrounded by a wet ditch. An external earthwork water battery had been built to increase the fire power. Located in the center of the fort was a timber barracks, built to accommodate up to 500 men. To shelter the men from bombardment the casemates and galleries were largely bombproof.

On the opposite side of the river, about 700 yards above, was Fort St. Philip, very irregular in shape and occupying a quadrilateral space of about 150 by 100 yards. Whereas Fort Jackson was fairly strong, St. Philip was relatively weak. Two external water batteries helped to add to its range of fire.

Both of the forts were armed with guns of inferior caliber, which were replaced as fast as better guns could be readied. Between seventy-five and eighty guns could be brought to bear upon the river but could not stop a task force of gunboats from passing unless the boats could be kept for some time under the fire of the forts. General Lovell pushed forward the construction of a raft, started by General Twiggs, that would obstruct the river, leaving a single opening that would admit only one vessel at a time.

R. F. Nichols, a New Orleans merchant, was hired to procure all the available chains, anchors, and cordage in the city. Assisted by a number of seamen and stevedores, the merchant took mooring chains from all the vessels tied up before New Orleans. The boats were then secured with smaller chains and with cordage. Some difficulty was encountered with several parties who tried to hide chains by placing them in the holds of their vessels or by sinking them in the river. Lovell assisted by ordering all the large chains and anchors to be had in Pensacola, Savannah, and other points.

The obstruction, completed in December, 1861, was placed just under the guns of both forts. It consisted of forty-foot-long cypress trees placed four or five feet apart and held by two-and-a-half-inch chains and by large timbers. The raft was fastened to trees on the left bank by chains and to the treeless right bank to capstans and huge anchors buried deep in the ground and buttressed by heavy timbers. Additional anchors attached to large chains were sunk in the deep water and attached all along the raft to help hold it in place. A steamboat and a number of skiffs were employed to remove the driftwood that piled up behind the raft faster than it could be removed. As advised by General Beauregard, a long boom was built to stretch across the Mississippi above the forts to divert the drift through the opening, but it was never put to use because it was impossible to find enough chains and anchors to fix it in position.

Other important posts in the exterior line of defenses guarding various coastal inlets were Fort Macomb and Fort Pike, guarding the approaches into Lake Pontchartrain and Fort Berwick on Berwick Bay. Macomb and Pike, brick and earth fortifications, were sent additional men and guns, but the caliber of both was in question.[20] One officer complained, "The discipline is awful, in fact there is none." [21] Beginning at Calcasieu Bay at the extreme southwestern end and moving eastward, there were a number of very small earth and timber forts mounting few guns and manned by troops ranging from one company to a small regiment. Lovell attempted to guard the rich cattle and agricultural areas from foraging parties and from light-draft enemy vessels. Trees were felled into the bayous, piles were driven into the beds of the streams, and chains and rafts were utilized, where possible, to keep out Federal boats. No major invasion attempt was anticipated from these quarters. The Mississippi was the logical ingress, but General Lovell felt that with the completion of the two ironclads, with fifteen thousand troops in the area, and with the maintenance of the interior and exterior lines of defense he could withstand any force the North could send against him.

Louisiana felt secure at the end of 1861. The Federal fleet would never be able to pass the forts; a land force would easily be driven out.[22] The first Confederate Christmas was described as being gay, despite the absence of loved ones away at war. There were fewer toys and imported articles, and more worship and prayer. New Year's Eve found the "socialites" of New Orleans engaged in a charity lottery in the beautiful ballroom of the St. Louis Hotel.[23] Too soon the complacent citizens of New Orleans would suffer a rude awakening.

PART TWO

THE CURTAIN OPENS: 1862

THE THREAT

THE NEW year dawned, and with it the threat of invasion became a reality. Word reached New Orleans in late December that a powerful Federal fleet was anchored off Ship Island in Mississippi Sound. Some citizens felt uneasy, but others believed the city impregnable.[1] Despite the optimism of General Lovell and of a large segment of the people of the Crescent City, Louisiana was not prepared to withstand a major attack by Union forces, and in the North secret plans to seize New Orleans were being perfected.

In his strength report of January, 1862, for Department No. 1, Lovell reported only 8,240 regulars available for duty in Louisiana. These men were spread along the entire coastal line from Mississippi to Texas, with the greatest concentration near New Orleans. There were only 158 heavy guns to protect this long line.

Governor Moore, through his adjutant general, notified Judah P. Benjamin that Louisiana, having placed some 20,000 troops in the field, was left without arms with which to supply the needs of local defense units. Of some 15,000 militiamen, only about half were armed and armed only with "the most miserable and unserviceable arms known in the civilized world." As the state had been called upon to furnish another regiment to the Confederate service, Moore urgently requested that weapons be sent to these men who were now awaiting muster.

Governor Moore tried to quiet the fears of apprehensive New Orleanians with a brave military show on Washington's Birthday. Over 25,000 men were paraded, but only 6,000 were armed in any manner whatsoever. A few thousand carried rifles; a few wore pistols; some were armed with sabers; but the majority had no weapon of any description. General Lovell had protested against the parade, because he thought the people would be deceived as to the actual strength of the forces, and he was right.[2]

Urged by the governor, meanwhile, the state legislature set to work to improve the militia forces and to guarantee more dependable state protection. On January 23 a new militia act was passed, ordering all free white male residents between eighteen and forty-five capable of bearing arms to enroll in the state militia. Civil officials, ministers, druggists, and Confederate employees were exempt. Militiamen were to be enrolled in each parish and were liable to three months' service anywhere in the state except when emergency dictated a longer period, up to six additional months.

A storm of protests against their subjects' being ordered to duty outside New Orleans was voiced by the English, French, Spanish, and other foreign consuls. In answer to an appeal made by Governor Moore, Benjamin advised: "Foreign residents are bound to do duty in defense of the city which is their home, but the President does not deem it politic to insist on them serving outside of the city defenses." Governor Moore quickly assured the consuls that no alien militiaman would be sent from the city.[3]

Not all opposition to the militia law came from the foreign consuls. There were other protests, especially after the governor amended the act with his Order 191, exempting one white man on each plantation where there were slaves. Brigadier General R. B. Todd wrote from Bastrop on March 10 to Major General Lewis, head of the state militia, saying that in the several northern parishes within his command it would be next to impossible to organize a militia force. "The population . . . , with the exception of the two parishes lying west of the Ouachita River, consists chiefly of planters who are slaveowners, their sons, and the overseers on the larger plantations, the non-slave owners . . . comprising but a small class of the population." These parishes had already contributed heavily to the Confederate army both from the planter and the nonslaveholding ranks. General Todd objected to the exemption of one white man on each plantation. Such action would reduce the patriotic contributions of the nonslaveowner, destroy harmony, and display inequality and injustice toward the less fortunate. Since many of the plantations were very small and had only a few slaves, the suggestion that "one man could conveniently take charge of several" was proposed.[4]

Already in Madison Parish, in General Todd's brigade area, some of the small farmers and overseers were saying that "a rich man's son's too good to fight the battles of the rich." Despite inept officers, the lack of arms, and adverse criticism, however, the militia went on drilling during March in this parish.[5]

In early April over in the Tenth Brigade, embracing parishes in northwest Louisiana, mounting "disaffection and disloyalty" in Natchitoches and Sabine parishes had caused the formation of secret societies and clubs. Members of these organizations refused to co-operate with the state or national military effort and openly expressed a desire to rejoin the Union. Governor Moore ordered the brigade commander, John B. Smith, to arrest the ringleaders and send them to the state militia· headquarters.

Foreign response to serving in the militia was mixed. Among the British opinion was divided. An attempt was made in February to convert a company of British merchants called the British Guards into a brigade, but there was poor response. Another company, the British Fusiliers, worked hard for the protection of New Orleans. The British Neutrality Association, organized in February, announced that their members would not bear arms for any purpose.

French citizens residing in New Orleans had been forming local defense units since April, 1861, and by February, 1862, despite frictions and schisms, there were some 2,600 French volunteers serving in the city militia units.[6]

By March, 1862, the Spanish citizens had raised a regiment of troops called the Spanish Legion. Another regiment called the Spanish Cazadores, composed of three Spanish, two Slavonian, one French, and one Italian companies, prepared to protect New Orleans from invasion. The Defenders of Louisiana, with hopes of forming still another brigade, completed one company by early February but attempts to raise a second received such poor response that French, Italian, and Portuguese citizens were invited to join. One battalion of the Cazadores was so well advanced in its training by mid-March that the men were sent to Camp Chalmette, where they joined forces with regular state troops, the First Brigade, commanded by Brigadier General Benjamin Buisson. These troops had been sent at the request of General Lovell to protect the approaches of the city from below.

By February fear of Federal invasion drove the foreign-born citizens of New Orleans to organize the European Brigade, consisting of four regiments of infantry, one cavalry troop, and the French Guard, an independent company with a total of 4,500 men. Heading this group was Brigadier General Paul Juge, Jr. Before the actual invasion attempt was made, this group was joined by two other European brigades, one of French citizens and another of Spanish, German, English, Belgian, Italian, Scandinavian, and Dutch citizens, bringing the total up to around 10,000 men. Valuable service was rendered by the three foreign brigades before and after the capture of the city.[7]

In the lower parishes, near the coast, fear of invasion caused heavier stress to be placed upon militia or local defense companies than upon units to serve the Confederacy. St. Martin, a parish which had contributed few volunteers, had little trouble in supporting a battalion of four hundred men for state service. The vulnerable coastal parish of St. Mary spent large sums on a battalion of local militiamen but sent only three companies to the regular army.

Along with the response to the militia and the already generous contributions of men to the Confederacy, during the first four months of 1862 Louisiana continued to raise and to send new organizations to areas in more dire need. On January 12, the Opelousas Guards were to depart for Camp Roman to join the Eighteenth Louisiana Regiment. The John Brown Rebels of New Orleans, forming for active duty at about the same time, offered arms, clothing, equipment, and a bounty of $60 to all who would join the company.[8]

In addition to the $50 offered by the Confederate government, bounties were offered to volunteers who would join new companies. Aid to needy families of the volunteers became more popular. Iberville Parish, desiring to fill her quota, offered $10 to each man who would muster into Confederate service. Anxious to complete a cavalry company, St. Charles added a lure of $40. Avoyelles Parish offered $30 to each soldier who enlisted and $75 to each cavalryman. To ease the financial burden each wife was to receive $12 monthly and each other dependent $3 monthly. Sabine, a poorer parish already burdened by military financing, continued a bounty system and voted $7 to each mother and wife and $2 for each child of a volunteer. Money was also provided for equipping members of the local militia. Madison Parish, a rich cotton area, in March offered $80 to anyone joining one of her new national companies. An additional $15 was to be paid each month to the soldier's family. Wives and children of men serving the Confederacy from West Feliciana were to receive from $10 to $40 depending upon the size of the family.

Concordia, a planter-dominated parish, displayed unusual Confederate patriotism in early March. A handsome bounty of $100 was of-

fered to any man who joined one of three designated companies forming for the duration of the war. A bounty of $50 would be paid to
those joining either of two companies being raised in the neighboring
parish of Catahoula. A $50,000 bond issue was voted to finance the
bounty program. At another meeting of the police jury on March
12, $40,000 was appropriated for the relief of the needy families of
volunteers in the parish.

In New Orleans so many troops had been drawn away from the
city by March that the *Daily Picayune* was filled with offers of $50
for each man who would volunteer for as little as three months' service. To take care of the dependents, the city would give the wife $25
per month and $3 for each child.

Occasionally a man already in the service would try to get out by
hiring someone to take his place. A member of the Catahoula Grays
serving in Columbus, Kentucky, offered $100 to anyone who would
act as his substitute. After conscription went into effect, newspapers
advertised for substitutes. A wealthy New Orleans draftee offered
a bounty of $100 and a complete outfit to any man who would go to
Virginia and take his place with the Orleans Cadets.[9]

The Confederate government, which already was offering a $50
bounty to all who agreed to serve for the war, amended this provision
in February, 1862. Too many of the trained and seasoned troops who
had volunteered for short terms were being lost through discharge.
To keep more of these men, a $50 bounty was offered to all who would
re-enlist for twelve months.[10]

Among the many new military companies formed in early 1862 for
Confederate service were the Carrollton Guards of Jefferson Parish,
who were sent forward to join Beauregard. The Calcasieu Invincibles,
in training at Camp Overton in Opelousas, prepared to leave for New
Orleans and active duty early in April. In March two more companies,
the Caddo Guards and the Caddo Pioneers, left aboard steamers for
New Orleans, and the Caddo Confederates and Dixie Rebels were organizing. In the adjacent parish of Bossier, the Bossier Cavalry, eighty-
one strong, completed its organization in March.

Claiborne Parish, which, like Caddo, had already sent many companies out of the state, raised two new companies, one in March and
one in April. The latter company went into training at Monroe and
in June was sent opposite Vicksburg to guard the west bank of the
Mississippi. The company formed in March went to Tennessee. March
also saw two new companies organizing in Concordia. These com-

panies, Company C and Company F of the Twenty-Fifth Louisiana Regiment, left Vidalia a short time later by steamboat for service in Tennessee.[11]

Kate Stone of Madison Parish reported that there was great excitement up in the northeastern part of the state late in February. "Men are flocking to Johnston's standard. . . . They are not waiting to form companies, but are going to join those already in the field." As soon as these men could gather some semblance of military gear, they would go to the river, hail the first upriver boat, and be off to help their comrades at Nashville.[12]

On the opposite side of the state the McLaurin Invincibles left Natchitoches for New Orleans in March, and the Chasseurs à Pied were in training for active duty. The Prudhomme Guards departed early in April for the duration of the war.

In south Louisiana the Allen Rifles began organizing on February 22 and enjoyed an overwhelming success after the men were treated to a big barbecue, accompanied by an impassioned address by Pierre Soulé. The citizens of Thibodaux and of Lafourche Parish were so fired with patriotic enthusiasm that a second company was quickly formed.

Since the outbreak of hostilities one year before, the manpower contribution as well as the material gifts from Louisiana to the Confederate army had been amazing. From all parts of the state men volunteered their services. Carroll Parish, with a white minority, was able to raise and finance six companies. Madison, another riparian, fertile parish, gave unstintingly of men and money. By mid-February four official companies of Madison citizens were in the service.

East Baton Rouge, Orleans, Rapides, and Caddo parishes were able to send large numbers of men from their urban centers, but, in proportion, their contributions were hardly more striking than those of other areas. Baton Rouge had sent eight companies, and New Orleans had furnished some one hundred and thirty companies. Alexandria and vicinity raised twelve volunteer infantry companies and two cavalry companies, and Shreveport and other towns in Caddo gave nineteen companies to the Confederacy in the first year.

Raising companies for the Confederacy depended on many factors. Urban centers naturally contributed more than sparsely settled piney woods parishes. In rich cotton plantation areas the response was far greater than in areas where small farms prevailed. Vulnerability to invasion and the strength of Union sentiment were other factors to be considered. In all, during the first year, Louisiana is estimated to have raised some three hundred and five companies for Confederate duty.[13]

Confederate forces in Kentucky and Tennessee badly needed strengthening. In February President Davis asked Governor Moore to send forward five-and-a-half regiments for the duration of the war. Governor Moore tried hard to co-operate with this request, but the path to success was far from smooth. The First Brigade of state troops from New Orleans was not anxious to join with Beauregard. These men did not want to leave the city, because of their families, their property, and their employment in vital industry. Only one company could be raised to go to Jackson, Tennessee.[14] General Lovell protested: "I regret the necessity of sending away my only force at this juncture, and feel sure that it will create a great panic here. . . ." Davis persisted and General Lovell was able to report to Judah P. Benjamin on February 27 that seven regiments and two batteries had already departed for Tennessee carrying five hundred shotguns and a million cartridges. The Twentieth Louisiana, originally mustered for state service, "not wishing to remain behind had organized for the war." This regiment would leave Louisiana in the next few days. These troops were outfitted by the state, and the Confederacy furnished them only with ammunition, transportation, and subsistence.

The people of New Orleans complained that the state had been stripped of its defenses, and General Lovell was accused of sending away all the troops "so that the city may fall easy prey to the enemy." Lovell called upon Governor Moore for ten thousand volunteers and militia for state service: "Raw troops, with double-barrel shot guns, are amply sufficient to hold our intrenchments against such troops as the enemy can send to attack them. Besides, I regard Butler's Ship Island expedition as a harmless menace so far as New Orleans is concerned." [15]

A more bizarre request emanated from General Beauregard's headquarters, and this call received an even greater response. To meet the shortage of metal suffered by the foundries trying to manufacture cannon, Beauregard asked Louisiana to contribute all her plantation bells. In answer to the call the Methodist, Baptist, and Presbyterian churches of Shreveport took down their bells and shipped them to New Orleans. Bells of every size and description—church bells, plantation bells, school bells—hundreds of them poured into New Orleans and were stored in the Custom House. After the fall of the city the bells were shipped to New York and sold at public auction.[16]

General Lovell tried to meet all of the demands made upon his department by the Confederate government. Despite the dire predictions made earlier by Braxton Bragg, Lovell proved to be a man of energy for the Southern cause. His formal office hours were from 9 A.M. to 3 P.M. From 3 P.M. to 8 P.M. he usually went on a personal inspection tour of the defense lines, foundries, shipyards, workshops, and camps, offering assistance and advice where necessary. After a hasty dinner the tireless commander would return to his office to labor far into the night over an endless pile of paper work.

The lithe, muscular, still young, brown-haired general evoked a feeling of confidence in the people. An excellent horseman who was visibly fond of his mount, Lovell rode with such a long stirrup that he appeared to be standing in his saddle; his upper body was ramrod-straight.

In compliance with a telegram from Secretary of War Benjamin, General Lovell in early January took possession of fourteen privately owned steamers at New Orleans. Benjamin instructed the department head to have the impressed vessels strengthened with iron casings at the bow for use as rams. Captains Townsend and Montgomery, sent by President Davis from Richmond to command two of the boats, and twelve other river-boat captains, to be chosen in Louisiana, were to select their own civilian crews. Inasmuch as these crews presumably knew little about guns, each boat was to have a single heavy gun, to be used only in case the enemy craft turned an unprotected stern toward the ram. A sum of $300,000 was to be set aside to outfit these vessels.

The river fleet was not to be a part of the Confederate navy, but was to be under the general orders of the military commander of the department in which the fleet served. The fourteen captains were to have almost complete freedom of action. General Lovell complained that "fourteen Mississippi captains and pilots would never agree about anything," and asked that one reliable man be put in charge. The two captains, Montgomery and Townsend, were sadly lacking in administrative ability and apparently never had heard of economy, system, or ingenuity. In readying the river fleet for action nearly $1,500,000 was expended.[17]

A more vexing problem dogged Lovell in the latter part of February. The raft between the two forts below New Orleans began to weaken and sag because of the huge mass of drift backed up against it. All available steamboats and skiffs were used to clear away the debris, but the river in flood stage kept far ahead of the clearing crews, and the task had to be abandoned. In the first week in March the main chains snapped. Lovell acted promptly. He appealed to the city council of New Orleans for $100,000 to be used in repairing the raft, but restoration was impossible. A new obstruction was fashioned, using parts of the wrecked raft and eight old schooners anchored in line and held by links of chains. As it was impossible to secure enough heavy chains, the second raft was far from satisfactory. Between forty and fifty fire rafts, piled high with lightwood, cotton, tar, and rosin, were placed above and below the raft to further deter enemy vessels. Two steam tugs were kept available for towing the rafts into the most effective positions. A great windstorm swooped down upon the vicinity of the forts on the night of April 10. The swollen storm-tossed waters whipped the fire rafts loose from their moorings and sent them crashing against the main raft. Some of the weaker chains parted, and the schooners were scattered. Hasty repairs were made, but the obstruction had suffered irreparable damage.

The raft was only one in a series of difficulties General Lovell had to face. Since late December the Confederacy had continued to drain Department No. 1 not only of troops but also of badly needed guns, ammunition, clothing, and supplies. Lovell complained in a letter of March 6: "New Orleans is about defenseless. In return we get nothing."

In December Lovell was ordered to send twenty-two heavy guns from his department to Tennessee and to South Carolina. This order was obeyed, even though compliance badly weakened the coastal defenses. In January the commander was forced to arm the fourteen confiscated river boats with one gun each. At the same time Lovell gave ten 42-pounders to the navy for the arming of the *Bienville* and the *Carondelet*. In addition to the guns, powder and crews were also furnished for these boats, which were to be used in Lake Pontchartrain and Mississippi Sound.

By April 1 the work of converting the fourteen river boats into rams was completed. Orders were issued from Richmond to send these boats upriver to Memphis and Fort Pillow, where, it was said, there was a greater need for them. Lovell, believing that there was greater danger of attack from below, detained six of the vessels and sent eight forward.[18]

As the attrition of Louisiana's defenses continued, Federal plans for the invasion of lower Louisiana reached a high point of development.

By March 8 troopships bearing New England volunteers, a detachment of the large army raised by Major General Benjamin F. Butler, had arrived at Ship Island and encamped. This group, the Fourteenth Maine and six companies of the Thirteenth Maine and the Twelfth Connecticut, were under the command of Brigadier General J. W. Phelps and were to be joined shortly by other troops.

And still the Confederacy did not let up on her demands. Louisiana was asked to send new reinforcements to Tennessee. Governor Moore did what he could. Proclamations were issued calling for five-and-a-half regiments to be raised by March 15. Each volunteer would be armed, outfitted, paid a fifty-dollar bounty, and transported to Tennessee at the expense of the Confederate government. The governor reported to Judah P. Benjamin on February 21 that Louisiana could furnish troops to Beauregard if the men were permitted to volunteer for short terms. Benjamin advised Governor Moore to accept armed men for six months' duty with General Beauregard. Groups from the state militia, including the Crescent Regiment, three companies of the Orleans Guard Artillery Battalion, and the Fifth Company of the Washington Artillery, volunteered to go to Tennessee in early March to join Beauregard for ninety days. The troops were outfitted by the state, Lovell furnishing ammunition, subsistence, and transportation. It was hoped that these men, once in the field, would remain indefinitely. President Davis continued to demand troops. On April 10 he insisted that more troops be forwarded to Beauregard. Governor Moore answered that he might be able to send unarmed troops. "I have no arms here except those General Lovell thinks we should keep." Moore continued to co-operate with Davis and by mid-April had sent 3,000 of the best armed state troops to reinforce the army in Tennessee.

On March 13 Jefferson Davis requested that martial law be declared in Orleans, Jefferson, St. Bernard, and Plaquemines parishes. The necessary orders were issued by General Lovell on March 15 and 18. All white males above sixteen living in these parishes were ordered to appear within six days before the provost marshals of their districts to register. Those claiming to be Confederate citizens were required to take an unconditional oath of allegiance to the Confederacy, and aliens had to swear to obey the laws of the Southern states as long as they remained in the Confederate states. "All persons . . . who are unfriendly to our cause, are notified to leave the district . . . without delay."

After too long a delay the city council of New Orleans became vitally concerned over local defenses. A Safety Committee, consisting of sixty men, was appointed in late February. Co-operation with state and government authorities was the stated purpose of the committee. The committee arranged with Governor Moore and General Lovell for an increase in the manufacture of rifles and cannon and furnished the necessary funds for expanding the foundry and factory facilities. The ironclad gunboat *Mississippi,* far behind schedule for completion, presented another problem. The committee offered the Tift brothers all the money they needed to complete the vessel; the offer to supply additional mechanics was refused. The Safety Committee sent agents all over the Confederacy to collect iron to use in plating the ship. A center shaft for the gunboat was found in Richmond and brought to the Tifts at the expense of the committee.

Wherever it could, the committee rendered assistance. The state navy department, it was discovered, was deep in debt and without credit. Some of the bills were paid by the committee, and other money was supplied for current needs. Agents were sent into the country to obtain food for the citizens of New Orleans. The food was sold at actual cost. The Safety Committee was always ready to help any man who tried to strengthen the city.[19]

The vast shipbuilding program that had been under way in the New Orleans vicinity since late 1861 continued. The *Louisiana* was still unfinished. E. C. Murray, a shipbuilder of twenty years' experience, encountered numerous unavoidable delays, including a wait for iron plating and timber, changes in design, strikes among the workers, and the slowness of the Leeds Company in transferring the engines from the *Ingomar* to the new ship.

On this floating fort New Orleans based much of her hopes of repelling an invasion. When the Navy department in April ordered the *Louisiana* sent upriver, General Lovell protested through the War Department and the *Louisiana* was retained. Secretary of the Navy Mallory still believed that the greatest danger to the Confederacy was an attack from above. On April 20, under pressing need, after the enemy bombardment had begun, the uncompleted *Louisiana* was towed on down to the forts to add her fire power to the job of dislodging the enemy mortars.

Also under construction in the city shipyards were the gunboat *Livingston,* completed in February, and the *Carondelet,* completed in March. The fleet commissioned by Secretary Mallory consisted of the

New Orleans, mounting twenty guns; the *Memphis,* eighteen guns; and the gunboats *Maurepas, Pontchartrain, Bienville, Livingston,* and *Carondelet,* each to carry six guns. Two others, the *Pickens* and the *Morgan,* were to mount three guns apiece. The ironclads *Louisiana* and *Mississippi* were each, when complete, to carry sixteen guns.

On the ironclad *Mississippi* all flat surfaces and straight lines were to be covered with three-inch iron plates, and the ship was to be 260 feet long and 58 feet wide. It was considered that it would be one of the strongest vessels in the world. Three powerful engines, driving three shafts connected with three propellers, would give the ship great speed. Unfortunately, the ship was never completed. In two more weeks the formidable vessel would have been ready. But time had run out. When the Federal fleet succeeded in passing the forts, the *Mississippi* was helpless; it could neither fight nor escape.

To the end, Mallory believed that the greatest threat to New Orleans would come from the upriver fleet of seven "tin-clads," then at Fort Pillow under Flag Officer Charles Davis. Disregarding the advice of some of his best naval officers, the Secretary of the Navy placed undue reliance upon the strength of Forts Jackson and St. Philip. Even as late as April, when David Farragut, commanding the largest fleet the United States had ever assembled, began bombarding the forts, Mallory was still convinced that the city would not fall. He continued to order ships, including the *Louisiana,* to proceed up to Tennessee.[20]

And still there were many in New Orleans who felt as Secretary Mallory did; the city was impregnable to Federal attack. An English resident of New Orleans reported: "Society . . . showed little sensitiveness to the great struggle in which we were engaged. Festivity was the order of the day; balls, parties, theatres, operas. . . . We felt too secure." Farragut's fleet was ridiculed, and the bombardment of the forts was a splendid show. Many journeyed down to watch the mighty spectacle.[21]

The charges against society were partly true. Carnival season was not entirely ignored. Seven huge Mardi Gras balls were held between February 22 and March 4, but they were mainly for charitable purposes. Motivated by a spy scare, Mayor Monroe prohibited all forms of street masking. "Mardi Gras passed off with a quietness never before known in New Orleans."

Interest in horse racing and the theater had long been keen in the city. The spring racing season, although somewhat curtailed, opened. On April 4 a large crowd went out to the Fair Grounds course to witness a $1,000 match race. Another race was scheduled for April 16. Harry Macarthy, the famous Arkansas comedian and author of the beloved song of the South, "The Bonnie Blue Flag," returned from a successful engagement in Richmond and appeared once more at the Academy of Music. Even while the forts below the city were under bombardment, this Irish comedian and musician, assisted by Miss Lottie Estelle, played to crowded houses.[22]

An event occurred on April 16 that would further weaken Louisiana in her time of crisis. In order to raise more men for the army, the Confederate Congress passed the first Conscription Act, making all able-bodied white male citizens between the ages of eighteen and thirty-five, with a few exceptions, liable to serve in the Confederate army for a period up to three years. A conscript had the right to hire a substitute to serve in his place. Newspapers decried the "substitute clause" and begged those eligible for the draft to volunteer before this honorable system was abolished. Bounties were not paid to conscripts.[23]

April was an especially busy month for General Lovell. Telegraph lines were completed, giving the department headquarters wire communications with Forts Jackson, St. Philip, Pike, Macomb, the Head of the Passes, Proctorsville, and Brashear City. Working through the citizens, the general attempted to gather enough flour and meat to last the city for sixty days. Trying everything, he reported a shortage of provisions to the new Secretary of War, George W. Randolph, and requested that flour be sent to New Orleans from Richmond. All attempts to accumulate enough food for a possible siege failed.

The general secured a few heavy guns from Pensacola and had them mounted in a new water battery near Fort Jackson. Sandbags from the city were sent to the magazines, water batteries, and casemates of the forts. A regiment of troops under Colonel Ignatius Szymanski was sent to Quarantine to prevent an enemy land force from moving above Fort St. Philip. Rising flood waters drove the men to the higher west banks, where they remained until subsequently they were forced to surrender. Sharpshooters were sent down both banks of the river to harass the Federal survey parties and to discourage pilots of enemy vessels. An appeal to General Beauregard for the return of the reconditioned ram *Manassas* was answered, and the vessel arrived in time to take part in the final action. Lovell placed Brigadier General Johnson K. Duncan in command of the entire exterior line of defense, which he controlled from Fort Jackson.

Lovell's department had been practically denuded of regular troops.

The general's appeal to Governor Moore for 10,000 militiamen for the defenses of New Orleans was answered by only 3,000 men, the rest having been sent to Beauregard. The two brigades of state troops under Generals Tracy and Buisson, state officers, were chiefly new levies. Less than 1,200 were armed with muskets, and the rest had only shotguns or were completely unarmed. When Lovell ordered a portion of the militia to Fort Jackson, the men mutinied and would not go until prodded aboard the transports by the bayonets of another regiment. Most of the troops were stationed at Chalmette, below the city along the interior line. No ammunition was issued to these state troops because rifles and shotguns were considered useless against gunboats, and because no land attack was expected. The insubordination of many of the men made Lovell hesitate "to put ammunition in their hands." However, 600,000 rounds of shotgun shells were stored in the camp arsenal. A battery of ten 32-pounder smoothbores and two 8-inch columbiads, recently turned out by the New Orleans foundries, were mounted on the Chalmette line, half on each side of the river, but only twenty rounds of ammunition were provided for each larger gun.[24]

And so the pitiful Confederate forces awaited the final blow. They did not wait long.

VII

THE QUEEN FALLS

MEANWHILE, the Federal fleet was preparing for action. David Farragut had arrived at Ship Island late in February, but so many immediate problems demanded solution that he could do little planning for the push against New Orleans. While he worked his way from under an avalanche of paper work, he had to direct and strengthen the blockade. Rotting ship hulls and worn ship engines had to be repaired. Boats had to be hauled over the bars and up the river passes. Medical supplies and coal had failed to arrive and had to be found. Finally, after an abortive try at negotiating Pass à l'Outre, Farragut was able by mid-March to maneuver through the Southwest Pass with the two sloops *Brooklyn* and *Hartford* and to join several of his gunboats at Pilot Town, a dismal village squatting on pilings driven into the river muck. By March 18 Commander David Porter, with his seven gunboats, had towed his twenty mortar schooners over the bar and up to the Head of the Passes. After two weeks of pulling and tugging, the last of the deep-draft sloops, the *Mississippi* and the *Pensacola,* were brought up with Porter's assistance.

Farragut's fleet, rendezvoused at Pilot Town, consisted of seventeen men-of-war mounting 165 guns, or 181 if howitzers were included. Porter's twenty mortar boats each claimed one 13-inch mortar. In addition, fifteen carried two 32-pounders, and the rest were armed with two 12-pounder howitzers each. The total guns carried by his seven steam gunboats was twenty-seven.

Several boats were sent out to survey and triangulate the area below the forts. Rags were tied to branches and poles along the banks to mark the best positions for the gunboats. General Johnson K. Duncan sent men out from the forts to remove the markers and to snipe at the survey crews. The Confederate sharpshooters were plagued with high water and often had to stand in water up to their waists when firing, and each of their shots was immediately answered by a rain of shrapnel from the gunboats. A great wind, accompanied by violent rain, on April 10 flooded the area and drove the sharpshooters back to the forts, and the survey crew completed its task in relative safety.[1]

The men in the forts were largely Northern men and foreigners, especially Germans and Irish. Some had been forced to come at the point of the bayonet; others had volunteered, hoping that the North would find it impossible to attack the forts at all. The forts were spic and span, and health conditions were good. Discipline was strict. Men guilty of insubordination or treasonable talk were usually punished by having a rope tied around their waists and then being dangled or floated for several hours in the "stinking ditch." As long as the Federal attack did not come, morale remained relatively high.

Meanwhile, Farragut's preparations continued. Following a suggestion made by Engineer Moore of the *Richmond,* a chain armor was fixed to the sides of the ships to protect the engines. Overlapping chain cables formed an almost solid sheet of armor around the boats. Sandbags were placed around the engines, around the guns, and above and below decks wherever added protection was needed. Rope nettings and hammocks were rigged over the decks to minimize injuries to the men from flying splinters and falling spars and rigging. To make the ships harder to spot during the day or night, river mud was smeared over the visible areas of the ships, including the rigging and the guns. Some of the ships painted their decks and gun carriages with whitewash so that gun crews would have greater visibility for handling their guns during a night assault. Whaleboats, provided with grapnels and chains, were prepared to tow fire rafts away from the vessels. Cheerfully, with infectious enthusiasm, Farragut visited his ships, directed the preparations, and won the admiration of everyone.

Porter's mortar fleet was moved up to a bend, where the small boats were stationed in line along the west bank, the nearest being some 950 yards below Fort Jackson and 3,700 yards from Fort St. Philip. Thick clumps of trees matted with vines made the boats practically invisible, and to make detection even more difficult, tree branches were fastened to the masts of the boats.

Porter's mortar boats opened up against the two forts at midmorning on April 18. Five of Farragut's gunboats were sent up within range of the Confederate guns to divert their fire away from Porter's more

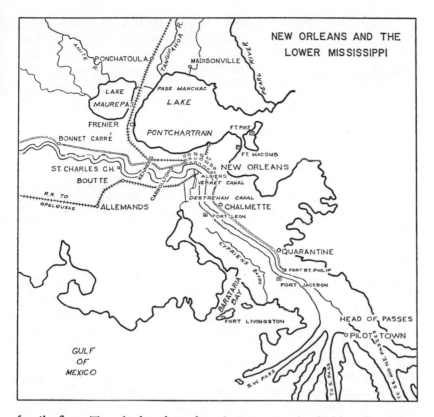

fragile fleet. Two lucky shots found targets in the hidden fleet. One shell passed through a mortar vessel, killing one man, and another boat was hit near the water line, but neither boat had to retire from action. In Fort Jackson mortar shells rained down upon the citadel. One heavy columbiad was dismounted, and the men were driven from the parapet guns and returned only when the Federal gunboats came closer. Porter's mortars set fire to the wooden barracks inside and outside the fort, and they blazed brightly far into the night. In the struggle to protect the magazines from the flames most of the men lost their meager clothing and all of their bedding. This, along with the flood waters and the falling shells, made life miserable for the defenders.

In the first day over 1,400 shells were fired at the forts. Faulty fuses caused many of the shells to detonate high in the air and others to fall far short of the target. However, according to Confederate reports, the first day saw the most effective firing accomplished by the mortars.

Early the next morning Porter resumed the bombardment. Again most of the shells missed the target, but seven guns were disabled at Fort Jackson. The Union navy did not escape injury. One mortar schooner was sunk, and the gunboat *Oneida* was struck twice, sending about fifteen men to sick bay down-river. All night and into the next day the mortars thundered away at the forts, and the forts occasionally returned the fire.

The strain was beginning to tell on the forts. Harassed by constantly falling shells, the men got little sleep, and the majority of the motley garrison became demoralized and restive. Porter's men were suffering too. For the past three days the men had eaten poorly and had gone with little rest. To give his men relief Porter divided up his boats into "three watches of four hours each," firing 168 times per watch or about 1,500 shells in a twenty-four-hour period. Between watches the exhausted crews and officers stretched out on deck and slept soundly while the mortars all around them fired away. Porter, however, was beginning to worry. Why hadn't the forts surrendered? He was almost ready to admit defeat when he learned from a deserter from Fort Jackson of the havoc his mortars had dealt. The commander took heart and redoubled his efforts.[2]

During the night of April 20 the wind quickened and the weather became cold. The mortars increased the tempo of firing to cover an attempt to destroy the chain raft. Captain Henry H. Bell took the gunboats *Itasca* and *Pinola* and moved up the river through the dark, windy night. As the ships neared the raft around midnight, they were discovered by the forts, and the water batteries opened a heavy barrage. Most of the shots sailed high overhead. A dash was made at the hulks, but no breach could be made. There were no guards near the raft and no lights; fire rafts were not used by the Confederates because of the high winds. After Bell's men slipped the chains with hammer and chisel from one of the schooners near the east side, the swift current and the freed schooner swept the *Itasca* toward the bank, where it grounded. The engines were strained, but all attempts to free the boat failed. Finally the *Pinola* came to the rescue. Once again free, the *Itasca* found herself running above the hulks and quickly reversed herself as a Confederate fire raft came drifting down. Swept along by the current, the *Itasca* plowed into the chain between the second and third schooners and broke it, leaving a hole large enough for the passage of the fleet.

The weather continued cold and windy on April 21. Throughout the day the mortars and gunboats kept up an incessant fire. Several guns were hit at Fort Jackson, and General Duncan worked swiftly to repair them. Two of the mortar vessels were struck but suffered little injury. There was no letup the next day. April 23 was clear, warm, and cloudless. Despite the concentrated mortar fire, Duncan used all of his men to make necessary repairs. General Lovell visited the forts and found Fort Jackson "much cut up" but suffering only four casualties. The heavy bombardment continued until noon, when there came a strange slackening of fire. Suspicion and speculation began to mount at the forts.

Standing ready to prevent Farragut's fleet from passing the forts were the forts themselves, Fort Jackson mounting around 95 guns and St. Philip about 52 guns, an assorted naval fleet, and 40 or 50 fire rafts. Four Confederate ships plus two Louisiana state boats, together carrying about 30 guns of various calibers and types, were under the command of Commodore William C. Whittle. Six of the mongrel River Defense gunboats, commanded by Captain John A. Stephenson, mounted around 12 guns. Seven unarmed steamers, serving as tenders and tugs, completed the immediate defenses. The forts and the twelve armed vessels, with a total firepower of 189 guns, stood against 46 ships, carrying 348 guns and 21 mortars.

There was great discord between the divided commands of the naval forces. Captain John K. Mitchell, the active commander of the Confederate naval ships, was also in command of the fire rafts. On April 23 General Lovell visited Commodore Whittle at his headquarters in New Orleans and begged him to order Captain Mitchell to send the ironclad gunboat *Louisiana* to a point one-half mile below the raft on the Fort St. Philip side, where she would be protected by a cross fire from the two forts and would be able to dislodge the enemy with her own guns and allow the forts to repair their injuries. After an argument, Whittle telegraphed Mitchell suggesting the change, but the *Louisiana* remained where she was, above Fort St. Philip. Her engines were not yet completed. Captain Mitchell had decided that the *Louisiana*'s portholes would not allow her guns sufficient elevation to reach the enemy mortars and gunboats and her thinly plated, flat upper decks would prove too vulnerable to plunging mortar fire.

The River Defense squadron proved unmanageable too. Lacking a competent commander, "unable to govern themselves, and unwilling to be governed by others, their almost total want of system, vigilance, and discipline, rendered them nearly useless and helpless when the enemy finally dashed upon them suddenly. . . ." During the fight, as before, the six river captains refused to obey any orders from a naval officer and cowardly fled up the river when the Federal fleet approached. The handling of the fire rafts proved disgraceful too.[3]

Farragut was a patient, kindly man. He had doubted the efficiency of the mortar fleet from the beginning but had allowed the over-confident Porter to try his hand at blasting the forts into submission. After more than five days and nights of bombardment there was still no sign of surrender. Farragut was through with waiting. He wanted to run by the forts under cover of darkness. Porter objected. Should the attempt succeed, the forts would be left intact, separating Farragut from the mortar fleet. The forts must be captured first and then the way to New Orleans would be clear. Farragut rejected Porter's idea and issued the necessary orders for running past the forts, personally supervising the last-minute details.

At dusk the process of maneuvering the vessels into battle order was begun. Arranged into three divisions, Captain Theodorus Bailey aboard the *Cayuga* was to lead off with his eight vessels and run up near the east, or right, bank past Fort St. Philip. The center division, composed of three ships, headed by Farragut aboard the *Hartford,* was to follow. Captain H. H. Bell, commanding the six ships of the third division from the gunboat *Sciota,* was to move up last, as close under Fort Jackson as possible.

After getting into line, the men were allowed to lower their hammocks and sleep a few hours. A calm settled over the fleet. At midnight, the men arose quietly and put away their gear. A heavy damp mist hovered over the water; the night was dark and chilly. The men took up their stations. Several hours passed. Nothing happened. During the wait some of the officers calmly played dominoes in their quarters.

Around 2 A.M. the signal was given, two red lights hoisted on the flag officer's ship. The first column encountered anchor trouble, and it was an hour later before Captain Bailey led his division through the breach in the chain raft, closely followed by Commodore Farragut aboard the *Hartford* and the other ships of the center division. Captain Bell then brought up the third division. As soon as the *Hartford* weighed anchor, Porter, with five of the mortar flotilla gunboats and accompanied by the *Portsmouth* from Farragut's fleet, moved up to within 1,500 yards of the water battery of Fort Jackson. The mortars were to open a heavy fire on the fort and drive the men from their guns.

The mortars opened the bombardment at 3:30 A.M., firing as rapidly as they could reload. Soon thereafter the men in the water battery and in Fort Jackson caught sight of the black indistinguishable masses moving slowly up the dark river. Not a light was burning; not a fire raft had been started. The battery and Fort Jackson opened fire almost simultaneously. Across the river Fort St. Philip added her thundering greetings to the Federal fleet.[4]

Captain Bailey in the lead ship, the *Cayuga,* moved up close under St. Philip, blazing away with grape and canister. The guns of the fort, trained on the mid-river, overshot the vital parts of the ship, injuring only the sails, rigging, masts, and spars. Engine trouble slowed down the *Pensacola* and delayed the rest of the first division. The *Cayuga* proceeded beyond the fort and engaged the ironclad *Louisiana,* tied to the bank, and the little ram *Manassas.* During this period the *Varuna* came up and briefly joined in the duel, firing a broadside at the enemy through the *Cayuga,* doing damage to it and to the enemy. The *Varuna* then disappeared. After helping to destroy three of the Confederate vessels Captain Bailey steamed on up the river in the *Cayuga* to attack the fortifications at Chalmette, despite the damages of some forty-two hits made upon his ship. Upriver the *Varuna* was overhauled by two Confederate ships and a deadly struggle ensued. Captain Bailey dispatched the *Oneida* to the assistance of the *Varuna.*

Confused by the excitement of battle, the deafening noise of hundreds of guns, the darkness itself, individual engagements with Confederate gunboats, and anxiety for the safety of its own vessels, the Federal fleet abandoned the prearranged order of passage. At the opening in the chain raft the *Brooklyn,* of the center division, rammed into the *Kineo,* of Bailey's division, and delayed the forward movement. The center and third divisions finally moved up on the left to attack Fort Jackson. At last a Confederate fire raft was released and came bearing down upon the *Hartford.* In the ensuing panic the *Hartford* grounded and was momentarily helpless. The *Mosher,* an unarmed tug, nudged a blazing raft against the side of Farragut's boat. Flames soon leaped halfway up the mainmast. Working frantically, some of the men extinguished the blaze while others continued to man their guns. A broadside shot sent the *Mosher* to the bottom. After a few minutes the *Hartford* worked its way free of the mud and moved over toward St. Philip, pouring shell after shell into the fort until passing out of range.

Porter, who had brought his gunboats in as close to Fort Jackson as he dared, waited under fire for fifteen minutes until the center had cleared his path of fire and then opened with shrapnel on the water battery and the forts. His mortars continued their heavy barrage from below. Only one of the gunboats was struck, the *Harriet Lane*, one man being killed and another injured. The *Portsmouth*, working in conjunction with Porter, was hit several times in the hull and rigging, leaving one killed and one wounded. When the last ship, the *Iroquois*, moved above, Porter retired his ships below.

After plowing into the *Kineo*, the *Brooklyn*, confused by the darkness and blinding smoke, overran one of the hulks of the raft and became temporarily entangled. The gunners of Fort St. Philip opened up on her. Hardly had she freed herself when the Confederate ram *Manassas* opened fire and struck her about five feet above the water line. Maneuvering about, the *Manassas* attempted to ram the *Brooklyn*, but because steam pressure was low, the ram gently butted the vessel and rebounded from the chain armor attached to the sides. The rebel gunboat *Warrior* next hove into sight and opened an attack, but a shell from the *Brooklyn* instantly set her afire and drove her ashore. Passing by St. Philip the *Brooklyn* gave and received a galling fire. For more than an hour and a half the *Brooklyn* was under fire. The damages were severe. Eight men were killed, and twenty-six were wounded.

The Federal flagship *Mississippi*, sighting the *Manassas*, tried to run her down. The ram commander, A. F. Warley, who had formerly served aboard the *Mississippi*, turned sharply to avoid the blow and in so doing struck a glancing blow on the port side of the Federal ship. The *Mississippi* reeled from the impact and temporarily grounded. The *Manassas* then disappeared. Above the forts, just as dawn was breaking, the *Manassas* was sighted a second time, and Captain Melancton Smith again bore straight for her. The *Manassas* dodged and found herself lodged on the bank. The *Mississippi* opened two broadsides on the impotent ram and wrecked her works. The crew crawled ashore and vanished in the swamps. Water flooded the boat, and she floated free. A few minutes later the drifting ram exploded and sank.

The heavy bombardment played upon the two forts by Porter's mortars and gunboats and by Farragut's fleet caused only temporary inconvenience to the Confederates. One participant reported that no guns were knocked out nor completely silenced in Fort Jackson nor the water battery. Despite the broadsides of grape, canister, shot, and shell the men stuck to their posts and fought until the enemy succeeded in moving out of range.

All of the Federal ships that made the attempt succeeded in passing the forts except three. The *Kennebec* fouled one of the schooners and became entangled in the chains of the raft. After a long struggle the gunboat floated free and made several fruitless attempts to pass the forts. When day dawned, the *Kennebec* found most of the fleet already above and retired below to safety. The *Itasca,* before Fort Jackson, was struck repeatedly. One shot entered the boiler, leaving a large hole and severing a steam pipe. Fear seized the captain as live steam filled the engine room and quarter-deck. All the men rushed from below and threw themselves flat upon the deck, and the ship was allowed to drift down-river. Out of range of the forts the pumps were manned, but the captain suspected that the craft would soon sink and beached the *Itasca* below the mortar fleet. The third ship, the *Winona,* like the *Kennebec* ran afoul of the chain raft. The *Itasca,* maneuvering through the obstacle, backed into the *Winona* while she was caught in the chain raft, causing a long delay. Freeing herself from the raft, the *Winona* attempted to move above, but daylight caught the hapless ship between the cross fire of the two forts and forced her to abandon the attempt to pass.[5]

When the mortars opened their heaviest fire on the forts, signaling a possible attack, the defending Confederate fleet anchored on both sides of the river above the cross fire of the forts, alerted their crews, and the upper boats built up their steam. General Lovell, who had hastened down from New Orleans to see that the *Louisiana* was moved to a more effective position down below St. Philip, arrived just as the engagement was beginning. As the fleet began to pass the forts, Lovell realized the hopelessness of the situation and ordered his boat to turn back to New Orleans. He barely eluded capture.

Bold, concerted action from the various divisions of the Confederate fleet was absolutely necessary. But it was not to come. The six rams of the independent River Defense fleet ignored the warning signs, and several failed to take any precautions. With the approach of the enemy vessels, those who had built up enough steam tried to run away. The others remained stationary, a target hard to miss. Without the slightest show of resistance, one by one the vessels were set blazing by enemy shells. Not one of them fired a shot in return nor attempted to ram a single enemy vessel.[6]

The passage of the forts did not put an end to the fighting. The speedy little *Cayuga* soon left the rest of the Federal fleet behind. Suddenly the ship was surrounded by Confederate gunboats. Captain Bailey opened his guns on the enemy vessels and succeeded in driving two ashore, where they rapidly burned to the water line. A short time later the *Varuna* and the *Oneida* dashed into the fray, freeing the *Cayuga* from danger. The *Varuna,* belching black smoke, ventured ahead of the rest of the fleet, overhauled the *Governor Moore* near Quarantine, and opened a withering fire of grape, canister, and shrapnel on her, killing many of the men. The state vessel, commanded by Beverly Kennon, ran down her tormentor, and twice the crashing, ripping noises echoed over the dark river. Another state gunboat, the *Breckinridge,* rammed the mortally wounded *Varuna* just as she reached the shore. The sinking vessel settled in the shallow water, where she was fired and abandoned by her commander.

Turning downstream, the *Governor Moore* prepared to do battle with the *Cayuga* but ran into the *Oneida* and six other Federal gunboats. As the Confederate ship rounded to as swiftly as possible, she was raked from stem to stern by the entire enemy squadron. The ship was riddled; her engines were disabled and her wheel ropes shot away. When the helpless ship was caught by an eddy and grounded, further resistance was useless. Out of a crew of ninety-three some fifty-seven had been killed and seventeen wounded. Kennon ordered the wounded brought on deck and the safety valve lashed down. When orders were issued to set fire to the ship, the wounded men were loaded aboard a longboat and the officers and crew took to their life preservers and abandoned the vessel. Only the commander, his pilot, and one seaman were left behind to carry out the destruction. The oil from the lamps was then emptied on mosquito bars and bedding, and the ship was soon a mass of flames. Kennon was surrounded by small boats from the *Oneida,* and he surrendered. Only seven men were able to escape to shore and through the swamps to safety. The rest of the men, caught in the water, were taken prisoners by sailors in dinghies from the various Federal gunboats. The Confederate navy gunboat, the *Jackson,* near the *Governor Moore* during the opening phases of the mortal conflict, fired only two shots and then fled in full cowardly retreat up the river.

With few exceptions the Confederate fleet had made a sorry showing. Self-destruction, lack of co-operation, cowardice of untrained officers, and the murderous fire of the Federal gunboats reduced the fleet to a demoralized shambles. Out of the River Defense fleet only the *Defiance* was saved. From the Confederate naval forces the *Louisiana,* the *McRae,* and the cowardly *Jackson* escaped. The tenders, transports, and fire rafts were almost all destroyed.

At dawn, sighting a Confederate camp at Quarantine, Captain Bailey anchored his gunboat *Cayuga* and ordered Colonel Ignatius Szymanski and his regiment to surrender. Farragut came up later and took over the captured post. Pressed for time, Farragut paroled the officers and over three hundred men after taking away their arms and equipment. He then sent a message to Commander Porter asking him to demand the surrender of the forts. Another message to General Butler requested that he bring his troops through Quarantine Bayou and cut off all possible land communications between New Orleans and the forts. Two gunboats were left at Quarantine to protect the troop landing, and crewmen were able to take the bodies of the dead ashore and bury them. The next morning, April 25, the fleet continued up the river.

Captain Bailey, with the *Cayuga,* far in advance of the slower ships, was first to sight the Chalmette and McGehee batteries, apparently abandoned, several miles below New Orleans. The *Cayuga* attempted to push on to the city, but as she came within range of the batteries, concealed gunners arose and opened a heavy fire. In rapid order fourteen shots tore into the vessel, and the *Cayuga* retired from action awaiting assistance from the ships below. The *Hartford, Brooklyn,* and the *Pensacola* steamed to the rescue and pasted the batteries with broadsides of grape, shrapnel, and shell. The Confederate guns were soon silenced and the crews were seen running in every direction.[7] Brigadier General Martin L. Smith, in command of all the interior lines of defense, was on the west side of the river directing the men of the McGehee gun emplacements. On the east side the Confederate forces were under Brigadier General Benjamin Buisson of the state militia. Both men had given up most of their ammunition and powder to the Confederate navy and shortly had expended their meager supply. The militiamen, without a single round of small-arms ammunition, were ordered to take cover in the woods. General Smith ordered the men of the McGehee line to make their way, by any means possible, to Camp Moore, on the east side some seventy-eight miles above New Orleans. Cut off from using the river and lacking wagons and teams, the guns and camp equipage had to be abandoned. On the Chalmette line the Confederate forces were ordered to move to New Orleans and board the Jackson Railroad for Camp Moore. The march was made through a heavy rain, and many of the men drowned their misfortunes in hard liquor. In the city a number of the soldiers deserted and others became so drunk they could not walk. The rest boarded the train and went on to Camp Moore.[8]

After a brief rest, the Union crews set about to clean their decks of the blood and mangled remains of the dead and wounded. Temporary repairs were made. About eleven o'clock anchors were raised, and Farragut and his fleet proceeded in triumph up the river. Along the way was evidence of panic. Boats loaded with flaming cotton and wrecked and burning dry docks went floating by. At one o'clock in the afternoon the Federal fleet began to anchor directly in front of the city, its guns at the ready position. Because of unprecedented high water the ships rode nine feet higher than the city level, and their guns could sweep the streets in any direction.

The levee was a scene of terrible destruction and conflagration. Torches had been applied to hundreds of bales of cotton, to warehouses loaded with tobacco and sugar, and to ships and steamboats anchored in the harbor. Nothing of value had been left for the invader. A pall of black smoke hung over the dismal, rainy sky. Wildly the alarm bell atop Christ Church tolled the dreaded news. Drums beat and soldiers milled around in wild confusion.[9]

On April 24, when news first reached the city that the enemy had succeeded in passing the forts, an English eyewitness reported: "People were amazed, and could scarcely realize the awful fact, and ran hither and thither in speechless astonishment." When they observed flames rising from the shipyards in Algiers and saw government officials destroying property that might be of value to the enemy, the dread truth was accepted. Shocked out of their dumb disbelief, many people joined in the destruction. Cotton was rolled from the warehouses, ships loaded with produce were boarded, and fire was set to the lot. Crowds of the city poor broke open warehouses and carried away baskets, bags, and carts spilling over with rice, bacon, sugar, molasses, corn, and other foods. What they could not carry away they attempted to destroy by dumping in the river, burning, or throwing into the open gutters. A mob broke into the powder and gun factories in the Marine Hospital and carried away rifles and ammunition. The city was in a frenzy of disorganized activity. General Lovell tried to restore order and busied himself with removing Confederate stores from the city. Horsemen, pedestrians, private carriages, and army wagons hurried from the city. All night long huge fires lit up the skies overhead.

The gunboat *Mississippi* still lay uncompleted in the shipyard above the city. Commander Whittle directed that the ship be towed to safety up the river and under no circumstances allowed to fall into the hands of the enemy. General Lovell made available two tugs, but they could not do the job and Commander Arthur Sinclair begged assistance from private shipowners. The appearance of the enemy put an end to the negotiations. Hurriedly a torch was applied to the ship, and the blazing vessel floated down past the Federal fleet at anchor before the city.[10]

The rain fell in torrents, but the howling mob did not disperse. At 2 P.M. Captain Bailey, accompanied by Lieutenant George Perkins, was sent ashore to demand the surrender of the city. The two men were forced to run a gantlet of angry men and women. Brandishing pistols, shaking fists, and waving Confederate flags, the rabble followed the officers, cheering for Jeff Davis and Beauregard and jeering Abe Lincoln. Occasionally someone threw a stone, but the aim was bad. Arriving safely at City Hall, the Union officers conferred with Mayor Monroe, who stated that he could not surrender since the city was under martial law and that he must await General Lovell. When General Lovell arrived, he refused to surrender and stated that he would withdraw his troops from the city and leave the final decision to Mayor Monroe. Outside, the infuriated mob kicked and beat on the doors and swore they would hang the two Union officers. While Pierre Soulé, a member of the council, tried to pacify the crowd, Captain Bailey and Lieutenant Perkins left from a rear entrance and returned safely to their ship.

On the same day (Friday, April 25), General Lovell ordered the Confederate troops and state militia, with the exception of the foreign brigades, to move from New Orleans to Camp Moore on the Jackson Railroad. As most of the freight cars were loaded with military supplies and guns, many of the men were forced to climb on top of the cars and were soon drenched by a new downpour. Safe from the rain in comfortable passenger coaches, the Confederate Guards (often called the Home Guard), a regiment of wealthy citizens enrolled in the militia, also awaited orders to move out. The dripping, bedraggled soldiers atop the freight cars vehemently complained of their lot and denounced the more pampered members of the state troops. At three o'clock the trains pulled out.

Aboard the passenger train the Home Guard, made up of rich and overweight old men, swore that they would rather die than live under Yankee rule. These men wore every conceivable type of clothing and carried muskets or shotguns they did not know how to use. Each time the train stopped, many slipped from the cars and began the long walk back to New Orleans, forgetting their vows and their fear of the Yankees. The remaining members of the Home Guard stuck out the trip and endured the hardships of camp life for several days, and then one by one they deserted and returned home.[11]

At eleven o'clock, April 26, Farragut and his men took time "to return thanks to Almighty God for His great goodness and mercy." The commander had just cause for his thanksgiving. Passing the fortifications with such small losses to his wooden ships and to his men constituted a minor miracle. Since the opening of the campaign the total casualties suffered by the Union navy had been only 39 killed and 171 wounded. The Confederates, too, despite the heavy bombardment, had lost only 11 killed and 39 wounded at the two forts. Losses aboard the Confederate and state ships numbered 74 killed and about the same number of wounded. However, far more serious, the Confederacy had lost control over the lower Mississippi, and it was only a matter of time before the Queen City would surrender. In the North Farragut became the hero of the hour.[12]

During the afternoon of the twenty-sixth, Farragut took a gunboat up to Carrollton, some eight miles above New Orleans, to examine fortifications located there. The Confederates had spiked all their guns and had burned the gun carriages. A long line of earthworks extended back from the river to Lake Pontchartrain. The entire area was deserted.

Earlier that day (April 26) a small party of Federal troops went ashore and raised the United States flag over the Mint. At ten o'clock Lieutenant Albert Kautz and Midshipman John H. Read, accompanied by a guard of twenty marines, were sent to reopen negotiations with Mayor Monroe. The Marine guard stirred up such dangerous excitement among the already belligerent crowd that the Marines returned to their ship and the two men proceeded alone through the hostile mob. Mayor Monroe and the city council still vacillated, and no definite decision to surrender could be reached. During the meeting several men, headed by the misguided patriot William B. Mumford, hauled down the hated flag from the Mint and tore it to bits in front of City Hall. While Pierre Soulé again pacified the hysterical mob, the two Union officers were slipped out a back door and spirited back to the river by fast carriage. The next two days, April 27 and 28, were spent in unsuccessful negotiations, but by this time the temper of the mob had changed and threats of violence abated considerably.

During the period of indecision, Mayor Monroe placed the city under the charge of General Paul Juge, Jr., and his European Brigade. A semblance of order was restored to the mad city. The arsonists and plunderers were subdued. The European Brigade quelled the mobs and prevented the destruction of the city.

The work of removing Confederate property from New Orleans still went forward. Lovell was seen often in the city directing the evacuation. Trains were kept running constantly, bringing out government stores and Louisiana state properties. Labor to load and cart the goods to the trains was hard to find. Many refused to work for Confederate money, and others refused because of fear of retaliation from the enemy. Some citizens volunteered their services free of charge. From the arsenal light artillery, shot, and shell was shipped; state-owned shoes, clothing, and blankets were removed; medical stores, some machinery, leather, hammers, new wagons, camp equipage, rifles, powder, and other valuable goods were shipped out. The machinery of the powder mills was removed and shipped to Vicksburg. Unfinished mortars and brass artillery pieces too heavy to move because of the labor shortage were either buried or dumped into a canal. Heavy field pieces mounted around the city could not be moved, and they were spiked.

Fearing that the Union forces would be able to cut off his troops stationed in the works along the coast of west Louisiana, General Lovell ordered the officers in command to destroy their guns and to join him at Camp Moore as soon as possible with all their small arms, provisions, and ammunition. Only the troops from Forts Berwick and Chene joined Lovell. At the other posts on the west, the demoralized men disbanded and returned to New Orleans. Following orders, the commanders at Fort Pike and the three other southeastern forts were successful in their evacuation.

It should be said in defense of General Lovell, often harshly criticized by some of New Orleans' leading citizens, that he had acted in the best interests of the city when he removed his troops; by so doing, he saved the city from destruction. It would have been a useless gesture to stand and resist the Federal might with unseasoned troops, many of them armed only with shotguns. However, when he learned that a large group of men wanted to defend the city, he returned on the night of April 28 and offered to bring back his troops and fight to the end. Mayor Monroe quickly saw the error of such a move and refused the offer.[13]

Down-river, David Porter and General Benjamin F. Butler were not idle. Shortly after the fleet had passed above, Porter silenced his mortars and gave his men a much-needed rest. Later in the morning the forts were asked to surrender, but General Duncan refused. Around noon Porter reopened the bombardment and continued it until late afternoon, when the mortars had exhausted their supply of shells. By sundown the mortar fleet and the other vessels had withdrawn out of sight down the river.

On April 26, Porter sent six of his mortar schooners out into the Gulf to the rear of Fort Jackson to cut off all supplies and the last avenue of escape. General Butler followed suggestions made earlier by Farragut and moved his steamers and most of his men to Sable Island, behind St. Philip. The Twenty-sixth Massachusetts Volunteers, accompanied by companies from the Twenty-first Indiana and the Fourth Wisconsin, some two hundred men in all, had boarded the light-draft steamer *Miami* and had moved within six miles of the fort when the *Miami* grounded in the shallow water. Transferring to thirty rowboats, the men traveled another four-and-a-half miles. Occasionally the water became too shallow even for the yawls, and the men jumped into the water and dragged the boats through the muck. Just below Quarantine, Lieutenant Godfrey Weitzel divided the men, keeping some on the east bank and sending the rest to the west side of the river. On the morning of the twenty-seventh, the Confederate garrisons found themselves surrounded.[14]

Inside Fort Jackson the rumor grew that New Orleans had fallen and that the garrison of the fort was to be sacrificed to the last man. Around midnight, open revolt broke out. Without warning, the men fell upon the guards and began spiking the guns, and some began to desert the fort. All attempts to quell the mutiny ended in failure. Officers who attempted to halt the spiking of the guns were fired upon by the desperate men. In a short time over half of the garrison left the fort, taking their firearms with them. Between 250 and 300 of the men surrendered to Butler's pickets opposite Quarantine. Only the St. Mary's Cannoneers, made up of planters, remained completely steadfast. The broken companies who remained had lost their fight. There was no use to resist any longer. A message was sent to the Union forces, offering to discuss surrender terms the following morning.

The next day, the twenty-eighth, a squadron of nine Union vessels, three of them gunboats, moved up and anchored near the forts. Resplendent in full dress uniform, the bearded Porter received General Duncan and his party aboard the *Harriet Lane* with solemn dignity. While considering the terms of capitulation, Porter missed the commanding naval officer and demanded that he be summoned. It was too late. The gunboat *Louisiana* was sighted floating down the river, her guns firing at random and flames shooting from her hold. Commander Mitchell, whose navy was not under the army command and who knew of the impending surrender, had decided to destroy the *Louisiana* rather than to allow the unfinished, but potentially dangerous, gunboat to fall into Federal hands. Nearing St. Philip, the boat blew up, showering the area with fragments, killing one Confederate officer, and wounding several others. The terrible explosion rocked the *Harriet Lane* but only temporarily interrupted the surrender proceedings.

In the surrender terms it was agreed that officers and men would be paroled and would be allowed to return to New Orleans after turning over the forts with all stores, ordnance, ammunition, and equipment. After the army officers returned to shore and hauled down their flag, Porter steamed up to the Confederate vessels, fired a shot, and demanded their unconditional surrender. Commander Mitchell complied, but Porter, rankling over the loss of the rich prize, the *Louisiana,* ordered the arrest of the Confederate naval officers. Later Farragut backed up Porter and sent them to a Northern prison.

Butler's troops, under Brigadier General John W. Phelps, who had been waiting aboard the sail vessels down near the mouth of the river, were now towed up to garrison the two forts.

Captain Bailey came up to New Orleans during the evening of the twenty-eighth with the welcome news that the forts had surrendered. Farragut made hasty arrangements to bring up some of General Butler's troops to occupy the city.[15] Farragut was through with Confederate delay and double-talk; formal possession of the city must be taken. On the twenty-ninth, Captain Bell, leading a detachment of sailors with two howitzers and a battalion of marines, landed and proceeded to the Custom House, where they raised the Union flag. The people watched in silence, cowed by the loaded guns. At City Hall the state flag was lowered, but the United States flag was not put in its place because this was not a Federal building. A dense, sullen crowd looked on but made no demonstration. The detachment returned to the ships unmolested.

General and Mrs. Butler arrived on May 1 aboard the *Mississippi,* along with fourteen hundred troops. Before them the city lay quiet, for when the citizens learned the fate of the city they lost heart. All bars, most of the stores, and all hotels were closed. Just before sundown Butler ordered his troops to debark. Forming their lines they moved off briskly when a regimental band struck up a lively march, "Yankee Doodle." [16] Marion Southwood, an eyewitness, stated: "Men, women, and children . . . went splashing through the mud together . . . to get first sight. As soon as they saw Butler, . . . every epithet which could be applied to the vilest was heaped upon him." [17] The unruly mob, pushing and cursing the invader, followed the column to the Custom House. Butler's brow was furrowed with anxiety, not from fear of the crowd but from fear that he would not be able to keep in step. The tone-deaf general wanted to impress the crowd with his military bearing. From the quarter deck of the *Mississippi*, Mrs. Butler, a former actress, watched the highly dramatic scene. Stationing the troops at the Custom House and at other prominent positions, Butler and his staff returned to the *Mississippi*. The city remained calm and serene that night.

Farragut, relieved of the onerous duties of playing watchdog to a truant city, now returned to his naval duties. Captain Thomas T. Craven, with seven vessels, was sent up the river to Baton Rouge to take the capital city.[18]

VIII

VICKSBURG, ACT ONE

WHEN GOVERNOR Moore saw that New Orleans would fall, he prepared to evacuate the capital and issued orders on April 25 calling for the destruction of all cotton in the areas in danger of enemy occupation. Those planters who could haul their cotton to safety in the interior did so, but those who lacked the time or the transportation facilities began to carry out the governor's order. At Baton Rouge on April 26, Negroes slashed open bales of cotton and set them afire. Along the levee flaming bales were rolled into the water to float downstream. Flatboats piled high with cotton were drenched in alcohol and whisky and ignited with blazing pine knots and set adrift. Neither cotton nor liquor was to be left for the invader.

All up and down the Mississippi cotton fires lit up the skies. At Donaldsonville sugar was destroyed along with the cotton. Along the levees, and atop Indian mounds in Tensas Parish, thousands of bales burned for days. In Madison Parish hundreds of thousands of dollars' worth of cotton smoldered and burned while planters sadly looked on.[1]

During the evening of May 7, Commander James S. Palmer, from Craven's detachment sent upriver by Farragut, proceeded to Baton Rouge aboard the *Iroquois* and demanded the surrender of the city. Receiving no satisfactory answer, Palmer landed a force on the morning of the ninth and claimed possession of the arsenal and barracks. There was no show of resistance.

Meanwhile, Farragut had decided that control of the river would not easily be accomplished, so he abandoned his plans to divide his forces and move against Mobile. Instead, he moved up to Baton Rouge, followed by General Thomas Williams and fifteen hundred of Butler's troops. Farragut ordered Commander S. P. Lee to proceed against

Natchez on May 13. Lee forced Natchez to surrender and pushed on to Vicksburg, with six gunboats and the troops under General Williams. Farragut joined Lee below Vicksburg on the eighteenth and immediately ordered the city to surrender. The order was refused.

Farragut was too late. The Confederates had mounted eight or ten heavy columbiads on the high bluff out of reach of the fleet's guns. Eight thousand men had been drawn quickly from Louisiana and Mississippi to man the citadel. General Williams, with his few troops, felt that an assault would be foolhardy. After due reconnaissance and consultation with his officers, Farragut abandoned the idea of an attack or an attempt at passing the forts. Leaving the six gunboats to harass Vicksburg, Farragut returned down-river. General Williams, short of rations, followed Farragut to Baton Rouge.[2]

Back before the capital city, James B. Kimball, the chief engineer of the *Hartford,* dumped his dirty laundry into a small boat manned by four sailors and started for a house near the wharf to find a washwoman. As the small party neared the shore, about forty guerrillas rushed down the levee and blasted the boat with buckshot, slightly injuring Kimball and two of the sailors. When Farragut learned of this, he ordered the *Hartford* and *Kennebec* to open fire. In the city the citizens panicked. With shells filling the air, women and children ran screaming into the streets trying to escape. Negro servants gathered up clothes and family silver and joined in the exodus. The cowardly guerrillas mounted their horses and took refuge among the fleeing, hysterical women and children. Surprisingly, only one woman was killed, three were wounded, and two drowned while trying to escape. The gunboats continued to shell the town as long as they thought they could see any trace of the guerrillas. Many houses near the river were pock-marked with grape and canister while others were riddled with shot holes. The beautiful Roman Catholic church, the Harvey House, and the stately capitol were the most heavily damaged.

As soon as the guns ceased firing, a small group of citizens rowed out to the *Hartford.* They apologized for the attack upon the dinghy and professed that the city had no control over the lawless guerrillas. Farragut assured the citizens, and later the mayor, that unless he were attacked again he would not fire into the city. If possible, he would give notice of his intentions so that the women and children could be evacuated.

The next morning (May 29) General Williams arrived with his troops from Vicksburg. Farragut gave Williams rations for three days and requested that he go ashore to protect "the lives and property of loyal citizens." The guerrillas had threatened to return and destroy Baton Rouge in order to keep the Federal troops from taking over. General Williams landed and took possession of the United States barracks and set up his artillery. Feeling that Baton Rouge was relatively safe, Farragut left two gunboats to aid General Williams and departed for New Orleans to obtain supplies.

Williams did everything to prevent an attack on Baton Rouge. No citizen was allowed to leave the city without a pass, and a pass could be secured only to bring back members of the family who had fled from the bombardment of May 28. The general hoped that if friends and relatives of Confederate forces remained, no attempt would be made to take the city. Guards were posted at every corner. Every day patrols searched the surrounding areas for guerrillas. The citizens found the Federal officers to be gentlemen, and not one enlisted man showed disrespect to any inhabitant. Many ladies who were short of food were given flour and other necessities by the occupation forces.[3]

A message from G. V. Fox, the Assistant Secretary of the Navy, awaited Farragut in New Orleans. Fox urged Farragut to abandon plans to take Mobile and to proceed to Memphis. Such a move might cut off all possible escape for Beauregard's army. Farragut lost no time in trying to carry out his orders. Urged by General Butler, Farragut summoned Porter from Ship Island. Butler promised tow vessels for the mortars and an army to help take Vicksburg and Memphis. Leaving a small force to protect Baton Rouge, General Williams embarked for Vicksburg.

Porter arrived at Vicksburg on June 20 with part of his mortar fleet. The next day the mortars began shelling the town. By the twenty-fifth, Farragut and his fleet, the rest of the mortar boats, and General Williams, with over three thousand troops, were ready to move against the city.[4]

Farragut learned that Commander Charles H. Davis had captured Memphis on June 6 and was coming down to Vicksburg. Meanwhile, Porter maneuvered his mortar boats into position on both sides of the river and opened an ineffective bombardment against the Confederate batteries and against Vicksburg itself. Farragut grew tired of waiting for Davis. In the early morning of June 28 signal lights were hoisted, and the two columns of gunboats began to move. At 4 A.M. Porter opened on the batteries, firing as fast as his gunners could reload.

The dark night and the thick acrid smoke made the batteries almost invisible to Farragut's men. Befuddled gunners fired more often at exploding mortar shells than at real targets. From high above, the Confederate gunners blazed away at the slow-moving fleet, splintering masts, damaging hulls, and finding human targets. Just after sunrise, however, less than two hours after the action began, all except three of the Federal ships had succeeded in reaching safety above the batteries.[5]

In compliance with instructions from General Butler, on June 27 General Williams began work on a cutoff canal a mile and a quarter long across a neck of land on the Louisiana side. It was the opinion of Butler and his advisers that a ditch four to six feet wide and about five feet deep would divert the channel of the river and that the rushing waters would dredge out a canal deep enough to admit any ship. There would be far less danger in using this route than in sailing directly under the guns of the city. If all went well and the expected "June rise" came, the course of the Mississippi would be diverted and Vicksburg would be left an inland city, with her batteries useless. Twelve hundred Negroes rounded up from nearby plantations were set to work cutting down trees, removing roots, and digging in the hard clay with shovels. Farragut awaited the results with keen interest.

The Negroes laughed and shouted at their work, thinking they were earning their freedom. While Williams' men wilted in the oppressive heat, the sweating Negroes flourished. The health of the troops suffered from lack of proper shelter. The sick list mounted. The transports were crowded and hot. By July 11 the ditch had reached an average width of eighteen feet and was thirteen feet deep, or about one-and-a-half feet below the level of the river. Preparations to let in the water were hastened, but suddenly the banks began to cave and the work had to be abandoned temporarily. After digging furiously for three days, Williams was disheartened to find the river falling faster than his men could dig. The general, however, thought that the canal would prove successful, and he prepared to gather up more Negroes and to work for three months, if necessary, to dig a real canal.

In the parishes along the river above and below Vicksburg some of the citizens began to move to Bayou Macon and beyond to escape a possible raid from the Yankees. Others, however, refused to acknowledge the presence of danger and continued to while away their time visiting, giving fish fries and picnics, and playing chess, backgammon, and cards. The continual roar of the cannons at Vicksburg eventually wore on nerves, and many of the planters began sending their Negroes into the interior, some taking them as far away as Texas. Press gangs sent out by General Williams ranged up and down the river, stripping the plantations of all able-bodied Negro men to work on the canal. The Negro men, lured by promises of freedom, gladly left their wives, children, homes, and masters for a life of hard labor and short rations, with only the trees for shelter at night. Occasionally the soldiers raided the plantations for food and for anything else that struck their fancy.[6]

Farragut had successfully run past Vicksburg but in so doing had accomplished very little. The Confederate guns were still intact. The citadel was as strong as ever and was growing stronger each day. In desperation Farragut appealed to General Henry Halleck to send him reinforcements from Corinth. Halleck failed to grasp the importance of taking Vicksburg and instead, when he broke up his army, sent men to join McClellan and reinforcements to Samuel R. Curtis and Don C. Buell. No troops were spared to be used against Vicksburg. Vicksburg would stand another year against the Union forces and would cost thousands of lives before it finally fell.

On July 1 Davis arrived at Young's Point, above Vicksburg, with four ironclad gunboats, four mortar vessels, and several auxiliary boats to join forces with Farragut. The gunboats and mortars of both Davis and Porter continued to throw their shells at the hillside batteries and into the city, but the rate of fire was greatly reduced. As usual, the importance of Vicksburg was being discounted, and on July 8 Farragut received a second dispatch from the Navy department ordering him to send Porter and twelve of his mortars to Hampton Roads. On the twelfth, Porter began the long two thousand mile trip to Virginia, leaving five of his mortars and the remaining steamers under command of Commander William B. Renshaw.

Farragut had much to worry him during the long, hot July days. The greatest and most immediate menace to his fleet was the recently completed Confederate ram, the *Arkansas,* which was anchored at Greenwood, up the Yazoo River. The *Arkansas* was 165 feet long and 35 feet wide, and wore an armor of railroad iron 4½ inches thick. Fore and aft the shields of the long, rakish vessel were slanted, but her side shields were perpendicular to the water.

Lieutenant Isaac N. Brown was under orders to take the *Arkansas* out of the Yazoo, past the Federal fleet, down the Mississippi into the Gulf, and on to Mobile to lift the blockade. The *Arkansas* entered the Mississippi just above Vicksburg on the morning of July 15 and began her run through the gantlet of the combined forces of Davis, Farragut, and the ram fleet under Colonel Alfred W. Ellet. The Union vessels were unable to build up sufficient steam and remained anchored or tied up in their original positions, pouring their broadsides into the ram. Shot after shot rained on the sides of the ram, loosening the iron plating. The boilers and smokestacks were riddled, and the steam pressure fell to twenty pounds. For an hour the *Arkansas* drifted slowly down the long line of Union gunboats, rams, mortars, and allied vessels, taking their fire and returning it with full measure. Miraculously, the *Arkansas* reached the protection of the upper batteries and was now safe to move directly to Vicksburg. When the *Arkansas* hove into view, the lower fleet panicked and fled downstream. One mortar caught fire and blew up. Infantry regiments camped on the Louisiana shore set fire to their stores, stampeded to their transports, and ran down the river. When they saw that the *Arkansas* did not intend to attack, they returned to their original positions.

At twilight Farragut took his forces down-river in two columns while Davis moved three of his gunboats into position to draw the fire of the batteries. But the dark, misty night and a change of positions made the Confederate ram impossible to locate until the Union vessels had moved too far beyond. When the last ship passed below, the *Arkansas* was still afloat, although her armor plate and one of her engines had been severely damaged.

Frustrated and angry, Farragut devised new plans for the destruction of the *Arkansas*. At dawn on July 22 the formidable ironclad ram *Essex,* commanded by Commander W. D. Porter, moved in to strike the *Arkansas,* still at anchor. The ships exchanged shots at close quarters, both were damaged, and the *Essex* was forced to seek refuge with the lower fleet.

Shortly thereafter, the ram *Queen of the West,* commanded by Colonel Ellet, appeared and ran head on into the *Arkansas*. Rebounding from the terrific blow, the *Queen* rushed in again and grounded. Freeing herself, the Federal ram made a third lunge at the *Arkansas*. The shock of the encounters shook up both vessels but did no real damage to either. However, by this time the *Queen* had been struck over twenty times by shot and shells and was much cut up. Colonel Ellet abandoned his attack and made a run for safety back to the upper fleet.[7]

Across the river, General Williams was digging away at a new ditch to divert the waters of the river and leave Vicksburg high and dry. The unacclimatized Northerners continued to suffer from the torrid midsummer heat and from swarms of malarial mosquitoes. Swearing men, alternately seared with burning fever and racked by chills, overtaxed every hospital facility. The supply of quinine was soon exhausted. Every inch of space aboard the transports had to be used as a sick bay, and men who were still well had to move to the shore. Only a few were able to find shelter tents and flies; the others "scrounged" for stray pieces of lumber and managed to erect crawl-in shelters. For weeks the men had nothing to eat but salt pork and moldy hardtack; there was no water to drink except the muddy waters of the Mississippi.

Williams showed little sympathy for the suffering of his men. An army career man, he had graduated from West Point and had rendered distinguished service with Scott in the Mexican War. Worshiping discipline, he was considered a martinet by his troops. Despite the oppressive heat and the debilitation of the troops, he ordered daily drills with full knapsacks.[8] Captain O'Brien of the Ninth Connecticut stated: "I saw men drop out of the line exhausted, and when we returned many of them would be dead. This drill and parading was done when the thermometer registered 110 to 115 in the shade." [9] Williams was disgusted with the frailties of his men, and he was determined to toughen them so that they could weather the broiling sun.

The toughening process failed. With each week the sick list increased by the hundreds. During mid-July 1,500, or about half the command, were confined to sick beds afloat and ashore. The mortality rate was fearful. From the Connecticut detachments present, some 350 men in number, 153 died during the campaign. Men who died were wrapped in an army blanket and buried without a funeral escort or any type of ceremony. The few men who remained well were used for picket duty and the supervision of the Negro work gangs; they could not be spared for the business of military funerals. The men became more and more despondent.

The commanding general was not discouraged; these were the fortunes of war. The Negroes were urged to dig faster. A portion of the labor force was used to convert the original canal into a defense line. The more the men dug, the faster the level of the river fell. The river men and Confederates ridiculed their efforts to turn the river through a man-made canal that started in an eddy, at the wrong angle. At last even General Williams despaired of success. On July 16 General Butler urged Williams to return down-river as soon as possible to blockade Red River and to help protect Baton Rouge. Williams prepared to abandon the canal project and to depart for Baton Rouge.[10]

Farragut, who had accomplished so little and who still smarted from his impotent efforts to knock out the *Arkansas,* was anxious to quit the area. Nearly half his crew was incapacitated, and daily more and more men succumbed to malaria or dysentery. His supply of coal and food was far from plentiful. Gideon Welles, who knew nothing of the imminent danger of the *Arkansas,* instructed Farragut to return to the Gulf, where he could render greater service. Flag Officer Davis was instructed to take over the defenses of the Mississippi.

No time was lost by Farragut in preparing for departure. Davis urged General Williams to remain, to help keep communications open between the upper and lower fleets, but Williams refused. General Williams reneged on his promise of freedom and deserted his Negro laborers. On July 24 Farragut's fleet, accompanied by Williams' fleet and men, departed for the lower river. The abandoned Negroes gathered on the levee; their shrieks of woe rang out over the water as the boats moved away. Davis, whose crews were also decimated by malaria, decided to leave Vicksburg, and on the thirty-first he retired with his gunboats and mortars to Memphis and Helena. Vicksburg was left to the Confederates, who quickly began to bring boats from the Sunflower River and to reopen commercial and military communications between Louisiana and Vicksburg. Only one gunboat, the *Essex,* under W. D. Porter, was left to patrol the river between Vicksburg and Baton Rouge.[11]

The fortunes of the Union fleet had reached a low ebb at Vicksburg. The campaign had been a hopeless failure for many reasons. The use of mortars had proven ineffectual against the hillside batteries; Farragut's and Davis' fleets had not always acted with dispatch and audacity when necessity demanded it; there were serious shortages of food and fuel; disease had taken a tremendous toll; and the canal idea had proved a fiasco. More important than these factors, however, were the failure of General Butler to co-operate fully by sending more men and the failure of Halleck to send any men at all. Halleck could have spared ten to twenty thousand men. Vicksburg could have been taken by assault while she had so few men in garrison. But what might have been did not happen. There would be another longer and more costly act to the drama of Vicksburg.

On July 26 General Williams arrived in Baton Rouge, and Admiral Farragut proceeded to New Orleans. The general stepped ashore with lively grace. His disciplined, erect body did not in the least reflect the terrible ordeal that had been his for over a month. His hair was neatly cropped, and his florid face was partially covered with well-trimmed whiskers and mustache. But with the men it was different. Their care-worn faces and their sagging, emaciated bodies clearly reflected the suffering they had known at Vicksburg. The procession of the sick, some borne on litters, some lodged in ambulances and wagons, and some staggering along on foot, made its way to various houses and buildings that had been confiscated for hospitals.

The men felt little respect for General Williams. Williams thought that any volunteer officer who went out of his way to make his men more comfortable was a would-be politician trying to drum up votes. Most of the men believed that the general considered a volunteer no better than a dog. General Williams was a stickler for petty regulations. In the enervating heat of Baton Rouge in late July he continued to hold regular drill and frequent full-dress inspections. Still weak from the rigors of the late and demoralizing campaign, more and more men sickened and died. The military cemeteries of the city had to be enlarged to accommodate the increasing number of dead. Nearly half of the entire garrison at Baton Rouge was on the sick list. Williams possessed courtly and gracious manners harking back to the days of chivalry, but his rigid discipline was not understood nor appreciated by the citizen-soldiers of his command.[12]

As soon as the Federal fleet took leave of Vicksburg, Major General Earl Van Dorn, a former classmate of Williams' at West Point, quickly assumed the offensive and ordered General John C. Breckinridge to lead an expedition to strike at Baton Rouge. The capture of this point would give the Confederates control over two points on the river and would open up Red River, from which badly needed supplies could be procured. Perhaps if Baton Rouge were held, the recapture of New Orleans might not be impossible. A small force of four thousand men left Vicksburg on July 27 by train for Camp Moore. As there were very few cars available, the men could carry only a little food, their arms, and ammunition. The troops arrived at Camp Moore on the evening of the twenty-eighth. While waiting for the *Arkansas* to be sent down to clear out the gunboats around Baton Rouge, the men languished at Camp Moore without shelter from the summer heat and rains, and many of them sickened. In a few days' time the epidemic reduced the ranks to about three thousand effectives. Receiving assurance that the *Arkansas* was on its way, Breckinridge started his men on a two-day march to Greenwell Springs on the Comite River.

The forced march was a nightmare. About one third of the men had no shoes, and the sandy road became almost unbearable to those who were barefoot. Some of the men were bare to the waist; some were dressed only in rags. Each man staggered through the blinding heat under the weight of a full pack. There was little water along the route of the march. Thirst-crazed men sighting a stagnant pond pushed aside the thick, green scum and drank greedily. Soldier after soldier, weakened by the heat, bad water, and dysentery, fell out and dragged himself to the shade of a tree or bush. Finally on Monday afternoon, August 4, Breckinridge and his men reached the Comite River, just ten miles to the east of Baton Rouge. Here the men were allowed to bathe and rest until 11 P.M., when orders were issued to move on to Baton Rouge. Word had arrived by messenger that the *Arkansas* would arrive before the city early the next morning and be ready to co-operate with the land forces in the attack.[13]

The Tennessee and Alabama troops had suffered especially. They were poorly clad, sickly, and worn out even before the march began. The Alabama, Mississippi, and Tennessee regiments were little more than small companies in size; one skeleton regiment had only forty-five men. "They marched in straggling order many of them lank, bent individuals, seemingly hardly able to support the burden of their blanket rolls and haversacks, but I noticed that their rifles were in perfect order, clean and shining."[14] Dysentery and the fatigue of the night march took additional toll among the troops. Around 4 A.M. the weary men arrived at the rear of Baton Rouge. Counting the troops in Brigadier General Daniel Ruggles' command from Camp Moore, Breckinridge had only twenty-six hundred men to carry into battle.

Some two hundred Partisan Rangers were employed to picket various roads leading into the town. During the night a few of these men moved too far to the front and ran into the enemy pickets, causing an exchange of shots. The Rangers rode back swiftly. Several enlisted men and one officer were killed, and others were wounded. The officer was A. H. Todd, half-brother of Mary Todd Lincoln. As soon as order was restored, Breckinridge placed his forces on the left and right side of the Greenwell Springs Road in a single line of battle. A small regiment of infantry, with one piece of artillery per division, was held in reserve. The alarm had been sounded. The element of surprise was gone. The Confederate troops waited in line for daylight to begin the attack.[15]

THE BATTLE OF BATON ROUGE

MAJOR GENERAL John C. Breckinridge of Kentucky, former Vice President of the United States and candidate for President in the election of 1860, was without military experience except for a short period in the Mexican War and his participation in the battle of Shiloh and the defense of Vicksburg. However, he could lead men and adapt himself to changing circumstances, and he was a man worthy of leading the attack against Baton Rouge.[1]

The Confederate forces, consisting of regiments from Louisiana, Mississippi, Kentucky, Tennessee, and Alabama, were divided into two divisions. Brigadier General Charles Clark of Mississippi, on the right of the Greenwell Springs Road, commanded the First Division, which consisted of one brigade under Colonel Thomas H. Hunt and one brigade under Colonel T. B. Smith, with Hudson's and Cobb's batteries. The Second Division, on the left of the road, led by Brigadier General Daniel Ruggles, a native of Massachusetts and a former U.S. Army officer, was comprised of the First Brigade on the right under Colonel A. P. Thompson and the Second Brigade under Colonel Henry Watkins Allen, with Oliver J. Semmes's battery between the two. Allen's left extended through a wood, resting on a large field. A squadron of cavalry, commanded by Captain Augustus Scott, was sent to the extreme left to observe and to prevent a flanking movement by the enemy. One small regiment and one gun were kept as a reserve for each division.

Meanwhile, on the Federal side there had been no napping. Hearing rumors of an intended attack, General Williams had made plans to repel it. As if by a miracle, many of the men in the hospitals found themselves recovering and rejoining their outfits. The powerful and magic tonic was the prospect of a fight. Only the day before, General Williams had personally reconnoitered the ground and had planned his various positions. And now, August 5, his troops stood in the gray dawn awaiting the attack. On the extreme left and to the north of the main part of the city, on the elevated right bank of Bayou Grasse, two sections of Captain Charles H. Manning's battery were deployed. On the south side of the Bayou and to the east and south, near the Penitentiary grounds, was the Fourth Wisconsin, with the rest of Manning's battery between them and the Ninth Connecticut. Farthest east, up near the crossing of the Bayou Sara and Greenwell Springs roads, was the Fourteenth Maine. Nearby, but on the right and south side of the Greenwell Springs Road, was Everett's battery. Next came the Twenty-first Indiana, which was stationed behind the Magnolia Cemetery and between Captain Charles Everett's and Captain Ormand F. Nims's batteries. The Sixth Michigan was on the extreme right near the juncture of Perkins and Clay Cut roads and to the west of the Catholic Cemetery and the race course. The Seventh Vermont stood behind the Twenty-first Indiana to strengthen the center, and the Thirtieth Massachusetts waited in reserve down near the state house, to support the extreme right. Brown's battery was also held in reserve in the rear. This disposition was made because the main Confederate attack was expected to come on the Federal left flank, where the *Arkansas* would help to cover the move. The two flanks of the Union depended upon the support of their gunboats in the river. The left was aided by the *Essex,* the *Sumter,* and the *Cayuga,* and the Federal right was supported by the *Kineo* and the *Katahdin.*[2]

Shrouded by a thick fog, the Confederate troops began their forward movement. General Breckinridge had ordered Lieutenant Colonel Thomas Shields of the Thirtieth Louisiana Regiment to take two companies of infantry and one of the dismounted Partisan Rangers, along with two guns from Semmes's battery, to the far left along the Clinton Road and, upon signal, to begin an attack upon a Federal battery thought to be posted there. The men marched all night. At dawn the signal, the sound of small-arms fire, was heard, and Colonel Shields, with his hundred and fifty exhausted men, moved forward on the double-quick. They found no Federal battery, and enemy pickets had fled, leaving various items of equipment hanging on posts, walls of houses, and trees. The Federal sentries halted and fired one volley from the shelter of a wood and then fled toward the Arsenal, nearer the river front.

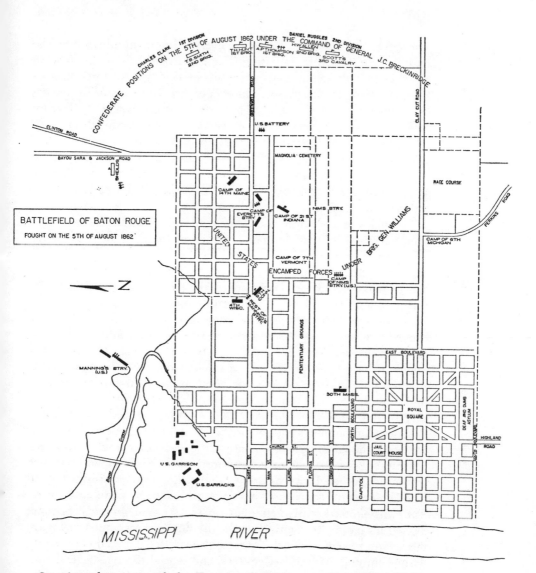

Battlefield of Baton Rouge — Fought on the 5th of August 1862

Spotting the camp of the Fourteenth Maine on his right, Shields ordered his men to advance slowly. The two pieces of artillery were placed in position to rake the street leading directly to the camp. The Maine regiment now appeared and halted the advance. Semmes's artillery, firing rapidly, caused the enemy to fall back, and Shields led his men to within 250 feet of the regimental camp of the Fourteenth Maine. Unfortunately, four artillery horses were wounded, and the rest refused to advance. Faced by overwhelming numbers, Shields's infantry was forced to fall back. The main body of the Confederate right wing, advancing toward the camp through the fog, mistook Shields's men for the enemy and opened fire upon them, fortunately doing little damage. Shields's infantry force was attached to the Twenty-second Mississippi by General Clark, and Colonel Shields was left with the artillery near the Clinton Road, a position he maintained until he retired by order of General Breckinridge at the end of the engagement. Clark drove forward, forcing the Fourteenth Maine to vacate their camp and move across the Greenwell Springs Road into the camp of the Twenty-first Indiana.

Through the dawn mist the Confederate left, General Ruggles' division, advanced in a single line. The men of the First Brigade moved across an open field. They were protected on the left flank by an impenetrable hedge of Chickasaw roses. At irregular intervals the men had to snake under, or clamber over, the fences lacing the field. Underbrush and briars tore at the men's clothes and flesh, temporarily impeding their forward progress. Suddenly the Twenty-first Indiana opened fire, and the Confederates, although they could see no one, returned the fire. The exchange lasted only a moment. The heavy fog hugging the ground prevented the smoke from the rifles from rising. Limited visibility was cut even more when the acrid smoke settled in thick clouds around the men.

A battery of Federal artillery, Nims's, then opened fire. General Ruggles sent Semmes's battery forward to dislodge the skirmishers and to silence the enemy guns. Using grape and canister at close quarters, Semmes's Louisiana Battery performed well. With a wild yell the entire line surged forward, firing rapidly. Enemy skirmishers poured from houses and from their positions behind trees, running back toward the protection of their guns on the Arsenal grounds. Semmes located his battery to the right of the division and continued to engage the enemy battery. Colonel Thompson's brigade advanced over fences, pushed through Magnolia Cemetery, and moved through several corn fields until they ran into a heavy fire from a wooded area. Here, for a considerable time, Thompson hotly disputed possession of the ground with the Twenty-first Indiana.

In the course of this exchange a portion of Clark's Division, on the right, was seen retreating. Thompson was assured by a mounted officer that there were orders for the entire Confederate line to fall back. Thompson obeyed this supposed order and fell back a short distance.

When the Indiana troops saw the movement to the rear, they raised a mighty cheer, increased their rate of fire, and started after Thompson's men. The Thirty-fifth Alabama and the Sixth Kentucky were so roiled over the premature shouts of the enemy that they rushed forward, without being ordered to do so, and checked the advances of the enemy. Colonel Thompson spurred his horse to the front of his men to lead the charge. A bullet found its mark, and the colonel fell from his horse. His wounds were serious, and he was borne from the field.

On the right, the Confederate First Division, under General Charles Clark, succeeded in pushing into the camp of the Fourteenth Maine. Lieutenant Colonel Thomas H. Hunt of the First Brigade re-formed his lines and attacked with renewed vigor, forcing the Fourteenth Maine from their second position and driving them through the Seventh Vermont encampment into a ravine on the south side of the Penitentiary grounds. Colonel Hunt fell from his horse with a shot through his thigh and was carried from the field. Suddenly an order of unknown origin was passed down the line to fall back. The Confederate troops were bewildered. The enemy was in retreat; why should they draw back? At this point General Clark rode up and ordered Captain John A. Buckner, who had taken over Hunt's brigade, to resume the advance against the Fourteenth Maine, which was now moving back toward its second position. The forward movement had hardly begun when General Clark was seriously wounded, and the men were ordered to retire to the cover of a small ravine in front of the Fourteenth Maine. They grumbled but finally complied. General Breckinridge rode up and rallied the men, ordering them forward once more. Leading the charge, General Breckinridge and his yelling troops drove the Federal forces from their positions and back near the Seventh Vermont camp, located in a grove fronting on the east of the Penitentiary grounds.

The Twenty-first Indiana, armed with breechloaders, was finally driven from its camp by the headlong drive of Thompson's brigade. The men took cover behind trees and hid in ravines to shield themselves. The force became somewhat disorganized. To add to the chaos, the Seventh Vermont, located behind the Indiana Regiment, opened up a deadly fire, killing many of the men of the Twenty-first and wounding others. The demoralized Vermont troops immediately gave way. In their retreat they met General Williams, who harshly demanded an explanation of their conduct. The Vermonters were severely reprimanded and ordered forward to the support of the Twenty-first Indiana. Williams then ordered the Thirtieth Massachusetts and two

sections of Nims's battery to support the Sixth Michigan on the far
Federal right. The Ninth Connecticut, Fourth Wisconsin, and one
section of Manning's battery were sent to aid the Twenty-first Indiana
but arrived too late.

The gunboats in the river were firing at the Confederate center, but
as the two forces drew closer to each other, it was necessary to suspend
fire. The contest in and around the encampment of the Seventh Vermont was bloody, for the men of Thompson's brigade, having exhausted
their supply of ammunition, used bayonets for hand-to-hand combat. For almost an hour the Federal center, the Twenty-first Indiana,
the Seventh Vermont, and a part of the Ninth Connecticut, held back
the Confederate advance. Several Federal officers were severely
wounded or killed. Among these were Colonel G. T. Roberts of the
Seventh Vermont, seriously wounded in the neck, and General Williams, shot through the chest. Williams died instantly, and Colonel
N. A. M. Dudley took over command of the entire Federal forces.
With Williams' death a certain amount of demoralization set in, and
the troops were withdrawn to a new position back nearer the Penitentiary area. Finally the entire center line began to break, and the
frightened Federal troops routed and fled to the protection of the guns
of the fleet on the river front near the United States Barracks and
Arsenal. They did not leave their place of safety during the rest of
the day. It was then ten o'clock in the morning.

On the Confederate left wing, while the First Brigade and Semmes's
artillery were advancing to the front of the Twenty-first Indiana, the
Second Brigade under Colonel Henry Watkins Allen, on the left,
moved steadily through heavy woods, briars, underbrush, cornfields,
and picket fences. A battery, supported by infantry, halted the Confederate advance. Several volleys were fired by Allen's men, and the
enemy scattered, taking its artillery with it. While in pursuit of
the retreating foe, the Confederates sighted another battery, supported
by the Sixth Michigan, on the extreme left near the juncture of Perkins
and Clay Cut roads, just below the race course. Taking this to be a
flanking movement and one which must be halted at all costs, Allen
ordered a movement to the left. At the command "Charge," the whole
brigade gave a great cheer and made a gallant charge. Seizing the
colors of Boyd's battalion, Allen rode full speed ahead. His men ran
after him, across an open field some three hundred yards wide. The
Sixth Michigan and supporting artillery raked the area with a murderous hail of rifle and artillery fire. Men dropped like leaves; Lieutenant

Colonel Samuel Boyd fell from his horse, shot through the arm. Allen pressed on and was almost up to the guns when his horse was hit and died instantly. Colonel Allen pitched to the ground, one of his legs shattered and the other riddled by grape and canister shot.

When the men of the Fourth Louisiana saw their beloved commander go down, they crowded around him and wept. Forming a stretcher of muskets, they bore him off the field. The demoralized regiment fell back in confusion, some of the men flinging away their arms. The enemy renewed the fire, and Boyd's battalion faltered and could not be rallied. The entire line broke and retreated in fright across the open field over which it had so bravely charged a short time before. In the shelter of a grove, Colonel Gustavus A. Breaux and Lieutenant Colonel S. E. Hunter, after a herculean struggle, rallied a sufficient number of men to form a new line. Semmes's battery was brought forward and, with rapid firing, was able to halt the enemy's advance. The Federal artillery and gunboats opened on the new position, and the right again gave way, followed by the entire line. The men, crying for water and ready to drop from fatigue and hunger, were utterly demoralized, and no entreaties from their officers could rally them again. This was the end of the fight for Allen's Second Brigade. Colonel Edward Crossland of the Seventh Kentucky Regiment was ordered to remain to support Semmes's battery, to cover the retreat of stragglers, and to assist those who were trying to recover the wounded. It was now around 10 A.M., and the August heat was unbearable. Many of the men began to search frantically for water.[3]

The citizens of Baton Rouge had been awakened at dawn by the fire of musketry and the deeper roar of the cannon. Rebel yells rent the air. Families with foresight had constructed bombproof shelters and now took refuge in them. As the battle neared, many persons panicked. Running pell-mell through the streets, the terror-stricken people discovered that only one avenue of escape remained, that to the south down the Highland and River roads. Men, women, and children, bearing whatever personal treasure they could seize, streamed through the dingy streets of "Catfishtown." The struggling masses poured out of the town, their wild flight stirring up clouds of dust. Some were hatless, some without shoes, some wore wrappers and coats over their night clothes. On they ran, through mounting heat and dust, some crying, some praying, some sick, but all with one common purpose—to escape the horrors of the bursting shells, the flying bullets, and the hand-to-hand fighting inside the city. South of the city the mob rushed into homes on plantations and farms. Feeling safe again, the hungry people became screeching, snatching animals. Storerooms were broken into, and while the food lasted, the townsfolk gorged themselves.

Watching from their bomb shelters, those who remained in town saw the men in gray spring over fences and swarm through the cemeteries, trampling graves, knocking over little crosses, and shattering larger monuments. They saw the streets fill up with Federal troops and Negroes when the Federal left wing gave way. Under the hill, down near the levee, the demoralized soldiers and frightened Negroes cowered, while their gunboats poured shells, grape, and canister into the streets of the city. All efforts made by the officers to rally their men failed. They would not return up the hill to face the victorious Confederates.[4]

Some three hundred miles above Baton Rouge, the ram *Arkansas* had completed her repairs and had hastily left Vicksburg, minus her ill commander, to reinforce the Confederate force in its attack on Baton Rouge. Lieutenant Henry K. Stevens, in his race against time, overtaxed his engines, and had to make several stops for repairs. Each delay forced Stevens to push his boat even more in order to be able to keep his appointment.

General Breckinridge strained his ears for the sound of the *Arkansas'* guns in action against the Federal fleet, but the sound did not come. Meanwhile, the gunboats and batteries near the barracks and arsenal poured a direct fire into Breckinridge's ranks. The men stood their ground, daring the cowering enemy to come up the hill and fight. These men were completely exhausted. They had marched all night and had been under arms for sixteen hours. For the last four hours they had fought hard. They had gone without sleep, without supper and breakfast, and had been out of water for hours. The troops had done all that could be done until the coming of the *Arkansas*. Breckinridge withdrew his troops to the suburbs in the east, where they found water in cisterns. Here they stayed the rest of the day, out of range of the gunboats. A detachment was sent back to destroy all of the camps and stores of the enemy. There were no transportation facilities at hand to use in carting away the rich prizes, so torches were applied to tents, and to quartermaster and commissary supplies.

While the troops and townspeople were waiting for news of the *Arkansas,* citizens from the surrounding area began to arrive with carriages and wagons to take the wounded to homes near by. Breckinridge's men had no picks nor shovels, and it was impossible to bury the dead.[5]

Just four miles above Baton Rouge the ram had developed new engine difficulties and was tied up to the bank. Hundreds of spectators in their carriages gathered along the river front, waving and smiling, happy in anticipation of a quick victory for the Confederacy. As they watched, enemy gunboats appeared.

The last engine trouble proved worse than expected, and when the enemy gunboats began their cautious approach, the *Arkansas* could not be moved. Several shots were exchanged by the two forces with little or no effect. Lieutenant Stevens ordered the crew ashore, set the ship afire, cut the moorings, and set her adrift. With flag flying high, the smoking, empty ship floated down upon the enemy. When the flames reached the shotted guns, they discharged. The fire finally reached the magazine, and the ship exploded. As the end of the *Arkansas* approached, many of the spectators wrung their hands and cried. The grimy, scantily dressed crew, some carrying only their guns and others burdened with knapsacks, moved through the crowd and made their escape.

Watching the death of the *Arkansas* from a safe distance were the two Federal gunboats, the *Essex* and the *Cayuga*. At no time had they shown a desire to move in close and do battle with the dread Confederate ram. What few shots were exchanged were fired from a distance of more than a mile and a half.[6]

At four o'clock in the afternoon Breckinridge learned of the fate of the *Arkansas* and abandoned all plans to resume the attack. Around dark he ordered his troops to withdraw to the Comite River. That night they traveled four miles and rested; the next day they reached the river and went into camp. An outpost was established at Pratt's farm, only five miles from Baton Rouge, but the Confederates were in no danger, as the enemy did not leave the city.

Federal reports, in comparison with available Southern sources concerning the battle of Baton Rouge, are few in number and short on information, even those in the *Official Records*. The Federal commanders in Louisiana usually wrote long, detailed reports concerning actions of far less importance and size than the Baton Rouge affair, but there was little the Union troops could point to with pride.

The two sides went into battle with almost equal numbers. General Williams with around 2,500 troops faced General Breckinridge with his 2,600 men. The opposing forces both suffered from the ravages of malaria and exposure. The Confederates had an advantage in that many of them were battle-seasoned veterans of Shiloh and defenders of Vicksburg, whereas none of the Union forces had ever been in battle and few had ever been under fire. On the other hand, Williams had eighteen guns, not counting those on the four gunboats, and the Confederates had only eleven. With better weapons and plenty of supplies, food, ammunition, and other advantages, the forces at Baton Rouge added no real glory to the Federal military record.

The battle had lasted only a short time, but the fighting had been severe. The Union had 383 casualties: 84 killed, 266 wounded, and 33 either captured or missing. Confederate losses were estimated to be 84 killed, 315 wounded, and 57 missing, a total of between 446 and 456. Having used up their energies and most of their resources, the Confederates had failed to drive the Federal forces out of the town. The obstacle of the gunboats, after the *Arkansas* failed to appear, could not be overcome.[7]

The day after the battle Negroes were set to work burying bloated, blackened bodies, now swarming with worms. For the next two weeks, men were kept busy with spades, picks, and axes building rifle pits and earth breastworks in anticipation of a second attack from the Confederates. Groves of massive oaks and magnolias, along with the trees that shaded the streets, were felled and laid across the leading streets to hinder an enemy advance. For nearly two weeks the work of building up defenses for Baton Rouge went forward. One third of the town was burned or torn down so that the gunboats, located above and below town, would have a clean sweep and be able to converge their fire on the rear and side approaches to the town. Colonel H. E. Paine of the Fourth Wisconsin, who assumed command on August 6, next shortened his lines and constructed strong entrenchments in the Arsenal grounds, placing twenty-four guns in position. Nothing was overlooked nor neglected to strengthen the position and to guard against a surprise attack.[8]

On August 13 Colonel James W. McMillan of the Twenty-first Indiana wrote General Butler that the town had been sacked by the troops. Most of the officers were indifferent or powerless to put a stop to it, and some of them even filled their own tents with fine furniture from plundered houses. McMillan bitterly complained of the lack of discipline everywhere.

General Butler, who had previously decided to hold Baton Rouge, after due reflection changed his mind. He feared above all else that the next Confederate target would be New Orleans and wanted to concentrate his men there to repulse the attack. He ordered Colonel Paine to burn Baton Rouge to the ground, in spite of an appeal by Lieutenant Godfrey Weitzel of the Engineers, who protested that the presence of large orphan and insane asylums would make this an inhumane action. Three days later, on August 19, Butler countermanded his orders and advised Paine to leave Baton Rouge as intact as possible. On further orders from Butler, Colonel Paine released the several hundred convicts from the Penitentiary and ordered them to enlist in the United States army.

Before departing, the unruly soldiers went on a new plundering rampage. Souvenirs, valuable books, silver, and art objects were collected. Swarms of Negroes were allowed to pass through the lines and to join the pillagers. Portraits on walls were slashed to ribbons. Vinegar, molasses, and anything that would stain or ruin walls, furniture, or floors was smeared over them. Mirrors were smashed. Dresses were shredded as they hung in armoires; fine china was broken; storerooms were robbed; and wrecked furniture was scattered through the houses and the yards. The once-beautiful town, with its shade trees felled, its streets littered with debris, and over one third of its houses burned or wrecked by the troops, was now a shocking sight. By Butler's order, Hiram Powers' statue of Washington and the books of the State Library were removed from the capitol. The statue was sent to the Patent Office in Washington, and Butler kept the books in New Orleans.

On the morning of August 21 the troops, with all their guns, equipment, and spoils, loaded aboard their transports and moved down to Carrollton, just above New Orleans, where they immediately began strengthening the defenses of Camp Parapet in anticipation of a Confederate move against New Orleans.[9]

Two gunboats, the *Essex* and the *No. 7*, remained before Baton Rouge and threatened to shell the entire town if Confederate forces entered. Almost immediately citizens who had fled during the battle began to move back into the shattered town.

Although the Confederate attack had failed to take Baton Rouge, the Breckinridge expedition did not end unsuccessfully. A few days after the battle of Baton Rouge, General Breckinridge carried out the wishes of General Van Dorn by occupying Port Hudson, between Baton Rouge and Bayou Sara, with troops under the command of General Ruggles. Port Hudson, unlike Baton Rouge, was one of the strongest points on the river, and batteries placed upon the bluffs could command the entire river front. Once more food, supplies, and men could be brought from the Trans-Mississippi region to Vicksburg and other points. Captain James Nocquet of the Engineers arrived and prepared positions for the guns being sent down by Van Dorn. On August 19, General Breckinridge left from Port Hudson for Jackson, Mississippi, taking a portion of his men. Ruggles remained and hastened the work on the fortifications.[10] General Butler and the Federal navy made no attempt to dislodge the Confederates from their new position until it was too late.

X

RULE OF THE BEAST

NEW ORLEANS was a changed city. From May 1 into December General Butler ruled over the city in the grand manner of a viceroy. "A . . . man of middle height, quick and nervous in his movements, . . . thin compressed lips, livid complexion, thin hair thrown back over his ears," the autocratic general was far from handsome.[1] He was inordinately proud of his fine teeth and smiled often, in a mechanical manner, as if to show his one outstanding physical blessing. Two vastly different eyes looked out from a massive head that seemed too large for his body. One enemy described his "cock-eyes" as "a good eye and an evil eye. Near to the evil eye there was something like a large, swollen projection on the cheek." [2] "General Butler, an eccentric, resourceful character, hardly inclined to suavity . . . was in no danger of allowing sentiment to interfere in his rigorous sense of duty." [3] Those who dared to oppose him were banished or thrown into prison, and their property was confiscated.

In his usual abrupt manner he issued his first proclamation, dated May 1, to the city newspapers for publication. The long but clearly worded order left few doubts as to what the people could expect.

According to General Order Number 1, New Orleans would be governed by martial law until the restoration of municipal authority. All persons in arms against the United States were to surrender to the Federal forces. Citizens were asked to renounce their allegiance to the Confederacy and to "renew their allegiance" to the United States. Newspapers, publications, and telegraphic communications were placed under rigid censorship. All taxes, except Federal and necessary local levies, were suppressed. Acts interfering with the law of the United States were to be tried by a military court; all other misdemeanors were to be tried by municipal authority. In order to further maintain order and to facilitate "normal" business activities, all street assemblies were forbidden; all places of business were ordered to register and to remain open; for the time being the use of local and Confederate money would be allowed; and the European Brigade was to remain active.

As promised, General Butler allowed Mayor Monroe and his council to continue operating the city government. Facing the municipal government, as well as the Federal authorities, were two very serious problems—a serious shortage of food, and the threat of flood by the swollen waters of the Mississippi. In a series of orders published early in May, the hungry populace was promised that flour, meat, and other foods would be provided. The free market was reopened, and Butler turned over a thousand barrels of beef to be distributed to the people. Butler promised that cargoes of cotton, sugar, and provisions would be allowed to come into the city from the interior if the owner came with the shipment. Further relief was given indigent citizens when Butler, on May 9, hired them to clean up the city and to make necessary repairs to the levees. On May 12 President Lincoln lifted the blockade on the city, and trade with Northern ports was gradually resumed and prices were lowered.[4]

But the relief system did not touch everyone. George Denison, the new Federal customs collector, wrote his mother on July 6: "Thousands in this city are almost starving for food, and well dressed men and women beg bread (frequently) from Uncle Sam's boys, to keep themselves and children from starving."[5]

Early in August Butler devised a new scheme for the relief of the destitute. He ordered the corporations, business firms, and private individuals who had contributed to the Committee of Public Safety (for a total of $1,250,000) "for the treasonable purpose of defending the city against the Government of the United States," to contribute $312,716 "for the purpose of providing employment and food for the deserving poor." Cotton brokers, who had advised planters not to ship their cotton to New Orleans after October, 1861, were to pay $29,200 into the relief fund.

Butler reported on September 1 that he was distributing about $50,000 per month in food and money to the whites and that his commissary was giving nearly double the amount of rations used by his troops to the Negroes. In addition, the charity hospital received $5,000 a month, and various orphanages and charity organizations were being supported.

Relief funds were nearly exhausted by early December, and Butler again ordered the "parties who had aided the rebellion" to contribute the same amount they had been assessed in August.

The Relief Commission report of December 1 stated that some 35,000 people were being given aid. From the total of nearly 11,000 white families some 2,000 were Federal soldiers' families, 7,869 were either foreign or native citizens who were not relatives of soldiers, and around 1,042 were families of Confederate soldiers. Items such as pork, beef, fish, split peas, bread, flour, sugar, coffee, rice, tea, and soap were being distributed at the free market. Nearly a quarter of the city's population was being supported by the Relief Commission.[6]

Because of the exigencies of war, sanitation had long been neglected. Intermingled with the perfume of myriads of flowers and shrubs were odors of a festering blight. Down near the levee the gutters were filled with stagnant water, covered with scum. Out at the new Basin, an artificial lake used as a port for steamers, the water was choked with refuse from distilleries and other filth.

The French Market, just off Jackson Square, was extremely dirty. Flies droned over the garbage and refuse that littered the place. Streaked with blood, grease, and mud, the market was a menace to the health of the city. Each of the five districts of the city had a market of its own, and each was filthy. Fearing for the health of his men, General Butler ordered an immediate cleanup campaign. Corps of men were hired to scour the streets, to flush the sewers, and to clean out the stagnant canals. In addition, Butler insisted upon sanitary conditions in both private and public premises and enforced a rigid yellow-fever quarantine against all incoming ships. As a result, New Orleans, for awhile, became one of America's healthiest cities.[7]

In Butler's order issued May 1 he had allowed the circulation of Confederate notes until other mediums of exchange could be provided. By May 16, a second order stated that all circulation of Confederate bonds and notes would cease by May 27, whereupon the banks asked their depositors to withdraw all Confederate notes before the final date. Angered, the general on May 19 stopped all payments of Confederate notes and said only United States Treasury notes, notes issued by the banks, or gold and silver could be used as legal tender. The use of shinplaster was made illegal, and the city began redeeming all that had been officially issued.

The heavy hand of Butler was felt acutely by the banks. Many found it difficult to continue in operation, crippled as they were by the loss of their specie to the Confederacy, the possession of Confederate notes rendered worthless by Butler's orders, and the general decline of business.[8]

From the beginning Butler looked upon the foreign consuls with suspicion and disfavor. He accused them of concealing Confederate property, aiding rebellion, and attempting to injure the prestige of the United States. The Netherlands consulate was seized and placed under guard. The English consul, George Coppell, was suspended because he refused to co-operate with the Federal government. Later by order of Secretary of War Edwin Stanton, Butler was forced to reinstate Coppell.

By early June, the State Department had been so heavily bombarded with heated protests from the foreign consuls in New Orleans that Secretary of State William Seward appointed Reverdy Johnson "to proceed to New Orleans, to investigate complaints of foreign consuls against certain military proceedings of General Butler." [9]

Negro spies informed Butler that Consul Amedée Couturié of the Netherlands had eight hundred thousand dollars in Mexican silver coins concealed in his liquor store. After investigation it was found that the money belonged to the Citizen's Bank, and Butler confiscated it, along with bonds and silverware belonging to private citizens. Secretary Seward immediately censured Butler for his act and apologized to the Dutch minister in Washington.

The officers and crew of the British warship, the *Rinaldo,* on a friendly visit to New Orleans in the summer of 1862, aroused the ire of the Federal navy through their expressions of sympathy for the Confederacy. On several occasions, curses to the Union and strains of the "Bonnie Blue Flag" were heard from aboard the British vessel. Farragut protested against the breach of neutrality and threatened to blow the ship out of the water. The British commander apologized and promised that these practices would cease immediately.

Difficulty and conflict increased between Butler and the foreign consuls. Butler's seizure of 3,205 hogsheads of sugar claimed by British, Greek, and French subjects brought a sharp rebuke from George Coppell. Butler told the British consul that this scheme to give aid to the Confederate cause could not be tolerated. Reverdy Johnson investigated the affair and, through President Lincoln, ordered Butler to restore the sugar to its owners. The Prussian ship *Essex,* carrying many cases of "rebel" bullion and plate, was refused clearance until the Confederate property had been unloaded. The strict quarantine maintained by Butler to guard against yellow fever delayed foreign commerce and brought many complaints to his headquarters from the foreign consuls. Butler's order demanding that all civilians turn over their arms to his office drew protests from Count E. Mejan. The French consul argued that the arms could not be seized because they were private property. Butler turned a deaf ear to such reasoning, and the French citizens turned in their weapons along with the other residents.[10]

When Butler finally decided to form Negro military units, he gave the consuls new grounds for argument. Many of the French and English residents owned slaves in New Orleans, although the practice was forbidden by their laws. Butler declared that all slaves owned by French or British subjects were therefore free. After much difficulty, the consuls were forced to admit the validity of Butler's action, and Butler proceeded to enroll a number of these Negroes in his Native Guard.[11]

Avendano Brothers, an old New Orleans firm controlled by Spanish nationals, was accused of running cotton through the Federal blockade and of importing guns and war munitions into the Confederate-held areas of the state. Around May 10, a Confederate blockade runner, the *Fox,* bearing $300,000 worth of arms, lead, powder, medical stores, and other contraband goods was captured while entering Bayou Lafourche. Investigation showed the Avendano Company was implicated, and Butler ordered the company to pay him the amount they had smuggled into the state on two previous trips of the *Fox.* After the Spanish consul made a futile protest against the order, the Avendano Company paid Butler.

Another consular dispute arose over the question of payment for Confederate uniforms and military cloth bought in several European countries. The money for payment, $716,196, had been withdrawn from the city banks when Farragut approached and had been deposited in the French consulate. False papers assigning the money to French citizens had then been drawn up. General Butler had investigated and sequestrated all the money in the consulate, including the clothing money. Without thorough investigation, Reverdy Johnson and Secretary Seward ordered Butler to return the funds to Count Mejan, the French consul.

The affair concerning Charles Heidsieck brought new difficulties between Butler and the French consul. Heidsieck was a French champagne manufacturer who came over to collect some debts and then hired out as a bartender aboard a vessel plying between Mobile and

New Orleans to disguise his mail-running activities. When he was arrested and imprisoned, Count Mejan proceeded to Washington and succeeded in getting him released by the War Department. A short time after the consul returned, Butler completed his investigation of French consular affairs and sent his findings to Washington. These papers led the French minister to dismiss Count Mejan.[12]

Consular wrath reached new heights over General Order No. 41 issued on June 10 by Butler's headquarters. All foreign-born who had resided in the United States for five years and who had not sought the protection of their government in that time were said to be citizens and must take an oath of allegiance to the United States.

A few days later most of the foreign consuls rendered a collective objection to the oath. Butler explained his order to them and warned the consuls that he would not tolerate any more collective "argumentative protests."

General Halleck informed Butler that the War Department was against the system. President Lincoln and Secretary Seward requested that Butler desist in requiring foreigners to take the oath.

Reverdy Johnson, the special investigator of the State Department, proved to be a thorn in the flesh of General Butler. Butler accused him of pro-Southern sympathies, arguing that Johnson always took the opposite point of view from himself. With too little investigation Johnson often recommended that Seward should reverse Butler's orders.[13] Seward, who wanted to remain on friendly terms with the foreign powers, championed every cause of the consuls. After about six weeks Johnson departed. In great anger, Butler wrote Seward on September 19: "Another such commissioner as Mr. Johnson sent to New Orleans would render the city untenable." [14]

Butler and his men were not allowed to exercise the peaceful occupation they desired. Die-hard Confederates continued to use every method short of actual violence to undermine the Federals. One of the most potent weapons was the threat of yellow fever. One diarist stated: "The People of the town are frightening them terribly with tales of yellow fever." So effective was the method that General Butler reported, "A panic seized many of my officers." Many of them began to apply for furlough and sick leave to escape the terrors of the dread scourge. To reassure his men, the general enforced rigid sanitation rules and a strict quarantine below the city.

The citizens further lowered the morale of the Yankee soldiers by social ostracism. "These people are treated with the greatest haughtiness by the upper classes and rudeness by the lower. They know how they are hated and hang their heads. Shopkeepers refuse to sell them." [15]

According to Clara Solomon's diary, many people felt "the air tainted" and the "soil polluted" by the very presence of the conquerors. She protested vehemently against the black crepe bows that many New Orleanians wore on their shoulders: "Our cause is not dead, it is only *sick*. We are conquered but not subdued, and our independence *will yet* be recognized by the leading powers of the world. The Yankees are here on a visit." [16]

From the beginning the city newspapers came under rigid censorship. The first victim was the *Daily True Delta*, seized by order of Butler for refusing to print his initial proclamation. On May 13 the offices of the *Bee* and of the *Daily Delta* were closed because they dared to condone the practice of the burning of cotton and the destruction of crops. The *Daily Delta* was taken over by the troops, who began publishing it as the official organ of the Union.

A few days earlier the *Crescent* had been forced to suspend publication because the owner and editor, J. O. Nixon, was in arms against the United States. On May 24 Butler ordered the *Estafette du Sud* suspended because an article published in the paper violated the May 1 proclamation. The next censorship victim was the *Commercial Bulletin*. The newspaper ceased publication on July 30, and its editor was sent to prison at Fort Jackson. The *Picayune* offended Butler with one of its editorials, and on July 31 Butler closed this newspaper. Most of the papers were allowed to reopen later but were so rigidly controlled that all color and interest were drained away.[17]

Churches of the city soon incurred the wrath of General Butler when they planned to hold a special day of fasting and prayer for the Confederacy. On May 13 Butler forbade all such meetings. On October 25 several clergymen were accused of being "Secessionists, Rebels, and enemies of the United States." They were placed under arrest for refusing to pray for the president and the officials of the United States. The Episcopal churches were closed, and their three ministers were sent to New York on October 26 under military escort.[18]

Teachers within the school system were accused of being "secession" and "abusive" to the United States. A short time after Butler moved in, the schools closed for the summer. Before the opening of school in the fall the entire educational system was revamped. Following the Boston system, a bureau of education and a superintendent was appointed. Old teachers of questionable loyalty were fired, and new Union supporters were hired. Pro-Southern schoolbooks were purged, and Northern schoolbooks replaced them.[19]

The women of New Orleans presented one of the biggest problems with which Butler was forced to cope. Many patriotic ladies insulted the Yankee soldiers, hoping to be arrested, thinking that arrest would raise the ire of the citizens and the paroled Confederate soldiers. Butler feared that the few Federal troops he commanded would not be sufficient to combat such a revolt. On May 15 Butler issued his famous General Order 28:

As the officers and soldiers of the United States have been subjected to repeated insults from the women (calling themselves ladies) of New Orleans, in return for the most scrupulous noninterference and courtesy on our part, it is ordered that hereafter when any female shall, by word, gesture, or movement, insult or show contempt for any officer or soldier of the United States, she shall be regarded and held liable to be treated as a woman of the town plying her avocation.[20]

This order seemed harsh and barbaric to Southerners everywhere. "The cowardly wretches," commented one lady. "Can a woman, a Southern woman, come in contact with one of them and allow her countenance to retain its wanted composure?"[21] But most of the women could and did refrain from further public demonstrations against the Yankee.

The publication of the "Woman's Order" excited violent opposition in the official ranks of the Confederacy and abroad. In the city, Mayor Monroe dispatched an angry protest to General Butler. The general tried to explain the order to the mayor, but Monroe was not convinced.

Since the first days of occupation, Monroe had clashed with the Federal authorities. Butler accused him of hindering the efforts to clean up the city, of dismissing the European Brigade and installing "thugs" to enforce the law, of sending food to General Lovell when the city needed it more, and in every way of failing to co-operate with him. In addition, Monroe was held responsible for the organization known as the Monroe Guards, a group of paroled Confederate soldiers who hoped to aid General Lovell.[22] With the mayor's heated opposition to the Woman's Order, Butler could no longer tolerate him. On May 16 Butler ordered: "John T. Monroe, late mayor of the city of New Orleans, is relieved from all responsibility for the peace of the city, and is suspended from the exercise of any functions, and committed to Fort Jackson without further orders."[23]

Mayor Monroe was not the only distinguished citizen to feel the strong hand of General Butler. Monroe's closest adviser, Pierre Soulé, former minister to Spain and former member of the Senate, was arrested on May 28 for "plotting treason against the United States Government" and was sent to prison at Fort Warren, Massachusetts. The chief of police, John McClellan, and Judge Kennedy, both accused of aiding the Monroe Guards, had already been sent to Fort Jackson. Six parole violators who had joined the treasonable Monroe Guards were sentenced to death. Through the intercession of two Union leaders in the city, J. A. Rozier and Thomas J. Durant, the death sentence was changed to hard labor on Ship Island for an indefinite time.[24]

The city government underwent a complete reorganization. Colonel George F. Shepley was appointed temporary mayor until the citizens could elect a man loyal to the United States. Captain Jonas H. French was named chief of police, and Major Joseph M. Bell was chosen to head the military courts, which were to try all violations of city and Federal laws.

Early in July Colonel Shepley received word that he had been appointed military governor of Louisiana by the President. In July Butler succeeded in having his friend promoted to brigadier general. Shepley, a Maine man, a graduate of Dartmouth, and a lawyer and district attorney, often acted with vehemence and impetuosity, but Butler found him easy to control.

All men who held any public office were required by Butler to take the oath of allegiance. Rather than give up their allegiance to the Confederacy, all officeholders resigned. The city council was abolished, and General Shepley appointed two committees of Union men to help him run the city.

President Lincoln, who was less than pleased with the military courts, in late October appointed Judge Charles A. Peabody of New York to head a provisional court system in Louisiana to hear all cases, civil and criminal. The judge was to set up the necessary rules and regulations and to appoint the necessary prosecuting attorney, marshal, and clerk for the court.[25]

In December, under direction from the President, elections were held to send two congressmen from the area under Butler's control to Congress. From the First Congressional District Benjamin F. Flanders, a stanch Union man, was elected. Flanders, a Dartmouth graduate from New Hampshire, had moved to New Orleans and in turn had become a teacher, a newspaper editor, a member of the city government, and a superintendent of schools in the first district; when the war came, he was an official of the New Orleans and Opelousas Railroad. After secession, Flanders remained a Union man and, under threats of violence, was forced to leave the South. After Butler occupied New Orleans, Flanders returned, was made city treasurer, and served until his election to Congress.

Michael Hahn, elected from the Second Congressional District, had migrated with his mother and several brothers and sisters from Bavaria and had settled in New Orleans in 1840. Hahn managed to secure an education and graduated from the University of Louisiana in 1851 with a law degree. During the secession crisis he had worked hard to keep Louisiana in the Union.

The two Louisiana congressmen were refused their seats because the election had violated the laws of the United States and of Louisiana. Finally in February the two were seated but were able to serve only fifteen days because their terms in the Thirty-seventh Congress came to an end on March 4.[26]

General Butler thrived in his legal empire. Besieged by mountainous problems, corruption, demands, pleas, threats, and chicaneries—the collective woes and spoils of a conquered city and province—a man of lesser political experience would have collapsed under the strain. Butler, however, did not weaken. Rarely did he allow purely military matters to clutter his mind or his desk. He dedicated himself to civil affairs and let others take care of the military campaigns, such as they were.

Throughout his tenure, the hand of Butler held a tight rein on the citizens of New Orleans. On May 8 Butler reported that he had just sentenced a man to three months' hard labor at Fort Jackson because he had dared to cheer for Jeff Davis. In his fervent desire to break up the display of Confederate sentiment, Butler had the man who had hauled down the United States flag from the roof of the United States Mint arrested, tried, and sentenced to death. On June 7 William Mumford was hanged at the scene of his crime before a large crowd.[27]

During the first days of occupation most of the stores and shops remained closed. Gradually a few stores reopened, but many of these refused to sell to the Yankee troops. After one shop owner was arrested and driven out of the city because he refused soldier trade, his goods were confiscated by order of General Butler. Fearing the same fate, more establishments resumed business and did not refuse to sell to anyone.[28]

Many citizens of the city were arrested and brought to face military justice. Charles H. Lee, a patriotic but often drunk citizen, was found guilty of insulting Union officers and soldiers and was sentenced to sixty days on Ship Island. Stephen Roberts of Baton Rouge was sentenced to life imprisonment at Fort Jackson for the attempted murder of Colonel J. W. McMillan, Twenty-first Indiana Regiment, a personal friend of Butler's. John W. Andrews, found guilty of displaying in the Louisiana Club a cross of human bones said to be those of a Yankee soldier, was sent to solitary confinement on Ship Island for two years, and Fidel Keller received the same sentence for exhibiting a human skeleton labeled "Chickahominy" in his bookstore window.

Despite the Woman's Order, some of the ladies still dared to flaunt their secession sentiments in the faces of the conquerors. Late in June a flag-wearing mania brought arrests and imprisonment to some of the women.

Early in July Mrs. Anne Larue, boldly displaying a secession flag on her clothing, caused a near riot that endangered a Union soldier's life. Convicted of the charge, Mrs. Larue was sent to Ship Island, where prison authorities were told to keep her apart from the other women for an indefinite period.

Both women and children delighted in provoking the authorities and did not seem to be frightened at the number of arrests.[29] A member of the Thirteenth Maine, stationed below at the forts, reported: "Large numbers of disloyal citizens were kept in confinement at the forts; mostly at Fort Jackson. . . ." St. Philip was also used, and from time to time many prisoners were transferred by ship to other forts and places of confinement.[30]

The most famous case involving a New Orleans lady of prominence was that of Mrs. Philip Philips, whose husband had served in President Buchanan's cabinet. Mrs. Philips was first accused of teaching her children to spit upon Yankee officers and had publicly apologized for the offense. On June 30, while the funeral of a Union officer was passing her house, she ran out on her balcony and broke into peals of laughter. For her disgraceful conduct General Butler sent Mrs. Philips to Ship Island for an indefinite period, during which time she was to be isolated and shunned by everyone. In mid-September he released her, after she swore not to give aid, comfort, nor information to the enemy. She was then allowed to proceed to Mobile, where Confederate society embraced her as a martyr.

The many manifestations of disloyalty from the people plus the absence of several thousands of his troops at Vicksburg and Baton

Rouge caused Butler to take greater precautionary measures. The provost marshal ordered that citizens must not assemble in the streets nor public squares. Congregations of more than three would be dispersed, and those who refused to leave would be arrested.

After the battle of Baton Rouge, fear of an imminent attack upon New Orleans was great. To help ensure the safety of the city, the citizens were ordered to turn in all their arms, and rewards were offered for reports of concealed weapons. Altogether some six thousand weapons were surrendered.[31]

The taking of oaths was pushed vigorously. It was reported on August 7 that 11,723 citizens had taken oaths of allegiance and that 2,499 foreigners had sworn oaths of neutrality. But this was not enough. On September 13 Butler ordered all neutral foreigners in the department to register so that they could be watched more easily.

Orders were issued on September 24 that all persons, male or female, eighteen years of age or above, who had ever been citizens of the United States and who still held allegiance or sympathy for the Confederacy must report to the nearest provost marshal by October 1. There they would register all their property and give their addresses, descriptions, and occupations. Certificates would then be issued proclaiming them enemies of the United States. Those who renewed their allegiance to the United States would be restored to full rights as citizens.

From Butler's point of view the orders were highly successful. Some 61,000 people took the oath of allegiance, and only 4,000 refused to do so. These "registered enemies" of the United States were to be allowed to cross the enemy lines, carrying with them personal clothing and not more than fifty dollars. They must never return to the department.[32]

Anxiety and suffering was not the lot of all of the citizens, nor of those soldiers lucky enough to be stationed in New Orleans. All who could afford it were able to find diversified entertainment. The theaters, the race track, and the incomparable restaurants did a thriving business.

Not all of the theaters closed when the Federal troops occupied the city. Most professional actors and singers were kept out by the war, but local talent helped to make up the deficit. Melodramas, operas, comic operas, ballets, and sister acts, all with casts made up of the available trained performers and amateur talent, attracted large audiences to the luxurious opera houses and theaters. Among the more popular offerings were Donizetti's opera, "Daughter of the Regiment," and "Christie's Minstrels." The latter was strictly an amateur production. In the fall and winter of 1862, the theaters and opera houses were sometimes the scene of a grand masquerade ball or of a lavish dance.

Hardly had New Orleans recovered from the shock of surrender before she resumed her interest in horse racing. Trotting races and match races were held periodically throughout the summer and into the fall. On May 14, 1862, there was a pacing match for a two-hundred-dollar purse at the Fair Grounds, and on the following day at the same course "Frank" and the favorite, "Gladiator," competed in a two-mile heat for a thousand dollars. Yankee and Confederate alike attended these matches.

The war and the occupation did not in any appreciable manner reduce the activities of the local *femmes de joie*. Union soldiers and civilian clients could find temporary consolation from their loneliness and troubles for a price. The *Daily Picayune* of May 7 lamented the fact that the streets were once again crowded with "abandoned women" and streetwalkers. The police were called upon to suppress their brazen activities. The women, lured from their brothels by the influx of Yankee soldiers, failed to heed this warning, and many were arrested and sent to the workhouse.

As long as these women did not patrol the streets in search of business, they seem to have been tolerated. Various controls were placed upon their activities, but all except the ordinance prohibiting streetwalking were repealed.[33]

The soldiers managed to find plenty of liquor. In June a young officer at Carrollton complained: "Since pay day there has been a bacchanalia of whiskey drinking. One-fifth of the regiment keeps drunk all the time." General Phelps, commanding the post, permitted the men to drink because he thought that "the men must have whiskey or die of country fever."[34] From time to time General Butler issued orders forbidding the public sale of liquor. Andrew Butler, the general's brother who joined the expedition without any official capacity, then forced the owners to sell their stock to him at a reduced price. Andrew's next move was to influence his brother to lift the ban.[35]

With plenty of capital and credit in his own and his brother's name, "Colonel" A. J. Butler led the parade of speculators who gathered like vultures in lower Louisiana. In addition to monopolizing the liquor trade, he had cattle brought in from Texas and flour from the North and realized a tremendous profit. Andrew, a jolly, fat man who could be as hard as nails where a dollar was concerned, quickly established a monopoly on all groceries, breadstuffs, medicines, and staples brought into the city. He also seized and operated a city bakery that was the only breadmaking establishment allowed in the city. Both Butlers, according to one lady, were "on the make," but the "Colonel" was not encumbered by official position, so it was he who attended to all the monetary details. Persons who desired special favors from the general soon learned that they would stand a better chance if they saw Andrew first.

With the backing of General Butler, Andrew could not fail to fatten his bank roll. In addition to the "legitimate" transactions he carried on, he was accused of accepting money for seeing to it that certain property was not confiscated; for receiving a "rake-off" on debts collected in New Orleans by Northern creditors; for accepting a share of the profits for medicines, salt, and clothing run through the Union lines into the Confederacy by others; and for taking handsome sums for securing the freedom of certain individuals in prison. Much of the sugar and cotton seized by the Federal troops was "auctioned off" to the "Colonel" at a ridiculous price and then shipped to New York and sold by him at a great profit. One English visitor to the city estimated that the "Colonel" had reaped between three million and six million dollars in profits from his business ventures. He thought the general was a silent partner and must surely share in the rewards.

Some nine river boats, intended for military use, were placed at the command of Andrew Butler. Escorted by a company of Federal infantry and armed with a pass signed by his brother, Andrew traveled deep into the enemy lines trading contraband medicines, salt, and military cloth for valuable cotton, sugar, and naval stores. Most of the troops objected to being forced to go on these trips, and many of them felt demoralized by the traffic with the enemy.[36]

George S. Denison, a Treasury Department agent in New Orleans, in his voluminous correspondence with Secretary Salmon P. Chase reported that illegal traffic with the enemy across Lake Pontchartrain was very heavy. Denison protested to General Butler, who answered that it was "the policy of the Government to get cotton shipped from this port, and for that purpose to trade with the enemy." Salt, a scarce item in the eastern part of the Confederacy, was a most profitable item of trade. After payment of two dollars per sack, an agent was given a permit by General Butler to carry six hundred sacks of salt across the lake. Four hundred of these were sold to the Confederate army at twenty-five dollars a sack, and the other two hundred were sold to citizens for thirty-six dollars per sack. The "Colonel" had not only received a handsome price but had gained an additional five dollars per sack for securing a permit to get the cargo cleared for shipment. Denison estimated that some ten thousand sacks of salt had been sent to the enemy from New Orleans by late August. In spite of the fact that speculators were aiding and abetting the enemy by enabling Confederates to buy vital goods out of New Orleans, General Butler and General Shepley continued to issue them permits. One speculator, D. D. Goicouria of New York, had made a profit of two hundred thousand dollars in four months. Goicouria had made a deal with the Confederates to swap ten sacks of salt for one bale of cotton. Goicouria told Denison that his friend "Colonel" Butler had already realized nearly a million dollars from his sugar speculation alone.[37]

For a brief period the general played a few hands in the speculation game himself, but official rebukes from Washington caused him to withdraw from active play. A politically ambitious man must use a measure of discretion. Through his "loans," his special orders, and his permits, all benefiting brother Andrew, General Butler was able to continue his trading by proxy.

Finding plenty of cheap sugar available at the levee, Butler's fertile brain had devised a plan to send some of the transports that brought his command down to Louisiana back North loaded with a ballast of sugar. Butler, who brought little money with him, borrowed one hundred thousand dollars in gold from a banker, Jacob Barker, and proceeded to buy some sixty thousand dollars worth of the sugar. The delighted merchants loaded the sugar on the transports without charge. Andrew Butler, who handled the transactions, was paid five dollars per hogshead for his trouble. Five dollars a hogshead would be paid to the government as freight for the use of the transports. By mid-May Butler had already shipped quantities of sugar, naval stores, and some cotton to his business agent, Robert S. Fay, Jr., in Boston.

In a letter to his business agent written on June 1, Butler stated that his brother had shipped sugar, molasses, pitch, and turpentine that he himself had bought with his own funds. Butler was willing for the government to have these stores as long as he was reimbursed for cost, freight, and other expenses. If the government did not claim the goods, then the agent was to sell them and place the proceeds in Butler's account. To pay himself for making all the arrangements and handling the goods, Andrew was sending some sugar home as ballast on a transport. The general pretended that he did not like such arrangements and vowed he would never "get in another such scrape."

The government chose to claim the cotton, sugar, and naval stores, and M. C. Meigs, Quartermaster General, authorized Fay to sell the goods at public auction. After paying Butler all expenses, the balance was to be deposited to the credit of the Treasury Department. Meigs mildly censured Butler. He felt that the general "ought not to be involved in private trade and profits arising out of his official power and position." Chase, the Secretary of the Treasury, also reprimanded Butler, advising him not to take advantage of his "military command to engage in mercantile speculation" by shipping goods North to his private account. "Be on your guard, . . . against the appearance of evil." [38]

Early in July the Federal Congress passed the Confiscation Act, and President Lincoln signed the bill on July 12. The act was made to order for the Butler brothers, and Andrew was given a new method by which he could enrich his coffers. Property belonging to Confederate civil or military officers was to be confiscated immediately. The rank and file and all the general abettors of rebellion were given sixty days in which to lay down their arms and resume their allegiance to the Union. Butler had already seized the property of General David Twiggs and moved his household into the Twiggs's mansion, having tired of the St. Louis Hotel. At the same time the home of John Slidell had been sequestered.

Armed with the Confiscation Act, General Butler began to seize the property of state and Confederate officers in the area he occupied. Sixty days later (September 24), as provided for by Congress, Butler began his real program of confiscation. Property belonging to the four thousand "registered enemies" of the United States who were forced to leave New Orleans and the property of soldiers fighting in the Confederate army was sequestered by Butler's order.[39]

Riper plums for plucking by the army and by a few favored speculators came on November 9, when Butler's General Order 91 sequestered all the sugar-rich Lafourche District west of the Mississippi River, with the exception of Plaquemines and Jefferson parishes. A commission of three officers was set up to take possession of all property of "disloyal" citizens. All who remained on their plantations and had not, nor would not, commit an act against the United States could keep their lands. Through the excellent management of Lieutenant Colonel J. B. Kinsman more than a million dollars' worth of property was confiscated in the Lafourche in six weeks time and sold at auction in New Orleans, the money being deposited to the credit of the United States.

Speculators without friends close to General Butler were thwarted by Lieutenant Colonel Kinsman, but those who dealt through "Colonel" Butler were able to do business as usual. Colonel J. W. McMillan of the Twenty-first Indiana Volunteers, who was working for Andrew, when blocked by Kinsman wrote the "Colonel" in November asking him to have his sugar and cotton released by the provost marshal and to send money for produce already shipped to him in New Orleans. McMillan informed Andrew that he was en route to the salt works and would begin salt shipments soon. The "public" auctions seemed to have been rigged from time to time, and "Colonel" Butler was able to buy sugar and cotton at absurdly small prices.

Andrew Butler, never one to leave a dollar unturned, was the first speculator bold enough to take over the operation of a confiscated plantation and, by using "free" Negro labor, to produce a bountiful crop of sugar. In the wake of his promised success the standing crops of several other plantations above and below New Orleans were taken over by other speculators. When the Lafourche District, from Berwick Bay to Donaldsonville, was occupied and many deserted or confiscated plantations fell into Federal hands, the Negroes found there were declared free and put to work for wages on these plantations. Provost troops were provided to guard the plantations and the free Negro laborers.[40]

A few weeks after the occupation of lower Louisiana began, General Butler had trouble with soldiers who engaged in private foraging and plunder. At Kennerville, several miles above New Orleans, a Wisconsin regiment committed a series of outrages "such as killing chickens, robbing sugar houses, insulting women, and disgracing the Flag and the Country." General Phelps was ordered to break up the practice and to post a guard to protect the inhabitants.[41]

Although Butler seems to have allowed members of his staff and his officer friends to seize property, to plunder, and to speculate, these privileges were not extended to other officers nor to any enlisted men. Orders were issued on May 27 prohibiting plunder for private use.

On June 12, after protests from a citizen, two men were arrested. In the investigation that followed, it was discovered that these two men belonged to a gang of seven who donned Federal military uniforms and, late at night, using forged authority of the commanding general, entered private homes, pretending to search for hidden arms and treasonable letters. Five of the men were rounded up and found guilty of plundering at least eight houses, taking money, watches, ladies' jewelry, and other valuables. Two were residents of New Orleans, and the rest were Yankees, one of whom belonged to the Thirteenth Connecticut. Butler issued orders sentencing four of the men to hang and sending the fifth, a minor, to Ship Island to perform hard labor for an indefinite period. Butler thought this object lesson would discourage future plundering.

He was wrong. The troops outside the city, away from the watchful eye of Butler, had a field day. One incident which occurred on September 10 was reported to the general by the navy. Three troop transports were sent to Donaldsonville, where they loaded sugar and other merchandise. One company of the troops forced its way into a mansion and took all the "wines, liquors, silver plate, and clothing belonging to ladies."

A few days later Butler issued General Order No. 74. As it had been reported that soldiers out on marches and expeditions sometimes entered houses and took property therefrom for their private use, it was ordered that any complaint of plundering from a peaceable citizen be investigated, the damages suffered totaled, and that amount "deducted from the pay of the officers commanding the troops." [42]

From the beginning, Butler felt that the troops in his command were inadequate for the task at hand. Receiving authority from Secretary Stanton to raise five thousand loyal recruits in Louisiana, Butler redoubled his efforts. To entice volunteers, recruits were promised thirteen dollars a month pay and a bounty of one hundred dollars.

Most of the paroled men from Forts Jackson and St. Philip who returned to New Orleans and found themselves without means of support enlisted in the army.

One Union man, Joseph P. Murphy, a citizen of New Orleans, requested permission to raise an infantry company "to strike a blow for the United States." Large numbers of Union men—Germans, Irish, French, and Americans—feeling the pangs of hunger begged to enlist. Recruiting offices were opened, and efforts to raise two regiments of infantry and one of cavalry were begun. Nearly all the early enlistments were men of foreign birth.

Confederate soldiers were urged to desert and to come to New Orleans, where they would be registered as paroled prisoners and given the right to join the Union army. To make up for men lost from disease, resignations, the fateful Vicksburg campaign, and other causes, Butler pushed the recruiting of troops in Louisiana. His original regiments were brought up to strength, and two new infantry regiments and four companies of cavalry were raised. Some of these Louisiana troops would serve the Union at Baton Rouge.

In late October the commander of the Second Louisiana Regiment complained that enlistments were falling off because "so many of the unemployed laborers are now being engaged by the planters to work their plantations in the place of negroes who run away." Wages were high, and the army could not match such payments. In November a group of Union men from Texas were brought to New Orleans and were busy forming a regiment of Texas cavalry.

The Negro problem had bothered Butler as much as or more than anything else. Runaway slaves and slaves from abandoned plantations poured into New Orleans, taxing the larder and patience of the army commissary. The homeless, unattached Negroes had to be fed and housed. Up at Carrollton, General Phelps, an ardent abolitionist, sent soldiers out to the plantations to lure slaves inside his lines. Citizens' protests were echoed by many of Phelps's own officers.[43]

One officer complained: "They are coming into camp by the hundreds and are a costly curse. They should be kept out or set at work, or freed or colonized, or sunk or something. . . . The live negro is a big problem." Soldiers resented the fact that the pampered Negro was given better tents, equal rations, and was allowed to tear down more fences for sleeping boards than were the soldiers. General Phelps had organized a few squads of Negroes and drilled them daily. One observer reported "their cattle-like movements are absurd." [44]

Not knowing what to do with so many Negroes, Butler at first returned the runaway slaves to their masters. But still the contrabands came. Some of them were employed as cooks, nurses, washwomen, and laborers. All had to be fed and cared for. General Phelps continued to welcome the Negroes. On May 23 Butler ordered the commander of Camp Parapet to exclude all unemployed Negroes and whites from his lines.

The Negroes remained where they were and still more joined them. The few available tents were long since exhausted, and the rest of the Negroes built huts of cane or rails that furnished only the most miserable shelter. Often at night music of a banjo and fiddle could be heard, and colored wenches could be seen "tripping the light fantastic toe" for the amusement of the officers and men. Often a soldier would seize one of these "sable nymphs" and lead her in a dance or to the privacy of his tent.[45]

General Phelps in mid-June suggested to Butler that the Negroes should be enlisted. Fifty regiments could easily be raised to carry on the fight for freedom and for the Union. Butler left the letter unanswered. In the meantime Phelps organized five companies of three hundred contrabands. The "swarthy, grizzled six-footer," known for his loose-jointed walk and his quick tongue, worked and sweated with his black neophytes. On he labored patiently with his simple charges, amusing them with his high-pitched, penetrating Vermont drawl. If one of his officers made an error, Phelps's face assumed a look of pain, and his body jerked spasmodically. The fine old man scoffed, swore, and instructed, but the amusing tones of his voice removed most of the sting.

Despite the ridicule heaped upon the Negroes by most of the white troops, they were beginning to look and act like soldiers. Late in July, General Phelps sent 150 contrabands down to General Neal Dow at Fort Jackson with the suggestion that they be given artillery training. Dow began training several gun crews and found the contrabands eager students. By August nearly 500 Negroes were employed as laborers in strengthening the two forts. Dow was confident that many of the Negroes could become good soldiers.

After waiting for about a month to hear from Butler, General Phelps sent a request to headquarters for enough arms and equipment for three regiments of Negro troops that he planned to raise at Camp Parapet. Butler rejected the proposal and suggested that the contrabands be used to fell the trees between the camp and Lake Pontchartrain and to strengthen the fortifications. General Phelps's abolitionist blood boiled. He refused to become a slave driver and tendered his resignation from the army. Butler refused to allow Phelps to resign and ordered the field commander to break up his Negro units and to use all the Negroes in working on the fortifications.

Phelps defied Butler's orders. He refused to use the Negroes as laborers. Butler submitted Phelps's resignation through channels, and an order was issued on August 23, stating that the President had accepted, and that the resignation had gone into effect August 21.[46]

Since the attack upon Baton Rouge, August 5, Butler had feared a Confederate move against New Orleans. When he was refused reinforcements from the North, Butler decided to resort to drastic action in order to build up his defenses. On August 22 he ordered that all former members of the Native Guard, which had been enrolled as a part of the Louisiana State Militia, would be given the right to enlist in the army of the United States. Such colored troops would be treated, paid, equipped, rationed, and armed like any white volunteer. All such persons were required to report to the Turo building on Levee Street to be mustered into service.

During the first week the place of muster was crowded with eager Negroes. In two weeks the first regiment was complete. Line officers were Negro, and field officers were white. Less than half the regiment was made up of free Negroes. The rest were fugitive slaves. Any physically fit Negro who swore that he was free was enrolled. Three regiments were quickly raised, and the officers from the second were chosen on the same basis as the first, but those of the third were chosen regardless of color. Most of the West Point officers objected to enlisting Negroes, and one of these, the newly promoted brigadier general, Godfrey Weitzel, refused to command Negro troops in an expedition to Donaldsonville and into the Lafourche District. Butler placed the Negro soldiers under another officer, and Weitzel remained in command. Weitzel, like the others, was eventually to see the advantage of Negro troops.

Two batteries of Negro artillery were raised, both having white officers. Two of the Native Guard regiments, after a period of training, were used as guards for the Opelousas Railroad between Algiers and Berwick Bay. As yet there was no official sanction from the President nor the War Department for the use of Negro troops. General Phelps, although he must have felt maligned by Butler, did his part in training the Negro recruits until his departure in early September. When the beloved commander took leave of his troops at Camp Parapet, he was given a rousing ovation. Many of his men thought he had been bullied out of the service by Butler.[47]

President Lincoln, in his Emancipation Proclamation, issued on September 24, gave support to some of the measures Butler had already pursued or planned to follow regarding the Negroes. According to the proclamation, beginning on January 1, 1863, all slaves within a state or part of a state "in rebellion against the United States" would be free. All slaves of persons in rebellion or of persons who rendered aid to the enemy who escaped inside the Union lines were to be free men. Since most of the slaves belonging to French and British subjects were free because their national laws forbade slavery, only about seven thousand slaves belonging to loyal Union men were kept in bondage in the areas occupied by the Federal forces.

Enlistment had not solved the problems of the Negro. Butler employed many colored laborers at the two forts below the city and at Camp Parapet to strengthen these works. In October he decided to work abandoned and confiscated plantations with the escaped and freed slaves for the benefit of the United States. Loyal planters in Plaquemines and St. Bernard parishes were permitted to hire Negro laborers to work every day except Sunday, ten hours per day, at a wage of ten dollars per month for each adult male and lesser amounts for women and children. Three dollars could be deducted for necessary clothing. The planters' responsibilities included feeding, housing, providing medical care, keeping time ledgers, and treating their laborers humanely. Suitable provost guards and patrols kept the peace, guarded the loyal planters, and supervised labor relations. The use of wage hands proved to be a success.[48]

Butler's days in Louisiana were numbered. On November 8 the War Department assigned command of the Department of the Gulf to General Nathaniel P. Banks. General Halleck promised Banks that he would be sent ten thousand additional troops; his first military operation was to be the opening of the Mississippi, in co-operation with General U. S. Grant.[49]

Butler hated Banks and was jealous of his political success and his "reputation of being the best general selected from civil life," although he possessed only "half the brains of Butler." Swallowing his bitter pill with a show of good grace, Butler welcomed his replacement to New Orleans.[50]

Two days later, December 16, Butler and Banks, along with their staffs, met at the headquarters in the Custom House, and Butler formally turned over command of the Department of the Gulf to General Banks. Next, Butler transferred the public property, amounting to nearly a million dollars. While waiting to take his leave, Butler spent much time in briefing the new commander on the civil and military affairs in the department.[51]

Gideon Welles, hearing that Butler had been superseded by Banks, doubted the wisdom of the change. Welles's opinion of the military abilities of both men was very low, but he did not question Butler's proven skill as a "police magistrate" in charge of civil affairs. Banks, he thought, did not have "the energy, power, or ability of Butler." He did have "some ready qualities for civil administration," but he was "less reckless and unscrupulous" and probably would not be able to hold a tight enough rein on the people. Welles believed that Secretary

Seward was behind the change and that the foreign consuls were responsible for his actions.[52]

Sickened by the despotic rule, the intimidation, and the graft and corruption, most people in the department agreed with the Treasury agent, George S. Denison, who wrote on December 18: "I cannot say I am sorry for the change. I like him [Banks] exceedingly. His advent here is generally hailed with enthusiasm." [53]

The handsome and dapper new commander immediately won the applause and respect of military and naval officers in New Orleans. David Farragut, who had found getting soldiers from Butler next to impossible, was pleasantly surprised when General Banks agreed with his suggestion that Baton Rouge should be reoccupied without delay. About half of the expeditionary force, some ten thousand men, under Brigadier General Cuvier Grover was ordered to accompany the *Richmond* and four of Farragut's gunboats up to Baton Rouge and to occupy the place. The mission was successfully accomplished on December 17.

General Banks delighted the people of the department and the foreign consuls with a series of orders that were previews of a more lenient regime. General Order No. 113 issued on December 20 stated that "permission to trade and travel within the military lines" would be granted through the new provost marshal general of the department, Colonel John S. Clark. No more fees would be charged for travel or trade permits, and no special privileges or monopolies would be granted nor recognized.

Planters from the west side of the river, regardless of "past political opinions or relations," were invited to ship their cotton, sugar, and other products to New Orleans, where they would bring a fair price. Slaves were advised to remain on their plantations for the time being and not to come into the Federal lines. Since Congress forbade the return of fugitive slaves, none could be returned to their owners. However, no more encouragement would be given to slaves to desert their masters.

Negro troops were dispatched by Banks to help strengthen the white garrisons of the forts and Ship Island. The majority of white troops would be concentrated for proposed moves up the river.

The conciliatory policy adopted by Banks brought new hope to the people in the occupied parts of the state. Banks ordered the release of all political prisoners; he forbade further public auctions of property; he continued to feed the destitute; those who wanted work were found a job; he ordered elections for two congressmen to be held; he restored many private homes and other private property; and he reopened the Episcopal churches of New Orleans.[54] It was clear that Banks was out to woo the good will of the people.

General Butler spent December 23 in taking leave of his troops and friends. The next day Butler and his wife entered a carriage and drove to the levee, where a large crowd gathered to see him off. Either Butler had with him in his personal effects, or he had previously destroyed, a portion of his records, including a book of "Letters-Sent," a "Special Order Book," and a "Special Permit Memorandum Book." These records were not turned over to Banks and were not recovered. Perhaps Butler was removing evidence that might be used against him at some future time.

After shaking hands with hundreds of people and taking leave of Admiral Farragut, Butler boarded an unarmed transport to begin the long journey home. As the boat pulled away from the wharf and headed downstream the people gave three cheers, and the flagship *Hartford* and a battery on shore fired a parting salute.[55] The "Beast" ruled no more.

SKIRMISHES
SECESSIA, AND EXPEDITIONS

AFTER THE fall of New Orleans, Governor Thomas O. Moore proceeded to Camp Moore to confer with General Mansfield Lovell. It was decided that conscripts should be enrolled immediately and that two new training camps should be established west of the river, one at Opelousas and the other at Monroe.

Cut off from General Lovell, who remained east of the Mississippi, Governor Moore began organizing companies of Partisan Rangers in the western part of the state. Men who enlisted with the Rangers were exempt from conscription as long as they served as Rangers. Although these troops were destined chiefly for state defense, they could be called into Confederate service. Louisiana had furnished thirty regiments of troops already fighting outside its borders. Since the lower part of the state had fallen into Federal hands, Louisiana had no ammunition, no cloth, no tents, no supplies—nothing but a few shotguns. Experienced officers must be sent by the Confederacy to organize and drill the conscripts, Rangers, and militia; money must be provided to subsist and pay troops destined for Confederate service; and tents, small arms, artillery, ammunition, clothes, and other necessities must be sent. There was not one single Confederate officer on duty in the state west of the river. To guard against further incursions of the enemy into the western part of the state, Governor Moore had around two thousand poorly trained militia.

General Beauregard, hard pressed for replacements, asked Lovell for some of his men at Camp Moore. Lovell replied that he had just sent two regiments and some artillery to Vicksburg and that he had only 2,600 men left, most of whom were new levies. If these men were withdrawn, the railroad would be opened up as far as Jackson,

Mississippi. This could not be permitted. Lovell was busy drilling the raw recruits and was trying to raise Partisan Rangers in Louisiana east of the Mississippi. On May 20, in answer to the urgent requests of Beauregard and of Governor Pettus of Mississippi, Lovell reluctantly sent two more regiments to Vicksburg.

On June 11 Governor Moore complained to Beauregard that Louisiana had been called upon to furnish three thousand conscripts to fill up depleted ranks of Louisiana units outside the state. Militia officers had already begun enrolling these men and would complete the job by July 1. Since there were no camps of instructions, no Confederate quartermaster, no funds, and no training officers, it was useless to call these men into service at the present. Beauregard should not expect reinforcements from Louisiana in the near future.

While Governor Moore was waiting for the slow wheels of the government to turn, he called the militias of three of the lower parishes, Terrebonne, Saint Mary, and Saint Martin, into active duty. Orders were issued to these troops on June 14 to keep the mouth of Red River open so that cattle could be sent across the Mississippi to the main Confederate armies.

Governor Moore next prohibited all private traffic and trade with the enemy. No passes into or out of enemy-held territory would be honored. Anyone not in sympathy with the Confederate cause was to be arrested. Only Confederate notes would be honored as currency. Despite the governor's orders cotton and other produce was shipped to New Orleans. The governor learned that large quantities of cotton were stacked along the banks of the Mississippi, Tensas, Ouachita, Black, and Trinity rivers within reach of the enemy, and he issued orders to burn the cotton or to move it to a place of greater safety.[1]

Since early May the area on the west side of the river from New Orleans, along the railroad over to Berwick City, had been occupied by a small force of Butler's men. Soon after they arrived, a party of four troops en route to Houma by wagon was ambushed by several armed citizens, and two of the soldiers were killed and the other two seriously wounded. This incident brought immediate reprisals. Four hundred soldiers moved into Houma and began a wholesale arrest of the citizens. The investigation of the murders lasted several days but failed to reveal the guilty parties. To frighten the citizens, the home of a Doctor Jennings was burned, two other houses were torn down, and the home and slave quarters of an outlying plantation were burned. The soldiers next began to seize sheep, cattle, mules, wagons, and saddle horses. Negroes began to desert their masters and to flock to the protection of the troops. The frightened citizens had no means of resistance, and many found it hard to stand by and see their country despoiled by a few hundred troops.[2]

A company of Federal soldiers on a reconnaissance in open flatcars near Lafourche Crossing was surprised by a group of Texans hidden in the bushes. The Texans fired into their midst with buckshot and killed forty-eight of them. The train immediately fled to New Orleans, and General Butler threatened to destroy all of Bayou Lafourche to avenge the attack.[3]

Nine companies of Partisan Rangers had been organized in the district west of the Mississippi by July 8, but they had no weapons other than their own shotguns. There was no excuse for this state of affairs. State property saved by Governor Moore from the Federal invader and shipped to Woodville, Mississippi, en route to the Red River, had been seized by order of General Van Dorn and carried to Vicksburg. Louisiana defenses had thus been stripped of 2,720 rifles, ammunition, one battery of artillery, camp equipage, saddles, and clothing. When Van Dorn refused to return the confiscated goods, Governor Moore and Louisiana members of the Confederate Congress appealed to Jefferson Davis to intercede and order the restoration of the guns and equipment to the state.

Governor Moore told Davis that around June 24 a party of soldiers sent down from Arkansas by General Thomas C. Hindman had visited Alexandria and had "seized private property, entered houses of private citizens, brutally practiced extortion and outrage and . . . spread terror among the people and disgraced the service." These men also terrorized Shreveport, took private property, and impressed Confederate supplies stored at that place as well as in Alexandria. The governor threatened that if these men dared to return, his marksmen might take care of them.[4]

Brigadier General Albert G. Blanchard, sent by the Confederate government, after much difficulty was able to cross over the Mississippi in a skiff at night and arrived in Monroe on July 12. He found no conscripts, no camp of instructions, and no arms. He discovered, too, that Louisiana west of the river had been divided into two military districts. The area south of Red River was under General P. O. Hébert, whose headquarters were located in San Antonio, and the northern part of the state was under General Hindman, with headquarters at Little Rock. Since communications were so slow, Louisiana had become an almost forgotten area, neglected and vulnerable to enemy advances. General Blanchard urged that money be sent to the department, as the people around Monroe would not sell their goods on credit. He also urged that the saline wells forty miles west and south of Monroe should be taken over and operated by the government to prevent salt "speculators from skinning us too much."

On July 14 General Blanchard issued his first call for conscripts. Men were to report to Opelousas with "a blanket, a knife, fork, spoon, canteen, haversack, tin cup and plate, also, a change of clothing."

Fourteen days later the Twenty-eighth Louisiana Regiment arrived in Monroe without a single gun. This regiment, made up of north Louisiana volunteers, had organized in May and had spent some two months drilling at a new camp near Vienna, to the west of Monroe. Blanchard begged Secretary of War George W. Randolph to get Van Dorn to release the arms he was holding at Vicksburg and to hasten the promised shipment from Richmond.

To guard the vulnerable matrix of streams that traversed the state and could be entered by going up Red River from the Mississippi, Governor Moore ordered Brigadier General John B. Smith, commander of the Tenth Brigade Louisiana Militia, to call the militia units of Natchitoches and Rapides to active duty. General Smith was to defend the areas along the Red, Black, Old, and Atchafalaya rivers from the enemy invasions.[5]

After three months of waiting, Governor Moore's request for a military commander was finally honored by the War Department. Richard Taylor, a favorite son of Louisiana, was detached from command of the Second Louisiana, promoted to major general, and ordered to Louisiana to enroll and conscript troops in the District of Western Louisiana of the Trans-Mississippi Department. Taylor was to command all troops south of Red River and was to prevent the enemy from using the rivers and bayous in the area. Troops were to be gathered and sent to fill up the ranks of Louisiana regiments serving in Virginia. After this, Taylor was to retain as many recruits as would be needed in the state. Light batteries of artillery were to be organized to harass passing enemy vessels on the streams. Partisan troops were to be made effective or else disbanded. The enemy was to be confined to as narrow an area as possible, and communications and transportation across the Mississippi River were to be kept open. Taylor arrived in Opelousas on August 20 to assume command of the District of Western Louisiana.[6]

A company of Partisan Rangers, "guerrillas" to the Yankees, for several weeks had been firing upon unarmed Union transports as they passed near Donaldsonville, a small town between New Orleans and Baton Rouge. Gunboats were sent to the town, and the citizens were warned that if another shot were fired the navy would bombard the area for six miles below Donaldsonville and nine miles above and would destroy every building on all of the plantations. The citizens appealed to the Partisans, but their appeals were ignored. Finally the transports were given an escort of gunboats, but they were still fired upon, although the shotguns and rifles of the Rangers were generally ineffectual against the gunboats. The irate naval commander, Admiral Farragut, ordered the bombardment of Donaldsonville as soon as it could be evacuated. All of the citizens of Donaldsonville and nearby Port Barrow "left their homes and went to the bayou, each house received two or three families from the small abandoned villages."

On August 9, after the battle of Baton Rouge, Farragut sent several gunboats down the river to Donaldsonville. Around eleven in the morning the bombardment began, and "at 12:30 a detachment of Yankees went to shore with fire torches in hand." [7] The hotels, warehouses, dwellings, and some of the most valuable buildings of the town were destroyed. Plantations above and below Donaldsonville were bombarded and set afire. After the boats withdrew, a citizens' committee met and decided to ask Governor Moore to keep the Rangers from firing on Federal boats. These attacks did no real good and brought only cruel reprisals against the innocent and helped to keep the Negroes stirred up. [8]

Rangers, or Partisan troops, and the militia continued to make trouble and work for Governor Moore. One group operating in the lower part of the state, the Prairie Rangers under Captain S. M. Todd, led one citizen to complain bitterly: "We could not fare worse were we surrounded by a band of Lincoln's mercenary hirelings. Our homes are entered and pillaged of everything that they see fit to appropriate to themselves." The letter referred to Todd's group as "Lawless wreches [*sic*]" and "Prairie Banditti." [9]

One of the militia officers, Brigadier General R. C. Martin, commander of the Fifth Brigade, added to the governor's woes by refusing to obey orders concerning the handling of Partisan troops and the militia of his district and by issuing counter orders to those of the governor. Martin was placed under arrest to await court-martial, and Major General John L. Lewis, head of all the state militia, took command of the Fifth and Ninth brigades.

When General Taylor took over the command of the District of

Western Louisiana in late August, he issued orders that all conscripts south of the Red River were to proceed to Camp Pratt, near Opelousas, with every necessity of a soldier except arms, ammunition, tents, and rations. Lieutenant Colonel R. E. Burke, C.S.A., was in command of the camp. All conscripts who had already enrolled in companies of Partisan Rangers were to be carried on the conscript rolls of their respective parishes.

Militiamen at Camp Pratt between the ages of thirty-five and forty-five were to be released from duty. All members of the militia between eighteen and thirty-five who were eligible conscripts were to remain at the camp for instructions and were transferred to conscript ranks by order of Governor Moore. An additional military camp was established at New Iberia. In every way Governor Moore was trying to co-operate with the new commander, Richard Taylor.[10]

In the parishes of northeast Louisiana bordering the Mississippi, a stigma was placed upon men who waited to be conscripted. Soon most of those who were eligible began to join new companies being formed. General Taylor reported that there were few conscripts to be had in north Louisiana because most of those eligible for the draft had already volunteered before the passage of the act. Of the few who were conscripted, about a hundred were sent to Vicksburg to fill up Louisiana regiments serving there. The dirty white conscript uniforms made them stand out from the others, and the volunteers ostracized them. Below Red River, despite the presence of the enemy in nearby areas, around three thousand men were enrolled as conscripts and sent to Camp Pratt. About two thousand of them were used to fill up skeleton regiments sent into Louisiana to join Taylor. The rest were organized, drilled, and finally sent to help defend Port Hudson. By December, conscripts brought into camp were very few. Most of them had to be hunted down in the woods and canebrakes by detachments of soldiers, who brought them in bound with rope or wearing chain and ball.

By late August General Blanchard had sent many of the troops at Monroe over to the Mississippi to stop the Yankee raids along the river front and to aid in landing guns and supplies from the eastern Confederate states, bound for General Albert Pike's Indian troops. Part of the Thirty-first Louisiana had been in this swampy area since June and had suffered greatly from measles and fever. On the night of August 18 a Confederate steamer, the *Fair Play,* loaded with guns and ammunition, pulled into Milliken's Bend. A Federal gunboat surprised the unloading operation and captured boat and cargo.

Late in August Federal gunboats dropped down from Lake Providence to a bend above Vicksburg and sent a detachment of men over to Tallulah, where they burned the depot of the Vicksburg, Shreveport and Texas Railroad and captured Confederate supplies awaiting shipment to the Indian territory. The Thirty-first Regiment stationed there made no resistance and fled for their lives.[11]

General Blanchard, with headquarters at Monroe (some 60 miles by rail from Tallulah and 105 miles by wagon road), had less than two thousand men to protect all of North Louisiana. Although the majority of the citizens west of the Ouachita were either younger than eighteen or older than thirty-five, they were anxious to serve the Confederacy, but some two thousand of them had to be turned down because there were no weapons.

The seven Federal ironclad gunboats and the five transports with troops stationed at Lake Providence constituted a major threat to the river front. The heavy sick list and lack of arms caused General Blanchard to recall most of the troops from the unhealthy swamp lands in October and to send them west of the Ouachita to the piney hills, where they recuperated for a month. In November some of the troops were sent to Jackson, Mississippi, and others were sent down to the Teche to join General Taylor.[12]

During late August, September, and October the Lafourche region saw renewed activity from Federal troops attempting to free the region of Southern troops. Two companies of the Eighth Vermont, numbering one hundred men, accompanied by Company B of the Second Regiment Massachusetts Cavalry, entrained at Algiers for Boutte Station where they left the cars and marched to Bonnet Carré Point near St. Charles Court House. A small force of the enemy was discovered, and the Union cavalry and two pieces rushed into action. The Southern troops took refuge in a cane field but were dispersed into the swamps by charges of grape and canister and escaped. Two Rebels were captured and one wounded. On the return march to the train the Federal troops collected a large herd of cattle, horses, sheep, and mules.[13]

Early in September a Confederate force set out to capture Boutte Station and Bayou des Allemands, which had been held by Federal troops since spring. The group was made up of part of a Terrebonne regiment of militia, a battalion of Rangers from Texas and Rapides Parish under Major James A. McWaters, and the St. Charles Militia, the whole command under Brigadier General John G. Pratt. En route the men saw the destruction that the Union forces had wrought in the nearby areas: "Nearly every place had been despoiled and plundered even to the huts of the poorest creole. We halted at General Taylor's place seven miles from Boutte . . . it was a complete wreck, the furniture smashed, the walls torn down, pictures cut out of their frames and . . . scattered over the floor, lay the correspondence and official documents of the old Genl. while President of the United States." The men found the Boutte deserted but soon ran into a company of seventy-five Federal troops aboard flatcars moving toward Algiers.[14]

Captain Edward Hall, of the Federal outpost at Bayou des Allemands, on September 4 sent a detachment of infantry and a howitzer on flatcars to guard a train bringing in supplies from Algiers. Near Boutte Station the Confederate force lying in ambush fired on the troops, instantly killing and wounding a number of men. A few minutes later, a thrown switch shunted the train onto a sidetrack and caused it to collide with an empty passenger car. The train from Algiers arrived just then, and Captain John S. Clark, overestimating Rebel strength at 1,000, deemed it wise to proceed with both trains back to Algiers. The Texas cavalry, it was stated, proceeded to strip the dead, wounded, and prisoners of their possessions and then moved with their prisoners toward Boutte Station, where they proceeded to hide in the dense bushes, flying a flag of truce above their hiding place. Captain Hall sent out a party to investigate, and when they failed to return a second party was sent. The Confederates, herding the captured men before them, moved up near the station and Captain Hall, seeing that he would have to fire into his own men, surrendered the post. The Federal casualties included 9 killed, 27 wounded, 155 captured, and 3 guns seized.

Encouraged by his success, Major McWaters moved his ragged cavalry force over to the Mississippi near St. Charles Court House, about twenty-five miles above New Orleans. Colonel James W. McMillan, with a portion of the Twenty-first Indiana Regiment and the Fourth Wisconsin, was sent by boat to land below the cavalry force while Colonel Halbert E. Paine with the Fourteenth Maine, Ninth Connecticut, and Sixth Michigan regiments and two sections of Thompson's battery landed above them. Gunboats were stationed on the river front to aid in the move. The Texas cavalry was hemmed in between the swamp and river, and the Indiana battery opened fire upon them. The Texans fled into the swamps and were followed by the attackers. Sloshing through mud and water up to their waists, the Federal troops found the cavalry horses tied to trees. The troops abandoned the pursuit and took out three hundred of the horses; a large number that could not be moved easily were shot. Fifty prisoners were taken, including several officers, and two Confederates were killed and three wounded. Shotguns, blankets, pistols, saddles, and other abandoned equipment were also captured. Butler breathed a sigh of relief and began preparing plans for a major expedition to clean out all the Lafourche area.[15]

The fruits of the first Confederate conscription act proved disappointing, and on September 27 the act was extended to include all men between the ages of eighteen and forty-five. These men were to serve for three years. Persons who were not liable to serve under the act could hire out as substitutes for those being conscripted. Draft dodgers, runaway conscripts, and deserters, numbering some eight thousand, were reported in the District of Western Louisiana in October.[16]

On October 1, Major General Taylor reported that the District of Western Louisiana had an aggregate of 5,840 men, including those present for duty and absent. These troops, made up of conscripts, volunteers, Partisan Rangers, and militia, numbered 3,425 infantry, 2,033 cavalry, and 382 artillery.[17] Nearly all of the men were poorly armed, but some of them were poorly equipped as well. A large portion of the Thirty-third Louisiana Regiment was "in a most deplorable state of destitution . . . being without blankets, shoes and tents. They have been compelled to sleep out in the open air, without any covering, for the last week, it having rained nearly every night." Many of the men were conscripts and looked forward to a tilt with the Yankees so that they could take winter clothes and shoes from them.[18]

Butler was finally ready to strike a major blow at the Lafourche district. Four light-draft gunboats were built and equipped and placed under Commander McKean Buchanan. The boats were sent via the Gulf over to Berwick Bay to stand ready.

Godfrey Weitzel, with some 5,000 troops loaded aboard seven transports, moved up to the deserted, smoke-blackened ruins of Donaldsonville on Saturday, October 25. The 850 Confederates in the area, commanded by Colonel W. G. Vincent, fell back to Napoleonville, where they were joined the next day by the Eighteenth Louisiana, the Crescent Regiment, and George Ralston's battery from Bayou Boeuf and Berwick Bay.

Two thirds of Donaldsonville was already in ashes, and the Union soldiers made havoc of the homes still standing. Window panes were smashed, furniture was wrecked, and the poultry yards were stripped of all the chickens and turkeys.

The next morning General Weitzel, with the majority of his troops, departed for lower Lafourche. The day was unreasonably cold, with ice in the puddles along the road. As the large force marched through the still-occupied plantation areas, the slaves became very excited and hard to handle. Many began to disappear at night, taking carts and mules, to follow the Union army.

Planters who could, attempted to move their Negroes beyond the temptation and reach of the Union forces. Many of the Negroes seemed delighted to go with their masters and set out bright and happy for Texas, but some of the slaveowners soon discovered that this joy was only a ruse. Each night groups of the male slaves would disappear until few were left. Many of the discouraged planters returned home, hoping that their remaining slaves would stay with them. A few of the luckier planters, although beset by hardships, did succeed in reaching Texas with many of their slaves and resumed their farming activities on rented lands.[19]

General Weitzel was appalled by the Negro problem. He complained that his train, swelled by conscripts, looked like a train of twenty-five thousand troops. Negro men marched along the flanks proudly carrying soldiers' knapsacks and ready to perform any task for their deliverers. Soldiers played practical jokes, and the more unscrupulous robbed their black wards of their valuables. Plantation carts loaded with black women, children, and household goods followed behind. There were not enough rations to feed the ever-increasing horde, so the Negroes foraged for their food, robbing henhouses, gardens, and pastures. When Federal gunboats appeared in Berwick Bay, the planters hastily loaded their Negroes in wagons to move them out of danger. The enemy came on so fast that the owners abandoned four hundred wagonloads of Negroes at Brashear City, and these contrabands swelled the ranks of their brethren already with Weitzel's army. On November 1 Weitzel complained to Butler: "I have already twice as many negroes in and around my camp as I have soldiers within."

Butler sympathized with Weitzel concerning the Negro problem. Weitzel was told that the conscripts who came into his lines were, according to the Conscript Act, free. Butler advised: "Put them as far as possible upon plantations; use every energy to have the sugar crop made and preserved for the owners that are loyal, and for the United States where owners are disloyal. Let the loyal planters make arrangements to pay their negroes $10 a month for able-bodied men . . . and so in proportion. Disembarrass your army of them as much as possible." [20]

Pillaging was not solely a Negro weakness. In the neighborhood of Centreville in St. Mary Parish, Yankee units swooped down on plantations, seizing sheep, hogs, cattle, chickens, horses, mules, bridles, and saddles. Buckets, pots, pans, dishes, silver, shoes, clothing—any thing of value was taken from the protesting owners. Negro men were persuaded to leave their masters and to become free men. [21]

Back at Donaldsonville, the First Louisiana Regiment under Colonel Richard Holcomb, left to hold the town, carried on the traditional habit of living off the country. While the neighboring plantations' supply of poultry and smoked meats lasted, these men ate well. To better hold the area Holcomb erected a fortification, christened Fort Butler, at Port Barrow near Donaldsonville. [22]

Brigadier General Alfred Mouton, a West Point graduate recently arrived in the department, relieved Taylor of some of his duties. Taylor proceeded to Red River to plan the building of defenses on the lower part of the river. It was not until he returned to Alexandria on October 31 that he received a communiqué from Mouton announcing that the enemy had again occupied Donaldsonville. Meanwhile, Weitzel, also a West Point man, had met Mouton in several skirmishes. The handsome, six-foot-four, twenty-six-year-old Union general, with his superior forces, steadily pushed General Mouton out of the Lafourche district.

As the Federal army was advancing down both banks of the Lafourche on October 27, Mouton found it necessary to take up positions on both banks of the bayou to avoid being outflanked. The Eighteenth and Crescent regiments, plus Ralston's battery and a detachment of cavalry numbering 539, were stationed on the right bank descending the bayou, and the Thirty-third Regiment, a company of the Terrebonne Regiment, Semmes's battery, and the Second Louisiana Cavalry numbering 853, held the left bank.

The Union column on the right, moving more swiftly than the left, met the Confederate forces around 9 A.M. and were checked briefly by Ralston's battery. With their commander wounded and captured and their ammunition gone, the battery fell back in confusion. Mouton now moved his entire force down above Labadieville, where they took up strong positions.

Around four in the afternoon, the Union right, consisting of the Eighth New Hampshire and Perkins' cavalry, still ahead of the left,

ran into a strong force of Rebel sharpshooters and two guns posted in
the woods and were abruptly halted in their advance. General Weitzel
had concentrated his strongest force on the left bank, expecting the
heaviest enemy resistance in that quarter, but Mouton, using the bridge
over the Lafourche at Labadieville, had switched most of his forces
over to the right bank. Weitzel discovered his error, after floundering
around in a dense cane field for over an hour. Two huge river flatboats had been towed down the bayou by mules and willing Negroes
to enable the forces to switch from bank to bank. Weitzel immediately
ordered the pioneers to cut the levee and to swing the boats end to
end across the bayou; at one end he stationed two 12-pound howitzers.
The surprised Confederates immediately opened fire on the pontoon
bridge. Most of the shells went high, but a few fell close and splattered
the Twelfth and Thirteenth Connecticut with muddy bayou water as
they dashed over to the opposite side. The Seventy-fifth New York
remained on the left bank to guard the bridge.

The Eighth New Hampshire was being pressed hard, and as the
new units moved into position they saw the Eighth slowly retreating,
their lines broken and somewhat disorderly. The men were confused
and entangled and fired at will, without waiting for orders, the men
in the rear ranks shooting over the heads of those in front or between
them. The Eighth rested on the bayou, slightly to the rear; the Thirteenth occupied the center; and the Twelfth took up position on the
far left. While the Eighth continued to blaze away at the unseen
enemy, the Twelfth and Thirteenth moved forward through thick
thorn bushes and over stumps and ditches. The Confederate batteries,
in their haste to fire, misjudged the range and lobbed their shells high
over the heads of the advancing troops. On they moved to a rail fence,
which they flattened by hitting it with their bodies. Many of the officers and men, under fire for the first time, bobbed and dodged at the
sound of every bullet or shell. Weitzel, wearing a sky-blue overcoat,
calmly smoked a cigar as he rode forward.

The Union officers pushed their men across a thicket of thorn
bushes, which struck fear in the hearts of the men. Orders were yelled
and echoed, "Center dress!" The inexperienced officers still believed
that the cause was lost if the men did not move into battle shoulder to
shoulder, with their lines in perfect order. As the Federals entered a
relatively open field, bound by the bayou levee on the left and dense
swamp forest on the right, the Confederates opened up a continuous

rifle fire. The sharp whir of bullets filled the air, puffs of dust kicked up along the ground, and clouds of blue smoke rose above the trees, but there was no enemy in view. The anxious Federal troops, when ordered to halt and fire by file from right to left by company, did not obey. Instead, they all fired in a volley toward the unseen enemy. Every man reloaded his rifle in record time, and without orders, several companies fell face down. Prodded up and onward, the men advanced, firing and loading as fast as possible, ignoring all commands to halt and dress the lines. As the ragged lines swept along, a swearing mania possessed the ranks, and the men, without knowing why, shouted obscenities at the tops of their lungs.

The first Confederates to show themselves were the Terrebonne Militia, who suddenly ran out of the forest on the west along a crossroad to reinforce the Confederate front. These men fired a sidelong volley at the Twelfth Connecticut and without joining the main line broke in confusion and headed for the safety of a nearby thicket. Mouton's center, the Eighteenth Louisiana and the Crescent Regiment, occupying a strong position in a drainage ditch behind a cypress fence, held their ground until the Twelfth Connecticut approached within a hundred yards of them. Suddenly all was silent, and a few minutes later swarms of dirty gray-uniformed men leaped out of their ditch and took off for the rear at a full run. Panic-stricken men ran over each other in their attempt to escape. The men of the Twelfth raised a shout of joy and redoubled their rate of fire. The Thirteenth sped forward, and the two regiments moved over the fence and across the ditch, following and firing at the already invisible enemy. The officers found it almost impossible to halt the headlong rush and even more difficult to quiet the riotous shouts of exultation.

The battle was not quite over. Mouton's left wing, the Second Louisiana Cavalry, appeared in the rear and began to attack the baggage guards. Unexpectedly, the Second Louisiana ran into the Eighth New Hampshire and suddenly gave up all ideas of fighting. The cavalry left by a circuitous route for Thibodaux. Perkins' cavalry, the Thirteenth Connecticut, and a section of artillery pursued Mouton's retreating forces toward the south for another half hour and then abandoned the chase.

The Union casualties at the battle of Georgia Landing, or Labadieville, were surprisingly small. Two officers and 16 enlisted men were killed, one officer and 73 men were wounded, and one officer and 4 men were captured or missing, for a total of 97. General Mouton claimed only 5 killed, 8 wounded, and 186 either captured or missing, although his forces were outnumbered two to one.

Mouton found that just at the time of the move from Donaldsonville, Butler had sent two other forces to bottle up the Confederates. Colonel Stephen Thomas took the Eighth Vermont Regiment and the First Regiment of Native Guards along the railroad toward Thibodaux. Later Butler sent the Second Regiment of Native Guards to join Colonel Thomas. Two shallow-draft gunboats were working their way into Berwick Bay. At noon on the twenty-seventh, Mouton, seeing that he must concentrate his forces, sent orders to Colonel T. E. Vick at Des Allemands to abandon his station and join him with the Lafourche Regiment of militia, numbering five hundred, and a detachment of three hundred men from the Thirty-third Regiment. At the same time the St. Charles and St. John militias were ordered forward. From Boutte Station and Vacherie the cavalry pickets were ordered to fall back on the main body. When these troops failed to arrive because of a mix-up in orders, Mouton decided to retreat until they did.[23]

Arriving at Thibodaux on October 28, Mouton burned the depot, bridges, sugar, and supplies he could not carry with him. The men were loaded aboard cars and sent to Brashear City. On the same day, Weitzel occupied Thibodaux. Meanwhile, back at Des Allemands, Colonel Vick burned the bridges and military property he had to leave behind and marched his men over the railroad bed to Terrebonne Station, where a waiting train took them to join Mouton. Many of the conscripts attached to Vick's command lagged behind and were later captured by the enemy. Vick brought only eighty-two men with him. The cavalry units arrived at Brashear on the twenty-ninth.

When the four small Federal gunboats appeared in Berwick Bay on Saturday evening at dusk, November 1, Captain E. W. Fuller, commanding the Confederate gunboat *Cotton,* ordered the steamers *Hart, Seger,* and *Launch No. 1* to go up the Teche to safety. The acting master of the *Seger,* I. C. Coons, purposely grounded his vessel, deserted his men, and fled, and the *Seger* fell into the hands of the enemy. After exchanging shots with the enemy, the *Cotton* retreated up the Atchafalaya to Bayou Teche.

Monday afternoon, November 3, the four Federal gunboats, mounting twenty-seven guns, came up the Teche, passed the weak obstructions sunk in the bayou by Mouton, and engaged the *Cotton* near Cornay's Bridge. For an hour and a half the squadron poured a steady fire into the *Cotton* and an artillery battery concealed behind a small earthworks. The *Cotton* and the battery returned the fire, doing serious damage to the enemy. The *Kinsman* was struck fifty-four times, and two men were killed and four wounded. The *Estrella* received three shots, which killed two men and wounded another, and the *Calhoun* received eight shots. The *Diana* was grounded but was later recovered and repaired. The *Cotton,* struck several times, suffered no real damage except two killed and one wounded. Giving out of ammunition, the *Cotton* retired.

The next day the *Cotton* returned to the obstructions and waited for the enemy boats to appear. Finally, Wednesday morning, the four boats approached cautiously but were bested in the ensuing duel and retired after an hour. Thursday the Federal gunboats came up again and threw shells at the Confederate gunboat for half an hour without doing any damage. The *Cotton* did not return the fire, and again the enemy withdrew to Berwick Bay and remained there.

General Richard Taylor returned to lower Louisiana on November 6 and found General Mouton entrenched near the confluence of the Teche and the Atchafalaya. All public roads were crowded, as frightened citizens were moving their families and Negroes to safety. Weitzel was now in possession of the Lafourche. Federal troops collected horses, mules, and sugar in large quantities. Planters who remained began taking the oath and were allowed to make contracts with the Negroes to finish their sugar crops.[24]

After Weitzel's successful campaign, General Butler created a new military district, the District of Lafourche, and named Weitzel to the command. Weitzel had considerable trouble with the undisciplined Negro troops. Usually the jail at Thibodaux contained a number of black soldiers "of whose behavior there are endless complaints of burning, stealings, ravishings, and lesser crimes." Many of the white troops believed that the "Native Guards" should be disbanded or placed "under iron rule, or to garrison some fort away from civilization."[25]

Slaves continued to desert their masters and to crowd into Thibodaux and other points held by Federal troops. If the owners tried to restrain them, some of the Negroes openly rebelled, tied up their overseers and masters, and left anyway. Occasionally these Negroes were tried in the provost courts but were usually released.[26] The planters who remained in the Lafourche "have generally taken the oath of allegiance and are up in camp often, looking after their live property, the ubiquitous negro, who comes and goes at his own sweet will, while the Government is protecting him and, too, the planter's property." [27]

Sugar speculators soon appeared in the district to purchase sugar. Some of the army officers were not too busy to join in the profitable trade. Cattle, mules, and horses continued to be seized from the plantations even though the owners had renewed their allegiance. Some of this property could usually be recovered by appealing to the provost marshal or to General Weitzel. A number of the planters were furnished military guards to curtail future depredations. [28]

The capture of New Orleans in the spring inspired several of the northwestern Louisiana parishes to form "committees of safety." The protection of the Red River Valley brought "committee" representatives from Bienville, Bossier, De Soto, Caddo, and Winn parishes, and from Harrison County, Texas, to Shreveport on November 22. It was decided that fortifications and obstructions must be built on the Red River. Nearly eighty thousand dollars was raised to finance the work. Committee delegates appealed to the planters to hire out their slaves to build the defense works. Owners would provide the worker with clothing, bedding, and tools and in return would be paid twenty-five dollars per month per man.

General Taylor had already begun a defense plan for the lower Red and the upper Atchafalaya. Colonel L. G. DeRussy, formerly of the Second Louisiana Regiment, an engineering officer, was placed in charge of building a fort on the Red about thirty-five miles below Alexandria. Another work was being erected at Butte-à-la-Rose on the Atchafalaya. This point, if it could be held, would give the Confederates free use of the upper Atchafalaya, and a way of transporting salt and other supplies to Vicksburg. [29]

Taylor's problems began to multiply as the year 1862 waned. Desertions, especially among the "Cajuns," became quite prevalent in the Teche region. Even in north Louisiana, near Minden, many robust-looking men claiming to be "discharged soldiers" were seen riding about. Taylor reported that a "large number of persons liable to military service . . . , deserters, enrolled conscripts who have failed to report, between the ages of eighteen and thirty-five, are to be found throughout the state." He ordered militia officers and parish sheriffs to arrest all men who could not prove legal exemption or absence from military service because of furlough or parole. Liberal rewards were offered for the apprehension of such men.

Exemption clauses of the Conscription Act had long caused trouble and jealousy. Overseers, plantation owners, local officials, Confederate officials, and workers in vital industries often took advantage of their rights. Orders were issued in December that "all shoemakers, tanners, blacksmiths, wagon-makers, millers and their engineers" must take a written oath that they were actively engaged in their habitual trade in order to remain out of the army. The act had also taken so many men from several areas that no able-bodied men were left to raise food for the destitute families. General Taylor allowed a number of men to return home for thirty days to provide for their families.

Governor Moore, feeling that Louisiana had been neglected too long, requested that President Davis order Louisiana troops back into the state or send other troops. This was done. H. H. Sibley's Brigade, together with Gurley's and Stone's regiments, arrived at Opelousas late in December.

The governor feared that Louisiana would soon be overrun with Federal troops and he took every possible precaution. Early in December he asked Brigadier General R. B. Todd, commanding the Eleventh Brigade in northeast Louisiana, to call into active service "the militia force of his brigade" and all men between eighteen and forty who were not subject to conscription. These men from Madison, Carroll, and Tensas parishes were to co-operate with Confederate authorities in helping to repel enemy attacks in that region.[30]

The state legislature, meeting in Opelousas in December and January, 1862–63, did what it could to build up the defenses. A law was enacted calling all white males between seventeen and fifty, whether permanent or temporary citizens, to serve in the militia. This legislature also authorized police juries to levy taxes and to call out able-bodied slaves to work on river defenses.[31]

On June 26 that part of Louisiana east of the Mississippi and the Gulf counties of Mississippi were designated the Department of Mississippi and East Louisiana by the Confederate government. General Daniel Ruggles was placed in command here. Partisan Rangers in the area were ordered to organize into battalions of at least five companies. These men were to be rigidly disciplined to prevent destruction of citizens' property and to be effective resistance to the enemy. The Federal troops at Baton Rouge in June and July periodically visited the surrounding area to burn homes, slave quarters, and sugarhouses; to plunder for cattle, horses, cotton, and sugar; or to arrest and insult citizens.[32]

Earl Van Dorn announced that he was moving his main forces

north and that therefore General Daniel Ruggles should send the Fourth and Twelfth Louisiana regiments to Vicksburg. Ruggles was to take command at Jackson, leaving about twenty-five hundred men under Brigadier General William Beall to hold Port Hudson.[33]

Since General Butler, after the evacuation of Baton Rouge, refused to station any troops in eastern Louisiana except in the area of New Orleans, the Confederates built up their strength at Pass Manchac and vicinity. On September 15, Major George C. Strong of Butler's staff, with three companies of the Twelfth Maine and one company from the Twenty-eighth Massachusetts, destroyed the Manchac bridge and moved on to Ponchatoula. Ponchatoula, headquarters for Confederate General M. Jeff. Thompson, was deserted by the defenders —the Tenth Arkansas, a battery of artillery, and a few home guards —after a weak resistance. Twenty freight cars loaded with cotton, sugar, and molasses were burned by Strong's men and the telegraph apparatus was destroyed. Twenty-one of Strong's men were wounded, ten of whom were left at Ponchatoula when the Federals retired back toward New Orleans. After the withdrawal, the Confederates returned and took over the town once more.[34]

The work on building up the fortifications at Port Hudson went steadily forward. Port Hudson occupied one of the strongest positions on the river, as well as one of the most important. It was thought that no Federal gunboat could pass the guns located on the bluffs, and holding this position would guarantee to the Confederates possession of the Mississippi northward to Vicksburg. Vital supplies from western Louisiana, Texas, and Mexico, via the Red River, could thus be safely shipped to the eastern half of the Confederacy.

Many of the troops stationed at Port Hudson were in rags and without shoes. Those lucky enough to have uniforms wore every variety of color and style. The men wore hats of every shape and fashion— straw hats, felts, caps—anything available. The barefoot, tattered army maintained a high level of morale and worked hard to give the enemy a proper reception.

The temporary commander, General Beall, reported fifty-five hundred men present for duty on December 2. Late in December Major General Franklin Gardner, a West Point graduate who had been with Taylor and Scott in Mexico and who had fought at Shiloh and in Kentucky, assumed command of Port Hudson.[35]

By order of General Banks Baton Rouge was reoccupied by some eight thousand Federal troops under Brigadier General Cuvier Grover on December 17. The town presented a desolate appearance; there were "black ruins standing everywhere," and many of the houses had been punctured by cannon balls. The streets, houses, camps, and levees soon swarmed with contrabands from nearby plantations. The Negroes were put to work cleaning up the battle debris and strengthening the fortifications.

As usual, the occupation troops resorted to marauding and plundering of an area that had already suffered heavily during the first occupation. General Grover issued strict orders that such practices must cease,[36] but official foraging was not forbidden. One of the soldiers reported that an "abundance of chickens, geese, milk, eggs, sweet potatoes" had been brought in. He boasted that they lived "off the fat of the land" and that "nearly all officers have taken fine horses." [37]

On the night of December 28, the beautiful Gothic capitol building was set on fire by careless troops occupying the place. All through the night the Baton Rouge skyline was lighted up by the bright flames. Despite the efforts of the Union commander to extinguish the fire, the next morning the building was a shell with only "blackened, scorched, and windowless walls" remaining.[38]

General Banks in December had 42,074 troops in the Department of the Gulf. Of this number 39,825 were in Louisiana and the rest were at Pensacola. Nearly one half of the force were nine-month men. This army was designated the Nineteenth Army Corps and was divided into four divisions. The first division was placed under Brigadier General Cuvier Grover, the second under Brigadier General W. H. Emory, the third under Major General C. C. Augur, and the fourth under Brigadier General Thomas W. Sherman.

With this army Banks was expected to help open the Mississippi as rapidly as possible. He then was to open up the Red River Valley, get control of Mobile, and secure a toe hold in Texas.[39] Great military feats were expected of the untutored and inexperienced political general, feats that would have stymied even the most seasoned Union commander.

PART THREE

UNVEXED TO THE SEA: 1863

XII

CANALS AND STALEMATES

THE CURTAIN was about to rise on a mighty drama far up the river at Vicksburg. Although General Banks had been named to play a major part, he preferred to produce, direct, and act in his own production downstream, leaving Grant, Sherman, and Porter to carry the stellar honors at Vicksburg.

Many changes and much spade work had taken place to make the project a success. In October, 1862, David D. Porter was placed in command of the Mississippi Squadron. Porter was given to exaggeration and boastfulness, accused by Stanton of being a "gas bag . . . , blowing his own trumpet and stealing credit which belongs to others," and goaded by ambition. He nevertheless possessed the qualities of abundant energy, recklessness, resourcefulness, and fighting spirit needed for the trying role ahead. Porter was assigned the task of aiding General John A. McClernand in opening the upper Mississippi. The choice of McClernand, a volunteer political general, pleased Porter, because he felt that all West Point men were "too self-sufficient, pedantic, and unpractical." [1]

Confederate Lieutenant General John C. Pemberton arrived in Jackson, Mississippi, on October 14 and assumed command of the Department of Mississippi and Eastern Louisiana. Pemberton was forced to reorganize his entire command, having inherited from his predecessor Van Dorn a beaten and demoralized army, fresh from the defeat at Corinth.

In the same month General U. S. Grant was given formal command of the opposing army with instructions to operate from the north and open the upper Mississippi. In early December Grant conferred with General Sherman at Grand Junction, and they planned a concerted move against Vicksburg. Grant would take his army by land down from West Tennessee to Jackson, Mississippi, and then move to the rear of Vicksburg. With the aid of Porter's fleet, Sherman was to go down-river from Memphis with his army and secure lodgment at Chickasaw Bluffs, north of Vicksburg, and aid Grant when he finally arrived.

Porter's Mississippi Squadron, after a long controversy, was strengthened in November by the addition of the ram fleet commanded by Brigadier General Alfred W. Ellet. Ellet's peculiar brigade, organized by the army, was to act as a marine force and to assist the navy in, breaking up guerrilla activity along the banks of the river. Porter insisted upon, and finally secured, full control over this army-marine group.[2]

Before McClernand arrived, Sherman was ready to start a down-river movement. Porter joined Sherman at Memphis, and on Saturday, December 20, the armada of transports got underway, headed by Porter's flagship, the *Black Hawk*. Stopping at Helena, troops commanded by Brigadier General Frederick Steele joined the expedition, giving Sherman some fifty regiments, ten batteries, sixty guns, and around thirty-two thousand men, including two divisions of new levies sent to Memphis by McClernand. Before dawn on Christmas day the troops reached Milliken's Bend, Louisiana, twenty miles by river above Vicksburg. Porter had arrived at the mouth of the Yazoo the day before. General A. J. Smith and his division, under orders to move down and seize control over the railroad opposite Vicksburg and to stop the flow of supplies from west of the river, landed at Milliken's Bend. The next day Sherman's other three divisions moved to join Porter at the mouth of the Yazoo.

Christmas morning a part of A. J. Smith's command, carrying light packs, set out for Dallas Station, some twenty-six miles inland along the Shreveport and Vicksburg Railroad. Arriving late in the day they destroyed one wooden railroad bridge two hundred feet long that spanned the Tensas River along with two smaller bridges. The next morning the work of destruction was pushed forward.

A small detachment of about forty Union cavalrymen moved to Delhi, ten miles distant, destroyed the railroad station there, captured some whisky, got drunk, and committed a number of outrages before straggling back to the main column. On December 26 the expedition moved back to the river through a light rain that made the ground very slippery and marching extremely difficult.

Although there were around a thousand Partisan Rangers, principally cavalry armed with shotguns, within striking distance of the Federal column, the Rangers allowed the enemy force of two thousand to move thirty-five miles inland, to destroy several cotton gins, railroad depots, railroad bridges, and Negro quarters of a plantation, and to take three hundred head of cattle, two hundred horses and mules, and seventy-five Negro slaves. Not a blow was struck, and not a Union soldier was lost on this raid.

Brigadier General A. G. Blanchard, at Monroe, became alarmed and called all the Partisan troops along the river to proceed to Monroe to escape capture. General Taylor, investigating the entire affair, pronounced it "disgraceful to the service in the extreme." Taylor stated that General Blanchard had failed to carry out orders and that this officer was completely incompetent for any command. However, until another officer arrived, Blanchard would have to be retained as commandant of camps of instructions in north Louisiana.[3]

The day after Christmas Sherman landed his main forces at Johnson's plantation in the lowlands between the Yazoo and Walnut Hills. Moving through a group of narrow lanes of swampy land between a matrix of bayous, Sherman pushed forward on December 27 and 28 to within striking distance of Chickasaw Bluffs.

The assault began on the morning of December 29. One brigade, after fearful losses, succeeded in crossing the broad, shallow bayou and took shelter under the farther bank, while lower down, another regiment crossed over only to cower in scooped-out mud caves along the bank. Porter's gunboats were of no use. Afraid to move up because of submarine mines, the naval guns could not reach their target. Under cover of darkness the Federal troops slipped back across the bayou, and Sherman retreated to higher ground. Sherman on January 1 abandoned the campaign, turning over his command to General McClernand, who had just arrived at Milliken's Bend.

Saddened by the loss of so many men and the failure of his Haines' Bluff (or Chickasaw Bluffs) expedition, Sherman proposed another expedition to the new commander, McClernand: Arkansas Post, a strong Confederate works fifty miles up the Arkansas River, should be taken to guard the Mississippi against attacks from the west side. McClernand was delighted, and the entire force, accompanied by Porter's fleet, moved up to Arkansas. After a naval bombardment of several days' duration, the troops assaulted and Fort Hindman surrendered.[4]

Grant, in the meantime, encountering seemingly insurmountable obstacles, had been forced to change his plans for the capture of Vicksburg. Establishing his main supply base at Columbus, Kentucky, and a secondary base at Holly Springs, Mississippi, Grant moved along the uplands toward the rear of Vicksburg. It was his idea to meet Pemberton in the field, defeat his army, and then easily take over Vicksburg. The plan failed when General Earl Van Dorn and General Nathan Bedford Forrest destroyed his supply and communications lines. Grant feared to continue his move, and he withdrew back to Memphis.

Grant was afraid to stand still. By his withdrawal he had committed himself to a river campaign against Vicksburg. Already denounced by the newspapers in the North, Grant must prove his worth as a commander. The Union desperately needed a new victory. Grant hastily organized the defenses of West Tennessee and on January 30 arrived in Louisiana to assume full command of the expedition. McClernand, William T. Sherman, and James B. McPherson were appointed corps commanders.

McClernand was angry with Grant for taking over his troops and assigning him to a less important position. The recently married general had brought his new bride along on the expedition to share with him the honor of a brilliant victory and the capture of Vicksburg.

According to instructions from Grant, McClernand landed his men along the levee at Young's Point. The men at Young's Point suffered from the heavy winter rains and lack of shelter. Tents were not issued to the troops because they were within range of the guns of Vicksburg, so the more enterprising men dug holes in the levee and covered them with their black rubber blankets. Floundering in knee-deep black mud and still exhausted from recent expeditions, numerous soldiers fell sick. Many cases of smallpox were reported. Hospital tents lined the back side of the levee and were crowded with thousands of sick men. Many died, and soon the levee was lined with new graves.

Grant instructed McClernand to resume work on the canal started by General Williams in the summer of 1862. President Lincoln believed the canal would work, and Grant felt obligated to try it. One of Williams' problems had been that his canal began in an eddy, from which the water could not be diverted with enough force to eat out a new channel. Grant therefore directed that a new opening be made where the current struck the bank with the most force.[5]

McClernand turned over the direction of the canal construction to Sherman. On January 25 Sherman wrote his brother, John: "The

River is now rising rapidly and already fills the canal, which is a narrow ditch—the water flows across it but thus far it shows no symptoms of cutting a channel. All my soldiers are busy day and night in throwing up a Levee on the inside of the canal to prevent the water overflowing in. . . . I have not much faith in the canal." [6]

Again on January 28, Sherman wrote: "Here we are . . . at Vicksburg on the wrong side of the river trying to turn the Miss. by a ditch, a pure waste of human labor." [7]

The men digging the canal shared Sherman's sentiments. One of these soldiers stated: "Every one almost who has seen the work says it will be a failure." Sergeant Cyrus F. Boyd complained of the rain, sleet, and frost and of working conditions: "The men do not relish the idea of having to *dig*. . . . Men have to work knee deep in mud and water The officers sleep until eight oclock and do not appear to care. . . . The men are often hurried off to work in the morning before they can get their breakfast and this makes them ugly and insubordinate There is but little discipline and the details go off swearing that they will not do anything and thus things go I do not believe our commanders know what we are here for But they will keep the men employed until they can *think up something*." [8]

Sherman complained to McClernand, "I have never seen men work more grudgingly, and I have endeavored to stimulate them by all means." Sherman had a corduroy road constructed across the swamp from the levee to the canal for easier travel to that point. The men worked with shovels to widen the canal by nine feet, throwing the earth on the sides to act as a levee, hoping it would prevent an overflow and would also serve as a parapet to help protect the workers. Sherman stationed riflemen and a few guns along the parapet for additional protection. Shovels and other tools were short, but details of a thousand men at a time were sent to work on the project.

Grant continued to push the work on the canal, using as many as four thousand men at a time on the project. Captain F. E. Prime of the Army Engineers was in charge of the construction. Negroes were rounded up around Lake Providence and transported to Young's Point to join the labor forces. [9]

Negroes were not only brought from upriver, but contrabands swarmed in from the back country, bringing with them horses, mules, carts, household goods, and every imaginable accouterment. Racial prejudice ran strong, especially among the Western men. One of Sherman's men reports, "The men in our camp treat them [the Negroes] worse than brutes and when they come into camp cries of 'Kill him' etc. are heard on every hand." [10]

Grant inspected the canal and decided that it could not be used— not enough water emptied from the river to make it navigable. He did not abandon the old canal construction, however. While the river was high and the land routes below and around Vicksburg were flooded, Grant was forced to try any plan that promised a measure of success. Speaking of his experiments in his *Memoirs,* Grant claimed that he wanted "to divert the attention of the enemy, of my troops and of the public generally." Grant's program caused the Confederates at Vicksburg to spread their forces, to shift their big guns to cover more territory, and to fortify the area from Haines' Bluff to Warrenton.

A second canal route in prospect was at Lake Providence, some sixty river-miles above. Lake Providence was a beautiful oxbow lake some six miles long, an old Mississippi river bed with an outlet through Baxter Bayou into Bayou Macon and thus into the Tensas, Ouachita, Black, and Red rivers. This long circuitous route of over four hundred miles might be used to get safely around the batteries of Vicksburg. Several other methods of getting to the rear of Vicksburg were also suggested and were soon to be tried.[11]

The Vicksburg campaign was to be the proving ground of two of the commanders, Grant and Sherman. Both men, under a cloud, would be made or broken by the measure of success with which they conducted the movement.

Sherman, a West Point graduate of 1840, had served as a colonel in Virginia and as a brigadier general in Kentucky, but he had yet to display any marked talents for leadership. Sherman, beset by hallucinations and unreasonable fears and finally contemplating suicide, had been relieved from command in Kentucky. He later began a new climb to success at Shiloh and Corinth under Grant. Still, if he muffed his Vicksburg assignment, which had begun unfavorably, he would rise no higher.

As a man, Sherman was an eccentric mixture of strength and weakness. Although he was impatient, often irritable and depressed, petulant, headstrong, and unreasonably gruff, he had solid soldierly qualities. His men swore by him and most of his fellow officers admired him.[12]

Grant, like Sherman, was on trial at Vicksburg. Grant, a man with a checkered military past, was at the turning point of his career. After his outstanding victory at Fort Donelson and the desperate battle of

Shiloh early in 1862, Grant had fallen from public attention and favor. Although he had done well in defending Memphis and had fought at Iuka and Corinth, for almost a year he was in a period of partial eclipse. His retreat from Mississippi and rumors that he was floundering in the overflowed lands of Louisiana and Mississippi and would probably fail in his Vicksburg campaign caused many people to assign Grant to a class with McClellan, Buell, and other Union failures.

Lincoln was besieged by critics who were out for Grant's scalp. Grant was accused of being a habitual drunkard, of needlessly wasting men in battle, and of committing stupid maneuvers. He was a witless, baffled, and bewildered commander. The President listened but chose to withhold judgment until after Grant had been given sufficient time to prove himself. After all, Grant was a fighting man, and commanders who were not afraid to fight were somewhat rare in the Union army at this time.[13]

As a person, Grant seemed to be "self-contained, simple-minded, and direct in all his thoughts and ways." He never cursed nor seemed to lose control of his temper.[14] Charles Dana, sent by Stanton to report on Grant's actions, found him to be modest, honest, and judicial. He was not "an original or brilliant man, but sincere, thoughtful, deep, and gifted with a courage that never faltered." Although quiet and hard to know, he loved a humorous story and the company of his friends.[15]

Many of Grant's and Sherman's difficulties stemmed from an unfriendly press. Thwarted contractors looking for a quick fortune, camp followers, and rival generals spread fake reports about the two generals, and news-hungry correspondents eagerly passed rumors along to the gullible public.

The correspondents found the protracted "ditch-digging" campaign extremely boring to watch and even less lucrative to write about. Many of the newsmen turned to buying cotton. Several of these men grew wealthy from cotton money, despite the keen competition from the army officers who stole cotton for their private gain and from the sharp speculators ranging the area.[16]

Despite the carping of the correspondents and of Grant's critics in the North, the ditch-digging at Young's Point still continued. To add to the woes and dangers of the troops engaged in the project, the Confederates placed batteries on the bluffs opposite the mouth of the canal and could rake two thirds of the canal with enfilade fire. From time to time Pemberton's guns would drop a shell into the working crews, leaving a few dead, others maimed, and all frightened. The rains continued to fall, and the weather remained cold. The sick list mounted. Epidemics of smallpox, measles, mumps, dysentery, and swamp fever raged through the camps. The "Dead March" became a familiar sound to the camp, but even burials were a special problem in these swampy lowlands. The army finally confined its burials to the sides of the levee, where the earth was dry enough to permit normal burials. The living soon found themselves hemmed in between the graves that honeycombed the levee.

Leaves of absence, resignations, and discharges were plentiful during the trying campaign before Vicksburg. Civilian officers, ranging from the bottom through full colonel, who could not take the hard military life, or were overly fearful of what was yet to come, or were too ignorant to fulfill their duties were allowed to resign. Chaplains who tired of the hardships, and who were not as successful in their religious work as they had expected to be, resigned and went home. Most of the enlisted men who were mustered out were either ill or under age. Many long leaves of absence were granted for health reasons upon the recommendation of a surgeon.[17]

Although Sherman's letters home continued to voice his doubts concerning the success of the canal, he continued to push the work as much as possible. The men strained to remove the hundreds of stumps and to widen the ditch to sixty feet. Sherman placed a six-gun battery below its mouth to try to discourage the fire of the Confederate batteries on the opposite side of the river.

To expedite the work two dredge boats were brought from Helena and Lake Providence early in March and put to work. The canal was deep enough by March 7 to promise success when a sudden rapid rise in the river broke through the levee protecting the upper part of the canal and submerged the canal, drowned work horses, and swept away all the tools. The men fled for their lives to the main levee; nearly two months of tremendous labor went for nought. The entire peninsula became a solid sheet of water.

The rising waters forced General McClernand to move the Thirteenth Corps on March 10 by steamer up to Milliken's Bend, "where fine camps were laid out on the broad, sandy cotton fields protected by a levee." Dry land, beautiful live-oak groves, spacious but abandoned houses—all of this seemed like paradise to the men who had weathered the watery hell of Young's Point.

Ranking officers took over the available mansions for themselves and turned over Negro huts to the surgeons to be used as hospitals. Many of the men were in need of the best medical attention after the grueling experience of Young's Point. Fatalities ran high. "The muffled drums were heard all day long, and the parting volleys at graves on the slope of the levee" did nothing to improve the morale of the men.[18]

Sherman's men took refuge on the levee and aboard transports anchored near Young's Point. While the troops were waiting to repair the damages to the canal, the two dredges continued to work, with the Confederate batteries throwing occasional shells at them.

On March 16 Grant ordered Sherman and his men to board steamers and to accompany Porter on his Steele's Bayou expedition into the Yazoo River. The purpose of the mission was to explore the feasibility of moving an army by this route to the rear of Vicksburg.

Admiral Farragut, who had successfully run past the batteries of Port Hudson a few days earlier, moved up south of Vicksburg and began to shell the lower Confederate batteries that were bothering the dredging machines. The enemy guns were not silenced, and the accuracy of their fire finally drove off the dredges. On March 27 the Young's Point canal was abandoned.[19]

Grant continued to explore other possibilities of getting within striking distance of Vicksburg. After a tour of the Lake Providence canal project early in February, Grant was very optimistic concerning the success of such a route. Sherman, who from the first had denounced the Young's Point canal, was enthusiastic in his endorsement of the new project.

The Ninety-fifth Illinois Regiment, first to arrive at Lake Providence on February 2, started work on the canal from the levee of the Mississippi to the lake less than a mile away. By the middle of the month much of the narrow ditch had been completed.

Major General James B. McPherson at Memphis was ordered to bring the Seventeenth Army Corps to join John McArthur's division at Lake Providence. A shortage of transports delayed McPherson for nearly three weeks and he did not arrive until late February.

Life at Lake Providence was relatively pleasant for the men. Abundance of good water, beautiful country, little danger, and some chance of recreation kept morale high. Even an order forbidding gambling or card playing caused little discontent, as the troops turned to horseshoe pitching and baseball for amusement. Of all the blessings at hand, the men appreciated the lake most of all. The sparkling expanse of water, lined with cypress trees festooned with Spanish moss and surrounded by beautiful plantations, had much to offer. Thousands of hot, dusty men shed their clothes at the end of the day and swam and bathed in the cool waters. Another favorite pastime of the enlisted men was to secure skiffs, or rowboats, or to contrive their own rafts, and paddle around in the lake. Fishing was good, and the soldiers' mess, with the excellent forage at hand, was enriched. When the wind blew, the waters of the lake rolled, and the men enjoyed riding the waves in their frail craft.

It rained often, and the men grumbled about the mud and flooded pup tents. This did not seem to hurt their health. Nearly every regiment reported a great improvement in the health of the men. The men foraged far and wide for fence rails to keep their bodies out of the ooze at night. These hard beds were softened with Spanish moss gathered from the trees. A greater cause for discontent was the lack of pay. After five months without pay the men with families worried about the welfare of their loved ones. Many threatened to desert.

Thousands of Negroes came to Lake Providence. Some came voluntarily; others were brought in by the army. They came loaded down with chickens, ducks, pigs, dogs, mules, and household goods. The men were immediately set to work digging on the canal and in clearing the timber from the bayous. The influx of contrabands helped to free most of the Union soldiers from the hated digging chores. Only a few troops were needed for supervisory duty. The released men were not allowed to be idle, however. The officers set up a new training program, and the men brushed up on company and brigade maneuvers.[20]

Discipline among the Western soldiers at Lake Providence was none too good. The men were often disorderly and disobedient, especially when there was no fighting. Many of the officers, drawn from civilian life and elected by their men, were not trained nor qualified to give proper leadership, and some of them did not rate the respect of the troops.

Whenever a soldier was caught committing some offense, his punishment was harsh. One of the men, a lad of nineteen, was accused of stealing forty-eight dollars from a comrade. Each evening for several evenings he was forced to march up and down in front of his regiment wearing a big black sign with the word "thief" painted in white letters while the band played the rogue's march. A number of the men were sentenced to hard labor in the penitentiary at Alton, Illinois, for the duration of their enlistment. Men who appeared in "non-regulation" uniform at dress parade or were found wearing their pants tucked in their boots were court-martialed and given humiliating penances. One man accused of cursing the President was forced to work dragging an iron ball and chain weighing over two hundred pounds. Drunks were sometimes sentenced to wear a ball and chain for thirty days.

A chaplain of the Seventy-eighth Ohio relates that the men of his regiment discovered a nearby frame cotton gin that promised material to keep the men off the damp ground for the night. The Seventy-eighth Ohio, joined by delegates from two other Ohio regiments, made "the boards and shingles . . . fly thick and fast." Some rogue set the wrecked building on fire, and it quickly burned to the ground. All of the men found with boards and shingles from this building were arrested, and the entire brigade was assessed two thousand dollars to pay for the building. Chaplain Thomas M. Stevenson had joined in this raid and was among those arrested. In his diary he expressed these sentiments: "If all rebel property was destroyed as soon as we came to it, this war would end much sooner than it will be the way things are carried on now." [21]

Carroll Parish was second only to Tensas in the production of cotton, and cotton was an all-important item to the army as well as to the speculators who swarmed into Lake Providence. Negro contrabands were rounded up from the plantations above and below the town and set to work picking the cotton on the abandoned plantations. General McPherson, commander at Lake Providence, signed contracts with speculators who agreed to pick, gin, and bale it for a one-half share. The army furnished the Negro pickers, and the contractor agreed to feed, clothe, and pay the contrabands a dollar per hundred. Several of the large plantations had up to a thousand bales of cotton still in the fields. A man named Kellogg from Memphis was the chief contractor and set up a gin at Lake Providence to bale every available pound of cotton. Fortunes were to be made. Cotton was bringing over a dollar per pound in New York and it could be procured here at less than a quarter a pound.

Army details were sent out in wagons to scour the countryside and in boats to search the river-front plantations for hidden bales of cotton. Speculators and cotton thieves roamed the area until their activities were halted.[22]

The narrow and tortuous Baxter Bayou, running out of Lake Providence on its northwest side, presented a tremendous problem to the army engineers. Huge, dense trees hung over the stream, and fallen timber had nearly choked up the channel. Winding in a west, south-west direction toward Bayou Macon, Baxter ran into lower ground and suddenly fanned out and disappeared entirely in a vast cypress swamp. For several weeks parties of Negroes and soldiers worked, cutting away the trees from the banks and clearing the stream of debris for a distance of five miles. Heavy rains caused the lake to over-flow, flooding much of the country and causing great difficulty and inconvenience to the work gangs. Men working with axes and saws in several feet of water tried to clear a passage for the boats through the cypress timber. All of the trees had to be cut under the water, as close to the ground as possible, for a distance of some three hundred yards before the entry to Bayou Macon was accessible. The levee at Lake Providence was to be cut so that a steamer could be brought down and a steam capstan could remove the rest of the logs and snags. Later McPherson intended to use a dredge boat to dig a channel from Baxter through the cypress swamp to Bayou Macon, a somewhat larger and deeper stream. From Bayou Macon the Tensas, Ouachita, and Red rivers were navigable for most boats, and Vicksburg would be safely bypassed.

Upriver at Ashton, just below the Arkansas line where Bayou Macon came to within three miles of the Mississippi, there was another possibility for a bypass below the guns of Vicksburg. By cutting the levee and flooding the open fields and a country road, passage from the river into the Macon could be made by any of the boats. The First Missouri Engineers were sent up by McPherson to carry out the job. On March 4, using powder borrowed from the fleet, they blasted several holes in the levee, and the flooded Mississippi rushed through the holes and ate out huge crevasses. The country overflowed, but the water never reached a sufficient depth at Ashton to be used. At Lake Providence the water backed up Baxter Bayou and drove the workers out. All of the camps were moved to the highest ground around the lake.

On March 16 McPherson set gangs of Negro laborers to digging two trenches thirty feet apart through the levee at Lake Providence, and just at sundown the waters came rushing through the break into the canal and into the lake. The swift, boiling current ran through the town and began to flood the land. McPherson transferred his men to higher ground at Berry's Landing, five miles above, as fast as the available transports could complete the job.

The Lake Providence canal route was not entirely abandoned, work being resumed after the flood waters had subsided somewhat. Mc-

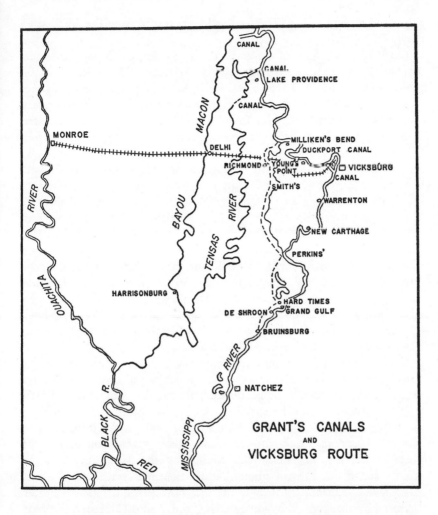

GRANT'S CANALS
AND
VICKSBURG ROUTE

Pherson was confident that the route would work. The Confederates had several groups of men stationed along the banks of Bayou Macon with a few pieces of artillery, to prevent the passage of the Federal boats. They were ready to fell trees across the channel and block the forward movement. By the end of March Grant had other plans for bypassing Vicksburg and the Lake Providence route was abandoned.[23]

Another of Grant's ideas to get to the rear of Vicksburg resulted in the Yazoo Pass expedition. Yazoo Pass in Mississippi, opposite Helena, Arkansas, had once been used by steamboats but no longer was used because a high levee cut off its entrance from the Mississippi River.

On February 3 a detail cut and blew up the levee. The racing waters opened up a channel through an old ditch into Moon Lake. Moon Lake connected with Yazoo Pass, which, in turn, joined the Coldwater River. The latter flowed into the Tallahatchie and the Yalobusha rivers, about two hundred and fifty miles below Moon Lake. The Confederates were busy after the levee was cut. They felled trees into the pass and blocked the channel for some twenty miles. After nearly two weeks of grueling labor Lieutenant Colonel James H. Wilson, the Federal officer in charge, and the accompanying troops opened up a route into the Coldwater. Finally on February 24 a combined naval and military expedition entered the break through the levee and after a slow, cautious move arrived at Greenwood, where the Yalobusha and Tallahatchie joined to make up the Yazoo. Here the expedition encountered a rude Confederate works of earth and cotton bales, mounting two heavy guns and a few lighter ones. The area surrounding the fort was submerged, and land approaches for troops were impossible. Aided by a shore battery the ironclads made two abortive attacks on March 11 and 13, but Fort Pemberton easily repelled them. A short time later the expedition was withdrawn to Helena.

Grant, who had heard nothing from the Yazoo Pass expedition, became worried. He did not know about the withdrawal, and he believed that the force must be rescued. It was decided to send Porter and Sherman as a relief expedition on another route and to set up a base above Haines' Bluff on dry land to the north of Vicksburg. With five gunboats and four mortar boats Porter started on March 15 through the network of bayous connecting the Mississippi and the Yazoo above the guns of Haines' Bluff. Sherman, with one division, took small transports through Steele's Bayou and followed Porter. Stymied by tree-choked bayous, shallow water, and Confederate sharpshooters, this expedition up Deer Creek was doomed to failure, and on March 27, to Grant's great disappointment, the forces drew back.[24]

Grant had yet another Louisiana canal scheme to be tried: a short canal from Duckport, on the river, into three bayous connecting with Bayou Vidal, which rejoined the Mississippi at New Carthage, between the Confederate batteries at Warrenton and Grand Gulf, a distance of some thirty-seven miles. He sent Captain John W. Cornyn of the Engineers with a detachment of three hundred men to survey the Duckport canal route. Cornyn reported that a canal from the levee of the Mississippi to Big Bayou would require an excavation three hundred yards long, fifty feet wide at the top tapering to twenty-five feet at the bottom, and fifteen feet deep. Big Bayou, choked with "heavy timber, drift-wood, logs, &c.," would have to be cleared, and some five hundred yards of the total distance of eight miles would have to be dug out and widened. Willow Bayou, up to a hundred feet wide at its widest point, with an average depth of five feet and banks ten feet high, could float almost any boat when flooded. The banks were found to recede lower down, and finally Willow Bayou disappeared into a swamp three miles in length. Ten-foot embankments would have to be built through the swamp to confine the waters. A small amount of timber would have to be removed below the swamp to connect the canal with Roundaway Bayou. Roundaway averaged seventy-five yards in width, had ten-foot banks, and was from ten to fifteen feet deep. If some timber were removed from the banks, Roundaway would be navigable.

Colonel G. G. Pride, assisted by Captain F. E. Prime, was placed in charge of construction, and on April 1 Grant ordered Sherman to send a thousand of his men by boat from Milliken's Bend to Duckport. Each day the men embarked at 7:30 A.M. and were relieved at 6 P.M. to return to the point of embarkation.

The labor force digging the canal was increased to thirty-five hundred men, and another strong detachment was set to work clearing out the bayous. The weather was relatively cool, and there were surprisingly few mosquitoes and gnats. The soldiers grew fat on the rich forage in the area. There was little doubt as to the practicability of the canal after the waters of the Mississippi had been released into it. By April 12 all of the hand digging had been completed. The next day the levee was cut, and shortly four steam dredges were moved in from the river to do the heavy work of digging out the swamp and deepening the bayous.

Grant sent to St. Louis and Chicago for as many barges and tugs as could be found. He planned to transport most of the men and some of the supplies through the bayou route to New Carthage and to send a number of large boats to run the Vicksburg batteries and join the expedition below. Several barges and tugs were run through successfully, but suddenly the river began to fall, and the water in some of the bayous sank to a depth of one foot. A few of the boats were grounded and left to corrode in the mud. A road was constructed to haul supplies to barges already beyond the low-water areas. By the end of April the river had fallen sufficiently for Grant to try an overland route that, unlike the canal routes, was to prove successful.[25]

XIII

VICKSBURG, ACT TWO

THE FEASIBILITY of Grant's new plan to move below the batteries of Vicksburg and Warrenton had already been tested in part.

On February 1 Colonel Charles Rivers Ellet of the Marine Brigade, on orders from Porter, started a run at 4:30 A.M. southward past the citadel in the *Queen of the West*. Although the *Queen* was struck by twelve enemy shells, she was little injured and was able to continue her southward move. Ellet, a headstrong teen-ager, was the son of Charles Ellet, Jr., and the nephew of the fleet commander, Alfred W. Ellet.

Below the mouth of Red River the *Queen* captured the empty steamer *A. W. Baker,* and a short time later the *Moro,* loaded with military supplies for Port Hudson, was seized. Entering Red River, Ellet intercepted the *Berwick Bay,* also loaded with supplies for Port Hudson. With his coal supply critically low, Ellet destroyed the three Confederate prizes and returned to the peninsula below Young's Point where he awaited instructions from Porter.

Porter on the night of February 7 floated a barge carrying a month's supply of coal down past the batteries to Colonel Ellet. The *Queen* was now ready to resume her mission of preventing military supplies from reaching Vicksburg and Port Hudson through Red River.

The *Queen,* accompanied by the *De Soto,* a small steam ferry, on February 10 passed below the Warrenton batteries without incident and proceeded to Red River. Two days later Ellet took the *Queen* down the Atchafalaya River. Intercepting a Confederate train of twelve wagons about six miles downstream, Ellet landed his men and destroyed them. At Simmesport seventy barrels of Confederate beef and one wagon loaded with ammunition were destroyed. On the return trip that night a group of civilians fired upon the *Queen*, injuring one officer. The next morning Ellet destroyed all of the buildings on three plantations near the scene of the attack.

Proceeding up Red River with his two boats, Ellet entered Black River on February 14 and surprised and captured the Confederate steamboat *Era No. 5*, which was carrying 4,500 bushels of corn. Leaving the *Era* well guarded, Ellet moved up to Gordon's Landing, which he found impossible to pass because of heavy fire from four well-placed 32-pounders. Ellet attempted to have his ship backed out of danger, but the *Queen* grounded within range of the Confederate batteries. Shot after shot rained on the helpless ram. The main steam pipe was shot away, and live steam made the boat untenable. Protective cotton bales were flung over the side, and the men and officers escaped and climbed aboard the *De Soto*, a short distance below. Confederate skiffs soon appeared and took possession of the abandoned *Queen*.

The overcrowded *De Soto* retreated but ran into one of the banks and fouled her rudders. When she drifted down to the *Era*, the *De Soto* was scuttled and burned. Ellet, fearing pursuit, fled in the *Era* down to the Mississippi. A short distance from Natchez Ellet met the ironclad *Indianola*, which had been sent below to reinforce him. The impetuous young Ellet had lost two boats and had had twenty-four men taken prisoner. Grant, fearing the *Era* might be captured by the enemy, a few days later ordered the boat to be sunk.

At Alexandria the Confederates hastily repaired the damages to the *Queen*, and an expedition, commanded by Major J. L. Brent, was organized to capture the ironclad *Indianola*. On the night of February 24 the *Indianola* was sighted opposite New Carthage, and although her armor and firepower were superior to theirs, the *Queen* and the *Webb*, with guns blazing, charged in to ram the Federal gunboat. Twice the cottonclad rams struck without damage. On the third pass the *Webb* cut a hole below the water line, and the *Queen* did serious injury to her stern. The *Grand Era*, loaded with infantry, rushed alongside, grappled the ironclad, and prepared to board. Captain George Brown appeared and offered to surrender. The Confederates tried to tow the prize down to the Red River, but the damages were found to be so extensive that the *Indianola* was run on a sandbar in ten feet of water. The captured crew was landed on the Mississippi side and sent to Jackson. A detail of one hundred men was placed aboard the *Indianola* to repair her, but when word came that two gunboats had passed the Vicksburg batteries en route to give aid to the *Indianola*, the rest of

the Confederate expedition abandoned the repair crew and fled down
the river. The orphaned work party, left to face the two enemy vessels
alone, burst three of the big guns, spiked the rest, and then blew up
the *Indianola*. In their headlong flight the Confederates had neglected
to save anything except the officers' wine and liquor stores. The far
more valuable guns, shot, shell, and powder were destroyed with the
Indianola.

The destruction of the *Indianola* was a costly blunder for the Confederates. The two gunboats were a myth. The sly, ingenious Porter
had fooled the overly cautious Confederates with a fake monitor, a
log raft three hundred feet long. From a distance it resembled the ram
Lafayette, complete with wooden guns, davited small boats, twin wheel-
houses, and mock smokestacks with iron pots burning tar and oakum
to produce a black smoke. The "monitor" was set free to drift by the
Vicksburg batteries, which poured a deadly fire into her, but to the
surprise of the gunners the audacious monster floated safely by without firing a shot. Porter's ruse worked. Brent's expedition fled, and
the *Indianola* was needlessly destroyed.

News of the capture of the *Indianola* reached Admiral Farragut at
New Orleans. Since Porter hesitated to use his gunboats on the heavily
armed stretch of the river between Vicksburg and Port Hudson now
completely under the control of the Confederates, Farragut decided to
run the batteries of Port Hudson with his fleet. With tremendous difficulty and great loss, Farragut succeeded on March 14 in taking only
two ships, the flagship *Hartford* and the tug *Albatross,* above Port
Hudson. With only two boats Farragut felt that he could not maintain
a proper blockade, so he hurried to Vicksburg to get reinforcements
from Porter. Farragut found the upper fleet engaged in the abortive
Yazoo Pass and Deer Creek expeditions, and it was not until Brigadier
General A. W. Ellet arrived at Young's Point with his Marine Brigade
that Farragut was promised any aid. Colonel Charles R. Ellet in the
Switzerland successfully ran past the batteries and joined Farragut's
patrol.[1]

General Grant had not been idle. In addition to his Duckport canal
project and his Mississippi expeditions Grant, on March 29, had ordered
General McClernand to begin moving his Thirteenth Corps along the
levees and banks of the bayous, through the flooded lands from Milliken's Bend to New Carthage, and below the Confederate batteries at
Vicksburg and Warrenton.

After marching over a boggy road for twelve miles, the Sixty-ninth Indiana and a section of artillery reached Richmond, on the banks of Roundaway Bayou, on March 31. A small Confederate force contested the advance, but the spirited fire of the Federal artillery and infantry drove the defenders from the area.

Continuing the march along the banks of the bayou, on roads barely above the water, the advance party moved on its way to New Carthage. Above that small settlement the bayou levee had broken in several places, flooding the road for two miles. An amphibious movement was mandatory, and boats had to be secured. Negroes revealed that a large flatboat was held by a Confederate picket eight miles down Bayou Vidal. General P. J. Osterhaus camped at Smith's plantation and on April 5 sent a detachment of the Third Illinois Cavalry and a group of willing Negroes to seize the boat. Small boats, skiffs and yawls, were found in the surrounding waterways, and others were built with lumber from confiscated homes.

Major Isaac F. Harrison, in command of the Confederate forces in the vicinity, had a force of only a few hundred men with which to hinder the move. At a camp of instructions, located on Lake Bruin about twelve miles below, there was one company of cavalry and one battery of artillery being held in reserve. A small body of pickets was stationed near New Carthage, and a third detachment was guarding the flatboat on Bayou Vidal.

The Negro guides led the Third Illinois Cavalry to the place where the flat was hidden. The Negroes were placed aboard and began paddling and poling the craft upstream. Major Harrison and a company of the Tensas Cavalry, composed of planters, fired upon the Federal detachment, and a noisy but ineffective contest ensued. While the short engagement raged, the flatboat made its escape. The next day (April 6) Osterhaus ferried his men across the flooded area and occupied New Carthage.

Osterhaus sent a picket from the Sixty-ninth Indiana to James's plantation along the levee below New Carthage, where a small squad of Harrison's men was encamped. The Confederates were easily routed, and Harrison had to pull all of his men down to Perkins' plantation.[2]

On April 8 at Berry's Landing, above Lake Providence, McPherson's corps was marched into an open field to hear an address from Adjutant General Lorenzo Thomas, sent into the area by the War Department. The venerable white-haired emissary startled the men by announcing that the government was now ready to arm the Negroes. Some of the men cheered, but more than a few of the Negro-hating, undisciplined Western men loudly hissed the proposal.[3]

All slaves remaining in the area were to be free. The able-bodied men were to be enlisted in Negro units, and the women, children, and those men unfit for military service would be placed on abandoned plantations, which would be leased for one year by the government to persons who would support the Negroes and pay them decent wages. The plantations would be protected by Negro troops as well as by white garrisons. The Negro units would be used for fatigue duty and to garrison the swampy, less desirable areas, freeing the white troops for more important work. All of the officers of the proposed Negro units would be white. Lesser officers could volunteer to lead Negro outfits and receive a much higher rank. White enlisted men with ability could become officers. In some of the divisions the response was overwhelming, and far more men volunteered to lead the Negro troops than were needed.

General Grant reported to Halleck that his corps commanders accepted "the new policy of arming the Negroes and using them against the enemy. . . ." Grant pledged that he would carry out the program to the best of his ability, and he kept his promise. Orders were issued to the various commanders to complete the organization of Negro regiments as swiftly as possible. Prejudice against Negro troops was to be stamped out, and the officers were to make their units as efficient as possible.[4]

A daring plan for the capture of Vicksburg had been suggested in January by James H. Wilson, one of the best engineering officers in the western army. Grant accepted the idea although, for various reasons, none of his military commanders, including Sherman, liked the proposal. The plan was simple. The batteries of Vicksburg would be run at night by gunboats and by transports, which would haul supplies below. As soon as the water receded enough, troops would be marched to a point below the batteries, be ferried across to the Mississippi side, and be moved overland to the rear of Vicksburg. By mid-April the flood waters were falling, and Grant was ready to make his combined land and amphibious move below.

Grant enlisted the aid of Porter, and final preparations were made to run the batteries. The navy would escort several steamers past the fourteen miles of guns. Porter prepared the steam transports for passage by lining the decks and machinery with bales of cotton and hay and sacks of grain. Barges loaded with coal, forage, and equipment were to be towed below by the transports.

At ten o'clock on the night of April 16, a moonless night, the squadron was set in motion. With no lights showing and with as little noise as possible, the boats got under way. Porter led off in the *Benton* and was followed at two-hundred-yard intervals by five other gunboats, the *Lafayette, Louisville, Mound City, Pittsburg,* and *Carondelet.* The transports, *Henry Clay, Forest Queen,* and *Silver Wave,* followed, towing their barges. The gunboat *Tuscumbia* came last.

The lead boats had already passed the upper fort when they were discovered. The roar of the guns on the hillside shattered the quiet night. The Confederates were holding a grand ball in Vicksburg, but they were not totally unprepared. A detail of Confederate troops swiftly rowed across the river and set fire to the railroad buildings and shacks at DeSoto, on the Louisiana peninsula, and huge bonfires were lighted on the Mississippi. The dancers left the ball to view the awesome spectacle, but as the gunboats began to lay shells in the streets the citizens fled from the city or took refuge in caves.

Grant, not wishing to miss the show, took his headquarters boat, the *Henry von Phul,* as close to the upper batteries as possible, and anchored in midstream. With him were Mrs. Grant, who had recently joined her husband at Milliken's Bend, their children, Grant's staff, and a battery of clerks.

The navy ironclads and gunboats ran close along the Vicksburg bank, and the transports moved near the Louisiana shore. For over two hours the action raged. The batteries bombarded the slow-moving targets, but little or no damage was done to the navy vessels, although each one was hit many times. One of the transports, the *Henry Clay,* was set on fire by a shell and burned to the water line. By two o'clock the boats were safely anchored at New Carthage along the Louisiana shore. The casualties were light; no one had been killed, and only fourteen had been wounded.[5]

Prior to the running of the batteries on April 16, McClernand had ordered the rest of the Thirteenth Corps to move down from Milliken's Bend to New Carthage. Many of the troops, overloaded with extra baggage, surplus clothing, and blankets, found the heat of the Southern springtime enervating and the going heavy. Gradually they began to unload themselves of their burdens. The line of march was soon strewed with abandoned articles of clothing, which later were gathered by slaves. As the days began to slip by, the slow-moving army encountered bad weather. Rains fell, turning the narrow, alluvial road into a slippery quagmire. From time to time the men were halted to repair a bayou levee or to reinforce the roads with additional logs so that the muddiest areas could be crossed. By April 25 the men had joined Mc-Clernand in the vicinity of New Carthage.

Major Harrison's small detachment of local troops had recently been reinforced from Grand Gulf, across the river, with 1,800 Missourians. At four o'clock on the morning of April 15 the Confederate troops attempted a pincer movement against McClernand's troops around New Carthage. The Missouri troops, led by Colonel A. C. Riley, drove in the Federal pickets at Dunbar's plantation on Bayou Vidal, some five miles below Smith's plantation. The Confederates slipped around the Federal force by wading across a flooded bayou and field and launched a new attack. When reinforcements arrived, the Confederate advance was turned and the Missourians were forced to retreat. Simultaneously with the Dunbar plantation action, a smaller group of Confederates under Major Harrison moved up the levee from below James's plantation and struck at McClernand's men along the Mississippi levee three miles below New Carthage. Harrison fought a delaying action, awaiting the Missouri troops, but when they failed to arrive he retreated below. The superior Federal forces failed to follow up their victory and allowed the Confederates to escape and set up a temporary defense works below, near the Mississippi. On April 17 Porter, upon the request of McClernand, sent the gunboat *Tuscumbia* to shell this position. The Confederate troops abandoned the works and moved to a new inland position on the west bank of Lake St. Joseph.

Grant and Dana, the morning after the running of the batteries, steamed down to New Carthage. After instructing McClernand to cross the river and take possession of Grand Gulf as soon as possible, Grant returned to Milliken's Bend to issue the necessary orders to his troops above Vicksburg to move below. McPherson, above Lake Providence, was to forward the Seventeenth Corps to Milliken's Bend and Richmond at once. One regiment was to be detailed to protect United States property on the plantations between Milliken's Bend and Lake Providence. As soon as Negro regiments could be fully organized and trained, they would relieve McPherson's men. Hospitals were established at Milliken's Bend and at Duckport, and all sick and disabled troops were to be left there. As the men convalesced, they would act as guards for their immediate area. The corps commanders were to collect all of the corn, fodder, cattle, and other needed supplies along the route of march. As soon as McClernand's men cleared the way, the Seventeenth Corps would follow, and Sherman's Fifteenth Corps would come down last.[6]

Grant saw that it would be impossible to haul enough rations to feed his tremendous army over the one narrow, almost impassable, road between Milliken's Bend and New Carthage, so he had six more wooden steamers prepared, protected as before, to run the Vicksburg and Warrenton batteries. Two barges, loaded with one hundred thousand rations, a forty days' supply of coal, medical supplies, and forage, were lashed to each boat. Around midnight on April 22, under a cloudy, dark sky, the expedition got under way. Again the Confederate guns blazed away at the slow-moving targets below, and the unarmed steamers, without naval escort, were impotent to return the fire. The lead ship *Tigress*, loaded with hospital supplies, was hit in the hull below the water line and sank on the Louisiana shore. The other five steamers were struck repeatedly but were able to pass by successfully with their barges. Two men were killed and only a few were wounded. Grant now had above Grand Gulf the supplies and transports he needed to make his crossing to the Mississippi side.

Grant moved his headquarters down to Smith's plantation, a few miles above New Carthage. Here he could personally direct the proposed movement across the river. The flood waters surrounding New Carthage made it impossible to use this area as a major staging area. After carefully scouting the region McClernand's men discovered a road from Smith's around Bayou Vidal to Perkins' plantation, about ten miles down-river from New Carthage. To make this road practical four bayou bridges had to be constructed, using boats and flats floated down from above and lumber torn from nearby houses. The men often had to work in water up to their necks. Two additional miles of road had to be hacked and cut through the swampy forest.

While the troops in the Milliken's Bend area were moving below over the muddy, rain-soaked bayou road, on April 25 Osterhaus sent two regiments of infantry and a cavalry detachment to reconnoiter the area from Perkins' place south along the curving banks of Lake St. Joseph to Hard Times on the Mississippi, three miles above Grand Gulf. En route, Colonel James Keigwin, commander of the expedition, ran into Harrison's small cavalry and artillery force blocking the way.

After light skirmishing and an artillery duel, Harrison was driven out and retired in the direction of the Tensas River swamp, and the Union detachment went on to Hard Times.

Like all the Union troops, McPherson's men were much taken with the lush beauty of the country through which they moved. Large comfortable one-story plantation houses, girdled with galleries and surrounded by fine lawns and well-tended gardens, were set in magnificent groves of moss-draped live oaks and magnolias. Despite orders from Grant and other commanders, many of the homes were entered by the enlisted men and some of the officers and were ransacked for things of value and for souvenirs. Wanton destruction was practiced by some. Pictures and portraits were slashed; rosewood chests were hacked to pieces; pages and leather bindings were torn from books; muddy feet were wiped on the velvet and brocatel upholstery of the chairs and sofas; feather mattresses were ripped open with bayonets and knives; and crystal chandeliers were sent crashing to the floor while soldiers danced madly around laughing and shouting, often inspired by the contents of a wine cellar. Negroes sometimes joined in the pillage. Too often the men maliciously then set a torch to the place, and the planter's home went up in flames. From Lake Providence to Bruinsburg the men foraged near and wide, taking chickens, vegetables, cattle, corn, and anything else of value. The army also carried on legitimate forage and gathered in thousands of bales of cotton hidden in the canebrakes.[7]

McClernand continued to try Grant's patience and temper with his carpings, criticism of fellow officers, delaying tactics, and near-insubordination. In violation of orders he had loaded himself down with tents and trappings when he moved below and had neglected to transport more vital supplies and food. To the detriment of swift movement he had brought his new bride to New Carthage and had continued his honeymoon at Perkins' plantation. Grant found it necessary to prod the bridegroom into action. To make way for McPherson's men moving down from Milliken's Bend, McClernand had to be pushed down to a new position.

On April 26 Grant ordered McClernand to move his men down and across the river and to attack Grand Gulf immediately. The next day McClernand's men were moved below by transports to Hard Times, about two miles across from, and above, Grand Gulf. One division of McPherson's men was also brought down. This troop movement was not completed until daylight of April 29. The rest of McPherson's men moved on foot from Perkins' place southward around Lake St. Joseph to Hard Times.

McClernand's men were reloaded aboard the steamers and barges on the morning of April 29 under orders to cross the river and seize a strong point on the Mississippi side after Porter's gunboats had reduced the batteries at Grand Gulf. About the same time the Confederate Missouri troops crossed over to Grand Gulf to aid in the defense of that post.

Porter began his attack at 8 A.M. with eight gunboats. For some five hours Porter's guns fired at the Confederate batteries nestled on the heights of Grand Gulf. McClernand's men crowded aboard the transports and watched the show, waiting for orders to make a landing on the Mississippi side. At 1:30 P.M. Porter withdrew from action, having used every weapon at his command without silencing a single gun. Porter's flagship, the *Benton,* was struck between decks by a shell, and nineteen of his men were killed and fifty-six were wounded.

Disembarking his men at dusk back at Hard Times, McClernand then marched them along the levee to De Shroon's plantation. Porter's fleet again engaged the batteries, allowing the transports and barges loaded with supplies to run past the batteries under the cover of darkness. On the morning of April 30 the troops boarded the transports and moved down-river from De Shroon's and crossed the Mississippi, landing on the east side at Bruinsburg, six miles below Grand Gulf. Porter used his gunboats as transports to ferry over the men. By 3 P.M. McClernand began moving along the road leading to Port Gibson. Port Gibson soon fell, and on May 3 Grand Gulf was evacuated by the Confederates.[8]

The swift final stages of Grant's Louisiana movement had kept Pemberton guessing. The line of fortifications from Haines' Bluff to Grand Gulf had to be maintained. Little did Pemberton expect that the main point of invasion would come from below. Grant had created several diversions to perplex and annoy the Confederates. In the middle of April he had started Colonel B. H. Grierson on a cavalry raid from Tennessee through the heart of Mississippi to Baton Rouge. This destructive raid deflected Pemberton's gaze eastward away from the river, struck fear into the hearts of the citizens, and somewhat demoralized the Confederate forces who failed to stop the move.[9]

Sherman's command was kept at Duckport, and half of Porter's fleet was retained above Vicksburg. Pemberton had no way of knowing where to expect the full weight of the Federal advance.

Grant's last diversion was to order Sherman, in co-operation with the upper fleet, to make a demonstration against Haines' Bluff to mask the real point of attack below Grand Gulf. Escorted by eight gunboats of varying sizes and descriptions, Sherman, on April 30, took a portion of one division, loaded on ten transports, and made a realistic show of force near Haines' Bluff. The gunboats moved near the batteries and opened a blistering but noneffective fire upon the works. The plunging fire of the Confederates did serious injury to several of the gunboats, but the ruse worked. Pemberton, who had just sent troops to reinforce Grand Gulf, recalled these men and rushed them to Haines' Bluff. Additional batteries were erected at this point. Before Pemberton saw his error, Grant had already landed thirty thousand men at Bruinsburg.

Orders were issued to Sherman to give up his demonstration and to move two of his divisions to Perkins' plantation, leaving the rest of his command at Young's Point and Richmond. He was to collect 120 wagons loaded with rations and send them to Grand Gulf. Troops at Helena and Memphis were to be brought down-river as quickly as possible. The remainder of the Seventeenth Corps was to be crossed over too. Sherman carried out all of his orders.

Grant was relieved. He was now safely on the east side of the river, was ready to strike deep into Mississippi, and to move to the rear of Vicksburg. He was entering the final phase of a long campaign, a campaign of misjudgments, outright blunders, delay, frustrations, death, fear, and timidities.

Once in Mississippi, Grant found himself. Boldly he left behind his base of supplies and moved into the middle of the state, subsisting himself as he went. What had started out as a miserable fiasco now became a brilliant campaign.[10] Errors would still be made; but once Grant abandoned his assault tactics and settled down to an orderly siege, Vicksburg's doom was sealed.

With Grant safely across the river, on May 3 Porter, with three of his gunboats, a ram, and a tug, went down to Red River to confer with Admiral Farragut. One gunboat and two tinclads were left at Grand Gulf. Anxious to be rid of the blockade duties of Red River and pressed by urgent business dealing with the Gulf blockade, Farragut left Porter in charge and went down the Atchafalaya aboard the *Sachem* to Brashear City and from that point by rail to New Orleans.

Taylor's army had retreated to Alexandria before Banks's superior forces. On May 4 Porter decided to move up to Alexandria and meet

Banks when he arrived. En route, sixty miles up the Red, Porter encountered the uncompleted Fort DeRussy, which was being stripped
of its guns and supplies by three wooden Confederate gunboats commanded by Captain John Kelso. The steamer *Countess,* hauling the
barge loaded with the guns, immediately got under way for Alexandria.
The *Grand Duke,* Kelso's flagship, opened fire on the three Federal
vessels, and a hot contest ensued. The *Cotton* was quickly disabled by
a Federal shell. The *Grand Duke* was struck a short time later and
set on fire. Kelso now decided to run for it, and the crippled *Grand
Duke,* with the disabled *Cotton* in tow, limped toward Alexandria.

Porter, noted for his bravery and dash, did not move in and complete
his kill. Instead he tarried to destroy the log-and-chain raft and did not
arrive in Alexandria until May 7. He found that all the gunboats and
supplies had been withdrawn up Red River toward Shreveport. The
rapids above Alexandria were too shallow for his ironclads to follow.
Union sympathizers welcomed Porter and Banks's advance guard,
which arrived later the same day. When Banks arrived, Porter turned
over the town to him and returned to Fort DeRussy, where he set
contrabands to leveling the earthworks. Porter dispatched Commander
S. E. Woodworth up Black River to capture the *Webb* and the *Queen
of the West.* Woodworth succeeded in destroying stores of sugar,
molasses, rum, salt, and bacon valued at nearly $300,000, but he failed
to capture the two ships.

The forward progress of Woodworth and his four boats on Black
River was blocked by Fort Beauregard on the heights of the little
town of Harrisonburg. After two days of bombarding the place, little
damage was done, and the gunboats retired down the river.[11]

Porter rushed back to Vicksburg to get in on the kill. Four ironclads
were left to blockade the mouth of Red River. One was stationed at
New Carthage and three at Warrenton. Walking across the peninsula
past Vicksburg, Porter once more boarded his flagship, the *Black
Hawk.* For amusement Porter played with his dogs and coaxed music
from a confiscated piano. His ship was a floating menagerie. In addition to the eight dogs, Porter kept a saddle horse or two and a cow
aboard ship.

A great vexation to Porter at this time was a shortage of trained
naval personnel. As new boats arrived from the shipyards above, he
had to distribute his experienced men evenly and make up his deficit
by enlisting soldiers and Negroes as sailors.[12]

Military action at Lake Providence in May centered around the

Bayou Macon area. Nine companies of the First Kansas Mounted Infantry and a hundred men from the Sixteenth Wisconsin, led by
Major William Y. Roberts, crossed over the Macon to Caledonia on the
morning of May 10. The Confederates, posted in a brick kiln, in heavy
timber, and in Negro quarters, were outnumbered five to one. They
were driven from their positions and fled toward the hills of Pin Hook
nine miles away.

Major Roberts divided his men into two columns, planning to en-
circle the Confederates. The Federal column moving along the banks
of Bayou Macon was ambushed near Lane's Ferry by Captain W. H.
Corbin and was temporarily routed. The column re-formed and rejoined the other column, however, and the entire Federal force moved
toward Pin Hook. Captain Corbin's small Confederate force was
joined by troops from Delhi and by the detachment at Floyd which
had been guarding the courthouse there. Colonel Frank A. Bartlett
assumed command of these forces, which numbered some 250 men.
The Confederates took cover in log cabins and behind trees and easily
repelled the first attack on their Pin Hook position. Rallying, the
Kansas and Wisconsin troops made another halfhearted attack. The
action of May 10 ended with the disorderly retreat of the superior
Federal forces back to Lake Providence. Losses were light on both
sides.

On May 9 Pemberton begged E. Kirby Smith, commander of the
Trans-Mississippi Department, to help relieve some of the pressure on
Vicksburg by attacking and destroying the Federal supply lines from
Milliken's Bend to New Carthage. Kirby Smith instructed Dick Taylor, reinforced by Walker's Texas Division, to move up the Tensas
and disrupt Grant's line of communications and to throw reinforcements across to Vicksburg if possible. Taylor reluctantly carried out
the order.[13]

General Henry E. McCulloch on the morning of May 31 debarked
his troops from transports and surprised the Federal camp at Perkins'
Landing. The defenders double-quicked to the levee and formed a
line of battle under the protection of their gunboat, the *Carondelet*.
For over an hour the Confederates stood under the fire of the gunboat. McCulloch ordered his artillery forward, and the fire drove the
Federal troops aboard their ships. With the gunboat, they dropped
down the river out of range. The retreating troops destroyed supplies
meant for Grant across the river.

One company of Major Harrison's cavalry on the morning of June 4 attacked a Negro camp of instructions on Lake St. Joseph. The small detachment, which numbered only 60 men, killed the white captain and 12 Negroes and captured some 875 others. Harrison continued his move and found all the Union posts abandoned from Carthage north almost to Young's Point. He was able to gather a supply of arms, medicine, and other supplies left behind by the enemy.

While awaiting the arrival of the rest of the Confederate forces, on June 6 Harrison learned that the Tenth Illinois Cavalry was en route to Richmond from Milliken's Bend. With a hundred men Harrison rode out to intercept them. Three miles away the enemy was discovered, and Harrison charged their line, killing eight and capturing twenty-five. The Federal force fled and was pursued back to the Bend.

Harrison's move destroyed the element of surprise and tipped off the garrison at Milliken's Bend that a major attack against that point was in the making. Brigadier General Elias S. Dennis appealed to Porter for gunboat protection. Porter answered the request with two gunboats, the *Choctaw* and the *Lexington*.

By a roundabout route General J. G. Walker's division, on June 6, moved to the vicinity of Richmond. Five miles above this place J. M. Hawes's brigade took the road leading to Young's Point to destroy the Federal camp there while McCulloch's brigade moved against Milliken's Bend. Horace Randal's brigade remained in reserve at the crossroads.

Between 2:30 and 3:00 on the morning of June 7, Harrison's cavalry, now serving as scouts for McCulloch, having approached within a mile of Milliken's Bend, were suddenly fired upon by the Federal pickets from behind a dense hedge. Many of the scouts broke and fled to the rear, throwing away their guns and losing their hats and coats. Mistaking Harrison's men for the enemy, the Confederate skirmishers fired at the retreating men and added to the confusion. Now without the benefit of the cavalry, McCulloch sent forward his skirmishers and drove the enemy pickets back.

Upon encountering strong enemy skirmishers, McCulloch ordered forward a portion of his command. The Confederates drove forward from hedge to hedge and ditch to ditch, through briars and tie-vines that made a regular military advance almost impossible. Twenty-five yards from the first levee, on the Union left flank, three brigades formed in line of battle and rushed the enemy posted behind the levee, driving him into the open space between the two levees. At the second levee nearest to the river the resistance stiffened. McCulloch fell back to the first levee and took up position there. The wounded were removed to the rear. An attempt against the Union right also was abandoned.

The two enemy gunboats raked the open areas with grape and canister, frightening the Confederates and forcing them to abandon another assault. General Dennis' defending forces consisted of the Twenty-third Iowa and the African Brigade, numbering in all 1,061 men. McCulloch went into action with 1,500 men. Many of the Negro troops were inexperienced in the use of a gun, and some had had only a few days of drill. As the Confederates charged up the first levee, most of the white troops and some of the Negroes in this line fled back to the second line of defense, leaving the Negro troops to defend the position. Hand-to-hand fighting with bayonet and clubbed rifle broke out between the Negroes and the Confederates. Many colored troops cowered below their cotton works and were shot in the head.

In this controversial encounter, charges and countercharges were later made against both sides. General Dick Taylor had ordered General Walker to take Milliken's Bend and drive the Federal forces into the river before they had a chance to escape to their transports and before the gunboats could go into action. Walker had chosen to remain behind with the reserves and had sent McCulloch, who displayed dash and bravery but, according to Taylor, had "no capacity for handling masses." The Confederates moved too slowly and were seized with a great fear of the gunboats, a fear which kept them frozen behind the protection of the first levee to which they had retreated.

McCulloch sent back some five miles to ask for reinforcements. Walker came forward just after noon with Randal's brigade but found that McCulloch had already withdrawn his troops. Walker ordered a general retreat back toward Richmond, instead of moving down to Duckport and Young's Point to aid General Hawes, as Taylor had instructed.

The Confederates captured 50 Negro soldiers and 2 of their white officers and brought back a number of horses and mules, small arms, and commissary stores. McCulloch's losses were light; 44 were killed, 130 wounded, and 10 were missing. General Dennis reported his total losses numbered more than 650. Of this number, about 100 were killed, and the rest were wounded and missing. Some of those reported missing straggled back into camp later on. Exact tabulations of losses on both sides are impossible.

Negro historians and those with a special interest in the success of the Negro as a soldier tend to exaggerate the bravery displayed by the colored troops at Milliken's Bend. The long-drawn-out hand-to-hand combat that is described by some of the partisan reports actually lasted only a few minutes. The Negroes did not all stand and fight. Many of them fled to the river bank when the first Confederate assault took place. Later, others quickly disappeared and hid out in the hedges. Some of the white officers who commanded Negro units absented themselves during the thick of the battle, then overpraised the performance of their black recruits in order to vindicate themselves. McCulloch's report concerning the Negro and the ferocity of the entire encounter must be weighed carefully. He failed in his mission, and he was trying to give excuses for his failure.

Whatever the truth may be, many of the Negroes did fight, and their service to the Union as outpost guards helped to free many thousands of white troops for the more important task of laying siege to Vicksburg.

General Hawes, who was to make a simultaneous predawn attack upon Young's Point while McCulloch took care of the post at Milliken's Bend, set out at 7 P.M. to cover the necessary twenty miles. This expedition numbered 1,403 Texans, plus a small detachment of Major Harrison's cavalry force to serve as guides. The night march over a good road moved along well until the force reached Walnut Bayou at 11:30 and found the bridge at this point destroyed. Hawes sent out scouts who floundered around for four-and-a-half hours, looking for a bridge only six miles away. When the bridge was found, the expedition resumed its march at four o'clock and spent the next six-and-a-half hours in covering fifteen miles.

It was not until 10:30 on the morning of June 7 that Hawes came upon a small picket of Negro troops, peacefully fishing, about two miles from their main camp. Hawes captured several of the pickets and drove the rest forward. After a reconnaissance reported the presence of three gunboats in the river before Young's Point, Hawes withdrew to the woods to his left rear without making an attack or firing a shot. A short time later the gunboats began shelling the area in front, and Hawes began a general retreat. Five hundred men claimed to be unfit for duty because of heat exhaustion, and two hundred of these stragglers had to be prodded from the shade and bushes later and taken back to the rear by Harrison's cavalry.

Taylor's instructions to seize the camp and send the captured property to the rear were forgotten. Nor did Hawes attempt to move up to Duckport, four miles above, and establish communications with

General McCulloch. No attempt was made to communicate with Vicksburg.[14]

Upriver at Floyd, parish seat of Carroll Parish, Colonel Frank A. Bartlett's Thirteenth Louisiana was reinforced by the Thirteenth Texas Infantry, giving him a total of nine hundred men. Taylor ordered him to march on Lake Providence and destroy the Negro camps of instructions in the vicinity and then push his cavalry below, breaking up the plantations held by lessees and Federal agents as far down as Milliken's Bend.

On June 9 Bartlett crossed Bayou Macon and moved over to Bunch's Bend on the Mississippi, capturing the Federal outpost at that point. Pushing down and around the western bank of Lake Providence with six hundred men, Bartlett met two companies of the First Kansas Mounted Infantry near Baxter Bayou. The Confederates captured nine army wagons loaded with supplies, thirty-six mules, and other enemy property. Driving the enemy forward, Bartlett moved to Bayou Tensas, one mile west of the town of Lake Providence. The bridge over the bayou had been destroyed, and an attempt was made to rebuild it.

Brigadier General H. T. Reid, commander of the post, sent the First Kansas and the Sixteenth Wisconsin forward to meet the Confederates. For an hour and a half the two forces fired at each other across the bayou, then at dusk Bartlett retired, leaving behind only a small group of skirmishers. Reid retired his main force and sent the Eighth Louisiana Volunteers (African descent) forward to the bayou. The remaining Confederates fired a few volleys into the underbrush on the opposite side before they withdrew to rejoin their command. Bartlett had overestimated the Federal strength (Reid had only eight hundred men) and made no attempt to cross the bayou lower down and flank the Union position. This he could have done, but instead he withdrew to Floyd.

Taylor attempted to place the blame for the failure of the mission upon his timid commanders, but it was Taylor himself who was largely at fault. By consolidating his forces he could have pushed over five thousand men against Milliken's Bend and Young's Point. As he did not trust his subordinate officers, he should have led his men into the field instead of remaining in the rear at Richmond.

Taylor decided to give up his campaign opposite Vicksburg and returned to Alexandria. However, he left Walker's troops in the vicinity for a while longer.

On June 8, from the rear of Vicksburg, Grant ordered Brigadier

General J. A. Mower to move his command from Haines' Bluff across the river to reinforce Dennis. Dennis was ordered to drive the Confederates from Richmond and to push on to Monroe.[15]

At the forks of the road near Richmond, Mower's command of six thousand men was joined by General Alfred W. Ellet, with two thousand men of the Marine Brigade. The Confederates, with half the Federal strength, waited for the attack behind a wide ditch fringed with clumps of willows. The Fifth Minnesota was sent forward as skirmishers while the other regiments formed a line of battle. Advancing across an open field, the Federal skirmishers had approached within thirty yards of cover when Walker's men opened up a heavy fire. The men of the Fifth Minnesota fell instantly to the ground, seeking partial shelter in the weeds and tall grass. For the next twenty minutes a sharp engagement ensued. The Eighteenth Texas Infantry charged the Union skirmishers and drove them back until they were met by the main body of Mower's and Ellet's troops. The Eighteenth Texas now fell back, pursued by the Fifth Minnesota and a portion of Ellet's command. The Confederates began to rake the open area with grape and canister. Mower sent two batteries forward, and an artillery duel followed that lasted for more than an hour. During this time Walker slipped his men across Roundaway Bayou, set fire to the bridge, and retreated along the road leading to Delhi. En route Brigadier General J. C. Tappan with his Arkansas brigade joined Walker.

The Federal cavalry forded the bayou and pursued the Confederate rear guard for six miles, capturing twenty-five stragglers. Mower rebuilt the bridge and burned Richmond to the ground, but instead of following the retreating Confederates to Monroe, he then returned to Young's Point, and Ellet's brigade returned to their boats.

Walker retired to Delhi and remained there until June 22, when he started on a new expedition against Goodrich's Landing, on the Mississippi between Milliken's Bend and Lake Providence. Traveling through the plantation region east of Bayou Macon, Walker broke up the plantations that were run by Union lessees and disloyal Southerners. On June 29 at Mounds plantation, about ten miles south of Lake Providence, Colonel W. H. Parsons, commanding two Arkansas regiments of Tappan's cavalry, encountered a fort, built on an ancient Indian mound, garrisoned by Negro troops who were used to furnish protection to the leased plantations. The sides of the mound had been strongly fortified and were next to impossible to scale without great loss of life.

Randal's brigade soon joined Parsons, and the entire force surrounded the post, demanding its surrender. Fearfully, the three white Federal officers agreed to surrender if they would be treated as prisoners of war. Suspecting that their Negroes under arms would be treated with barbaric cruelty, the officers nonetheless offered to surrender them unconditionally. The terms were accepted by the Confederates, and the 3 officers, plus two companies of the First Arkansas Volunteers (African descent), numbering 113 men, were captured.

Walker moved to the vicinity of Goodrich's Landing, continuing to destroy plantations. General Reid dispatched the First Kansas Mounted Regiment from Lake Providence to drive the Confederates away, but the superior Confederate cavalry drove the Kansans back to Lake Providence. At this point the armed steamer *Raine,* of Ellet's Marine Brigade, appeared and fired her small guns at the Confederates, who beat a hasty retreat. The men aboard the *Raine* landed and followed the Confederates for a short distance, rescuing several hundred contrabands left behind by the hastily retreating Arkansas cavalry.

That night, June 29, Porter sent all of Ellet's command to reinforce Goodrich's Landing. Arriving at 2 A.M. on June 30, Ellet found the countryside lighted up by the burning mansions, slave quarters, and cotton gins set afire by Walker's men. Ellet disembarked his infantry, cavalry, and artillery and set out at daylight in pursuit. He discovered the Confederates resting on the opposite side of Tensas Bayou, some twelve miles inland. Walker made a halfhearted attempt to cross the bayou and turn Ellet's right flank, but the Union skirmishers and artillery thwarted this plan, and Walker slowly retreated.[16]

On July 11 Walker boarded railroad cars and moved to Monroe on the Ouachita, where he remained until July 19, when he was ordered to Alexandria.[17] Despite the ragtag appearance of the troops, the ladies of Monroe gave them a most hearty welcome. Some of the men wore homespun pants with the knees out, a Texas penitentiary cloth jacket, and a ragged straw hat. Others wore a black shirt and "breeches" made from castoff blankets. Most of the men wore hats of one description or another. Some of these were woolen pyramids covered with assorted buttons, topped by a red tassel.

While Grant's forces were driving inland through Mississippi to the rear of Vicksburg, Porter ordered the gunboats from below to bombard the forts and city. Along the peninsula on the Louisiana shore before Vicksburg Porter had mounted guns on scows, flatboats, and platforms. Other naval guns were mounted inland behind earthworks, and the Marine Brigade, along with army detachments, operated these batteries. With his mortars and upriver gunboats Porter did what he could to aid Sherman's command in the assault from the north side.

The assault made by Grant on May 22 ended in failure, and the Union army settled down to siege warfare, which continued for more than forty days—from May 22 to July 4. By mid-June Grant's strength had been swelled by reinforcements to over 85,000 men. While the army dug trenches and tunnels and tried to sap the works, Porter's gunboats, mortars, and land guns made life unpleasant inside the citadel, if not always dangerous.[18]

Inside the besieged city the closely confined troops were becoming restive. They saw no hope for relief, and all hope of victory was gone. One private wrote General Pemberton on June 28: "Our rations have been cut down to one biscuit and a small bit of bacon per day, not enough to keep soul and body together, much less to stand the hardships we are called upon to stand." He warned Pemberton, "There is complaining and general dissatisfaction throughout our lines. Men don't want to starve, and don't intend to. . . . If you can't feed us, you had better surrender us. . . . This army is now ripe for mutiny, unless it can be fed." [19]

The end had come. To resist any longer was useless. Capitulation terms were arranged, and Grant took over the city on July 4. The fall of Vicksburg caused great jubilation in the capital and all over the North. Grant's star had now ascended to great heights. Soon he and his commanders and Porter would receive rich rewards for their parts in the campaign.[20]

Except for Port Hudson, the Mississippi was now completely in Federal hands. The Confederacy had been split apart; never again would the eastern half benefit to any great extent from the resources of Louisiana, Texas, and Mexico. In a few days the Mississippi would run "unvexed to the sea."

XIV

TIME OF INDECISION

GENERAL BANKS had inherited from his predecessor in New Orleans the burdensome duties of controlling a major city and adjacent territories. Unlike Butler, he had adopted a conciliatory attitude toward the people. The citizens of New Orleans found the new regime a pleasant relief from the harsh rule of "Beast" Butler.

The Banks, with their fashionable clothes, bodyguards, servants, and stylish airs, were comparable to royalty. Mrs. Banks had her weekly receptions at the St. Charles and all the "best ladies appear[ed] there in lace and diamonds." Many of the confirmed Confederate ladies whose husbands were given jobs by the new commander seemed to be won back to the Union. However, the dapper general was soon to experience some of the disorders, snubs, insults, and threats with which Butler had so effectively dealt. Banks found it imperative to alter his policy and to become more stern with the populace.

George S. Denison kept Secretary Chase well informed concerning Banks's activities. Denison found the new commander "thoroughly honest" but vague and unwilling to express his convictions. Banks took definite action against a group of the Butler regime swindlers and army speculators, but Denison found him "to be no judge of men." Most of Banks's staff were highly inexperienced, some "of little ability," and some, "objects of ridicule." Conciliation, inefficiency, inexperience, and hesitation characterized most of the proceedings in the department.

Denison reported that Jews, speculators, and camp followers accompanied Banks to New Orleans and that more were arriving each day. These unscrupulous men seemed bent on becoming millionaires overnight, regardless of whom they hurt in the process.

The Treasury agent complained that New Orleans could no longer be considered a Union city. Loyalty was growing weaker by the day.[1] The schools in the city, poorly attended, were branded hotbeds of "rebellion." Many of the children refused to sing "national airs." The instructors were accused of instilling "the poison of rebellion and treason in their young minds."[2]

Many citizens of the city delighted in provoking the Federal officials by singing "The Bonnie Blue Flag," cheering for Jeff Davis, cursing Lincoln, wearing Confederate uniforms, or otherwise displaying sentiment for the success of the Confederacy. The courts were tied up with cases of "seditious conduct" during the first few months of Banks's administration. The *Daily Delta* was ordered closed by Banks on February 8 for its lack of co-operation.[3]

Planters within and near the Union lines were invited to bring in their cotton, sugar, and other produce to sell in New Orleans, but they hesitated because under Butler the military commission through which such goods must pass was "a dishonest plundering concern." Banks reassured the planters, and soon goods once more began to move into the city. On supplies and goods sent to the plantations or to some other port the Treasury Department collected a five per cent tax. All permits to trade had to be approved by the provost marshal's office in New Orleans. The military authorities collected a two per cent tax on goods sent upriver or into the interior and collected five dollars on each bale of cotton for the hospital fund.[4] These taxes were not excessive, and the profitable trade did increase.

The contraband problem proved troublesome to Banks. Several large contraband camps were located at Camp Parapet above New Orleans in January. From time to time military details were sent upriver to collect Negroes on abandoned plantations and bring them back to these colonies. Soldiers were detailed from several companies to help the officers govern and feed the contrabands.

In all the camps, at first, the Negroes were allowed freedom of movement and no guards were posted. Women and children were kept in camps separate from the men, and after their day's work able-bodied Negro men who were working at the fortifications visited their women or attended all-night religious revivals held in the swamp. Many of the men could not do their work properly when they returned to the job after a night without sleep, and consequently white sentries at the engineer camp were ordered to shoot any Negro who tried to leave without a pass.

The laborers were divided into gangs of a hundred and twenty-five each under two enlisted men, and this group was subdivided into squads of twenty-five under a Negro straw boss. Often the white soldiers, to pass the time, played soldier with their gangs and drilled them without arms. The Negroes liked this activity and tried hard to follow instructions.

As the task of feeding and controlling so many Negroes in the camps became more difficult, a shortage of labor on the government plantations and other plantations caused Banks to make radical changes. He announced that no more Negroes would be hired from the plantations and that those already in the contraband camps, with the exception of the engineer camp, would be returned to the plantations. The Negro could choose the plantation on which he wished to work, but once he had made his choice he must remain for a year. If he ran away, he would be returned by force. The planter would pay the Negro a small fixed wage or divide up one-twentieth of the yearly profits among the Negro laborers. Officers and enlisted men would be detailed to see that the Negro behaved himself and carried out his duties. This labor system caused George Denison to charge Banks with re-establishing slavery, but it restored the labor supply, and prospects of a good crop in 1863 in the vicinity of New Orleans became much brighter.

In addition to the abandoned plantations already operated by the government, Banks instructed his quartermaster to secure additional plantations "suitable to the production of vegetables for the use of the troops." These plantations would be supplied the necessary mules, wagons, implements, and other requirements for a successful crop.

When Banks assumed command of the department, he found three Negro regiments in existence, but he never put them into active service. He seemed to be against enlisting any more Negroes, an opinion which was urged upon him by some of his West Point officers who were strongly prejudiced against colored troops. Banks's New England soldiers disliked particularly the Negro officers who commanded the Negro regiments. Banks claimed that these regiments were so demoralized "and engaged in controversy with white troops" that they were next to useless. Many of the officers, both black and white, were "unsuited for duty" and of "discreditable character."

Gradually Banks's timorous approach to the question of using Negro troops and of raising new levies began to change. Butler's three colored regiments were reorganized and were led by white officers only. Most of the "noncoms" were white too. In February, authority to raise a

One of the mortar boats used by David D. Porter in the bombardments
of Fort Jackson, Fort St. Philip, Vicksburg, and Port Hudson.

Major General Mansfield Lovell, commander of Confederate forces at New Orleans until its fall, April, 1862.

Lieutenant General Edmund Kirby Smith, commander of the Trans-Mississippi Department.

Major General Benjamin F. Butler, in command of the occupation forces in New Orleans, May–December, 1862.

Major General Nathaniel P. Banks, leader of Union forces in major Louisiana campaigns.

Advanced Union gun emplacement at the siege of Port Hudson.

Gunboat *Signal* towing materials for the series of dams built to deepen the Red River and release Porter's fleet.

The ram *Arkansas* is destroyed by her commander, to prevent capture. Her failure to reach Baton Rouge helped lead to the defeat of Breckinridge.

Banks's army crosses Cane River, March 31, 1864, in the advance on Shreveport. Sketch by C. E. H. Bonwill.

The battle of Pleasant Hill, April 9, 1864. Sketch by C. E. H. Bonwill.

The occupation of Baton Rouge. The Union flag is raised over the state capitol, December 17, 1863.

The *Osage* before Alexandria. This river monitor, one of the most powerful naval vessels then afloat on western waters, played an important role in Porter's Red River expedition.

Library of Congress

fourth regiment of Native Guards was issued, and the ranks were quickly filled. By March Banks was organizing the First Regiment of Louisiana Engineers. Unemployed Negroes were to be enlisted, but under no circumstances was the plantation labor system to be disrupted by enlistment of the workers. The colored troops and noncommissioned officers would be paid considerably less than the white enlisted men.

A second new regiment of infantry was begun shortly thereafter. When the Federal forces opened up the Teche in April, a large number of colored recruits had been secured, and on May 1 Banks announced that he planned to raise eighteen Negro regiments of infantry, artillery, and cavalry. Brigadier General George L. Andrews, a West Point graduate, was put in command of the colored troops. Before the war ended, more than twenty-four thousand Negro soldiers had been enrolled. Louisiana furnished more colored troops to the Union army than any state.[5]

In a desperate attempt to protect the interior of the state from Banks at New Orleans and from Grant's army before Vicksburg, the state legislature, meeting in extra session at Opelousas, passed an act calling for the enrollment of up to twenty thousand men who were not in the service of the Confederate States. Early in January Governor Moore issued orders that all white men between the ages of seventeen and fifty, citizen or resident, except certain state and local officials, professors and students of the military academy at Alexandria, and men who had been clergymen for at least seven years before this act, would be enrolled. Each man would be paid sixteen dollars per month and a bounty of fifty dollars at enlistment, and he or his heirs would be given eighty acres of land at the end of the war.

For the families of officers and enlisted men who needed assistance, the legislature voted to pay the wife ten dollars per month plus five dollars per month for each child under twelve. Parents of soldiers would also be given ten dollars, and brothers and sisters under twelve would receive five dollars per month.

The response to the inducements was apparently small, because the state militia headquarters at Alexandria on February 14 informed all those eligible for state service that they had only until March 1 to volunteer. Those who were drafted would be given no land and no bounty, but would receive eleven dollars pay per month. Those who failed to report within ten days after March 1 would be arrested and tried as deserters and, if convicted, sentenced to death.[6]

To provide the state treasury with more funds, the legislature passed Act No. 32, authorizing the state to issue special notes bearing no interest and redeemable one year after peace was restored. These notes, in denominations of five dollars to one hundred dollars, would be used in all business or state transactions.

Another act of importance approved by the legislature in January empowered the governor to conscript slave labor to build military defenses. For each male slave between the ages of eighteen and fifty so employed, the owner would be paid one dollar per day per slave. At no time would more than half of the slaves of an individual owner be conscripted. If the slave were killed or incapacitated while performing military labors, the owner would receive just compensation.[7]

The "Tax in Kind" act passed by the Confederate Congress in April, 1863, by the end of the year brought still greater discontent to the already dispirited Louisiana farmer. Of the present year's crop, every farmer was to deliver to a Confederate agent fifty bushels of Irish potatoes, fifty bushels of sweet potatoes, and one hundred bushels of corn or fifty bushels of wheat. Before March 1, 1864, the farmer must also contribute one tenth of his new crop of grains, Irish and sweet potatoes, hay, sugar, molasses, cotton, wool, peas, beans, peanuts, and tobacco. In addition one tenth of the cattle, horses, and mules would be taken, and one tenth of his cured bacon to help feed the army.

Because of Banks's successful move up the Teche, the legislature had to move to Shreveport, and here in June the militia act of January was considerably softened. Men who failed to report for duty were to be court-martialed and, if found guilty, were to be fined from fifty to five thousand dollars or imprisoned from ten to ninety days. After paying the fine or serving time, the person would then be placed in the militia.

Volunteers would be enlisted for terms of three months to a year. The pay would be eleven dollars per month. Refugees from enemy-occupied parishes, editors and workers necessary to publish existing newspapers, men with very large families to support, overseers on plantations where the owner was serving in the army or where employed by widows and minors, indispensable railroad men, millers, and certain tanners were allowed to be exempt, in addition to men in categories exempted in the January act.

Regardless of Confederate and state laws and penalties, hundreds of poor whites took to the swamps in order to escape military service with the army or with the militia. These "Jayhawkers" or draft-dodgers were most plentiful in the Catahoula swamps and hills and along the Pearl River in the parishes east of the Mississippi, but there were some in almost every parish. Regular Confederate and state scouting parties were sent out, often with dogs, to round up these culprits. Officers on furlough often organized parties to hunt down slackers. Most of the Jayhawkers were armed and desperate, and it was not unusual for the hunter and the hunted to kill each other.[8]

Earlier, this same legislature had appropriated $500,000 to pay for the hire or loss of slave property "while employed on public works." To aid destitute refugees driven out of the lower part of the state, $300,000 was provided. No individual would receive more than fifty dollars. An act prohibiting the distillation of spirituous liquors from grain, sugar, molasses, or cane juice was approved, to conserve needed food products. Violators would be fined $5 to $15,000 and imprisoned up to twelve months. This act did not apply to distilleries manufacturing liquor for medicinal purposes for the Confederate States government.

With refugees from the river parishes and lower Louisiana streaming into the interior, to Monroe, to Shreveport, to the hill country, and into Texas with what slaves, clothing, food, household goods, and treasures they could carry, it was necessary not only for the state, but also for inland towns, to aid the less fortunate refugees. To assist soldiers, their families, and displaced persons, various charity affairs were promoted in Shreveport and vicinity. At the end of December, 1862, the "Confederate minstrels" gave two performances in Shreveport to raise money for patriotic purposes.[9] A tableau presented in Mansfield on New Year's night added $295 to the funds. Ladies of the Springridge community on January 29 planned a *tableau vivant* in their church. Admission was a dollar or a pair of socks. The Shreveport Ladies Aid Society in late March announced a "Grand & Fancy Dress Ball, Mon. Eve. Apr. 6th at A. W. Miller's Ball Saloon . . . Tickets—Each gentlemen $10." In late April the patriotic students of the Mansfield Female College presented a vocal and instrumental concert.[10]

Federal military operations in late December and throughout the early months of 1863 were marked with timidity and hesitance. Banks was busy with civic matters and allowed his commanders much leeway in conducting their cautious probing into the interior.

Under instructions from Washington to secure a foothold in Texas, and urged by Farragut and Butler, Banks in late December, 1862, had sent a small force to occupy Galveston Island, which had been seized by the navy in October. On New Year's Day the Confederates attacked and captured the land forces, consisting of 260 men, and destroyed or captured the transports and naval vessels. The next day reinforcements arrived, but finding the place in Confederate hands, they returned swiftly to New Orleans.[11] Banks had lost his feeble footing in Texas by sending too few men too late.

With fifty-six regiments, twenty-two of which were made up of green nine-month men whose terms expired in May, July, and August, and with his 30,000 men spread out in the numerous posts from Pensacola to Texas on the Gulf, along the Mississippi to Baton Rouge, and in the fortifications on Berwick Bay and Lake Pontchartrain, Banks claimed that he could muster an offensive force of only 14,000 men. Like too many of the Union commanders, he grossly overestimated the Confederate strength opposing him. Believing that Port Hudson was defended by 18,000 men and that no less than 15,000 Confederates occupied the Teche country, Banks felt that his forces were inadequate for his several objectives.

To help Grant open up the Mississippi, Banks would have to take Port Hudson. Instead of a direct assault, Banks decided to move inland toward Red River, along the network of bayous, so that he could cut off all supplies for Port Hudson and bypass it. To accomplish this move, Brigadier General Godfrey Weitzel, with 4,500 men at Berwick Bay, was instructed to destroy the Confederate force along the Teche and then move over to the Atchafalaya River up to Butte-à-la-Rose and take this fortification.

On Bayou Teche near Pattersonville, to the west of Brashear City, the Confederates, under the command of Brigadier General Alfred Mouton, occupied an extensive earth fortification called Fort Bisland. Working in conjunction with the troops to keep the Union forces from using the bayou route was the gunboat *J. A. Cotton,* which was partially clad in railroad iron.

On December 31 and again on New Year's Day the Federal gunboats had come up the Teche and had fired at the *Cotton* without effect. Following these feeler movements, on January 13 Weitzel moved up the Teche and unloaded at Pattersonville. His force was made up of seven regiments of infantry and sufficient artillery and cavalry support, loaded aboard four light-draft gunboats under Lieutenant Commander Thomas McKean Buchanan. Forming in line of battle, the men slept on their arms that night under the cover of the gunboats.

With his much smaller force, Mouton took up position in his rifle pits and awaited the coming attack. At eight o'clock the next morning the action opened with a hot artillery duel between the Federal gunboats and the *Cotton*. Weitzel sent the Eighth Vermont up the east bank of the Teche to clear out any Confederate forces on that side. Then he formed the bulk of his command in line of battle on the west side. The Eighth Vermont on the east side and the Seventy-fifth New York on the west side were instructed to send forward sixty volunteers to move up both banks and attack the gunners aboard the *Cotton*. The artillery and cavalry were sent around various plantation roads and came up to aid the volunteers, regular skirmishers, and gunboats in the attack. Captain Edward W. Fuller returned the increased fire of the Federal gunboats and blasted away at the attacking land forces with the field pieces aboard. Despite his brave resistance the gunboat was shot up, his pilots were killed, several of his officers and crewmen were killed or wounded, and Fuller himself was injured in both arms. Working the wheel with his feet, Fuller backed up the Teche out of range of the gunboats and beyond the reach of the infantry and artillery. The Federal gunboats could not follow because an obstruction erected by the Confederates blocked the narrow channel. Despite his injuries, Captain Fuller brought the *Cotton* downstream again to enter the fight, but again he was driven back to cover.

The Eighth Vermont on the east side, faced by only a small defending force, was able to drive the Confederates from their rifle pits and, aided by the cavalry, to round up forty-one prisoners. On the west bank Weitzel's main force proceeded cautiously through a rain of shell, grape, and canister from the *Cotton* and the few pieces of Confederate artillery. Most of the Union regiments hit the dirt, seeking all available cover. About four o'clock in the afternoon the advanced infantry skirmishers were driven from their forward position by Mouton's artillery, and following this, there was only very light skirmishing between the two forces. The outnumbered Confederate infantry played little part in the day's action.

That night a heavy rain fell, and the wind blew "unmercifully." Weitzel's exhausted men lay down in the mud and water in cornfields, shivering in the cold, until they were called early in the morning to begin removing the obstructions in the Teche so that the gunboats could advance. Hardly had the work commenced when the bayou waters were lighted up by the flames of the *Cotton,* afire and floating downstream. Mouton knew that eventually the obstructions would be removed and that his small force could not hold its position nor protect the gunboat, so after taking off the guns and ammunition, he had the *Cotton* set afire. She burned to the water line and sank, making another obstacle for the Federal gunboats.

Weitzel exchanged a few shots with the Confederates on the morning of the fifteenth and then considered that his mission, to destroy the *Cotton* and open up a possible bayou route above Port Hudson, had been accomplished. He now ordered his command to return to camp at Brashear City. Federal casualties were light; one lieutenant and five privates were killed and twenty-seven enlisted men wounded. The navy suffered the loss of Lieutenant Commander Buchanan. Fifty Confederate prisoners were taken, and the dead and wounded were estimated to be treble those suffered by the Union forces.[12]

Although the troops were plagued with cold and mud, the line of march back to Brashear "was as hilarious as a bacchanal procession." [13] Flushed with victory, the men forgot discipline, and many fell out of rank and began to raid the plantations along the way, stripping them of chickens and pigs, and setting fire to some of the homes. Weitzel allowed his men to enjoy their victory, and his praises were sung by everyone.[14]

While Banks was still searching for a possible bayou route to take him above Port Hudson, Farragut learned of the capture of the *Queen of the West* and the *De Soto*. The admiral quickly saw that he must move his gunboats above Port Hudson to destroy these captured boats, to blockade Red River, and to patrol the Mississippi from Port Hudson north to Vicksburg. Farragut asked Banks to make a demonstration with his army before Port Hudson while his gunboats ran the batteries; Banks agreed. New Orleans was stripped of most of its forces, Emory's division was recalled, and a force of seventeen thousand men was gathered at Baton Rouge early in March.

Banks left Baton Rouge on Friday, March 13, with twelve thousand troops bound for Port Hudson. Five thousand men remained behind to guard Baton Rouge.

Leading off was a detachment of cavalry, "clanking and clattering along." Then came the general's staff, mounted on fine horses, with regimental flags flying. Following was another cavalry troop and the artillery, accompanied by their noisy ammunition wagons. The infantry and the division's baggage wagons brought up the rear.[15] The green troops, many of whom had never before been on a long march, loaded themselves down "with overcoats, rubber and woolen blankets, dress coats, extra shirts, towels, brush and blacking, three day's rations, one hundred rounds of ammunition, guns and equipments, a canteen of water," and anything else they felt was essential for an active campaign. The men, excited by the prospects of battle, gave voice to their spirits by heartily cheering the officers and by singing their favorite camp songs.[16]

As the columns moved past plantations and farms, men slipped from the ranks and raided the area, despite strict orders against pillage. Some dared to enter the houses to snatch food from the table and to steal jewelry and small art objects. Negro porters and cooks, a half dozen accompanying each company, joined in the illegal foraging.

As mile piled on weary mile, the marching troops grew more and more quiet. Fewer troops left the columns to forage. The hot sun beat down on the men moving through the dust-choked roads hemmed in by tall trees and rank vegetation. The plodding soldiers began to turn red, and sweat rolled down their bodies. Caps were pushed back, pants were rolled up; desperately the men tried to keep cool.

The oppressive heat caused the overloaded men to relieve themselves of blankets, shelter tents, shoes, and even entire knapsacks. Most of the soldiers tossed their dead chickens, turkeys, and other plunder into the bushes and ditches. A number of officers who were wearing bulletproof vests began to shed their heavy iron armor, adding it to the castoff equipment and the carcasses of pigs and fowls that now littered the route of march.

Hot, footsore troops began to falter and, finally, to drop out of ranks to seek shelter in the shade. The relative order that had prevailed when the march began now practically disappeared. The neophyte officers could do little with their undisciplined, headstrong civilian soldiers.

Arriving before Port Hudson, Banks took up positions from five to ten miles from the nearest Confederate gun. As his cavalry neared Port Hudson, the Confederate cavalry began a game of cat and mouse. The Confederates would appear and then suddenly retreat, trying to lure the Federal cavalry closer. As usual, Banks grossly overestimated the Confederate force, believing the garrison to contain between twenty-five and thirty thousand men, although actually there were only a few more than he had in his expedition. He meant only to divert the attention of the Confederates while Farragut ran the batteries and had no intentions of assaulting the works. Gardner, on the other hand, entertained no idea of leaving his fortifications to face Banks. Most of the Federal troops were ordered to bivouac for the night, but hardly had they settled when their rest was shattered by the cracking and booming of the guns from the forts, gunboats, and mortars.[17]

Farragut had arrived in Baton Rouge on March 11 and immediately stripped his ships for action. To protect his engines and the vulnerable sides of his ships, chain cables were strung around. By Friday afternoon he was ready, and his fleet moved upriver. Saturday morning, March 14, Farragut reached Profit Island, within sight of Port Hudson. The six mortar schooners were placed behind trees, within firing range of the forts.

Banks informed Farragut that the army would be in position ready to create a mock attack on the rear of Port Hudson after midnight. Banks later claimed that Farragut agreed to attempt the passage in the early dawn, but whatever the agreement, Farragut moved out at 10 P.M. Gardner and his men expected the action. The Confederate batteries waited silently until the ships moved up within range, and then their guns blazed away at the slowly moving targets. A huge bonfire on the west side was lighted by a Confederate detachment, and Farragut's ships stood out in bold relief, easy targets for the cliffside gunners. Finally the Union naval guns scattered the burning wood, and most of the action took place in darkness.

Soon a dense cloud of black smoke settled over the river, making visibility even more difficult. The lead ship, the *Hartford,* with the gunboat *Albatross* lashed to her port side, grounded under the batteries. With the aid of the *Albatross,* the *Hartford* got free and proceeded with little difficulty above the batteries. The Confederate guns, from eighty to a hundred feet above the river, were not depressed sufficiently and most of their shots sailed harmlessly over the *Hartford.*

The *Richmond,* the next ship to enter the gantlet, succeeded in reaching the last battery. Then a plunging shot ripped into her engine room, filling most of the ship with live steam and lowering the steam pressure, so that the boat could make no headway against the current. When her consort, the gunboat *Genesee,* could not move both boats upriver, the two turned and retreated to safety below. In the confusion, the gun crews aboard the *Richmond* fired into the *Mississippi,* who was just beginning her run.

Next in line was the *Monongahela* and her escort gunboat, the *Kineo.* The *Monongahela* ran aground, and the *Kineo* slipped her moorings. The *Kineo* secured a line to the *Monongahela* and after straining and tugging for twenty-five minutes, finally succeeded in freeing the grounded vessel. Suddenly the *Kineo's* rudder jammed, and she drifted helplessly with the current. The *Monongahela* attempted to pass on above, but her engines stopped and she floated downstream under a heavy barrage from the shore batteries. Many shots found their mark, and the *Monongahela's* casualties were heavy.

Through the thick smoke and the deafening roar of the guns the last ship, the ancient side-wheeler *Mississippi,* felt its way through the dark, firing occasionally at the flashes from the guns along the bluffs. Nearing the last battery, the *Mississippi* grounded. After a half-hour of fruitless strain the ship still remained stuck in the mud while more and more Confederate shots found their mark. A shell set fire to one of the storerooms, and Captain Melancton Smith ordered that the ship be abandoned. Near panic developed, but sufficient order was restored to allow the removal of the wounded to the ships below. Other members of the crew were sent to the western shore. After setting fire to the ship in several places, shotting the guns, and cutting her water pipes, Captain Smith and his executive officer, George Dewey, boarded a small boat and moved through the hail of shells down to the *Richmond* below. As the flames mounted higher aboard the *Mississippi,* an unbridled rebel yell rang out from the bluffs above.

The stern of the stricken ship gradually filled with water, lifting the bow free from the mud. The blazing vessel floated down the river toward the fleet below. Wild confusion ensued. Hastily the disabled gunboats were towed to safety by the others. The mortar schooners cut themselves loose from their cables and scurried down the river. When the flames reached her magazine, the *Mississippi* exploded with a deafening roar. Momentarily the dark skies were as brilliant as day. Then there was dead silence.

Despite the terrific bombardment Confederate losses were negligible. Only one man was killed, and nineteen were wounded. Not one gun was damaged, and little harm was done to the parapets. Farragut's total losses were fairly heavy: ninety-nine men were reported killed or missing; forty-eight were captured; one hundred and thirty-eight were wounded. Wasting no time, Farragut proceeded with the *Hartford* and the *Albatross* upriver to Vicksburg to beg Porter for some of his gunboats with which to set up an effective blockade of Red River.[18]

When Banks learned that two of Farragut's gunboats had successfully run the batteries, he ordered the gradual withdrawal of the troops back to Bayou Monte Sano, where they would encamp and await further orders. The reserve was ordered to move out first. Immediately rumors spread like wildfire, and terror seized the men. Word was circulated that the forward troops had been fighting desperately and, having been defeated, were now in full retreat. The two infantry brigades, a part of the artillery, and the quartermaster teamsters who were well in the rear fell all over themselves in the rush to get out of the area. They covered the first five miles on the double-quick. The sultry heat and the excessive fear made many of the troops ill, but they did not fall out. The fear of being captured kept them going. To lighten their load many threw away their remaining equipment and ammunition.

Banks's main force withdrew much later in a leisurely manner. They had heard no rumors, and they knew that no real engagement had taken place. There was no humor in the ranks. The men were sullen. They were retreating without firing a shot at the enemy. They could not understand why they were retreating.

General Banks rode by with his staff. The day before he had been a popular man with the troops. Today was different. A dead silence greeted him as he passed each unit.

For the next several days Banks's weary, demoralized troops retreated through heat and dust that eventually gave way to heavy rains and thick mud.

On March 16, the sun came out and all of the men moved into the higher ground along Monte Sano Bayou. Here they disrobed and washed their mud-coated clothes and bodies and caught up on their sleep.

Once more rested, the troops began to pillage far and near, taking what they wanted to eat or to keep as a souvenir. Tuesday, March 17, General Banks ordered all the sugar, cotton, cattle, mules, horses, and other necessities to be collected and brought in for the use of the army. His usual orders against private foraging were, as usual, ignored.

After more than a week of foraging the troops were ordered back to Baton Rouge.[19] A man from the Fiftieth Massachusetts reported that "in the wake of the army . . . there followed a procession of contrabands and mules and wagons loaded with the personal chattels that had been the property of a rebel planter the day before."[20]

For the time being the Confederate troops at Port Hudson resumed the life they had been following before. When not drilling nor engaged in military pursuits, the men resorted to various *divertissements*. A favorite pastime was drinking corn beer. Every company had its own crude brewery. Louisiana rum was more potent and desirable, and nearby planters, unable to sell their sugar, turned out a great deal of this item. Details were sent out from Port Hudson to destroy the distilleries, and guards were ordered to seize all rum being smuggled through the ranks, but much rum got to the men regardless of official action. Two handwritten one-sheet newspapers, the *Mule* and the *Woodchuck,* were put out daily. These rival papers satirized various officers and men. Visits from planters' daughters helped to break the monotony of camp life. Staff officers who were lucky enough to have horses were able to attend balls, banquets, picnics, and to visit the young ladies, but since the distances were too great for walking most of the post had to forgo these pleasures. Fiddle players helped enliven things at night.[21]

Pending a general movement up the Teche, on March 21 Banks sent Colonel Thomas S. Clark of the Sixth Michigan up the Jackson Railroad to destroy a bridge at Pontchatoula. At the same time Colonel F. S. Nickerson of the Fourteenth Maine was sent to destroy enemy communications along the Jackson Railroad and the bridges across the Amite River.

The Confederate mounted pickets withdrew after a light skirmish, and the coast was clear to Ponchatoula. Moving in line of battle the Sixth Michigan swept into the town. Women and children scampered about, begging for protection. There was no Confederate force to be found, and suddenly all discipline crumbled. The men went wild, and they were joined in the orgy of pillage by their corpulent commander, Colonel Clark. First the depot was sacked, and the men grabbed up bundles and boxes they found stored within. The next targets were the two small stores in the village. The doors were battered in, and the blue-coated soldiers rushed in. The liquor supply was quickly confiscated. The post office was next. Mail bags were slit open, and letters and newspapers soon littered the streets. The Turkish-clad Zouaves, the One Hundred Sixty-fifth New York, came up the railroad and joined in the pillage, raiding the Masonic Hall and taking the silver stars, squares, and other emblems. Private homes were broken into, and everything of value—fine coverlets, wine, and women's clothes—was removed. Soon the neat little village was in a shambles.

Colonel Clark was disappointed to find no cotton in Ponchatoula, but he consoled himself by gathering all of the mules and wagons in the vicinity, loading them with valuable turpentine and resin and with the plunder of the village, and sending them back to Wadesborough to be loaded aboard waiting schooners. The citizens of the town who remained behind were administered the Federal oath of allegiance and promised protection by the officers.

After burning a railroad bridge over a bayou just outside Ponchatoula, Colonel Clark, on March 25, retired three miles south of the village along the railroad. Six companies were left behind in the town
as pickets. On the evening of the twenty-sixth a Confederate force, led
by Lieutenant Colonel H. H. Miller and consisting of four hundred
men, attacked Ponchatoula and drove out the Sixth Michigan. The
Federal troops set fire to the stores in the depot and set a torch to the
town before leaving. Screened by the smoke they withdrew to the
main force below. Miller and his men quickly put out the fires and
reoccupied the town.

Colonel Clark built up a strong fortification of railroad ties, iron
rails, and earth but was driven from this position by Colonel Miller.
Retiring five miles down the track, Clark erected a stronger fortification, and for the remainder of March the Union troops occupied the
miserable camp along the Jackson Railroad. The Confederates made
only a slight pretense of attacking the positions. Around April 1, the
command was moved down to Manchac, eleven miles below Ponchatoula.

The expedition along the Amite River led by Colonel F. S. Nickerson was blocked by Major W. H. Garland, in command of a small
Confederate force. After light skirmishing Nickerson withdrew his
troops. The cowardly Clark suddenly abandoned his troops around May
1 and returned to New Orleans with two schooners of cotton, captured
by the New York Zouaves, and his booty from Ponchatoula.

Later, when an attack against Port Hudson grew more imminent,
his troops were withdrawn from Manchac. Several officers, headed by
Lieutenant Colonel Edward Bacon of the Sixth Michigan, brought
formal charges against Colonel Clark, charging him with "conduct un-
becoming an officer and gentleman," "conduct prejudicial to good order
and military discipline," "neglect of duty," and "misbehavior before
the enemy." These accumulated charges embraced being "drunk and
unfit for duty"; indecent exposure and conduct with a Negro woman;
indulging in private cotton speculation while endangering the lives
of his troops; stealing money, silverware and household goods; and
cowardice and neglect of duty on the Amite River and at Manchac.
Before any official hearing could be held, the Port Hudson campaign
developed, and Colonel Clark was still employed as the commander of
the Sixth Michigan.[22]

BY THE BACK DOOR

E ARLY IN February Lieutenant General E. Kirby Smith was
assigned command over the entire Trans-Mississippi Department.
Kirby Smith, a West Point graduate, a hero of the Mexican War with
fifteen years' service in the United States army, had displayed great
ability at Manassas and had added to his prestige in the Kentucky
campaigning. Only thirty-seven years of age, his rise in the Confederate army had been very rapid.

On March 7 Kirby Smith assumed control of the Trans-Mississippi
and set up his headquarters at Alexandria. Without wasting time, he
set about familiarizing himself with his command.[1] In a short while
Kirby Smith found his small force taxed by demands for the relief of
Vicksburg and by Banks's drive up the Teche.

After a relatively quiet period, the Union forces were ready to resume the offensive. Weitzel sent the gunboat *Diana* on a reconnaissance
of the Grand Lake area above Berwick Bay. Two companies of infantry were sent along to protect the expedition. After exploring the
various lakes and inlets the *Diana* turned toward Berwick Bay. In
search of adventure, the gunboat commander violated orders and
moved into a second channel of the Atchafalaya which passed Pattersonville. He expected to fire a few shots to frighten a secessionist widow
who owned a large sugar plantation and also to intimidate a small
group of Confederates thought to be in the area.

Lying in ambush was the Valverde battery, a detachment of cavalry
attached to Sibley's Texas Brigade, and a few men from the Twenty-
eighth Louisiana Regiment. The cavalry first showed itself by dashing
alongside the boat. A shot from one of the *Diana*'s guns felled several
of the horses and riders and sent the others flying to the cover of a

woods nearby. From the bushes the line of waiting riflemen and hidden artillery opened a deadly fire upon the small gunboat, driving the gunners from their pieces and forcing the infantry to seek shelter between decks. For nearly three hours the *Diana* withstood the murderous fire as she tried to make her way back to safety at Berwick Bay. Cannoneers and infantrymen who dared to expose themselves on deck met almost instant death or serious injury. Hunks of flesh and splats of slippery blood and gore soon littered the decks. Bloodcurdling rebel yells blended with the sound of rapid firing from the rifles and artillery pieces. The *Diana's* steering mechanism and one of her steam pipes were shot away, and the boat became unmanageable. The sound of firing carried to Fort Buchanan at Berwick Bay, and the gunboat *Calhoun* was sent to aid the *Diana*. Unfortunately, the *Calhoun* grounded and could not get free until it was too late. With escape impossible, and in order to stop the carnage, Lieutenant Harry Western raised the white flag of surrender. The overjoyed Confederates rowed out to the crippled vessel in sugar coolers and took possession.

Thirty of the men aboard the *Diana* were killed or seriously wounded, and 120 men and officers were captured. The *Diana,* mounting five heavy guns, was repaired by the Confederates and added to Taylor's little fleet of gunboats on the Teche.[2]

By March 25 Banks had begun the first phase of his Teche campaign. General Grover was ordered to proceed from Baton Rouge by transport to Donaldsonville and to march along the Lafourche to Thibodaux. After debarking Grover's brigade, the river boats returned to Baton Rouge to take Emory's brigade to Algiers, where they would travel by rail over to Berwick Bay. General Augur was left to guard Baton Rouge, with 4,500 infantry, including three regiments of Negro troops, three batteries of artillery, and two companies of cavalry. To assist him, five gunboats and six mortars guarded the river approaches.

General Banks arrived at Brashear City on April 8 and found the troops ready to push forward. The next day Weitzel began crossing the bay to Berwick City and as soon as this ferriage could be made General Emory's brigade began crossing.

Grover began embarking his men, horses, artillery, and supplies on the afternoon of April 10 but moved so slowly that he did not complete the task until the night of April 11. The general plan of attack was for Grover to move by transports through Grand Lake to Indian Bend, near Franklin, and attack the Confederate rear while the main force made its assault against the fortifications at Bisland, below Franklin. Grover's departure was delayed by a heavy fog until mid-morning of April 12.

Banks did not wait for Grover. Around noon on April 11 the main column moved forward, Weitzel in the lead. The Confederate skirmishers fell back slowly but no real engagement was sought. Banks was killing time until Grover could depart.

Light skirmishing and deceptive cavalry maneuvering occupied the next morning, but when word arrived that Grover at last had moved out Banks ordered a stronger forward movement along both banks of the Teche. The hot, humid weather and the terrain quickly tired the men and slowed them down. The panting, sweating men moved across the drainage ditches and the deep furrows of the cane fields. Near four o'clock an artillery duel broke out and lasted until nightfall. The main force was drawn back out of range of the Confederate artillery and slept on its arms. The bloodthirsty mosquitoes fed freely upon the exhausted men.[3]

When Brigadier General Alfred Mouton arrived at Camp Bisland on April 10, he found the Confederate line of entrenchments on the west bank of the Teche completed, but no fortifications built on the east side. He immediately collected all the Negroes in the area and Saturday morning, April 11, set them to work. Night and day, part of the time under enemy fire, the troops and slaves worked until Monday morning, April 13. Because of a heavy barrage from the enemy artillery on that day, it was necessary to send the troops into line and the unsupervised, frightened Negroes fled to the rear before they completed the works.

Well aware of Grover's expedition to his rear, Taylor ordered Brigadier General H. H. Sibley and his Texas Brigade, on the west bank of the Teche, to open an attack at daybreak on April 13. The object of this move was to throw the enemy back in confusion and to force Banks to recall Grover to reinforce him. After issuing his orders, Taylor rushed to direct the rear guard in trying to prevent Grover's landing behind the main Confederate force. Contrary to orders, Sibley did not begin the attack.

Bisland, between Pattersonville and Centreville, was a line of simple breastworks across the narrow necks of dry land which extended on both sides of the Teche. Impenetrable cypress swamps and canebrakes flanked the short line on either extremity, and a strong redoubt served each side as an observation and command post. Along the Teche, which ran through the right center of the Confederate line, fields of knee-high sugar cane, laced with deep drainage ditches, stretched on either side back to the swamps. Mouton's Louisiana troops and A. P. Bagby's Seventh Texas Mounted Volunteers occupied the east bank. This line, nine hundred yards long, was held by only 1,500 men, one third of whom were members of Bagby's cavalry. On the west side General Sibley commanded a force of about equal strength.

After the heavy fog lifted and the day turned fair and bright, Banks ordered his whole line to move forward. The *Diana,* commanded by Captain Oliver J. Semmes of the Confederate artillery, came below the main line of defense and poured a heavy fire into the left center of the advancing Federal line. The *Diana,* masked by a screen of trees, was struck by a lucky shot fired from a thirty-pounder Parrott gun. The shell pierced the plating which guarded the boilers and exploded, killing two engineers and wounding five crew members. Serious damage to the engines forced Semmes to withdraw for repairs.

General Mouton, on the east bank, set up his command post in the parapet of the redoubt, from which he could observe the enemy movement and at the same time easily direct his troops. Colonel Bagby's Seventh Texas cavalry, dismounted and stationed 500 yards to the front and on the extreme left flank in a woods fronting on the lake, held Colonel O. P. Gooding's skirmishers in check. On both sides of the Teche a slow, general forward movement began at ten o'clock. The main point of Federal contact on the east side was against Mouton's left, held by Bagby. Mouton sent about 250 men from V. A. Fournet's battalion, a portion of the Eighteenth Regiment, and a detachment of sixty men from E. Waller, Jr.'s battalion to reinforce Bagby. The small group successfully resisted the onslaught of five Federal regiments until sundown, when Bagby was forced to yield slightly. Gooding claimed that two Confederate officers and eighty-four enlisted men were captured. Bagby was painfully injured in the arm.

Along the rest of Mouton's line, two of Gooding's regiments pressed slowly against the center and three regiments against his right, resting on the bayou. The Confederates kept up an incessant rifle and artillery fire against the cautious advance. By nighttime the superior Federal forces were within storming distance of Mouton's works and orders to fix bayonets were issued by both sides. The Confederates waited, knowing that they would be engulfed by the overwhelming numbers, but the attack did not come.

On the west bank, simultaneously with Gooding's movement, Weitzel, on the left, and Halbert E. Paine, on the right, moved forward against Sibley. Timothy Ingraham's command acted as a reserve for both. Heavy artillery caused Weitzel to send the Seventy-fifth New York, with the One Hundred Fourteenth New York, to the canebrake at the far left to flank the Confederate right. Twice the New York troops tried to break through but were held in check by the Fifth Texas Mounted, a portion of Waller's battalion, and the Twenty-eighth Louisiana, aided by the Semmes and Valverde batteries. About three o'clock Sibley attempted a flank movement over the soft swampland through the canebrake. Suddenly the Rebel yell rang out from the dense growth of cane. The startled Federal left rallied to stop the Texas troops who were trying to flank their left. Into the swampland and impenetrable canebrake rushed the Texans and New Yorkers. Unable to see or to reach the other, each force fired in the general direction of the other without gain to either side. By nightfall Weitzel and Paine were preparing for a general assault along the entire Confederate works on the west bank.

A composite picture of the battle of Bisland, or Bethel's Place, is one of intense artillery action and short forward movements by the infantry. On both sides of the Teche the infantry forces advanced slowly over the rows of sugar cane, trying at all times to keep their lines straight. When the Confederate fire became too intense, the men were ordered to lie down. The dry drainage ditches served best as cover, and the infantry spent most of the day in these many ditches watching the artillery show. The sides of the ditches were lined with blackberry bushes and while waiting for orders to advance the troops ate berries. Screeching shells sailed overhead. Rifles cracked and their bullets went whizzing and zipping through the air. The din of battle continued without letup all day. The artillery did the fighting, while the infantry did little more than support its batteries. The Union losses were in no way commensurate with the amount of powder expended. From an aggregate of 224 casualties, 3 officers and 37 enlisted men were killed and 8 officers and 176 men were wounded. The Confederates made no report on their losses.[4]

Banks had not pressed his attack to the maximum but had contented himself with holding the Confederates in position. All day long he awaited news from Grover's flanking expedition as he had ordered a general assault as soon as Grover had successfully landed. When this word did not come until late afternoon, Banks decided to postpone storming the works until early the next morning. The weary men were withdrawn to a safer position and went into bivouac.

Around noon on April 12 Taylor had sent Colonel W. G. Vincent and the Second Louisiana Cavalry Regiment to Verdun's Landing, about four miles to the rear of Bisland. Vincent was to observe the movement of Grover's gunboats and transports in Grand Lake and to prevent a Federal landing. Two sections of Cornay's battery were sent to assist in this work. Vincent, contrary to orders, had placed a small picket at Hudgins' Point and another at Charenton above and had bivouacked his main force on the west bank of the Teche. As a result, Grover was able to begin debarking his troops at Hudgins' on the morning of April 13, a task which was not complete until late afternoon. When Taylor, at Bisland, learned of this, he dispatched Colonel James Reily with the Fourth Texas to help Vincent stop Grover's advance.

That night at nine o'clock a message from Colonel Reily informed Taylor that Grover had crossed the Teche and had driven Vincent's cavalry down to Caroline's plantation, about a mile and a half below Franklin. With only 4,000 men, Taylor was faced by more than three times this number on his front and was also outnumbered to his rear. He decided to evacuate his Bethel, or Bisland, earthworks, to cut his way through Grover's army, and to move to safety at New Iberia, some thirty-five miles to the northwest. Wagons containing quartermaster, ordnance, medical, and commissary stores, as well as the sick and wounded, were started on the road to Franklin. The infantry and artillery were to move above as soon as possible. The Fifth Texas, Waller's battalion, and one section of Semmes's battery, serving as rear guard, were to hinder Banks's forward movement until Taylor could move through Grover above.

The entire Confederate command, with the exception of the rear guard, silently abandoned Bisland. It was not until 3 A.M., April 14, when the rear guard began preparations to leave, that Banks even suspected such a move. The men were aroused and ordered into line. An hour later orders to assault the works were issued. At daybreak the entire Federal line swarmed over the works, only to find the place empty. Instead of trying to catch the retreating Confederates, the jubilant men were allowed time to have breakfast. Banks then started in pursuit of Taylor, but the stubborn Confederate rear guard prevented rapid progress.[5]

Taylor hurried from Bisland on the night of April 13, picked up Reily, and moved one mile east above Franklin to join Vincent. Major F. H. Clack, with his Louisiana battalion, soon arrived from New

Iberia. In Nerson's Woods (Irish Bend) in front of McKerall's plantation, facing east, Taylor formed his line of battle and awaited Grover's attack. On the bank of the Teche, and slightly to the front, Taylor posted Clack's battalion and two guns from Cornay's artillery. Clack's men were to act as skirmishers. Next was Reily, and on the extreme left, resting on the impassable swamp, was Vincent and the remaining two guns belonging to Cornay.

Early on the morning of April 14 Grover began moving around the Crescent Bayou road toward Franklin, where he expected to join Banks and completely hem in Taylor's small army. Birge, with Rodgers' battery, led the column, followed by Dwight, with Closson's battery, and Kimball, with Nims's battery, brought up the rear. Suddenly Birge's skirmishers, to their surprise, ran into Clack's battalion, and the advance was halted.

The Confederates had every advantage of concealment, whereas the Federal position had little to offer. The muddy sugar-cane field traversed by drainage ditches made a forward movement very difficult. On the Federal left was the Teche; on the right was the swamp; and in front was Nerson's Woods, where the Confederates were posted.

Birge quickly formed the remainder of the Twenty-fifth Connecticut in line of battle and sent it across the field through the foot-high cane toward the Confederate left. This regiment advanced to within a hundred yards of the trees where the men lay down in a shallow ditch. The Twenty-sixth Maine was sent to the left of the Twenty-fifth Connecticut and the two regiments opened a withering rifle fire from the open ditch against the concealed enemy. Cornay's two guns near the bayou were highly effective for awhile until Birge sent a section of Rodgers' artillery to divert the Confederate attention. Along the line leading from the swamp to the bayou the One Hundred Fifty-ninth New York was placed to the left of the Twenty-sixth Maine, and the Thirteenth Connecticut formed between the main road and the bayou on the extreme left.

To Taylor's great relief, Colonel Henry Gray and his Twenty-eighth Louisiana Regiment arrived at Franklin around seven o'clock and were rushed to bolster the extreme left of the Confederate line.

A number of Reily's men were killed and injured, and early in the action, Colonel Reily himself fell mortally wounded. The leaderless Texas men "grouped together like so many badly scared boys" until a Major Hamilton stepped forward to take over command.

Taylor now ordered his entire line to charge Birge's men. As the screaming Confederates rushed out of the woods across the drainage ditches, they poured a murderous fire into the One Hundred Fifty-ninth New York, the most forward regiment. An order to retreat was issued and quickly carried out. The retreating New Yorkers swept over the frightened Twenty-sixth Maine and Twenty-fifth Connecticut, and a general rout took place.

The Thirteenth Connecticut, nearest to the Teche, moved across the open field and into the grove, pushing Clack back slightly and forcing a temporary withdrawal of Cornay's two guns. This advance was halted by Grover's orders to retire and re-form brigade battle lines. The Thirteenth Connecticut brought back sixty Confederate prisoners.

Shortly after Birge's brigade was driven back, General Dwight came up from the rear and formed two lines, with the Sixth New York and Ninety-first New York in front, and the Twenty-second Maine, First Louisiana, and One Hundred Thirty-first New York behind them. Dwight drove against the Confederate left, pushed them back to their original positions, and captured seventy men.

As soon as possible Birge re-formed his brigade and, after a long delay, a cautious advance of the entire division was ordered by Grover. The gunboat *Diana* was brought up the bayou from Franklin by Captain Semmes to help protect the Confederate right. Her guns helped to make the already timorous Grover even more cautious.

General Mouton arrived at Franklin around eight o'clock and was placed in command of the troops holding out against Grover. Taylor moved into Franklin to push the supply trains and troops from Bisland over a cutoff road to New Iberia.[6]

Colonel Thomas Green, commanding the rear guard of the retreat from Bisland, slowly retired, holding Banks's forces back as long as possible. Taylor issued orders that the crippled *Diana* be abandoned and burned and that Mouton should evacuate his troops before Green entered Franklin.

These plans went awry. General Sibley, without consulting Taylor, ordered Green to rush to Franklin before the enemy above cut off his only road of retreat. Green complied with these orders, entered the cutoff road, and set fire to the only bridge over Choupique Bayou. Weitzel's advance moved into the lower part of Franklin as the last of Green's men quit the upper part of town.

When Mouton learned of the situation at midday, he secretly retired his men under the cover of the *Diana's* guns and, taking a short cut, was just able to get the last of his men across the burning bridge before it was completely destroyed.

Banks rode into Franklin and conferred with Weitzel. After a long delay, during which prisoners were questioned, Weitzel moved to the cutoff road while Emory moved around the Teche to block Mouton's retreat. Too much time had been spent. Riding up to the bridge, Weitzel found it impassable, and Emory found that Mouton had made good his escape.

Captain Semmes kept up a steady fire from the *Diana* long after Mouton's departure. Then, according to orders, he fired his ship and attempted to escape overland with his crew. They were all captured a short time later. Weitzel, a former classmate and friend of Semmes at West Point, placed a nominal guard over his prisoner, and subsequently Semmes managed to escape.

The Confederate transports used on the lower Teche were all burned to keep them out of enemy hands, with the exception of a hospital boat, the steamer *Cornie*. Taylor had provided wagon ambulances for the sick and wounded, but Sibley failed to transfer these men to the wagons. He ordered the *Cornie* to try to pass through the enemy lines flying a hospital flag. Sibley had erred again. The *Cornie* and all aboard were captured.

General Grover, after Taylor's early morning charge, became so fainthearted in his movements that he did not discover the withdrawal of Taylor's men until 2 P.M. Moving down toward Franklin Grover met Emory coming up the bayou road. The painful truth then dawned. Grover realized that he, with over 5,000 troops and a vastly superior artillery, had been held at bay by barely a thousand men, while Taylor's main force had escaped. His overcaution had even allowed the rear guard to withdraw. The muddling Grover had failed to land his men high enough above Taylor, and finally, he had allowed the Confederates to slip through the only hole in the area.

The battle of Irish Bend, or Nerson's Woods, was over. Grover had suffered 353 casualties. Six officers and 43 enlisted men were killed while 17 officers and 257 enlisted men were wounded. Thirty men were listed as missing. Taylor never made a casualty report, but 21 officers and men, including Colonel Reily, were left dead on the field of battle. Thirty-five Confederate wounded were captured by Grover.[7]

Banks was stymied. The bridge across the bayou was burned and could not be rebuilt until the next day. The only way to reach Taylor was via the roundabout bayou route, but before his tired men could cover this ground, all hopes of bottling up the Confederate force would be gone. Banks ordered his men to bivouac for the night.

While Banks's army, on April 14, was displaying such a lack of coordination and was engaging in dilatory tactics, the Federal navy enjoyed a signal victory in the nearby waters of Grand Lake. The *Queen of the West,* taken from Charles Rivers Ellet, shortly before, had been ordered by Taylor to come down the Atchafalaya to help the *Diana* drive off the Federal gunboats. A company of infantry was placed aboard the *Queen* and a regiment aboard her consort, the *Minna Simma.* The ram and steamer had then proceeded to Grand Lake. At 5:15 on the morning of April 14, the *Estrella, Arizona,* and *Calhoun,* the gunboats which had escorted Grover above Bisland, had opened a long-range fire on the *Queen.* Approaching within three-quarters of a mile, the *Queen* opened a rapid fire on all three gunboats. Forming his boats in a semicircle, Lieutenant Commander A. P. Cooke of the *Arizona* closed in on the *Queen.* The *Queen* steamed for the *Arizona,* intending to ram her, but sighted the *Calhoun* bearing down upon her. Captain E. W. Fuller, uncertain of his actions, stopped his engines. The three gunboats showered the motionless *Queen* with shot and shell. Suddenly a puff of white rose from the decks of the ram, followed by dense black smoke and flames. One of Cooke's shells had struck a box of ammunition, setting the decks and rigging afire. A mad scramble now took place aboard the burning ram. The men threw cotton bales overboard and then jumped into the water. Cooke ordered an immediate cease-fire and lowered his boats to save the men from drowning. In the confusion the *Minna Simma,* which was some distance to the rear, made her escape. Ninety men were rescued, but some thirty were drowned. Cooke managed to remove the five guns from the burning ram before the flames grew too high. After the *Queen* drifted for some time, the fire finally reached the magazine and she ended her brief career in a mighty explosion which rocked the Federal gunboats.[8]

Following his hasty withdrawal from Franklin, Taylor placed General Sibley at the head of the column. To the Louisiana foot soldiers the retreat was a hellish experience. After hard marching, Taylor's men reached Jeanerette, about twelve miles below New Iberia.[9] In describing the first day, April 14, Arthur W. Hyatt of Clack's battalion reported:

Thus we had marched about twenty-six miles in fifteen hours and fought a battle in the bargain. But such terrible hard marching I never witnessed before. Our feet are all blistered and swollen, and we have had scarcely anything to eat—what with hunger, thirst, mud, rain, marching, fighting, *dust,* etc., etc., we are perfectly worn out.

That night the weather turned unusually cool and the men got very little sleep.[10]

At daylight Taylor's still weary, footsore troops resumed the race to safety. They arrived in New Iberia at 3 P.M. where they were allowed to rest for an hour. Taylor found the gunboat *Stevens*, commissioned by the Confederate navy, still unfinished and unfit for action; therefore, he ordered her destruction. The boat was towed two miles below the town, set afire, and sunk in the channel to obstruct the passage of the Union gunboats. Resuming the march, Taylor moved to Camp Pratt and went into bivouac. The next day, April 16, he pushed his men twenty more miles to Vermilionville, where they crossed the Vermilion Bayou, and, after burning the bridge and posting a section of artillery on the heights and sharpshooters along the upper bank, the men were allowed to rest until the following afternoon.[11]

As Taylor retreated, his army grew smaller and smaller. A number of his men lived in the area through which they now traveled and many of them slipped away to visit their families. Many of the Louisiana men were conscripts and were serving under duress. Taylor reported: "Nearly the whole of Lieutenant-Colonel Fournet's battalion, . . . deserted with their arms, remaining at their homes." Taylor lamented the lack of discipline among his troops and reported: "From Sibley's brigade also a very considerable number have straggled off and returned to their homes in Texas." Colonel James P. Major was ordered to Niblett's Bluff, on the Sabine River, to collect the stragglers and deserters trying to get into Texas.[12]

Banks, after giving his men an afternoon and night of rest at Franklin, during which time a pontoon bridge was laid, crossed over the stream on April 15 and took up the chase. His cavalry advance skirmished lightly with the small rear guard of Texas cavalry under Colonel Green. That night Banks bivouacked near Jeanerette. Early the next morning the march was resumed and the command, after hard skirmishing, proceeded to a point just above New Iberia, where they encamped.

Some of the men confiscated a large batch of Louisiana rum in the village and made things lively, especially in General Dwight's brigade. After a struggle, the drunk and riotous men were quieted and the weary troops, except for a detachment of Grover's brigade, settled down for the night.

At midnight Grover dispatched Colonel W. K. Kimball with the

Twelfth Maine, the Forty-first Massachusetts, a section of Nims's battery, and one company of the Twenty-fourth Connecticut to destroy the Avery Island salt works, ten miles to the southwest of New Iberia. On this small island in May, 1862, a mine of pure rock salt had been discovered, and in the intervening months it had produced over 22,000,000 pounds of salt for the Confederacy. This valuable mine had been well protected until Banks began his push up the Teche. After his all-night march Kimball advanced to the beautiful little island and, without opposition, burned eighteen buildings, smashed the steam engines and mining equipment, scattered 600 barrels of salt awaiting shipment, and brought away a ton of gunpowder left behind by Taylor's men. Two days later Kimball rejoined Grover at Vermilion Bayou.[13]

On the morning of April 17 Grover, joined by Gooding's brigade, took the left-hand road leading almost directly to Vermilionville, or Lafayette, while Weitzel took the right hand road which followed the winding path of the Teche. That afternoon Grover arrived at the Vermilion Bayou only to find the bridge in flames. General Dwight sent forward Closson's and Nims's batteries, supported by skirmishers. The Federal skirmishers were driven back by the two sections of Faries' and Valverde's batteries. The Federal artillery continued its fire until nightfall, but the shells exploded too high and to the rear of the Confederates' position. Under cover of darkness the Confederates retired and rejoined their batteries at Opelousas, twenty miles beyond. Grover spent the next day building a bridge across the bayou, and Banks gave his men a much-needed rest.

Chasing Taylor up the Teche was no picnic for Banks's men. The agony of blistered feet soon turned the troops into a snarling, swearing pack. They cursed the general for ordering them to march; they swore at each other because the torment of their comrades seemed to intensify their own pain. Line officers found it impossible to keep the men in marching order. Hundreds threw themselves down in the dust and refused to budge.

Some of the footsore men found an answer to their marching problems. They slipped out of the column, seized horses, and rode along in comfort. Soon every plantation and farm along the route was rifled of its horses, mules, buggies, and carriages. Hour by hour the men became more scattered, and in the confusion, the various companies and regiments began to lose their identity. Immediate action was taken. One company of the One Hundred Fourteenth New York was posted ahead and ordered to stop every man and officer "who was riding with-out authority, arrest him," and take his horse or vehicle.

Suffocating clouds of dust, stirred up by thousands of marching feet, added to the miseries of the men. They resembled an army of gray-brown ghosts with their eyelashes and hair loaded with dust, their faces a mask of grime and sweat, and their blue uniforms soon the color of the ground over which they marched. On raw blistered feet, through the swirls of blinding dust, the soldiers were pushed toward Lafayette.

The men's bodies were always damp in the April heat in their thick woolen uniforms. Many of the troops suffered from ground itch. White, pus-filled pimples covered the skin, producing an unbearable itching. To get relief the men scratched themselves until the blood ran. Their bodies soon were pocked with scabrous sores.[14]

After noon on Friday, April 17, Taylor pushed on toward Alexandria, destroying all of the bridges along the way. On Monday he sent his entire cavalry force, with the exception of Waller's battalion, to the open prairie, west of Opelousas, to attack the enemy flanks and to harass the rear and thus slow down Banks's forward movement. By April 23 the main Confederate force was encamped at Lecompte, eighteen miles below Alexandria.

Crossing the Vermilion and Carencro bayous on April 19 in a driving rain, Banks's men, now somewhat rested, "plodded along, singing and joking in the jolliest of humors." Despite the water and mud Banks moved on to Opelousas.

The main force went into bivouac just beyond the town while all of the cavalry, a section of artillery, and the Thirteenth Connecticut pushed up to Washington, on Courtableau Bayou six miles above. The men found Opelousas a beautiful town boasting several churches, a fine convent, and a large courthouse. Washington, on the other hand, while larger and more thriving than Opelousas, was "squalid and dirty." The men soon began to refer to Washington as "Niggertown" because of its filth, its ugly buildings, and its large number of black inhabitants.[15]

On the same day that Banks occupied Opelousas, Lieutenant Commander Cooke, with his gunboats *Estrella, Calhoun,* and *Arizona* accompanied by four companies of the Sixteenth New Hampshire from Brashear City, captured Fort Burton at Butte-à-la-Rose on the Atchafalaya. Sixty men of the Crescent Regiment, two heavy guns, and a supply of ammunition were taken. The New Hampshire troops now took over the desolate, miserable post which controlled the Atchafalaya.

The last of Taylor's bayou fleet, the steamer *Ellen,* was captured at Barre's Landing on the Courtableau on April 22. To ensure his supply lines from Brashear to Opelousas, Banks sent the Fourth Massachusetts to Berwick Bay to replace the Sixteenth New Hampshire, now at Butte-à-la-Rose, and the One Hundred Seventy-fifth New York was stationed at Franklin, while the Twenty-second Maine bivouacked at New Iberia. General Dwight held Washington; Grover occupied Barre's Landing; and Weitzel and Emory remained at Opelousas.

Banks's unduly long stay at Opelousas, which allowed Taylor to make good his escape, had come about not only because he wanted to ensure his communications along the Teche, but also because he was waiting for Grant to send him 20,000 men from Vicksburg. With reinforcements, he felt sure that he could take Port Hudson. Pressing civil affairs took Banks back to New Orleans on April 25, and he did not return to Opelousas until May 1.

In the meantime, most of Banks's men whiled away the time in drill, picket duty, and in government foraging.

With the approach of the Federal troops up the Teche on April 24, E. Kirby Smith issued orders transferring his headquarters, the Trans-Mississippi, from Alexandria to Shreveport. General Taylor, with his greatly reduced forces, occupied Alexandria and vicinity.[16]

William A. Seay, Superintendent of the Louisiana Military Seminary at Pineville, across from Alexandria, found the job of holding the cadets in the classroom fruitless. The school had opened for its fourth session in November, 1862, with 112 students. The undisciplined young cadets with their enthusiasm for war were a continuous source of trouble. Around April 1 the cadets decided to close the school. They broke into the kitchen, smashed all the furniture, and seized all the cutlery, dishes, pots and pans, dumping them into the well. Most of the students then went home to volunteer. Professor Seay was able to keep a few students until April 23, when the excitement of the approach of Banks's army caused him to close the school and send the cadets home to fight.[17]

Banks, on May 4, ordered Dwight to move toward Alexandria from Washington, and on the same afternoon Weitzel left from Opelousas. Emory's division followed the next morning. Meeting no opposition, the army moved swiftly over the dry, dusty roads, arriving at Governor Moore's plantations below Alexandria on May 7 at six o'clock in the evening. Earlier, the cavalry had been sent forward to Alexandria to reconnoiter the area.

On May 6 Taylor had withdrawn his main forces from Alexandria and had beat a hasty retreat toward Natchitoches. Porter, who had succeeded in reducing the works at Fort DeRussy, stole the march on Banks and, early in the morning of May 7, took over Alexandria with his gunboats. Later in the day Banks's cavalry burst into the town and were amazed to find Porter already in possession.[18]

Banks was greatly disappointed to learn that Porter held Alexandria, but he determined to push on to the town although his tired men had already marched more than twenty-five miles that day. A regimental race developed between the Eighth Vermont and the Seventy-fifth New York and helped them to forget their weariness. "For four or five miles, singing, shouting, laughing, joking, our boys crowded on faster than my horse could walk," one of the officers of the Seventy-fifth New York reported. Weitzel marched his men into town around eight o'clock, and after they had received a full ration of liquor, they were allowed to enjoy a long night's sleep.[19]

On the afternoon of the following day, Emory's brigade moved up to Alexandria. Emory's men marched through the town, stepping smartly to the music of regimental bands and with flags flying, to bivouac on the grassy banks of Red River above.

Porter, who disliked Banks, reported that as soon as Banks arrived he posted guards over everything and declared martial law. Porter turned over Alexandria to Banks and left to rejoin Grant. Leaving the gunboat *Lafayette* at Alexandria to aid Banks and posting the *Pittsburg* at Black River, Porter proceeded with the rest of his fleet back to Vicksburg.[20]

Taylor kept up his retreat toward Shreveport. His tired, dispirited men continued to desert. One of Taylor's line officers, Arthur W. Hyatt, wrote in his diary: "Friday 8th [May] . . . reaching the banks of Cane River. . . . We are now on a regular race from the enemy, and are bound for Grand Ecore. . . ." Three days later Hyatt wrote: "Monday, May 11th We have now retreated two hundred and eighty miles. Natchitoches is quite a 'town,' and the galleries were crowded with pretty women, who waved us a kind reception as we passed through the town."[21]

Banks was in a quandary. Should he follow Taylor up Red River to Shreveport, or should he proceed to Vicksburg to reinforce Grant, or should he move against Port Hudson?

From the beginning the Teche campaign was marred by plunder and pillage. Banks and his officers had, as usual, issued orders prohibiting such actions, and as usual, the undisciplined troops had chosen to disobey them.[22]

Moving from Bisland to Franklin, a soldier of the One Hundred Fourteenth New York wrote: "The men soon learned the pernicious habit of slily leaving their places in the ranks, when opposite a planter's house, to 'appropriate' a chicken, or 'confiscate' a pig, or 'gobble' a few turnips and radishes. Oftentimes a soldier can be found with such an enormous development of the organ of destructiveness, that the most severe punishment cannot deter him from indulging in the breaking of mirrors, and pianos, and the most costly furniture. Men of such reckless dispositions are frequently guilty of the most horrible desecrations. . . ."

The One Hundred Fourteenth New York, following in the wake of Banks's army, "saw fences torn down and burned, houses rifled, fields trampled over, and carcasses of butchered cattle." [23]

Some of the planters and small farmers who lived along the Teche often flew an English or French flag over their houses, hoping that this claim to foreign protection would spare their property.[24] The soldiers "regarded the exhibition of a foreign flag as a direct insult, and the inmates of such houses had very little mercy shown them." [25]

Lieutenant William H. Root of the Seventy-fifth New York Regiment wrote in his diary on April 15: "A guard is posted over every house of more than two chimneys till the cavalcade passes to keep the soldiers from taking anything, though the smaller houses of the poor are left unguarded." Evidently these guards were very lax because Lieutenant Root reported some three hundred soldiers had already been arrested for confiscation of "secesh" property.[26]

Many of the citizens, most of whom had never before seen a Yankee soldier, expected the worst from the invader. Describing their reaction, the Reverend George H. Hepworth wrote: "Some cried, some cursed, some whined; and some overcome with fear, hid themselves in the woods, leaving everything to the tender mercies of the army." [27]

Negroes were responsible for much of the plunder and pillage. Negro camp followers and officers' servants roamed the plantations and small farms without hindrance, bringing in their booty to camps each afternoon. Soldiers often invited the resident Negroes to take food, clothing, fine furniture, horses, or whatever they wanted from their masters.

The guilt for most of the pillage committed by the army was placed upon stragglers. It was estimated that some five hundred soldiers remained in the rear without permission after the army had passed, to enjoy the spoils of the rich countryside.[28]

Attempts to break up the forbidden pillage were made through wholesale arrests, but it was General William Dwight who found the most effective deterrent to such practices. A private from the One Hundred Thirty-first New York was caught taking clothing from a home. Dwight summarily ordered that the man be executed. While the brigade looked on, the private was led before a firing squad and shot to death. Later General Grover ordered that in the future no man could be executed without a proper court-martial. Banks backed up Dwight's severe measures, but no more men were shot.

Faced by limited supplies and a long supply line, Banks lived off the country as much as possible. He, too, wanted to pay for the campaign through the seizure of property. Banks wrote General Halleck on May 4: "I have deemed it expedient, in order to prevent the reorganization of the rebel army and to deprive the rebel Government of all possible means of support, to take possession of mules, horses, cattle, and the staple products of the country—cotton, sugar, and tobacco." Citizens loyal to the Union were to be compensated for all products seized by the United States. By May 4 Banks reported that "20,000 beeves, mules, and horses have been forwarded to Brashear City, with 5,000 bales of cotton and many hogsheads of sugar."

Operating from Opelousas, Washington, Barre's Landing, Franklin, New Iberia, and Alexandria, detachments of Banks's men gathered cotton, vegetables, molasses, rum, sugar, saddles, bridles, horses, mules, cattle, corn, and sweet potatoes. Negroes were mounted and assisted in driving in the cattle and horses found hidden in the woods and swamps. Between eight and ten thousand bales of cotton were collected. It was estimated that the Teche and lower Red River regions were stripped of legitimate forage valued at more than ten million dollars. These goods, along with thousands of Negroes, were sent by wagons and boats back to Brashear City for safekeeping.[29]

The effect of the Union army upon the Negroes during Banks's first Red River expedition was overwhelming. As the troops moved up to Alexandria, the Negroes crowded the roadsides to watch the passing army. They were "all frantic with joy, some weeping, some blessing, and some dancing in the exuberance of their emotions."[30] All of the Negroes were attracted by the pageantry and excitement of the army. Others cheered because they anticipated the freedom to plunder and to do as they pleased now that the Federal troops were there.[31]

John H. Ransdell wrote from Elmwood plantation, just below Alexandria: "The arrival of the advance of the Yankees alone turned the negroes crazy. They became utterly demoralized at once . . . restraint was at an end. All business was suspended and those that did not go with the army remained at home to do *much worse*. No work was done and the place swarmed with negroes from other places." [32]

Provost troops left behind by Banks to restore law and order and to help the loyal citizens with their labor problems had their hands full. Stragglers from the Union army often made the Negroes quit work under a threat of being shot. Owners were often so frightened that they did little to get the Negroes to resume their labors. Provost marshals urged the Negroes to return to their former plantations where they would work for wages. In most cases these efforts were successful. However, bands of Negroes below Franklin became very unruly, and it was necessary for the occupation troops to take measures against them. An officer of the Twenty-second Maine reported: "While here the regiment done good service in suppressing the negro insurrections that prevailed in St. Mary & the other adjoining Parishes." [33]

When Banks decided to evacuate the area and move against Port Hudson, he sent what Negroes he could to Brashear but the vast majority remained on the plantations. Without the protection of the Federal army, the Negroes were forced to return to work. Some refused to work and were shot; some were soundly thrashed; and all of them began to act better. Many of the runaway Negroes slowly returned to their masters and resumed their old way of life.[34]

Late in April Banks learned that Brigadier General Daniel Ullmann had been sent to New Orleans by the War Department to raise a brigade of Negro troops. Banks at Opelousas, on May 1, proposed the formation of the Corps d'Afrique to consist ultimately of eighteen regiments, representing all arms. To organize, discipline, and instruct this corps, the best officers of the Nineteenth Army would be temporarily or permanently assigned. Banks welcomed Ullmann, informing him that he already had five regiments of Negroes, numbering a thousand men each, and that he had collected enough able-bodied recruits in the Teche campaign to fill an additional two or more regiments. These recruits and other regiments, except for the Corps of Engineers, who could be spared from special duty would be turned over to Ullmann's command.[35]

Correspondence between Banks and Grant had, from the beginning, been unsatisfactory to both men. Some of the dispatches had taken over a month to reach their destination. Misunderstandings, undated dispatches, and the failure of the Lake Providence canal route had added to the confusion and had led to the failure of co-operation between the two commanders. It was not until Banks arrived at Alexandria that he received his first direct communication from Grant. By this time it was too late. Grant had already crossed the Mississippi and had fully committed himself to the reduction of Vicksburg.

On March 23 Grant had written to Banks stating that he would send him twenty thousand men to aid in the reduction of Port Hudson if he could secure sufficient light draught vessels and provided the Lake Providence route proved successful. This message did not reach Banks until April 10 at Brashear City. He immediately assured Grant that he would be at Port Hudson by May 10, but this message did not reach Grant until May 2, after he had already crossed the river.[36] On April 14 Grant sent another dispatch to Banks in which he stated: "Am concentrating my forces at Grand Gulf. Will send an army corps to Bayou Sara by the 25th to co-operate with you on Port Hudson." This undated letter reached Banks below Alexandria on May 5. Banks thought Grant meant May 25 and wrote that he probably would be at Port Hudson by that time.[37]

Banks was now certain of success. But then on May 12 he received a communiqué from Grant, written on the tenth, which shattered his immediate hopes and plans. Instead of sending troops, Grant requested Banks to come to Grand Gulf and aid him in the Vicksburg campaign.

Banks wrote Halleck that he did not have sufficient transportation to join Grant and, even if he had, he did not want to leave Port Hudson and Mobile in his rear. He could not abandon all the Negroes, cotton, horses, mules, and supplies that he had collected and he prophesied the recapture of New Orleans if he went to the aid of Grant. Since he had counted on transportation to be sent down-river by Grant, Banks felt that he did not have enough boats to move down Red River and cross over the Mississippi above Port Hudson. Also, the task of establishing communications with Baton Rouge and New Orleans from above might take too long or might seriously endanger the success of the campaign. Pessimistically he concluded that he would have to retrace his steps—returning over four hundred miles to Brashear, New Orleans, and Baton Rouge—and attack Port Hudson from below.

After reconsideration and careful reconnaissance Banks decided against the retrograde movement and resolved to move a few of his men and supplies by the available river transportation. He would have to take most of his troops and supplies overland by way of Simmesport. Writing to Grant on May 13, Banks promised that he would embark twelve thousand men and proceed up the Mississippi to Grand Gulf and would join Grant in ten or twelve days. Later Banks changed his mind again and committed himself fully to the Port Hudson campaign.

From the beginning Halleck had urged Grant and Banks to join forces. When he learned of Banks's "eccentric movements" at Alexandria, he expressed his disappointment and his belief that "serious disaster might befall Grant unless the two forces be united between Vicksburg and Port Hudson on the east side of the river." He even considered authorizing Banks "to assume the entire command as soon as you and General Grant could unite."

Still unwilling to renounce all possibilities of securing aid from Grant, on May 13 Banks sent General Dwight by steamer up to Grand Gulf, there to move inland, to find Grant, and to request in person the needed assistance. Finding Grant busy with the battle of Champion's Hill, Dwight sent a dispatch back to Banks before he had actually seen Grant. The message did not reach Banks until around May 20 at New Orleans. Misinterpreting the wording and believing Grant would send twenty thousand men to Bayou Sara by May 25, Banks gave up all plans of reinforcing Grant and decided to proceed immediately with his assault on Port Hudson.[38] The die was cast. Both generals went their divergent ways and were destined not to meet until after the close of their separate, and equally successful, campaigns.

Around the tenth of May, while Banks mulled over various plans of action at his encampment in Alexandria, General Dwight's brigade and attached troops were sent to catch the retreating enemy and to reconnoiter the area for a possible movement against Shreveport. The men marched some forty or fifty miles over dusty roads to the "piney woods" region but did not sight Taylor's army. Dwight's troops were preparing to push farther into the desolate region when word arrived that a movement toward Port Hudson was underway. The men began the long trudge back to Alexandria.[39]

Grover's troops were the first to leave Alexandria. The next day, May 15, Paine followed on the road to Cheneyville and Simmesport. Weitzel and Dwight pulled out of Alexandria on May 17, followed at a safe distance by a small Confederate force composed of Colonel W. P. Lane's regiment, fresh from Texas, Waller's battalion, and a detachment from Sibley's brigade. Early on the morning of the twentieth the Confederates attacked Weitzel's pickets but were driven off and pursued back to Cheneyville by the Federal cavalry, the Fourth Wisconsin, recently mounted, and the Twelfth Connecticut. On May 22 Weitzel started the move from Murdock's plantation to Simmesport, arriving there the next day.

Banks earlier had gone by steamer to New Orleans. Back in the city, he placed Emory in command of local defenses and ordered Sherman, Dow, and Nickerson to proceed upriver to join Augur below Port Hudson. Banks rushed back to Simmesport, arriving on May 21. The same day he began a move to Morganza, some twenty miles by river to the west of Bayou Sara. Transports were waiting and as fast as the men could be moved they were carried across the Mississippi to Bayou Sara.

Bayou Sara, once an important river port, was now a blackened skeleton of chimneys arising from rubble heaps. Federal gunboats had wrecked a terrible revenge upon the town following the guerrilla attacks upon the Federal navy and shipping in the river. Leaving the decaying, lifeless village behind, Banks soon posted his men around Port Hudson.[40]

PORT HUDSON, MAY 27

IN APRIL, except for a few cotton raids and foraging expeditions, things remained relatively quiet around Baton Rouge after Banks started his Teche campaign. With so little to do, the men in garrison began to complain. Army rations came up for criticism. Salt pork, a staple issue, was said to be "soft, oily, and maggoty." New England troops wondered why the quartermaster could not supply them with salt herring or mackerel. The men complained bitterly that only officers could purchase liquor. They grumbled, too, about the lack of reading matter and other entertainment. A theater had been established which used soldier talent and offered comedies, musicals, and vaudeville revues. It was "quite well patronized by officers and negroes," but since few enlisted men had any money, most of them could not attend.

The day of the jubilee had indeed come to the contrabands who crowded into Baton Rouge. The provost marshal allowed the Negroes to move into abandoned houses. The colored women often boarded white officers at ten dollars a week and washed their clothes, charging a dollar for each dozen pieces. Their men hired out as day laborers to the army; a few kept restaurants; others joined the army. Never before had they known such wealth and luxury.

Two regiments of Negro troops, along with the hundreds of laborers, were employed in fortifying the town. Each day more and more of the Negroes joined the army and drilled enthusiastically.[1]

The great event of early May was the arrival of Colonel Benjamin H. Grierson from Tennessee with the Sixth and Seventh Illinois Cavalry. Grierson and his men had "swept down like a whirlwind" from Tennessee through the length of Mississippi into southeastern Louisiana.[2] Their main objective was to pull Pemberton's attentions eastward away from the river while Grant moved on the Louisiana side below Vicksburg. Grierson destroyed railroads and telegraphic communications and took mules, horses, forage, food, and anything of value from the area. In this brilliant and costly raid, covering some eight hundred miles in seventeen days, the Union officer eluded capture and dazed the Confederate commanders with his daring and dash.

Gardner dispatched cavalry, infantry, and artillery detachments from Port Hudson to intercept Grierson before he could reach the road from Tangipahoa to Baton Rouge. They arrived too late; Grierson had already passed. C. C. Wilbourn's camp, the Confederate outpost near Baton Rouge, was caught by surprise and a number of prisoners were taken, all the tents destroyed, and ammunition, guns, stores, and documents seized. The raiders, moving toward Baton Rouge, surprised a cavalry unit of Miles's Legion, which was picketing Roberts' Ford at the Comite River, and captured more than forty of the Confederates along with their horses and accouterments. At 3 P.M. on May 2 Grierson and his saddle-weary men were given a rousing reception as they rode triumphantly into Baton Rouge.[3]

When Grant pushed his troops across the river into Mississippi, Pemberton immediately began to call in all available forces with which to defend Vicksburg. On May 4 he ordered Gardner to join him with five thousand men. Brigadier General W. N. R. Beall was to be left in command of his brigade and the heavy artillery at Port Hudson. Gardner at once sent three brigades and on May 8 left Port Hudson with Samuel B. Maxey's brigade. The day before, Pemberton had received a telegram from President Davis which read: "To hold both Vicksburg and Port Hudson is necessary to a connection with Trans-Mississippi." Pemberton immediately sent a wire to Gardner, which reached him at Clinton, ordering him to return with two thousand of his men to Port Hudson. General Joseph E. Johnston, who did not see eye to eye with either Pemberton or Davis, ordered Gardner to abandon Port Hudson and move to Jackson, Mississippi. When Gardner received this message, Federal troops had already moved up from Baton Rouge. Gardner planned to evacuate his post on the night of May 24 but found it impossible. Now completely invested, Gardner prepared to hold his position against heavy odds.

On May 8 the mortar boats of the lower Federal fleet were brought up within five miles of Port Hudson and in the afternoon they opened fire on the river batteries. After getting their range, the mortars remained silent until just before midnight, when they began a regular bombardment which was to continue until June 18. Early the next morning the eleven Confederate river batteries replied. During some forty-three days of bombardment the Confederate artillery claimed to have lost only four killed and three wounded.

For several weeks General Gardner had labored to build up a food reserve at Port Hudson. In addition to gathering supplies on the east side, he drew three hundred beeves, four hundred sheep, and four hundred bushels of corn from across the river, despite the presence of the upper and lower Federal fleets.[4]

General Augur, receiving orders from Banks on May 18 to move the major portion of his troops to the rear of Port Hudson, two days later left Baton Rouge. Colonel Charles W. Drew was left in command of the Fourth Louisiana Native Guards at Fort Williams inside the town.

Early on the morning of May 21, Augur moved toward the junction of the Plains Store and Bayou Sara roads to pave the way for Banks's landing. As the advance cavalry under Grierson approached the woods marking the southern edge of the Port Hudson plain, it encountered a detachment of the Fourteenth Arkansas Infantry, led by Colonel F. P. Powers, a small cavalry force, and Abbay's Mississippi Battery. Brisk skirmishing now followed. By ten o'clock the main Federal force had moved up to the plain, but found the way blocked by the brisk fire from the Mississippi battery. Dudley sent forward some of his artillery and attempted to dislodge the Confederate guns. For two hours the artillery duel continued. For most of the Federal troops, this was their first time under fire, and they ducked and dodged at the sound of the shells shrieking overhead. When wounded men and bleeding horses were seen coming from the front line, many of the troops felt their first great fear of battle.

At noon General Gardner ordered Colonel W. R. Miles to proceed with four hundred men and Boone's Louisiana Light Battery to relieve Powers, who was being hard pressed by the greater Federal force. Taking a long detour through the woods, Miles was able to move up undetected. All was now quiet. Dudley moved his men to the Port Hudson road and ordered his command to bivouac for the night. The Forty-eighth Massachusetts was sent up the road to support one section of artillery. The other Federal regiments bivouacked below Plains Store on the Bayou Sara road. Hardly had the command begun its bivouac when rapid artillery fire was heard in the front. The Forty-ninth Massachusetts and the One Hundred Sixteenth New York were ordered immediately to go to the support of the Forty-eighth Massachusetts. They had gone but a short distance, when a heavy musketry fire opened on their immediate front and a horde of panic-stricken troops broke through the bushes into the ranks of the Forty-ninth, causing great consternation.

Colonel Miles threw out two companies on his right under Major James T. Coleman and three on the left under Lieutenant Colonel F. B. Brand. Coleman first drew the fire of the Federal artillery section, but rushing through an apple orchard, he charged the guns, killed the horses, and scattered the gunners. The terrified Forty-eighth Massachusetts immediately broke and stampeded to the rear. Colonel William Bartlett of the Forty-ninth Massachusetts ordered his men to hold their position, and when the Confederate artillery fire became too hot, he ordered them to lie down. With so few men, Coleman found it impossible to advance his line.

Possessed by a mounting terror, the Forty-eighth Massachusetts rushed back past the One Hundred Sixteenth New York. This regiment, hemmed in by the dense forest, had no knowledge of the situation to the front, but firmly held its ground. Later, forming in line, the regiment advanced. Meanwhile, Colonel Brand had flanked the entire three regiments and had come up behind the One Hundred Sixteenth New York. Brand opened a heavy volley of musket fire upon the regiment. Immediately the One Hundred Sixteenth about-faced and returned the fire. Yelling at the tops of their lungs, the men of the One Hundred Sixteenth rushed toward Brand, driving him out of the forest, across an open field, and into another belt of woods. A second charge dislodged the Confederates and ended the battle of Plains Store.

Faced by an overwhelmingly superior force, Colonel Miles withdrew his men within the entrenchments of Port Hudson. Miles counted his losses and reported eighty-nine killed, wounded, and missing. The Union forces reported 100 casualties: 15 men killed, 71 wounded, and 14 captured. A much larger number of men were temporarily missing before the report was issued, but were apprehended trying to slip back to Baton Rouge and brought back to the front.[5]

At 2 A.M., May 22, Banks and Grover landed unopposed at Bayou Sara and were followed by the rest of the troops from Morganza as fast as transports could be provided. A cavalry detachment sent out by Augur soon appeared at Bayou Sara with news of the battle of Plains Store and Banks was informed that Augur was at the moment engaged in a new skirmish with the Confederates. Despite a violent storm, Banks pushed forward to Augur's assistance, only to find the skirmish ended.

Banks and Grover then bivouacked on Thompson's Creek, northwest of Port Hudson. Paine soon followed and camped one mile in the rear of Grover at the Perkins plantation. T. W. Sherman, who had come up from New Orleans, reached Springfield Landing on the same day, May 22, and posted his men on Augur's left and to the south of Port Hudson. By nightfall of the twenty-second, Port Hudson was virtually surrounded.[6]

The next few days Banks spent in reconnoitering the Confederate line. A Confederate cavalry and an infantry force commanded by Colonel I. G. W. Steedman of the First Alabama was assigned the task of making this reconnaissance as ineffectual as possible. Heavy skirmishing between the rival forces continued until the night of May 24, when Steedman fell back behind his fortifications.

Steedman immediately realized the weaknesses of the works in the sector assigned to him. On the left, for a distance of three fourths of a mile to within five hundred yards of the Mississippi, there was not a rifle pit dug nor a gun mounted. A hasty appeal to Gardner brought the chief engineer, all of the available tools, and Negro laborers to the area, and through the night the task of filling in the gap was pushed. By morning four guns were mounted on Commissary Hill, and a series of rifle pits had been started. Tuesday the Negroes sweated to complete a line of shallow rifle pits to protect the left wing. Tuesday night two heavy pieces of artillery were moved from the river batteries and mounted on the rear left line. In open areas earthworks had to be constructed under fire from enemy sharpshooters.

On Monday, May 25, Paine's, Weitzel's, and Dwight's brigades, led by Weitzel, pushed through the woods and attacked the position held by the First Alabama, but nothing was gained by either side. Lower down on the Confederate right, Colonel W. R. Miles successfully turned back two strong attacks made by Augur's infantry and cavalry. This same day Negro troops were advanced to Sandy Creek and set to work on a pontoon bridge which they completed the next day. A detachment of the Seventh Illinois Cavalry, two companies of the Thirty-first Massachusetts, and a section of artillery proceeded to Thompson's Creek and there seized two steamers, the *Starlight* and *Red Chief,* a flatboat, and twenty-five prisoners. This capture helped to disrupt Confederate transportation.

Already Steedman had lost forty men in killed, wounded, and missing. After reinforcing his line of skirmishers in anticipation of an early morning attack, he ordered his men to sleep on their arms. Banks earlier that night had sent a formal demand to Gardner asking him to surrender the post and thus avoid further shedding of blood. Gardner flatly refused. There was little doubt now that morning would bring a general assault.

Some two miles above Port Hudson the Mississippi River abandoned its southward course and curved in an eastwardly direction, striking the high bluff on which the village had been built and then turning south again. The bluff extended a few hundred yards above Port Hudson and then dropped off into a ravine, beyond which was a narrow, saw-tooth ridge. A short distance away was Sandy Creek, which meandered over a large portion of the Confederate enclosure. To the northwest was an extensive marsh and dense canebrake. Through this swamp ran Thompson's Creek.

A mile and a half below Port Hudson the bluff was gashed by a ravine some three hundred yards wide. The ravine followed a winding course in a northwesterly direction toward the village.

Inland and east of the village a plateau extended to large fields, through which ran roads to Jackson, Clinton, Bayou Sara, and Baton Rouge. Northward, the ground dropped off into a series of ravines covered with heavy woods, until it reached Sandy Creek. A railroad ran through the area to Clinton, several miles to the northeast.

Two and a half miles below Port Hudson, near Ross Landing, an irregular line of parapet and ditch was begun. This line, describing a slight arc, traversed a series of broken ridges, ravines, and plateaus for three quarters of a mile from the river. For the next mile and a quarter the line followed the wide level plain of Gibbon's and Slaughter's cotton fields. The next quarter of a mile led through deep, irregular declivities and, three quarters of a mile beyond, through fields and hills to a deep gorge, traversed by a branch of Sandy Creek. The semicircular line ran for another mile and a half along the swamp to the river above the village. This line had only reached the broken ground at the Clinton road on the north when Banks began his siege. The area beyond was considered impassable and had been neglected until Colonel Steedman discovered that although military operations here would be difficult, attack was imminent. Gardner rushed to fill in the vulnerable gap with shallow rifle pits and gun emplacements. The breastworks on the south were well built, but those on the northern extremity were of the most expedient construction. Inside the works was a narrow ditch with small caves scooped out along its sides to shelter the men from enemy fire. Hospitals nestled in the deep ravines.

Along the inland line twenty-two pieces of field artillery and redans
were distributed. On the Confederate left wing there were nine batteries;
on the center there were eight; and on the right wing there were five
guns. During the long siege several heavy guns were switched from
the river front to the land defenses and simulated guns made from
logs were put in their positions along the river to deceive the Federal
fleet.

Defending the water approaches were eleven embrasures, each built
in the form of a pentagon-shaped arc. In three of these, pivot guns could
be used to cover the river or could be swung around to use against land
forces in the rear. There were thirty guns ranging in caliber from a
4-inch Parrott to a 10-inch Columbiad. These guns were able to sweep
the river and pour a plunging fire into an enemy ship trying to run the
gantlet.

Although the proper defense of the works called for at least 15,000
men, General Gardner had less than half this many troops, about 7,000,
inside Port Hudson after Pemberton began to draw them off to
strengthen the defenses of Vicksburg. Some 1,200 additional Confederate
troops were located at Clinton and other nearby areas.

Gardner placed Colonel Steedman in command of the left wing and
all the river defenses. Later this command was taken over and ably
executed by Lieutenant Colonel M. B. Locke. There were so few
men to hold the left wing that they were stationed five feet apart in
single file. Beall defended the center, and Miles commanded the right
wing.

The Union line, stretching some six miles from one bank of the
river to the other and describing an arc to the front of the Confederate
forces, was held on the extreme right by Weitzel, then by Paine and
Grover, with Augur in the center and T. W. Sherman on the extreme
left wing. At Port Hudson, General Banks had between 30,000 and
40,000 men under his command between May and July of 1863. That
figure, of course, varied from day to day, and the effective strength was
something less than that.[7]

Above and below, in the river, the Union navy helped to complete
the investment of Port Hudson. Below, off Profit Island, Farragut
commanded five gunboats and the mortar fleet. Around the bend, above
Port Hudson, Commander James S. Palmer was in charge of five additional gunboats. Small Federal picket boats at night roamed the river
to spy on Confederate activity. Banks had requested Farragut to use
his mortars at night to prevent the enemy's rest.

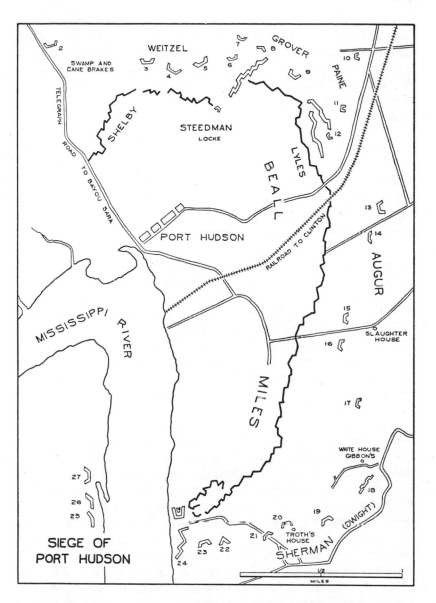

Although the Union forces did not attempt another reconnaissance in force on May 26, they were far from idle. In every regiment men were kept busy preparing fascines (bundles of sticks and branches about six to eight feet long, tied with grapevines) to be carried to the ravine in front and thrown in to facilitate the crossing of the main force. Much time was spent in canvassing the regiments for volunteers to serve in the "forlorn hope" group. One half of these men were to run out of the woods with their fascines, poles, or planks, bridge the ditch in front of the Confederate breastworks and then return to safety while the other half crossed the bridge and stormed the works at the point of the bayonet.

That night Banks called together his division commanders to plan the assault of the next day. The morale of the officers and men of the Nineteenth Army Corps had reached a new high. They were all confident that Port Hudson would be taken.

Brigadier General Richard Arnold was assigned command of the reserve artillery and was to open fire at dawn on the Confederate works. During a concerted attack all along the line, Weitzel was to drive into the works. If the opportunity presented itself the other division commanders were to force their way into Port Hudson too. While a specific time for the grand assault was not set, it was understood that the movement would be simultaneous.[8]

As the soft dawn light began to seep through the dense magnolia forest, the Federal artillery opened up all along the line. Gardner's guns answered the furious cannonade but soon slowed down to conserve ammunition. From the river the guns of the navy joined in the crescendo, hurling shot and shell toward the water batteries and into Port Hudson itself.

In the dense woods Weitzel waited. At six o'clock he was sure that Grover and Augur on his left had already begun their assault although he could not see them nor could he communicate with them through the intervening forest and thickets. Forming his men in columns of brigades, he advanced through the magnolia forest toward the front. Colonel Jacob Van Zandt, commanding Dwight's brigade, led off followed by Colonel Stephen Thomas, leading Weitzel's brigade. With regimental banners held high the blue-coated troops marched out of the shadows of the forest into the sunlight. On the immediate left, Brigadier General Halbert E. Paine sent forward the second brigade of his division, led by Colonel Hawkes Fearing, to support Weitzel. Paine's third brigade under Colonel O. P. Gooding was held in reserve.

The ravines and woods in front of the Confederate works were occupied by Steedman's outpost and skirmishers under Lieutenant Colonel

M. B. Locke. As soon as the enemy came within range, the fighting became severe. The thin scattering of Confederate sharpshooters, firing rapidly from the cover of logs, ravines, and trees, cut a deadly swath through the massed advancing column. On they came. Closing ranks, they stepped over their dead and wounded. Running, sliding, and slipping down the embankments, Weitzel's and Paine's men entered the broken ground and maze of fallen timber, forcing the Confederates back. After more than an hour of furious fighting, Locke was forced to retire his men behind the main works. As soon as the skirmishers had reached safety, the four guns on Commissary Hill opened fire on Weitzel's men. Thomas' brigade found its sector easier to traverse, and it moved ahead of Van Zandt. Deploying his men in a regimental line from right to left (the One Hundred Sixtieth New York, the Eighth Vermont, the Twelfth Connecticut, and the Seventy-fifth New York), Thomas moved forward. Because of the rugged terrain Van Zandt drifted too far to the right, and Paine quickly moved in to fill the gap. In front of Steedman's works, felled timbers, laced and crisscrossed in the ravines, made any type of attack difficult if not impossible. Thomas found his advance slowed to a snail's pace. Any of his men who ventured beyond the cover of the ravines and trees was greeted by a withering fusillade of rifle fire, shrapnel, canister, and shell. Inching their way through the labyrinth of brush-choked ravines, creeping low over the hills, and climbing over the fallen tree trunks, they found it impossible to keep ranks. Weitzel finally reached and held a ridge some two hundred yards from Steedman's works. Sharpshooters left the ridge, crept up near the Confederate batteries, and began to snipe at the cannoneers with deadly accuracy. The fallen timber furnished good cover for the sharpshooters. Several charges against the works were tried by individual units, but they were driven back with fearful loss. On the left, Colonel Fearing of Paine's division ordered his front line, composed of the One Hundred Thirty-third and the One Hundred Seventy-third New York, to charge, but their line was soon broken and scattered. The Eighth New Hampshire and Fourth Wisconsin, composing the second line, swept forward over their fallen comrades and succeeded in driving the enemy skirmishers from their outer fortifications across the eroded ground and the slash into their works. When support failed to come up, Fearing's most advanced troops were forced to retreat to a more sheltered position.

Here they continued to fire for the rest of the day whenever a Confederate gunner or rifleman showed his head. Fearing's casualties were heavy, but so were those of the Tenth Arkansas which occupied the position directly in front of him. Sweating pioneers labored to open up entrance lanes through the abatis and thicket-clogged ravines for the artillery. Soon Duryea's, Nims's, Haley's, Bainbridge's, and Carruth's batteries were placed on the ridge beside Weitzel and were opening up on Steedman's position.

On the left, some six hundred yards away and slightly to the rear of Weitzel, Paine had advanced his men. Grover on Paine's left, sent two of his regiments, the One Hundred Fifty-ninth New York and the Twenty-fifth Connecticut, by a roundabout route to aid Weitzel. Slowly scrambling through a ravine cut by a branch of Sandy Creek, these two regiments made their way to the foot of a high bluff just to the left front of Paine. Forming at its base, the two regiments, shouting at the tops of their lungs, rushed up the steep hill to its crest, where they were met by a murderous flank fire from Steedman's rifles. The two regiments, only thirty yards from the works, were forced to fall back and seek cover.

By this time a portion of Thomas' men had crossed another arm of Sandy Creek and, after driving back the skirmishers, had moved up a hill on Weitzel's right, where they began constructing a fortification by rolling logs into position. Later this works was named Fort Babcock in honor of the commander of the Seventy-fifth New York. By noon all of the Confederates had been driven in, and during the afternoon Thomas' sharpshooters to the front made life grim for Steedman's men.

General Dwight, who had assumed command over the colored troops on the far Federal right earlier in the day, sought to create a diversion for Weitzel by ordering Colonel John A. Nelson, with his two Negro regiments, to move against the extreme Confederate left where the line bent back southward toward the river. This segment of the line nestled atop a steep bluff surveying the low land adjacent to the sugarhouse, where Foster's Creek was crossed by the telegraph road. On this bluff was Colonel W. B. Shelby with six companies of the Thirty-ninth Mississippi. To the front and at a lower elevation was a second imposing bluff extending from the main elevation for four hundred yards then returning in an abrupt right turn to the parent bluff. This formidable, natural outwork was occupied by Lieutenant T. C. Rhodes and one of Shelby's companies plus fifteen men from Wingfield's Battalion, a total of sixty men. Two batteries of six field guns were ranged along the line, and from the river front the traverse Columbiads covered all approaches to the outwork.

Around seven, Nelson ordered the First Louisiana Native Guards, made up of free Negroes of French extraction, forward followed closely by the Third Louisiana Native Guards, composed of former slaves. Two pieces of artillery were sent across Thompson's Creek, but as they were being placed in position, a single Confederate gun on the heights opened up with solid shot upon them. So effective was the fire that the guns were hastily limbered and withdrawn back across the creek after firing only one shot. From the bluff behind the lower ridge the field artillery now opened with shrapnel and shell upon the Negro troops as they floundered across the creek and up the opposite bank. The Negroes filed to the right under a cover of willows, formed their battle lines, and began advancing. From the lower ridge Rhodes and his sixty men opened a rapid rifle fire upon their clearly visible targets, throwing the Negroes into confusion and disorder. On they came, a horde of screaming, shouting blacks. When they were within two hundred yards of the extreme Confederate left, the Columbiads from the river opened an enfilade fire. Then all of the guns began to fire canister, and without orders, Shelby's infantry on the bluff began blazing away as fast as they could reload. The Negroes fired one volley, but as the shot began to drop thick among their ranks, the First Regiment broke in great disorder and fell back upon the Third Louisiana Native Guards, then in the process of fording the creek. Some of the Negroes held their ground and attempted to swim across a pool of backwater from the river to the base of the bluff. The few who made it were mowed down by the riflemen. All attempts to halt the frightened, demoralized troops failed. They thrashed wildly across the creek and fled to the sugarhouse beyond the north bank, where they were finally halted. After some difficulty the two regiments were re-formed, and their white officers awaited new orders from Dwight, but orders never came. They waited until nightfall and then retired.

This portion of the battle had the distinction of being the first engagement of any magnitude between white and Negro troops in the war. Just a few more than 1,000 Negroes, without support, were ordered to take one of the strongest natural positions along the entire line. Their conduct surprised their worst critics in the Union ranks, and their bravery and dash more than pleased their strongest supporters. Evaluations of their conduct vary widely, however, and there seems to be evidence both of unusual bravery and of unjustified cowardice. Since the Third Regiment of Native Guards barely got into action, about 500 men bore the brunt of the battle, and among these there were 308 casualties—37 killed, 155 wounded, and 116 missing—the highest percentage of losses of the day. Not a single man was lost by Shelby.

To divert a Confederate concentration on Weitzel's front, Grover sent his three regiments, the Twelfth Maine and Thirteenth and Twenty-fifth Connecticut, against the west face of the bastion at the northernmost point of the finished Confederate line. This point of attack was some five-eighths of a mile to the left of Weitzel's position. As with Weitzel and Paine, these regiments found it impossible to maintain their organizations in the slash and underbrush, and soon the lines became a confused mass of men from separate commands. Despite heavy losses, a few of the men pushed on to the parapets but the lethal fire from above drove them back. The men took cover wherever they could find it, realizing after three hours that their isolated efforts were fruitless.

Now came a lull. Weitzel continued to hold the advanced positions he had seized but made no new attempt to assault the works. Grover now joined Weitzel for a conference, and the two decided to wait until Augur assaulted the center or Sherman moved against the left before they renewed their drive on the right.

Augur was ready. His men waited under arms for the command to move forward, a command which would be issued as soon as Sherman put in his men. Unable to understand the delay, Banks rode to Sherman's headquarters and found the general and his staff seated in his tent calmly eating lunch. Enraged, Banks gave Sherman a dressing down and rode back to his headquarters to send his chief of staff, Brigadier General George L. Andrews, to replace Sherman. When Andrews arrived, he found Sherman astride his horse ready to lead his men into battle. Keeping silent, Andrews allowed Sherman to retain his command. At a quarter past two Sherman moved out.

On the right, the Fourteenth Maine, its men acting as skirmishers, was followed in column of regiments by the Twenty-fourth Maine, the One Hundred Seventy-seventh New York, and the One Hundred Sixty-fifth New York. These troops, under Nickerson, moved out of the forest into the clearing to the front. His right terminated on the road running past the smoldering ruins of the Slaughter plantation house. Immediately on the left, General Dow, with the Sixth Michigan leading, followed by the Fifteenth New Hampshire, Twenty-sixth Connecticut, and One Hundred Twenty-eighth New York, advanced to the front. Dow's extreme left extended down to the Gibbons' house. Sandwiched between the two brigades rode Sherman with his entire staff.

Beall, in command of the Confederate center, around two o'clock began to detect signs of an imminent attack. Hasty preparations were made to repulse this assault. At best, Beall had only a thin line of defenders, and at certain points there were stretches with no men at all. Some of his men had been sent earlier to strengthen Steedman but could not be recalled in time. Quickly Beall called upon Colonel Miles on his right for assistance. Miles's Legion barely arrived in time to meet the assault. Each man was armed with a rifle and a shotgun.

Sherman's men charged out of the woods on the double-quick onto the level plain stretching hundreds of yards to the front. Slightly to the front of his command rode General Sherman and his staff. A pioneer corps made up of three hundred Negro engineers led the way, carrying green, rough poles about six inches thick and up to twenty-five feet long. These poles were so heavy that several Negroes had to shoulder them. The "forlorn hope," made up of volunteers from the several regiments, followed the Negroes, carrying planks two inches thick, a foot wide, and five feet long. Without protection, the Negroes were to advance over the open field near the Slaughter house to the wide ditch which supposedly lay at the foot of Beall's works and there to place their poles in position, about four feet apart. Then the board carriers would move up, lay their planks in position, and thus form a bridge to the base of the parapet. There was no abatis, and except for a few shallow plantation ditches crossing the fields, the way was smooth. When the Federal advance got within range, Beall's artillery ran its guns into position and opened up a shower of grape, shot, and canister. One of the first casualties was General Sherman. Down went his horse. The general rolled clear, but one of his legs was shattered. He was carried to the rear. Moments later two members of his staff were shot from their horses.

The increased tempo of the Confederate guns caused great confusion in the Federal ranks but failed to halt the advance. Four rail fences lay across the fields, and as the troops moved toward the parapet, these fences were charged and flattened, adding to the confusion of commands. The frightened Negroes, prodded by the white plank carriers, struggled halfway across the field in the face of the terrible fire. Seeing some of their comrades fall, all of the Negroes threw down their poles and fell flat on the earth. No amount of urging could rally them. Some darted to the rear like frightened rabbits, and others hid behind any cover they could find. The "forlorn hope" now threw away their useless boards, and they too sought cover in the ditches and behind stumps and began to fire back at the enemy.

Each of Beall's infantrymen carried sixty rounds of ammunition and, as Sherman's men drew nearer, the Confederates fired their rifles as fast as they could reload. The cannoneers loaded their pieces with double charges of canister and fired into the face of the advancing enemy. Running short of grape and shot, some of Beall's men gleaned spent bullets and scraps of iron from the parapet. Cutting the sleeves from their shirts and underwear, they dumped the scrap metal into them, tied up the ends, and loaded these bags into the guns. The blazing guns caused the blue-coated ranks to waver and break. Again and again the men were rallied, but each time they tried to advance, they suffered heavy losses.

One of Nickerson's regiments, the One Hundred Sixty-fifth New York Zouaves, in their red, baggy pantaloons and tasseled red caps charged across the extreme right of Slaughter's field. Their bright uniforms made easy targets, and they were mowed down by the score. On they came until they approached close to the works. They were ordered to lie down, but before this order could be executed, their colonel was felled by a bullet. The men now broke and fled some six hundred yards to a ditch in the rear.

When Sherman fell wounded on the field, the command of the left wing should have been assumed by Dow, but before he learned of Sherman's injury, Dow himself suffered a similar fate. He was struck by a spent ball, and his arm became so swollen he could not handle his horse. Dismounting, he proceeded on foot until he was struck in the left thigh by a rifle ball and had to be helped to a hospital in the rear. Nickerson, next in order of command, inherited the title, but in the heat of battle no one bothered to notify him. Consequently, for a long period there was no commander to assume complete control. As the afternoon wore on, officer casualties became heavier. Colonel Cowles of the One Hundred Twenty-eighth New York was killed. Two successive commanders of the One Hundred Sixty-fifth New York were cut down. Lieutenant Colonel Abel Smith was mortally wounded, and Major Carr was seriously wounded. There would be others before the fight closed.

By now most of the order was gone. Isolated regiments and companies charged and recharged without success. Men began to act on their own initiative, loading and firing whenever a target appeared on the parapet. All were now seeking shelter, hiding behind stumps and fallen trees on the field or diving into the big ravine on the right which led up to the enemy's works. Dow's men, who were nearer the woods, by 4:30 P.M. were able to fall back to their original position. Some of Nickerson's men, singly and in groups, made it to the safety of the deep ravine, and others remained on the field, lying down behind the logs and stumps until nightfall. From the safety of the woods in the rear General Andrews, who had now taken command, attempted to form his men for a new assault but was unable to rally a sufficient number. Sherman's efforts had accomplished nothing but slaughter for his men.

The Plains Store road led across the field to a sally port flanked by sharp angles. The Confederate infantry and artillery were able to cover the entire area with a concentrated fire. The field in Augur's front was about an eighth of a mile long and wide. A skirt of woods bounded the east and south; there was an open area to the north; and on the west was the breastworks. Little of the field was smooth. Part of the area to the front was covered with big stumps and felled trees inter- laced with a heavy undergrowth. Over this formidable abatis, in the face of the enemy fire power, Augur's men were expected to charge and take the Confederate works. The road was the only place along the line where the going was smooth.

As soon as Augur heard the noise of Sherman's attack on the left, he put forward his division. Chapin's brigade ranged across the Plains Store road, and Dudley's brigade was held in reserve. On the left side of the road skirmishers from the Twenty-first Maine led off, followed by the "forlorn hope" column of two hundred volunteers under Lieutenant Colonel O'Brien of the Forty-eighth Massachusetts. The One Hundred Sixteenth New York, the Forty-ninth Massachusetts, the Forty-eighth Massachusetts, the Second Louisiana, from Dudley's brigade, and the remainder of the Twenty-first Maine were deployed from right to left on the right side of the road.

All was quiet until the advance had completely emerged from the woods along the road, then all hell broke loose. Grape, canister, shot, and shell filled the air and dropped among the heavily burdened fascine bearers. The thud of metal striking flesh, sharp outcries of the wounded, and the gasps of the dying could be heard above the cannons' roar. Wheeling to the right off the road, the forlorn hope began advancing across the field. As they moved forward, the field became more rough. Crossing a deep ditch they approached the abatis. With their unwieldy bundles the fascine bearers attempted to climb over or to go around the felled timber. Every move was made with the greatest difficulty. Confederate sharpshooters took unerring aim from the parapet ahead. A hail of Minié balls, solid shot, and canister thinned the ranks of the bearers and of the storming party with every step. Now, within forty rods of the enemy, the bearers began to toss aside their fascines and to drop down under the cover of the stumps and slashings. The skirmishers followed suit, occasionally rising to fire a shot at the men ranged along the breastworks.

The main columns now left the woods and advanced on the double over the small smooth area to the broken ground ahead. The Confederates increased their rate of fire, and dozens of blue-coated men went down in the soft dust. The advance slowed considerably on reaching the log-choked area, and soon the main line of attackers became inextricable from the storming group. Colonel Chapin, in a dress coat and white Panama hat, was clearly marked as a commander and was shot through the brain. Unlike Weitzel and Sherman, Augur patterned his personal action after that of Grover, remaining far back in the shelter of the magnolias and making no attempt to lead his men personally. Only one of Augur's officers rode into battle, Colonel W. F. Bartlett, who had only one leg. Like Sherman, Bartlett was soon cut down.

The fire became so severe that soon the main line, including the officers, began to drop behind every available shelter in the shallow ravines. The Confederates slackened their fire, and about an hour later, Colonel O'Brien sprang up, waving his sword and ordering his men to charge. Less than a dozen men responded, and in a half minute O'Brien fell dead. The few men who had risen now lay down again. This was the last attempt to storm the works on May 27.

Augur's men hugged the ground, not daring to raise their heads. The fallen timber was strewn with bloody corpses and with the wounded. The groans of those who had been hit added to the fear of those who were yet uninjured. Everyone suffered heavily from the burning sun and from extreme thirst. None of the troops got beyond the abatis. Augur had failed.

At five o'clock all firing ceased. A stick topped with a white handkerchief had mysteriously risen from one of the ravines within the abatis. While an investigation was being made to determine the origin and purpose of the white flag, the Confederates laid down their rifles and crowded atop their parapets to see what was going on. A number of the Union troops rose up from their shelters and fled back to the woods. Stretcher bearers appeared and began moving their bleeding burdens off the field. It was soon discovered that the flag had been raised by a colonel from one of the New York regiments who found himself in a precarious position to the front of the rest of the troops. Upon hearing this, the Confederates resumed their fire and kept it up until dark.

With the coming of night the medical corps and details from various regiments began to roam the abatis looking for the wounded. Singly and in small groups all along the line the Union troops left their hiding and found their way to the rear. Whisky was passed out by some of the commanders to their men as they came in.

A fire broke out in the abatis, and the wounded who still had not been carried from the field were in danger of being roasted alive. As the flames began to mount, the Federal troops shuddered over the plight of their fallen comrades, but they were afraid to venture into the area again. Slipping out of their works, the Confederates extinguished the fires, partly out of humanity and partly to preserve their own protective abatis. "The piteous cries of 'water,' 'water,' from hundreds of the enemy's wounded, and the groans of the dying now touched with deepest sympathy those with whom they had but today been locked in deadly strife," reported a man from the First Alabama. Risking the fire of the Union pickets, a number of Confederates carried canteens to the fallen enemy. When a report came that many excellent Enfield rifles had been abandoned on the field, the Alabama men swarmed out and picked up these rifles.[9]

The night held other horrors yet. In their tents to the rear the surgeons worked feverishly all night with the wounded. A man from the Forty-ninth Massachusetts described the scene: "On the operating table were the victims, whose shrieks of agony, but partially deadened by chloroform, illy prepared the wounded all around them for *their* hours of martyrdom. Seeing the doctors with sleeves rolled up, splashed with blood, here a pile of booted legs, there a pile of arms, was more trying than the horrors of the battlefield."[10]

The next morning the Confederates opened the fire, but soon after, Banks raised a flag of truce and requested permission to care for his wounded and to bury his dead. All was quiet. While Federal officers and men roamed the fields and abatis searching for their fallen comrades, they made hasty surveys of the Confederate works. After interring their own dead, the Confederates mounted the parapet and chatted with the Federal search parties. The dark, sunburned Southerners, dressed in filthy reddish homespun and wearing wool hats with broad brims, watched the burial details. Immense trenches were dug near the Confederate works, and into each one of these the burial parties piled a hundred bodies and covered them over. Some of the dead were missed in the tangled abatis, and no attempt was made to bury the horses and animals that had been killed. These bodies, human and animal alike, lay in the hot sun until the stench became unbearable. Soon the buzzards gathered.

Wherever Banks held an advanced position, he set large details of men to work on a series of breastworks behind which his men could stand and fire safely at the enemy. Gun emplacements were also deepened and buttressed, in violation of his truce with Gardner.

At 7 P.M. the white flags were withdrawn and all men disappeared. For an hour a heavy fire was opened by both sides, and periodically through the night the Union batteries continued to throw shells toward the Confederate works.

May 27 was a terrible Union blunder. The failure of the commanders to charge simultaneously the thinly held Confederate works cost them heavily. This piecemeal attack allowed the Confederates to shift their men from one point to another and to repel any new attack. The lack of clarity in Banks's orders was partly responsible, but at least one of the division commanders, Sherman, who opposed the assault, willfully chose to misinterpret his instructions and to delay his attack until he was personally ordered to get under way. It was then too late to save the day.

Banks totaled his losses. Out of an effective force of 13,000 men the Union had suffered 1,995 casualties. A total of 293, including 15 officers, were killed; 1,545 were wounded, of which 90 were officers; among those missing were 2 officers and 155 enlisted men. Almost as serious in outcome was the fact that the strong confidence that the men had felt a short time before was now destroyed. They would never again respect the ability of General Banks and some of the other officers as greatly as they had in the past. By comparison, Gardner had suffered little from the assault. He had lost only about 235 in killed, wounded, and missing out of just over 4,000 effectives. Even more important, the morale of the Confederate troops soared to new heights after the abortive Federal assault.[11]

The bloody repulse of May 27 convinced Banks that he must resort to siege tactics and dig or construct gradual approaches toward the breastworks. He immediately called in all of the troops that he had left behind to guard the Teche and the Atchafalaya. General Emory at New Orleans was ordered to send "all armed negro troops now at N.O. . . . to Springfield Landing immediately." On June 1 Banks directed the provost marshal at Baton Rouge to send him "all the able bodied negroes in, and around Baton Rouge, that can be spared. Also all the stragglers that can be found." General Ullmann was requested to "forward to this point all the troops which he has raised whether armed or unarmed. . . ." [12] To build up his strength Banks begged Grant to lend him 5,000 or 10,000 men. With such additions he expected to reduce Port Hudson in one day.

Since Banks had suffered heavy casualties among his officers, some commands from the company level through that of the division had to be shifted or strengthened. Banks, too, had to assign positions along the line to the newly arriving troops. The disposition of the Federal force now had Weitzel on the extreme right, Grover next to him, followed by Paine and Augur. Dwight, who had been given Sherman's division, was on the extreme left.

Banks allowed most of his men a short period of rest. On May 30 detachments of contrabands were set to work throwing up breastworks to shelter the artillery. The Confederates were also busy constructing new works to protect their guns. Throughout the next few days there was much cannonading on both sides, and the pickets and sharpshooters kept up a continuous fire. On either side, when a man carelessly showed himself, a shower of rifle balls tore up the ground around him. Every night the mortar boats threw hundreds of shells into Port Hudson. By day the gunboats took over and kept up a constant, harassing fire.

By June 1 siege operations were begun in earnest. The woods were filled with axes, shovels, picks, wheelbarrows, and other tools. Timber was felled, hewed, and lugged to the front to be used in building platforms and breastworks. Night and day for the next two weeks all of the regiments were engaged in digging rifle pits and zigzags, constructing breastworks and covered ways, and mounting guns. In places, the Federal works were within seventy-five yards of the Confederate line. The Confederates, too, continued to strengthen their works. Rarely now did the Confederates fire their cannon. They were conserving ammunition.

Life for the Federal soldier settled into a routine. The cycle consisted of one day of duty on the parapet and two days off. On the right, tiers of logs were laid along the crest of the low ridge. Notches were cut in the logs to provide portholes for the sharpshooters and observers. Cotton bales were often rolled up to the front and, behind this protection, the men began digging rifle pits, with a capacity of a dozen men, behind these log works. The pits were made deep enough to conceal standing men. Leading from the pits to the rear was a trench of the same depth to allow the men to pass freely without being exposed to enemy fire. These breastworks were six or more feet high on the inside and from thirty to a hundred feet long, the length being determined by the number of guns to be placed there. There were no tents in the front lines, but the Federal troops built lean-tos of branches in the gullies to shelter themselves from the burning sun. When it rained, they threw their rubber blankets over the roof to keep dry. Some of the men dug holes in the sides of the hills and ravines and spread their rubber sheets over the mouths of these caves.

Sutlers were not long in following the Union men to the front and were soon supplying them with cheese, tobacco, and gingerbread at inflationary prices. The men found a vendor with plenty of whisky, and business was brisk.

Constantly in the open and exposed to the hot rays of the sun, many of the troops began wearing wide-brimmed straw hats. Unfortunately, the Confederates found these hats good targets, and the men had to return to their regulation caps, which gave no protection to the back of the neck. The men in the ravines and trenches near the front suffered from lack of exercise and of good drinking water, and from the horrible odor of the half-buried bodies.

Although there were mosquitoes at Port Hudson, the men did not find them as bloodthirsty as those in the Teche region. The most troublesome insect was a small black bug, a snapping beetle, which would crawl into the ear of a sleeping man, driving him from his nap in a crazy frenzy of pain. Most of the soldiers soon learned to thwart these bugs by stuffing their ears with cotton each night.

All cooking had to be done some three quarters of a mile in the rear, and the food was brought to the front and distributed to the troops by Negroes and band members. They crossed the open fields unmolested by the Confederate sharpshooters. Coffee, hard tack, and fried salt meat were the chief staples served.

The men became dirty and ragged beyond belief. All clothing except that on their backs was left behind at Brashear, Baton Rouge, or Camp Parapet. There was only a small supply of warm, brackish swamp water to drink, and no water for washing clothes or skins. Almost every day and sometimes at night rain fell, and the soldiers received a soaking that temporarily relieved their uniforms of some of the grime and mud. When the sun came out, the men stripped, wrung out their soggy clothes, and threw them over a bush to dry. Shaving was next to impossible, since there was no water and no barber tools. Hair grew long and often went uncombed for a week or more. Some of the men had blankets, but many had lost theirs or tossed them away on a forced march.

To relieve the deadly monotony of trench life, the men slept, talked, or played cards, and a number of the regiments resorted to nightly sessions of hymn singing. General Paine was annoyed by the practice and ordered the Forty-ninth Massachusetts, camped near his head-quarters, to stop singing hymns. General Augur, located near the Negro camp, allowed the Negroes to sing and dance as much as they liked. There was some jealousy between the Negroes and whites be-cause some of the Negroes had their wives or women with them and the white troops did not.

Gradually the siege works moved forward, forming a tighter ring around the Confederate works. Negro engineers rolled cotton bales up to the front and advanced the saps closer to Gardner's fortress. Planks and cotton bags were placed over trenches and ravines, forming covered ways close to the parapets.[13]

Outside of Port Hudson, the Confederate cavalry and mounted in-fantry was doing what it could to relieve the Federal pressure on the besieged post. In the latter part of May, Colonel F. P. Powers of the Fourteenth Arkansas learned that a foraging expedition under a cavalry escort, numbering four hundred strong, had been sent by Banks toward Clinton. Powers posted his men in the edge of the forest along the road, and a mountain howitzer was masked to cover the approach. As the unsuspecting expedition approached the ambush, a howitzer shell burst over their heads, and with a bloodcurdling Rebel yell the Con-federates charged the enemy. The bewildered cavalry escort fired a few shots and then "skedaddled," leaving forty new wagons, their teams, and their drivers to the Confederates.

A few days later Powers sent Major Thomas R. Stockdale with his battalion of mounted Mississippi troops to make a feint against Banks's rear at Port Hudson. Stockdale struck the camp of the Fourteenth New

York Metropolitan Regiment, eight hundred strong, mostly foreigners, which had arrived three days before from New Orleans. At this early hour most of the camp was still asleep, and the wild rush of Stockdale's two hundred and fifty men caught them completely unprepared. The Confederates fired into the tents, screaming like wild Indians as they rode by. Some of the foreigners were able to escape, but those who were surrounded were so demoralized that they went down on their knees begging for mercy in a foreign tongue. Prisoners were quickly disarmed and sent back to Clinton.

Powers, who had accompanied the expedition, remained behind with Stockdale to strip the camp. A torch was set to the tents, and as the blaze mounted Grierson's cavalry appeared. His mission accomplished, Powers retreated to Clinton, and Grierson did not attempt to stop him. A large number of horses, fine McClellan saddles, cavalry sabers and pistols, ammunition, wagons, and quartermaster stores were brought back by Powers.

On June 3 Grierson, with about 1,200 troops, set out for Clinton to break up Logan's stronghold. The Federal cavalry pushed across the Comite River and moved to Pretty Creek, where Logan and Powers waited with their main force.

With Cage's Louisiana Battalion and Garland's troops, Colonel Powers detoured through the swamps and struck at Grierson's left flank and rear, causing great disorder. When the Federal center wavered and bent back, Stockdale charged down the road, while Griffith's dismounted troops filed through the woods directly against the front. Panic gripped the Federal forces, who erroneously thought themselves greatly outnumbered, and a rout now took place. After losing a number of his men, Grierson finally halted a portion of his troops and reformed them, but was unable to stop the Confederates. When night put an end to the engagement, Grierson had withdrawn beyond the Amite and set up a strong position. For several days Grierson waited here for reinforcements from Banks.

General Paine on June 5 left Port Hudson with 4,000 men and strong artillery support to join Grierson. Grierson's cavalry pushed into Clinton on June 7 but found the town deserted. Logan had withdrawn ten miles to the north. Grierson burned the railroad depot, a warehouse containing several hundred hides, a small supply of corn, a machine shop, a locomotive, a crude woolen mill, a cartridge factory, a supply of ammunition, and several hundred barrels of Louisiana rum.

Paine and Grierson returned to Port Hudson late on June 8 with their mission only a partial success.[14]

All day long and into the night, on June 10, the gunboats and artillery kept up a relentless bombardment against Port Hudson, indicating to the Confederate garrison that an attack might come at any time. Banks ordered a night reconnaissance all along the line to force the enemy artillery to unmask so that his batteries could knock them out. Another motive for the move was to familiarize his men with the ground before launching his next general assault.

Around one o'clock the regiments were ordered to fall in and keep silent. Through the dark the men stumbled, fell down steep banks, floundered about the abatis, and moved into the ravines near the foot of the Confederate works. Scratched and bleeding, the bewildered men awaited orders. Few knew what was expected of them because they had received no order other than to advance. Around three o'clock a driving rain drenched the struggling men and turned the clay banks into slippery mud slides. The Confederates discovered the movement and opened a vigorous rifle fire but refused to unmask their artillery.

Two Maine regiments, the Twelfth and Twenty-second, operating under the impression that they were to assault the works, were able to slip through the darkness into a gorge among the abatis and to move within the Confederate line.[15] This brought them into deep ravines filled with the offal of hundreds of butchered cattle, refuse from a slaughter pen on the bluff high above. A Confederate officer wrote: "The men got separated and lost while bogging and floundering in this awful putrid mess. They came straggling through our thin line, and were captured in detail. The greater number scrambled back to their own lines. Those captured were hideous, stinking objects and glad to get a chance to wash up." [16]

Colonel Steedman, in command of the Confederate left wing during Banks's night reconnaissance, was having his troubles. The Tenth Arkansas, occupying a vital position within three hundred yards of a Federal battery of six guns and two mortars, began to talk of mutiny and surrender. Steedman finally calmed them down and got them to remain at their posts. Colonel Miles had found the Ninth Louisiana Battalion (Partisan Rangers) untrustworthy. When placed on outpost or picket duty, they began to desert to the enemy. Miles placed a guard over them.

During the darkness and rain many of the Federal troops fell back behind their lines. They considered the entire maneuver to be stupid and suicidal. Near dawn, when the gray, misty light began to appear, the Federal troops who remained in the abatis opened fire from the cover of the fallen timber. When the sun finally rose, orders were shouted along the line to retire, but the troops found it difficult to comply. Many of them raised up and were mowed down by the Confederate sharpshooters. A few were able to spring up and run full speed back to safety. Two Confederate guns were run up and peppered the area with grape and canister. An entire company of skirmishers threw down its arms and fled in terror. Steedman later collected these rifles. The Federal artillery made short work of the two Confederate guns, leaving them total wrecks. Some of the soldiers, afraid to expose themselves, hid in their holes and behind stumps and logs all day. That night they withdrew to their lines.

The early morning attack of June 11 had been another mistake. Nothing constructive was accomplished. The Federal morale was lowered, and the faith of the men in Banks and his staff was further weakened. No complete official figures concerning the losses of June 11 were ever issued by either side, but Banks was thought to have suffered more than two hundred casualties.[17]

Talking with Confederate prisoners and deserters helped Banks to decide that digging his way into Port Hudson would take too long. He learned, too, that the Confederates were much weaker and more demoralized than he had expected. Deserters informed Banks that the garrison had only enough corn meal to last a few more days. There was still some unground corn, but the grist mill, which was powered by a jacked-up locomotive, had been struck and the mill stones broken. The mill had been moved into a ravine, where repair efforts were frantically being pushed. There was still a five-day supply of beef, plenty of peas, sugar, and molasses.

Banks, who had overestimated the strength of the garrison, learned that Gardner had around 4,000 men, which included 3,200 infantry and 800 artillery. The command still hoped that Johnston would be able to send reinforcements. Most of the men were anxious for the siege to end so that they could return home. A few were still confident of victory. Thirteen guns remained mounted on the river front, two of which were traverse guns. Two 24-pounder Coffin guns, two Tennessee 24-pounders, and two 12-pounder Blakely guns had been transferred to the breastworks. By June 12 one Blakely gun had been knocked out and one of the Coffin guns disabled. The Tennessee guns were placed where the railroad crossed the works, and the remaining Coffin gun was mounted on Beall's front near the Slaughter house. There were four batteries of light artillery along the breastworks, with plenty of ammunition but a serious shortage of caps.

By the evening of June 12 Banks had completed most of his plans for another general assault. A naval battery of 9-inch Dahlgrens was posted on the left flank, and a number of mortars were removed from the schooners and set up at intervals along the line. His trenches, cotton fortifications, bombproofs, and covered ways had been advanced nearer the enemy. New weapons, the Gatling guns, with twenty-four rifle barrels each, loaded and fired by a crank, were set up on the right wing.

Just before noon on Saturday, June 13, the gunboats, mortars, and artillery opened a terrific bombardment upon Port Hudson. Farragut, who had complained that his ammunition was running low, was assured by Banks that the general assault would take place the next day. After an hour Banks ordered a cease-fire, and again a formal request to surrender the post was sent to General Gardner. As expected, Gardner refused. A short time later the bombardment resumed and a slow fire was continued for the rest of the day.

As early as June 10 Banks had ordered each brigade to choose new fascine bearers, pioneers, bridge details, and skirmishers. No volunteers were called for; instead, the men where chosen by lot. Troops were busied with filling three-foot-long bags with cotton to be used as shields from the enemy bullets and then used to span the ravines and ditches. The parties were ordered to practice carrying, assembling, and laying pontoon and dry-land bridges so that they could bridge the ravines under heavy fire. Parties of pioneers would then use their shovels, axes, picks, saws, and other weapons to cut gaps in the Confederate breastworks so that the Federal artillery could be run inside.

Late on the night before the new assault, Banks called his division commanders to his headquarters for final orders. Grover's division, reinforced with two other regiments, was to make the main attack on the Priest Cap, a fortification near Slaughter's house under the command of Colonel N. A. M. Dudley. A short time after 3:30 A.M., Dwight was to use two regiments and try to work his way into the Confederate works on the extreme Federal left near the river. At 2:45 A.M. Augur was to begin bombarding his front and thirty minutes later was to feint an attack with his skirmishers, but if circumstances proved favorable he was to convert it into a real attack.[18]

PORT HUDSON, JUNE 14

AT THE appointed time, early Sunday morning, June 14, the artillery opened its mighty chorus along the entire Federal line. A dense fog hung over the air, muffling even the thunder of the big guns. Around four the first wave of the assault started its forward movement.

The main attack had been entrusted to Grover, who now commanded the entire right wing. Grover had chosen Paine's division for the heaviest work, with Weitzel's brigade acting as support. Colonel Halbert E. Paine insisted on leading his column. He led off with seventy pioneers carrying axes, shovels, hatchets, pickaxes, and other tools. In their footsteps came a storming party of four hundred men, carrying their long, cotton-stuffed bags, and with them came the engineers who were to carry their balks and chesses forward to bridge the big ditch. As skirmishers, the Fourth Wisconsin and Eighth New Hampshire led off, accompanied by the Fourth Massachusetts who carried hand grenades fashioned from 6-pounder shells. The Thirty-first Massachusetts, carrying their cotton bags, came next. Moving out last was the main force, the rest of Gooding's brigade, Fearing's brigade, and Ingraham's brigade led by Ferris. Nims's artillery waited at the rear of the column to move into the enemy works as soon as the line could be breached.

Paine's column was assigned a sector which offered the least protection of all. The field and the road were slightly rolling, and there were no trees, no deep ravines, and few stumps and underbrush to shelter the skirmishers. In a voice rising above the roar of the artillery, Paine ordered his columns forward. Before leaving the woods and entering the plain, the regiments became mixed up, but on they moved at quick time. When they approached within one hundred yards of the works, the Confederates opened a heavy fire with their rifles and guns.

Bullets singing through the air found their human targets. The skirmishers rushed on with a shout, but with each yard their numbers were reduced. The storming party threw down their bags, forming a crude breastworks behind which they crouched for the rest of the day. The bridge crew threw away their materials, and the pioneers abandoned their tools and sought every available inch of shelter. The main column behind advanced within range of the Confederate riflemen and suddenly stopped. Dropping to the ground, they too burrowed low behind the scanty natural shelter. Some of the men from the Eighth New Hampshire and Fourth Wisconsin succeeded in crossing the ditch and began climbing the parapet. Some were shot as they climbed, rolling back dead and wounded into the ditch. A few successfully scaled the parapet and crossed into the Confederate line but were quickly captured.

Only a few of the grenade carriers reached the parapet and were able to toss their grenades inside the works. They had cut their fuses too long, and to their dismay the Confederates threw most of the grenades back over the parapet.

The advance was driven back to the cover of a small ridge, where the men waited for the main body to advance. Paine succeeded in rallying the advance for a new charge, but hardly had he uttered his command when he was shot down. The concerted charge never came off. Individual regiments attempting to move forward suffered such heavy losses that they quickly abandoned the effort. All day long Paine's men, scattered in groups over the field, remained pinned to the ground. Paine, with a bullet in his thigh, could not be rescued. Periodically he tried to rally his men for another assault but found it impossible. The main assault had failed miserably.[1]

By seven, Weitzel had moved his men through the woods to Paine's left and was ready to attack the right side of the Priest Cap. Deployed as skirmishers were the Twelfth Connecticut and the Seventy-fifth New York. Following came the Ninety-first New York, carrying the heavy hand grenades; the Twenty-fourth Connecticut, carrying two long cotton bags weighing thirty pounds each; Weitzel's main column; and, in the rear, the division's artillery.

Weitzel's only approach was through a series of gorges cut by branches of Sandy Creek. Where these gorges approached the Confederate works, the banks of the ravines grew more steep and the depth increased. Near the works the arm of the creek and its ravine took a sharp turn to the north and united with Big Sandy Creek and a wider, deeper ravine at the foot of the works. From the bastion on the right, the Priest Cap on the left, and the works in front, the Confederates could sweep the ravine with a deadly fire. It was through this main ravine that Weitzel decided to launch his attack.

Moving to the right of the Jackson road over the rough ground and through the timber into the ravines, Weitzel made his way safely toward a narrow ridge leading to the main ravine in front of the works just north of the Priest Cap. Near the end of the ravine the Twenty-fourth Connecticut, carrying the cotton bags, balked and refused to move forward. After half an hour of hard talking by the officers the recalcitrant regiment again moved forward, and the entire column proceeded to the foot of the ridge, where they formed. Yelling wildly, the men charged up the hill onto the ridge. There they were greeted with a heavy rifle fire. Many of the troops were dropped by the Confederate sharpshooters, and the rush ended at the crest of the hill. Only a few succeeded in crossing the hill and the main ravine. These few, when they attempted to climb up the breastworks, were shot down or driven back into the ditch, where they lay among the dead and wounded, sheltered by logs, and afraid to move. At one point on the ridge, cotton bags were piled by some of the men of the One Hundred Sixtieth New York to form a breastworks, but this failed because the cotton was set on fire by rebel bullets. Under a heavy fire the main column charged up the ridge, but they were stopped before they reached the crest. Word was sent back to Grover for reinforcements, and Colonel Morgan, with two brigades from the First Division, was sent forward. The reinforcements encountered great difficulty in the covered way leading to the open space before the ridge. Since it was crowded with skulkers, hospital aides, and the wounded and dead, a long delay resulted. Casualties among the regimental officers mounted higher; with each loss the men became more demoralized and scattered. Not a single staff officer, general, or officer of high rank went near the parapet all day. Weitzel, Grover, and most of the brigade commanders sent in substitute officers and relayed their orders to them through aides. One such temporary commander, Colonel Simon G. Jerrard of the Twenty-second Maine, who took command of Grover's First Brigade when Colonel Holcomb was killed, refused to make a new charge when ordered to do so by Colonel Morgan and one of Grover's aides. Jerrard tersely replied that he had tried to rally the men but only a few answered his call and that he would not foolishly lead them to certain slaughter. If they wanted another assault, then Grover should come forward and lead it. Later Jerrard claimed that Morgan lay drunk behind a log during the battle and issued stupid orders that endangered the lives of all his men. (Several days later, Dwight, who was Jerrard's immediate commander, had Banks issue a dishonorable discharge without giving Jerrard a hearing.) The main column remained pinned to the ridge, afraid to advance or to retreat, until after dark.

Poor leadership, lack of proper planning, the failure to make a mass assault, lack of discipline, especially among the nine-months men— these factors that had helped cause the defeat on May 27 were duplicated on Sunday, June 14.

General Augur, in the center, was under orders to feint an attack to his front in an attempt to draw the Confederate troops away from the right and left, where the main assaults would take place. Skirmishers were sent forward before dawn to creep as near the Confederate works as possible, and upon signal, the sharpshooters and all the artillery were to open a concentrated fire on the enemy. After two hours, additional skirmishers were moved forward, and they added to the clamor of the mock attack. Utilizing good cover, few of Augur's men were lost, and after remaining on the field under the broiling sun, the men were withdrawn after nightfall.[2]

In command of the Federal left was General William Dwight, the most hated officer in the Department of the Gulf. One of his regimental commanders described him as being "short, prissy, red-faced, pig-headed, . . . with a singular slope from the top of his head, both ways, to his belt. No forehead; wide mouth, [and a] neck larger than his head."[3] Another critic spoke of him as "a man not distinguished for courage or sobriety," who showed his prowess by ordering his officers under arrest.[4] The jug-shaped general, who had been forced to resign from West Point under questionable circumstances, considered himself a military authority and made everyone under him recognize the fact or be punished. His cruelties, his besotted despotism, his insane show of power, and his military ineptitudes were strangely tolerated by Banks because, it was rumored, General Banks was in debt to Dwight's father, a wealthy Bostonian, and could not redeem his debts.

Dwight's men heard Farragut's guns on the river open with one of the heaviest bombardments they had yet launched against Port Hudson. A little later the early morning hours were disturbed by the opening of the artillery fire along the line. When rapid rifle fire joined the heavier chorus of the big guns, the men knew that Paine had begun his assault. When his rifle fire slowed and almost stopped, they knew the assault had failed. Using the same guide, the sound of the firing, they checked off Weitzel and Augur. They too had failed. The appointed hour for Dwight's attack had long passed, and still the men awaited orders.

After daylight the order came. The Sixth Michigan and the Fourteenth Maine were ordered to the extreme Federal left for the purpose of storming the Confederate works near the river. The two regiments crossed a muddy ravine and climbed up a narrow ridge near the edge of the river. About a quarter of a mile to the right was the high, well-fortified bluff called the Citadel. The Fourteenth Maine, followed by the Sixth Michigan, moved along the bank toward this point. Cannoneers inside the Citadel trained their guns on the advancing column and waited. After leaving the bank, the Union troops would have to cross an open valley completely covered by a direct fire from the Citadel and by a cross fire from a redoubt up the valley. If they succeeded in crossing this area, they would then have to scale the precipice, one at a time, up a winding path under the muzzles of the Confederate sharpshooters. A few Confederate riflemen fired slowly at the men atop the ridge, some of whom were hit by the flying bullets. Immediately orders to halt were issued, and the two Union regiments hugged the cover of the hillside. About an hour later an aide recalled the two regiments, and the Sixth Michigan was sent forward to support a battery while the Fourteenth Maine was held in reserve.

Colonel Thomas S. Clark, in command of the First Brigade of Dwight's division, had started his main column forward simultaneously with the attempt on the far left. Skirmishers with cotton bags, grenades, and rifles moved forward on the double, accompanied by the One Hundred Twenty-eighth New York. Immediately following came the Fifteenth New Hampshire and the Twenty-sixth Connecticut. As they moved in columns of companies over the Mount Pleasant road below the Troth house, they were sighted by the enemy, who poured shot and shell into their ranks. The skirmishers advanced to a deep ravine choked with felled trees and a dense growth of vines and briars. Here they froze behind their cotton bags until the main column came up. With the appearance of the main force, the Confederates opened up every gun, firing as rapidly as possible. The exposed columns scattered, threw themselves down the banks of the ravine, and took refuge behind the slashing. Clark's men remained safely under the cover of the logs until dark, when all except the skirmishers were withdrawn.

Nickerson's brigade on Clark's right, led by Colonel Lewis Benedict, attempted to move through an open field to Clark's assistance, but a few rounds from Miles's artillery drove the brigade back. Re-forming and moving forward again, some of the men managed to reach the abatis, where they took cover for the rest of the day. Dwight's assault was so weak, so poorly planned, and so badly executed that it could hardly be considered an assault.

When darkness fell, the commanders began to remove their troops from the blood-stained field. Tired, sick, wounded, and hungry, the men began to straggle in. A few of the troops who held advanced positions were left all night without food and blankets.

As the Federal troops withdrew, they could hear the jubilant Confederates celebrating their victory. Bugles and drums, joined by the voices of hundreds of "Rebs," filled the air with the "Bonnie Blue Flag" and other Southern airs. Some of the Confederates adopted a more solemn method of celebration. Groups of men gathered in prayer circles and for more than an hour sang their favorite hymns and prayed for guidance. In the Federal camps the scene was quite different. Officers and men talked in subdued tones about their failure and sadly tallied their losses.

There was just reason for mourning and regret among the Union troops. They had lost 1,792 men, 203 killed, 1,401 wounded, and 188 missing. Officer casualties, as on May 27, had been especially high. In comparison, the Confederate losses were light; 22 were killed and 25 wounded, for a total of 47. A number of Confederate guns were dismounted by the furious bombardment. To take their places, 13-inch mortar shells were rigged up as bombs to be exploded at the approach of the enemy. Men in the lines were also furnished hand grenades to help make up the deficit in fire power.[5]

The next day, June 15, dawned bright and beautiful and, except for a few light showers, remained clear. At intervals the Federal land batteries and the flotilla on the river opened fire on Port Hudson. In the early morning Colonel John L. Logan, from Clinton, disturbed several outlying camps by suddenly dashing into their bivouac areas with his Confederate cavalry. He captured over a hundred prisoners, a number of Negroes, teams and wagons, arms, and a supply of salt. Ten of Banks's men were killed, but Logan made off unscathed with his booty.

At noon Banks treated the men to a hearty meal of fresh boiled beef, bacon, hardtack, and fresh coffee with sugar, their first substantial food in nearly forty-eight hours. Details of Negroes were sent onto the battlefields to recover the dead and wounded, but enemy fire drove them from the area. In the afternoon Banks sent forward, under a flag of truce, an appeal to General Gardner requesting permission to send medical and hospital supplies within the works to be used by the wounded Federal prisoners and by the Confederate wounded if desired. Gardner granted the request and stated that some wounded and dead Federal troops lay just outside his breastworks, but that they could not be given succor because Banks's sharpshooters fired upon all Confederate details who tried to climb down into the ditch. Gardner expressed his surprise that Banks had failed to request a truce to enable him to care for his dead and wounded. Like Grant at Vicksburg, Banks refused to ask for a truce, and scores of Union wounded died unnecessarily.

For three days the dead and wounded remained on the field unattended. Finally the effluvia from the decomposing bodies became so offensive that the Confederates asked for a truce, agreeing to deliver the Union dead to Banks. Details of Confederate troops, gagging from the horrible stench, collected the bloated, blackened, fly-blown bodies and turned them over to Federal details for burial.[6]

After two bloody repulses, Banks still had not learned his lesson. Two days after the losses of June 14 the general called for a thousand volunteers to serve as a storming party in a new assault. The response was far from satisfactory; only around three hundred men volunteered. Most of these men came from the Thirteenth Connecticut and from two colored regiments. It was agreed that Colonel H. W. Birge of the Thirteenth Connecticut would lead them. A separate camp was laid out for the volunteers, where they were showered with attention while undergoing special training for their dangerous mission.

To make such an attack easier and to safeguard his men, Banks resorted to every procedure, orthodox or bizarre, that was suggested by his commanders. Night and day, but especially at night, work was pushed on the siege fortifications at four main points along the line. Most of the labor was performed by thousands of raw Negro recruits, aided by detachments from the various regiments. The main approach led from Battery No. 12, on Paine's front, several hundred yards north of the Jackson road, and followed the meandering ravines to the top of the hill, which was only a few yards away from the Priest Cap. With hard digging, a trench or ditch was extended out to the left along the general line of the Confederate works. The distance from the works ranged from twenty to forty-five yards.

On Grover's front, some two hundred yards on the right of the main sap, near Battery No. 8, a zigzag was dug from the ravine toward Steedman's stronghold. Because of the relative directness of this route, all digging had to be done from behind cotton bales and hogsheads filled with dirt or cotton. Slowly the line inched closer toward the works. Any attack in this quarter would have to make use of sap rollers until the main ditch was reached.

A great trench was extended from Battery No. 20, north of Troth road, around Mount Pleasant, and almost to the riverbank on the extreme Federal left. This covered way connected five different batteries, including Battery No. 24 with seventeen guns. Most of the batteries were crescent-shaped and had thick walls of cotton bales, clay, logs, and sandbags. They were large enough to accommodate many guns, several hundred sharpshooters, and a command post. A cover of logs, vines, and other materials helped to shade the men from the hot rays of the sun. From this line near the riverbank five covered saps led across the ravine onto the high hill where the Citadel was located. At the closest point the saps were only ninety-five yards from the Confederate works. While the work was in progress, the Confederates did little firing, apparently saving their ammunition.

A secondary approach was constructed to the northeast, on the left of Gibbons' field, which ran from the ravine in front of mortar battery No. 18 and paralleled a Confederate outwork some 375 yards away. This approach was largely for show and would not prove to be a practical point from which to launch an assault.

A fourth major approach was dug by the Twenty-first Maine from the ravine near the Slaughter house to Battery No. 16. The distance from the zigzag to the works at its closest was some four hundred yards.[7]

While Banks's men were building their siege works, the Confederate troops strengthened their parapets with additional sandbags made from sheets, fine linen tablecloths, calico, homespun, and dress silk —from every available scrap of cloth. At places along the line where there was danger of the Federal troops breaking through, a second line of defense was dug to the rear. Night and day, the soldiers remained on duty behind the breastworks until the end of the siege. All able-bodied men were needed. Some of the men worked with spade and ax while others served as sharpshooters to watch the enemy movements.

As the weary June days wore on, both sides suffered. Life in the trenches was sheer torture. The stifling air, the burning sun, the high humidity, the lack of proper food, and the constant vigilance and duty took their toll. Heat exhaustion and sunstroke, malaria, and diarrhea felled many of the troops on both sides. The number of men fit for duty dwindled with each passing day. The Confederates, short of everything, suffered most. Their supply of quinine and other medicines was exhausted. Their wounded had to undergo operations and amputations without an anesthetic. Confederate food stocks grew smaller and smaller, and the men were reduced to half rations. Since there were no reserves to take their places on the front, the men had to remain in the trenches and snatch what rest they could.

At several points along the line an informal truce, which lasted over a week, was arranged on June 16 by the enlisted men. Both the Confederate and the Union troops constructed their works in full view of the other without danger of being fired upon. The working parties exchanged banter and occasionally slipped out of their trenches and met halfway between their lines. Banks's men exchanged small amounts of tobacco, coffee, and newspapers for sugar, molasses, canteens, and the few things the Confederates had. When high-ranking Confederate officials learned of the practice, they ordered an end to fraternizing, but because their ammunition was short, they allowed the informal truce to continue a while longer. Elsewhere along the line there was no truce, and the opposing sharpshooters fired at each other all day. At night both sides sent out raiding parties with hand grenades and rifles. The Confederates made several attempts to burn the cotton-bale works of the enemy. Closer and closer the Federal approaches crept toward the Confederate parapets while the Confederates strengthened their defenses. Trip-torpedoes were set in the most vulnerable spots on the Confederate line.

Affairs grew quieter at Port Hudson during the late June days. While the Federal artillery was being placed in new positions, there was little firing. The Confederates, short of primers and ammunition, had to conserve what little they had to repel a major assault. The mortars in the river, having expended most of their shells, ceased firing on June 18, and the gunboats fired only on rare occasions.

At Battery No. 11, to the northwest of the Priest Cap, Grover had succeeded in pushing his sap to within thirty yards of the ditch in front of the Confederate works. On the night of June 28 Colonel O. P. Lyles was sent by Gardner with the Eighteenth and Twenty-third Arkansas regiments to hold this position. In the afternoon of June 29 Lyles succeeded in setting fire to the cotton bales being used as sap rollers by the Union details in their approach to the works. At six o'clock on the same evening Grover sent out a storming party from the Federal trenches to sweep down into the exterior ditch before the breastworks and to drive in the few Arkansas troops who manned an outwork in the area. One detachment of troops attempted to scale the parapet and a few succeeded, only to be slaughtered by the alert Confederates. Later that night a second assault drove forward into the ditch and succeeded in tossing a few hand grenades inside the works, but little harm was done. The Confederates attached fuses to 12-pounder shells, lighted them and threw them over the parapet to roll down a wooden gutter into the enemy ranks in the ditch below. Grover withdrew his men before morning. The move was a failure, like all previous attempts.

During the affair Colonel Lyles had difficulty with the undisciplined Eighteenth Arkansas, who refused to obey his orders. Had Grover pushed his first attack, before reinforcements arrived, he could have breached the defenses and moved into Port Hudson.

Bailey's cotton-bale fortress on the far left was completed, the battery was emplaced, and the guns began a bombardment of the Citadel on June 26. Three days later, just before sundown, General Dwight ordered Nickerson to take the One Hundred Sixty-fifth New York and the Sixth Michigan and charge the position. A deep zigzag trench, or sap, led from the battery to the foot of the Citadel hill. The Zouaves and Michigan men had just begun to climb the hill when the enemy opened with a heavy rifle fire from above. Finding shallow depressions in the hillside which gave them some shelter, Nickerson's men lay down, not daring to rise. The long night passed, and as dawn approached, the men left their hiding places one by one and slipped back into their trench. Those with the best cover remained until noon the next day, when, driven by thirst and heat, they made a desperate but successful dash for the safety of the zigzag.

Late that afternoon Dwight, drinking heavily, appeared and ordered the same two regiments to charge the Citadel again. As instructed, the men charged by twos from their trench and attempted to run up the hill into the muzzles of the Confederate rifles. Many fell dead or wounded, but a few succeeded in entering the works, only to die instantly. The suicidal "whisky charge" was halted by orders from General Banks, and Dwight, who had boasted that Port Hudson would be his that night, bitterly cursed the two regiments as they returned to their positions behind the line.[8]

Colonel Powers, at Clinton, planned a coup that he thought would demoralize the Federal troops at Port Hudson and at the same time bring valuable information to the government in Richmond: he would attempt to capture one of the generals before Port Hudson. A small party of Confederate scouts surrounded the plantation home of a Mrs. Cage, where General Neal Dow had lived since being wounded on May 27. Under a bright moon the scouts entered the gate of the high board fence surrounding the yard and found Dow astride his horse ready to gallop to safety. Covered by carbines and pistols, Dow peacefully surrendered and was quickly sent on his way to Richmond.

Colonel Powers was mistaken; there was no one who mourned Dow's fate. The hyper-critical, sanctimonious, ex-Quaker from Maine had earned the hearty dislike of his men. His antiliquor crusade at Camp Parapet had ended all peddling in camp and had deprived the men not only of liquor but also of milk, fruit, candy, and newspapers. Although Dow had strict scruples about liquor, he was one of the worst pillagers among the Federal officers, taking whatever he wanted for his own use. Up to now he had displayed little ability as a field commander, and his loss would not be felt by the Nineteenth Army Corps.

A few miles below Port Hudson was Springfield Landing, Banks's main supply depot. On the night of July 2 Colonel Powers with his cavalry and mounted Partisans moved from Clinton to destroy this important post. Carrying bottles of turpentine and a supply of matches, Powers' men caught the pickets napping and charged into the dark camp. Amid the resulting confusion, the Confederates set fire to huge mounds of bales, barrels, and boxes. The scene grew wilder as the flames mounted, and Powers' men tore around the camp giving full voice to the fearful Rebel yell. Several hundred Negroes and the entire Sixteenth New Hampshire scattered in every direction, some rushing to the safety of steam boats in the river. In their great panic, twenty-one of the Negroes were drowned trying to crowd aboard the boats. The gunboats and mortars opened fire on the camp without doing much damage to the attackers. Finally the One Hundred Sixty-second New York rushed to the scene and, aided by the light of the fires, succeeded in killing several of Powers' men. Now greatly outnumbered, Powers attempted to fight it out, but his men became so scattered that he ordered a withdrawal. Fear of Grierson's cavalry also hastened the return to Clinton. The raid had been a great success; over a million dollars worth of stores had been destroyed.[9]

Banks was in a quandary. The enlistments of twenty-two regiments of his nine-month volunteers were beginning to expire and by the end of August all would have expired. This would leave him with only thirty-seven regiments, or around ten thousand men, to be used in the defense of his far-flung department and in future campaigns.

Already many of the nine-month men were grumbling and were refusing to do hazardous duty. The first regiment to show open mutiny was the Fourth Massachusetts. Banks had the regiment lined up, took away its colors, forcibly disarmed the men, stripped several officers of their rank, and ordered a court-martial for the ringleaders. Later, addressing his entire command, he strongly denounced all the short-term volunteers and threatened them with death or hard labor on Dry Tortugas if they refused to do their duty in the future. All except one hundred members of the Fourth Massachusetts returned to duty.

Following the example set by the Fourth, the Forty-eighth Massachusetts refused to go into line to relieve the One Hundred Sixteenth New York. Colonel E. F. Stone rallied most of the rebellious men and marched them off into the line, leaving only one mutinous company behind. General Paine ordered the company to report to his headquarters. The defiant company marched with loaded guns to the command post, where they were surrounded by two other companies with cocked pieces. One by one Paine called out each man and asked him if he still refused to do his duty. Only three stuck to their decision and were quickly placed under arrest. The rest quietly moved off to join their regiment in the rifle pits. The Fiftieth Massachusetts planned to mutiny at the same time, but after dire threats they were convinced that they should enlist for another two weeks. Banks in a special order thanked them for their show of patriotism.

On July 8 Banks detached the Fourth, Fiftieth, and Fifty-second Massachusetts, the Twenty-sixth Connecticut, and the Twenty-second, Twenty-fourth, and Twenty-sixth Maine from their divisions and ordered them into garrison duty while they awaited transportation home. The nine-month men still remained restive and demanded to go home immediately. On July 20 one company of the fractious Fiftieth Massachusetts refused to perform its light garrison duties. The company was immediately arrested, shipped to New Orleans, and sent later to Ship Island to begin a sentence of hard labor for the duration of the war. Later, on July 29, the nine-month men at Port Hudson marched aboard the steamer *Omaha* and headed home.[10]

After more than forty days of bloodshed, backbreaking labor, sharp-shooting, filth, mud, heat, dust, boredom, and suffering, the sun-blackened men on both sides were sick of Port Hudson. The rains ceased, the creeks dried up, and washing one's clothes and body became impossible. While on the line the men could not shave, and hair on their faces and heads grew long and became matted with filth and dust. Uniforms drew up and faded in the sun and rain, were torn by the brambles and bushes, and soon were worn out. Lice began to infest the unwashed ranks, making life miserable yet at the same time giving the men something to do.[11] Charles McGregor, one of the men of the Fifteenth New Hampshire wrote: "At all times men could be seen with their vestiments removed, sitting in shady nooks and busily occupied in this war of extermination." On July 2 McGregor wrote: "We have got the ground itch, and are all lousy. Our chief recreation is eating hardtack, scratching and hunting lice." [12]

The food situation, although far from good with the Union troops, was increasingly worse for Gardner's men. By the end of June the last beef ration was issued. On July 1 a wounded mule was butchered as an experiment, and the tender, juicy meat was found to be palatable. Horses were also slaughtered, but the men preferred mule meat. Big wharf rats infesting the place were killed by the men and were considered delicious eating. As the supply of corn diminished, cowpeas were issued, but the hard, indigestible peas caused stomach disorder, and the men refused them. There was plenty of sugar, molasses, and salt, and the men concocted a type of beer from corn, sugar, and molasses. Barrels of the beer were kept on the line, and the soldiers drank it in preference to the putrid water they were furnished. Coffee was not to be had, and they brewed "coffee" from parched rye, parched wheat, and from dried, parched sweet potato, parched meal, and parched sugar, while the supply of these items lasted. In lieu of tobacco the men chewed and smoked leaves, vines, and barks.[13]

As the siege moved into July the Federal troops continued to push their saps and zigzags closer toward the Confederate works. On the Union left relations between the opposing troops remained friendly. When the officers ordered the men to fire, they called to each other, "Get down out of sight there, I'm going to fire now." In his diary, Colonel Willoughby M. Babcock claimed that the Southerner fired "on the Negroes on all occasions" and that often he shouted out to the white soldiers guarding a work party: "Hello! Yank, Get down there. I want to shoot that d——n nigger!" [14]

July 4 saw all of the Federal camps in a holiday mood. No operations were planned, and much of the day was spent in listening to the reading of the Declaration of Independence and to short patriotic speeches.

Most of the batteries fired national salutes, using blanks, but a few aimed their guns at the parapets and saluted the Confederates with live shot. Liquor and wine were distributed, and the men enjoyed their independence holiday.

Captain Joseph Bailey, Dwight's untutored engineering officer, began a vast tunnel under the Citadel hill on the far left near the river. Negroes slowly dug out a subterranean chamber, passing the dirt from hand to hand out to the rear. Thirty barrels of powder were then placed inside to blow up the Citadel. The Confederates did not attempt to counter-mine, because a strong interior works a quarter of a mile to the rear would prevent Dwight's men from entering Port Hudson even if the Citadel were blown up.

A second tunnel was started on Grover's front on the right near the Priest Cap. Confederate engineers here began digging a countermine. By July 7 the mine under the Priest Cap was completed and twelve hundred pounds of powder placed inside. At dawn on July 9 Banks intended to explode the mines under the Citadel and the Priest Cap, and his forlorn-hope details were to rush into the breach, followed by the main army. Port Hudson would then be his.[15]

But his preparations were unnecessary. On July 7 a gunboat arrived at the upper fleet bringing news of the surrender of Vicksburg on July 4. The navy wildly cheered Grant, and every gun in the upper fleet fired a salute in honor of the victory. Later in the day, when the lower fleet received the word, its guns and men joined their voices in the celebration. Just before eleven that morning, Colonel Kilby Smith of Grant's staff carried the glad tidings to General Banks. The troops along the line joined in the tumultuous celebration. With tears stream-ing down their sun-baked faces, the men began to cheer. The long-silent bands began to fill the forest with strains of "The Star-Spangled Banner." The Confederate troops were puzzled and hastened to their posts, expecting a new assault. The news of Grant's victory was shouted across the lines, but Gardner's men refused to believe it. Later, messages were written on paper attached to a stick or a shell and thrown over the parapet. Now the Confederates were convinced, and hundreds of them crowded the parapets and moved down into the area below to mix and mingle with the jubilant Union men. A few hours before most of them had been trying to kill each other—now they were friends. They shook hands; they swapped stories of the siege; and they joked and gibed with each other.

Just after midnight General Gardner sent out a party, requesting a copy of the communiqués from Grant so that he could verify Pemberton's surrender. Banks complied, and throughout the rest of the night both commanders were busy exchanging notes and making necessary arrangements for discussing surrender terms the next morning.

At 9 A.M. on July 8, Colonel I. G. W. Steedman, commanding the left wing, Colonel W. R. Miles, commanding the right wing, and Lieutenant Colonel Marshall J. Smith, in charge of heavy artillery, were sent by Gardner to meet with Banks's commission, consisting of General Charles P. Stone of Banks's staff, General Dwight, and Colonel Birge. In the shade of a beautiful grove of magnolias, the officers amiably discussed the terms of surrender, enjoying an ample supply of Bordeaux wine. An agreement was reached by two o'clock that afternoon, and the Confederate commission returned to Port Hudson.

The terms demanded unconditional surrender. Gardner must turn over Port Hudson with its garrison, munitions, armaments, public funds, and materials of war to Banks. The officers and men would be treated as prisoners of war, and personal property could be retained by the owner. After the men stacked arms and grounded their colors, they would line up near the village for formal surrender ceremonies the next day at seven. Proper medical care would be given to the Confederate sick and wounded.

Fraternization between the enlisted men of the opposing armies continued during the day while the officers were in consultation. Lively trading was carried on. Bowie knives were swapped for tobacco, bacon for wooden canteens, coffee for Confederate buttons, and hardtack for corn cakes. The one item which the Confederates possessed in large quantities was corn beer, and they freely shared this with Banks's men. The Confederate officers generally stood aloof and, when questioned, proudly replied that they would be ready to fight again as soon as they could be paroled or exchanged.

Late in the day Banks sent a wagon train of provisions into Port Hudson to feed the half-starved garrison. Joyous shouts greeted the arrival, and for the first time in many days the men enjoyed a good meal. A still greater cheer was raised when their officers told them that they would soon be going home.

The next morning, July 9, at seven o'clock, General George L. Andrews rode into Port Hudson, accompanied by Birge's forlorn-hope group. Next came picked regiments from all the divisions. The various bands, playing "Yankee Doodle" and other lively marching tunes, lifted the spirits of the Union troops even higher, and they marched proudly into the village. General Gardner waited, with his soldiers drawn up in line. The simple surrender ceremonies were soon over. At the order "Ground arms" the battle-weary Confederates piled their rifles in front of them, and Gardner offered his sword to General Andrews, but it was refused. The Confederate flag was hauled down, and the Union flag was raised on the staff while the bands played and the guns roared a salute. General Banks made a short speech commending the garrison for its gallant defense and promising the men paroles. A cheer went up and the ceremonies ended. All officers were to be held as prisoners until an exchange could be arranged and some of the officers were sent to New Orleans while others were sent to Memphis and to the north. As soon as paroles could be worked out, the enlisted men were allowed to return to their homes.

Banks found that the long siege against Port Hudson had been very costly. From May 23 to July 8 he had lost 4,363 men, including 45 officers killed, 191 wounded, and 12 captured or missing. Among the enlisted men 663 were killed, 3,145 wounded, and 307 captured or missing. Those men who died from natural causes from the long exposure and other hardships were not counted in these totals.

Since no complete returns were ever made by the Confederate authorities, the exact number of casualties at Port Hudson cannot be determined. The chief surgeon's report showed a total of 623 casualties, 176 killed and 447 wounded. Not included in the list were the losses at Plains Store, which numbered 12 killed and 36 wounded. Captain C. M. Jackson, one of Gardner's staff officers, on July 9 reported that some 200 men had been killed, between 300 and 400 wounded, and around 200 had died from sickness. According to Federal reports, General Gardner had surrendered 6,340 prisoners of war to Banks, 405 officers and 5,935 enlisted men.[16]

Gardner had defended Port Hudson to the utmost of his ability. After more than forty days of merciless pounding from the fleet and the land batteries, his men were exhausted and dispirited. Improperly clothed, sheltered, and fed, they sickened and there was no medicine for them. Hope that Johnston would send relief grew fainter as each day of the siege progressed. As Gardner's meager supply of ammunition was nearly exhausted, many of his guns were wrecked, and his food stock was dangerously low, the news of the surrender of Vicksburg decided the fate of Port Hudson.

THE TECHE
THE MISSISSIPPI, AND TEXAS

O N THE west side of the river Confederate military affairs in April and May had been far from happy. In April Taylor had been driven out of the Teche to Alexandria, and in May he had been forced to flee to Natchitoches while Banks occupied Alexandria. Reinforced by two brigades from Texas and J. G. Walker's division from Arkansas, Taylor was ordered by Kirby Smith to proceed to northeast Louisiana to help relieve the pressure on Vicksburg. The attempt had failed, and Taylor had returned to Alexandria in early June, leaving Walker in northern Louisiana.

At Alexandria, Taylor began preparations for a campaign to disrupt communications between Banks and New Orleans. Recruiting new forces and reorganizing his old, Taylor divided the three thousand men into two detachments. One detachment, consisting of the forces of Alfred Mouton and Thomas Green, was to collect every available boat and move down the Teche and attack Brashear City. The second detachment, three regiments of Texas cavalry under Colonel J. P. Major, was ordered to proceed to the Atchafalaya, thence to Plaquemine, and finally to join Mouton before Brashear.

Colonel Major, with his force of some three hundred cavalry, caught the small Federal detachment at Plaquemine by surprise on the morning of June 18. Eighty-seven men of the Twenty-eighth Maine under Lieutenant C. H. Witham were captured, and a supply of commissary stores was seized. Proceeding to Bayou Plaquemine, Major destroyed the grounded steamboat *Lasykes* and demolished the steamer *Anglo-American,* after capturing the officers and crew. A short distance below, the *Belfast* was captured and was burned. A little after nine the gunboat *Winona,* out of Baton Rouge, learned of the attack and began to shell the enemy, forcing Major out of the area.

Moving down the Mississippi, Major hit Bayou Goula at daylight on the nineteenth and there took possession of Federal quartermaster and commissary stores. Over a thousand laborers were rounded up on the government plantations, and the Negro men were taken, whereas the women and children were left behind. Learning that the Federal force was too strong to risk an attack on Donaldsonville, Major sent Colonel W. P. Lane, with a portion of the troops, through the swamp to strike at Thibodaux and to cut all railroad and telegraph communications. With the rest of his men Major skirted Donaldsonville and moved over to the Lafourche road en route to Thibodaux and Brashear.

Disorder prevailed at Brashear among the undisciplined Federal troops and convalescents, and the weak commander, unable to cope with the situation, asked to be relieved. General Emory, whose command embraced the Teche and Lafourche regions as well as New Orleans, sent Lieutenant Colonel Albert Stickney of the Forty-seventh Massachusetts to take command. A gunboat was also sent from New Orleans to help defend Brashear.

Stickney proceeded to "straighten out" the post. He determined to show the men what discipline was, drilling them unmercifully under the burning sun. At night they were marched out and left to sleep on their arms, fighting mosquitoes until dawn. Expeditions were sent out aboard a steamer and gunboats to scout the surrounding lakes and streams and to forage. The artillery was ordered to keep up a continuous bombardment on the empty village of Berwick and the desolate shore above. The men knew no rest, and in about ten days, the killing pace put over half of them on the sick list. Stickney rode among them astride a black charger, issuing petty orders and finding fault with trifles while he neglected building up the defenses. The morale of the garrison began to sag further under the rule of the martinet.[1]

Learning that Major's forces were en route down the Lafourche, on June 20 Emory warned Colonel Stickney and directed him to move to Lafourche Crossing after leaving proper protection at Brashear and Bayou Boeuf. Colonel Thomas W. Cahill, with all the men he could collect, sped to the support of Stickney, leaving only 250 troops to protect New Orleans.

At Thibodaux on June 20 Lane's yelling Confederates caught several provost guard companies by surprise. The Federal troops seized every available horse and mule and fled toward Lafourche Crossing four miles away. Men on foot ran alongside the detachment of cavalry. Plantation guards joined the terror-stricken hegira as it swept by them. The Confederates drove the guards to the very muzzles of Stickney's guns. Firing rapidly, the Federal artillery turned the attackers, but for an hour Lane's men deployed and reconnoitered before returning to Thibodaux with around a hundred prisoners.

Back in town the ragged, hungry cavalrymen celebrated and feasted at the expense of the United States. They raided commissary and sutlery stores and seized whisky rations from the quartermaster. Saturday night in Thibodaux was a scene of wild debauchery fired by issue liquor and local "red-eye."

The orgy continued into Sunday, but near sundown Major succeeded in rallying his drunken command and set off to attack Lafourche Crossing. A terrible thunderstorm broke, and rain fell in torrents. The men, well fortified with alcohol, rode through the storm seemingly oblivious to the discomforts and dangers of the expedition.

Stickney now had some eight hundred men, having been joined the night before by the Twenty-sixth Massachusetts from New Orleans. He awaited the attack from the cover of the Lafourche levee, from the railroad embankment, and from shallow rifle pits dug in the exposed areas. His available guns were concentrated along the front of the levee from which he expected the attack.

At 6:30 P.M. the Confederates rode within sight and unlimbered a 12-pounder howitzer, which began to throw shot and shell into the works. Stickney's artillery replied as fast as it could fire, and soon the Confederate howitzer was silent. The rain had now ceased, but the ground was soft and slippery. At seven, led by Colonel Charles L. Pyron, some 200 men began a charge against the Federal front. Most of the Confederate forces were dismounted, but some of the more audacious, or perhaps drunken, rode boldly up to the cannons, only to be dropped from their saddles. The hot rifle fire, and especially the accurate artillery work of Major Morgan Morgan of the One Hundred Seventy-sixth New York, halted the first wild charge and sent Pyron's men reeling back. After Pyron rallied his men, a second charge was sent forward but was again repulsed. Several minor attempts against the flanks were driven back. For a third time battle lines were formed, and the Confederates afoot and mounted drove forward with a wild yell as if to overrun the guns. Firing swiftly, but without taking careful aim, some of the Confederates swept over the embankment into the midst of the riflemen on line and sent some of them hurrying to the rear. Re-forming, the infantry was pushed forward through the glue-like mud. A few hand-to-hand encounters occurred, but the effective artillery fire prevented the main Confederate force from entering the works, and the few who did enter were either killed or driven out. Night had now come, and no amount of effort could force the Confederates to attack again. Mounting their horses, they rode off toward Thibodaux, leaving their dead behind.

The next morning the Confederate dead were collected by the Federal troops, hauled to Thibodaux, and there turned over to Major. Stickney claimed that his losses were light, 8 killed and 41 wounded. The Confederate losses were shrouded in mystery, as usual, but conservative estimates report at least 50 killed, over 60 wounded, and 16 missing.

At eleven the next morning, June 22, Colonel Thomas W. Cahill arrived with the rest of the troops from New Orleans, and Stickney, after turning over the command at Lafourche to him, returned to the city. That same day Emory received the Fifteenth Maine from Pensacola and sent them immediately to Cahill.[2]

General Mouton, on the Teche, had collected forty-eight skiffs and flats. On the night of June 22 Major Sherod Hunter and 325 volunteers rowed, with oars muffled, down the Teche and the Atchafalaya and landed the next morning in the rear of Brashear. At the same time, Brigadier General Thomas Green slipped into the ruins of Berwick City and into a woods just below the west bank of the bay with three battalions of cavalry and mounted infantry and two batteries.

Just before dawn the Federal garrison was suddenly awakened by the guns of the Valverde battery firing from across the bay. The Union batteries concentrated their fire upon Green while the gunboat *Hollyhock* was backed down the bay out of danger by her cowardly commander.

At Brashear there were 700 men, of whom only 400 were effective. The rest of the troops, 300 convalescents, had been left behind earlier by some thirty regiments. In command of the post on the morning of June 23 was Major R. C. Anthony of the Second Rhode Island Cavalry.

Under the cover of Green's heavy artillery fire the real intent of the Confederates was masked. Hunter's men waded up to their waists through swampy country in the rear of Brashear. Hunter then formed his men in order of battle, dividing his command into two columns. One, made up of men from various cavalry units from Louisiana and Texas, was ordered to charge the fort and camp on the left of the depot, and the right column, composed of men from Baylor's Texas Cavalry, was to assault the fort and sugarhouse above and on the right of the depot. The two columns, with about the same distance to cover, were to unite at the railroad buildings.

The Federal garrison soon recovered from the shock of Green's bombardment from the west shore. They saw that Green had few men and no means at hand of crossing the bay to attack Brashear. Their artillery was vastly superior to Green's. With nothing to fear, most of the men drifted out of the fort and returned to their camps.

At this point Hunter's men leaped out of the woods and ran across the open fields of ploughed ground and stubble between the bay on the left and a belt of timber on the right. No attempt had been made to guard this section. The swamp was considered impassable. Before the startled, unofficered, and straggling squads could form any line of defense, the left column of the attacking force reached the cover of an orange grove near the almost vacant camps of the Twenty-third Connecticut and One Hundred Seventy-sixth New York and began firing into the tents. A few of the Union troops attempted to make a stand, but before they succeeded, the Confederates were upon them. The bewildered and untutored men began to drop back toward the shelter of the town, occasionally halting to fire a single shot.

Hunter's screaming troops swept down upon the convalescent camps and soon had the terrified men running to and fro looking for shelter. Few of the convalescents attempted to resist and few could have; they were, for the most part, unarmed. The charging, yelling "Rebs," firing as swiftly as possible, shot down a number of the unarmed men as they milled about. The smoke and confusion was so great that it was impossible to distinguish between those who were resisting and the sick noncombatants.

Isolated squads of Union soldiers tried to halt the advance into the village, but they were either shot down or sent flying to cover. The greatest resistance came from the railroad depot area, but by ten o'clock in the morning the fighting had ended and the garrison surrendered to Hunter. The weeks of harsh discipline and fruitless marches and the neglect in organizing the troops to meet an attack had portended the fall of Brashear long before the actual event.

Hunter's losses were very light—3 killed and 18 wounded. He claimed that 46 of the Federals were killed, 40 wounded, and 1,300 prisoners, eleven guns (24-, 30-, and 32-pounders), 2,500 rifles, 2,000 Negroes, over 200 wagons, hundreds of tents, and a huge quantity of quartermaster, commissary, and ordnance stores were captured. No Negro troops were captured; they had fled through the woods when Green began his bombardment.

In celebration of their victory the Confederate troops began to loot the town and the camps. They were looking for souvenirs, for clothes to replace their rags, for food and for liquor. Soon they were well fed and a number were drunk. For the first time since his arrival in the department Taylor had an abundance of supplies.

On the same day (June 23) Green crossed the bay with a portion of his troops and rode off to attack another Federal garrison at Bayou Boeuf. On June 24, Taylor came down to Brashear with Mouton's men. The men were allowed to take what clothes, arms, and equipment they wanted. Privates were soon preening themselves in Federal officers' uniforms, complete with sword, belt, and sash.

The enlisted men captured at Brashear were given parole and, with haversack and blanket, were allowed to march back to Algiers. The officers were made prisoners of war and were, for the time being, kept at Brashear.[3]

Lieutenant Colonel A. J. H. Duganne of the One Hundred Seventy-sixth New York had arrived from Brashear on June 22 and had immediately set to work fortifying Boeuf Crossing. A detachment was sent out and returned with entrenching tools and hundreds of contrabands from nearby plantations. The Negroes were set to work digging rifle pits while the soldiers gathered all available materials which could be used in the construction of rough breastworks. Hundreds of refugees from surrounding plantations, both white and black, crowded into the area for protection.

On the night of June 23 two locomotives arrived with a report of the fall of Brashear and the dread news that Green was now moving toward Boeuf Crossing. A council of officers was called by Duganne, and it was decided to surrender the post without a fight.

Immediately the large sugarhouse and surrounding sheds, containing much of the personal baggage of the men at Port Hudson, arms, and other military supplies, were burned.

The next morning at daylight, June 24, a small scouting party sent out by Green appeared, and Duganne agreed to surrender the post. Four guns, ammunition, small arms, a few stores, and 435 officers and men were captured. The Negroes, numbering 3,000, were returned to their owners. All enlisted men were paroled, and the officers were marched back to Brashear to join the officers captured there. Later the captive officers were marched off to prison at Tyler, Texas.

Thibodaux, abandoned by Major, was immediately reoccupied by Federal troops. On the afternoon of June 24 terrified Negroes and whites raced into the town announcing that 3,000 Confederate cavalrymen were en route to attack Thibodaux and Lafourche Crossing. Colonel Cahill ordered an immediate retreat. The bayou bridges were burned, three field guns were destroyed, and as many of the men and horses as possible were loaded aboard the cars and ordered to move to Raceland. Here, followed by rumor, the wild flight was resumed. Ammunition was destroyed, horses abandoned, and four field pieces were left behind. Following on the heels of the Federal troops came Waller's and Pyron's battalions. They chased Cahill's command back to Algiers. By July 1 the Confederates occupied Boutte Station, twenty miles from New Orleans, and were planning to occupy the city if the opportunity presented itself.[4]

Taylor turned over his command to General Mouton and hurried to Alexandria to bring down Walker's division to join the other forces. Mouton, on June 26, ordered Green's and Major's brigades to move to Donaldsonville and to take that place.

At Donaldsonville, Fort Butler, a star fort mounting six 24-pounders, was protected on one side by the Mississippi and on the other by Bayou Lafourche. A deep, brick-lined moat surrounded the works. The earth parapet was high and thick and covered with a luxurious turf. The sides flanking the river and bayou were given additional protection by a strong log stockade extending from the levees to the water. Built to accommodate 600 men, the fort was held by only 180—two companies of the Twenty-eighth Maine and convalescents from several regiments. Major Joseph D. Bullen was in command.

On the night of June 27, Green moved up to within a mile and a half of the fort and dismounted his men. Major Denman W. Shannon of the Fifth Texas Mounted Volunteers was sent around the fort to the river, a mile above, and just after midnight on the morning of June 28 advanced down along the Mississippi levee to the stockade, between the levee and the water's edge, driving out the enemy pickets. He succeeded in pushing some of his men over the stockade, and the rest moved through the shallow water around the log fence and into the fort.

Green began his main attack at 2 A.M. in order to keep the gunboats from sighting his advance. Phillips' regiment, under Colonel Major, surrounded the fort and began to push toward the works simultaneously with Major Shannon. Colonel P. T. Herbert's regiment flanked the two end ditches and tried to pick off the gunners and their sharpshooters on the parapet. The Fourth Texas, led by Hardeman, became temporarily lost and did not begin its attack on the Lafourche side stockade until nearly daylight. By some error no guide was sent to lead Colonel Lane, and his regiment did not get into action.

Shannon and Phillips succeeded in getting through and around the stockade between the river and the levee but, to their surprise, they encountered a deep ditch inside the levee separating them from the works. Unable to cross the ditch, the Confederates pried loose some of the bricks from the side and threw them at the enemy atop the parapet. The Federal troops returned the missiles in full measure. A number of men were injured by the flying bricks but more deadly was the rifle fire from the fort. The Confederates yelled continuously during the attack, helping the riflemen find their targets in the dark.

The gunboat *Princess Royal* now drew up before the works and began throwing shells to the right of the fort into a skirt of woods and over the fort along the bayou. Later, she began firing grape and shrapnel at the Confederates on the river side of the stockade. Toward daylight the *Winona* and *Kineo* appeared and joined the *Princess Royal* in firing upon the Confederates.

As day began to break, the Rebel yells began to die out, and the fire began to slacken, finally ceasing. Green ordered his men to retire. Along the banks of the bayou and the river, inside the stockade, and near the edge of the woods lay the Confederate wounded and dead.

The numbers engaged in the action at Fort Butler vary with each report. Banks said that 225 Federal troops defended the fort which was attacked by 800 Texans. Green had several hundred men in the rear who did not get into the fight. The losses, too, are hard to determine. The Confederates said that they lost 40 killed, 114 wounded, and 107 missing, a total of 261 casualties. Federal reports claimed that they captured 130 prisoners and killed and wounded some 350 men, and that only 8 of their men were killed and 15 wounded.

Green, after mourning his losses, left the Fourth, Fifth, and Seventh Texas regiments to watch the fort. Several batteries, numbering some twenty guns, and Major's cavalry brigade were ordered to the Mississippi to harass the shipping. The cavalry and artillery units covered an area some twenty miles along the river, and from July 3 until after the fall of Port Hudson not a single transport succeeded in going up the river from New Orleans except those under heavy convoy. One gunboat, the *New London*, was so shot up that she was run ashore and abandoned. Several other gunboats and transports were also injured and suffered casualties while the Confederates remained safely behind the cover of the levee.[5]

Shortly after the formal surrender ceremonies at Port Hudson, Weitzel's and Grover's troops were transferred by transports to Donaldsonville. The two Federal divisions, one on each side of the bayou, now faced General Green. Major's brigade, consisting of four regiments numbering 800 effectives, and two sections of artillery were recalled from the river and posted on the east bank of the Lafourche. Green took up position on the west bank with his three regiments, 750 effectives, and two guns. That day (July 11) and the next, minor skirmishing occurred between the opposing forces.

On the morning of July 13 Grover sent his troops on a forage mission down along both banks of the Lafourche to Cox's plantation, some six miles below Fort Butler. N. A. M. Dudley and his brigade, with Charles J. Paine's brigade, a troop of cavalry, and two batteries of artillery, marched down the west bank while Colonel Joseph S. Morgan, acting brigadier, moved Grover's division down the east bank. The skirmishers unexpectedly bumped into Green's pickets and were driven back. Green deployed his men on the west side and, moving through a large cornfield stretching from the bayou across to a swamp on the west, attacked the two flanks with his largest force. Captain H. A. McPhaill, with detachments from the Fifth and Seventh Texas Cavalry, moved along the banks of the bayou, knocking out the artillery and cutting up the infantry support. With the Fourth Texas Colonel G. J. Hampton charged Dudley's right wing and succeeded in turning it while Lieutenant Colonel P. T. Herbert charged Dudley's front. The entire force on the west bank was driven back. Dudley's forces reformed several times, but each new stand became weaker, and the Union troops fell back several miles and were joined by Paine. They now made a more resolute stand.

On the east bank, Colonel Morgan was attacked by a small force of about 400 men under Colonel Major simultaneously with the attack on Dudley's columns. Joseph Morgan, who had been accused earlier of misdirecting an assault along his sector of the line (on June 14 at Port Hudson) because of drunkenness, was again drinking heavily on July 13, and under attack he fell back in panic, his men running full speed to the rear through the cornfields and willow thickets. The hot, sultry day took its toll, and many of his men fell from heat exhaustion, to be picked up later as prisoners by Major. With Morgan's retreat, Major's artillery was now free to bombard Dudley's forces across the bayou and to help drive them back.

General Grover appeared on the scene and ordered both columns to fall back under the protection of the guns of Fort Butler. The battle of Cox's Plantation was a sorry, humiliating affair for the Union forces. Green's entire force, numbering only around 1,200, was able to beat back a force three times as large with a loss of only 33 men: 3 were killed and 30 wounded, 6 of whom later died. Grover lost a total of 459 men, 56 killed, 217 wounded, and 186 captured or missing. In addition, he lost three pieces of artillery, a number of Enfield rifles, ammunition, provisions, camp equipage, and a number of wagons and teams.[6]

Most of the blame for the repulse was placed upon Colonel Joseph Morgan, and in September this officer was court-martialed in New Orleans. He was found guilty of "Misbehavior before the enemy" and "Drunkenness on duty" and was sentenced "to be cashiered and utterly disqualified from holding any office or employment under the Government of the United States."[7]

Mouton sent orders to Green at Donaldsonville to fall back to Berwick Bay, where the command would be consolidated. Learning that Federal gunboats would soon arrive at Berwick, Mouton moved up the Teche to Franklin, where he went into camp.

Two Federal gunboats were sent to Berwick Bay and gradually Weitzel transferred his men from Donaldsonville to Brashear and Thibodaux. For the next few weeks the men were given a long rest, making only a few foraging expeditions to gather food and to hunt for horses and firearms among the Southern sympathizers in the area. An occasional minor skirmish with Taylor's pickets helped to relieve the monotony.[8]

With the opening of the river, Grant sent down beef, forage, steamboats, and anything else requested by Banks. On July 25 Major General Francis J. Herron, with a small division of 3,605 men and 18 guns, was sent from Vicksburg to Port Hudson. At the end of the month Grant, following orders from General Halleck, sent the reorganized Thirteenth Army Corps to Carrollton to join Banks. This corps of 14,712 men and officers was to replace the twenty-one nine-month regiments whose term had expired or would expire in August.

With the arrival of the Thirteenth Corps Banks had to make a number of changes. Major General William B. Franklin, recently arrived from the North, was given immediate command over Banks's own Nineteenth Army Corps. General Weitzel took over the First Division, Emory commanded the Third, and Grover the Fourth. There was no Second Division. The Thirteenth Corps was placed under Major General C. C. Washburn with Benton, Herron, Lee, and Lawler commanding the divisions and Colonel John J. Mudd controlling the cavalry brigade.[9]

As his next military move, Banks suggested to the War Department that he, Grant, and Farragut attack Mobile. He believed that this important post could be taken easily. Because of the "Mexican and French complications" in Mexico and Texas and for "reasons other than military," General Halleck ordered Banks to concentrate on planting the Union flag somewhere in Texas and leave Mobile until later. Halleck suggested that a combined military and naval expedition up Red River, from Alexandria to Natchitoches or Shreveport and on into northern Texas, would be the easiest method of getting into Texas. Banks disagreed. He thought the route too difficult and dangerous, and since the final decision as to the route of attack was left to his discretion, he decided upon "a movement by the coast against Houston, selecting the position occupied by the enemy on the Sabine as the point of attack." Banks argued that a landing could be made at Sabine Pass and the troops moved swiftly to Houston, where all of the railroad communications in Texas would be brought under Federal control.[10]

On September 2 General Grant with his staff arrived in New Orleans to consult with Banks concerning the proposed move against Texas. Like Banks, he thought Halleck's proposed Red River expedition into Texas was a waste of valuable time. Ever the perfect host and appreciative of the theatrical, Banks showered the hero of Vicksburg with a round of receptions, banquets, soirees on the levee, and nightly band serenades. On September 5 a grand review was arranged for Grant at Camp Carrollton, eight miles above New Orleans. After inspecting the troops Grant, Banks, and their staffs began the return to New Orleans. Grant was riding a fine, unbroken horse that taxed his good horsemanship, particularly inasmuch as he was well fortified with liquor. The spirited steed, well in advance of the cavalcade, suddenly shied at the sight of a carriage and fell to the ground, throwing Grant free. The next officer in line did not see the accident and rode over the unconscious and prostrate general with his horse. Grant was discovered by members of the staff, who carried him into a nearby inn. After an examination it was discovered that his thigh was badly injured and that he could not move his leg. For nearly two weeks Grant could not be moved.[11]

The Texas expedition set sail from New Orleans on September 5. Major General W. B. Franklin was in command of the entire movement. The troops included two brigades from Weitzel's First Division and two brigades from Emory's Third Division, plus five batteries of artillery and two squadrons of the First Texas Cavalry. Lieutenant Frederick Crocker, who had served for months in the West Gulf blockade and knew the Sabine Pass area, was chosen to head Franklin's naval support. Crocker had four shallow-draft gunboats in his squadron.

To transport the troops there were ten ocean steamers and six river steamers. All of the boats were grossly overcrowded, old, rotten, and unseaworthy. Leading off the expedition was General Weitzel, who sailed from New Orleans on September 4 escorted by the *Arizona*. Franklin followed close behind.

Lieutenant Crocker with his four gunboats escorted the transport *Charles Thomas,* bearing Weitzel and the Seventy-fifth New York, into the Sabine in the early morning of September 8. After hasty reconnaissance the rest of the expedition was signaled to enter.

At a turn in the river one-half mile below Sabine City, where the stream's channel divided into two parts, separated by a shifting sandbank, was located a small earthworks mounting four to six guns. One company of Texas artillery numbering just over forty men, under the temporary command of Lieutenant Richard W. Dowling, held the post.

Just before dawn the *Sachem,* accompanied by the *Arizona,* both with guns blazing, steamed up the eastern Louisiana channel and soon came under the fire of the fort. Almost immediately a shot from Dowling's guns struck the main steampipe of the *Sachem,* and she was enveloped in a cloud of steam. Amid the screams of the scalded, dying men, the injured vessel hauled down her colors and ran up the white flag. Speeding up the Texas channel, the *Clifton* was shot through her boilers and grounded. Twenty minutes later this ship was also surrendered.

Weitzel and Franklin watched the entire action but made no attempt to land troops and to attack the small fort while it was occupied with the gunboats. When the two gunboats were disabled and a third grounded, signals were hoisted to retire, and the frightened army commanders, after throwing overboard 200,000 rations and 200 mules, retreated down the stream, crossed over the bar, and re-entered the Gulf.

This disgraceful and disorganized expedition had cost the Union heavily. In addition to the two gunboats, the Confederates had captured 350 prisoners and had killed or wounded 50 men without losing a man. The defending force of some forty. raw Irish recruits of the Davis Guards had turned back a force of some 6,000 men.

After his miserable retreat, Franklin set sail back to New Orleans, disregarding Banks's orders to make a landing along the coast. The trip was a nightmare. Heavy winds and giant waves tossed and pitched the small transports, sending them into dizzy rolls and spins. Many of the frightened troops got drunk, and others swore and threatened to mutiny. Many were seasick, and the decks were soon foul, slippery, and dangerous.

At last the ordeal ended, and the men disembarked safely at Algiers on September 11. They were disgusted and ashamed and cursed Franklin and the navy for botching the expedition through their lack of co-operation and poor leadership.[12]

After the humiliating retreat from Sabine Pass, Banks still did not abandon the idea of gaining a toe hold in Texas. He could not afford to. Halleck's strong appeal could not be ignored, although low water in the Atchafalaya and the Red rivers and the Federals' inability to maintain a long supply line made it impossible to use Halleck's suggested route at this season. Banks decided instead to move up the Teche to Lafayette or Vermilionville, over the grass plains to Niblett's Bluff, and into Texas. Emory's and Weitzel's divisions of the Nineteenth Army Corps, under the command of Franklin, supported by Washburn's and McGinnis' divisions of the Thirteenth Corps, under Ord, were concentrated at Bisland on the lower Teche in preparation for the new move to Texas. At New Iberia the cavalry division of General Albert L. Lee guarded the front.

Herron's division, 2,500 strong, sen. down by Grant, was stationed at Morganza to prevent the Confederates from operating in the upper Atchafalaya. Major General N. J. T. Dana, due to the illness of Herron, assumed temporary command of the division on September 28. An advanced detachment, under Colonel J. B. Leake, of nearly 1,000 Iowa, Indiana, and Missouri infantry, plus two regiments of Illinois cavalry and a section of artillery, held a position at Sterling's plantation, some seven miles from Morganza on the road to the Atchafalaya. Leake's men were to reconnoiter the area constantly and keep back the Confederate forces.

At 3 P.M. on September 28 General Thomas Green began crossing the Atchafalaya with Waller's and Rountree's cavalry battalions and Semmes's battery. After dusk a drenching rain began to fall, but the crossing continued. By 1 A.M. on the twenty-ninth all the troops were safely on the east bank, and at daylight Green began his forward movement. Mouton's and Speight's infantry brigades took a muddy trail through the swamps leading to a juncture with the main road behind Sterling's. The rest of the force, Waller's and Rountree's cavalry, the artillery, and the three Texas Mounted Volunteer regiments moved over the main state road to Fordoche bridge in front of Leake's position.

The cavalry reached the bridge by 11 A.M. and began skirmishing with the Federal pickets at that point. Half an hour later a brisk fire was heard in the rear of Sterling's place. General Green pushed forward through the plowed fields, now deep in mud, driving the enemy's advance cavalry back. One mile from the bridge at Norwood's house, Rountree found the Federal cavalry drawn up in line of battle. Rountree charged; the enemy scattered and disappeared through the turnrows and through a secret lane leading around the Confederate trap back to Morganza. Major H. H. Boone took the two battalions of Confederate cavalry to Sterling's and rode down the enemy artillery. The engagement now ended, and the Federal infantry was rounded up as they fled in the rain over the muddy fields and through the wet bushes.

Federal losses amounted to more than 500, with 16 killed, 45 wounded, and 462 taken prisoners. Green claimed he lost only 121 men, 26 killed, 85 wounded, and 10 missing. Green added two 10-pounder Parrott guns, two new ambulances and a hospital wagon, medical stores, many small arms, and clothes to his train. Colonel Leake was caught napping and had paid the penalty.

General Dana sent out a force from Morganza to rescue Leake's men and to disperse the Confederates, but the heavy rains, the deep mud, and the fear of the unknown number of the enemy caused the loss of so much time that Mouton and Green were able to make good their withdrawal.

Early in October General Franklin began a slow movement from Bisland toward Opelousas and Washington. At the same time General Edward O. C. Ord, reinforced by General S. G. Burbridge's division, left Berwick and on October 14 joined Franklin at Carencro Bayou.

Franklin now had 19,500 men for the overland move against Texas. Taylor, with about half the Federal strength, fell back slowly to Opelousas, fighting several minor skirmishes with Franklin's men. The Federal forces pushed into Opelousas and took possession of the surrounding territory, which they continued to occupy until the end of the month.[13]

Back in New Orleans, after a brief visit to Franklin on the Teche, Banks began organizing a second Texas expedition to go by water. Under the command of General Dana, the Second Division of the Thirteenth Army Corps, the Thirteenth and Fifteenth Maine, and the First Engineers and Sixteenth Infantry Regiment of Negro troops left New Orleans on October 26 for Texas. Early in November this expedition landed at Brazos Santiago and proceeded to occupy Brownsville and Point Isabel. Several other points in the interior and along the coast of Texas were occupied in the next month. Banks sent most of the remainder of the Thirteenth Corps to Texas. At last he had a weak foothold in Texas.[14]

General Franklin, who had graduated from West Point in 1843 at the head of his class, had upheld the promise of a brilliant military career fighting with Scott in the Mexican War. In the Civil War he had taken part in the battle of First Bull Run and in the Peninsula Campaign but had come under a cloud after the serious Federal losses at Fredericksburg. General Ambrose E. Burnside blamed the defeat largely on Franklin and requested that Franklin be dismissed from the army. No action was taken, and after months of remaining idle he was sent to Banks in Louisiana in the summer of 1863. In the disgraceful Sabine Pass affair and in the handling of the new overland Texas expedition, Franklin still failed to live up to his earlier promises. He wasted too much valuable time through long rest periods and personal indecision. By the time he finally reached the upper Teche region, he found the waters in the bayous at a low stage and no longer suitable for navigation. By the end of October he had abandoned the idea of marching across the Louisiana plains and began a slow retreat by detachments toward New Iberia. Taylor's men followed, skirmishing with the divided Federal forces.

At noon on November 3, in camp near Grand Coteau on Bayou Bourbeau, General Burbridge was caught napping by two brigades of Confederate infantry and cavalry led by Thomas Green. Green's men suddenly swooped down upon Burbridge from all directions before he could form his troops. After a near rout, a short and bloody contest

was fought in the woods, and a portion of the Federal troops succeeded in escaping to General McGinnis, three miles in the rear. Green's
slightly superior forces caused great damage to Burbridge. Out of 1,625
men from the Thirteenth Corps with detachments from the Nineteenth Corps, 716 casualties were suffered. Twenty-five were killed, 129
wounded, and 562 were captured. Green's killed and wounded were
slightly less and only 53 of his men were missing. Green also succeeded in capturing one gun, a number of small arms, and a great
deal of camp equipage. Reinforcements were rushed forward to Burbridge, but after a hot skirmish, Green retired with his prisoners and
booty.

The next day, November 4, Franklin resumed his march, fighting
minor skirmishes every day or two until he arrived back at New Iberia
on November 17 and went into camp. Within a few days the Thirteenth
Corps men were shipped to Texas. Until the end of November Taylor's
men continued to harass the Federal troops along the Teche, and in
turn, Franklin's cavalry periodically raided weak Confederate positions,
capturing several hundred men.[15]

While Taylor's main force remained in the vicinity of the Teche,
a portion of his men were sent in mid-November to join Walker's Texas
Division near Morganza. Batteries were installed along the levee of
the Mississippi to fire upon all enemy craft that tried to run by. Several
gunboats and transports were fired upon, but the only steamer to suffer
severely was the *Black Hawk,* which was burned to the water line.

On December 15 James M. Hawes's and Randal's brigades of Walker's command were moved to Marksville, to go into winter quarters.
Scurry's brigade remained near Simmesport to protect the Atchafalaya.
The Texas men at Marksville built wooden huts to shelter themselves
from the icy winds and rain. At night, after the usual camp routines,
the men amused themselves around their campfires with practical jokes
and group singing or sat listening to the music of a regimental band.
Some of the soldiers often gathered under an arbor of boughs to dance
jigs, reels, and doubles to the music of several fiddles. On the opposite
side of the camp another arbor served as a church. There at night,
with the area lighted by pine knots, men listened to the exhortations
and prayers of the preacher and sang favorite hymns.

Mouton's men left Walker and were ordered to march to Monroe.
The miserable troops moved through mud, rain, and severe cold and
finally reached Monroe on December 27. The townspeople gave the
tired soldiers a hearty welcome. Life along the banks of the Ouachita

was little improved, however, complained A. W. Hyatt in his diary: "Weather bitter cold. and all our tents left behind. One blanket on a frozen ground is too ridiculously thin."

Banks's men, in temporary winter quarters at New Iberia, during December found the weather each day more and more severe. The dreary days dragged by, and the men grumbled as they plowed through the freezing rain and deep mud in performing the regular routines of camp life.[16]

MINOR ENGAGEMENTS
AND REORGANIZATION

WHEN VICKSBURG and Port Hudson fell, military action in the northern and eastern parts of Louisiana was somewhat curtailed but did not cease entirely.

The village of Vidalia, across from Natchez, an important shipping point for cattle and other supplies from the Trans-Mississippi to the eastern part of the Confederacy was invaded on July 14 by two hundred mounted infantrymen led by Major Asa Worden of the Fourteenth Wisconsin. This detachment succeeded in capturing the rear of Kirby Smith's ordnance train on the Trinity road, fifteen miles from the river. A large supply of muskets, cartridges, and ammunition was taken.

At Goodrich's Landing, just below Lake Providence, on July 29 a group of Confederate Partisan Rangers surprised two companies of Negro troops, sheltered in a small fort located on an Indian mound, and took some two hundred prisoners. The Rangers spent the rest of the day burning cotton gins, plantation houses, and Negro quarters on plantations occupied by Federal lessees and "Union" Southerners along the river and in the back country. Porter ordered the Marine Brigade to Goodrich's Landing, and on the morning of July 30 the brigade moved on foot to Tensas Bayou, where they were halted by a hot fire from the Confederates who were drawn up in line of battle.

On August 9 an assault was made against Lake Providence by Captain John McNeil with some seventy mounted men. To McNeil's surprise, the gunboat *Mound City* was tied up before the town and began to throw shells at the attacking force. McNeil fled, leaving behind several dead and wounded.

Later in the month (August 20) Brigadier General John D. Stevenson, with the Third Division of the Seventeenth Army, the Third

Brigade of the Sixth Division of the Seventeenth Army, and three batteries of artillery, plus a battalion of cavalry, embarked from Vicksburg on an expedition to Monroe. The purpose of this expedition was to clear out the Partisans and to break up the reported troop encampment at Monroe. After debarking at Goodrich's Landing, Stevenson moved toward Bayou Macon, skirmishing lightly with small Confederate forces. Cavalry detachments were sent against the towns of Floyd, Monticello, and Delhi. These troops succeeded in taking several prisoners and in destroying a few supplies and wagons.

Crossing the Macon on August 24, the Federal troops found themselves "in a land of plenty" in which the people were still at home. At the beginning of the expedition Stevenson had issued strict orders against foraging, but there was more than ever before.

At Oak Ridge, a small hamlet of six or seven houses some twenty-five miles northeast of Monroe, stubborn resistance was shown by a small Confederate force before it could be dislodged.[1]

Minor skirmishes continued as Stevenson pushed on to Monroe, arriving on August 28. Forewarned, Brigadier General Paul O. Hébert had withdrawn his small command from the town, crossed the Ouachita, and headed for Shreveport. At Monroe, as at Oak Ridge, the Federals found a number of hospitals crowded with sick Confederate troops. Hébert left behind only a small amount of commissary stores and forage. Stevenson in his report stated: "I found the inhabitants well disposed, and many expressions of satisfaction at the occupancy of the place by the Federal Army."

Crossing the Ouachita, Stevenson found five thousand bales of cotton in flames, set afire by Hébert as he withdrew. No other cotton had been burned in the area west of Bayou Macon. The area was "in a high state of cultivation, with immense crops of corn and cotton maturing, and vast numbers of cattle fattening in the cane-brakes and swamps." His mission accomplished, Stevenson left Monroe on August 28 and returned to the Mississippi River, arriving back in Vicksburg on September 2.

The next foray into north Louisiana got under way from Natchez on September 1. The Seventeenth Wisconsin, led by Brigadier General M. M. Crocker, crossed the river to Vidalia and without delay moved inland toward Trinity on the Black River. That night the Confederate steamer *Rinaldo* was taken after a short artillery duel and was destroyed. For the rest of the night Crocker skirmished with the few troops stationed at Trinity.

Federal reinforcements, including Gresham's brigade and several companies of mounted infantry, were rushed from Natchez and moved to Harrisonburg on the Black, which was reported to be the main Confederate point of concentration. On the same day Crocker moved toward Harrisonburg, skirmishing with enemy pickets for some nine miles.

When Lieutenant Colonel George W. Logan, commanding Fort Beauregard at Harrisonburg, learned that a large Federal expedition was on its way to attack the place, he lost his reason and decided to evacuate the post, although he knew that Colonel Horace Randal, with his Texas brigade of 1,100 men, was en route to reinforce him. At 1 A.M. on September 4, Logan slipped out of the fort and started on his long trek to Alexandria. Randal appeared a short time later, and after lightly skirmishing with the Federal forces above Harrisonburg, he too slowly retired toward Alexandria.

Around midmorning Crocker's troops began the occupation of Harrisonburg. They found that Logan had destroyed a large amount of ammunition and commissary stores, had burned a number of small arms, and had hastily tried to render useless the eight guns left behind. Crocker removed two of the guns and further demolished the remaining six that could not be moved. Leaving Harrisonburg, Crocker marched back to the Mississippi.

A Confederate force of some two hundred cavalrymen appeared suddenly at Vidalia on the morning of September 14 and began to cut its way through the Negro pickets. The place was being held by forty men of the Thirtieth Missouri Infantry, a small detachment of Negroes from Farrar's regiment, and a company of pontoniers. Swooping down upon the pontoniers, the Confederates began to fire upon the men, to pillage the tents, and to free the mules. The Thirtieth Missouri was rushed forward to the defense, and the Confederates were steadily driven back. As swiftly as river transportation could be found, General Gresham sent over from Natchez two regiments of mounted infantry and two of regular infantry. The Federal mounted infantry set out in pursuit of the retreating Confederates, lightly skirmishing with them until they came up with the main body of the Confederate cavalry. The Confederates made no other attempt to attack, and the Federal troops remained at Vidalia without trying a real counterattack.[2]

Vincent's Louisiana cavalry forces inhabited the Black River area until the end of the year. Just above, between Waterproof and St. Joseph, Major Isaac F. Harrison's mounted Partisans roamed the region. Between Lake Providence and Milliken's Bend and to the west, the Negro troops were kept in a constant state of turmoil by bands of mounted Confederate guerrillas.

These guerrillas, consisting of two companies of Quantrill's Missourians who had been driven from their home state, had been sent by Kirby Smith to disperse the speculators and cotton thieves in northeast Louisiana. John Jarrette, commanding these irregular troops, managed to intercept several wagon trains that were collecting cotton and to frighten the Negro troops along the Mississippi. Alfred W. Ellet's Marine Fleet and Federal gunboats were kept busy trying to drive out the guerrillas and to protect leased plantations.

Although Jarrette succeeded in arresting and hanging a number of speculators and spies and in stopping cotton raids, word got back to Kirby Smith that the guerrillas were guilty of committing robberies and other atrocities against citizens, and Jarrette was ordered to get out of the region. Once more the raiders and speculators had a free hand. Toward the end of 1863, Captain Joseph Lea, also formerly with Quantrill but supposedly of unimpeachable character, was sent by Kirby Smith to break up Federal and jayhawker activities on the river. He raided Federal camps and leased plantations, hit at straggling detachments, and succeeded in breaking up the Marine raids.[3]

On August 2 General George L. Andrews, in command of Port Hudson, sent a detachment of 250 colored infantry and 50 cavalrymen from the Third Massachusetts and a section of Vermont artillery to collect Negroes to build up the Twelfth Regiment of the Corps d'Afrique. Fifty contrabands were gathered, but on August 3 around 5 p.m., while trying to find others, Colonel John L. Logan with 500 men surprised the Federal force at Jackson. After a short skirmish the Negro troops fell back and then fled in a complete rout. Logan claimed he took "two Parrott guns, horses, ten wagons with commissary stores, killing, wounding, and capturing not less than 100 Yankees and a large number of negroes in arms." Logan stated that he lost only 12 men killed and wounded.[4]

From the beginning Kirby Smith's problems had been legion. Procuring arms and other military supplies was the most serious. Always short of funds, Kirby Smith instructed his tax agents to collect all taxes due the government. His military commanders were ordered to impress any property needed after agreeing to pay schedule prices, according to authority granted by the Impressment Act of March, 1863.

Funds from Richmond were requested, but little money was sent. Pay vouchers were issued in lieu of cash.

Since most of the arms had to be procured in Europe, the money problem was a part of the arms problem. Louisiana had cotton, and Europe desired cotton above all else. Since railroads were few, Kirby Smith resorted to the wagon train, manned by troops, to move cotton into Texas or Mexico for export. He hoped to replace these soldiers with slave teamsters hired from planters so that the troops could be returned to active duty.

Kirby Smith thoroughly reorganized the Trans-Mississippi Department, trying to make it as self-sufficient as possible. Various surveys were made to discover the total economic resources of the country. By purchasing cotton at a small cost and selling it abroad for gold, Kirby Smith was able to import the necessary machinery from Europe to set up machine shops and factories and to better exploit the saltworks of Louisiana. Most of Texas had escaped the ravages and dangers of Federal invasion, so this area could produce sufficient cattle, grain, and other commodities to feed the rest of the department, provided adequate transportation to haul them and adequate funds to purchase them were found. To aid him in his work, Kirby Smith created several bureaus and agencies.[5]

All of these special bureaus had problems, but the Conscript Bureau had more than its share in trying to provide adequate troops for the field. Conscript officers were sent into every parish, and as soon as the enemy quit an area these officers moved in and began drafting all men between eighteen and forty-five who were eligible under the Conscription Act of September, 1862. The substitution clause of the act allowed any person who was called the privilege of hiring anyone exempt from military service to take his place.

Anticipating action from the Confederate government, Kirby Smith on July 19 issued an order that substitutes, who were already hard to find, no longer would be received in the department. As expected, the Confederate Conscription Act was amended at the end of December, prohibiting substitutes altogether.

Conscription was as unpopular in Louisiana as elsewhere in the South. Drafting a man was one thing; keeping him in the army was another. The Shreveport *Semi-Weekly News* on June 19 carried a series of notices offering thirty dollars reward for the return of deserters. Kirby Smith attempted to solve the desertion problem in late August by issuing orders granting a pardon to all officers and men who were then A.W.O.L. if they returned to duty before September 30. Deserters who had already been convicted and sentenced would be freed from prison to return to the field, provided that they were not two-time offenders.

General Taylor, under orders from Kirby Smith, had sent five companies into the north-central red-hill parishes of Winn and Jackson to round up deserters, to arrest conscripts who failed to report, and to break up any jayhawker groups in the area. In Union Parish, just above Jackson Parish, draft-dodgers and deserters joined together to resist the details sent to bring them in. After a struggle these men were subdued and captured. In November Kirby Smith, who evidently was discouraged with the poor response to his lenient orders, directed that all men who shirked their military duty would be hunted down and forced into camp. Those who tried to escape the conscript hunters would be shot down. The terrain of Louisiana, with its many canebrakes, swamps, and hills in which to hide, made such an order difficult to carry out.

Desertions among the Texas troops under Taylor's command were especially heavy. Among Mouton's men on the Teche, wholesale desertion had set in, and little concern was being shown over it. On September 22 only 200 men reported for duty out of an entire brigade. Brigadier General Henry Watkins Allen reported in mid-October that some 8,000 deserters and draft-dodgers were still at large in the area. In eastern Louisiana 1,200 or more deserters and conscripts were hiding out in Livingston, Ascension, and St. Tammany parishes.[6]

Various persons were still exempt from conscription. In addition to many public officials and ministers, all who were employed by the niter and mining bureau or in hauling ordnance or cotton were not to be bothered by the enrolling officers. Agents, owners, and overseers on plantations using thirty slaves or more were made subject to conscription in September. Certain tanners and shoemakers were exempt, but in Shreveport, because they were charging "exhorbitant prices," they were ordered into conscript camps.

The Confederate government in June, 1863, approved a militia law calling "all between 17 & 50 not subject to Confederate service, to be armed by State and subject to call of the Governor, Exemptions same as for Confederate Service." None of these men would be called into active duty except when extreme danger threatened, nor would they be sent to serve outside their own states. State troops were solely under the control of the governor, and Kirby Smith had little to say in their affairs.

In addition to the local defense units that sprang up in the area east of the Ouachita, in early September a company of volunteers, ineligible for conscription, was organized at Homer, in Claiborne Parish, northeast from Shreveport. In lower Louisiana, around Opelousas, groups of citizens banded together to combat jayhawkers in the area.[7]

Conditions in the Florida parishes of Louisiana went from bad to worse after the fall of Port Hudson. In late December it was reported that "stragglers, deserters and paroled prisoners" were "roaming the country, preying upon citizens and trading with the enemy." The few troops in the region were "utterly demoralized and scattered," and they too were trading with the enemy.[8]

A plague of jayhawking struck all parts of Louisiana in the latter part of 1863. In Union, Winn, and Jackson parishes in north-central Louisiana troops were sent by Kirby Smith to break up these bands, but the few troops detailed were never enough. In the vicinity of Opelousas five Confederate soldiers were attacked and killed in early August. Later in the same month a posse of soldiers and citizens hunted down the jayhawkers, but when they came face to face with the desperadoes, the posse "fled in all directions." Five hundred soldiers were then sent to the area, but evidently they too failed, because the jayhawker and runaway-Negro atrocities and murders still continued. The bold jayhawkers announced that there were "about 25 citizens they intend [ed] to slay."[9]

Down in St. Mary Parish in May a white jayhawker incited a group of Negroes to rise up against their masters. The frightened citizens quickly formed a local vigilance committee and, assisted by thirty-five soldiers, broke up the rebellion. The white ringleader and fifty of the Negroes were hanged.

In the area just across the river from Baton Rouge jayhawkers were also active. In civilian dress, Federal uniforms, and Confederate uniforms, they would strike suddenly, take what they wanted, commit murder if any dared oppose them, and then ride off to their hiding places.

Before and after every battle or campaign or when conditions became too difficult, refugees began to move from the troubled areas. Many planters moved out into the interior and toward Texas when Grant moved into northeast Louisiana and began his drive toward Vicksburg. Delhi and Monroe were overcrowded with these refugees until they moved on westward. Strong Union sympathy was encountered in both towns.

Traveling between Monroe and Minden through the piney hills, the refugees found the poor people living there very hostile. Many refused to sell food or shelter to the refugees and treated them with contempt.[10]

Refugee life in Texas had many drawbacks. A number of persons who went into Texas returned to Louisiana, "stating that they were so harshly treated there that they could not remain" and that "extortion in prices of all necessities were practised upon them." [11]

Shreveport, connected by wagon train with Brownsville and Mexico, continued to receive a limited supply of consumer goods as well as munitions of war. Advertisements in the Shreveport *Semi-Weekly News* in May, June, and July announced that scarce items such as shoes, cloth, flour, buttons, and coffee had arrived and were ready for sale.

Goods running the blockade brought fancy prices. Kate Stone, a refugee from Madison Parish, reported that her mother spent "nearly a thousand dollars" for "five or six dresses." A plain cotton dress cost $200, and a velvet mantle or poplin dress "cost some $1,500."

Items purchased for Governor Moore's plantations at Alexandria were proportionately high. A pound of tea cost $25.00, five papers of pins cost $9.00, a cake of soap over $4.00, a skein of thread $2.00, a box of hairpins $1.00, a gallon of castor oil $70.00, and a gallon of whisky $60.00.

In late August a soldier in New Iberia bought three cotton figured shirts at $15 each. He spent another $90 for a coat and vest. Boot blacking, a very scarce item, cost $100 a box.[12]

Trade with the enemy was frowned upon from time to time, and sometimes was forbidden by both sides. When the Confederates were hard pressed for supplies, trade regulations were often relaxed. The United States Treasury Department strongly endorsed trade in the conquered regions, especially in cotton. General Grant did not favor such trade, believing that the enemy would be aided, the war would be prolonged, and that Federal officers and troops might become demoralized, if not corrupt, by such trade.

In September the Mississippi River was completely open to trade, "subject only to such limitations as may be necessary to prevent the supply of provisions and munitions of war to the enemies of the Country." Cotton or other products could be brought to military posts along the Mississippi "without restraint." Persons within Federal-occupied regions could bring or send their goods to designated posts and receive up to forty per cent of the payment in family supplies or part, or all, in bank notes. No trade was to be conducted with sections outside the Union lines. Treasury agents were to regulate trade, to collect "internal revenue and duties," and to receive all "abandoned or captured property" except purely military supplies.[13]

Trade regulations had been violated before and, despite new restrictions, would be violated again. Poorly paid treasury agents could be bribed to issue trade permits for almost any item anywhere in Louisiana, and they sometimes accompanied speculators outside the lines to lend an air of validity to the illicit trade. Even the military winked at certain violations. Cotton poured into New Orleans from all parts of the state. From March to the first of November 30,500 bales were shipped north from New Orleans, and some 8,000 bales awaited shipment.

Following the fall of Port Hudson, a number of wealthy citizens began to buy up all the cotton they could find in the vicinity of Amite, in eastern Louisiana. A large supply of cotton was bought and shipped to Baton Rouge and New Orleans. The proceeds were then used to buy goods that were brought beyond the Federal lines and sold at high prices to the citizens of the Florida parishes. Confederate money was refused; the speculators would accept only Federal currency or cotton for the goods. These influential citizens did not hesitate to take the Union oath, required before they could trade in Baton Rouge or New Orleans. Hundreds of others of less prominence were also engaged in traffic with the enemy. Supplies of rope and bagging were sent out from Baton Rouge to be used in baling loose cotton. The cotton was cleared for shipment by the Confederate military authorities at Camp Moore, and so much was going through that two large steamers were leaving Baton Rouge daily for New Orleans. Occasionally guerrilla bands would seize the cotton and force the owners or speculators to pay them fifty dollars or more a bale as ransom or to divide the cotton with them before they would release it.[14]

Kirby Smith had done what he could to build up industry in Texas, Arkansas, and Louisiana, but private enterprise was needed, too. Private tanners and shoemakers were turning out their wares both for civilians and for the army, but they were never able to supply enough leather nor shoes. A match factory was opened early in 1863 at Natchitoches by an enterprising citizen.

Salt, which had become one of the most precious commodities in the Confederacy, was not neglected in Louisiana. Salt licks in the north-western part of the state, principally in Bossier, Bienville, and Winn parishes, were overrun by slaves, white families, and commercial interests.

The largest of these licks was King's Salt Works, located on Lake Bistineau. Here up to fifteen hundred men were engaged in salt-making. Water was taken from the brine wells and springs and boiled in huge pots and pans and the wet salt then further dried in the sun. As the war continued, the price of salt increased, and more and more people engaged in the salt industry.[15]

With military fortunes still in a state of flux and many areas under Federal control or under threat of invasion, the citizens of Louisiana found little time to aid needy soldiers or their families. In late March, however, a series of tableaux was given by the ladies of Shreveport, and six hundred dollars was raised. On May 1 these same patriotic ladies were "busy as bees making clothing for volunteers." To acquire containers for medicines, citizens were "asked to bring in all old bottles." "To benefit soldiers families" the philanthropic ladies of the city in late September gave a concert which brought in fifteen hundred dollars.[16]

The lessee system, which had been tried by Butler and had proved successful, was imported into northeast Louisiana, the Teche, and all along the Mississippi. Most of the planters in the northeast fled inland taking as many of their slaves as possible with them. The long line of abandoned plantations was then leased by the army and treasury agents to carpetbaggers and to Southerners who took the oath of allegiance. Since the necessary Negro labor, farming implements, and mules were provided by the army, lessees were responsible only for feeding and clothing the Negroes until the harvest, when they paid off their obligations to the army and to their laborers. Yearly expenses ran between $5,000 and $30,000 on a plantation of a thousand acres, while profits might run higher than $200,000. There was little trouble in finding lessees for the plantations.

During the siege of Vicksburg Grant was unable to give complete protection to the plantations. Six white regiments and several regiments of Negro troops were left in Louisiana. These, aided by the gunboats, were not enough. As soon as he could, Grant sent additional troops to the region, and guerrilla activity from Bayou Macon and the Tensas was impeded for a while.

When Vicksburg was surrendered, many planters in the region along the Mississippi between Vicksburg and Port Hudson abandoned their land and fled inland, leaving their crops to be gathered by Negroes in the Union army labor depots or by speculators. Some Negroes farmed small pieces of land on their own, and in some cases as many as a dozen Negro families farmed co-operatively and divided their returns when the harvest was in. By 1864 there were thirty Negro lessees around Milliken's Bend.

In late June several visits were made by Confederate troops to the area below Lake Providence. They took all of the mules and horses, seized some of the Negroes, and frightened the rest. A few of the lessees were made prisoners and taken into other parts of the state or into Texas. These raids during the critical growing season greatly disrupted affairs, and many plantations grew up in weeds before new laborers and mules could be found. During 1863 the Union lessees rarely made as much as half of the regular cotton crop and most made less. In certain areas the army worm helped cut down on the yield.

Many of the white lessees showed far less regard for their hired Negro laborers than the most negligent planter had shown for his slave. Negroes old, or infirm, or too young were weeded out and sent to Federal contraband villages and camps located along the river, where they had to be cared for by the provost marshals. In 1863 few lessees paid their labor except in food and clothing. For these items they often charged the Negroes five times the actual value, and at the end of the year the Negro was told nothing was due him. Some lessees realized up to $80,000 profits, paid their labor nothing, and then boasted of their ability to swindle the Negro. A few lessees used their plantations for shipping out stolen cotton or for illegal trade. Provost marshals and labor agents often were bribed to shut their eyes to malpractices carried on by the lessees.

Negro labor was often hard to control. The Negroes, considering themselves free, believed that they did not have to work if they did not want to, even though they had signed labor contracts. Withholding food and docking the pay helped to stabilize the Negro, but did not work as a cure-all. Pigs, cattle, and sheep were slaughtered without the permission of the owner, and food was frequently stolen. Soldiers sometimes had to be called in to restore order or to make the Negroes go back to work. On government-operated plantations without overseers, laborers were usually idle and often raided productive plantations, threatening the lives of the lessees and the white owners.[17]

Leased plantations were plagued not only by Confederate troops and guerrillas but also by the Federal army and by recruiting officers. In September the superintendent of plantations, G. W. Cozzens, complained that various plantations "have suffered severely from having the able-bodied hands forced at the point of the bayonet from the plantations for conscription; mules and carts . . . have also been taken by officers and soldiers without hesitation, notwithstanding the order issued by General Banks that property on these places should not be interfered with." [18]

By September, however, Banks ordered that all "able-bodied men of color between the ages of twenty and thirty years, employed upon Government or private plantations, [would] be detailed for military service in the Corps d'Afrique." No one could recruit Negro troops for any other unit, and only those who had the written approval of the superintendent of recruiting and the commissioner of enrollments could recruit for the Corps d'Afrique. These troops were to be used primarily to protect the leased plantations from invasion. [19]

The Corps d'Afrique by October had finished recruiting twenty infantry regiments, and General Daniel Ullmann was given command of the First Division, of two brigades, but the Second Division, also of two brigades, never functioned as a real division. Its first brigade was detached by regiments to garrison Forts Jackson, St. Philip, and other fortifications.

A white officer serving with a detachment sent to the Teche in October to gather colored recruits, reported that the Negroes were "wild with joy and eager to become 'Linkum Sogers.'" To give the Negro soldier greater confidence and pride, General Ullmann decided to establish schools for his black recruits. He petitioned the American Christian Association for teachers. These Northern instructors reported that within six months around five hundred soldiers had been taught to read and write, and others were showing promise. Everything possible was done to erase the prejudices against Negro troops, but the program was never completely successful.

A complaint by inspecting officers against Negro units was the lack of proper sanitation. Dirty camp areas, filthy uniforms, unbuttoned coats, improper uniforms, sloppy cook sheds, and dirty or improperly located sinks were often reported. [20]

The lack of discipline found among some of the Negro troops often could be blamed on their inefficient, lazy, or corrupt officers. In December a battalion of Negro troops below New Orleans was reported "committing depredations and terrorizing the whites in and about that section." Their officers could not, or would not, control them. A white company was sent to the area, and while the Negroes were engaged in a showdown inspection and separated from their arms, the white troops subdued the rebellious Negroes, arrested the ringleaders, and restored order to the battalion.[21]

In order to give the colored troops the best leadership possible, General George L. Andrews, commander at Port Hudson, created a school for the white officers and personally supervised the instructions. Thus one of the original weaknesses of the Negro units was greatly improved. No effort was spared to set and maintain a higher, more uniform standard among the colored troops.[22]

Despite the careful screening and retraining of most of the white officers, some of the older officers of Negro units continued to give trouble. One such officer was Lieutenant Colonel Augustus Benedict of the Fourth Regiment Corps d'Afrique. From August to December this sadistic officer ruled over his Negro regiment like an omnipotent tyrant, freely administering cruel and unusual punishments upon his naïve black charges. One of his fellow officers reported that he had "frequently seen him at Fort Saint Philip, at guard-mounting, strike men in the face with his fist and kick them because their brasses were not bright or their boots not polished." On another occasion, for an equally minor offense, another black soldier was stripped and spread-eagled on the ground with his hands and feet firmly tied to stakes. Molasses was then smeared on his face, hands, and feet to attract the ants. For two days this cruel, inhuman treatment was continued.

On December 9, while in charge of the retreat ceremonies at Fort Jackson, Benedict became angry with two drummers who had turned out without coats. He seized a mule whip and began to flog the two Negroes. The Negro troops watched the beating without moving, but as soon as Benedict had spent his anger and had left the parade ground an angry shout went up, and the men rushed to the armory, seized their weapons and ammunition, and began firing into the air. "One man proposed to 'kill all the damned Yankees.'" Some of the crazed Negroes rushed outside the fort and excited the two companies stationed nearby, and they too joined in the aimless fire. Thinking that Benedict had taken refuge on a steamer tied up near the fort a large group rushed toward the boat screaming: "Kill him, shoot him; kill the son of a bitch. . . ." Working frantically, the company officers succeeded in quieting the men and in persuading them to go to their quarters.[23]

Despite the fact that many Federal officers and white enlisted men remained prejudiced against the Negro in the Federal army, his value as a plantation guard and as an engineer soldier was so great that colored recruiting was increased. Before the end of the war there would be more than 24,000 Negroes enrolled in the Federal army in Louisiana.[24]

PART FOUR

THE RED RIVER CAMPAIGN: 1864

XX

THE CAMPAIGN OPENS

THE DOLDRUMS of military and political activity came to an end in the first quarter of 1864. Louisiana acquired a new, more vigorous Confederate governor, and the Federal commander increased Union political activity in the occupied areas. Military ennui was shattered by a campaign that in size and daring dwarfed any previous military activity confined solely to the state.

Far up Red River, on January 26, at the courthouse in Shreveport, the invalid hero of the battle of Baton Rouge, Henry Watkins Allen, was inaugurated Confederate governor to succeed Thomas O. Moore. Still racked with pain from his war wounds, Allen dramatically hobbled to the rostrum on his crutches to deliver an address that not only stirred his immediate audience but inspired the entire South when it was published in the Confederate newspapers.

In his long, impassioned message the new governor requested permission to create a special "State Guard" to be used in those border parishes "where neither military or civil law" existed. These men would remain at home until raids or invasions threatened and would then be called, serving at no time longer than sixty days.

The legislature, *en rapport* with Allen, tried to fill this and the many other requests made in the inaugural address. Later the new governor was allowed to raise a state guard of two battalions to maintain law and order, to arrest deserters, and to co-operate with the Confederate army against the enemy. East of the Mississippi in the area often harassed by the enemy, Allen was permitted to raise one company of special guards.

The special militia system was strengthened by the legislature in subsequent weeks with acts providing severe punishments against sedition, desertion from state-guard service, and the harboring of deserters. Allen retained authority over the militia only a short time, however, for the Confederate congress amended the conscription law by changing the age limits to seventeen and fifty. Such a law overlapped the state militia, and the governor gave up his control over the militia and guard units.

Welfare measures recommended by Allen were also approved by the legislature. A law was passed authorizing the governor to take proper action in preventing illegal impressment by Confederate agents. Other relief acts, quickly approved, included an act allowing Allen to purchase medicine and to distribute it to the needy, an act allowing him to purchase cotton and wool cards for distribution, an act to provide eleven dollars per month for disabled soldiers, and an act allowing provisions and other essentials to be purchased from the Confederate officers or from private citizens for distribution to the needy. The sick and the wounded soldier was not forgotten. New hospitals were created, and generous aid from the legislature and from civic philanthropy helped to support these institutions. To conserve needed grain and sugar, the legislature gave Governor Allen a stronger prohibition act.[1]

The matter of trade with the enemy was a vexing problem for the governor, as it had been for a long time with the Confederate commanders. Although Allen believed that private trade could lead to the demoralization of the citizens, he did not hesitate to make state contracts with traders who trafficked with the Union men in New Orleans. On February 19 the governor signed a contract with Edward Jacobs of Shreveport in which Jacobs agreed to bring $200,000 worth of cotton cards and $200,000 worth of medicine within the Confederate lines from New Orleans. The state would deliver to Jacobs, at an appointed place, sufficient cotton to cover the amount of the purchases and the expense of delivering the goods, along with the necessary clearance papers and permits. The agent was to deposit $50,000 with the governor as a fourth of the profits he might realize from the sale of the cotton. This system evidently did not work satisfactorily, as Allen canceled the contracts on October 17, 1864.[2]

Despite his bodily frailties, Governor Allen continued to be a dynamo of positive action. He established a system of state stores, foundries, and factories. Quinine and drugs were smuggled through the lines from New Orleans or brought in from Mexico. State laboratories were set up to manufacture turpentine, castor oil, carbonate of soda, and medicinal alcohol. Arrangements were made with Kirby Smith to transfer to the state very large amounts of cotton and sugar, collected by the Confederate authorities as tax-in-kind, until the huge Confederate debt to Louisiana was paid. This cotton was then shipped by wagon trains from Louisiana into Mexico, where it was swapped for shoes, machinery, dry goods, pins, coffee, tobacco, flour, cotton cards, paper, medicine, and other necessities the state could not raise nor manufacture. The state stores sold these goods and state-produced goods to those who could pay and gave them to those who could not. By accepting either state or Confederate money in payment, Allen helped to restore the value of the money in the state. Citizens who had claims against the government for impressed, bought, stolen, or destroyed property were investigated, and if their claims were legitimate, Allen tried to collect from Richmond. Zealously he guarded the civil rights of the citizens from infringement by the military authorities.

Like Kirby Smith on behalf of the military, Allen did everything possible to make the state self-sufficient. A factory for manufacturing cotton cards and wool cards was erected at Minden. The governor ordered a survey of Louisiana minerals and, finding the ore of poor quality, bought a fourth interest in the Davis County, Texas, Iron Works. He gave state protection and supervision to the salt works. A foundry for the manufacture of cooking utensils was established. Private industry such as meat-packing, tanning, and shoe-manufacturing was encouraged.

Not only did the citizens of the state enjoy the fruits of Allen's economic measures, but the Missouri troops, exiled from their home state, were cared for by Allen's philanthropy. He encouraged talented citizens of Shreveport to give a series of plays, concerts, and tableaux for the benefit of these needy men. Through his ingenuity, tact, and energy, Allen succeeded in raising the morale of the people and in helping to strengthen the Trans-Mississippi Department.[3]

Until early spring the Trans-Mississippi Department lines "extended from the Indian Territory, through Arkansas, to the Mississippi and down to the mouth of the Red River, thence to the Atchafalaya to Berwick Bay, and from there by the coast to the Colorado." Kirby Smith, from his Shreveport headquarters, massed his forces in three main bodies. J. Bankhead Magruder at Matagorda faced Banks's main Texas concentration. In Arkansas, Sterling Price kept watch on Frederick Steele at Little Rock. Taylor, in Louisiana, guarded the series of streams leading into the interior of the state on the west side of the Mississippi.[4]

Richard Taylor, the commander of the District of West Louisiana, was forced to scatter his meager troops over most of the state. In January the disposition of his command was as follows: Brigadier General Mouton with the Second Infantry Division operated along the Ouachita near Monroe; in the Sub-District of North Louisiana Brigadier General St. John R. Liddell commanded; a Texas brigade under Brigadier General Camille Polignac occupied Harrisonburg.

Camille Armand Jules Marie, Prince de Polignac, was a tall, grave young Frenchman who had been given an unruly Texas brigade. The rough Texans at first had refused to serve under the "Damn frog-eating Frenchman," but his own ability to swear, his bravery, and his attention to the welfare of his troops won them over. They grabbed their noses when he appeared, and called him "General Pole Cat," but they were ready to follow wherever he led.

Kirby Smith leaned heavily upon Dick Taylor. The two men did not always see problems in the same light, but their differences of opinion did not produce an open schism until the closing phases of the Red River campaign. Taylor was extremely popular with the people of Louisiana; he was Jefferson Davis' brother-in-law; he was possessed by military and political ambitions; hence, Kirby Smith treated him with consideration and diplomacy.

Taylor objected to the price schedules approved by Kirby Smith's department. In January he complained of a shortage of corn. Corn was selling for $3.00 a barrel on the market but the army schedule would allow only $1.50 to be paid. Planters, naturally, refused to sell to the army, saying that they had only enough corn for their own use. If the army attempted to impress the corn, the planters hid it, sold it to the enemy, or shipped it beyond the reach of the impressment officers. Taylor stated that low prices and impressment "alienates the affections of the people" and that in the future many would "plant no more than they themselves require." Taylor then complained that he had received no salt meat nor bacon for his troops during the fall and winter. The government purchasing agents in Texas had failed to furnish any cattle from that area. With Kirby Smith's permission, Taylor sent one of his officers to Texas to try to secure the necessary meat supply. Meanwhile, he began impressing cattle on the prairies, but soon the disgruntled inhabitants began driving their herds out of the region and selling them to the enemy for Federal dollars rather than accepting promises to pay in depreciated Confederate paper. In some areas armed bands of citizens drove out the impressment officers.

Taylor said that leather, another short item, had been entered on the price schedule of the army at less than half the real market value. As a result, tanners were refusing to cure any more hides, and nothing could be done to force them to do so. Taylor suggested that an upward revision of the price schedule would help to clear up many of his shortages and would make the people more content.

Kirby Smith and his various bureaus were doing what they could to meet the demands of the army for guns, ammunition, and equipment. In Shreveport, in four Texas towns, and in one Arkansas town, the clothing bureau had established shoe factories, which were supplying ten thousand pairs of shoes a month to the department. Hat factories were operating at the same places and were turning out as many as thirteen thousand caps and hats per month. Foundries, laboratories, and shops were set up in Shreveport by Kirby Smith's Ordnance Bureau to manufacture ammunition. They could produce up to ten thousand rounds per day for small arms and lesser amounts of shot and shell for the artillery. Additional machinery had been ordered from Europe to expand the production of existing factories and for new factories being planned.[5]

Cotton and the question of trade with the enemy took much of Kirby Smith's and Taylor's time that should have been devoted to their military duties. In the rich Ouachita valley region around Monroe many citizens traded with the enemy at Vicksburg when Confederate troops were not there to stop them. Near Washington and Opelousas, areas that had been stripped clean of cotton the year before, large stores of cotton were moved from the interior to the navigable bayous by private citizens to be sold to the Federal cotton speculators. On January 16 Colonel W. G. Vincent was sent by Taylor to take possession of the cotton for the army. Vincent, with an inadequate force, remained in the area to try to prevent future private trade with the enemy.

Cotton contracts, similar to those Allen made with agents in Texas, were signed by Taylor with speculators from New Orleans and the North in order to secure needed supplies from the areas under Federal occupation. Finally Taylor ordered that no more contracts be signed. He believed the practice was unnecessary, as Banks had relaxed trade relations so much that those who chose to could bring up supplies, and after they did, fair exchanges could be arranged. Goods suitable for army use would enter the lines but would be placed under guard until Confederate officials arrived to inspect them and to receive them.

Lieutenant Colonel W. A. Broadwell, head of the Cotton Bureau with headquarters in Shreveport, in his report of March 15 informed Kirby Smith that the bureau had purchased over 80,000 bales of cotton in Louisiana. The cotton east of the Ouachita, numbering 18,926 bales, was so located that it could not be removed nor properly cared for. At Monroe there were 9,017 bales that could not be moved. Cotton purchased in St. Landry, Avoyelles, and Rapides parishes numbered 11,356 bales. Some of this cotton had been captured earlier by the enemy, and some of it had been burned by the Confederate troops. Around 2,000 bales had been handed over to Taylor, who had sent it to Niblett's Bluff for shipment into Texas. In the vicinity of Natchitoches 12,556 bales of Confederate cotton were stored. Nearly 2,000 of these bales had recently been sent into Texas. At Shreveport 28,505 bales had been purchased, and 10,602 bales had been shipped to Texas to procure army supplies from Mexico.

In March all cotton east of the Ouachita and south of Alexandria was ordered burned with the exception of a few bales to be left to help subsist the loyal families in the area. The serious shortage of transportation precluded the possibility of removing the cotton to safety when Banks's troops began to move into the area. Trade with the enemy along the Mermentau and Calcasieu, to the southwest through the inlets from the Gulf, could not be broken up because Taylor lacked an adequate cavalry force to send into this region.[6]

Jayhawking in the early part of 1864 was proving even more troublesome than illicit trade. In St. Landry Parish, around Opelousas, jayhawkers began to make daring daylight raids "robbing the inhabitants in many instances of everything of value they possessed, but taking particularly all the fine horses and good arms they could find." Conscription in the area came to a standstill. Any man who wanted to stay out of the army had "only to go within the lines of the jayhawkers to be perfectly safe from the officers of the law." Those conscripts who did not join the lawless group refused to leave home until adequate steps were taken by the state or the army to protect their families from the jayhawkers.[7]

In the swampy area around Catahoula Lake and Little River a number of jayhawkers were "committing depredations on citizens and defying civil & military authorities." When pursued by the cavalry, they were able to elude capture by taking to the swamps. Taylor suggested that packs of "negro dogs" should be used to round up these hated men.[8]

Taylor directed Major R. E. Wyche of the Louisiana State Troops and Polignac at Harrisonburg "to scour this portion of the country thoroughly," and to shoot "every man found with arms in his hands, against whom reasonable suspicion exists of a determination to resist the laws. . . . Such men must not be arrested." Any man "capable of bearing arms, of whatever age, who [could not] give substantial proof of his loyalty to the Government" was to be arrested and brought to Taylor's headquarters.[9]

Another group of desperadoes, not jayhawkers, was causing great destruction and fear in northeast Louisiana. They were members of Quantrill's gang. All too often these men turned upon loyal citizens and took whatever they wanted. If anyone resisted, he might be shot down in cold blood or hanged. Taylor tried to put a stop to these outrages, and by the middle of February had arrested one of the officers of the gang and seven men. However, the Red River campaign interfered with the completion of the job, and this lawless band, often dressed in Federal uniforms, continued to terrorize both the enemy and the loyal Confederates for many more months.[10]

Richard Taylor on February 1 ordered Polignac to raid the Vidalia area to secure needed horses and mules. Polignac sent a detachment of some five hundred cavalry and began an early evening attack on Vidalia. Lieutenant Colonel H. A. McCaleb, with the Second Mississippi (Colored) Heavy Artillery Regiment, was sent over from Natchez with nearly five hundred men to reinforce the garrison there. These Negro troops were hurried to a front position on the road leading toward Trinity. The Confederates dismounted and moved forward on foot to the attack. The advance was halted when four Union gunboats began throwing shells into the ranks of Polignac's men.

In mid-February Polignac tried again, and this time he succeeded in breaking up leased plantations along the river and along Lake Concordia. He brought off a number of mules, a supply of cattle, some Negroes, and much food.

At Waterproof, some thirty miles above Vidalia, a garrison of three hundred Negro troops was attacked on February 13 by some eight hundred men from Harrison's cavalry regiment under the leadership of Captain Eli Bowman. The Federal gunboat *Forest Rose* opened fire from the river and drove Bowman back with a loss of seven killed and four prisoners. Captain Anderson lost five Negroes killed, six wounded, and several missing.

The next afternoon and night Bowman resumed the attack, driving in the pickets and pressing hard against the main force. The *Forest Rose* rapidly shelled the Confederates and again they fell back in confusion.

During the night Bowman was joined by Harrison's cavalry and infantry. At seven-thirty on Sunday morning, February 15, Harrison, now in command, tried to storm the town, but again the effective fire of the *Forest Rose* held the Confederates at bay. Another assault by Harrison's reserves suffered the same fate as the first. When three additional gunboats appeared, Harrison called off the attack and retreated toward Harrisonburg. The Confederates' unreasonable fear of gunboats had been insurmountable, and Waterproof remained in Federal hands.[11]

The need for Negroes and for horses caused Taylor to issue orders to Generals Liddell and Walker similar to those he had given to Polignac. Liddell on January 28 was ordered to collect some two hundred and fifty horses, "one hundred good large mules for artillery purposes," and "all able-bodied negroes" in the parishes of north Louisiana, "particularly west of the Washita river," where there had been no enemy raids. Only the mules and horses necessary for crop purposes would be left. Proper vouchers would be given for all the draft animals impressed.

General Walker was ordered to hire or impress at least one hundred able-bodied Negroes and send them to Alexandria to serve as stevedores. These Negroes were to be taken from Pointe Coupee and West Baton Rouge parishes. Later, when an enemy advance became almost certain, Taylor cleared out the Atchafalaya country of all wagons, horses, and mules that might fall into enemy hands. Protests of the owners fell upon deaf ears. Taylor was determined to leave as little for Banks as possible.[12]

Always short of men, Taylor probed every available quarter of the state for additional troops for immediate and future use. Paroled men were ordered into camps for additional training and to await future service. General Liddell, using Harrison's cavalry, was ordered to round up and force the parolees in north Louisiana into camp. South of Red River, Colonel Vincent was collecting the paroled men as fast as his mounted detachments could bring them in. Liddell was informed that the country between lower Little River and Red River was infested with draft-dodgers who should be rounded up and forced into service.

Intelligence reports concerning Federal troop movements confirmed the previous speculations of Taylor and Kirby Smith "that the line of Red River would be the line of his principal attack. . . ." In an attempt to prevent Porter and his gunboats from co-operating with the land forces, in January Taylor stepped up the work of strengthening Fort DeRussy, some thirty miles south of Alexandria. Every available Negro was pressed into service, but many of them tired of the heavy labor and ran away. Those planters who had failed to furnish their quotas of slaves for the work of defending the area were to be forced to do so.[13]

Although by the end of 1863 Banks occupied several points in Texas, General Halleck was still far from satisfied. He had not yet surrendered his ideas of the previous summer concerning the most effective route of operations against Texas. On January 4 Halleck wrote Banks: "Generals Sherman and Steele agree with me in opinion that the Red River is the shortest and best line of defense for Louisiana and Arkansas and as a base of operations against Texas." The general in chief ordered Banks to "operate in that direction" as soon as there was "sufficient water in the Atchafalaya and Red Rivers." Steele's army from Arkansas, some of Sherman's men in Mississippi, and Porter's gunboats would join Banks in the movement. Banks had strongly objected to the use of this route but was reassured when Halleck wrote on January 11: "The best military opinions of the generals in the West seem to favor operations on Red River. . . ."[14]

On January 16 Banks, worn down by argument and anxious to please, bowed to Halleck's decision. He really desired to join Sherman and Farragut in a move against Mobile, but since Halleck ordered otherwise, he again agreed on February 25 to operate in conjunction with William Tecumseh Sherman and Steele against Shreveport.

The sudden reversal of Banks's opinion concerning the Red River campaign was due not only to Halleck's pressing demands and to the promise of aid from Sherman but to other factors—politics and cotton. With an eye on the forthcoming election, Lincoln had strongly urged Banks to hold a constitutional convention, draft a new constitution, and bring Louisiana back into the Union as soon as possible. Lincoln wanted Louisiana's electoral votes. Unknown to Lincoln, Banks himself aspired to the Republican nomination in 1864. If he failed to bring Louisiana back into the Union, Lincoln might remove him from command, which would probably weaken his political chances.

William Seward, Lincoln's Secretary of State, for diplomatic reasons insisted that Banks move in force into Texas. All Confederate foreign trade going through that state could be halted, and the possibility of Napoleon III's sending aid to the Confederacy through Mexico would be stopped.

The desire for cotton played no small part in Banks's decision. He learned that tens of thousands of bales of cotton were stored in western Louisiana and that for a price he could pick up this cotton and ship it safely to New Orleans. If he helped to relieve the cotton famine in New England, influential textile-mill owners would be more ready to support him politically. Through the sale of the cotton the government would be greatly enriched, and Banks would gain much publicity.

On March 1 Sherman traveled from Vicksburg to New Orleans to confer in person with Banks. The meeting was disappointing to both commanders. After learning that Banks intended to command the expedition and that McClernand, who had been assigned to the department in January, might also take part, Sherman gracefully refused to go, saying that Grant needed him; however, he promised to send ten thousand of his best troops along with Porter's flotilla to join Banks on March 17 at Alexandria. Steele, it was understood, would move from Little Rock to Monroe and join forces with the expedition near Shreveport.

Banks was caught up in a swirl of military, social, and political affairs. As the three-year enlistment terms of the older regiments of the corps were soon to expire, the men were offered a bounty and a thirty-day furlough at home if they would re-enlist for another three-year period. Every one of the nineteen regiments and six batteries of the Nineteenth Corps accepted the offer. Four new regiments, the Twenty-ninth and Thirtieth Maine, the One Hundred Fifty-third New York, and the Fourteenth New Hampshire, were sent to Banks. Two batteries, the First Delaware and the Seventh Massachusetts, were assigned to the Nineteenth Corps. The War Department, realizing that a large cavalry was needed for the Red River campaign, sent seven new cavalry regiments into the department from the North. Seven more infantry regiments were mounted, swelling Albert L. Lee's cavalry force to nineteen regiments. The Nineteenth Corps was then shuffled, and the First, Third, and Fourth divisions were compressed into two divisions. The new First Division was headed by Emory (replacing Weitzel, who went north on special duty), and the Second Division, by Grover.

Orders were issued to suspend operations at Galveston, and Cameron's and Ransom's divisions of the Thirteenth Corps were called back to join Franklin on the Teche. Small detachments were left in Texas to hold Brownsville and Matagorda Bay. Except for garrisons at New Orleans, Port Hudson, Baton Rouge, Donaldsonville, Pensacola, and Key West, Banks concentrated his troops on the Teche. On the evening of March 13 the cavalry advance moved out on the road to Alexandria. On March 15 Emory and Ransom began their march up the Teche. Grover brought the Second Division of the Nineteenth to Alexandria by steamer.[15]

Politically, Banks had a finger in the local pie. An election for governor was to be held near the end of February. Interest in the coming event was stimulated by rallies, speeches, and grand torchlight parades. Election day (February 22) passed off in good order, and Michael Hahn, Banks's candidate, won with ease. General and Mrs. Banks held a victory celebration that evening, a bal masqué, at the New Opera House.

At sunrise on March 4 a salute of one hundred guns reminded the people that Louisiana's first Union governor would be inaugurated on that day. All the bells of the city were rung simultaneously. Around midmorning a tremendous throng packed Lafayette Square to witness the ceremonies.

Michael Hahn found himself a governor without a legislature and without a constitution acceptable to the Union supporters. Just before setting out on the Red River campaign, Banks ordered that an election be held soon to choose delegates to a constitutional convention. He was so confident of success in his expedition that he stipulated that all forty-eight of the parishes might choose delegates to the convention.[16]

When Kirby Smith received word of Sherman's visit to Banks in New Orleans, he was convinced that the two would co-operate in a drive against Red River. Taylor, with only seven thousand men, sorely needed reinforcements, and on March 5 General Thomas Green's division was ordered to move from Texas to Alexandria. The next day Major General J. B. Magruder was told to send all troops possible to Louisiana from Texas. On March 15 Debray's regiment, excepting three companies, was ordered by Magruder to proceed to Alexandria. The three detached companies were to go to Galveston to relieve the men of Major's brigade so that they could rejoin their regiment in Louisiana. Previously, on March 7, General Camille Polignac had been instructed by Taylor to move his brigade to Alexandria without delay. General Liddell was left with his small command to cover the defenses of the Ouachita and Black rivers.

At 6 P.M. on March 10 A. J. Smith, with fifteen regiments of infantry and two batteries of light artillery from the Sixteenth Army Corps, and six regiments of infantry and one battery of artillery from the Seventeenth Corps, sailed from Vicksburg for Red River, accompanied by Ellet's Marine Brigade. Immediately after arriving, on March 11, Smith received a wire from Banks "stating that the heavy rains had so delayed his column that he would not be able to reach Alexandria before March 21. . . ."

Porter conferred with Smith and informed him that Taylor had built

a strong fortification and river blockade halfway between the mouth of
the Red River and Alexandria; before the gunboats and transports
could proceed to Alexandria, this fortification had to be taken. The
two officers agreed to act in conjunction with "the army in the rear
by land and the navy by river." Porter immediately sent nine of his
gunboats into the Atchafalaya, followed by Smith's transports. The
remainder of the gunboats proceeded up the Red to remove the river
obstructions. They were to await the arrival of the troops, or until
Porter could come up, before they bombarded the fort.

At 3 A.M. on March 14 Smith began his overland move toward Fort
DeRussy. At Mansura Smith learned from disloyal citizens that the
bridge across Bayou De Glaize had been burned, that General Walker
had moved most of his command forward to join William R. Scurry's
brigade, and that these forces were waiting five miles to the west, where
it was expected Smith would try to cross the bridge over the bayou.
Instead of moving against Walker, Smith tore down a cotton gin and
used the timber to bridge the bayou at Mansura. Using the bridge and
a small ferry boat, Smith crossed the bayou and moved to the north
and west, thus going around Walker and leaving him on his left.

About a mile and a half below Fort DeRussy A. J. Smith halted his
men and, after posting Brigadier General Thomas Kilby Smith to protect his left flank and rear from Walker, ordered Mower to send out
skirmishers and to move forward with the First and Second brigades
of the Third Division of the Sixteenth Corps, followed closely by the
Third Brigade. The Confederate artillery opened fire with five guns
on the line as it came within sight of the fort. Just before sunset Mower
ordered his men to charge, and the first two brigades rushed forward
through a thin and scattered fire. The rapid fire from Mower's skirmishers forced the Confederate infantry to keep down. With a rush
the Federal troops swarmed over the parapet and fell upon the enemy.
Amid the ringing shouts of Mower's men the garrison immediately
surrendered. Mower lost only 3 killed and 35 wounded; he captured
10 guns and around 250 prisoners, killed 5 men and wounded 4.

Walker's division fell back to Evergreen, about thirty miles below
Alexandria, where it was joined by Mouton's division, made up of
Polignac's brigade of Texans and Gray's Louisiana Brigade.[17]

As soon as Kirby Smith learned that the combined military and
naval expedition from Vicksburg had entered the Red River area, he
immediately ordered General Price in Arkansas to send all of his in-

fantry to Shreveport. General Maxey in the Indian territory was to join Price with all his forces, including the Indians. Magruder was ordered to send "all disposable infantry detachments in Texas" toward Marshall and to strip the coastal defenses to an "absolute minimum," sending the cavalry to Taylor at Alexandria. General Liddell was instructed to proceed with his command from east of the Ouachita toward Natchitoches.[18]

As Porter made his way slowly to DeRussy by the longer Red River route, he found his way blocked by a formidable raft of timber and by great piles driven into the river bed. This piling had collected hundreds of floating logs. Hawsers were fastened over the piles, and the gunboats, by backing away, pulled up the giant stakes, freed the log jam, and broke loose the raft in two hours.

Porter proceeded upriver toward Alexandria that night after taking the captured artillery pieces aboard. After giving the men of the Sixteenth Corps a much-needed rest following their thirty-mile march and assault on the fort, A. J. Smith sent them aboard the transports on the evening of March 15 to occupy Alexandria. Brigadier General Thomas Kilby Smith's command of the Seventeenth Corps was kept behind to dismantle the fort and to destroy the magazines and casemates.[19]

Great excitement possessed Taylor's troops at Alexandria when they learned of the capture of Fort DeRussy. On March 15 all the steamboats were loaded with government stores and were ordered to move above the falls out of reach of Porter's gunboats. As the last boat was struggling to escape over the shoal, a gunboat appeared and fired a few harmless shots. The pilot became so excited that he grounded the steamer, and to keep it from falling into enemy hands, it was burned. Taylor withdrew Mouton's and Walker's forces and proceeded along the Natchitoches road to Carroll Jones's plantation, two days' march away, where he expected to stay until Green's cavalry from Texas could join him. Vincent's cavalry, below on the Teche watching Franklin's forces, was ordered to join Taylor, leaving only flying scouts along the enemy flanks. Carroll Jones's plantation was a forage depot located only twelve miles from Bayou Rapides and Cane River. From this area Taylor could draw additional supplies from several other depots and could watch Porter's fleet along Red River. On March 19 Vincent's Second Louisiana arrived and joined Taylor.[20]

Mower's troops, accompanying Porter, peacefully occupied Alexandria. Two days later, on March 18, Kilby Smith's troops came up and joined in the occupation. Banks still had not arrived. While waiting for Banks most of the troops rested and enjoyed Alexandria.

The first portion of Banks's expedition, one hundred men from Lee's cavalry, arrived in Alexandria on March 19. The next day the main body of the cavalry division entered the town and went into camp. At the same time Banks's chief of staff, Brigadier General Stone, and several other members of Banks's staff arrived by steamer from New Orleans.

On March 20 Taylor sent the Second Louisiana Cavalry, led by Vincent, into the Bayou Rapides valley to push as close to Alexandria as possible. Scouting parties sent out by A. J. Smith skirmished briskly with Vincent's troops during the twentieth and on the next morning. Taylor sent Edgar's battery of light artillery to strengthen the cavalry. Vincent went into camp on Henderson's Hill, some twenty-three miles above Alexandria. The hill commanded the junction of the two bayous, Rapides and Cotile.

On the morning of March 21 General Mower, with the First Division and one infantry regiment and a battery of light artillery from the Third Division of the Sixteenth Corps, plus the First Brigade of Lee's cavalry division, set out for Henderson's Hill to dislodge Vincent. Arriving that night, Mower left three infantry regiments, one artillery section, and the cavalry in front to occupy Vincent's attention. Using deserters and jayhawkers as guides, he took two infantry regiments, one section of artillery, and the Sixteenth Regiment of Indiana Mounted Infantry, to skirt around the left to the rear of the hill. The night was wild and stormy. Rain interspersed with hail and sleet beat upon the troops. Capturing couriers from both Vincent and Taylor, Mower learned that the hill was being held by one small cavalry regiment. He also learned the countersign, and after capturing Vincent's pickets, he moved forward and quickly surrounded Vincent's men, taking them in detail around their campfires without firing a shot. Vincent and a few of his men succeeded in escaping, but Mower took over two hundred prisoners, two hundred horses, and all of Edgar's guns. The next day Mower marched back to Alexandria.

From March 13 almost to the end of the month, Franklin was busy moving his forces from the Teche up to Alexandria. As usual, orders were issued prohibiting straggling, private plunder, arson, and the destruction of private property. Again there were those who violated these orders. Governor Allen reported that the soldiers left a wake of broken windows and "charred ruins and decay." Negroes were completely demoralized, and many of them followed the army to Alexandria. Those who remained on the plantations worked poorly or refused to work at all. Men dressed as Confederate soldiers moved behind the army committing crimes and "requisitioning" produce and equipment, supposedly for the army. Negro soldiers and Federal gunboats terrorized the citizens along the lower Teche by threatening to destroy their towns unless they were paid a bribe. Even with all these acts of vandalism the movement to Alexandria was reported to be one of the most orderly ever made by the Union army.[21]

Political affairs well in hand, Banks left Major General J. J. Reynolds in charge of the defenses of New Orleans, Lafourche, and Baton Rouge and proceeded to Alexandria aboard the steamer *Black Hawk,* arriving on March 24. During the next two days General Franklin's command arrived from below. Since word had arrived from McPherson in Vicksburg demanding the return of the Marine Brigade to patrol the Mississippi, Alfred W. Ellet, with his 3,000 troops aboard his transports, departed on March 27.

During the interim before Banks's arrival at Alexandria, Porter had whiled away the time collecting cotton. He sent his gunboats and barges between Alexandria and the mouth of Red River to bring in cotton, which was selling in the northern markets for more than a dollar a pound. Still operating under the general prize law of the navy, Porter seized three hundred bales of Confederate cotton from warehouses in Alexandria and marked it "U.S.N. prize." Taking bagging and rope from the warehouses, the admiral sent his sailors far into the surrounding country to search for unginned cotton. After it was found, it was hauled in confiscated wagons to be ginned and baled and brought back to the gunboats. When cotton was found near the river, the sailors merely rolled the bales down to the waiting boats. Porter and some of his officers personally joined in the game of "the fast buck" by landing their horses and riding out into the interior to scout for cotton. They also seized molasses and wool as prizes. The coal from the gunboat barges was unloaded, and the "prize" cotton was put aboard and shipped to the admiralty court at Cairo. Porter took all cotton wherever he found it, cotton belonging to the Confederate government, cotton belonging to "rebels," and cotton belonging to "loyal" citizens. The relentless search netted the navy some three thousand bales by the time Banks arrived on the scene.

General Banks was furious with Porter when he learned that the admiral was scouring the interior for cotton. Since he had no authority to stop Porter's speculative activities, Banks could only try to beat him to the remaining cotton. Army wagons were sent out in large numbers to collect the cotton. Thousands of bales were brought in by the troops and stored for future shipment. Jealous of the abundant transportation facilities of the army, unprincipled navy men stole army wagons and teams at night, repainted the wagons and branded the mules with navy initials, and drove deep into the country in search of cotton.

Rumors were circulated that Porter was a partner in the speculative affairs of the firm of Butler and Casey because of his friendship with its agent, a "Mr. Halliday." Porter had honored a pass held by Halliday and refused to sign passes held by other speculators or even to listen to their appeals. When it was proved that Halliday's pass was signed by none other than Lincoln, the rumors ceased. Banks, too, became the target of the rumormongers. It was whispered that Banks, before leaving New Orleans, had held a conference with former Governor Yates of Illinois at which time Yates had proposed that Banks enter the presidential race in November. In return for Yates's political support, Banks supposedly agreed to allow a group of the ex-governor's cotton-speculator friends to accompany the expedition in order to purchase cotton. A part of the profits was to be used to finance the political campaign, and the rest was to go to Yates and his friends. Yates denied that any such agreement had ever entered his mind.

In his instructions of January 4 Halleck stated that one of the purposes of the Red River expedition was to secure the large quantities of cotton in the area. Perhaps this fact helped to start the rumor that a "tacit understanding" existed between the Union and Confederate authorities, permitting trade in cotton as long as no cotton was seized by force. Whether or not this was true, many of the army and navy officers claimed that Porter's unbridled seizures forced the Confederates to begin burning or hiding their cotton. In denying the charge, Porter claimed that the Confederates had already begun to burn the cotton before he took a single bale.

A number of civilians did go up to Alexandria with the army. About a dozen of these men were known for their past speculation in cotton, but less than half of the group enjoyed any success in buying cotton. Some of these men came with passes from Lincoln, but there was no proof that Banks had given any permits to these speculators, nor did he give them any assistance in securing cotton. Banks was far too busy with legitimate military and political affairs to have time for speculators.

Soon after Banks came to Alexandria, small groups of men began to drift into town from the piney-woods area. These ragged, desperate men had been hiding in the woods for months, fighting off small groups of conscript hunters and dodging large Confederate parties who came with bloodhounds to track them down. These jayhawkers, each with a score to settle with the Confederacy, gladly took the oath of allegiance and volunteered to act as mounted scouts and spies for the Union army. The services of over five hundred were accepted. Negroes, too, by the hundreds, male and female, young and old, flocked inside the Union lines. Two recruiting stations and training camps were opened, one at Alexandria and the other at Fort DeRussy, and nearly six hundred colored volunteers were accepted for army service.[22]

While waiting for the Red River to rise so that he could go on to Shreveport, Banks busied himself not only with recruiting and with collecting cotton for the United States but also with political matters. The oath of allegiance was administered at Alexandria, and some three hundred voters were registered. According to Banks, on April 1 "an election of delegates to the constitutional convention was held at Alexandria, by the request of citizens of the parish of Rapides. No officer or soldier interfered with or had any part whatever in this matter. It was left exclusively to the loyal citizens of the parish of Rapides." [23]

Within the occupied areas elections of delegates to the constitutional convention went forward. On March 28 elections took place in New Orleans. A few days later elections were held at Alexandria and at Marksville, and as soon as the Union army occupied Grand Ecore elections were held there. None of these elections in any way impeded the progress nor materially affected the outcome of the Red River campaign.[24]

Near the end of March Porter attempted to negotiate the shallow rapids at Alexandria. The gunboat *Eastport,* mounting a full head of steam, started over the shallow strip but grounded in the shoal water. For the next three days large groups of soldiers, manning hawsers, pulled and dragged the ship over the falls, completing the task on March 26. The hospital boat *Woodford,* next to follow, was wrecked in the attempt and had to be destroyed. Three more days were spent in dragging and working the next five boats over the shallow stretch, and it was not until April 3 that the last of the thirty transports and twelve light-draft, relatively weak tinclads chosen to accompany the army to Shreveport succeeded in getting above the falls. The rest of the fleet was either left behind at Alexandria or sent back into the Mississippi.

The day that Porter succeeded in getting his first gunboat above the falls, March 26, General Banks ordered A. J. Smith to march to Cotile Landing, some twenty-one miles above Alexandria, and there to wait for the transports. At Cotile on April 2 Smith loaded his men aboard the transports and proceeded up the Red to Grand Ecore, four miles from Natchitoches, where they went into camp on the night of April 3.[25]

Banks had not intended to leave a garrison at Alexandria, but "conditions on the river and the inability of the transports to pass the falls made it necessary to establish a depot of supplies at Alexandria and a line of wagon transportation from the steamers below to those above the falls." To protect the depot and the transports, General Grover and his division were left at Alexandria. Banks thus lost the services of some 3,000 of his men in the move toward Shreveport.[26] A part of this loss was made up by the arrival from Port Hudson of Dickey's brigade of some 1,500 colored troops. By the end of March Banks had around 30,000 men and 90 guns, not counting Porter's forces, ready to push on to Shreveport. As soon as Steele joined him from Arkansas, Banks would have an army of some 44,000.

Despite orders from Grant and appeals from Banks, Steele delayed his departure from Little Rock. It was not until March 23 that he finally moved toward Arkadelphia with around 8,000 men and sixteen guns. There he was to be joined by Thayer's forces of some 4,000 men and fourteen guns from Fort Smith.[27]

Just before leaving Alexandria, Banks received a dispatch from General Grant dated March 15 in which Grant said: "I regard the success of your present move as of great importance in reducing the number of troops necessary for protecting the navigation of the Mississippi River. It is also important that Shreveport should be taken as soon as possible. This done, send Brig. Gen. A. J. Smith with his command back to Memphis as soon as possible." Banks was warned that if the move took longer than the time Sherman had allowed Smith to be away then Banks was to send him back anyway, "even if it leads to the abandonment of the main objective of your expedition." If Shreveport was captured, Banks was to hold the city and Red River with the necessary troops and return the rest of his command to New Orleans.[28]

Undaunted by Grant's order, Banks proceeded with the campaign plans. General Lee, on March 28, left Alexandria, followed by Franklin,

Emory, and Ransom and the main supply train. Lee's cavalry rode along the Red River some forty miles above Alexandria to Monett's Ferry, where the ever-changing Red had taken a new channel to the east, leaving an old river bed that was now a separate stream called Cane River. Encountering a small Confederate force at Monett's Ferry, Lee skirmished with the enemy and, after driving them off, crossed Cane River and proceeded to Cloutierville, where he again encountered light resistance on March 29. Recrossing the Cane, Lee moved on to Natchitoches and occupied the town on March 30 after driving off a small opposing force. Following the same route of march, Franklin entered Natchitoches on April 2 and went into camp. A. J. Smith's command, aboard the transports, and a part of Porter's fleet arrived at Grand Ecore the next night. Banks arrived aboard his steamer a short time later.[29]

Several soldiers on the expedition kept diaries or later wrote their impressions of the journey. One man reported: "From the day we started on the Red River expedition, we were like the Israelites of old, accompanied by a cloud (of smoke) by day, and a pillar of fire by night." A company of Confederate cavalry had been left behind to set fire to the cotton along the Federal route. Flames spread from the cotton to outhouses and sometimes set slave cabins and white residences on fire. As long as the army moved through the cotton belt, it was greeted with the smoldering ruins of gin houses and piles of half-burned cotton. In the beginning heavy rains drenched the army, and the muddy roads slowed down the marching men as well as the supply trains. Leaving the plantation area, the men marched for two days through the piney-woods area. No rain had fallen here, and the narrow, winding road, deep in dust churned up by rolling wagon wheels and thousands of marching feet, made visibility and breathing difficult. The tall virgin pines shrouded the road in a deep gloom, cutting off the air and holding the dust around the moving men. A high wind moaned among the tree tops.

Leaving the piney woods, the army re-entered the rich alluvial lands of Cane River and again the sight of burning cotton greeted them on the horizon.[30] Approaching the prosperous town of Natchitoches, Franklin closed up ranks, and "with colors flying and bands playing" the army moved through the streets to the bivouac areas.

On March 22 and 23 Taylor withdrew his wagon trains and Mouton's division to Beasley's plantation from which point he could cover the road to Natchitoches and Many. After Lee crossed Cane River, Taylor ordered his small group of cavalry to move toward Natchitoches and to slow down the advance of the enemy. The infantry forces were sent by way of Fort Jesup to Pleasant Hill. Proceeding to Natchitoches on March 30, Taylor received his first reinforcements from Texas, the Fifth Texas Cavalry numbering 250 men, under Colonel A. J. McNeill. The next day the Seventh Texas Cavalry, led by Lieutenant Colonel P. T. Herbert and numbering 350 men, arrived. Of the 600 Texas troops, 175 men were unarmed.

Ordering General Liddell to post Harrison's brigade with a battery of artillery just above Campti on Red River, Taylor sent the Fifth Texas as reinforcements. While Vincent's small cavalry group harassed Lee's advance toward Natchitoches, Taylor withdrew and proceeded to Pleasant Hill. He arrived there on April 1 and was joined by Walker's and Mouton's divisions on the same day. Lee drove into Natchitoches a few hours after Taylor retired. That evening General Thomas Green arrived from Texas and joined Taylor. Taylor was informed by Green that Colonel X. B. Debray with his cavalry regiment, his trains, and two batteries was moving up from Many to Pleasant Hill.

On March 24 Price's infantry division from Arkansas, numbering some five thousand men, arrived in Shreveport. Finding the ammunition they brought with them to be defective, Kirby Smith detained the division and chose not to send them to Taylor until a good supply of ammunition could arrive. Meanwhile, Price's men were reorganized into two smaller divisions and placed under the commands of General Thomas J. Churchill and General Mosby M. Parsons.[31]

Richard Taylor was spoiling for a fight, but Kirby Smith wanted to delay as long as possible. Kirby Smith estimated that Banks had brought with him a force of over fifty thousand, whereas Taylor thought he had only half this number. Kirby Smith informed Taylor that Steele had left Little Rock on March 24 and was marching toward Washington, Arkansas, with ten thousand men and twenty-four guns. If Steele continued to move swiftly, Kirby Smith thought it would be better to take Price's division and rejoin with the remainder of Price's infantry and cavalry force and fight Steele above. If victorious, Taylor could then be sent a much larger force of around thirteen thousand instead of five thousand. When Taylor read this dispatch, he was furious with Kirby Smith and in his answer of March 30 he wrote: "I respectfully suggest that the only possible way to defeat Steele's movement is to whip the enemy now in the heart of the Red River Valley. Price's command could have been here on the 28th, and I could have fought a battle for the department to-day. To decline concentration when we have the means, and when the enemy is already in the vitals of the department, is a policy I am too obtuse to understand." The next day Taylor continued his bitter tirade against Kirby Smith's failure to send Price's division and against the slowness of Green's movements. "Had I conceived for an instant that such an astonishing delay would ensue before re-enforcements reached me I would have fought a battle even against the heavy odds. It would have been better to lose the State after a defeat than surrender it without a fight."

Kirby Smith urged Taylor to continue using caution before attacking Banks's superior forces, and he requested that Taylor hold himself in readiness to move against Steele if the need arose. Taylor answered on April 4: "Action, prompt, vigorous action is required. While we are deliberating the enemy is marching. . . . We may lose three states without a battle. Banks is cold, timid, easily foiled. . . . Steele is bold, ardent, vigorous. If he has anything like the force represented he will sweep Price from his path. He is the most dangerous and should be met and overthrown at once." Taylor reported that all was quiet on his front and that Banks probably would be occupied for many days in collecting supplies. Meanwhile, Taylor stood ready to leave at once to strike at Steele.[32]

Porter's fleet, which arrived at Grand Ecore on April 3, waited for four days for the water to rise sufficiently to push on upriver. Leaving his six deepest draft gunboats behind, on April 7 he shoved off for Springfield Landing, about 110 miles above Grand Ecore, with six of his tinclads, followed by T. Kilby Smith's division aboard twenty transports. The transports also carried a huge supply of food, ammunition, and military supplies for the main army. Smith was instructed to make a reconnaissance from Springfield and to open the road leading to Mansfield if possible.

Contrary to Taylor's expectations, Banks resumed his movement against Shreveport on April 6. Instead of making a reconnaissance to find an existing river road which would have afforded him plenty of drinking water and the additional protection of the gunboats, Banks chose a shorter, more traveled road that left the river to the west and traversed another great piney-woods area almost all the way to Shreveport. Since he did not expect Taylor to make a stand before reaching Shreveport, Banks felt reasonably safe. It was his intention to occupy

Mansfield and control all the roads in the area by the time Porter reached Springfield Landing. Banks, however, made a grave error; he took a road that led him directly into a Confederate trap.

Lee's cavalry and supply trains led off from Natchitoches, followed at intervals by the Nineteenth Army Corps. On April 7, A. J. Smith, after seeing Porter off, moved from Grand Ecore and joined Banks's rear column. The colored brigade, under Colonel W. H. Dickey guarded the main wagon train, and Gooding's cavalry brigade protected the left flank and the rear. On the same day Banks had turned over the command of Lee's movements and of the army to General Franklin.

As the army moved along the narrow road, up and down small hills and through ravines shaded by the towering pines, rain fell now and then, impeding the progress of the supply trains and slowing up the troops. So sure were the Federal commanders that Taylor would not make a stand before reaching Shreveport that few precautions were taken. The advancing column stretched for twenty miles in a loose organization, with long lines of supply wagons separating the units. On April 7 Banks's men reached the little summer resort village of Pleasant Hill.[33]

Taylor, low on forage and food, had already withdrawn his forces to Mansfield. Here, on April 5, he was joined by Kirby Smith. The two generals discussed the necessity of a campaign against Steele. Kirby Smith had already sent Churchill's and Parsons' divisions from Shreveport to Keatchie, which was within supporting distance of both Taylor and Shreveport. Again Taylor reassured Kirby Smith that since Banks was so timid and slow, a general engagement would not take place before Steele was met and defeated in Arkansas. Kirby Smith then returned to Shreveport and wrote a letter to Taylor, saying that if an engagement seemed imminent he was to be notified and he would come down at once.

General Lee, on April 7, moved his main cavalry force toward Mansfield. Slowly Major's pickets gave way before the advance, but during the afternoon at Wilson's farm, three miles above Pleasant Hill, Major took a more firm stand. To Lee's surprise the Confederates, with a wild yell, charged against the numerically superior Federal force. Richard Taylor and Tom Green arrived on the scene with Green's forces, and after two hours of brisk skirmishing with heavy losses on both sides, Green, now in command, fell back to Carroll's mill, eight or nine miles beyond Pleasant Hill, where he adopted a more stubborn resistance. The Federal cavalry forced Green to fall back to within five miles of Mansfield. Lee now went into bivouac for the night ten miles below Mansfield.

Lee was puzzled. Never before had the Confederate cavalry made such a bold stand. He was much worried over the caliber and ability of his amateur troopers. One half of his ten regiments, until a short time before, had been infantrymen, and most of them still were unable to handle their horses properly. Even more worried that his huge wagon train might seriously encumber his advance, Lee failed to follow the retreating Green.[34]

Taylor immediately wired Kirby Smith, reporting that the action might be "merely a reconnaissance in large force" and asking whether he "should hazard a general engagement at this point. . . ." Later Taylor stated incorrectly that he had informed Kirby Smith of his intentions "to fight a general engagement the next day if the enemy advanced in force unless ordered positively not to do so." If Banks was allowed to move through Mansfield, three possible routes to Shreveport would be open to him, and no longer could Taylor confine the enemy to one narrow road. Hasty preparations were made by Taylor for the next day. The Arkansas and Missouri troops under Churchill and Parsons were ordered to move early the next morning from Keatchie to Mansfield.[35]

MANSFIELD AND PLEASANT HILL

Beginning AT dawn on April 8, Walker's and Mouton's infantry divisions moved into position some three miles below Mansfield. Walker's division, made up of Scurry's, Waul's, and Randal's Texas brigades, held a position on the right of the road leading to Pleasant Hill. On his right were two regiments of cavalry, Buchel's and Terrell's, commanded by Brigadier General H. P. Bee. Mouton's division, consisting of Mouton's own brigade of Louisianians commanded by Henry Gray and Polignac's Texas brigade, occupied the left side of the road with a division of dismounted cavalry, under Brigadier General James P. Major, made up of Major's own brigade and Bagby's brigade. A little to the rear, Debray's cavalry regiment was held on the road. Two batteries, Haldeman's and Daniel's, were posted on the right with Walker, and Cornay's and Nettles' batteries were with Mouton on the left. Up front with the cavalry advance was McMahan's battery, which soon was to be withdrawn to the rear to act as reserve. The entire effective Confederate force at Sabine Crossroads, according to Taylor, totaled 8,800 men. Due to the wooded conditions of the area, it was impossible to use all of the guns. Taylor's line of battle rested on the edge of the woods and fronted on a cleared field, eight hundred yards wide and twelve hundred yards long, which stretched out on both sides of the road leading from Pleasant Hill. Across the sloping field was a fence separating it from the dense forest. Here Taylor waited for Banks to advance.[1] At ten-thirty that morning one of Taylor's men wrote in his diary: "The line of Battle has just been formed, and we are ready and eager to meet the damned rascals."[2]

Already General Lee, commander of the Federal cavalry, had discovered that mounted men were next to useless in the heavily wooded, hilly terrain. At Wilson's farm and again at Carroll's mill, on the afternoon before, Lee's troops had been forced to dismount and skirmish as infantry before they were able to drive off Taylor's cavalry outposts. Lee found that leaving the horses behind, advancing on foot, and then returning for the horses after dislodging the enemy was too time-consuming. He begged General Franklin for a brigade of infantry to help him dislodge the Confederates. Franklin refused the request because his infantry was tired after its day's march and could not be expected to keep up with the cavalry movements. He also feared that an infantry force might precipitate a battle before he could close up ranks. In the late evening of April 7, Banks arrived at Franklin's headquarters and ordered him to send forward the infantry reinforcements requested by Lee. Colonel W. J. Landram was sent with Emerson's brigade to join the cavalry. At 5 A.M., April 8, after a two-hour march, Landram arrived at Lee's headquarters.

After sunrise on April 8, Lee, pressing hard against Taylor's cavalry advance, drove them in and advanced in strength against the Confederate left, only to be sent reeling back by the Eighteenth Louisiana. The men of one regiment of the First Cavalry Brigade dismounted, led by Colonel Thomas J. Lucas, were now sent forward by Lee as skirmishers, followed by the two regiments of Landram's command drawn up in line of battle. Encountering stiffer resistance than anticipated, Lee then sent forward the other two infantry regiments, while the cavalry covered each flank. That afternoon, around one o'clock, Lee had driven forward to the large clearing near the crossroads where Taylor waited for him on the opposite side.

General Ransom, who had left Pleasant Hill around five that morning, was just going into bivouac for the day when he was ordered by Franklin to take Vance's brigade forward to relieve Emerson's exhausted men. Just before noon Ransom started out.

Around 1:30 P.M. Lee ordered Landram to send the Nineteenth Kentucky forward as skirmishers with the rest of Emerson's brigade in close support. Green's advance guard fell back across the open field and into the woods beyond. Landram took up a position on the crest of the hill.

Franklin saw the need to close up his long column and had ordered the head of the column to move only a short distance and to go into camp; the rear was to move up within supporting distance of the front as rapidly as possible.

When General Banks arrived on the scene, he realized that Taylor was waiting in force on his immediate front. Ordering Lee to hold his position, Banks sent word to Franklin to bring up his column. Ransom arrived and joined the cavalry and infantry forces. For several hours a running fire was kept up, but Taylor refused to unmask his position or to reveal his full strength to Banks. Issuing the necessary orders to the Nineteenth Corps and joining with Cameron's division, General Franklin rushed to the front, arriving there at 4:15 P.M.[3]

Banks and Franklin misunderstood a shift of units on the Confederate left and decided that Taylor intended to concentrate his greater force in that area, in preparation for a flanking movement against the Federal right. Immediately Franklin began to shift some of his units to halt the movement. Observing this, Taylor anticipated a turning movement from Banks's right, and he began to build up his strength on his left. Terrell's cavalry regiment was moved over to the left to reinforce Major, and Randal's brigade, from Walker's division, was shifted from the right to strengthen Mouton. Next, Debray's regiment was brought forward and deployed on both sides of the road.[4]

Shortly after four o'clock, having completed his deployment, Taylor stated that he became "impatient at the delay of the enemy in developing his attack, and suspecting that his arrangements were not complete, I ordered Mouton to open the attack from the left."[5] Riding in front of his men, General Mouton led his brigade of Louisianians and Polignac's brigade of Texans across the open field and down the hill into a ravine that was swept by a murderous fire from muskets and artillery. With his men dropping about him, Mouton rallied his troops, swept over a fence, and up another hill into the woods held by the enemy. Screaming at the tops of their lungs, the Confederates charged up to the guns that were now throwing grape and canister. The gunners turned and fled to the rear. On his horse, Mouton made a perfect target, and a Federal marksman dropped him from his saddle. The gallant Polignac now rode forward and took over the command. With tears of grief and rage in their eyes, the yelling men followed Polignac. They ran on through the deadly hail, determined to avenge the death of their leader. For awhile, Landram's division held steady and took a terrific toll on the advancing Louisiana and Texas men. Down went James Beard, commander of the Crescent Regiment, and Colonel Leopold Armant of the Creole, or the Eighteenth Louisiana, Regiment. Losses continued to mount. The Crescent Regiment sustained two hundred casualties, and Mouton's division lost about one third of its total strength.

Major's division (consisting of his and Bagby's brigades, the Louisiana Cavalry Brigade under Vincent, and Terrell's regiment, the latter two dismounted) moved forward on Mouton's left and, keeping pace with the main assault, was able to turn the enemy's right flank. Randal's brigade supported Mouton's right. Taylor, sitting astride his horse and smoking a cigar, watched the progress of the movement on the left. He found Mouton's charge "magnificent" and was pleased to see "the gallant Polignac" press "stubbornly on" after Mouton fell. Randal impressed Taylor with his "vigor, energy, and daring." Thomas Green, who was later placed in command of the entire movement of cavalry and Randal's infantry on the left side of the road, "displayed the high qualities which have distinguished him on so many fields," Taylor reported.

With the attack on the left well under way, Taylor ordered General Walker to send Waul's and Scurry's brigades forward on the right side of the Pleasant Hill road. At the same time General Bee, on Walker's right, was to push forward with Debray's and Buchel's cavalry and gain Banks's rear. Scurry was ordered to drive in, turn the enemy's left, and take up position on the high road beyond the main Federal line of battle. Moving through the dense woods and a swamp, Bee was unable to make much headway, but the infantry brigades on his left and those across the road drove the enemy before them.[6]

When Mouton's charge began, Landram brought up Lieutenant Pinckney S. Cone's Chicago Mercantile and Martin Klauss's First Indiana, posting them on the ridge near the center, so they could fire to the right and to the left. Over on the Federal left, Dudley's dismounted cavalry fell back before the Confederate cavalry that had succeeded in flanking Dudley's brigade. Nims's battery was left unprotected. Cone's and Klauss's batteries by now were under such a heavy fire from Walker's infantry that Ransom ordered the guns withdrawn to safer ground. Walker's Texans, cursing and screaming, pushed through the Third Massachusetts Cavalry Regiment and swept up the hill, forcing back the Sixty-seventh Indiana and Twenty-third Wisconsin. Nims, who had lost over half his artillery horses, was forced to leave three of his guns on the field. Cone and Klauss were lucky enough to fall back with all their guns. Walker's men turned Nims's three abandoned guns on the retreating Wisconsin and Indiana men.

Now Ransom ordered Landram to pull his men back to a safer position in the dense woods beyond the clearing. These orders never reached some of the regiments on the right, including the One Hundred

Thirtieth Illinois and the Forty-eighth Ohio, who stubbornly held their ground until completely surrounded by Major and Randal. Sustaining heavy losses, the Illinois and Ohio troops were forced to surrender. Both Vance and Emerson, who were wounded, were taken prisoners with their brigades. Ransom, hurrying toward the rear, was wounded and had to be helped to an ambulance.

Falling back to a second wooded ridge, Landram worked swiftly to restore the confidence of his frightened men and to set up a second defensive position. Cameron's division (the Third Division of the Thirteenth Corps) now arrived from below, and he joined his 1,300 men with Landram. General Franklin, who had accompanied Cameron, took over command of the Federal forces and succeeded in pushing the Confederates back to the clearing. Realizing that he would not be able to hold on indefinitely against Taylor's superior force, Franklin rushed an order back to William Emory to bring up the First Division of the Nineteenth Army Corps and to set up a line of defense at the first adequate clearing. Franklin rode to the front to observe and to better direct his forces. He had hardly arrived when his horse was shot from under him; he himself was injured in the leg and had to be moved to the rear. After a short but bold stand, the entire Federal line began to waver and to give way before Taylor's forces. A general retreat now began, and nothing could be done to rally the men in spite of the efforts of the commanders. Lucas' and Dudley's cavalry did what they could to slow down Taylor. The Confederate cavalry, for the most part dismounted, could not move up fast enough to inflict much damage to the retreating forces.

About a mile in the rear of the Federal lines, the cavalry wagon train, hearing the sounds of the raging battle, had attempted to turn on the narrow road and had succeeded only in blocking the way. A group of wagons became hopelessly mired in a small creek, further cutting off the escape of most wheeled vehicles. The fleeing artillery became ensnared in the mass of wagons, and seventeen more guns had to be abandoned. The terror of the fleeing infantrymen was magnified when they came upon the roadblock; like scared rabbits, they detoured through the woods, tossing aside blanket rolls, canteens, rifles, and all other items that encumbered their flight. Sweating, swearing, and sobbing men broke through the trees, skirted the blocked passage, and returned to the road to join with the horses and wagons moving to the rear. All semblance of order had disappeared.[7]

When General Emory received Franklin's orders to bring his men to

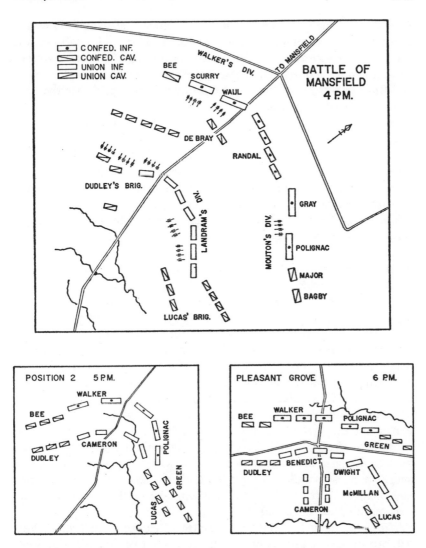

the front, he moved out as soon as possible. Encountering Ransom's ambulance, Emory learned of the repulse from the wounded officer. A short distance beyond, a swarm of camp followers and stragglers, followed by the horde of terror-stricken men of the Thirteenth Corps, swept around Emory's column crying that all was lost. Emory ordered his men to fix bayonets and to push through the mass of fugitive Negroes, cavalry, infantry, wagons, and ambulances. Double-quicking his

men, Emory finally reached ground on a ridge that would allow him
enough room to deploy his troops in line of battle. The small clearing
was a farm, enclosed by rail fences and cut through by a narrow crossroad, a ravine, and a small creek, some two or three miles from Lee's
and Ransom's original front. In the distance Emory could see the Confederates rapidly approaching.

But the onrushing Confederates, tempted by the stalled wagons,
stopped to investigate and to sample the wares, giving Emory a chance
to complete the formation of his lines at Pleasant Grove. He deployed
the One Hundred Sixty-first New York as skirmishers across his entire
front, formed McMillan's brigade on the right, Dwight's in the center
to hold the road, and Benedict's on the left.

Their curiosity satisfied, the Confederates moved forward, re-forming
their line and advancing rapidly against the Union skirmishers. Green,
Polignac, Major, Bagby, and Randal drove against the Federal right,
and Walker, Bee, and Scurry pressed against the left. Emory called in
the One Hundred Sixty-first New York, and as they retired, the Confederates, yelling wildly, rushed after them. The main force of the
attack hit the center of the line, but Dwight's men held fast, sending
the Confederates reeling back with a furious point-blank fire. Now
the Confederates tried to turn the right flank. The pressure was so
hard against Dwight's right that several of his regiments faltered momentarily. McMillan was now deployed at a sharp angle on the far
right. Again the Confederates were checked.

At this stage of the battle there was no roar of guns. In his swift
movement Emory had left his artillery and trains behind. Taylor was
without his batteries, too. The mass of wagons had stopped Taylor's
guns as they had blocked Ransom's. This was a fight between infantry
and dismounted cavalry using rifles. Only the sharp crack of the rifles
and the zing of the bullets, mingled with the thud of flying feet and
screaming voices, disturbed the air.

With lines re-formed, the Confederates now tried to turn the Federal
left, but Benedict's lines held and the third stage of the fight, the battle
of Pleasant Grove, was over. The entire action had lasted only twenty
minutes. Darkness now engulfed the battlefield. Emory with his five
thousand men had snatched back a remnant of honor for Banks on this
inglorious day. Taylor, however, had succeeded in driving Emory some
four hundred yards beyond the creek and went into camp with a supply
of water for his men assured.

Banks's advance on Shreveport had been brought to a jarring halt.

Taylor had fought on ground of his own choice against a divided army sent forward in detachments against him. Franklin had erred when he had refused to allow Lee to leave behind his huge baggage train. Not expecting an attack short of Shreveport, Banks had allowed his forces to be strung out along the narrow, wooded road for some twenty miles; he had then been unable to close up in order to bring a sufficient force against Taylor at any one time. The combined units met by Taylor in the three stages of the battle more than equaled his strength, but he was able to defeat each by detail before reinforcements appeared.

Compared with the small numerical strength taken into the fight, Banks's losses in the battle of Mansfield were very heavy. From a total loss of 2,186, 115 were killed, 648 were wounded, and 1,423 were captured. Taylor reported that he had taken 20 guns, thousands of small arms, and over 200 wagons. As usual, Confederate reports of losses were hazy and unreliable. Taylor claimed that he lost altogether around 1,000 men.[8]

After darkness brought a halt, Emory's men retired a short distance and went into bivouac in line of battle. The night was chilly, and the men were without blankets. They were not allowed to light fires for warmth nor for cooking, and their only food was hardtack washed down by a little water. The screams of the wounded and the moans of dying comrades on the battlefield in their front were all too audible. The men remembered it as a night of misery.[9]

Banks held a hasty council of war with his commanders. Supplies, food, and water were seriously short, so it was decided to fall back to Pleasant Hill, where A. J. Smith and his fresh troops could reinforce the army. Here, too, would be found more open ground and a better defensive position. There were few facilities for the moving of the wounded, but every available conveyance was pressed into service— horses, mules, a few ambulances, artillery caissons, carts, and wagons. Even so, most of the wounded had to remain on the field with the surgeons left behind to care for them. The demoralized and defeated Thirteenth Army Corps was rounded up, formed into skeleton companies, and moved out as silently as possible over the gloomy, pine-shrouded road leading to Pleasant Hill. Around midnight the rear guard of the Nineteenth Army Corps moved to the rear. All night long the retreat continued.

Taylor granted his exhausted men a well-deserved rest after their victory at Mansfield. Early the next morning he moved up his artillery and fired a few rounds into the Federal position of the night before.

Receiving no response, he sent his cavalry scouts forward to reconnoiter. They found that the enemy had slipped away the night before. Around dawn Taylor sent the cavalry forward to pursue Banks and followed with his infantry, which had just been reinforced by Churchill's division from Keatchie. The road to Pleasant Hill was littered by burning wagons, abandoned knapsacks, arms, and cooking utensils. Federal stragglers and wounded were met by the hundreds and were quickly rounded up and sent to the rear.

Banks, too, allowed the men of the Thirteenth and Nineteenth army corps a period of rest following their all-night hike. The day was peaceful and bright, and after a hot meal the men stretched out on the ground in line of battle and fell asleep. Banks spent much time arranging the battle lines to give the best possible defense. During the morning a few of Taylor's cavalry approached to reconnoiter. Following behind Green's cavalry came Churchill's, Parsons', Walker's, and Polignac's men. It was noon before the last of Taylor's infantry column approached Pleasant Hill. The men of Churchill's division were so fatigued by their long march that Taylor granted them several hours rest before making another move. The Federal cavalry was sent forward to halt the advance, and minor skirmishing between the rival cavalry forces took place during much of the afternoon. Around four o'clock Taylor was ready to attack the strong Federal position.

Pleasant Hill, a piney-woods summer resort consisting of a dozen or more houses clustered along a cleared knoll, offered Banks many advantages as a battlefield, but because of the great distance from the main supply base at Alexandria and the serious lack of sufficient drinking water for an entire army, Banks could not hold this position for any length of time. During the one day, April 9, most of the rain water stored in the cisterns was depleted. Without making a final decision concerning the future of his campaign, Banks sent his wagon trains, convoyed by most of Lee's cavalry and Dickey's brigade of the Corps d'Afrique, on the way toward Grand Ecore. At the same time messengers were sent to Porter and Kilby Smith to tell them of the battle and to instruct them to fall back to Grand Ecore.

Colonel William T. Shaw with his brigade from Mower's division, Sixteenth Army Corps, was placed out front in a skirt of woods squarely across the road from Mansfield. The Twenty-fourth Missouri was stationed on the right on a small ridge with one battery of the Twenty-fifth New York artillery posted just in front. The Fourteenth Iowa bisected the road. Moving in line to the left were the Twenty-seventh and Thirty-second Iowa regiments. Dwight's brigade, the First Brigade of Emory's division, Nineteenth Army Corps, held the extreme right flank along a wooded ravine that ran generally parallel with the main road. A battery of artillery, Grow's, occupied a hill between Dwight and Shaw. Brigadier General James McMillan's brigade was sent to Dwight's right rear to act as reserves. The Third Brigade of Emory's division held a dry ditch in a slight depression west of the Logansport road and to Shaw's left rear. Benedict had a light cover of small trees on his front, but his left was clear and exposed. Closson's battery was posted on an elevated spot behind the Thirtieth Maine to enable it to fire over Benedict's men. Shaw's two flanks were left unprotected and wide gaps existed between this brigade and Dwight; there was an even wider gap between Shaw and Benedict.

Some four hundred yards to Benedict's rear were Mower's two divisions, under A. J. Smith, in position to cover the roads leading to Fort Jesup, Natchitoches, and Blair's Landing. Hebard's battery was to the right of Smith's main force. Cameron held the extreme left flank on the Fort Jesup road but, through some misunderstanding of orders, abandoned this position and retired to the rear to protect the wagon train. When the battle opened, he was several miles below Pleasant Hill. A detachment of 1,000 men, taken from various cavalry regiments and commanded by Colonel Thomas J. Lucas, was ordered by Franklin to watch all the possible approaches open to the Confederates.[10]

Around four in the afternoon Taylor had completed his battle lines and was ready to move forward. East of the Mansfield road were two brigades of cavalry, Debray's and Buchel's, under General Bee, supported by Polignac's division that had suffered so greatly in the Mansfield action. On the Confederate right, west of the Mansfield road, was Walker's Texas Division. On his right flank were the Arkansas and Missouri divisions under Parsons and Churchill with three regiments of cavalry. Major's and Bagby's dismounted brigades were sent to the far Confederate left to seize and hold the crossing at Bayou Pierre, thus cutting off the possibility that Banks might escape in the direction of Blair's Landing, or the possibility that the army detachments with Porter's fleet might join with Banks.

At 4:30 P.M. Taylor ordered General Green to open a heavy artillery fire across a cleared field upon a battery located on a hill along the Mansfield road. The purpose of this action was to mask Churchill's movement on the right. The Valverde battery led off and for a short time swapped shells with the New York battery. When the two other

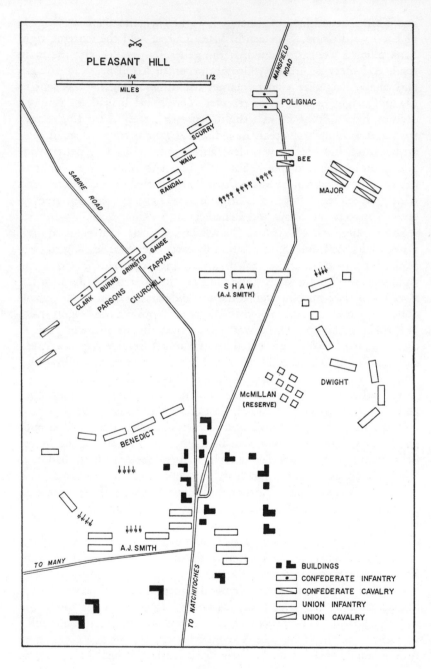

PLEASANT HILL

Confederate batteries came into position and began firing, the Federal battery panicked. Leaving two of their guns behind, they made a wild rush to the rear with their horses and remaining guns. Green advanced his guns into the open field within two hundred yards of the Federal infantry's position on the wooded hill, but when the enemy fire became too heavy, he withdrew them.

Churchill, with the First and Second divisions of Arkansas and Missouri troops under Brigadier Generals J. C. Tappan and Mosby M. Parsons, was ordered by Taylor to make a detour to the right of the road leading to Sabine and to turn the enemy's left flank; after an hour and a half's march through the woods he arrived at the point designated by his guide. Forming his line of battle with the Missouri division under Parsons on the right and the Arkansas division under Tappan on the left, Churchill began his forward movement. After advancing a short distance, Churchill discovered that he was not far enough to the right and ordered his command to move by the right flank. Again, because of the undergrowth, Churchill had failed to move far enough to the right for a flanking movement. Shortly before five o'clock Churchill drove in the skirmishers and hit Benedict's Third brigade of the Nineteenth Army Corps on the left flank and diagonally across the front. Running down the slope, the Arkansas and Missouri men, deployed in two lines, delivered a heavy fire and fell upon Benedict's men in the gully. Without taking time to reload, the Confederates began striking at the enemy with the butts of their rifles. For a brief time hand-to-hand fighting held sway. The swiftness of the advance and the fury of the attack demoralized Benedict's men and the line began to crumble. Beginning with the One Hundred Sixty-fifth New York, followed by the two other New York regiments, the line broke and fell back in great disorder to the hill above the ditch. The Thirtieth Maine, except for two companies, held its position until the pressure on its front and the envelopment of both of its flanks forced the unit to retreat up the slope to the rear under heavy fire. The Confederate advance on the left, owing to a dense thicket and a low abatis piled up by the enemy, was not able to keep up with the right. Colonel Francis Fessenden of the Thirtieth Maine succeeded in partially re-forming a portion of the Third Brigade and sent another volley into the Confederate ranks. Without halting, the Confederate line swept forward, and Benedict's command broke again and fled to the rear in great confusion. In the woods to the right of A. J. Smith's troops, a portion of the Third Brigade was again rallied and formed into a new line of battle. Churchill rushed over the fields into the town of Pleasant Hill, failing in his moment of triumph to see A. J. Smith's troops in line of battle on his right.

After routing Benedict's left, Parsons became careless and left his right flank open to attack from Colonel W. F. Lynch's unseen Illinois regiment, which was hiding in a skirt of woods. As Parsons' men approached, Lynch and the men of the Fifty-eighth Illinois rose up, fired a quick volley, and began charging forward. The Missourians began folding in upon themselves. The lines disintegrated, and the Illinois troops, yelling like savages, drove Parsons' men back into the ditch in front, capturing four hundred of them there. The frenzied Missouri troops now broke completely and ran up the hill in the rear through the ranks of the dismounted Texas cavalry. The Texas troops, who had no love for the Missourians, taunted them for being cowards but nothing could halt the headlong flight. The Missourians made for the cavalry horses belonging to the Texans, stole them from the guards, and rode beyond danger. Scurry's brigade, which was supposed to cooperate with Churchill but failed to do so, now formed in line and drove the surprised Illinois troops back a quarter of a mile until they struck the full force of A. J. Smith's advancing lines.

Churchill's attack was a signal to General Thomas Green to begin his cavalry charge. Bee, with Debray's and Buchel's regiments, in columns of fours, rode swiftly forward down the Pleasant Hill road toward the enemy lines. Before Bee could reach a point close enough to deploy and charge, a body of the enemy, concealed behind a fence perpendicular to the enemy's line of battle, swept his command with a terrible cross fire at close range. Men toppled from their saddles, wounded horses screamed in anguish, and for a moment pandemonium reigned. Bee's men took temporary shelter on the right in a series of small ravines studded with young pines until they recovered from the shock of the unexpected attack. Bee rallied his men but in the process had two horses shot from under him. Colonel Debray was injured when he fell from the saddle of his dead horse. Shaw's front line now joined in the fire along with the ambuscade, but Debray was able to withdraw his men safely to the rear leaving, however, about a third of them killed or wounded on the front. Buchel, a former Prussian soldier who followed Debray in the attack, was able to draw back in time to avoid the ambuscade. Moving to the left, he dismounted his men and moved forward on foot to attack the hidden Federal regiment. Buchel succeeded in driving this regiment back to its line, at the cost of his life. Bee now withdrew his men to the rear.

During this time, General Walker had formed his division and was moving across the field in two lines against Shaw's entire front. Hidden by the woods and a rail fence, Shaw held his fire until the first line was within easy range, and then the entire line opened fire and stopped the first line of attack. Walker's men returned the fire, but after sustaining severe losses the first line fell back in disorder. Heedless of its losses, the entire second line advanced over its dead and wounded comrades and began bending in Shaw's front, Major's dismounted cavalry at the same time pressed hard against Shaw's right.

On Shaw's left Benedict had been driven back by Churchill, and the Confederates had passed in the rear of Shaw's left flank. Another group of Confederates, Major's troops, had succeeded in passing around his right flank and were firing into his right rear. Dwight, on Shaw's right, did nothing to aid him. General A. J. Smith, seeing Shaw's peril, ordered him to fall back. Shaw ordered the Fourteenth Iowa, Twenty-fourth Missouri, and Twenty-seventh Iowa to withdraw but, because of the difficulty of communications through the pine thicket, the Thirty-second Iowa was left to get out the best way it could. The thick brush and the heavy fire on the flanks caused a great deal of confusion, but Shaw succeeded in escaping with most of his men through a narrow passage. His losses for the day were the heaviest at this point. Although the Thirty-second Iowa was virtually surrounded, Walker's men failed to close in for the kill and this regiment remained in the front position until after sundown. Just as dark began to fall, Shaw, who had fallen behind Smith, succeeded in re-forming his battered regiments.

At the onset of the struggle between Shaw and Bee, General Dwight had shifted the First Brigade, Nineteenth Army Corps, farther to the rear, leaving Shaw's right flank vulnerable to attack. After Bee withdrew his men from Shaw's front, he moved over to the Confederate left and joined with the remainder of the cavalry command. The dismounted cavalry was joined by Polignac's division, under the command of General Green, and moved forward against Dwight's right and right center. General Major took his brigade around Dwight's far right flank and drove the enemy in to his hastily constructed breastworks of rails and fallen pines. For a short while the fighting was close and hot, but Major soon found it impossible to dislodge the enemy from his improvised works, nor could he outflank him. The position, paralleling the Mansfield road, was such that a portion of Buchel's command was firing into Major's men, and, without realizing that they were shooting at their own comrades, Major's troops returned the fire. Polignac now started to Major's assistance but, at the same moment, Lane's regiment on the extreme left was ordered to reinforce Major. It was beginning to grow dark, making it impossible to distinguish friend from foe, and when Lane's men approached within three hundred yards of Major they opened fire upon his command. Caught between the fire of the enemy on the right and Lane on the left, Major had to quit his position. As his men were leaving some of Polignac's troops opened upon them, mistaking them for the enemy. Before the mixup could be straightened out, it had become so dark that a new attack was impossible.

On his left, Dwight shifted his men to repulse Walker's troops who were beginning to break through Shaw's lines. Shaw, with some artillery now and a portion of his command, came rushing through Dwight's position on the way to the rear. For a time Dwight's brigade was almost surrounded by Confederate troops.

On the front, General Walker, joined by some of the dismounted cavalry, and on the Confederate right Scurry, with his brigade, were pursuing Shaw's and Lynch's retreating forces. A. J. Smith now sent the main body of the Sixteenth Army Corps into action. Portions of Shaw's, Lynch's, and Benedict's demoralized troops were rallied on the right of Smith's main body and moved forward against the advancing Confederates. General McMillan, who had been held in reserve behind Dwight, was ordered by General Emory to the left to support Benedict's faltering line. McMillan immediately took command of the Forty-seventh Pennsylvania and was moving to the left when a volley from the enemy, who had broken through from above, sent the Pennsylvanians reeling back upon the One Hundred Sixtieth New York and the Fifteenth Maine. Re-forming a part of the Forty-seventh Pennsylvania, McMillan then advanced with this regiment, accompanied by the Fifteenth Maine and the One Hundred Sixtieth New York. McMillan's brigade, acting in conjunction with Smith's command, now drove the Confederate lines steadily back.

Mower, in immediate command of A. J. Smith's troops, with the aid of McMillan relentlessly drove forward against the advancing Confederates. The fresh Federal troops now turned the tide of defeat into victory. Steadily Scurry, Walker, and the other Confederate troops began to give ground and to fall back to the low ground and the ditch where they put up a brave but useless resistance. General Walker was painfully injured in the groin and was ordered by Taylor to leave the field. General Polignac was ordered to the front to reinforce the line but did not arrive in time to render any real assistance. When darkness fell Taylor's men had been driven from the ditch and from the open ground back into the woods. The withdrawal bordered on a rout and, despite all efforts to stem the retreat, the Confederate officers' efforts were fruitless. Darkness brought a halt to all the fighting. Both Union and Confederate units became confused and entangled and it was impossible to continue the struggle.

That night Taylor's infantry forces fell back some six miles to a bayou while most of his cavalry continued on to Mansfield where there was adequate water and forage. Taylor, with a remnant of Debray's cavalry, remained near the battlefield where he was joined a few hours before midnight by Kirby Smith, who had ridden down from Shreveport.

The losses on both sides were very heavy. The Union suffered 1,506 casualties, 152 killed, 859 wounded, and 495 captured. Taylor reported a total loss of around 1,500 men. Both Banks and Taylor claimed to have been faced with overwhelming enemy forces but, in truth, the opposing forces were nearly equal. Taylor had just above 12,000 men while the Union forces in action were not larger than 13,000.[11]

XXII

"SKEDADDLE"

GENERAL BANKS called a meeting of his commanding officers and, after long consultation, it was decided that the army should fall back without delay to the Red River to reorganize and perhaps to find another route to Shreveport. The water supply was seriously low and would be depleted before morning. Without water for men and horses a resumption of the battle at Pleasant Hill the next day was out of the question. Since no word had been received from Porter, it was reasoned that the low stage of the river would seriously impede the transportation of food, supplies, and forage above Alexandria and probably would prevent the gunboats from reaching Shreveport. Already Emory had exhausted his food supply. Banks in no way could plan the rest of the expedition without Porter's co-operation. Still under the impression that Taylor had a superior force and that immediate aid from Steele could not be expected, the majority of Banks's officers decided in favor of retiring to Grand Ecore. There the fleet and Kilby Smith's command would rejoin Banks, and a final decision would be made concerning the fate of the expedition. Banks overlooked the possibility that Taylor's forces were demoralized and weary to the bone from the long marches, from two major battles, and from heavy losses. Had he pushed forward the next day, Taylor probably would have retired and Banks could have driven on to Shreveport.[1]

When orders were issued to the troops to prepare for the retreat, the men of A. J. Smith's command generally condemned General Banks. One soldier reported that "curses were loud and deep" and many begged to stay on and follow up the battle of the day before. Smith was so astounded when he learned of the impending retreat that he rushed to Banks and begged him to rescind the order. When the commanding officer refused, Smith hurried angrily to Franklin and proposed that Banks should be relieved of his command and that Franklin should take over. Franklin turned a deaf ear to the mutinous suggestion.[2]

Until the final order to move out was given, the exhausted men tried to get what rest they could. The night turned very cold, and the shivering troops found sleep impossible. The majority of the wounded remained where they had fallen without water, blankets, or any attention, and as always after a battle, their groans were clearly audible to the troops nearby. Shortly after midnight the army began retiring over the lonely road through the pine barrens toward Grand Ecore. Emory led the column and Mower brought up the rear.

Late on April 10, after a hard march, most of the army had arrived at Grand Ecore, the river landing for Natchitoches. The place, consisting of eight or ten houses located on a high bluff on a bend of Red River, was considered to be a strong defensive position. As soon as the army was rested it was put to work digging a line of entrenchments and throwing up breastworks. Trees were felled and crisscrossed and a formidable works was constructed.

To the great surprise of Taylor's cavalry scouts the next morning after the battle of Pleasant Hill, they found that Banks had secretly retreated during the night. General Bee entered Pleasant Hill a short time later and was soon approached by several surgeons who had been left behind by Banks to care for the Federal wounded. Bee refused to consider the surgeons as prisoners of war and allowed them to go about their work, offering them any assistance they required.[3]

The Confederate wounded, victims of both battles, were moved into Mansfield where they were given shelter in the churches and other public buildings, as well as in private homes. Describing a visit to one of the hastily contrived hospitals, one lady wrote in her diary: "Oh what a dreadful sight. Our poor men just lying on the floor in cotton. And such an odor. . . . There are more than a thousand wounded . . . every private house full. Sent five pillows to the hospital."[4] The ladies not only gave freely of their homes, scanty food, and linens, but also helped to nurse the wounded of Confederate and Yankee alike.

When Taylor rode into Pleasant Hill, he sent Bee's cavalry in pursuit. Bee followed for some twenty miles without firing a shot and captured a number of prisoners who had been unable to keep up with the swift pace of the retreating army. Taking up positions in the surrounding pine hills, Bee's men in the next week were to make frequent patrols into Natchitoches to guard the town and to spy upon Banks at Grand Ecore.

Taylor, Bee, and other commanders were certain that Banks's Red River expedition had already been defeated. In discussing the future of the campaign, Kirby Smith and Taylor agreed that since there were no available supplies below Natchitoches and since only a part of the force could be employed in pursuit of Banks, that most of the troops should be used to stop Steele's advance in Arkansas. Taylor requested permission to accompany the Arkansas expedition and, after placing General Polignac in command of the troops who were to drive against Banks's retreating army, he prepared to leave for Arkansas.[5]

Banks anxiously awaited news from the fleet. Shallow water, poor pilots, countless curves, and unseen snags caused transports and gunboats to ground often and they had to be pulled off by the other boats. Porter, therefore, did not arrive at his destination, Springfield Landing, until a full day after his appointed time.

The fleet reached Loggy Bayou, a short distance above Springfield Landing, around 2 P.M. on April 10 but found the river at this point blocked by a large Confederate steamer, *New Falls City,* which had been filled with sand and mud and sunk to block the channel. A short time later a messenger sent out by Banks arrived on the scene. The courier informed T. Kilby Smith and Porter that the Union army had been repulsed two days before at Mansfield. Smith now gave up trying to reach Mansfield, and Porter left the *New Falls City* untouched and began to withdraw down the river.

General Liddell, on the east bank, followed the retreating flotilla all day on the eleventh, his sharpshooters firing occasionally upon the men who carelessly exposed themselves. Little harm was done. On April 12 the gunboats and transports found the going much more difficult. Many of the transports were crippled with unshipped rudders and broken wheels.

A Confederate cavalry force of several regiments, led by General Tom Green, suddenly arrived from Pleasant Hill. At Blair's Landing, the port for Pleasant Hill, several of the transports and gunboats grounded or suffered such damages that they could not proceed. T. Kilby Smith quickly gathered guns from three of his transports, landed on the opposite shore, and opened upon Green. The Confederate artillery horses were killed, and the hot fire forced the gunners to change positions often, pulling their fieldpieces by hand. Green's sharpshooters, deployed along the bank and sheltered by cottonwoods, began to pour a steady fire into the boats in their front. Smith's men were posted on the hurricane decks and were well protected by cotton bales, hay, and sacks of oats, which cut down on the Federal casualties. The grounded gunboat, *Neosho,* succeeded in freeing herself, steamed down around the bend, and fired charges of canister all along the west bank. The *Lexington, Hindman,* and *No. 13* joined in the fray, sweeping the banks for two miles along the river with grape and canister. All except five of the transports had proceeded below to safety, and Smith's casualties were small.[6]

General Green was audacious in the extreme. One of the Texas men writing of this affair stated: "Colonel Green was a man who, when out of whiskey, was a mild mannered gentleman, but when in good supply of old burst-head was all fight." Green charged boldly down the bank to the edge of the water in the face of the gunboats "with a raw Texas regiment (Wood's) that had never been in a fight before." Green, well fortified with Louisiana rum, "with a yell told them that he was going to show them how to fight."

The charge against the gunboats was made on horseback. "Green was killed well in advance, a cannon shot taking the top of his head off. Three hundred riderless horses ran off the field. Three hundred Texans lay on the field . . . Four hundred escaped. . . ."[7] Porter wrote in his diary: "Every man we picked up had his canteen half full of whiskey. [They were] well set up with it or they wouldn't have attacked."[8] Drunk or sober, foolish or not in waging the attack, Green was a valuable man, and General Taylor lamented him.

The action came to a sudden halt around six o'clock. Green's men had fallen back in disorder. His guns were silent. Just at dark Porter ordered a resumption of the down-river movement.

General St. John R. Liddell, who had followed the fleet from the east bank of Red River for several days, harassed the flotilla all the way to Campti. On the evening of April 13, in answer to Porter's plea, General A. J. Smith, with two brigades, crossed over the river to the east side and marched twelve miles to Campti, arriving there the same night. Here Smith found some of Porter's gunboats tied up, awaiting the arrival of the transport fleet. It was the knowledge of Smith's arrival at Campti that prompted Liddell to retire and to thus make possible the safe passage of the transports on April 14.

Most of the gunboats and transports proceeded to Grand Ecore, and later in the day, A. J. Smith marched back there. As Smith's troops departed, they set fire to the few remaining houses in Campti. By

April 15 all of the gunboats and transports were back safely at Grand Ecore, although many of them were pocked by shot and shell, and many had suffered minor damages from snags and frequent groundings. Kilby Smith had lost only two men killed and eighteen wounded, and Porter had only one man injured.[9]

Banks consulted with Porter on April 15, and the admiral expressed confidence that the expected rise in the river would come and that the move toward Shreveport could be resumed. Banks assured Porter that he definitely intended to advance. To strengthen his forces, he ordered General McClernand to leave Texas with all the white infantry that could be spared and to rejoin the Thirteenth Army Corps in the field. Birge, with three regiments, came upriver from Alexandria and joined Emory on April 13 at Grand Ecore. Nickerson's brigade came up from New Orleans to reinforce Grover at Alexandria. Banks sent a special messenger to Steele in Arkansas asking for his immediate co-operation.

Porter was wrong. Instead of rising, the river continued to fall. Without consulting Banks, Porter began to move his fleet below to Alexandria.

Banks anxiously awaited word from Steele, but he heard nothing. Without Steele, he considered his forces inadequate to advance farther. Both Grant and Sherman had issued deadlines for A. J. Smith's return to the Mississippi, and Grant had renewed his pressure. Without Smith, Banks felt that he would be so grossly outnumbered by Taylor that even a successful retreat would be impossible. Writing to Halleck and Grant, Banks pleaded that the safety of the fleet as well as that of the army depended upon retaining Smith beyond the time limit. Porter begged Sherman, in a long letter written on April 14, to let Smith remain. Sherman gave his consent.

With Porter in retreat and with a falling river making the hauling of supplies from Alexandria most difficult and the co-operation of the navy impossible, Banks began to see the handwriting on the wall. Definite information was finally received from Arkansas that Steele would not arrive. The fear that he would lose Smith still gnawed at Banks's confidence. For the time being, until Porter could complete the movement of the fleet from Grand Ecore to Alexandria, Banks abandoned all hopes of moving against Shreveport and resolved to remain for a time longer at Grand Ecore. An eventual retreat was inevitable.[10]

On April 12 Kirby Smith wrote Taylor: "Steele is bold to rashness, will probably push on without thought of circumspection. To win the campaign his column must be destroyed." Kirby Smith feared that Steele would be able to accomplish what Banks had failed to do. He assured Taylor that Banks "was so crippled that he cannot soon take the offensive." Banks would probably retreat to Alexandria, but since Taylor's troops would be forced to conduct a campaign through a country denuded of supplies, it would be useless to try to stop the retreat. Kirby Smith instructed Taylor to send him, without further delay, Churchill's command and three additional brigades. On the same day Taylor asked Kirby Smith to send him "all the infantry re-enforcements you can" after Steele had been defeated.

On the morning of April 13 Kirby Smith came down to Mansfield to visit Taylor. Again he pointed out the necessity of dealing with Steele without delay but Taylor tried to convince him that Steele would retreat as soon as he learned of Banks' defeat. After failing to change Kirby Smith's opinion, Taylor offered to take his infantry to General Sterling Price and serve under him to defeat Steele. He then expected to return to Louisiana to complete his campaign against Banks. Early on April 14 Taylor sent Walker's, Parsons', and Churchill's divisions on the road to Shreveport. On the same day, Taylor sent Polignac's division toward Natchitoches to support Bee's cavalry against Banks. On the night of April 14 Taylor went to Shreveport. Kirby Smith refused his offer to take the troops to Price, and he was left in command at Shreveport with permission to join his men at Natchitoches if he chose. Kirby Smith informed Taylor that Steele had changed his route and was pushing toward Camden. On the morning of the twentieth Taylor left for Natchitoches to assume command of the troops there.[11] Kirby Smith had already proceeded into Arkansas to join Price, who was engaged in stopping Steele.[12]

With most of Porter's gunboats before Alexandria and the rest on their way, Banks was ready to begin his retreat to Alexandria. All offers to render additional aid to Porter were refused. T. Kilby Smith's transports had already been sent below under a sufficient guard.

There was no real excuse for the Federal retreat. Banks did not know that Taylor had sent most of his infantry to Price in Arkansas and that he had less than 2,000 men of Polignac's division and around 3,000 cavalry, plus William Steele's small Texas cavalry brigade, under John A. Wharton, which had recently joined him. Had Banks known these facts and had he possessed the proper will, he could have moved forward and seized Shreveport.

Late in the afternoon on April 21 Banks was ready to leave for Alexandria. General Franklin was placed in charge of the move. A rapid march was expected, with the enemy contesting the entire way. To hasten the movement, the men were stripped of all superfluous blankets, overcoats, and extra clothing. These were burned in huge piles. After dark great fires were built to guide the wagons and men around the stumps leading from the village. Soldiers fired a large warehouse and the flames spread to other buildings. A lurid light lit the way for miles. All hopes for secrecy of the retreat were gone. The cavalry corps, now commanded by General Richard Arnold since Lee's removal, led off.

Soon Taylor's men were hot in pursuit. Every day, for many hours, the rear guard commanded by A. J. Smith was forced to halt and give battle.

Franklin drove his main column forward without mercy. The forced march was felt necessary to gain possession of the river crossing at Monett's Ferry before the Confederates cut them off. Through the heat and dust the men drove on, taxing their energies almost beyond endurance. Stragglers began to drop out by the hundreds, disregarding the danger of capture by the Confederates. In less than twenty hours Birge's men had covered more than forty miles. That evening at seven, Birge went into bivouac two miles beyond Cloutierville. By 3 A.M. on April 23 the rest of the column arrived.

The road from Grand Ecore to Cloutierville was lighted by burning buildings. Every mile saw a new fire springing up on the horizon. The western troops, A. J. Smith's men, who were far less disciplined than the eastern troops, were blamed for the wanton destruction.

Franklin got his men under way early that morning and proceeded to the river crossing, but found that the Confederates had arrived before him and were contesting the crossing with artillery and small arms from the bluffs on the opposite side. Franklin's wound began to pain him terribly, and he turned over his command to General Emory.[13]

On April 21 General Bee was ordered by Taylor to go below on Red River with his cavalry division and one battery to prevent transports from bringing supplies to Banks at Grand Ecore. On April 22 he skirmished with the advance Federal column and then retired to the south side of Monett's Ferry to join Major's division guarding the crossing. Not realizing that the entire Union force was en route for Alexandria, he was surprised on the morning of April 23 when Banks appeared in his front. Bee and Major, with their cavalry and four batteries of artillery posted on the bluffs, were determined to hold the crossing. General Bee assigned the right to Bagby, the center to Major, and the left to Debray. He understood from the engineers that Cane River was fordable only at one point. Here he established his main position. The right of the main position, with its high, abrupt bank, could not be scaled and the left, with its timbered hills protected by impassable swamps, lakes, and ravines, had complete protection. Expecting the attack from the direct front, Bee massed his greatest strength opposite this point. Terrell's brigade was sent to Beasley's plantation to look after the cavalry supply base there.

General Emory, now in command, considered the position too strong for a frontal attack, and a detachment of cavalry under Lieutenant Colonel Joseph Bailey and Colonel Edward J. Davis was sent around the Federal left flank through the thick canebrakes and swamp to search for a ford, which they failed to find. General H. W. Birge with Emory's third brigade supported by two regiments from the Thirteenth Corps under Cameron and a few mounted men of the Thirteenth Connecticut, was sent two or three miles on the right flank above the crossing to find if the river could be forded and whether it would be possible to sweep in on the Confederate left.

To divert attention from Birge's movement, Emory ordered his First and Second brigades to make a fake demonstration against the crossing. Closson's guns were advanced across the flat ground and opened a steady fire against the Confederate positions on the ridges opposite. A spirited artillery duel now opened between the opposing forces without apparent damage to either.

Birge moved at a snail's pace through the thick timber and impenetrable brakes and across the swamp. A ford was found, and Birge's men waded across Cane River through muddy water up to their waists. Moving by the right flank through a marshy stretch of woods, then across an open field, through a deep bayou fronted by a swampy thicket to the crest of a bluff, and then in a semicircle for about a mile to a small clearing at the foot of a high hill, Birge finally approached the enemy position in the late afternoon.

Colonel Fessenden was ordered by Birge to take the hill. After a hasty reconnaissance it was found that the left flank of the Confederate position was well protected by a lake and a marsh and that the right was protected by a deep ravine. Fessenden, therefore, prepared to charge against the front. The troops were deployed in line of battle with the One Hundred Sixty-fifth New York on the right, the One

Hundred Seventy-third New York, the Thirtieth Maine, and the One Hundred Sixty-second New York to its left. Moving over one rail fence, the men charged nearly a quarter of a mile over the open field and over a second rail fence and some fallen timbers to the foot of the hill. Fessenden re-formed his lines and, at the head of his brigade, led his men up the steep sides, despite a galling fire from the three regiments of enemy cavalry under Colonel George W. Baylor. Colonel Fessenden was severely wounded in the leg and the command of the brigade fell to Lieutenant Colonel J. W. Blanchard of the One Hundred Sixty-second New York. The four regiments succeeded in gaining the tree-studded hill and fired a volley after Baylor's fleeing men. His troops somewhat scattered, Blanchard halted the regiments for some twenty minutes to re-form for another advance. Again moving forward, the brigade had advanced another half mile when a deep ravine was encountered. A right flank movement was made at this point by the First Louisiana and the Thirteenth Connecticut, who heretofore had brought up the rear. Filing into an open field, the two regiments encountered a deadly fire from the enemy, who had taken a second position on another hill. The advance moved to a ditch in the middle of the field and lay down while Blanchard changed fronts and drove against the second hill, only to find it evacuated. Blanchard filed by the left toward the main crossing one mile away. Not a sign of the enemy could be found. Baylor, under Emory's artillery fire from across the river and outnumbered by Birge's men on his front, began to retreat. In the assault Birge had lost a total of 200 killed and wounded. Fessenden's brigade had lost 153 of this total. Bee reported a total loss of only 50 men.

As soon as Emory heard the first sound of Birge's rifles, he sent forward five guns under Closson to knock out the guns placed directly in front of the crossing. Skirmish lines were deployed as if a frontal attack was planned. A detachment of Confederate cavalry, seeing the guns so near, charged down the hill and rushed over the stream to capture the battery. The One Hundred Sixteenth New York, supporting the battery, quickly drove them off. The Second New York Veteran Cavalry, dismounted as skirmishers, rushed forward in pursuit, crossed the stream, and seized the heights above the crossing on the opposite side.

Bee beat a hasty retreat southward to Beasley's, about thirty miles away on the Fort Jesup Road. As soon as Birge came to the crossing, Emory sent out three regiments of cavalry to follow the retreating

Confederates. In the dusk and ensuing darkness, the Federal cavalry mistook a small rear guard detachment for Bee's main force and pursued it for miles along the road to Alexandria while Bee succeeded in making his escape. The action at Monett's Crossing had cost the Union around 300 casualties, while Confederate losses were much lighter.[14]

Taylor immediately blamed Bee for losing Monett's Crossing and held him responsible for allowing Banks to escape. He censured Bee for sending Terrell's brigade to Beasley's to look after the supply base when this had already been taken care of by Taylor. He condemned him for taking no steps in constructing breastworks and for massing his main force in the center instead of on the flanks. Too, Bee was severely criticized for withdrawing his force to Beasley's instead of attacking Banks as he moved through the pine woods toward Cotile, heavily encumbered by his supply trains and artillery. Taylor added that Bee "displayed great personal gallantry, but no generalship."

After Bee's retreat, the Negro engineer brigade was ordered forward to lay a pontoon bridge across Cane River. A little after dark the bridge was ready, and the crossing continued all night and well into the next day. The rear guard, A. J. Smith's troops, was closely pressed by Wharton's cavalry during the morning, but after an hour's struggle the Confederates withdrew. The last of the rear guard crossed over Cane River at 2 P.M. on April 24, and the pontoon bridge was taken up. Moving rapidly over the hot, dusty roads by way of Henderson's Hill and along Bayou Rapides, the head of the column reached Alexandria early in the morning of April 25.[15]

Banks's army, moving from Grand Ecore to Alexandria, left a trail of destruction in its wake. One cavalry soldier from Massachusetts, in describing the scene, reported that "the country was in flames. Smith's men made a clean sweep. Buildings were burning on every hand."[16] Some of the Union soldiers condemned this action and were ashamed. An Eastern soldier remorsefully reported: "The wanton and useless destruction of valuable property has well earned his [Smith's] command a lasting disgrace."[17]

There is little wonder that Taylor reported as early as April 24: "The destruction of this country by the enemy exceeds anything in history. For many miles every dwelling-house, every negro cabin, every cotton-gin, every corn-crib, and even chicken-houses have been burned to the ground; every fence torn down and the fields torn up by the hoofs of horses and wheels of wagons. Many hundreds of persons are utterly without shelter."[18]

In his report on the conduct of the Federal troops on their return to Alexandria, Governor Allen stated: "They sacked private dwellings, . . . they grossly and indecently . . . insulted the unprotected females. . . . They shattered crockery, glass-ware, and mirrors, strewing the floor with their fragments. . . . they dashed to pieces and burned for fuel costly articles of furniture. . . ." They violated the tomb "and stripped the dead"; they "fired volleys into peaceful citizens"; resorted to "arbitrary arrest of peaceful citizens"; and they even "robbed negroes of watches, food, money, etc." [19]

Even General Franklin was mortified by the "indiscriminate marauding and incendiarism" committed on the march. The day after his arrival at Alexandria he published an order condemning these atrocities as being "disgraceful to the army of a civilized nation" and offered a reward of $500 "for such evidence as will convict the accused of incendiarism before a general court-martial. . . ." [20]

The Federal withdrawal was not all fatigue, dust, and destruction. From Cane River to Alexandria thousands of Negroes with all of the household goods they could lug on their backs or balance on their heads joined the retreating columns. These contrabands, of all colors, ages, and sizes, fell in principally with A. J. Smith's rear column. Most were on foot but a few lucky ones rode mules or rode in carts loaded with clothes, pots, and babies. These Negroes proved to be a source of amusement and were also useful as porters to help carry packs and spoils. One Western soldier reported: "Many of the soldiers formed an acquaintance with some one of these swarthy damsels and they marched along side by side in apparent entertaining conversation. . . ." [21] Some of the Western boys, after sacking houses and plantations along the route, garbed themselves in stolen ladies bonnets and dresses and cavorted in and out of the lines mimicking Southern ladies. [22]

Late on April 26 General McClernand arrived from Texas with most of the reinforcements requested by Banks. McClernand's men, in their bright new uniforms, were a great contrast to the faded, dusty, and ragged men who had just returned from up Red River. The reinforcements were cocky and full of confidence, whereas Banks's men were morose and downhearted after having learned the taste of defeat. They knew that they had failed.

The Federal army was soon convinced that its stay in Alexandria would be a long one. The troops were allowed to make themselves as comfortable as possible. Lumber and tools were foraged, and the men busied themselves by building wooden tent floors, benches, and furniture. Regimental details were set to work enclosing Alexandria with a zigzag line of fortifications. The soldiers of the Sixteenth and Seventeenth corps occupied areas along the main roads several miles in front of the fortifications and were often forced to skirmish with Taylor's men.

Banks, indeed, did intend to make a protracted stand at Alexandria. Porter's fleet was stuck above the falls and could not be destroyed nor abandoned. Banks knew that he could not advance again until there was a rise in the river. To add to his worries, Major General David Hunter arrived on April 27 bearing orders from Grant, written ten days before, instructing him to turn over his command to the next in rank, return to New Orleans, and begin preparations for a campaign against Mobile. Banks was to end the campaign immediately and return A. J. Smith's troops to the Mississippi. General Halleck later backed up Grant's order. Hunter, seeing the hopeless situation of the fleet, returned to Grant and convinced him that Smith should be left with the expedition until the navy could make its escape. Banks did not know, however, that on April 22 Grant had wired Halleck "asking for the removal of General Banks" and that Lincoln was even then pondering the question.[23]

Porter's fleet at the falls just above Alexandria was in a precarious position. Unless a rise in the river came soon, the boats would have to be destroyed. Early on the morning of April 24 General Liddell pushed his small cavalry command into Pineville and began firing into the gunboats on the opposite side, but could do little damage with his small arms. Dropping back upriver, Liddell sent a squadron to Montgomery's Point, a regiment to Deloach's Bluff, and the remainder of his men to Bush's place to await the rest of Porter's fleet, still upriver.

The gunboat *Eastport,* after running afoul of a torpedo, had finally been refloated and sent down-river by Porter. On April 26 she became hopelessly grounded on a log jam fifty miles below Grand Ecore, near Montgomery's. Porter, with two tinclads, rushed to the rescue but no amount of effort could release the vessel and she was blown up.

In the early evening Lieutenant Colonel J. H. Caudle, with two hundred sharpshooters and Captain Florian Cornay's battery posted near the junction of Cane and Red rivers, opened fire on the gunboat *Juliet* and one of the pump boats. The *Juliet* was crippled and the pump boat was struck in the boiler, sending up a cloud of live steam. The injured gunboat, hidden by the shower of steam, was able to make good her escape. The loss of life aboard the overcrowded pump boat was appalling; some two hundred men were killed or seriously scalded by the explosion and the jets of live steam. The boat drifted to the bank and the survivors were quickly made prisoners. Porter's flagship, the *Cricket,* suffered thirty-eight hits and twenty-five men were killed or wounded, but he finally succeeded in running by the battery.

The next morning the gunboats *Hindman* and *Juliet,* lashed together and followed by the remaining pump boat, attempted to run past the battery. Both boats were struck repeatedly, becoming separated and unmanageable. They floated past the batteries bumping both banks but, fortunately, not grounding. The pump boat fared a worse fate. Riddled with shot and with the pilot gravely wounded, the boat was quickly captured by the Confederates. Taylor withdrew his batteries to conserve ammunition and left sharpshooters on both sides of the river to follow the gunboats down to Alexandria.

Taylor sent Polignac's division to hold McNutt's Hill and a brigade of cavalry with one battery was pushed around Alexandria to David's Ferry, near Marksville, to keep Banks from communicating with the Mississippi. Another squadron of cavalry had been sent to Simmesport to block the escape of runaway Negroes. Vincent's cavalry still on the Teche was ordered to proceed to Marksville and Simmesport. General Liddell moved down near Pineville. On April 31, around sunrise, Liddell surprised a Federal cavalry reconnaissance force of some 2,000 by falling on its rear and flanks. The Union cavalry was driven back in great confusion to Pineville. For the next few days Liddell watched the Federal troops transfer goods below the falls to Alexandria and watched them begin trying to get the gunboats below. On May 6 Taylor sent an order across the river to Liddell ordering him "to harass the enemy constantly at Pineville and in their works at the falls, the failure to do so being inexcusable. . . ." The next day he sent a conflicting order, commanding Liddell to take most of his troops below Wilson's plantation, near Major's command, on the opposite side. Liddell left one company to watch the Federal activities and, before moving below, sent in his resignation to Taylor. At Wilson's on May 10 Liddell received his orders from Taylor relieving him of his command.[24]

At Alexandria, Porter's troubles were only beginning. From all appearances, there was no hope that his stranded gunboats could get below the falls for months. The falling water had laid bare a ledge of rocks extending for almost a mile. In places the water was only four feet deep while the heavy gunboats required at least seven feet. The current, running up to ten miles per hour, narrowed to almost nothing here and there along the channel. A plan to dam the stream and raise the water level at least seven feet was proposed by Lieutenant Colonel Joseph Bailey, an acting engineer on Franklin's staff. Franklin gave his approval and so did Porter, after some hesitation. Banks, too, fully co-operated with Bailey. Porter, who hated Banks, was prompted to state: "To General Banks personally I am indebted for the happy manner in which he forwarded this enterprise, giving it his whole attention night and day, scarcely sleeping while the work was going on. . . ." [25]

Over three thousand men were detailed to work on the dam. On the Pineville side opposite Alexandria large detachments of New York and Maine regiments plus many Western troops from the Thirteenth Army Corps were set to work felling trees, hauling them a short distance to the river, and floating them into position. Some of the men quarried stone above the dam and loaded it aboard barges to be brought down. The trees were placed fifteen or twenty abreast pointed toward the opposite bank and weighted down with bags filled with dirt and stones. Successive layers formed a crisscross pattern and were made tight with sand, bricks, and brush. Gradually the Pineville side began to expand out into the river. Night and day the task went forward despite the backbreaking labor, the heat, and the danger from the swift current. The men often worked in water up to their necks.

On the Alexandria side two Negro regiments commanded by Colonel George D. Robinson and an additional detail of four hundred men from Dickey's colored infantry brigade began work building a crib dam from the bank out to meet the tree dam. Houses were torn down and additional lumber was taken from warehouses and a mill to furnish timber for the cribs. The navy blacksmiths helped to make bolts to hold the cribs together and, after deeper water was reached, navy boats helped to move the cribs into position. Stones from the quarry, bricks torn from buildings, and heavy machinery taken from sugar mills and cotton gins were then thrown into the cribs to hold them in position. Finally the two wings dammed most of the 758 feet from shore to shore, with the exception of a gap about 150 feet wide. To narrow the gap, four large coal barges, weighted down with stones and bricks, were sunk alongside the crib and tree wings. The water level above was raised sufficiently to float the lighter gunboats over the shoals.

Sunday, May 8, after eight working days, the *Osage, Neosho,* and *Fort Hindman* passed the upper falls and moved down to the pool formed by the dam. The next morning around five two of the coal barges were swept away by the swift current. For some reason, only one vessel above the falls, the *Lexington,* was ready to move when the barges gave way. Porter ordered the *Lexington* to make a run for it. Steaming at full speed into the churning waters of the gap, the *Lexington,* after rolling wildly and grounding briefly, swept safely into the deeper waters below. The exultant voices of the watching men resounded over the river. The *Neosho* stalled her engines near the opening and was swept helplessly through the gap, suffering a hole in her bottom which was quickly repaired. The *Osage* and *Hindman* came through safely.

According to Banks, Porter had done little or nothing to lighten the draft of his heavier gunboats until after the barges gave way. Had he done so, all of his boats could have safely passed below on May 9.

Bailey and his details, inspired by the partial success of their first attempt, cheerfully went to work at the upper falls to construct a new crib wing from the southwest bank and a tree dam from the Pineville side similar to the first dam. A diagonal bracket dam of logs was constructed just below to confine the waters into a narrower channel. After working three days and nights the water level was raised sufficiently to try another passage below.

In the meantime, Porter had removed a portion of the armament, plating, cotton, and supplies and thus had considerably lessened the draft of his vessels. On May 11 the *Carondelet, Pittsburg,* and *Mound City* passed over the upper falls safely and proceeded to the first dam. On May 12, the *Ozark, Louisville,* and *Chillicothe* and two tugs safely negotiated the upper rapids and that evening and the next morning all of the boats successfully passed through the gap in the dam. With his fleet now safely below the falls, Porter rapidly reloaded his vessels and prepared to move as quickly as possible to the Mississippi. The army had labored hard and long to free the fleet but, except for the quartermaster, the navy had done little to aid itself.

While a portion of Banks's army was busy building dams, Lawler's brigade and A. J. Smith's men were forced to skirmish heavily with Taylor's cavalry forces below Alexandria.

On May 1 Colonel George W. Baylor, with a division of cavalry from Major's brigade and J. A. A. West's battery, was just getting into position at Wilson's Landing on Red River, some thirty miles below

Alexandria, when an enemy transport, the *Emma,* passed by. As West's guns were not yet ready, Isham Chisum's cavalry gave chase and, after two miles, the transport surrendered. In violation of Taylor's orders, Baylor burned the transport instead of sinking it to block the channel.

Two days later (May 3) Baylor caught the transport *City Belle* as she headed up the river with 700 officers and men aboard. Hardeman's regiment opened fire upon the transport with small arms while West's battery moved into position. The second shot from the Parrott rifle struck the *City Belle's* boiler, sending up a heavy shower of steam. Men began jumping overboard to escape being scalded. The boat was beached, and Baylor took most of the One Hundred Twentieth Ohio Regiment captive. A number had been killed, some had drowned, and only a few escaped through the woods.

On May 5 two Union gunboats and a transport were sighted moving down from Alexandria. The enemy succeeded in passing the upper section of artillery and then approached Baylor's second position. The transport *John Warner,* in the lead, was disabled by the first shot. The men of the Fifty-sixth Ohio, being furloughed home, were badly shot up and the survivors were taken as prisoners when the transport finally surrendered. The gunboats rushed forward and opened up on the shore with their Parrott guns, rifled Dahlgrens, and howitzers. The gunboat *Covington* caught fire and was abandoned by her crew, who rowed to safety on the opposite bank under a heavy fire from the sharpshooters. The gunboat *Signal* continued to pour broadsides at Baylor's battery, but Baylor's riflemen were so effective with their Enfields that the *Signal* was forced to close her portholes and surrender. Most of the crew, from both the *Signal* and the *John Warner,* escaped through the woods. The *Covington* blew up. After removing the ammunition and armament from the *Signal,* she, along with the transport, was sunk across the channel by Baylor. Red River was for the time being closed to the outside. Major strengthened his position at Wilson's Point and Bagby, with Bee's former division, held Fort DeRussy. A road was cut to connect Major and Bagby, in order that a swifter concentration of troops could be supplied to either officer. From May 5 there was no communication between Alexandria and the Mississippi. Seven Federal transports approached Fort DeRussy from below on May 6. Three were loaded with troops from Matagorda and the others carried supplies. When Bagby's batteries opened fire, the transports fled back down the river.

Taylor was being pressed hard below Alexandria and practically all of his command had been switched below. After eighteen days of continuous fighting, Taylor begged the Trans-Mississippi headquarters for artillery horses and ammunition of all types and for two good regiments of cavalry to reinforce Liddell's small force on the north side of Red River. He reported that all forage and subsistence had been removed beyond Banks's reach and that strict orders were given to destroy cattle and anything useful that might fall into enemy hands.[26]

On May 10 Taylor reported to the adjutant general in Shreveport that: "On several occasions we have forced the enemy from strong positions by sending drummers to beat calls, lighting campfires, blowing bugles, and rolling empty wagons over fence rails." With only 6,000 men he felt he had to resort to every subterfuge. He claimed: ". . . the end is drawing near. Banks's cavalry is almost destroyed. His troops are disheartened, sullen, and disinclined to fight. He is short of provisions and almost entirely without forage. Sickness prevails to an unprecedented extent. . . ."[27]

With some of Liddell's men destroying bridges and felling trees to block all roads leading from Pineville east to the Ouachita and the Mississippi and with the strong force below on Red River, Taylor felt that he had Banks trapped. The gunboats and transports would soon be caught by lower water and would be his. Banks could do nothing but surrender.

While Banks was away on his campaign, cotton speculators around Alexandria continued their operations. Army transports were sent to New Orleans loaded with cotton. The navy, even during the retreat from Grand Ecore, continued to gather cotton. When the ill-fated expedition returned to Alexandria, Porter claimed that Banks sent out army wagons to bring in cotton which was loaded aboard transports desperately needed to remove public stores to safety.[28]

On May 9 Banks informed the Quartermaster that all transportation facilities would be needed "to transport the material of the army and the property of the Government, and the freight of private individuals not connected with the army cannot be taken under any circumstances whatever." The next day Banks ordered: "All cotton on the transports at this place will be taken off to make room for Government stores. No more sugar will be taken until all other Government stores are loaded."[29] Detachments were put to work immediately removing the cotton and loading army stores aboard. The cotton was thrown in piles along the levee.

With the fleet safely below the rapids, Banks issued orders for the army to move out early on May 13.[30] For several days a part of the army had been busy laying waste to the area. One soldier reported that on one day he had "counted nineteen sugar plantations burning" and that later he saw the ruins of many more. He claimed that these fires were set by jayhawkers who took "this opportunity of revenge on the rich planters and their cruel overseers." [31] This charge may be partly true, for even the Confederate army had its hands in the destruction. To get revenge against the turncoat lieutenant governor, J. Madison Wells, a raid was made on his plantation along the Boeuf on the night of April 22 "destroying all of the cotton (2000) bales, his buildings, and confiscating all the mules, beeves & in other words *cleaned him out!*" [32]

When the Federal army returned to Alexandria, it was understood among some of the commanders that should it be necessary to withdraw, the town would be burned. Banks testified before the Joint Committee that he "did not see any necessity for firing the town. I knew there were a good many Union people there and I gave instructions to General C. C. Grover to provide a guard for its protection, . . . which he did." [33] For two days and nights before the evacuation the town was protected by the One Hundred Thirteenth New York Regiment, "who faithfully and efficiently" guarded the city. They were relieved on the morning the army departed by a cavalry detachment of five hundred men.[34] The cavalry was ordered to police the town "to prevent any conflagration or other act which would give notice to the enemy of the movements of the army." [35]

To the music of the bands, the men stepped lively as they began their departure from Alexandria early on the morning of May 13. Lawler led off the infantry, followed by Emory, while A. J. Smith's men brought up the rear. The route of march followed the river bank as far down as Fort DeRussy in order to cover the removal of the gunboats and transports.[36]

Despite Banks's orders, Alexandria was set on fire "and, as the last of the army moved eastward, the city was wrapped in flames." [37] Citizens claimed "the burning and plundering was the work of the 16th and 17th Corps," (A. J. Smith's men), who "fired a store on Front Street." A strong wind spread the flames rapidly from one building to the next.

. . . men entered the yard with a tin bucket and mop, and sprinkled the fencing and out-buildings with a mixture of turpentine and camphene. . . .

At many points persons were seen, belonging to the Army, in the act of setting fire to the houses.

During the conflagration of the buildings they were entered by gangs of soldiers and pillaged of everything valuable. . . . Many officers were conspicuous in their exertions in behalf of suffering citizens, and to them was due the saving of a number of dwellings.

Governor Allen reported that witnesses described the "Court house, Episcopal Church, Methodist churches burned and every building upon twenty-two blocks." Prowling army stragglers were seen robbing the citizens of some of their belongings that they had rescued from the fire.[38]

Banks was still in Alexandria when the fire broke out. He later told the Joint Committee that the "fire broke out in the attic of one of the buildings on the levee" inhabited by either soldiers or refugees, "and it was not in human power to prevent their setting their place on fire when they left." He had ordered out the colored engineers and other troops to stop the fire, but because of the long drought the buildings and trees were so dry that very little could be done.[39]

Pandemonium reigned; frightened cows bellowed and charged through the flaming streets; squawking chickens with scorched wings tried to fly out of danger. Hundreds of women, children, and old people ran through the streets, trying to carry a few of their belongings to safety. When the heat became unbearable, they dropped their loads and fled to the levee. Thieves ran from house to house and even along the levee taking whatever they wanted from the shocked people. By noon the most congested parts of town were destroyed. An attempt to blow up a church in the path of the fire only succeeded in helping to spread the flames.

A part of the fleet still remained at the docks. Some of the ammunition and ordnance transports, tied up within a few yards of the fire, quickly cast off and started down to safety.[40] Huge piles of cotton burned and smoked at the wharves and along the banks. Admiral Porter, who had not yet departed, expressed sympathy for the suffering people but felt that "the burning of Alexandria was a fit termination of the unfortunate Red River expedition." [41]

Steele's cavalry division followed the Federal rear guard while Harrison, reinforced by Likens' regiment, accompanied the retreat on the opposite side of the river. Harrison's main object was to harass the fleet. Polignac, Major, and Bagby in Banks's front and on the flank skirmished lightly with the advance cavalry. On May 14 skirmishing occurred at Wilson's Landing and the next day at Marksville, but Taylor made no real attempt to halt the retreat. The transports and Porter's fleet proceeded on to the Atchafalaya to await the army.

On the broad rolling plains of Avoyelles, before Mansura, on the morning of May 16 Taylor formed his battle lines to contest the further progress of the Federal army. Bagby and Major, with nineteen guns, held the right and Polignac, with two of Debray's cavalry regiments and thirteen guns, held the left. At dawn brisk skirmishing opened along the line. Around 6 A.M. the main Federal force moved up to "the broad, open prairie, smooth as a billiard table" and formed their lines. Mower took position on the right, Kilby Smith next to him, Emory the center, and Lawler on the left. Arnold's cavalry took up position in columns on the flanks. The artillery was stationed at vantage points between units. The batteries on both sides kept up a continuous roar and the smoke rose straight up and held like a column in the motionless air. The duel lasted for almost four hours. Across the broad treeless plain the men of both sides could see every maneuver made by the others. Several halfhearted attempts were made by Arnold's cavalry to turn Taylor's right, but Taylor easily fell back and re-formed his lines. Taylor's men were stretched over a long thin line while Banks, with at least ten thousand more men, presented several lines of battle. At 10 A.M. a general Federal advance was ordered against the center and the left. Hopelessly outnumbered, Taylor fell back in good order and left the road to Simmesport open to Banks. Losses on both sides were negligible. It had been a grand spectacle of movement and fire with little damage to anyone. The greatest suffering came to Banks's men, who were short of drinking water.

On the morning of May 17, at Moreauville, Wharton's troops attacked and drove in the rear guard of cavalry. Debray, with two regiments and a battery, was hidden in ambush in the woods a short distance away. As A. J. Smith formed his lines to drive off Wharton, Debray suddenly rose up and enfiladed the surprised line. A number of Smith's men were killed and Wharton succeeded in taking many prisoners. At the same time Colonel W. O. Yager, with his regiment and the Second Louisiana, struck the Federal wagon train near Yellow Bayou, scattered the Negro guards, killed a few white officers, and destroyed some of the property. Yager could not bring off the wagons as the Sixteenth Corps was posted along the only available side road. Brisk fighting continued until dark, when Smith and the entire rear guard retired across Yellow Bayou.

Taking advantage of the divided Federal forces, on the morning of

May 18 Taylor decided to make one last bold attack on the enemy's rear before he could cross over the Atchafalaya. In the vicinity of Norwood's plantation, near Yellow Bayou and Bayou De Glaize, Taylor formed his entire command in line of battle. Major's cavalry division was dismounted and posted on the right while Polignac's troops held the left. Confederate skirmishers moved forward against the cavalry pickets located in a belt of timber. Swiftly the pickets were driven back on the Sixteenth and Seventeenth corps. The entire Confederate line was ordered forward. Yelling wildly, the Confederates rushed into the woods. General Mower, who was in command of the Federal rear guard in the absence of A. J. Smith, with only three brigades of infantry and one cavalry brigade was under orders from Banks to hold his position at all costs until the Thirteenth and Nineteenth army corps were safely across the Atchafalaya. Moving forward, Mower drove the Confederate pickets before him until he came to a dense thicket of briars interlaced with dead trees. He pushed his way through the thicket and found Taylor's men moving forward on the opposite side of a field. Taylor opened up with twelve guns. Two Federal batteries, one on the right and the other on the left, were brought forward. Hidden behind the thicket, Mower completed the placement of his line. Major's division advanced in columns on the Federal left and Polignac's division in line of battle moved on Mower's front. The Federal cavalry on the left gave way and Major's troops got in the rear of the left flank. Polignac's troops on the front moved up to the thicket and, after a few rounds of canister and a bayonet charge, Polignac was driven back in confusion. Mower shifted one battery of artillery and most of his men to face the enemy on the left flank. The battery opened up with double-shotted canister, and Major was pushed back with heavy losses.

As the morning moved into afternoon, the weather grew progressively warmer. The sweating Federal troops had consumed the little water they had with them long before. There was no more to be had. Men began to fall out from sunstroke and heat exhaustion. Mower withdrew beyond the thicket and gave his weary men a brief rest. He then slowly re-formed his line and advanced again through the briars and over fallen timbers, only to discover that the Confederates had rallied and had just begun to enter the thicket a second time. A quick desperate struggle with bayonet and rifle ensued and the Confederates once more were driven back into the open field. On the left, Major's men again drove in the Federal cavalry and again, after leaving heavy skirmishers facing the open field, Mower shifted his main body and drove Major back. The last charge had set the thicket afire so that an impassable wall of fire prevented the advance of either side. Taylor had had enough. He now withdrew and did not make another attack. Mower reported his losses as 38 killed, 226 wounded, and 3 missing, for a total of 267. Taylor had 30 men killed, 350 wounded, and over a hundred of Polignac's men captured, for a total loss of some 500.[42]

Taylor knew by now that he could not prevent Banks's escape. On May 18 he wrote Colonel S. S. Anderson, the assistant adjutant general: "The campaign will probably close today at Simmesport. . . . Nothing but the withdrawal of Walker's division from me has prevented the capture of Banks's army and the destruction of Porter's fleet. I feel bitterly about this, because my army has been robbed of the just measure of its glory and the country of the most brilliant and complete success of the war." The next day he wrote: "The limits of human and equine endurance have been reached." He reported that he himself was "suffering from sickness and exhaustion" but that he would cross the Atchafalaya, set up his batteries on the Mississippi, and blockade the river. Later he intended to move into the Lafourche and confine Banks to New Orleans.[43]

At the Atchafalaya, the ingenuity and native engineering ability of Colonel Bailey was again called upon. He was asked to construct a bridge across the river so that the troops, horses, artillery, and wagon trains could be moved over rapidly. Bailey, with his usual energy, brought twenty-two of the transports into line, anchored and lashed them abreast, and connected them with gangplanks and boards, forming a continuous roadway. The first units of the Thirteenth and Nineteenth corps began crossing on May 19. The next day A. J. Smith's command crossed over and the bridge was immediately dismantled. After loading the wounded, sick, and exhausted aboard the transports, the entire fleet steamed toward the Mississippi while the army marched toward Morganza on the banks of the river where they would be reorganized and refitted.

A. J. Smith's command left Banks at Red River Landing on May 21. Many of the Easterners breathed a sigh of relief to see the last of the Sixteenth and Seventeenth army corps. The rough Westerners had not been easy to live with, to put it mildly. Smith arrived back at Vicksburg on May 23 but found that he was already too late to join Sherman's spring campaign. Until sent to Missouri, Smith remained at Vicksburg.

From the flaming town of Alexandria to the banks of the Mississippi the arsonists of the Federal army continued their work. Plunderers were not idle either. The villages of Marksville and Mansura, although not burned, were thoroughly sacked by the stragglers and by the hordes of Negroes who trailed along with the army. The citizens were insulted, abused, and robbed of their food or whatever struck the fancy of the plunderer.[44]

Soon after his arrival at Simmesport, Banks was joined by Major General E. R. S. Canby. Grant, through his numerous requests for Banks's removal from command, had won a partial victory. Halleck had written him on May 3 stating: "General Banks is a personal friend of the President, and has strong political supporters in and out of Congress. There will undoubtedly be a very strong opposition to his being removed or superseded." To remove Banks, Lincoln would "require some evidence in a positive form to show the military necessity of that act." On May 7 Lincoln made his decision. Canby was "assigned to the command of the Military Division of West Mississippi," which embraced the Department of the Gulf and of Arkansas. On May 18 Canby took over command from Banks. Banks still retained the titular control of the Department of the Gulf, but it was understood that his duties in the future would be purely civil.[45]

The failure of the Red River campaign could largely be laid at Banks's door, but there were many who shared in this failure. Seward, desiring a toe hold in Texas, had convinced both Lincoln and Halleck that inestimable diplomatic advantages over French-held Mexico would be gained. Halleck, backed up by Sherman and joined by Porter, had picked the Red River route over Banks's protests. At Grand Ecore Banks had failed to make a proper reconnaissance to find a river road that would give him naval protection. Instead he struck out inland and moved into Taylor's trap at Sabine Crossroads. The long interior march through the pine barrens had necessitated long supply trains. Franklin, in overall command, had been wrong in insisting that the wagon train remain with the cavalry in front of the infantry. Lee's cavalry, fairly weak at best, should not have been allowed infantry reinforcements, which helped to bring on the battle of Mansfield. Neither Banks nor Franklin had expected Taylor to make a stand short of Shreveport since he had consistently retreated up to that point. They erred in allowing the infantry columns to become so widely separated, forcing the Federal army to fight in details and in so doing meet defeat. The retreat from Pleasant Hill to Grand Ecore was a serious error on Banks's part, although it was endorsed by most of his commanders. A drive against Taylor's demoralized forces after Pleasant Hill would have led him into Shreveport. Banks's military ineptitude, Steele's case of the "slows" and his failure to co-operate with Banks, the falling river, the difficulty of sending supplies for great distances, Porter's anxiety for the safety of his fleet, the imminent departure of Smith's troops—all of these things added to the final failure. Banks had little or no control over some of these factors, but he failed to do all that he could have done. Porter, Franklin, A. J. Smith, and many of the men held Banks, the political general, entirely responsible for the failure of the campaign.

THE QUIET PERIOD

RICHARD TAYLOR at Alexandria, ill and worn out from the late campaign, still brooded over Bank's escape and with each passing day laid more of the blame at Kirby Smith's doorstep. He was a bitter man. In a series of blistering letters he struck out at his superior commander. He harshly criticized Kirby Smith for heading the Arkansas expedition and for bungling the job. Again he repeated the charges that Kirby Smith alone was responsible for letting Banks get away because he had arbitrarily robbed Taylor of his best troops. He refused Kirby Smith's offer of a promotion and refused to command the Missouri expedition then under consideration. Taylor claimed that Kirby Smith's top-heavy bureaucracy would doom any campaign to failure. He denounced the Conscript Bureau and the entire Quartermaster Bureau as being incompetent and next to useless. Kirby Smith attempted to placate Taylor, but at the same time he let him know that he objected to his insubordination. By May 28 Taylor wrote that he was very discouraged and asked Kirby Smith to remove him from command. On June 5 he tossed restraint to the wind when he wrote, "The grave errors you have committed in the recent campaign may be repeated if the unhappy consequences are not kept before you. After the desire to serve my country, I have none more ardent than to be relieved from longer serving under your command."

His patience at an end, Kirby Smith issued an order on June 10 relieving Taylor of command and placing Major General John G. Walker in charge of the District of West Louisiana. Taylor was ordered to Natchitoches until Jefferson Davis could be informed of the move. The next day Kirby Smith wrote to Davis and enclosed three of Taylor's letters along with the removal order.[1]

Taylor, after six weeks of idleness, and waiting "the pleasure of the President of the Confederate States" received orders at Natchitoches on July 18 to cross the Mississippi promptly and assume command of the Department of Mississippi and East Louisiana. Infantry that could be spared by the Trans-Mississippi Department would follow Taylor as soon as possible.

On July 28 Kirby Smith ordered Taylor to move to Alexandria, to take command of two infantry divisions, and to "cross the Mississippi River with as little delay as possible." Kirby Smith immediately ordered a pontoon train of twenty-five boats to proceed to Alexandria. At Alexandria Walker prepared eighteen more, making a total of forty-three, capable of ferrying 1,000 men across the river at a time.

Lieutenant Colonel H. T. Douglas of the Engineers presented a plan to Taylor, offering to bridge the Mississippi with pontoons so that the troops could cross "en masse" with "subsistence, artillery, and trains." Taylor endorsed Douglas' suggestion, but Kirby Smith did not. He regarded the scheme as "impractical and visionary" and thought that it would cause a delay of more than two months. He felt that the first plan would be more efficient and could be executed in greater secrecy and with less trouble. By dismantling the artillery and by swimming over the necessary horses, four batteries could be crossed over. Taylor was irked by Kirby Smith's proposals, and when the crossing continued to be delayed he fumed. His anger rose to new heights when Kirby Smith would not allow him to choose the staff officers who would accompany him.

Taylor finally planned to cross the river without the troops, but Kirby Smith positively forbade him to do so. Taylor argued that "the impracticability and impossibility" of crossing with troops at this time had come about because the enemy had learned of the plan and had stationed gunboats at twelve mile intervals between Vicksburg and the mouth of Red River with other gunboats regularly patrolling between these stations. "Already several hundred desertions from the infantry corps have taken place," Taylor reported. He felt that the desertions were due to the fact that the soldiers had not been paid in a year, to the inactivity of the troops for two months, and to the fact that most of the familiar field officers were absent or had been shifted in their commands. Taylor informed Kirby Smith that he was no longer under him and that as soon as Davis ordered him to move he would, if he thought it the best policy.[2]

In late July Walker's men were moved near Harrisonburg on Black River where they remained in camp for nearly a month. On August 25 they received orders to get ready to cross the Mississippi. Moving to the Tensas, these troops were joined by the pontoon train and Polignac's division. Many of the men deserted in order to escape crossing the river.[3] Earlier, on August 22, Kirby Smith had sent word to Taylor "to immediately suspend the movement of the troops across the Mississippi River." Taylor was to send the two divisions to Monroe and he was "relieved from the command" and was to cross the river alone.[4] A few days later Taylor happily carried out the order and, according to his report: "On a dark night, in a small canoe, with horses swimming alongside, I got over without attracting the attention of a gunboat anchored a short distance below." [5]

A number of changes in command in the Trans-Mississippi had been ordered by Kirby Smith on August 4. Major General S. B. Buckner had been assigned command of the Department of West Louisiana and J. G. Walker was returned to Texas. J. B. Magruder was transferred to Arkansas.

One of Buckner's first duties in Louisiana was to send out his cavalry to hunt down the hundreds of men who had deserted when they learned that they were to cross the Mississippi. The deserters were to be informed of the abandonment of the crossing and were to be promised that if they would return voluntarily they would not be punished. Buckner, after visiting his commanders, reported that "in at least one instance . . . an open mutinous outbreak under arms, encouraged, . . . by a few officers" had taken place and that the ringleaders were being tried. The leaders were tried and shot, and all those who refused to return were to be shot too.

Kirby Smith now renewed his interest in an Arkansas-Missouri campaign. Price was sent from Camden toward Missouri. En route he was joined by Marmaduke's and Fagan's divisions and by Shelby's cavalry. Now with some 12,000 men, Price in mid-September moved into Missouri to recruit loyal Missourians and to seize supplies, stores, and mules.[6] A few days before, Walker's old division and a few attached Western troops had reached Arkansas from Louisiana. With supplies so scarce in the Red River area, Kirby Smith in November ordered Forney's and Polignac's divisions to take up winter quarters near Minden.

The pressure from Confederate commanders east of the Mississippi and from the War Department in Richmond was to continue during the winter of 1864–65. Both Kirby Smith and Buckner believed a large scale crossing of the river too difficult, if not impossible. There were few supplies near the river; the Mississippi was too high; Federal gunboats were patrolling the river too closely; and there was not sufficient artillery available to protect such a crossing. The Louisiana senate joined Kirby Smith in protesting against sending troops from their department into the East. Governor Allen opposed the crossing, and public opinion in general was against the move.[7]

Kirby Smith during the course of the Red River campaign, and after, was faced by many problems. Sufficient soldiers in the field was one of the most vexing of these problems.

After Banks's retreat, Colonel Louis Bush of the Fourth Louisiana had been ordered by Taylor to clear out all the enemy forces, jayhawkers, and deserters from southern Louisiana "with very little delay or hesitation." Those persons of St. Landry, Calcasieu, Vermilion, Lafayette, St. Martin, and St. Mary parishes liable for military service were ordered "to come forward and join the Louisiana infantry regiments on duty in the state on or before the 1st day of June, 1864; otherwise they [would] be considered and treated as jayhawkers and shot down on sight."[8]

In response to the order, recruits began to appear and in a short time Bush had increased his small force to six hundred, but he was still handicapped by a shortage of arms. These men went into camp near Franklin and were given extensive training. After a short time they became effective soldiers and periodically during May and June they raided the Federal outpost on Berwick Bay which was held by twelve hundred Negro and two hundred white troops. The Union garrison soon became afraid to forage far afield, and it was little wonder that the citizens along the Teche wanted the Fourth Louisiana to remain.[9]

In mid-August, Henry Watkins Allen was beginning to talk about the conscripting of free Negroes into the Confederate army. In late September the governor communicated his ideas to the Secretary of War, James A. Seddon. "The time has come for us to put into the army every able-bodied Negro man as a soldier." Allen concluded: "He caused the fight, and he will have his portion of the burden to bear. We have learned from dear-bought experience that Negroes can be taught to fight, and that all who leave us are made to fight against us. I would free all able to bear arms and put them into the field at once."[10] No immediate action was taken by the Confederate government on this suggestion.

The question of parolees gave Kirby Smith a number of new problems. In May his headquarters issued an order stating that "prisoners captured before January 1, 1864, including officers and men of the Vicksburg capture, are declared exchanged." In late July he ordered all Vicksburg prisoners to report for immediate duty.[11]

One of the parolee camps was set up at Pineville, near Alexandria, under the command of Colonel Szymanski. Walker reported exchange prisoners from Vicksburg and Port Hudson were "coming in slowly and unwillingly, but by vigorous measures and some necessary examples of severity I have hopes of being able to put a good brigade (as to numbers) into the field." [12] Many of the men arrived in camp in rags and tatters and without shoes. These necessities were taken care of promptly. Other similar camps were established at Natchitoches, Vienna, and Shreveport. Toward the middle of October, Kirby Smith had around 5,350 men of all arms in the Department of West Louisiana.[13]

The supply situation in Louisiana was very grave in the second half of 1864. Armies of any size no longer could expect to live off the country. Texas, on the other hand, had plenty, but many of the people there began to demand payment in specie and refused to accept Confederate paper money. The subsistence office at Paris, Texas, with 200,000 pounds of bacon and flour on hand was ordered by Kirby Smith to send much of this supply to Louisiana. This was not done because there was no transportation available. On July 12 Kirby Smith ordered that one half of the wagons used in overland commerce must be volunteered for army service or they would be impressed. Only wagons that were exempt from impressment, those used to haul cotton, would not be affected.

Cotton was the open-sesame to procuring goods from Europe through Mexico. Kirby Smith on June 1, 1864, instructed his purchasing agents to impress one half of the cotton in the department if they could not purchase this amount at the schedule price. The dire need for military stores made impressment mandatory if all other methods failed.

In November reports of the destitute condition of some of the troops were still coming into Confederate headquarters at Shreveport. Later in the same month, the inspector general reported that the ration situation was still grave and the supply of clothing and shoes was far from adequate. Much of the blame, he stated, could be laid at the soldiers' own door. Many troops were taking their issued clothing and were selling it to civilians at high prices. In conclusion, the inspector reported that the stationery supply had become so short that units often could not furnish higher headquarters with copies of their orders.[14]

Under the authority of an act of the Confederate Congress, dated April 21, 1862, which allowed the purchase of cotton from producers to be sold at home or abroad, 121,036 bales had been purchased in Louisiana by October 30, 1864. Nearly $8,000,000 had been expended, each bale costing just over $64. The authorities, with no idea of immediate sale or shipment, scattered the Confederate cotton on various plantations. Confederate agents occasionally visited to inspect it. Only a small portion of the cotton was shipped abroad or sold to the enemy.

Estimated losses of Confederate cotton in Louisiana through the end of October, 1864, were 43,443 bales. This figure included that captured by the enemy, stolen, burned by the Confederates, and that used for military fortifications. Another 24,328 bales had been sold to the enemy or shipped abroad to help ease the pressing need for supplies. Still on hand in Louisiana were 53,265 bales. No estimate of the number of bales collected through tithe or impressment could be made.[15]

By December Kirby Smith had decided on the policy of destroying all the cotton in Louisiana. Governor Henry Watkins Allen protested vigorously. He argued that "a government has the right to destroy its own property" and that "if it is necessary to keep private property out of the hands of the enemy, the government should buy and pay for it, thus placing its right to destroy it beyond question."

Allen believed that no real benefit had been realized from destroying the cotton in the first place. Most of the cotton in the state belonged to small farmers who had been stripped of most of their cattle, grain, horses, and mules either by the enemy or through impressment by the army. These people had little more than their cotton left. Allen preferred to see a few speculators make money rather than to leave widows, orphans, and others destitute.

Since the government had gathered large supplies of cotton in the Ouachita Valley and had sold much of it directly to Federal agents, it would be unfair to burn the few bales of cotton belonging to small farm owners when these were often their only medium of exchange for use in the purchase of supplies.[16]

Canby, who replaced Banks, was also having his troubles with cotton. On July 26 President Lincoln wrote to him: "Frequent complaints are made to me that persons endeavoring to bring cotton in strict accordance with the Trade Regulations of the Treasury Department, are frustrated by seizures of District Attorneys, Marshals, Provost Marshals and others, on various pretenses, all looking to black mail and spoils, one way and another." Lincoln asked Canby to break up this practice.[17]

The need for money was desperate in the Department of West Louisiana. Many of the soldiers had not been paid in more than a year. Kirby Smith, in December, begged President Davis to send additional funds as soon as possible. With millions of dollars in outstanding debts yet to be paid, it would be impossible to secure public credit in the future. Procuring supplies for the army would later become practically hopeless. Kirby Smith felt that impressment without the ability to pay the citizens was unfair and illegal.

The money situation was worsened by counterfeit Confederate bills that began to appear in increasing numbers in the department. Counterfeiters had been busy for the past two years and had succeeded in helping to devaluate the paper currency. The use of Federal greenbacks, although forbidden, was also harming the value of Confederate currency. Blockade runners and others were beginning to refuse payment in Confederate bills and were demanding greenbacks.[18]

Living conditions in many parts of Louisiana were becoming more difficult for the civilian population as well as for the soldiers. After the close of the battle of Mansfield, in early April, the citizens of that area did what they could for the wounded soldiers left behind by Taylor. Fish fries, picnics, checkers, dancing, church services, song fests, craw-fishing, parties, and other entertainments were provided. By May, the people of Mansfield were "almost reduced to starvation" and could give the recuperating soldier only a little bacon and corn bread to eat. Eggs, when available, were selling for $2.50 a dozen; corn brought $2.50 a bushel. Meat sold for around $2 per pound. Few could afford to pay such prices. By the end of June eggs were $5 a dozen and there was no meat, sugar, butter, nor flour at any price.

Living costs in Shreveport, as well as in other places, continued to rise. By early August a pound of butter cost $5, eggs $5 a dozen, beans $2.50 a quart, melons $5 apiece, and a single apple sold for 50 cents. Room and board at the hotel cost $20 a day. Even the one-way fare on the makeshift stage from Shreveport to Alexandria had risen to $240.[19]

In reporting on conditions in late June around Alexandria, Colonel George W. Guess of Walker's command wrote: "Not only every vestige of food in the whole country has been destroyed, but nearly every town and house has been burned. The clothing of helpless women and children has been burned and they are in the woods without food, shelter or clothing. There are many . . . who are actually living on blackberries."[20] Prices in Alexandria were exorbitant. A soldier reported in mid-November that butter cost $10 a pound, bacon $5 a pound, flour

$3 a pound, and a bushel of meal was $10. "All wear homespun, and shoes made of cloth or some few have shoes of leather, which they tan and make themselves." [21]

The citizens of Opelousas, who had suffered greatly when Banks passed through on the way to Red River, had tried to resume a normal life afterwards. A band of jayhawkers, led by a Dr. Dudley, increased their difficulties by launching a series of raids in the area. A citizens' council was organized in mid-April and succeeded in routing the jayhawkers. The Fourth Louisiana Cavalry, under Colonel Bush, continued to flush out the jayhawkers and to restore peace in the area. After Bush's cavalry was withdrawn in August, the jayhawkers resumed their activities. Another citizens' council, aided by a few soldiers, again broke up the jayhawker gang.

In September and October the jayhawkers came from hiding and resumed their regime of rape, murder, and pillage. A new home guard was raised in November but the jayhawkers, now led by a slave named Bernard, continued their reign of terror. In mid-December the home guard had had so little success that the jayhawkers were becoming bolder and were daily increasing in numbers.[22]

Jayhawkers in northeastern Louisiana were especially active in the early part of 1864. General Liddell sent one company of his cavalry into the Tensas area to clear them out. Bob Taliaferro, leading a company of desperadoes, was intercepted near Black River and, after a running fight and the loss of eleven men, Taliaferro's gang scattered into the swamps. In the parishes north of Tensas, Captain Joseph C. Lea and his guerrillas did much toward the end of the year in ridding the area of the feared and hated jayhawkers.[23]

Many people in Louisiana did not forget the soldiers who were helping to defend the state, even though they themselves were suffering from shortages of every type. The Reverend James Earl Bradley of Opelousas took charge of a drive to raise three thousand dollars for needy soldiers. By early December he had succeeded in raising more than that amount and, in addition, had collected numerous articles of clothing.[24]

Some of the people around Alexandria remembered the great sacrifices of the man in service. On Christmas Eve the ladies of Prairie Roberts entertained for the soldiers in the area with a "magnificent dinner, and sung a few appropriate songs such as 'When this Cruel War is Over,' 'The Poor Soldier' & several others." The table "groaned under the weight of good things. We had any number of splendidly stuffed turkeys—young pigs stuffed—ducks—chickens—capons—cakes —candies of all descriptions—puddings—pies &c." [25]

Up in Shreveport, the recently organized Glee Club, composed of older male civilians and a few officers and men from the army, held a benefit performance on October 15 to aid the needy Missouri troops. The vocal and instrumental performance was a huge success, with more than five thousand dollars being raised. This popular group was called upon again to give a second benefit at the Gaiety Theatre in mid-December.

By December, social affairs were beginning to pick up around Shreveport. A grand tableau was held at Spanish Lake near the city. Several tableaux were planned for Shreveport in January to raise money. Dances and supper parties were being held in honor of the soldiers in December. Below at Natchitoches, tableaux were planned for early January and a money raising concert was scheduled for later in the month. Both Shreveport and Natchitoches were becoming more lively. Eggnog parties and other social affairs during the Christmas holiday season lifted the morale of civilians as well as that of the soldiers. [26]

Aid to the families of soldiers and others who were destitute bothered the Federal authorities just as it did the Confederate citizens. The original assessments made in 1862 by General Butler, against the men who had subscribed $1,250,000 "for the defense of New Orleans against the United States," had been used up, but the need for funds had not been removed. Canby ordered the original subscribers to pay an additional $250,216.25 to further relieve the poor. [27]

General Edward Richard Sprigg Canby, who relieved Banks at Simmesport, soon after taking over his new command sent Banks to New Orleans to look after civil affairs while he made a tour of inspection of his department.

Canby lacked the social amenities of Banks, appearing to most people as stern and taciturn. George S. Denison, a Treasury agent in New Orleans, wrote on June 23: "Gen. Canby is very active, but his work makes no great show as yet, because it is conducted too quietly & without ostentation. Canby is a tall man of thoughtful and kind face—speaks little & to the point—thoroughly a soldier & his manner is very modest & unassuming & sometimes even embarrassed." [28] By late July Denison informed Chase that Canby was "becoming popular—more perhaps because he snubs Banks . . . than for any other reason."

Poor Banks! From a star part he had been demoted to the role of a supporting actor. He was a military commander without any troops to command. Denison, who had found reason to admire Banks in the past, now, like many others, found reason to criticize him. He stated that Banks had become "very unpopular, especially with the army who attribute to him alone the miserable failure on Red River." The state Constitutional Convention, called by Banks, in public opinion "stands no higher than Banks himself." Denison reported that the delegates were making fools of themselves.[29]

As planned by Banks, the Constitutional Convention convened early in April at Liberty Hall, New Orleans. Ninety elected delegates were qualified to revise and amend the state constitution. Orleans Parish was represented by sixty-three delegates and twenty-seven came from the fifteen parishes under Federal control.[30]

One of the first actions taken by the delegates was to approve payment of "$10 per diem" to each member. Denison reported that only a few of the delegates were intelligent. The great majority were inexperienced and ignorant. The treasury agent, who was becoming more strongly pro-Negro, reported: "Prejudice against the colored people is exhibited continually—prejudice bitter and vulgar" and "the whole policy respecting the colored people is ungenerous and unjust." [31]

After nearly four months of heated debate, the convention completed its work. The efforts to abolish slavery altogether in Louisiana were voted down. Negro suffrage was partially side-stepped; however, one article in the constitution did grant the legislature the right to enfranchise "citizens of the United States, [who] by military service, by taxation to support the government, or by intellectual fitness, may be entitled thereto." Every male, white, twenty-one years of age, who was a citizen of the United States, who had lived in his parish for three months, and who had resided within the state for a year would be given the right to vote.[32]

The new constitution was submitted to the people on September 5 and, in a small vote, was ratified, 4,484 for to 789 against. At the same time, members of a new state legislature and representatives to Congress were also chosen. Despite the poor turnout and strong evidence that the elections were largely rigged, President Lincoln, urged by Banks, accepted the new state government. The five representatives and two senators who reported to the Thirty-eighth Congress in December were forced to cool their heels for several months and in the end were not granted their seats. Congress adjourned in March and the disappointed Louisiana delegation returned home. The state legislature met in New Orleans in October but soon discovered that the real power of the government still rested in the hands of the military authorities.[33]

New Orleans had changed but little. A newly arrived hospital chaplain reported that New Orleans was the most wicked city in the country. He complained of the cheap amusements afforded by the theaters, saloons, beer gardens, and cockpits, all of which were open on Sunday night. There were, he stated, "eleven hundred and sixty-five places, where the public could purchase rum." There also were "houses of ill-fame where unblushing licentiousness [went] on day and night." Equally destructive to the morals of the people were army-licensed gambling houses. The Reverend Mr. Gregg stated that rebel sympathy still flourished within the city.[34]

A new arrival from the North in June complained bitterly of the high prices of food and lodging. He was convinced that much of the corruption of the army was due to the fact that army pay would not support an officer even in the most modest manner.[35]

Mrs. Banks did what she could to enliven the social scene in the absence of her husband. She entertained at lavish dinner parties and sponsored tableaux. On the night of April 12 Mrs. Banks held a *tableau vivant,* entitled the "Spirit of 1866," for the benefit of Union soldiers and their families. She played the role of the Goddess of Liberty surrounded by all of the states of the reunited country. Little did she realize that only a few days before her husband had met with a severe repulse in the vicinity of Mansfield and would soon abandon his expedition.[36] By July 4 the city had sufficiently recovered from the shock of the Red River fiasco to again put on a mammoth concert, complete with anvils and artillery.[37]

Banks's troops, upon reaching Morganza on the Mississippi in late May, were ordered into camp to await reorganization and a final disposition of the units. The unbearable heat drove the men to construct arbors and bowers to shield themselves from the sun. In a short time an orderly city of tents and company streets stretched along the banks of the river between the water and the levee. Early in the morning and in the late evening the troops were called out for drill periods and gymnastic sports, but most of the day they were free. They spent much of their time lounging in their tents and in the shade, wearing as little clothing as regulations would allow. Some of the men braved the sun and went fishing, or swimming, or visited the sutlers' tents. For more than a month the sweating troops lazed away the long, hot summer days with only an occasional review or alarm to break the monotony.

The heat and the excessive rainfall began to tell upon the troops who were facing their first summer in Louisiana. Epidemics of scurvy, chronic diarrhea, swamp fever, and smallpox began to take an appalling toll. Many times a day the death march sounded, and new victims were carried to their graves along the river bank.

Near the end of June Canby began reorganizing his troops at Morganza. The First and Second divisions of the Nineteenth Corps remained much as they were, but seventeen regiments of the Thirteenth Corps were used to form a new Third Division for the Nineteenth Corps.

Canby, like Banks, was ordered to move against Mobile as soon as he could get ready. But Canby proceeded too slowly, and Grant, in the meantime, had suffered such heavy losses in the Wilderness that he ordered Canby to postpone the attack on Mobile and to send the Nineteenth Corps without delay to Hampton Roads.

At the end of June Canby began moving the First and Second divisions to Algiers and on July 3 the first of the troops moved below New Orleans on the way to the Gulf. The last regiment left for Virginia on July 20. Some of the best regiments of the Nineteenth Corps were left behind in Louisiana along with the newly activated Third Division, the corps headquarters, all of the cavalry, and the artillery. Major General Joseph J. Reynolds was named the new corps commander.[38]

Although Grant had called a temporary halt to the projected expedition against Mobile and had moved most of the Nineteenth Army Corps, General Canby still believed that he would soon be able to collect enough troops in his department to aid Farragut against Mobile. In late July he sent two thousand troops, under Major General Gordon Granger, by ocean vessels to Mobile Bay. On August 8 Fort Gaines was captured and later, on August 23, Fort Morgan surrendered.[39]

Even then Mobile could not be occupied by the available Federal forces for Canby could not send any more troops from his department. Yellow fever broke out in New Orleans in September and by October a number had died and there were over a hundred cases in that city alone. The newspapers kept quiet about the epidemic, but the dread news could not be kept from the soldiers. Denison wrote his uncle on October 8, "Some of the fellows grow weak in the knees and suddenly

remember some very important business in the North." The yellow-
fever epidemic caused the Federals to abandon their attempts against
Mobile for the present.[40]

To raise more troops to replace some of the men sent to Virginia
and to Mobile and to give additional local protection, on July 30 Canby
issued an order for "all able-bodied males, between the ages of eighteen
and forty-five within the lines of occupation in the Department of Arkansas and the Gulf and the district east of the Mississippi River" to
enroll immediately for service in the militia. Neutral foreigners would
be enrolled and used "whenever necessary as a local police or con-
stabulary force."

On August 2 Banks ordered that "all able bodied colored men between 18 & 40 will be enlisted for the military service of the U.S., ⅕
of men liable to conscription to be exempt . . . [and] laborers taken
from plantations by this order to be returned temporarily when the
harvesting [is] ready." [41] Canby on October 15 authorized General S.
A. Hurlbut (who had taken over temporary control of the Department
of the Gulf when Banks had gone on a visit to the North in September) "to raise two regiments of colored volunteer infantry in the city
and vicinity of New Orleans." [42] A hundred dollar bounty would be
given to each volunteer.[43]

The Red River campaign, which necessitated the concentration of
most of Banks's and Taylor's forces in that one area, left few troops
available for action elsewhere. Except for a few minor raids and skirmishes the military scene remained relatively quiet in other parts of
Louisiana during the expedition.

In the early part of 1864, Captain Joseph C. Lea of the Missouri
guerrillas resumed operations east of the Ouachita. Lea, with two hundred men, moved into Tensas Parish on the Mississippi. At 4 A.M. on
March 21, Lea came on a crude fortification held by four hundred of
Alfred W. Ellet's marines. Lea inflicted heavy casualties and drove the
marines to the banks of the river where they took refuge aboard their
boats. A Federal warehouse near the levee, filled with powder, lead,
groceries, medicines, cloth, and other goods intended for trade in
cotton, was seized by Lea. Under constant bombardment from the
boats, he slowly began to remove the valuable stock. Several times the
marines landed and tried to drive off the Confederates but instead
were driven back themselves. Finally, after three days, Lea succeeded
in loading seventy-five captured Federal wagons, a number of sleds,

and cotton carts gathered from the area. He then fell back and sent the captured stores on the way to Shreveport.

During April Ellet's marines raided plantations along the river for cotton. Lea, with his casualties and with the absence of a portion of his men detailed to the wagon train, could not stop all of these raids nor could he break up the traffic between the enemy and the citizens of the area.

Word got back to Kirby Smith that Lea's men were plundering plantations belonging to loyal Confederates as well as to Federal lessees and that they were stealing Negroes, horses, mules, and cotton and were selling these to the Federal army or to anyone who would buy. Lea, in June, was summoned to Shreveport to answer these charges. After some delay, he cleared his name and was sent by Kirby Smith to take charge of all the country east of the Ouachita.

On August 26 Captain Lea, with two hundred of his guerrillas, made a costly raid on the plantations leased by H. B. Tibbetts and Company in the area below Lake Providence. They murdered two white scouts, a white overseer, a white clerk, and several Negroes and took away many supplies. Lea, with his headquarters on Bayou Macon, had terrorized the area with his periodic raids from Tensas Parish north to Arkansas. Colonel A. Watson Webber of the Fifty-first Regiment U.S. Colored Infantry, commander of the Federal post at Goodrich's Landing, sent an expedition of 230 mounted Negro troops, under Major C. H. Chapin, to drive Lea from the region.

Proceeding by way of Lake Providence to Ashton, Chapin crossed Bayou Macon to the west on August 30. Continuing down the Macon, several plantations were raided and the houses burned. Arriving at the village of Pin Hook, Chapin left only one house standing. Several Confederate soldiers were encountered near Floyd and they were shot down. At sundown the Negro troops entered Floyd and, within a few minutes, had stripped the place of all its valuable goods and had set fire to four-fifths of the town. Most of the residents along the Macon were left destitute.

In mid-September Lea attacked a Negro garrison at Horseshoe Bend on the Mississippi. The Confederate guerrillas charged a series of covered ditches and were driven back three times. Two gunboats on Lea's flanks added their lethal fire to that of the colored infantry. After a desperate fourth charge, Lea gained a ditch and, despite the heavy fire, succeeded in driving the Negroes to the gunboats. The

Federal losses numbered 195 killed, 72 wounded, and 63 captured. Lea lost 80 men in killed and wounded. He returned to his headquarters on Bayou Macon with his prisoners and two hundred stands of arms.

On September 18 Lea moved down to Lum's plantation on Willow Bayou, in Madison Parish, to break up a band of jayhawkers and Negroes who were holed up in the impenetrable cane and cypress swamps in the area. This band, made up of draft dodgers, deserters, and runaway Negroes, often left the swamps to rob, kill, or capture anyone who passed by on the road. Dressing sixty of his men in captured Federal uniforms, Lea succeeded in tricking the outlaws. The leader of the desperados, a huge black, welcomed the supposed Federal troops. Suddenly, Lea's disguised men fell upon the surprised gang and began to slaughter them. Lea rushed up with the rest of his command and in a quick but bloody struggle killed 130 of the group. The few who escaped never again returned to ravage the area.

For the duration of the war, Lea spent some time in Mississippi and Kentucky but occasionally would return to northeast Louisiana to continue his operations.[44]

Early in June, before he replaced Taylor, General Walker had sent Major J. L. Robinson with a squadron of cavalry east of Black River "to break up the plantations of Federal lessees and to destroy supplies of forage" collected for shipment to Morganza. Robinson's expedition destroyed several large corn depots and all of the cotton gins being used "by the Yankees and disloyal planters" and captured many mules and horses. He had driven to within four miles of Vidalia. Here he began a skirmish with a regiment of enemy cavalry but succeeded in returning safely back across Black River.[45]

Near New Orleans and Baton Rouge, where there were few guerrillas, most of the lessees went unmolested.[46] However, in late August many complaints had been heard from plantations "worked by loyal men" in the vicinity of the Federal picket lines of Baton Rouge and Port Hudson. Union soldiers were accused of "wandering about at will, and helping themselves without stint to whatever could be found." In Ascension Parish, along the river south of Baton Rouge, a planter, W. R. Hodges, complained in September that several raids had been made by guerrillas on the three plantations which he was operating with some five hundred hired hands. He boasted that his crops were good, but unless a small detachment of soldiers was sent down to guard the parish his and other crops would be ruined by guerrillas.

General Canby by December was not too hopeful for the future of the lessee system unless certain changes were made. He believed that the plantations should be subdivided and more lessees should control. The Negro male laborers should be mustered into the army for better discipline and should be issued guns and ammunition to defend the place when attacked. Although the labor system "greatly embarrassed military operations" and was too much of a burden on the army and the Treasury department, Canby felt that it could not be abandoned. He feared that the Negro would become completely demoralized.

In his annual report dated February 1, 1865, Thomas W. Conway, Superintendent of the Bureau of Free Labor, informed General Hurlbut that in the past year there had been 1,500 "plantations under cultivation by military orders" and that there had been some 50,000 freedmen on the plantations "who were managed by the bureau." Conway reported that on twelve plantations he "found it necessary, . . . in order to secure payment of wages, to make seizures either of the produce or other property belonging to hirers, or of funds from merchants and others who had received produce without regard to the lien of the laborers." From these seizures he had collected over $22,000.

The bureau had supported an average of 1,000 freedmen during the year, furnishing them with rations, clothing, fuel, and medicines. The entire cost of this program was $113,426.40.

Wages due Negroes, who had been conscripted on the plantations before final settlement, were collected and paid wherever possible by the bureau. In some thirteen parishes in lower Louisiana nearly $12,000 due former laborers now serving in the army was collected.

The superintendent reported that the "old planters" in matters of wages to the freedmen "paid them more promptly, more justly, and apparently with more willingness than have the new lessees from other parts of the country." A few wealthy Northerners, however, who had come to settle in the area had "done better for the freedmen than any others" because they did not desire to milk the land and the ex-slave and then leave. Such men, stated Conway, treated the laborers humanely and gave "cheerfully to their educational, religious, and social welfare." He concluded that "order was brought out of chaos" and, considering everything, that the free labor system had "been successful in its time and in the objects intended by it."

Military operations in Louisiana after the Red River campaign were greatly curtailed. Both sides, sapped of much of their strength, had to spend time in rebuilding their forces. Most of the military action consisted of small expeditions, raids, and guerrilla activity.

On the east side of the river, the Second Illinois Cavalry was sent from Baton Rouge to the Amite River on July 24 to break up a Confederate camp in the area. They fell upon the Confederate camp and routed some three hundred troops. Captain H. R. Doyal re-formed his surprised men and skirmished heavily with the enemy. Major Franklin Moore fell back to the Amite, where he formed a line of battle. Doyal drove against this line, losing twenty-five men in the attempt. The Confederates retired and Moore returned to his post.

Colonel John S. Scott, in command of the Confederate forces at Clinton, in search of spoils, skirted the strong Federal posts at Port Hudson and Baton Rouge and, on the morning of August 5, hit the Union camp at Doyal's plantation on the Mississippi, some thirty miles below Baton Rouge. Moving over a back road, he filed through a cornfield and a skirt of woods and completely surrounded the camp before the Federal force realized he was there.

Major S. P. Remington, faced by four pieces of artillery and a brigade of cavalry, decided to make a run for it. With only 206 members of the Eleventh New York Cavalry present for duty, the men were ordered to cut through Scott's line and ride as swiftly as possible down the levee road to the telegraph station. As the Federals moved forward, three of the Confederate guns opened with shot and shell, but little damage was done because of incorrect range. The Federal cavalry "charge was impetuous and spirited" and Scott's men, who expected Remington to defend his stockade, were so surprised that they allowed the Federal cavalry to break through their center.

Scott rounded up all the Federal troops left in camp, totaling ninety-two enlisted men and two officers. He also captured 130 horses and a great deal of camp equipage.

The next day, August 6, a force of mounted Confederate infantry attacked the pickets belonging to Major Richard G. Shaw's command at Plaquemine. Shaw reported that two men from the Eighth U.S. Colored Artillery were killed and three were captured. After suffering about the same losses, the Confederates retreated toward the squalid settlement of Indian Village. The three Negro soldiers were shot by their captors a short time later.

Major General F. J. Herron, commanding the District of Baton Rouge and Port Hudson, determined to rid the Clinton area of Scott's men. General S. P. Lee, leading a detachment of cavalry from Port Hudson on August 23, encountered Scott's troops around midnight near Redwood, seventeen miles out. A sharp encounter ensued and Scott retreated toward the Comite River.

Herron, with an infantry force, left Port Hudson on the evening of August 25 to join Lee at Clinton. When the Federal forces reached Clinton, Scott departed for Mississippi. After seizing a few bales of cotton, some cattle, and a number of Negroes, Herron returned to Baton Rouge.

On the west side of the Mississippi, General M. K. Lawler, commanding the forces at Morganza, sent out a scout force of seventy-five men to Williamsport on September 15. A regiment of Confederate cavalry intercepted the detachment and killed or captured more than half of the group. To prevent the Confederates from moving into the Atchafalaya region, Lawler sent a heavy cavalry force to intercept them. By early October over eight thousand Federal troops were in the Atchafalaya to guard the area.

General Albert L. Lee left from Baton Rouge with a division of cavalry on October 5 to make another raid on Clinton and vicinity. At Greensburg Lee destroyed a tannery containing two thousand sides of leather. Here, too, he seized a large supply of quinine and other stores. Moving to Osyka, Mississippi, he destroyed many valuable Confederate supplies. Moving back into Louisiana, he raided Camp Moore where he burned barracks and other buildings and a large supply of clothing and cloth. He returned to Baton Rouge on October 9 with 150 prisoners and 200 horses and mules. In his report he stated: "endless niggers have followed us in." [47]

At the end of November Lee paid another visit to Camp Moore with a large force. The post was caught by surprise and a number of prisoners were taken. The rest of the camp was completely destroyed.

Until the end of the year minor raids and skirmishes occurred in the vicinity of Doyal's plantation, around Morganza, at Bayou Sara, and near the Atchafalaya. Little was accomplished by either side. [48]

In an attempt to improve the pride and efficiency of the colored troops, the special schools begun earlier were continued. The Christian Commission sent an ex-mayor of Boston, J. V. C. Smith, to distribute slates, pencils, necessary supplies, books, and other reading matter. Since most of the Negroes "were destitute of the most rudimentary knowledge," learning to sign their names was their chief accomplishment in these schools. It filled the Negro soldier with great pride to sign his own name to the payroll instead of having to make his mark.

There was hope that some few could be taught to read the Bible and the Constitution in due time.

Early in the year Banks had made provisions for the education of the colored children. In each one of the police and school districts there was to be at least one school established for the instruction of all colored children under the age of twelve. In New Orleans by the end of 1864 there were nine of these schools operating, with an average attendance of 2,400. The American Missionary Association sent down twenty teachers. Some of these teachers worked with colored regiments but the majority taught in the schools for children.[49] In northeastern Louisiana the usual school for colored children was a rough leaky shed with the barest furnishings. The lady mission teachers were socially ostracized and could find only the most miserable of living accommodations. Not all of the opposition to the "nigger" schools came from the Southerners. Yankee provost marshals sometimes refused to help establish or guard these schools and in Tensas and Concordia parishes Northern lessees would co-operate with the schools only when forced to do so. The students ranged in age from four to forty, were poorly clothed, loved to fight, and were "extremely filthy, their hair filled with vermin." Religious instruction, with readings from the Bible and prayers, was emphasized while reading from primers and studying spelling and writing rounded out the course work. The program stressed "a maximum of memory and a minimum of reasoning." The schools sponsored by the Christian societies were gradually taken over by a board of education and supported by special property and crop taxes. These schools operated primarily along the Mississippi and few, if any, were established in the interior.[50]

White public schools continued to operate in New Orleans, and in addition, there were several day academies and boarding schools operated by the Catholic orders which offered instructions to all faiths at three to five dollars per subject. There were also boarding and day schools for young ladies and private commercial colleges offering instructions to young men, from the age of eight, as well as to adults. Outside of New Orleans, in both the occupied and Confederate areas, only a few private schools, usually denominational, continued to operate.[51]

The fall season saw an increase in amusements being offered in New Orleans. In September the Varieties Theatre opened its theatrical season. The annual fall racing season at the Fair Grounds began later in the month. At the Masonic Hall a Dr. Beale offered a "Grand Scenic

Spectacle and Marionette Show." In late October the Academy of Music resumed with a variety program and "parlor entertainment" featuring a "female actress." The St. Charles Theatre began its winter season with a company of bareback riders. Other new forms of entertainment were offered by a shooting gallery and the Phoenix House, which was New Orleans' "oldest established restaurant," which now not only featured the "best food and drink" but also "6 new Ten-Pin Alleys—the best in the world." In December S. B. Howe's Great European Circus began an extensive run and featured "a caged living lion, lady riders, clowns, tableaux." [52] The Union Clubs, with their meetings, balls, and other activities,·helped give the people more to do.[53]

General Canby soon felt that the rash of gambling in New Orleans was beginning to demoralize his officers and men and was an unwholesome influence on the entire population. To curtail this practice, all gambling houses were ordered to close by November 1.[54]

Thus the year 1864 came to an end. Military activity had dwindled to almost nothing in Louisiana. In Confederate Louisiana the people, with their trials and tribulations, were sick of war. The new year, 1865, would either make or break the success of Confederate opposition.

PART FIVE

THE CURTAIN CLOSES: 1865

XXIV

EVENTIDE

LIFE IN most of Confederate Louisiana became more monotonous and dull with the new year. With many people taking refuge in Texas and other parts, those who remained were either too busy or too poor to bother with social affairs. A citizen of Bastrop reported that Christmas and New Year's passed with an absence of parties and festivities.

Social conditions were even worse in the Lafourche region. Here the few citizens who remained were under a constant threat of a new invasion by the Union army. Each day their Negro laborers were becoming more impudent and harder to manage. In fact, it was becoming dangerous to travel around to visit because armed Negroes roamed the area and often shot at white people on sight.[1]

Shreveport, as the headquarters for the entire Trans-Mississippi Department, had its armies to help enliven the local social scene. Ladies from Shreveport and vicinity would visit the surrounding camps daily to view soldier life and to spread cheer. During visiting hours regimental bands added to the festive mood.

On February 18 thousands of spectators rode out to the camp area to witness a gala review followed by a mock battle. Generals E. Kirby Smith and J. B. Magruder participated. Forming lines of battle, skirmishers firing rifles were first advanced. The artillery then joined in and the opposing lines advanced, firing as they came. The soldiers were quite pleased with their realistic show as "some fair ladies screamed, and down the cheeks of others coursed tear-drops. . . ." After the sham battle the troops and visitors "repaired to tables, where a bountiful and substantial repast was spread." The food was followed by a series of short patriotic speeches.[2]

Private F. D. Pitts, bugler for the Chicago Mercantile Battery, reported a lively time in New Orleans in January. He attended a number of plays and enjoyed a circus performance. To vary the routine, on January 11 he "got tight on bad whiskey." In the middle of the month he went to Baton Rouge and there participated in a soldier-produced "Nigger Show Minstrel" which played to a packed house. While at Baton Rouge he attended the circus and played baseball, receiving five dollars for the latter.[3]

Beginning after January 1 the Sabbath scene in New Orleans underwent a radical change. All theaters, bars, and gambling places were to remain closed. General Hurlbut, for his blue laws and for his efforts to close down all gambling houses, was highly praised by the chaplains of the department, but probably became less popular with the men of the army.

Charity and politics still added color to the New Orleans social scene. Several "Fancy Dress Balls" to benefit widows and the destitute were given in January by the various fire companies. Another "Grand Masked & Fancy Ball" to enrich charity was held in mid-March. The Orleans Theatre in late May offered a concert to the public to raise money for soldiers' aid.[4]

To celebrate the adoption of emancipation by Missouri and Tennessee, Governor Michael Hahn declared January 24 to be a holiday. By early morning the principal streets of New Orleans were crowded with both blacks and whites, many of whom wore "red, white and blue." All public buildings were decorated with bunting and the national colors. At noon a salute to the Union was fired and all of the bells in the city were rung. Military bands played throughout the day, and the evening brought the usual political speeches from the governor and his staff, highlighted by a series of transparencies.

On March 4, a great city parade was held to celebrate Lincoln's second inaugural and to welcome a new governor to office. Governor Hahn had been elected in January to the United States Senate, and his Lieutenant Governor, J. Madison Wells, took over. The city police and fire departments paraded through the bunting-draped streets while band music enlivened the scene.

"Grand Mass Meetings of the National Rights League" with fiery orations from local and imported politicians drew large throngs of Negroes to Economy Hall in March and May.

Mardi Gras at the end of February enjoyed a brief revival. Several parades were held, but evidently the usual masking and other festivities were missing as no particular notice was paid the event by the newspapers.

When word arrived in New Orleans on April 15 that Lee and Johnston had surrendered, people crowded Lafayette Square to celebrate. The war had not ended in Louisiana but the people knew that the Trans-Mississippi could not hold out much longer.[5]

Political affairs in occupied Louisiana entered troubled waters after Wells took over as governor in March. He proved to be a turncoat to many of the rabid Unionists and carpetbag politicians who had helped to elect him. The new governor was determined to run the entire political show himself. Late in the month, Mayor Stephen Hoyt, a friend of both Banks and Hahn, was removed, and Dr. Hugh Kennedy was put in his place. Kennedy, the former editor and owner of the *Daily True Delta,* a supporter of secession, and a strong advocate of keeping the former aristocracy in power, was opposed by the strong Union men. Wells stated that he made the change because he thought an old citizen could better understand the problems of the city.

Mayor Kennedy immediately earned the enmity of the city laborers by cutting their wages. Carpetbag politicians called a protest meeting, and Doctor A. P. Dostie, a radical leader, harangued the crowd and "called upon the people to seek redress" against the "outrageous" conduct of both the mayor and the governor.[6]

In mid-March General S. A. Hurlbut wrote Lincoln a letter in which he denounced the state legislature as being "entirely useless, very expensive, and liable to do serious harm." The legislators, according to Hurlbut, had long since used up all available public funds and were "simply increasing public debts." He complained of the unreasonable tax burden, both local and Federal, and urged "the most rigid economy, the abolition of useless offices, and the simplification of the machinery of government."[7]

General Banks, who had gone North in September, 1864, did not return until April, 1865. Once again in New Orleans, Banks set out to get rid of Kennedy. On May 5 he ousted Wells's mayor and appointed Colonel Samuel M. Quincy of the Seventy-third U.S. Colored Infantry as the acting mayor. Wells did not surrender without a fight. He hastened to Washington to confer with President Johnson and soon won his support. On June 4 Banks was recalled from the department, and Canby took over the full political reins. General Canby saw eye to eye with Wells and reappointed Hugh Kennedy as the acting mayor.

Wherever he could, Governor Wells restored political power to the old guard and removed the radicals from office. The New Orleans police helped to carry out the governor's removal orders and, for the time being, the radicals were curbed.[8]

In January General Canby informed all speculators that goods held by persons outside the Union lines could be brought within the lines under certain restrictions and, therefore, it would be unnecessary for them to resort to illegal traffic. Trade on Red River, because of the apparent desire of the Confederate commander to continue it, was peaceful and safe. Canby in mid-January saw "no present objection to vessels going up that river for the purpose of procuring cotton."

In February Kirby Smith authorized General Buckner to issue permits to those who wished to carry on cotton trade with the enemy. This action was excused by Kirby Smith as being a "military necessity." Each person with such a permit was required to pay fifty dollars per bale to a district officer, the money to be credited to the War Department. Among those granted this right was Major John Adams, who was given permission to take 1,000 bales down Red River to trade with the enemy.

Governor Allen later in the month was authorized to secure and export all cotton he could find south of Red River beyond the permanent Confederate lines which was liable to capture by the Federal forces. The money procured would be used entirely for the state.

Under the impression that Federal troops were going to attempt to invade and gain possession of the Ouachita region, the Trans-Mississippi headquarters at Shreveport issued orders to the cavalry in that area to burn all the cotton, "especially that held by Calderwood and others suspected of disloyalty."[9]

The expected Federal occupation did not take place, and Union boats continued to come up the Ouachita to Monroe to trade. On March 8, two boats engaged in the cotton trade were doing a thriving business swapping coffee, liquor, dry goods, and money for cotton. Confederate officers were accused by a citizen of encouraging the trade and of fraternizing with the enemy, eating their oysters, and drinking their liquor.

Late in March four Federal steamboats under a flag of truce were on the Ouachita for trade purposes. The boats carried trade permits from Shreveport and were furnished Confederate guards. Citizens for miles around brought in their cotton to trade for scarce items. Farmers from as far away as Homer "hurried their cotton to Monroe to trade with Yankees."[10]

Since the occupation of the Mississippi Valley, "the products of insurrectionary districts" were subject to Federal military taxes of five dollars for each bale of cotton, or a proportional tax on other products. The money thus raised by the military authorities was used "to the care of freedmen, refugees, and other charities, or to sanitary and municipal purposes." For several months General Canby had failed to collect this tax and the cotton business had greatly increased. Only a small tax of fifty cents a bale, to cover trade protection expense, was collected. On March 2 Canby announced that he was ready to resume the full five dollar tax.

Kirby Smith followed a vacillating policy concerning the cotton trade. On March 4 he wrote a speculator, A. R. McDonald: "I have positively prohibited the exit of cotton in the direction of the enemy lines and the introduction of goods within our own, yet as you have acquired large quantities of cotton from our citizens under the promise of export privileges, you will be allowed to complete your arrangements and export the cotton . . . [provided] it will be shipped to Europe without payment of a revenue tax to the U.S. Treasury." Other trade permits were granted speculators to carry cotton down the Atchafalaya.

On March 8 Kirby Smith wrote the Confederate States Treasury agent, P. W. Gray, that he had "determined not to sanction any system of trade through [the] lines with the enemy. . . ." A few hundred bales of cotton belonging to the state and located on the Ouachita, and about 400 bales of government cotton used to procure supplies were the only bales allowed through the lines at that time. The closing of the lines to the trade was partly dictated by the fall in cotton prices and partly by a desire to shut off trade with the enemy. Smuggling cotton through the Atchafalaya area continued despite strenuous attempts to break it up.

Still fearing invasion, Kirby Smith late in March ordered all planters not to plant more cotton than was necessary to meet their Confederate and state taxes. He did not want the Union army to make a rich haul in confiscated cotton.

Tax problems, along with trade, caused Kirby Smith much vexation and worry. On January 2 Kirby Smith reported "that unauthorized persons are collecting the 'tax in kind' " and he ordered "that only regular officers and agents on 'tax in kind' duty, . . . can give valid receipts to a producer for his tithe tax." Any officer or soldier who collected the tithe without authority would be immediately arrested.

Impressment, too, was becoming more of a problem. According to an act passed by the Confederate Congress in February, 1864, "every article impressed must be paid for at the time of impressment." Kirby Smith reported to Secretary of War James A. Seddon that his department was "practically without funds and without the means of procuring them" and therefore could not pay off any of the impressment vouchers. As a result, the government credit rating no longer existed and the people holding "unpaid certified accounts for large sums" did not wish to extend any more credit for their goods. The Louisiana legislature had enacted "stringent laws against illegal impressment," and any new impressments by the army would be "resisted by force" by the state officials and the people. Tax collectors were hounding the citizens for their tax payments, while these same people held millions of dollars of certified vouchers for impressed goods that still had not been paid. It was unfair, and widespread "discontent and dissatisfaction" was the end result. Payment to the people, even if fractional, for their impressed property must be made before any more goods were procured.

The need for money was made even more desperate because the pay department owed over $50,000,000 to the soldiers "for bounty, clothing, money, and pay proper." Some of the soldiers had not been paid a dollar in more than two years. Kirby Smith had made repeated appeals to the Treasury Department for funds but without success. He now appealed to the War Department to procure and send thirty to forty million dollars so that the soldiers could be paid a part of the amount due. He believed such "funds would greatly relieve the soldiers and improve their efficiency." [11]

The lack of money was made even more serious by the steep rise in prices. Price inflation in Shreveport, the gateway to goods from Texas and Mexico, was alarming. Flour sold for up to $2.25 a pound, lard around $2.00 a pound, salt $25 a bushel, whisky $85 a gallon, and a prime slave brought $7,500.[12] Prices must have been higher in other parts of the state.

Governor Henry Watkins Allen continued to aid the citizens not only through greater imports but through established state-owned industries. The various salt works in Louisiana were more fully exploited by the governor. At Minden a factory turning out cotton and wool cards was in full operation early in 1865.

In 1864 Dr. Bartholomew Egan was appointed by Allen to set up a laboratory for the manufacture of medicines. Egan bought out the Mount Lebanon Female College and nearly a hundred acres of land in Bienville Parish, and here began to turn out large quantities of excellent turpentine. A good grade of medicinal whisky was also distilled. Egan, too, produced a large amount of castor oil and a quantity of opium. The native wild white poppy produced an opium equal in strength and effectiveness to the imported product.

In addition to the Mount Lebanon medicinal laboratories, by March, 1865, Governor Allen was operating for the state a second turpentine distillery, a second whisky distillery, a factory turning out carbonated soda, a second laboratory for the manufacture of indigenous medicines, two cotton cloth factories, a foundry, the enlarged cotton card factory at Minden, and the Davis County Iron Works.[13] On April 1, due to a growing shortage of iron and fuel, the governor appealed to the people to bring in their "old castings and charcoal" to the state foundry in Shreveport. In return they would receive "plows, plow points, . . . scooters, skillets and ovens." [14]

According to General Orders No. 7, issued by Hurlbut on February 8, all plantations within the lines must be duly registered if operated by the owner or by another private individual. Peace and good order must be maintained. All freedmen being cared for by the government who were able to work would be forced to make a labor contract. Home farms and colonies for those unable to work would be located in several areas—one in St. Charles Parish, one near Baton Rouge, and one at Thibodaux. All labor contracts would be supervised by the Superintendent of Freedmen or his agents. Wages per month, after March 11, would be $10 for a first class male and as low as $2 per month for girls under fourteen. To help finance the freedmen labor system and to help support the aged and helpless, a poll tax of one or two dollars would be collected "from each planter for every hand employed . . . on the 1st day of June." Efforts would be made "to collect the same poll tax from all colored persons not on plantations. . . ." [15]

Both lessees and private owners found the labor regulations onerous. In March a Northern co-lessee of two plantations in Concordia Parish complained of the regulations and "red tape" and stated that he had a mind "to damn Mr. President." [16] Alexander F. Pugh, a large sugar planter who operated his own plantation near Thibodaux, complained that the Negroes and the federal officers took up too much time in negotiating new labor contracts. Part of the delay was occasioned by the fact that the Negroes were dissatisfied with the settlements from the past year, and additional delays were brought about because of changes in labor rules and regulations. On April 14 Pugh wrote in his diary: "I have agreed with the negroes today to pay them monthly

wages. It was very distasteful to me, but I could do no better. Every-
body else in the neighborhood has agreed to pay the same and mine
would listen to nothing else." [17]

Near Morganza, a Captain Carmouche in February had succeeded
in raising a company of eighty men and had begun "to stop all persons
in this parish from planting who [were] 'cultivating on the Yankee
principle,' all who [were] disaffected toward the Confederates, . . .
and to take away all their mules."

Planters in the Confederate areas of Lafayette, Vermilion, and St.
Landry parishes were ordered by Confederate officers to make "their
hands do faithful work." The planters must plant "as much corn as
possible for the support of the citizens and such detachments of [the]
army as may be necessary for the protection of this country." Planters
were warned "not to plant more cotton than . . . [that] required to pay
their State and Confederate taxes." Those who failed to work their
Negroes properly or who planted too much cotton would prove their
"indifference and disloyalty" to the cause.[18]

The month of January brought no major military action, but there
were a number of minor skirmishes fought by small Federal detachments who were sent out to stop Confederate recruiters, smugglers, and
foragers to the west and northwest of New Orleans.

One such expedition, consisting of a portion of the Second New York
Cavalry led by Colonel Morgan H. Chrysler, left Morganza on January
12 and scoured the lower part of Pointe Coupee Parish and Iberville
Parish as far as Plaquemine. They found the swamps flooded and all of
the bridges swept away by unusually high water. After collecting nine
prisoners, twenty-one horses, sixty-seven mules, a large quantity of
percussion caps, powder, and some Confederate mail, the expedition
returned to Morganza on January 15.

Four days later a scout of fifty men from the Third Rhode Island
Cavalry left Donaldsonville to pursue and capture a band of some two
hundred Confederate guerrillas. After a light skirmish the Confederates
rode off into the swamps and escaped. On January 23 the hunted became
the hunter. Williams' guerrillas attacked a detachment of Third Rhode
Island Cavalry acting as couriers near Plaquemine. The Federal cavalry,
being slightly outnumbered, refused to counterattack. The sergeant in
charge of the detail used the flat side of his saber to good advantage
and forced the reluctant men forward. After two minor skirmishes the
sorry Union cavalry horses played out and the couriers and guards quit
the fight and returned to Plaquemine after losing five men, one seriously
wounded and four captured.

Thirteen couriers from the Third Rhode Island, while again attempting to travel from Plaquemine to Donaldsonville on January 24, were once more intercepted by twenty-four of Williams' guerrillas near Bayou Goula. The first fire wounded two of the cavalrymen and the sergeant in charge immediately surrendered without firing a gun.

Colonel Willard Sayles, on January 27, in attempting to carry out instructions from New Orleans to "clear the country between Donaldsonville and Plaquemine of the enemy," sent out a detachment from the Eighteenth Colored Infantry under the command of Major William A. Hatch. A cavalry force from the Third Rhode Island was sent out two days later. This group broke up a guerrilla camp and burned a small supply of corn. Intercepting a small group of Confederates, a running skirmish was fought, but the enemy escaped into the swamp carrying with him a number of horses and mules taken from leased plantations. The chase continued for several days but, because of a myriad of bridgeless bayous swollen with flood waters, the going was slow and dangerous. The Confederates escaped across Grand Bayou and the chase was abandoned. Except for destroying two camps, gathering a few firearms, beef, and wood, little permanent good was accomplished by the overcautious leader of the expedition.

With over five hundred men stationed at Donaldsonville and a nearly equal number at Plaquemine and within reinforcing distance from Morganza, where nearly three thousand troops were encamped, the Federal forces were making a sorry show against the small bands of Confederates in the area around Donaldsonville. In March crevasses developed in the levee in West Baton Rouge Parish, and the flood waters overflowed much of the area, bringing a temporary halt to skirmishing in the region.

Colonel John L. Rice started from Bayou Boeuf Station on April 4 with a detachment of a hundred men aboard twenty-two small boats. They moved into Bayou Natchez, an area known to be a rendezvous for "cotton speculators, smugglers, mail carriers, Confederate quartermasters, &c." Rice arrested several civilians engaged in contraband trade and speculation and seized a quantity of quinine, morphine, flannel drawers, shirts, cloth, thread, pens, and other assorted items. Eleven prisoners were taken—one lieutenant, seven privates, and three civilians. Later Rice met a small group of Confederates near Napoleonville and succeeded in killing, wounding, or capturing ten men.

Guerrilla captains continued to recruit men and to make periodic raids in the Lafourche district during April and the first half of May. A Captain Brown, operating between Plaquemine and Donaldsonville with only a handful of men, constantly harassed and embarrassed a much larger Federal force. With elusive cunning he managed to escape every trap laid by the Union commanders.

Colonel Chrysler was sent out from Morganza with five squadrons from the Second New York Cavalry to scout the area around False River for Confederate recruiting officers. Marching through blinding rainstorms the expedition reached New Roads early on the morning of January 31. Here five officers were discovered hiding in closets, under houses, and one was partly buried in a hole. These officers belonged to Colonel Scott's command, which consisted of three well-mounted and well-armed regiments. Scott, operating around Morganza and below, was able to obtain many of his supplies from Baton Rouge. Here Federal officers gladly exchanged food, clothing, and other necessities for cotton smuggled across the river by Scott's men.

During the first two weeks of February Confederate activity around Morganza was very heavy. Small groups of regular troops and guerrillas would suddenly spread out over the entire parish of Pointe Coupee, scouring the area for conscripts, horses, and mules.[19]

Brigadier General Daniel Ullmann, now in command at Morganza, on February 8 ordered Colonel Chrysler to send several cavalry units to drive out the conscript hunters and guerrillas. A Confederate force of only 180 men, some of them green recruits, was encountered near Grosse Tete. The hopelessly outnumbered Confederates gave way and took refuge in the canebrakes and swamps where the New York men dared not go. The Confederates followed the Federal cavalry almost all the way back to Morganza, ambushing them wherever swamp or other cover was adequate. Two Confederate prisoners were taken and one man was killed, but Chrysler had come out second best, having lost five men captured and one wounded. The abortive expedition, like so many others, showed how cautious the Federal troops were becoming.

In February a change was made in the designations of the Union-occupied areas of Louisiana. The district including Morganza, Port Hudson, and Baton Rouge thereafter would make up the Northern Division of Louisiana and would be commanded by Major General F. J. Herron. The Southern Division of Louisiana, retained by Brigadier General T. W. Sherman, embraced the country within "the Defenses of New Orleans."

It was not long before General Herron discovered the proclivity of General Ullmann for a fast dollar and his inefficiency as a military commander. Herron, on February 26, relieved Ullmann of his command at Morganza and ordered him to New Orleans. Herron explained to General Hurlbut, who now temporarily commanded the Department of the Gulf, that Ullmann had "not been in condition for several days to give his best attention to the duties devolving upon him. . . ." Herron felt that a besotted commander was no fit person to leave in charge of such an important post.[20]

The parishes of West Baton Rouge, upper Iberville, and lower Pointe Coupee in late February were reported to be "infested with unorganized bodies of jayhawkers." They were guilty of many crimes against the people of the area as well as firing on the laborers repairing the levee and upon Federal steamboats in the river. Federal officials and Confederate authorities deplored the lawless actions of these men and both parties desired to break up jayhawking. Captain W. B. Ratliff, who commanded an advanced Confederate post in the Grosse Tete area, arranged a truce in mid-March with General Herron during which he proposed "to capture or drive away these [jayhawkers] with his own forces," provided no Federal military force was sent below Morganza nor north of Plaquemine for the next ten days. The Union commander agreed to the truce.

On the east side of the Mississippi there was practically no military activity above Baton Rouge until March. A Federal expedition from Baton Rouge, sent out by General Herron, moved toward Clinton on March 5, skirmishing heavily with an inferior Confederate force. Federal losses were two killed and five wounded. Five Confederates were killed and an unknown number wounded. The Federal cavalry, numbering some 1,500, pushed twenty miles above Clinton in order to discourage future Confederate activity in the area.

In northeast Louisiana, which was now a part of the Department of Mississippi, St. Joseph in Tensas Parish served as the chief route across the Mississippi. Such a strong force of Confederate cavalry occupied the Mississippi side opposite St. Joseph that all Federal attempts to close the transit in January ended in failure.

In late January an expedition of some three thousand cavalrymen, led by Colonel E. D. Osband of the Third U.S. Colored Cavalry, embarked from Memphis for northeastern Louisiana. Landing in southeastern Arkansas, Osband struck out in a southwesterly direction, foraging as he went.

Moving into Louisiana, Osband set up headquarters temporarily at Bastrop where "foraging details brought in a large number of horses, mules, and negroes." Learning that Colonel A. J. McNeill was camped near Oak Ridge with eight hundred Confederates, Colonel Osband sent his Third Brigade to the area, to find less than sixty men at the place. When McNeill's men heard the approach they fled and scattered in the swamp, leaving most of their horses. Several prisoners were taken along with some good mules and horses.

On February 3 two squadrons of the Fourth Illinois Cavalry were ordered to Prairie Mer Rouge, east of Bastrop, where the troopers "burned about 200,000 bushels of corn, some cotton, and brought in several horses, mules, and negroes."

Another detachment of four hundred men pushed on to Monroe but "found the place nearly deserted, all Government property having been moved by Harrison across the Washita River." Foraging parties were sent over to the Macon.

Torrential rains and extreme cold plagued the expedition from the beginning. On February 11 all of Osband's command embarked for Memphis, having lost ten men—one killed, two captured, and seven left behind because they were too ill to ride. He had lost 203 horses, 49 mules, a few carbines and pistols, and other equipment due to the mud, cold, and carelessness of his men. He had captured 276 good horses and 358 mules. Nearly 450 Negroes were brought out, 200 of whom were promptly inducted into the army. Osband took 44 prisoners "and a large number of deserters and refugees [were] brought in."

The expedition had failed in its major objective, "the destruction of Harrison's command," because he had moved west of the Ouachita and there was no means available of crossing the flooded river. Osband felt certain that there was nothing to worry about concerning Harrison's future operations east of the Ouachita. He boasted that "no squad of men . . . can live anywhere we have been. The people have neither seed, corn, nor bread, or the mills to grind the corn in if they had it, as I burned them wherever found. . . . I have taken from these people the mules with which they would raise a crop the coming year, and burned every surplus grain of corn. . . ." [21]

Kirby Smith learned in January that a heavy troop concentration was gathering in New Orleans. He believed that the enemy intended to start "immediate operations against either Mobile, Galveston, or Red River. . . ." Confederate troops were shifted in the Trans-Mississippi to better guard the Red River and Texas. J. H. Forney's division at Minden was ordered to east Texas where it would be able to go immediately to Houston or Natchitoches, and Churchill's division was moved to Minden to take up winter quarters. At Alexandria, General Buckner's headquarters of the District of West Louisiana, a strong force made up of Louisiana, Missouri, Arkansas, and Texas men occupied winter quarters. In the area between Alexandria and Opelousas, Brigadier General Joseph L. Brent and his forces stood ready to absorb the first shock of an attack from Brashear City or Donaldsonville.

Richmond had not given up the idea of transferring a portion of the Trans-Mississippi forces to the east side of the Mississippi. There was a strong feeling, fanned by the carping of Dick Taylor and the prolonged idleness of the troops west of the river, that E. Kirby Smith left much to be desired as a commander. A movement was under way to replace him with Braxton Bragg.[22]

Jefferson Davis, on January 31, telegraphed Kirby Smith to move a portion of his men east of the river as soon as possible. The telegram was not received at Shreveport until February 23, and Kirby Smith answered it a few days later. "It is physically impossible to cross troops over the Mississippi at this season. When the streams fall and the river bottoms become passable the attempt will be made if the enemy's operations here permit. This will not be before June." Kirby Smith still feared that the Federal forces massed in New Orleans might take advantage of the high water and invade the Red River valley. On March 7 he expressed his willingness to co-operate fully "with the armies east of the Mississippi" by moving a part of his men to the east side and by making a new drive into Missouri.[23]

The morale of the troops in the Trans-Mississippi was in a bad state. Private Morgan from North Louisiana, stationed near Alexandria, wrote to his wife on January 24, 1865: "The Armey hear is very much demoralized." A few days later he wrote: "The boys is praying . . . in camps and wee see them nelt don all about in the woods praying for pease. . . . Wee have prayer meeting every night in the company. . . ."[24]

Federal spies echoed the news of demoralization in the Department of West Louisiana. A report dated January 24 stated that "great discontent and insubordination exist among the rebel forces mainly on account of lack of pay, scantiness of rations, and the destitution of the soldiers' families. Desertions occur daily. If captured the deserter is treated with rigor. Military executions take place weekly—on Fridays. Fifteen men have been shot at one time recently for desertion. One brigade at Alexandria is said to have mutinied not long since. Thirty-five of the ring-leaders were shot."[25]

A soldier from the Second Louisiana Cavalry stationed near Alexandria wrote his girl on February 12: "Missouri and Ark. troops are deserting daily and going home to fight no more. An order was issued sometime ago—to furlough one soldier out of two in each company. A

whole Texan Brigade was being furloughed according to the order.
The balance concluded that it would be 2 years before they got furloughs so the whole Brigade deserted & went home. Every night as
many as 6 and sometimes 12 soldiers desert from the Infantry and go
home or with the Yankees. The plan of shooting still goes on—and
as many as 5 & 6 are sent to their long accounts every week."

On March 1 the same soldier wrote: "The state of things now in
this D'pt. approaches nearer to mutiny than anything I can say. Our
food is the poorest of beef & musty meal. . . . The affairs are badly
managed—yes—in a horrible condition." [26]

In an attempt to break up the wave of desertions in Louisiana a regular
furlough system was announced by Kirby Smith in March. Up to ten
per cent of a company's "total present for duty" was entitled to a furlough at one time. Executions of deserters also helped to dissuade others
from deserting. Kirby Smith tried to placate his soldiers with more and
better food. In mid-March orders were issued to the planters that they
must supply the troops in their districts. If they did not, the troops
would have to be withdrawn or rigid impressment would have to take
place.

Bands of deserters and jayhawkers were reported to be "infesting
the country north of Red River and between the Black and Mississippi
Rivers" in March. General J. L. Brent ordered a detachment of cavalry
into the area to clear it out. Along the Ouachita around Monroe deserters
and stragglers were becoming so plentiful that a special detachment
was sent from Alexandria to round them up.[27]

General Canby was pleased that demoralization of the Confederate
forces had set in. In a general order of January 8, desertion was encouraged. According to the order: "Deserters from the enemy will not
be drafted, and if enlisted will not be assigned to local organizations,
but will be sent in detachments . . . to be assigned to regiments serving
on the Indian frontier." Later, in March, another Federal order promised
fair treatment to all deserters and refugees who came within the Federal
lines. Again the deserter was promised that he would not be conscripted
and that he could sell his horse and other equipment to the army. If
he wanted to serve in the army he could be sent to another department
or if he needed employment the army would help him find some type
of work.

The troops were not alone in their growing loss of hope for the
future. Kirby Smith on February 1 wrote to a friend who was on his
way to Mexico asking him "to make known to His Majesty the Emperor,

that in case of unexampled catastrophe to our arms and the final over-
throw of the government, . . . it is my fixed purpose to leave my native
land and seek an asylum in Mexico." He was ready to render his
"humble services and such influence" as he could bring to bear in the
services of Maximilian. If liberal terms of colonization and military
service were granted to Southern soldiers, Mexico might profit greatly
in case of "possible collision between the Imperial Government and
the United States. . . ."

The need of greater manpower in the field, always a problem in
Louisiana, was tackled anew by Kirby Smith in February, 1865. General
Orders No. 77 announced that "all details granted . . . to persons between the ages of eighteen and forty-five are hereby revoked, and all
such men, . . . together with those within the said ages, who hold
furloughs or temporary exemptions by reason of pending applications
for detail will be promptly assembled at camps of instruction and ap-
propriately assigned among the armies for service."

Late in March, General Orders No. 28 stated that all men within
the proper age limits who were found fit for field duty would be
assigned to the field, and those found fit only for staff duty would be
detailed to that duty. Those unfit for any duty would be issued a proper
certificate by the medical examining board.

The Federal commander, too, was always on the lookout for more
men for the army. On January 8, General Canby ordered "a draft of
one in seven" to be "made in the Departments of Arkansas, Mississippi,
and the Gulf on the 15th day of February" unless the quotas were filled
by volunteers. Troops so raised would be assigned to units already organized. Any person who had come into any of the departments who
had not fulfilled his military obligations would be drafted.[28]

The great concentration of Federal troops at New Orleans which
tied Kirby Smith to a restricted area was being gathered to proceed
against Mobile and not against the Ouachita, Red River, or Texas as he
had feared. The Sixteenth Army Corps under A. J. Smith arrived from
Nashville about March 1 and, along with the troops that made up the
reorganized Thirteenth Corps, were completely outfitted from the depots
in New Orleans. In February, March, and April the troops were transported to Dauphin Island and other environs of Mobile as swiftly as
available ships could carry them. The successful Mobile campaign,
which drained away the best available Union troops from Louisiana,
prevented any major Federal military action in Louisiana in 1865.[29]

XXV

SURRENDER

TIME WAS running out in Louisiana just as it was elsewhere in the Confederacy. News from Lee in Virginia in early April was all bad. Even now, however, a soldier stationed in Shreveport reassuringly wrote to his wife on April 14 that despite the bad news, "I firmly believe that we will yet achieve our independence." [1]

The soldier's confidence for the future was soon to be shattered. On April 9 Lee had surrendered to Grant at Appomattox, and ten days later this news reached Louisiana. Many of the people in Shreveport rushed to convert their Confederate money into specie at a fabulous rate of exchange. Wild inflation set in, and it was necessary late in April for the governor to sell corn meal to the needy at $5 per bushel. The inflated regular market price had long since soared beyond the pocketbooks of the poor.

On April 20 the first news of the assassination of Lincoln reached Louisiana.[2] The newspapers of New Orleans were framed in large black bands. A Unionist reported: "Gloom hung over the city like a sombre pall. Public business was suspended. Public schools were closed, flags at half mast." [3] April 22 was set apart as a day of special mourning and all houses and places of business were draped with black crepe. Bells tolled mournfully. Schools remained closed for one week.[4]

In Baton Rouge, as in New Orleans, all business came to a standstill. Public buildings were draped in black, and the churches of the city held special service in honor of the dead president.[5]

On April 21 Kirby Smith announced to the soldiers in the Trans-Mississippi Department that Lee had surrendered and that the fate of the Confederacy, although seemingly disastrous, was not yet hopeless. He told his troops: "With you rests the hopes of our nation, and upon your action depends the fate of our people." He called upon them to "prove to the world that your hearts have not failed in the hour of disaster" and asked them to "sustain the holy cause" and to "stand by your colors." The department still possessed "the means of long-resisting invasion," and hope for aid from abroad should not be abandoned. "The great resources of this department, its vast extent, the numbers, the discipline, and the efficiency of the army" would lead to "securing the final success of our cause."

After hearing the announcement of Lee's disaster, the troops received their commander's appeal with mixed feelings. Some were dejected and talked of mutiny; others felt, like Kirby Smith, that the war could be continued.[6]

On April 26 a public meeting was called in Shreveport at which the tenor of several speeches was to continue the fight. Plans were made to send a representative to Havana to consult with Jefferson Davis. Davis and his cabinet were expected to escape to Cuba and later would be brought to the Trans-Mississippi via the Rio Grande. The capture of Davis in Georgia a few days later killed this plan.[7]

On Saturday, April 29, a special mass meeting was called by Governor Allen. A citizen who attended the "large and enthusiastic war meeting" reported that "a great amount of patriotism and valor were let off in the shape of eloquent speeches. . . . I fear it was all but whistling to keep the courage up." The letter expressed a fear that the department soon would be forced to surrender and concluded with a lament: "Oh! my country! where are those eloquent pens and tongues that led you into this difficulty. Gaunt fear stalks over the land . . . My country!" [8] Governor Allen, one of the speakers, asked the people to be patient, to persevere, and to give all of their strength to remaining independent.

Conditions around Shreveport went from bad to worse. Robberies and other depredations became so prevalent that a special military patrol had to guard the city. Kirby Smith and his staff found it dangerous to go about the streets at night unguarded.[9]

In late March a scheme was formed to convert one of the steamers used on Red River for transport and mail service into a ram and then to slip the ram out into the Gulf to serve as a blockade-runner and raider. Command of the *Webb* was assigned to Lieutenant C. W. Read of the Confederate Navy. With the assistance of Kirby Smith, Read quickly converted the unarmed steamer into an ocean-going ram. A bulkhead of pine lumber twelve inches thick completely surrounded the engine room and 190 bales of cotton were arranged as a shield to further protect the engines. Three guns, a 30-pounder Parrott and two iron 12-pounders, were mounted on the boat. The *Webb* left Shreveport on April 7 for Alexandria. A pilot, George Price, familiar with the waterways of lower Louisiana, was picked up below Alexandria. He was to take the *Webb* through the Atchafalaya to the Gulf and then to Cuba, but when he discovered the vessel drew too much water he informed Read that the Atchafalaya route could not be used.

Lieutenant Read decided instead to make a dash for it down the Mississippi past the forts into the Gulf. Just off the mouth of Red River were four Federal gunboats. Three hundred miles lay between the mouth of the Red and that of the Mississippi, and at regular intervals Federal ironclads patrolled the river. To prevent these gunboats from being alerted, a detail of soldiers was to cut the telegraph lines as far down as Plaquemine, and Read planned to cut the wires below that place. He did not want to risk an encounter with any gunboat on the way down unless it blocked his path. A torpedo attached to a long pole on the bow would be used to clear the path. To carry out this daring scheme the elements of speed, surprise, and time were all important. Since the two forts would have to be passed during the daylight, Read must prevent the forts from being warned.

The night of April 23, at 8:30, carrying signal lights used by the Union navy, the *Webb* left the Red and moved slowly out into the Mississippi, passing the four Federal gunboats. It was not until the *Webb* was nearly out of range that one of the boats suspected the true nature of the vessel and fired one shot toward the ram which fell far short of its target. The *Webb* picked up speed but stopped every ten or fifteen miles to send a party ashore to cut the telegraph wires.

Just above Fort Parapet, guarding the upper river approach to New Orleans, Read hoisted a United States flag, remembering to keep it at half-mast in honor of Lincoln's death, and building up a full head of steam, he began passing New Orleans at noon on April 24.

The unexpected appearance of the vessel flying the Union flag led the gunboats to mistake the *Webb* for an army transport, and no attempt was made to hail her. When they discovered their error, the gunboats fired several shots at the swiftly moving vessel, three of which struck her, one in the bow just above the water line. This shot dislodged the torpedo, swinging it under the bow and endangering the vessel. Read halted, cut the torpedo loose, and resumed his mad flight. Two other shells struck the *Webb* but did no damage.

The gunboats at anchor could not give chase until they had built up steam. The *Hollyhock* was the first of the four gunboats to get underway. Far in the distance the *Webb,* now flying a Confederate flag, could be seen. About twenty-five miles below New Orleans the ram unexpectedly met the *Richmond* coming up the river. Caught between two gunboats, Read decided to destroy his vessel. Running the *Webb* ashore, he set her afire, and she soon blew up. One man who was too slow was killed by the explosion. Over half the crew was captured later in the swamp, but Read and a few others managed to escape.[10]

General John Pope, Federal commander of the Division of the Missouri, wrote a letter to Kirby Smith on April 19 enclosing a copy of the correspondence between Lee and Grant leading to the final surrender of the Confederate forces in Virginia. Pope was ready to grant the same terms of surrender to Kirby Smith. The Trans-Mississippi commander was told that future resistance would be useless, since the great armies east of the Mississippi now could be thrown west of the river and Kirby Smith would be overwhelmed. Pope asked Kirby Smith to avoid needless bloodshed, devastation, and misery by accepting the surrender terms.

Colonel John T. Sprague brought Pope's letter down the Mississippi to the mouth of the Red and, after some delay, was allowed to proceed to Shreveport. Sprague talked freely with Kirby Smith and other commanders, but found that the Confederate leaders desired more liberal terms than had been granted to Lee.

On May 9 Kirby Smith wrote General Pope that the "propositions for the surrender of the troops under my command are not such that my sense of duty and honor will permit me to accept." He regretted that the "communication should have been accompanied by a threat" and that any offer for "personal considerations" was made.

The same day that he refused Pope's offer, Kirby Smith wrote to the governors of the states in the Trans-Mississippi—Allen of Louisiana, Pendleton Murrah of Texas, Harris Flanagin of Arkansas, and Thomas C. Reynolds of Missouri. He reported that his army still remained strong and well equipped and that despite "the disparity of numbers" his men could outweigh the differences "by valor and skill." He offered to continue the defense of the department provided "perfect concord of the civil and military authorities" and the complete support of the people could be secured. He closed by requesting that a special governors' conference be held in which the governors would help him decide upon the future policies of the department.

The governors' convention was held as suggested and on May 13 drew up an agreement to guide Kirby Smith's future actions. The Trans-Mississippi commander was advised to "disband his armies in this department; officers and men to return immediately to their former homes or such as they may select . . . and there to remain as good citizens, freed from all disabilities, and restored to all the rights of citizenship. . . ." Other terms to be incorporated in a surrender agreement were embodied in the governors' letter. Allen, Flanagin, and Guy M. Bryan (who represented Texas at the meeting because of the illness of Murrah) concurred in this agreement. Governor Reynolds stated that if the people and the authorities should decide to continue the war then Missouri would "stand by them faithfully to the last." If they decided to end the war then Missouri would be ready in a short time to obey the decision.

Kirby Smith on May 15 informed Colonel Sprague that since the governors of the department had decided in favor of surrender—provided "certain measures which they deem necessary to the public order and proper security of their people" were accepted by the Federal authorities—he felt it his "duty to support those views." He then enclosed a memorandum in which he reminded Sprague that since the Confederate army in the department was still "well appointed and supplied, not immediately threatened, and with its communications open, . . . it is the determination of the military authorities not to submit to ignominious terms." Next he listed five propositions he considered reasonable and necessary before a military peace could be arranged. Sprague received the various communications and headed down-river.[11]

While Kirby Smith talked with Colonel Sprague and the governors met in Marshall, Texas, demoralization of the troops grew stronger. A citizen of Shreveport, a Mr. Wise, on May 8 wrote former Governor Moore in Texas that "the clouds thicken around us from every quarter, every countenance is filled with despondency. . . ." Wise reported that he had "no confidience [sic] in Smith." [12]

There were many, both civilian and military, who shared Wise's sentiments in regard to Kirby Smith. Sarah Dorsey wrote that he "never had been popular with either the people or soldiers," although he was a "gentleman, sincere, upright, and pioused, and dashing soldier in the field." Many thought that he was too modest and gentle and too easily influenced and manipulated by "often unworthy subordinates."

During the peace parley, in the camps around Shreveport there were rumors that Kirby Smith wanted to continue the war but that Governor Allen was in favor of immediate peace. The perplexed soldiers became frightened and began to desert by the hundreds. After the years of hardship and deprivation the bitter pill of surrender was hard to swallow. Many soldiers, bereft of reason, began to pillage the Confederate depots and quartermaster warehouses. When they found millions of dollars in Confederate issue, the memory of the long period without pay enraged them. They broke open huge boxes and found a great supply of new clothing. They cursed the Quartermaster department for its negligence, carelessness, inefficiency, and corruption. Angrily they began stripping the government stores and warehouses, rationalizing that this was government property and that since the government owed them back pay, they had the right to take what they wanted.[13]

A soldier stationed at Camp Boggs near Shreveport on May 10 reported that the men who "gathered in groups everywhere, . . . both officers and men, swore fearful oaths never to surrender. The humiliation was unbearable." The Quartermaster Department opened its doors and issued rations in huge quantities including such delicacies as coffee and other items not seen by the soldiers in years. Ammunition, rifles, and military stores were loaded on wagons and sent to Texas. Shreveport was crowded with citizens anxious to learn all they could of the peace negotiations.

By May 13 "troops began to leave for home, openly and unmolested." The Third Louisiana, which was one of the few regiments not ravaged by wholesale desertions, was enraged on May 18 when a rumor was spread that, since Louisiana troops could not be trusted, the dependable Missouri troops would soon relieve them of all their duties. The indignant Louisianians threatened to desert en masse but leading citizens, including Governor Allen, begged them to remain. The rumor became a reality when that afternoon a Missouri regiment surrounded the Third Louisiana and told them that they had been sent to guard them. That night the Third carried out its threat. By the next morning most of the men were gone, taking with them government wagons, mules, and horses. They loaded themselves down with linen and cotton cloth, ready-made clothes, buttons, thread, leather, and other scarce items found in the government warehouses. No one tried to stop them. Some of the clerks in the warehouses began to aid the pillagers by issuing goods in such large quantities that they could not take everything with them.

Conditions grew worse. Official furloughs and discharges were issued to the Louisiana troops still remaining on May 20. Many men were seen riding off in government wagons and on horses, and those less lucky floated down the river on pontoons or started walking home.[14] A few of the footsore men appropriated stray horses or mules they found along the road or entered a planter's pasture and jayhawked a mount.

Sunday, May 21, dawned bright and hot. From early morning the streets of Shreveport overflowed with soldiers and civilians. Few officers were to be seen and it was reported that Kirby Smith and his staff had deserted Shreveport. Government depots stood wide open, and the soldiers and citizens were seizing whatever goods they could lay their hands on. Speculators eagerly bought large quantities of the plunder, paying in silver only a fraction of the actual value of the goods. The streets were littered with abandoned goods and with scattered government papers. Suddenly the Missouri soldiers appeared and began to restore order. Goods were seized from the pillagers and speculators and stored for safekeeping in the courthouse.[15]

A young soldier, returning from a three-day pass to his camp just above Mansfield, on May 11 found the camp practically deserted. Officers told the soldier that the men had mutinied the day before, bending their rifle barrels around trees, "driving their bayonets into the ground and swearing they were going back home regardless of the consequences." The few soldiers who remained were given their discharges and started toward home.[16]

Near Natchitoches, Hays's division of the Twenty-sixth Louisiana was ordered to march to Mansfield on May 13. Despite the careful picketing and double guard details, the command began to fade away. The cause was already lost, and some of the men saw no reason to remain. Arriving at Mansfield on May 19 they found that the government stores had already been pillaged, and since the division was very short of supplies, the officers decided to disband the unit temporarily and allow the men to go home and await further orders there.

Early on the morning of the twentieth, the troops proceeded to appropriate the meager supply of food, weapons, powder, horses, wagons, and other property of the government until the Twenty-sixth Louisiana Regiment was detailed to halt the pillaging and to restore order. As a closing ceremony the men and officers of the Twenty-sixth and Twenty-eighth Louisiana gathered around the flagpole and lowered the colors. While the regimental band played a solemn dirge, the colors were torn into small pieces, and each man was given a small piece to keep. No one spoke, but tears welled in the eyes of the silent men. The Twenty-sixth stuck together as a unit and marched homeward in perfect order until the men came to their respective homes or had to turn off on another road.

At Alexandria the wave of demoralization spread swiftly. Beginning early in May large groups of men deserted each night, taking their arms and large supplies of ammunition. By mid-May those who still remained at their posts were beginning to weaken. The country was filled with armed deserters, and the loyal soldiers wondered if they should not be at home to protect their families.

Dispatches from Magruder, Walker, and other commanders in Texas informed Kirby Smith that the troops in Texas were deserting in wholesale lots; entire organizations were disbanding, and the men were going home on stolen horses or in government wagons loaded with public property. To check the mass desertions and to rally the Texas forces, Kirby Smith decided to change the headquarters of the Trans-Mississippi to Houston, Texas. On May 18 he quietly departed from Shreveport, leaving Lieutenant General Simon Bolivar Buckner in control with orders to move all the troops to Houston.

While en route, Kirby Smith learned that Walker's command had disbanded at Hempstead, Texas, on May 20. Pushing on to his new headquarters, Kirby Smith arrived in Houston on May 27, only to find that the entire army in Texas had disbanded a few days before.[17] On May 30 he wrote Colonel Sprague: "Abandoned and mortified, left without either men or material, I feel powerless to do good for my country. . . . The citizens and soldiers alike, weary of war, are ready to accept the authority and yield obedience to the laws of the United States." He closed by begging the United States to adopt "a conciliatory policy" toward the people. He told Sprague that he intended "to go abroad until the future policy of the United States Government toward the South is announced" and he could safely return to his family.[18]

Shortly after the departure of Kirby Smith, the Arkansas and Missouri troops began to defect, refusing to march toward Houston. All hope of continuing the war was now gone, and the officers in Louisiana began to plan for surrender.[19] On May 23 three commissioners sent by Major General Harry Hays (the new commander of West Louisiana) arrived in Baton Rouge to arrange the terms of surrender for the district. Before this commission could accomplish anything, a second group from Shreveport, consisting of Buckner and Price, arrived at Baton Rouge, picked up General Brent of the first commission, and proceeded to New Orleans. Canby conferred with these three men on May

25 and assured them that he would accept no terms except those allowed by higher Federal authority.

On May 26 General Buckner signed the surrender terms in New Orleans for the Trans-Mississippi Department. Conditions set forth in the terms of the convention included in part: (1) "All acts of hostility on the part of both armies are to cease from this date." (2) The officers and men were "to be paroled until duly exchanged. . . ." (3) All property of the Confederate Government was to be turned over to the United States officials. (4) All officers and men could return home. (5) "The surrender of property will not include the side arms, or private horses or baggage of officers" or enlisted men. (6) According to the Executive Order of April 29, "all 'self-disposed persons' who accept in good faith the President's invitation 'to return to peaceful pursuits' are assured that they may resume their usual avocations, not only without molestation, but, if necessary, under the protection of the U.S. troops. . . ." [20]

When Buckner signed the surrender terms, he knew nothing of the disintegration of the Texas forces, and he insisted that Kirby Smith must sign before the terms became valid. A copy of the articles of surrender was rushed by the U.S. steamer *Fort Jackson* to Galveston, and here aboard the vessel on June 2 Kirby Smith signed.

On the same day Governor Henry Watkins Allen, deciding that he had finished his work and learning that Federal plans were under way to punish all military and civil leaders in the Confederacy, prepared to start on the long journey to exile in Mexico. Before leaving he addressed a long letter to the people of Louisiana begging them to keep the peace and "submit to the inevitable" and "begin life anew" without whining or despair. The crippled governor then got into his ambulance while a group of friends, tears streaming from their eyes, told him good-by.

After signing the articles of surrender, General Buckner returned to Shreveport and immediately began to reorganize his Missouri troops. One thousand men were picked, outfitted with new uniforms, horses, pack mules, tents, rifles, and cannon and were led by Buckner into Texas. He, too, feared Federal punishment and was attempting to escape to Mexico. Marching through Texas, he encountered several strong groups of former Confederates who had turned into desperadoes, and he was forced to defeat them. A number of former Confederate leaders, both civil and military, including Henry Watkins Allen, Governor Reynolds of Missouri, Generals Kirby Smith, Magruder, Bee, Price, and others joined with Buckner and moved into Mexico. There they attempted to colonize and rehabilitate themselves, with varying degrees of success.[21]

On May 22 President Johnson signed an order relieving Banks of all his duties in the Department of the Gulf. The same order assigned Major General P. H. Sheridan to the command of the Division of West Louisiana, including the territory "west of the Mississippi, south of the Arkansas River." At the end of the month General Canby sent General Herron to Shreveport with four thousand troops. He was met at the mouth of the Red by Sheridan. Five thousand troops were ordered down from Little Rock, and the nine thousand were to garrison Alexandria and Shreveport. Canby remained in command of the Department of the Gulf.

A Federal order issued on June 3 reached Shreveport and was published in the newspaper on June 10, stating that slavery was at an end. Negroes were warned that although they were free, they must not abuse this freedom.

General Herron's occupation troops began arriving in Shreveport on June 6. Upon landing, one of the first actions taken by Herron was to order the city to clean up the littered streets. Soon both black and white laborers were set to work. Negro occupation troops were brought up to Shreveport on June 20, and the white troops were either sent back to New Orleans or to Natchitoches and vicinity.[22]

Trade on Red River was reopened, and goods of every description began to arrive. The wharves were lined with boats and supplies. By June 24, the local newspaper reported that "stores [were] springing up all over," and that there were not enough buildings to house all those wanting to open. Coffee houses and liquor dealers were reopening. The resumption of legitimate cotton trade sent the price down to 26¢ per pound. Coffee which had sold for nearly $2 per pound now could be had in any amount at 36¢ per pound.[23] The main trouble with the revival of trade was that most people had only worthless Confederate money, so many were hungry in the face of plenty.

Lieutenant Commander J. H. Carter on June 3 met Commander W. E. Fitzhugh of the Federal navy and surrendered the entire Confederate naval forces on Red River. Carter turned over the ironclad *Missouri,* the only naval vessel still left on the Red or its tributaries. The *Missouri,* built on a formidable plan, was in a wretched condition. Poorly seasoned timbers made her leak badly. Mounting only two small guns and two 32-pounders she had hardly been a challenge to any of the Federal gunboats. A small amount of naval property at Shreveport was taken over by Fitzhugh. Friendly relations were established between the rival navies, and the six officers and eighteen men who surrendered were quickly paroled and allowed to return home.[24]

During the war Louisiana had contributed more than her share to the Confederacy. It was estimated that she had given about 56,000 men to the Confederate Army and with re-enlistments had furnished up to 65,000. A total of 982 companies had been raised in the state. Some six hundred military engagements, mostly skirmishes, had taken place in Louisiana. Only three states, Virginia, South Carolina, and Georgia, had suffered more destruction and casualties than Louisiana during the war. It was estimated that around one fifth of the Louisiana men enrolled in the army had died in battle or in hospitals.

Louisiana had lost more than manpower. The war had robbed the state of one third of its economic wealth—its slave property. An estimated $170,000,000 had been swept away by abolition. The river parishes, the center of slavedom, were the most seriously hurt by this loss, and many planters were forced to give up much of their land and to work a restricted area with their own hands in order to live. Some turned to trade for a living. At least half of the horses, mules, sheep, cattle, and pigs had disappeared during the conflict. Two thirds of the farm equipment and machinery for making sugar had been destroyed or had rusted beyond repair. In 1865 the sugar plantations, numbering 1,200 in 1861, were reduced to 180. These surviving plantations were hard pressed to pay their laborers or to replace destroyed, worn out, and very expensive equipment.

While the sugar industry probably suffered most, the cotton planters had more than their share of grief and misery. The desolate countryside, with many homes burned and with those homes and buildings still standing in a sad state of repair, little resembled the once-wealthy plantation region. Weeds grew where once endless acres of cotton, corn, and sugar cane flourished. At least one third of the land could not be put back into cultivation for several years. Levees had crumbled, rivers overflowed the lowlands, cattle and pigs were scattered in the brush and swamps. Entire villages had been burned or were turned into ghost towns. Land values had shrunk one third or more and mortgage foreclosures were frequent. Rich man and poor white were made to suffer for many more years. Even the Negro, to whom freedom had meant so much, was to find that the blessings and privileges of independence often brought hardship, suffering, and dubious benefits.

The banking system was in a state of ruin. The once-strong banks of New Orleans, having sent most of their gold to the Confederate government, were left with now-worthless Confederate paper and credits that would never be redeemed. Many of the older mercantile firms were in financial ruin or were struggling to exist. Over one half of the former wealth of the state had been swept away by the war. Only speculators, Union sympathizers, and carpetbaggers seemed to have adequate money, which they loaned at ruinous rates of interest.[25]

A planter, E. W. Moore, living at Washington, Louisiana, wrote to his uncle on July 2: "The closing of the war this section of the country having been subjected to the ravages of both armies for the last two years leaves us all in a very exhausted and ruined condition and I anticipate much suffering—as for myself—I have been completely ruined my lands the only thing remaining is totally valueless—my stock has been nearly destroyed and every source of revenue completely dried up. . . ."[26]

The war was over and Louisiana entered a new era. Reconstruction was just beginning.

REFERENCE MATTER

NOTES

CHAPTER I

The House Divides

1 *Proceedings of the Louisiana State Convention, Together With the Ordinances Passed by Said Convention and the Constitution of the State as Amended* (New Orleans, 1861), 5–12; Baton Rouge *Daily Advocate,* January 27, 1861; Jefferson Davis Bragg, *Louisiana in the Confederacy* (Baton Rouge, 1941), 32–33; William E. Highsmith, "Louisiana During Reconstruction" (Ph.D. dissertation, Louisiana State University, 1953), 10–12.

2 New Orleans *Daily Crescent,* January 28, 30, 1861; West Baton Rouge *Sugar Planter,* February 2, 1861.

3 New Orleans *Daily True Delta,* January 24, 1860.

4 *Ibid.,* April 24, 28, May 2, 1860; New Orleans *Daily Picayune,* March 7, 1860; New Orleans *Daily Crescent,* May 7, 31, July 2, November 2, December 4, 1860; Baton Rouge *Weekly Gazette and Comet,* September 15, October 12, 1860; Baton Rouge *Daily Advocate,* September 29, October 8, 15, 18, 1860; Alexandria *Constitutional,* August 20, September 8, 15, 1860; False River *Pointe Coupee Democrat,* October 6, 1860; Plaquemine *Gazette and Sentinel,* September 22, 1860.

5 New Orleans *Daily Crescent, Daily Picayune, Daily True Delta, Bee;* Baton Rouge *Daily Advocate, Weekly Gazette and Comet;* Alexandria *Constitutional;* False River *Pointe Coupee Democrat;* Plaquemine *Gazette and Sentinel;* September, October, November, 1860. These newspapers carried political news clipped from other papers over the state.

6 New Orleans *Daily Crescent,* December 4, 1860; Willie M. Caskey, *Secession and Restoration of Louisiana* (Baton Rouge, 1938), 14–15; Henry Clay Warmoth, *War, Politics and Reconstruction; Stormy Days in Louisiana* (New York, 1930), 35.

7 New Orleans *Daily Crescent,* November 12, 26, 1860.

8 Baton Rouge *Daily Advocate,* November 19, 23, 1860; False River *Pointe Coupee Democrat,* December 1, 1860; Plaquemine *Gazette and Sentinel,* November 24, 1860; Frederick William Williamson and George T. Goodman (eds.), *Eastern Louisiana, A History of the Watershed of the Ouachita River and the Florida Parishes* (Louisville, 1940), II, 538; Lilla McLure and J. Ed Howe (eds.), *History of Shreveport and Shreveport Builders* (Shreveport, 1937, 1951), II, 8.

9 Ellis Family Collection, Department of Archives, Louisiana State University; Fannie A. Beers, *Memories. A Record of Personal Experience and Adventure During Four Years of War* (Philadelphia, 1888), 227; Plaquemine *Gazette and Sentinel,* November 17, 1860.

10 Baton Rouge *Daily Advocate,* November 19, 1860; New Orleans *Daily Crescent,* November 26, December 4, 1860; Albert D. Richardson, *The Secret Service, the Field, the Dungeon, and the Escape* (Hartford, 1865), 49; Caskey, *Secession and Restoration of Louisiana,* 18–20.

11 New Orleans *Daily Crescent,* December 11, 1860; Baton Rouge *Weekly Gazette and Comet,* December 12, 1860; Governor T. O. Moore's message, in *Documents of the Second Session of the Fifth Legislature of the State of Louisiana,* 1861 (Baton Rouge, 1861).

12 New Orleans *Daily True Delta,* December 15, 1860; Bragg, *Louisiana in the Confederacy,* 22–27.

13 Plaquemine *Gazette and Sentinel,* December 15, 29, 1860, January 12, 1861; New Orleans *Daily Crescent,* December 6, 1860, January 3, 1861; New Orleans *Daily Picayune,* January 8, 1861; J. K. Greer, "Louisiana Politics, 1845–1861," *Louisiana Historical Quarterly,* XIII (October, 1930), 640, 641.

14 Annual Report of the Adjutant General, in *Documents of the Second Session of the Fifth Legislature of the State of Louisiana,* 1861, pp. 9–11; New Orleans *Daily Crescent,* November, December, 1860, January, 1861; Williamson and Goodman (eds.), *Eastern Louisiana,* II, 538.

15 *The War of the Rebellion: A Compilation of the Official Records of the Union and Confederate Armies* (Washington: 1880–1901), Ser. I, Vol. I, 489–90, Vol. LIII, 610, cited hereinafter as *Official Records* (unless otherwise indicated all citations are to Series I); William Miller Owen, *In Camp and Battle with the Washington Artillery of New Orleans* (Boston, 1885), 3–4; New Orleans *Daily Crescent,* January 11, 1861; Robert Aertker, "A Social History of Baton Rouge, 1860–1865" (Master's thesis, Louisiana State University, 1947), 11–13; Baton Rouge *Daily Advocate,* January 12, 1861; Napier Bartlett, *A Soldier's Story of the War* (New Orleans, 1874), 11; W. H. Tunnard, *A Southern Record* (Baton Rouge, 1866), 22.

16   M. A. DeWolfe Howe (ed.), *Home Letters of General Sherman* (New York, 1909), 187.
17   *Official Records,* I, 489, 491, 495–96.
18   The Papers of William T. Sherman, VIII, IX, Manuscript Division, Library of Congress, Washington, D.C.; Howe (ed.), *Home Letters of General Sherman,* 187.
19   New Orleans *Daily Picayune,* December 12, 1860; New Orleans *Daily Crescent,* January 14, 1861; Plaquemine *Gazette and Sentinel,* January 12, 1861; McLure and Howe (eds.), *History of Shreveport and Shreveport Builders,* II, 9; Bragg, *Louisiana in the Confederacy,* 51; Thomas O'Connor, *History of the Fire Department of New Orleans from the Earliest Days to the Present Time* (New Orleans, 1895), 140, 153–66.
20   New Orleans *Daily Crescent,* January 26, 1861; Caskey, *Secession and Restoration of Louisiana,* 29.
21   Thomas O. Moore Papers.
22   *Official Journal of the Convention of the State of Louisiana,* 1861 (New Orleans, 1861), 5, 12, 20, cited hereinafter as *Journal of the Louisiana Convention,* 1861; Bragg, *Louisiana in the Confederacy,* 30.
23   New Orleans *Daily Crescent,* January 24, 26, 28, 1861; Alexandria *Constitutional,* February 2, 1861.
24   *Official Records,* LIII, 614–15; West Baton Rouge *Sugar Planter,* February 9, 1861; Bragg, *Louisiana in the Confederacy,* 30–32.
25   *Official Records,* LIII, 616; *Journal of the Louisiana Convention,* 1861, pp. 17, 18, 231; Roger W. Shugg, *Origins of Class Struggle in Louisiana* (Baton Rouge, 1939), 167–69; Baton Rouge *Daily Advocate,* January 27, 1861.

CHAPTER II

An Ounce of Prevention

1   *Journal of the Louisiana Convention,* 1861, pp. 19–24, 34–48, 235–41, 248–61; John Rose Ficklen, *History of Reconstruction in Louisiana* (Baltimore, 1910), 19; Bragg, *Louisiana in the Confederacy,* 39–40.
2   Caskey, *Secession and Restoration of Louisiana,* 34–35.
3   Eliza McHatton-Ripley, *From Flag to Flag* (New York, 1889), 10, 13; Caroline E. Merrick, *Old Times in Dixie Land* (New York, 1901), 31.
4   J. Thomas Scharf, *History of the Confederate States Navy From Its Organization to the Surrender of Its Last Vessel* (New York, 1887), 22; *Official Records,* I, 489, 492, 497.
5   Bragg, *Louisiana in the Confederacy,* 54.
6   *Ibid.,* 53; West Baton Rouge *Sugar Planter,* February 9, 23, 1861; Ellis Family Collection; Liddell Family Papers.

7   Special Report of the Military Board, February 14, 1861, in *Documents of the Second Session of the Fifth Legislature of the State of Louisiana,* 1861, pp. 4, 7; Edwin Albert Leland, "Organization and Administration of the Louisiana Army During the Civil War" (Master's thesis, Louisiana State University, 1938), 26.

8   New Orleans *Daily Crescent,* January 22, February 25, 26, 28, March 29, April 5, 1861; Leland, "Organization of the Louisiana Army," 26, 50, 53–54; Plaquemine *Gazette and Sentinel,* January 12, April 27, 1861; Alexandria *Constitutional,* May 11, 1861; Ella Lonn, *Foreigners in the Confederacy* (Chapel Hill, 1940), 101, 102; O'Connor, *History of the Fire Department of New Orleans,* 140, 153–66.

9   New Orleans *Daily Crescent,* February 13, 1861; New Orleans *Daily True Delta,* February 13, 1861; Lyle Saxon, *Fabulous New Orleans* (New York, 1928), 1–6; Perry Young, *The Mistick Krewe, Chronicles of Comus and His Kin* (New Orleans, 1931), 49.

10 T. Harry Williams, *P. G. T. Beauregard, Napoleon in Gray* (Baton Rouge, 1954), 45–50; Alfred Roman, *The Military Operations of General Beauregard in the War Between the States 1861 to 1865* (New York, 1884), I, 8, 13, 15–18; *Official Records,* I, 500–501; Baton Rouge *Weekly Gazette and Comet,* February 14, 1861; Alexandria *Constitutional,* February 23, 1861.

11 Scharf, *History of the Confederate States Navy,* 28; W. W. Lester and William J. Bromwell, *A Digest of the Military and Naval Laws of the Confederate States* (Columbia, 1864), 41.

12 Leland, "Organization of the Louisiana Army," 27–28.

13 John S. Kendall, *History of New Orleans* (Chicago, 1922), I, 236–37; Highsmith, "Louisiana During Reconstruction," 54; Bragg, *Louisiana in the Confederacy,* 43–46.

14 *Acts Passed by the Fifth Legislature of the State of Louisiana, Second Session, 1861* (Baton Rouge, 1861), 113. Cited hereinafter as *Louisiana Acts.*

15 Van D. Odom, "The Political Career of Thomas Overton Moore, Secession Governor of Louisiana," *Louisiana Historical Quarterly,* XXVI (October, 1943), 1005–1006; New Orleans *Bee,* March 29, April 18, 1861; Thomas Ewing Dabney, *One Hundred Great Years, The Story of the Times Picayune from Its Founding to 1940* (Baton Rouge, 1944), 117; *Official Records,* LIII, 667, 669, Ser. IV, Vol. I, 211; "Historical Militia Data on Louisiana Militia," April 1–20, 1861, typed copy in Louisiana State University Library of W. P. A. Original in Jackson Barracks, New Orleans, 35; Beers, *Memories,* 227.

16 *Official Records,* I, 1, Ser. IV, Vol. I, 221–22; New Orleans *Daily Crescent,* April 13, 15, 1861; H. C. Clarke (comp.), *The Confederate States Almanac and Repository of Useful Knowledge for 1862* (Vicksburg, 1862), 88–90.

17 Weeks Family Papers.
18 *Official Records,* LIII, 675; Leland, "Organization of the Louisiana Army," 30, 59–61, 68, 70–71; Plaquemine *Gazette and Sentinel,* April 28, 1861; Liddell Papers.
19 Tunnard, *A Southern Record,* 25, 31; William Watson, *Life in the Confederate Army Being the Observations and Experiences of an Alien in the South During the American Civil War* (New York, 1888), 127, 141–42, 158, 387; Colonel A. I. Powell, Q.M., to Maj. Gen. John L. Lewis, June 22, 1861, in Executive Communications, Louisiana, 1860–64, Chapter VIII, Vol. CXL, War Records Division, National Archives; F. Jay Taylor (ed.), *Reluctant Rebel; the Secret Diary of Robert Patrick 1861–1865* (Baton Rouge, 1959), 30–31; New Orleans *Daily Crescent,* May 10, 1861; *Official Records,* LIII, 679–80; New Orleans *Daily Picayune,* May 12, 1861; Baton Rouge *Gazette and Comet,* June 12, 1861.
20 Frederick R. Taber Papers.
21 Frank E. Vandiver (ed.), "A Collection of Louisiana Confederate Letters," *Louisiana Historical Quarterly,* XXVI (October, 1943), 951.
22 Charles James Johnson Papers.
23 Ellis Collection.
24 John McGrath, "In a Louisiana Regiment," *Southern Historical Society Papers,* XXXI (1903), 109–12.
25 Johnson Papers.
26 McGrath, "In a Louisiana Regiment," *loc. cit.,* 112.
27 *Ibid.,* 109; Robert A. Newell Papers; J. A. Small, *Memories of the Civil War as Experienced by an Old Veteran* (n.p., n.d.), Pamphlet, 2.
28 Johnson Papers.
29 Watson, *Life in the Confederate Army,* 164.
30 Ellis Collection.
31 Frank L. Richardson, "War As I Saw It," *Louisiana Historical Quarterly,* VI (January, 1923), 92.
32 Newell Papers.
33 Taber Papers.
34 Ellis Collection.
35 John and James Durnin Papers.
36 Silas T. White Papers.
37 Wendell Holmes Stephenson and Edwin Adams Davis (eds.), "The Civil War Diary of Willie Micajah Barrow, Sept. 23, 1861—July 13, 1862," *Louisiana Historical Quarterly,* XVII (July, 1934), 437, 445.
38 Gras-Lauzin Family Papers.
39 New Orleans *Daily Crescent,* April 16, May 7, 15, 28, July 6, 1861; Clara E. Solomon, "Diary of a New Orleans Girl, 1861–1862," typed copy in Louisiana State University Library, 7; McLure and Howe (eds.), *History of Shreveport and Shreveport Builders,* I, 31.
40 Owen, *In Camp and Battle,* 10–12.

41 Bartlett, *A Soldier's Story of the War,* 16–21.
42 McGrath, "In a Louisiana Regiment," *loc. cit.,* 115–16.
43 New Orleans *Daily Picayune,* June 7, 1861.
44 *Official Records,* LIII, 690, 692; *Dictionary of American Biography* (New York, 1928–36), XIX, 83, cited hereinafter as *D.A.B.; The South in the Building of the Nation* (Richmond, 1909–13), XII, 485.
45 *Official Records,* LIII, 739.
46 New Orleans *Daily Delta,* May 24, 1861; New Orleans *Bee,* May 26, 1861.

CHAPTER III

The Armed Camp

1 D. W. Harris and B. M. Hulse (comps.), *The History of Claiborne Parish, Louisiana* (New Orleans, 1886), 173, 180, 185, 192–95; John G. Belisle, *History of Sabine Parish, Louisiana* (Many, La., 1912), 149–51; J. Ed Howe, "Progressive History of Bossier Parish, 1843 to 1950," 10, bound with McLure and Howe (eds.), *History of Shreveport and Shreveport Builders,* II; Leland, "Organization of the Louisiana Army," 87–88; McLure and Howe (eds.), *History of Shreveport and Shreveport Builders,* I, 32; Louisiana newspapers, June, 1861—February, 1862.
2 New Orleans *Daily Delta,* July 15, 26, 1861; New Orleans *Daily Picayune,* July 19, 1861.
3 Lester and Bromwell, *Military and Naval Laws of the Confederate States,* 49.
4 "Historical Militia Data on Louisiana Militia," 117.
5 Bragg, *Louisiana in the Confederacy,* 249.
6 New Orleans *Daily Delta,* June 18, 1861; Leland, "Organization of the Louisiana Army," 66–68.
7 Edwin W. Fay, *The History of Education in Louisiana* (Washington, 1898), 76, 162; Merrick, *Old Times in Dixie Land,* 28–30.
8 Liddell Papers.
9 New Orleans *Daily Delta,* November 21, 1861.
10 Walter Lynwood Fleming, *Louisiana State University, 1860–1896* (Baton Rouge, 1898), 104–106, 112, 121; Sherman Papers, IX, 1159.
11 Leland, "Organization of the Louisiana Army," 59; Opelousas *Patriot,* July 13, October 5, 1861; New Orleans *Daily Picayune,* June 8, 1861; *Official Records,* LIII, 745; New Orleans *Daily Crescent,* September 30, 1861; Plaquemine *Gazette and Sentinel,* June 1, 1861; Alexander F. Pugh and Family Collection, Diary, 1861–1864; Liddell Papers.
12 Lonn, *Foreigners In the Confederacy,* 100–14; Leland, "Organization of the Louisiana Army," 58; Shugg, *Origins of Class Struggle in Louisiana,* 172.

13 John Q. Anderson (ed.), *Brokenburn, The Journal of Kate Stone 1861–1868* (Baton Rouge, 1955), 14–16; J. Fair Hardin, *Northwestern Louisiana* (Louisville, 1939), II, 59; Sidney A. Marchand, *The Flight of a Century (1800–1900) in Ascension Parish, Louisiana* (Baton Rouge, 1936), 151; Lonn, *Foreigners in the Confederacy,* 109; New Orleans *Daily True Delta,* November 10, 1861.

14 New Orleans *Daily Picayune,* April 18, 1861; New Orleans *Commercial Bulletin,* May 2, 1861; Leland, "Organization of the Louisiana Army," 45; Shreveport *Daily News,* July 18, 1861; Lonn, *Foreigners in the Confederacy,* 100, 109, 111; McGrath, "In a Louisiana Regiment," *loc. cit.,* 103.

15 New Orleans *Daily Picayune,* January 22, 1861; McGrath, "In a Louisiana Regiment," *loc. cit.,* 103; Lonn, *Foreigners in the Confederacy,* 102, 109.

16 New Orleans *Daily Picayune,* June 5, December 27, 1861; *Official Records,* XV, 480–81; Lonn, *Foreigners in the Confederacy,* 100–109, 112; McGrath, "In a Louisiana Regiment," *loc. cit.,* 103.

17 New Orleans *Bee,* June 3, 1861; New Orleans *Daily Delta,* October 2, 1861; Leland, "Organization of the Louisiana Army," 50, 52.

18 U.S. Census Office. 8th Census, 1860, *Population of the United States in 1860* (Washington, 1864), 615. Cited hereinafter as *Eighth Census, 1860, Population.*

19 New Orleans *Bee,* June 3, 1861; New Orleans *Daily Picayune,* July 4, 1861; Lonn, *Foreigners in the Confederacy,* 100.

20 Leland, "Organization of the Louisiana Army," 43–44; Milledge L. Bonham, Jr., *The British Consuls in the Confederacy* (New York, 1911), 172–74; Lonn, *Foreigners in the Confederacy,* 401, 402.

21 New Orleans *Bee,* April 26, 1861; Baton Rouge *Gazette and Comet,* April 25, 1861; West Baton Rouge *Sugar Planter,* June 15, 1861; Joseph T. Wilson, *The Black Phalanx* (Hartford, 1888), 481–82; *Eighth Census, 1860, Population,* 190–93.

22 Shugg, *Origins of Class Struggle in Louisiana,* 118, 119; Wilson, *The Black Phalanx,* 482; New Orleans *Daily Delta,* December 28, 1860; Benjamin Quarles, *The Negro in the Civil War* (Boston, 1953), 38–39.

23 New Orleans *Daily Crescent,* April 24, 1861; *Official Records,* XV, 556; Leland, "Organization of the Louisiana Army," 78–79; New Orleans *Daily Picayune,* February 8, 1862.

24 Anderson (ed.), *Brokenburn,* 17; Howe, "Progressive History of Bossier Parish," *loc. cit.,* 10.

25 Leland, "Organization of the Louisiana Army," 31–32; New Orleans *Daily Crescent,* July 1, 1861; Lester and Bromwell, *Military and Naval Laws of the Confederate States,* 51–52.

26 *Louisiana Acts,* 1861, 173.

27 Bartlett, *A Soldier's Story of the War,* 12–13; West Baton Rouge *Sugar Planter,* April 27, 1861; Baton Rouge *Gazette and Comet,* April 27,

1861; McLure and Howe (eds.), *History of Shreveport and Shreveport Builders*, I, 31; Henry Rightor (ed.), *Standard History of New Orleans, Louisiana* (Chicago, 1900), 154; Leland, "Organization of the Louisiana Army," 19–21; New Orleans *Daily Crescent,* April 26, 1861.

28 Robert Dabney Calhoun, "A History of Concordia Parish," (Part V), *Louisiana Historical Quarterly,* XVI (January, 1933), 107; Williamson and Goodman (eds.), *Eastern Louisiana,* I, 142.

29 Corinne L. Saucier, *History of Avoyelles Parish, Louisiana* (New Orleans, 1943), 406–407.

30 Howe, "Progressive History of Bossier Parish," *loc. cit.,* 7; Leland, "Organization of the Louisiana Army," 91; Belisle, *History of Sabine Parish,* 113; Alfred Flournoy Papers; New Orleans *Daily Picayune,* June 19, July 4, 1861; Plaquemine *Gazette and Sentinel,* April 27, 1861; Alexander F. Pugh Family Collection, Diary, 1861–64; Bragg, *Louisiana in the Confederacy,* 57.

31 Leland, "Organization of the Louisiana Army," 18–23, 88; New Orleans *Daily Delta,* June 20, 1861; Quarles, *The Negro in the Civil War,* 38–39; McLure and Howe (eds.), *History of Shreveport and Shreveport Builders,* I, 31; Grace E. King, *New Orleans the Place and the People* (New York, 1902), 378.

32 John D. Winters, "Confederate New Orleans, 1861–1862" (Master's thesis, Louisiana State University, 1947), 33; New Orleans *Daily Crescent,* May 6, July 6, 22, 1861; Kate M. Rowland and Mrs. Morris L. Croxall (eds.), *The Journal of Julia LeGrand, New Orleans 1862–1863* (Richmond, 1911), 37; Marion Southwood, *"Beauty and Booty," The Watchword of New Orleans* (New York, 1867), 13, 14, 17.

33 Robert T. Clark, "The New Orleans German Colony in the Civil War," *Louisiana Historical Quarterly,* XX (October, 1937), 990, 1013; New Orleans *Daily Crescent,* May 20, 1861.

34 Bragg, *Louisiana in the Confederacy,* 87–91; Dabney, *One Hundred Great Years,* 134–35; Southwood, *"Beauty and Booty,"* 77–78; New Orleans *Daily Crescent,* October 4, December 7, 1861, May 2, 1862; Rowland and Croxall (eds.), *The Journal of Julia LeGrand,* 37; New Orleans *Daily Picayune,* January 2, 1862; Rightor (ed.), *Standard History of New Orleans,* 154.

35 Baton Rouge *Gazette and Comet,* May 18, November 27, December 14, 1861; McHatton-Ripley, *From Flag to Flag,* 13–16; West Baton Rouge *Sugar Planter,* July 6, August 24, 1861.

36 McLure and Howe (eds.), *History of Shreveport and Shreveport Builders,* I, 31–33, 204; Shreveport *Daily News,* June 27, November 1, 1861.

37 Flournoy Papers.

38 Natchitoches *Union,* December 5, 1861; Shreveport *Semi-Weekly News,* December 31, 1861.

39 Alexander F. Pugh Family Collection, Diary.

40   New Orleans *Daily Picayune,* August 1, 1861.
41   Anderson (ed.), *Brokenburn,* 47, 52, 55, 56, 59.
42   Bragg, *Louisiana in the Confederacy,* 92; Shreveport *Daily News,* August 29, 1861; McHatton-Ripley, *From Flag to Flag,* 17.

CHAPTER IV

Blockade and Naval Preparations

1   Scharf, *History of the Confederate States Navy.* 23, 28, 31, 36, 240.
2   *Official Records of the Union and Confederate Navies in the War of the Rebellion* (Washington, 1894–1922), Ser. I, Vol. IV, 156–57, cited hereinafter as *Navy Records* (unless otherwise indicated all citations are to Series I); James Russell Soley, *The Blockade and the Cruisers* (New York, 1883), 27.
3   A. T. Mahan, *The Gulf and Inland Waters* (New York, 1883), 3–4; Scharf, *History of the Confederate States Navy,* 240–41.
4   Frank Lawrence Owsley, *King Cotton Diplomacy* (Chicago, 1931), 32, 36, 43–47, 51, 90–91, 146–47; Flournoy Papers.
5   Rightor (ed.), *Standard History of New Orleans,* 519, 566–71; John C. Schwab, *The Confederate States of America 1861–1865: A Financial and Industrial History of the South During the Civil War* (New York, 1901), 238.
6   *Navy Records,* IV, 188–89.
7   David Dixon Porter, "Private Journal of Occurrences During the Great War of the Rebellion," Manuscript Division, Library of Congress, 48, 109, 114, 116–18, 121, 125–28; *Navy Records,* IV, 188–89, 190–91, 193, 695, 703; Richard S. West, Jr., *The Second Admiral, A Life of David Dixon Porter 1813–1891* (New York, 1937), 97–99; James M. Morgan, *Recollections of a Rebel Reefer* (Boston, 1917), 49; Soley, *The Blockade and the Cruisers,* 121; David Dixon Porter, "The Opening of the Lower Mississippi," in Robert U. Johnson and Clarence C. Buel (eds.), *Battles and Leaders of the Civil War* (New York, 1887), II, 23. Cited hereinafter as *Battles and Leaders.*
8   Scharf, *History of the Confederate States Navy,* 36; *Battle-Fields of the South, from Bull Run to Fredericksburgh* (New York, 1864), 180–81; Morgan, *Recollections of a Rebel Reefer,* 49, 51–55, 61; H. Allen Gosnell, *Guns on the Western Waters* (Baton Rouge, 1949), 35–36; *Official Records,* LIII, 739.
9   Soley, *The Blockade and the Cruisers,* 132.
10   *Ibid.,* 29, 129–32; *Navy Records,* XVI, 683, 685, 738–39; Scharf, *History of the Confederate States Navy,* 274–77; Morgan, *Recollections of a Rebel Reefer,* 55–58; Gosnell, *Guns on the Western Waters,* 38–43; Mahan, *The Gulf and Inland Waters,* 5; David D. Porter, *Incidents*

and Anecdotes of the Civil War (New York, 1885), 67–68; Frank Moore (ed.), *The Rebellion Record: A Diary of American Events with Documents, Narratives, Illustrative Incidents, Poetry, etc.* (New York, 1864–68), II, 367–71

11 Scharf, *History of the Confederate States Navy,* 274; Gosnell, *Guns on the Western Waters,* 43; Morgan, *Recollections of a Rebel Reefer,* 58; New Orleans *Daily Crescent,* October 13, 14, 1861; New Orleans *Sunday Delta,* October 13, 1861; New Orleans *Daily Picayune,* October 13, 1861; New Orleans *Daily Delta,* October 16, 1861; Soley, *The Blockade and the Cruisers,* 132; Alcée Fortier, *A History of Louisiana* (New York, 1904), IV, 7.

12 Scharf, *History of the Confederate States Navy,* 249; *Navy Records,* XVI, 774–75, 794–96; Owsley, *King Cotton Diplomacy,* 258–60.

13 Solomon, "Diary," 7–66, 74, 77, 78, 125–32; New Orleans *Daily Crescent,* October 2, November 9, 1861; Eliza McHatton-Ripley, *Social Life in Old New Orleans Being Recollections of My Girlhood* (New York, 1912), 275; Shugg, *Origins of Class Struggle in Louisiana,* 171; Bragg, *Louisiana in the Confederacy,* 76–77.

14 West Baton Rouge *Sugar Planter,* November 2, December 7, 28, 1861; Plaquemine *Gazette and Sentinel,* July 6, 1861; Shreveport *Semi-Weekly News,* November 11, 1861.

15 Shreveport *Semi-Weekly News,* November 11, 1861; McLure and Howe (eds.), *History of Shreveport and Shreveport Builders,* I, 33.

16 Rightor (ed.), *Standard History of New Orleans,* 578; Schwab, *A Financial and Industrial History of the South,* 124–31; *Journal of the Louisiana Convention,* 1861, p. 281; Solomon, "Diary," 68; New Orleans *Daily Crescent,* September 16, December 20, 1861; Lonn, *Foreigners in the Confederacy,* 343; George W. Cable, "New Orleans Before the Capture," *Battles and Leaders,* II, 18.

17 Winters, "Confederate New Orleans," 113.

18 West, *The Second Admiral,* 109–14; Porter, *Incidents and Anecdotes,* 65–66; Gideon Welles, *Diary of Gideon Welles Secretary of the Navy Under Lincoln and Johnson* (Boston, 1911), I, 116–17, 134; Charles Lee Lewis, *David Glasgow Farragut: Our First Admiral* (Annapolis, 1943), 13.

CHAPTER V

The Pace Quickens

1 Saucier, *History of Avoyelles Parish,* 214–15; Helene Dupuy Diary, April 12, 1861—April 13, 1865; Hardin, *Northwestern Louisiana,* II,

59; Opelousas *Patriot,* September 14, 21, 1861; Belisle, *History of Sabine Parish,* 152; *Official Records,* LIII, 739.

2   *Official Records,* VI, 740–48, LIII, 739, 742, 744–45.

3   Shugg, *Origins of Class Struggle in Louisiana,* 172.

4   War Department Collection of Confederate Records, Chapter VIII, Vols. CXL, CXLI, CXLII, War Records Division, National Archives; Adjutant General's Annual Report, November 22, 1861, in "Historical Militia Data," 56, 59, 61.

5   War Department Collection of Confederate Records, C, Chapter VIII, Vol. CLI, Special Orders, 1st Division, Louisiana State Troops, January–December, 1861, War Records Division, National Archives, Washington, D.C.; Calhoun, "History of Concordia Parish," *loc. cit.* (Part V), 110; Baton Rouge *Gazette and Comet,* November 15, 1861; Natchitoches *Union,* November 28, 1861; Harris and Hulse (comps.), *The History of Claiborne Parish,* 199–202; Shreveport *Semi-Weekly News,* November 14, 1861.

6   Adjutant General's Report, November 22, 1861, in "Historical Militia Data," 61; Baton Rouge *Gazette and Comet,* November 15, 1861.

7   Winters, "Confederate New Orleans," 112–13.

8   New Orleans *Daily Picayune,* April 2, June 16, 1861, February 8, 28, 1862; New Orleans *Daily Crescent,* February 8, 1862; William H. Russell, *My Diary North and South* (Boston, 1863), 231.

9   Solomon, "Diary," 48.

10 U.S. Census Office. 8th Census, 1860, *Manufactures of the United States in 1860* (Washington, 1865), xxi, xxv, lxvi, lxxiii, 191; cited hereafter as *Eighth Census,* 1860, *Manufactures;* New Orleans *Daily Crescent,* January 7, February 16, April 26, May 31, June 12, September 16, 1861; New Orleans *Daily Picayune,* June 16, 1861; Charles Gardner (ed.), *Gardner's New Orleans Directory for 1861 Including Jefferson City, Gretna, Carrollton, Algiers and McDonogh* (New Orleans, 1861), 2, 32; Nathaniel C. Curtis, *New Orleans: Its Old Houses, Shops, and Public Buildings* (Philadelphia, 1933), 59.

11 *Official Records,* VI, 560–63, 584, 621, 639, 760, 769.

12 *Ibid.,* 592, 790; New Orleans *Daily Delta,* December 29, 1861; New Orleans *Daily Crescent,* February 7, 1862.

13 Morgan, *Recollections of a Rebel Reefer,* 55; Fortier, *A History of Louisiana,* IV, 10.

14 *Official Records,* VI, 621, 627; Jefferson Davis, *The Rise and Fall of the Confederate Government* (New York, 1881), II, 225.

15 *Eighth Census,* 1860, *Manufactures,* 196–201, 203.

16 McLure and Howe (eds.), *History of Shreveport and Shreveport Builders,* I, 12, 33–34; Hardin, *Northwestern Louisiana,* II, 154–55.

17 *Official Records,* LIII, 748–49; Sarah A. Dorsey, *Recollections of Henry*

Watkins Allen, Brigadier General Confederate States Army, Ex-Governor of Louisiana (New York, 1866), 68.

18 Moore Papers.
19 Dorsey, *Recollections of Henry Watkins Allen,* 68; *The South in the Building of the Nation,* XII, 116; *D.A.B.,* XI, 441.
20 *Official Records,* VI, 512, 557–60, 564, 581, 639, 774–75, XV, 413–16; Davis, *The Rise and Fall of the Confederate Government,* II, 213; Liddell Papers.
21 Ann E. Spears Papers.
22 *Official Records,* VI, 556–57, 559–61, 593, 774; Dorsey, *Recollections of Henry Watkins Allen,* 87, 90–91; *Battle-Fields of the South,* 182; Southwood, *"Beauty and Booty,"* 19.
23 New Orleans *Daily True Delta,* December 25, 1861; New Orleans *Daily Picayune,* January 2, 1862.

CHAPTER VI

The Threat

1 New Orleans *Daily Crescent,* January 11, 1862.
2 *Official Records,* VI, 637, 791, 819, LIII, 775–76; Louis A. Bringier Family Papers; Dabney, *One Hundred Great Years,* 142.
3 "Legislative Acts of Louisiana Militia 1857 to 1865," typed copy in Louisiana State University Library, 50–66; "Historical Militia Data on Louisiana Militia," 66, 95–101; *Official Records,* LIII, 786; Bonham, *The British Consuls in the Confederacy,* 181.
4 *Official Records,* VI, 850–52.
5 Anderson (ed.), *Brokenburn,* 95, 97.
6 *Official Records,* Ser. II, Vol. II, 1422; Leland, "Organization of the Louisiana Army," 43–44, 47; Lonn, *Foreigners in the Confederacy,* 112.
7 Juan Miangolarra Papers; Leland, "Organization of the Louisiana Army," 50–51; New Orleans *Commercial Bulletin,* February 25, 27, March 18, 1862; New Orleans *Bee,* February 24, 1862; Lonn, *Foreigners in the Confederacy,* 113–14.
8 Leland, "Organization of the Louisiana Army," 98–99; Opelousas *Le Courrier des Opelousas,* January 4, 1862; New Orleans *Daily Picayune,* Jan. 7, 1862.
9 New Orleans *Daily Picayune,* January 7, February 11, March 9, 12, 1862; Leland, "Organization of the Louisiana Army," 31; Saucier, *History of Avoyelles Parish,* 407; Belisle, *History of Sabine Parish,* 113; "West Feliciana Parish Military Board Minute Book 1862–1863,"

Department of Archives, Louisiana State University; Calhoun, "History of Concordia Parish," *loc. cit.,* 108–109.

10 Lester and Bromwell, *Military and Naval Laws of the Confederate States,* 52.

11 New Orleans *Daily Picayune,* March 5, 1862; Opelousas *Le Courrier des Opelousas,* April 12, 1862; Shreveport *Semi-Weekly News,* January, 1862, March 7, 14, 1862; Hardin, *Northwestern Louisiana,* II, 116; Harris and Hulse (comps.), *History of Claiborne Parish,* 205–20; Calhoun, "History of Concordia Parish," *loc. cit.,* 110.

12 Anderson (ed.), *Brokenburn,* 93.

13 Natchitoches *Union,* March 20, April 3, 1862; Winchester Hall, *The Story of the 26th Louisiana Infantry, in the Service of the Confederate States* (n.p., n.d.), 2; New Orleans *Daily Crescent,* February 21, 1862; Leland, "Organization of the Louisiana Army," 96; McLure and Howe (eds.), *History of Shreveport and Shreveport Builders,* I, 32–33.

14 *Official Records,* VI, 823; Shreveport *Semi-Weekly News,* February 21, March 4, 1862; Letters Received, Louisiana State Troops, 1862, Chapter VIII, Vol. CXLIII, War Records Division, National Archives.

15 *Official Records,* VI, 823, 825, 847.

16 Opelousas *Courier,* March 15, 1862; Shreveport *Semi-Weekly News,* April 4, 1862; Natchitoches *Union,* September 25, 1862; T. Harry Williams, *P. G. T. Beauregard,* 122–23; James Parton, *General Butler in New Orleans* (Boston, 1864), 283.

17 *Official Records,* VI, 595, 809, 811–12, 817, LIII, 770; Cable, "New Orleans Before the Capture," *Battles and Leaders,* II, 18; Scharf, *History of the Confederate States Navy,* 250; *Navy Records,* XVII, 159–60.

18 *Official Records,* VI, 512–13, 561–62, 591, 841, 861, 864–65, I, 522–23; Scharf, *History of the Confederate States Navy,* 250.

19 *Navy Records,* XVIII, 56–57; Shreveport *Semi-Weekly News,* February 21, March 4, 1862; New Orleans *Daily Delta,* March 2, 1862; *Official Records,* VI, 561, 575–77, 830–31, 837, 847–48, 856–57, 860–61, 872.

20 *Official Records,* VI, 513, 878; Scharf, *History of the Confederate States Navy,* 266–70, 300.

21 *Battle-Fields of the South,* 182–84.

22 New Orleans *Daily Picayune,* March 2, 5, 6, 23, April 5, 16, 22, 24, 1862; Dabney, *One Hundred Great Years,* 142.

23 *Official Records,* Ser. IV, Vol. I, 1095–96; Lester and Bromwell, *Military and Naval Laws of the Confederate States,* 57; Shreveport *Semi-Weekly News,* April 22, 1862; Calhoun, "A History of Concordia Parish," *loc. cit.,* 109.

24 *Official Records,* VI, 513, 561, 563–64, 595, 878–79.

CHAPTER VII

The Queen Falls

1 *Navy Records,* XVIII, 35–50, 57, 64–65, 67–68, 88, 109, 135–36, 263–
 64, 391; Porter, "Private Journal," 231–34; Fletcher Pratt, *Civil War
 on Western Waters* (New York, 1956), 77–78, 80, 83; Lewis, *Our
 First Admiral,* 25–28, 33.
2 *Navy Records,* XVIII, 48–49, 133–36, 156, 364–67, 391–92; Lewis, *Our
 First Admiral,* 33–35; Porter, "Private Journal," 244–45; *Official Rec-
 ords,* VI, 524–26, 546.
3 *Navy Records,* XVIII, 135, 367, 525–26, 383, 391, 442; *Official Records,*
 VI, 514, 526–27, 564–65, 569, 590, 603, 611–13; George B. Bacon,
 "One Night's Work, April 20, 1862," *Magazine of American History,*
 XV (March, 1886), 305–307; George Dewey, *Autobiography of George
 Dewey, Admiral of the Navy* (New York, 1913), 58–59; Pratt, *Civil
 War on Western Waters,* 86; Lewis, *Our First Admiral,* 38; Scharf,
 History of the Confederate States Navy, 251–52, 278–79, 300.
4 Loyall Farragut, *The Life of David Glasgow Farragut, First Admiral
 of the United States Navy, Embodying His Journal and Letters* (New
 York, 1879), 219–20, 224; *Navy Records,* XVIII, 145–46, 155, 160, 166,
 367; "History Set Right," Reprint from *Army and Navy Journal,* July
 17, 1869 (New York, 1869), 12; Gorham C. Taylor, *Notes of Conversations With a Volunteer Officer in the United States Navy, On the
 Passage of the Forts Below New Orleans April 24th, 1862 and Other
 Points of Service on the Mississippi River During that Year* (New
 York, 1868), 9; Lewis, *Our First Admiral,* 54; William B. Robertson,
 "The Water-Battery at Fort Jackson," *Battles and Leaders,* II, 100.
5 *Navy Records,* XVIII, 142, 154–57, 168, 170–72, 175, 182–85, 197, 198,
 218, 224–27, 294, 367; "History Set Right," *loc cit.,* 4–5; Dewey, *Autobiography,* 64–71; Robertson, "The Water-Battery at Fort Jackson," *loc.
 cit.,* 100.
6 Beverly Kennon, "Fighting Farragut Below New Orleans," *Battles
 and Leaders,* II, 77–80; *Official Records,* VI, 510, 636; *Navy Records,*
 XVIII, 294.
7 *Navy Records,* XVIII, 157, 171–73, 198, 305–309; *Official Records,* VI,
 528–29; Kennon, "Fighting Farragut Below New Orleans," *loc. cit.,*
 87–88; Scharf, *History of the Confederate States Navy,* 299; Mahan,
 The Gulf and Inland Waters, 85; George E. Belknap (ed.), *Letters of
 Capt. Geo. Hamilton Perkins* (Concord, 1886), 70.
8 *Navy Records,* XVIII, 285; *Official Records,* VI, 553, 585; Butler Family
 Papers (C), Part III; Sanders Family Papers; John Roy Diary; Hall,
 The Story of the 26th Louisiana, 7.

9 *Navy Records*, XVIII, 157–58, 198; Belknap (ed.), *Letters of Capt. Geo. Hamilton Perkins*, 70; Dorsey, *Recollections of Henry Watkins Allen*, 104; Southwood, *"Beauty and Booty,"* 19; Benjamin F. Butler, *Autobiography and Personal Reminiscences of Major-General Benj. F. Butler; Butler's Book* (Boston, 1892), 370; *Battle-Fields of the South,* 185–86.

10 *Official Records*, VI, 576, 609, 615; *Battle-Fields of the South,* 185–86; Cable, "New Orleans Before the Capture," *loc. cit.,* 18.

11 *Navy Records*, XVIII, 154; New Orleans *Daily Picayune*, April 26, 1862; Belknap (ed.), *Letters of Capt. Geo. Hamilton Perkins,* 70–71; Cable, "New Orleans Before the Capture," *loc. cit.,* 21; Morgan, *Recollections of a Rebel Reefer,* 75–77; Hall, *The Story of the 26th Louisiana,* 8–9.

12 *Navy Records*, XVIII, 152–55; *Official Records*, VI, 550; William T. Meredith, "Farragut's Capture of New Orleans," *Battles and Leaders,* II, 72–73; Lewis, *Our First Admiral,* 62–63; Dewey, *Autobiography,* 73.

13 *Navy Records*, XVIII, 153–55; *Official Records*, VI, 515–17, 586–87, 592, 606, 615, 634, Ser. II, Vol. III, 613–15; New Orleans *Daily Picayune*, April 27, 1862; Rowland and Croxall (eds.), *The Journal of Julia Le Grand,* 40–42; Albert Kautz, "Incidents of the Occupation of New Orleans," *Battles and Leaders,* II, 91–95; Southwood, *"Beauty and Booty,"* 19; Marion A. Baker, "Farragut's Demands for the Surrender of New Orleans," *Battles and Leaders,* II, 97.

14 *Official Records*, VI, 504, 529, XV, 447; *Navy Records*, XVIII, 142; Porter, *Incidents and Anecdotes,* 48–49; Porter, "Private Journal," 283; Benjamin F. Butler, *Private and Official Correspondence of Gen. Benjamin F. Butler During the Period of the Civil War* (Norwood, Mass., 1917), I, 426; E. S. S. Rouse, *The Bugle Blast* (Philadelphia, 1864), 132.

15 *Official Records*, VI, 505, 508, 531–33, 614, XV, 428–37, LIII, 524–25; Butler, *Private and Official Correspondence,* I, 427–28; Dorsey, *Recollections of Henry Watkins Allen,* 103–106; Davis, *The Rise and Fall of the Confederate Government,* II, 219; Porter, *Incidents and Anecdotes,* 49–55, 71; West, *Second Admiral,* 142; John W. De Forest, *A Volunteer's Adventures* (New Haven, 1946), 15; Dewey, *Autobiography,* 74–75; *Navy Records*, XVIII, 159.

16 Baker, "Farragut's Demands for the Surrender of New Orleans," *loc. cit.,* 98–99; Kautz, "Incidents of the Occupation of New Orleans," *loc. cit.,* 93; *Official Records*, VI, 506; George N. Carpenter, *History of the Eighth Regiment Vermont Volunteers, 1861–1865* (Boston, 1886), 34; Wickham Hoffman, *Camp, Court and Siege* (New York, 1877), 23–24; De Forest, *A Volunteer's Adventures,* 18; New Orleans *Daily True Delta,* May 1, May 2, 1862; New Orleans *Daily Picayune*, May 2, 1862; Parton, *General Butler in New Orleans,* 279–81.

17 Southwood, *"Beauty and Booty,"* 41–43.
18 De Forest, *A Volunteer's Adventures,* 18; Parton, *General Butler in New Orleans,* 281–82; Butler, *Private and Official Correspondence,* I, 438; Lewis, *Our First Admiral,* 81.

CHAPTER VIII

Vicksburg, Act One

1 Bringier Papers; Shreveport *Daily News,* May 2, 1862; *Official Records,* VI, 883; Sarah Morgan Dawson, *A Confederate Girl's Diary* (Boston, 1913), 17–18; Dupuy Diary; Dorsey, *Recollections of Henry Watkins Allen,* 281–82; Anderson (ed.), *Brokenburn,* 100–101, 103.
2 *Navy Records,* XVIII, 473, 491–92, 519, 520; Lewis, *Our First Admiral,* 81–83; G. Mott Williams, "Letters of General Thomas Williams," *American Historical Review,* XIV (January, 1909), 317.
3 *Navy Records,* XVIII, 515–16, 520, 706–707; Dawson, *A Confederate Girl's Diary,* 39–51, 53–73; Watson, *Life in the Confederate Army,* 388–89; Aertker, "A Social History of Baton Rouge," 26.
4 Porter, "Private Journal," 333, 339–55; Lewis, *Our First Admiral,* 85, 91; *Navy Records,* XVIII, 557, 576; Francis Vinton Greene, *The Mississippi* (New York, 1882), 21; West, *Second Admiral,* 146–49; Butler, *Private and Official Correspondence,* I, 562–63; Roland Chambers Diary; G. Mott Williams, "Letters of General Thomas Williams," *loc. cit.,* 322.
5 Lewis, *Our First Admiral,* 94–101; West, *Second Admiral,* 154, 156; *Navy Records,* XVIII, 588, 713–14, XXIII, 231–34; Thomas R. Markham Papers; Wm. C. Holbrook, *A Narrative of the Services of the Officers and Enlisted Men of the 7th Regiment of Vermont Volunteers (Veterans), from 1862 to 1866* (New York, 1882), 18; A. D. Kirwan (ed.), *Johnny Green of the Orphan Brigade, The Journal of a Confederate Soldier* (Lexington, 1956), 42–45; John B. Pirtle, "Defence of Vicksburg in 1862—The Battle of Baton Rouge," *Southern Historical Society Papers,* VIII (June and July, 1880), 325–26; Farragut, *The Life of David Glasgow Farragut,* 275.
6 *Official Records,* XV, 27–28, 31–32; G. Mott Williams, "Letters of General Thomas Williams," *loc. cit.,* 322–23, 326; Butler, *Private and Official Correspondence,* I, 595–96; Benj. F. Butler Papers, 1862, Manuscript Division, Library of Congress; Kenneth P. Williams, *Lincoln Finds A General* (New York, 1949–59), IV, 11; Anderson (ed.), *Brokenburn,* 114–32.
7 *Navy Records,* XVIII, 595, 630, 632, 651, 678–81; Butler, *Butler's Book,* 455, 457, 458; Greene, *The Mississippi,* 18; West, *Second Admiral,* 160–61; J. P. Knox Family Papers; Porter, "Private Journal," 366–67;

John Johnson, "Story of the Confederate Armored Ram Arkansas," *Southern Historical Society Papers,* XXXIII (1905), 2–4; Scharf, *History of the Confederate States Navy,* 303–307, 310–29; Markham Papers; George W. Gift, "The Story of the Arkansas," *Southern Historical Society Papers,* XII (1884), 48–54, 115–19, 163–70; Thomas W. Knox, *Camp-Fire and Cotton-Field* (New York, 1865), 201–203; Albert Theodore Goodloe, *Some Rebel Relics From the Seat of War* (Nashville, 1893), 187–88; Warren D. Crandall and Isaac D. Newell, *History of the Ram Fleet and the Mississippi Marine Brigade in the War for the Union on the Mississippi and Its Tributaries* (St. Louis, 1907), 98–103, 113.

8 G. Mott Williams, "Letters of General Thomas Williams," *loc. cit.,* 304–306, 324–25; Holbrook, *A Narrative of the 7th Regiment, Vermont,* 22–23; W. A. Croffut and John M. Morris, *The Military and Civil History of Connecticut During the War of 1861–1865* (New York, 1868), 310.

9 Thomas H. Murray, *History of the Ninth Regiment, Connecticut Volunteer Infantry, "The Irish Regiment" In The War of the Rebellion, 1861–65* (New Haven, 1903), 111–12.

10 Holbrook, *A Narrative of the 7th Regiment, Vermont,* 23, 25, 26, 28; Croffut and Morris, *The Military and Civil History of Connecticut,* 310; Murray, *History of the Ninth Regiment, Connecticut,* 111; G. Mott Williams, "Letters of General Thomas Williams," *loc. cit.,* 324–26; Knox, *Camp-Fire and Cotton-Field,* 198; Hoffman, *Camp, Court and Siege,* 45–46, 48; *Official Records,* XV, 31; Butler, *Butler's Book,* 463.

11 *Navy Records,* XVIII, 595, XXIII, 235, 237, 239, 240–41; Crandall and Newell, *History of the Ram Fleet,* 118; *Battle-Fields of the South,* 416; Knox, *Camp-Fire and Cotton-Field,* 203; Edward Bacon, *Among the Cotton Thieves* (Detroit, 1867), 15.

12 Edward Bacon, *Among the Cotton Thieves,* 6–7, 13–15; Knox, *Camp-Fire and Cotton-Field,* 203–204; Holbrook, *A Narrative of the 7th Regiment, Vermont,* 36–37; Murray, *History of the Ninth Regiment, Connecticut,* 114; G. Mott Williams, "Letters of General Thomas Williams," *loc. cit.,* 306.

13 *Official Records,* XV, 16–17, 76–77, 785–86; Scharf, *History of the Confederate States Navy,* 332; Kenneth P. Williams, *Lincoln Finds A General,* IV, 13; John Smith Kendall, "Recollections of a Confederate Officer," *Louisiana Historical Quarterly,* XXIX (October, 1946), 1081.

14 Kendall, "Recollections of a Confederate Officer," *loc. cit.,* 1082.

15 *Official Records,* XV, 77; Pirtle, "Defence of Vicksburg," *loc. cit.,* 329; Dorsey, *Recollections of Henry Watkins Allen,* 77, 90, 132.

CHAPTER IX

The Battle of Baton Rouge

1 *D.A.B.,* III, 7–10.
2 *Official Records,* XV, 39, 51–52, 77–78, 83, 90–91, 100; Murray, *History of the Ninth Regiment, Connecticut,* 115; Dorsey, *Recollections of Henry Watkins Allen,* 135; Croffut and Morris, *The Military and Civil History of Connecticut,* 310; Hoffman, *Camp, Court and Siege,* 48; Richard B. Irwin, "Military Operations in Louisiana in 1862," *Battles and Leaders,* III, 582–84.
3 *Official Records,* XV, 42, 48–52, 54, 74, 78–79, 84, 91, 92, 100, 102–107; William E. S. Whitman and Charles H. True, *Maine in the War for the Union* (Lewiston, Maine, 1865), 320–21; Kendall, "Recollections of a Confederate Officer," *loc. cit.,* 1084–88; Benj. F. Butler Papers, Manuscript Division, Library of Congress; Holbrook, *A Narrative of the 7th Regiment, Vermont,* 61–106; Hoffman, *Camp, Court and Siege,* 49–50; Dorsey, *Recollections of Henry Watkins Allen,* 136, 140–41; Croffut and Morris, *The Military and Civil History of Connecticut,* 310–11; Richard B. Irwin, *History of the Nineteenth Army Corps* (New York, 1892), 39.
4 McHatton-Ripley, *From Flag to Flag,* 32–35, 50; Kendall, "Recollections of a Confederate Officer," *loc. cit.,* 1088–89.
5 *Official Records,* XV, 79, 83, 99; Dorsey, *Recollections of Henry Watkins Allen,* 141–42; Kendall, "Recollections of a Confederate Officer," *loc. cit.,* 1089.
6 Scharf, *History of the Confederate States Navy,* 332–34; Pirtle, "Defence of Vicksburg," *loc. cit.,* 331; Gift, "The Story of the Arkansas," *loc. cit.,* 205–12; Kenneth P. Williams, *Lincoln Finds a General,* IV, 13–14; Benj. F. Butler Papers, Sept. 1862, Manuscript Division, Library of Congress; *Official Records,* XV, 17–18, LIII, 531–32; Dawson, *A Confederate Girl's Diary,* 148–53; Welles, *Diary,* I, 88, 145; Butler, *Butler's Book,* 483.
7 *Official Records,* XV, 51, 79–80; Kendall, "Recollections of a Confederate Officer," *loc. cit.,* 1089; Irwin, *History of the Nineteenth Army Corps,* 34–35, 38–39; Kenneth P. Williams, *Lincoln Finds a General,* IV, 13; Irwin, "Military Operations in Louisiana in 1862," *loc. cit.,* 584.
8 Edward Bacon, *Among the Cotton Thieves,* 30–31; McHatton-Ripley, *From Flag to Flag,* 49; *Official Records,* XV, 550–51; Murray, *History of the Ninth Connecticut,* 126–27; Irwin, "Military Operations in Louisiana in 1862," *loc. cit.,* 584.
9 *Official Records,* XV, 53, 130, 553, LIII, 533; Butler, *Butler's Book,*

484, 488; Benj. F. Butler Papers, Manuscript Division, Library of Congress; Edward Bacon, *Among the Cotton Thieves,* 31; Dawson, *A Confederate Girl's Diary,* 174; McHatton-Ripley, *From Flag to Flag,* 45, 48–50; Irwin, "Military Operations in Louisiana in 1862," *loc. cit.,* 584.

10 *Official Records,* XV, 80–81, 130–31, 555, 797, 800; Lemanda E. Lea Papers.

CHAPTER X

Rule of the Beast

1 W. C. Corsan, *Two Months in the Confederate States, Including a Visit to New Orleans Under the Domination of General Butler* (London, 1863), 22–23.

2 Watson, *Life in the Confederate Army,* 410–11.

3 Dewey, *Autobiography,* 78–79.

4 *Official Records,* VI, 421, 717–21, 725, XV, 447; New Orleans *Daily Delta,* May 4, 1862; New Orleans *Daily Picayune,* May 5, May 6, June 18, 1862; Butler, *Butler's Book,* 378, 383, 646, 647; Parton, *General Butler in New Orleans,* 304; Salmon Portland Chase, *Diary and Correspondence of Salmon P. Chase,* in *American Historical Association Annual Report . . . for the Year 1902,* II (Washington, 1903), 297.

5 George S. Denison Papers, Vol. II, Manuscript Division, Library of Congress.

6 *Official Records,* XV, 462–63, 538–39, 558, 607; Parton, *General Butler in New Orleans,* 309–21; Benj. F. Butler Papers; Benjamin F. Flanders Papers; Shugg, *Origins of Class Struggle in Louisiana,* 187.

7 New Orleans *Daily Picayune,* May 11, 1862; Butler, *Butler's Book,* 395, 400–403; *Historical Sketch Book and Guide to New Orleans and Environs,* (New York, 1885), 259; Russell, *My Diary North and South,* 249; *Official Records,* XV, 462–63.

8 New Orleans *Daily Delta,* May 4, 1862; *Official Records,* XV, 426; New Orleans *Daily Picayune,* May 21, May 22, 1862; Rightor (ed.), *Standard History of New Orleans,* 601; Parton, *General Butler in New Orleans,* 415–16; Stephen A. Caldwell, *A Banking History of Louisiana* (Baton Rouge, 1935), 96.

9 New Orleans *Daily Delta,* May 13, 1862; New Orleans *Daily Picayune,* July 13, 1862; Bonham, *The British Consuls in the Confederacy,* 182; Benj. F. Butler Papers, 1862, June 1–15; Butler, *Private and Official Correspondence,* I, 553; *Official Records,* XV, 471.

10 Benj. F. Butler Papers; Butler, *Butler's Book,* 505; Butler, *Private and Official Correspondence,* I, 490–95, 556–59; *Official Records,* XV, 471, 479, 549; Dewey, *Autobiography,* 82–83; Farragut, *The Life of*

David Glasgow Farragut, 306–307; New Orleans *Daily Picayune,* July 17, 1862; Chase, *Diary,* 316; Milledge L. Bonham, "The French Consuls in the Confederate States," in *Studies in Southern History and Politics* (New York, 1914), 98.

11 Rouse, *The Bugle Blast,* 155–56.

12 Parton, *General Butler in New Orleans,* 389–90; Benj. F. Butler Papers, August, 1862; Bonham, "The French Consuls," *loc. cit.,* 101–102.

13 *Official Records,* XV, 479, 483, 497, 557; Butler, *Butler's Book,* 470; New Orleans *Daily Picayune,* June 19, 1862; Benj. F. Butler Papers, June 16–30, 1862; Parton, *General Butler in New Orleans,* 356, 373, 379.

14 Bernard C. Steiner, *Life of Reverdy Johnson* (Baltimore, 1914), 58.

15 Rowland and Croxall (eds.), *The Journal of Julia Le Grand,* 44; Butler, *Butler's Book,* 398–401.

16 Solomon, "Diary," 197–99.

17 New Orleans *Daily Delta,* May 3, 1862; *Official Records,* XV, 421–22, 439, 533; New Orleans *Daily Picayune,* May 17, 1862; Butler, *Private and Official Correspondence,* I, 476; G. Mott Williams, "Letters of General Thomas Williams," *loc. cit.,* 316; Parton, *General Butler in New Orleans,* 435.

18 War Department Records, Book 26, General and Special Orders, Feb. 26, 1862 to June 18, 1862, War Records Division, National Archives; *Official Records,* XV, 428; New Orleans *Daily Picayune,* May 17, Dec. 18, 1862; Benj. F. Butler Papers.

19 Flanders Papers; Parton, *General Butler in New Orleans,* 435; Emily H. Reed, *Life of A. P. Dostie* (New York, 1868), 46.

20 Butler, *Butler's Book,* 416–17; *Official Records,* XV, 426; New Orleans *Daily Delta,* May 16, 1862.

21 Solomon, "Diary," 209.

22 Butler, *Butler's Book,* 420; *Official Records,* LIII, 526–27, Ser. IV, Vol. III, 616–17; Benj. F. Butler Papers, May, 1862; Parton, *General Butler in New Orleans,* 329; Kendall, *History of New Orleans,* I, 280.

23 New Orleans *Daily Picayune,* May 21, 1862; Butler, *Private and Official Correspondence,* I, 497–500.

24 Butler, *Private and Official Correspondence,* I, 431, 499–500, 571–74.

25 New Orleans *Daily Picayune,* May 21, June 9, 1862; Parton, *General Butler in New Orleans,* 336, 450, 452–53; *Official Records,* XV, 1, 483, 581–82; *D.A.B.,* XVII, 78–79.

26 Butler, *Butler's Book,* 523; Chase, *Diary,* 297; Flanders Papers; Bragg, *Louisiana in the Confederacy,* 274–75.

27 De Forest, *A Volunteer's Adventures,* 9; Butler, *Private and Official Correspondence,* I, 452–53; Benj. F. Butler Papers, May, 1862; *Official Records,* XV, 465, 469; New Orleans *Daily Picayune,* June 8, 1862.

28 G. Mott Williams, "Letters of General Thomas Williams," *loc. cit.,* 315–16; Benj. F. Butler Papers, May, 1862.

29 War Department Records, Book 27, Special Orders, War Records Divi-

sion, National Archives, p. 75; War Department Collection of Confederate Records, Ch. VIII, Vol. CXLIV, War Records Division, National Archives; Parton, *General Butler in New Orleans,* 442; Butler, *Butler's Book,* 512–13; New Orleans *Daily Picayune,* June 28, July 2, July 17, 1862; De Forest, *A Volunteer's Adventures,* 30.

30 Edwin B. Lufkin, *History of the Thirteenth Maine Regiment From Its Organization in 1861 to Its Muster-Out in 1865* (Bridgton, Maine, 1898), 46.

31 *Official Records,* XV, 510–11; New Orleans *Daily Picayune,* July 1, July 25, 1862; Parton, *General Butler in New Orleans,* 438–39, 441–42, 463–66; *Battle-Fields of the South,* 189; Benj. F. Butler Papers, September, 1862.

32 Parton, *General Butler in New Orleans,* 462; *Official Records,* XV, 571, 575–76; New Orleans *Daily Picayune,* May 1–December 31, 1862; Highsmith, "Louisiana During Reconstruction," 79.

33 New Orleans *Daily Picayune,* May 4–October 29, December 13, December 16, December 29, 1862; Herbert Asbury, *The French Quarter, An Informal History of the New Orleans Underworld* (New York, 1936), 357.

34 De Forest, *A Volunteer's Adventures,* 29.

35 Porter, "Private Journal," 371.

36 Parton, *General Butler in New Orleans,* 303–304, 409–11; Robert S. Holzman, *Stormy Ben Butler* (New York, 1954), 39, 92–95; Corsan, *Two Months in the Confederate States,* 34–35; Loreta Janeta Velazquez, *The Woman in Battle* (Hartford, 1876), 242; Porter, "Private Journal," 372; Chase, *Diary,* 321, 341–42.

37 Chase, *Diary,* 321–38.

38 Butler, *Butler's Book,* 384; Parton, *General Butler in New Orleans,* 407–409; Butler, *Private and Official Correspondence,* I, 490–95, 612–13, 632; Benj. F. Butler Papers, June, 1862.

39 Parton, *General Butler in New Orleans,* 467–68; Ficklen, *History of Reconstruction in Louisiana,* 35–36, 39; *Official Records,* XV, 571; New Orleans *Daily Picayune,* September 24, 1862.

40 Butler, *Butler's Book,* 521–22; Parton, *General Butler in New Orleans,* 581–84; Benj. F. Butler Papers, November, 1862; Corsan, *Two Months in the Confederate States,* 35; Porter, "Private Journal," 372; Chase, *Diary,* 329–30.

41 Dept. of the Gulf, Gen. Benj. F. Butler, Book No. 1, 219, War Records Division, National Archives; *Official Records,* XV, 22, 422.

42 *Official Records,* XV, 445, 478, 568–69, 573–74; New Orleans *Daily Picayune,* June 15, 1862; Butler, *Butler's Book,* 448–49.

43 *Official Records,* XV, 441, 493, 499, 555–59, VI, 535; New Orleans *Daily Picayune,* May 15, 1862; George G. Smith, *Leaves From a Soldier's Diary* (Putnam, Conn., 1906), 24; Benj. F. Butler Papers, May, October, November, 1862; Butler, *Private and Official Correspondence,*

I, 494, 516–21; Homer B. Sprague, *History of the 13th Infantry Regiment of Connecticut Volunteers, During the Great Rebellion* (Hartford, Conn., 1867), 54–55; Chase, *Diary*, 311; Rouse, *The Bugle Blast*, 154; De Forest, *A Volunteer's Adventures*, 35; George S. Denison Papers, Vol. II, Manuscript Division, Library of Congress.

44 John M. Stanyan, *A History of the Eighth Regiment of New Hampshire Volunteers* (Concord, New Hampshire, 1892), 107.

45 New Orleans *Daily Picayune*, May 29, 1862; De Forest, *A Volunteer's Adventures*, 26–27, 39; Butler, *Private and Official Correspondence*, I, 514; Smith, *Leaves From a Soldier's Diary*, 35.

46 Quarles, *The Negro in the Civil War*, 115; De Forest, *A Volunteer's Adventures*, 9–10, 39–40; Neal Dow, *The Reminiscences of Neal Dow* (Portland, Maine, 1898), 672–73; *Official Records*, XV, 534–37; Benj. F. Butler Papers, August, 1862.

47 *Official Records*, XV, 556–57, 621–22; Wilson, *The Black Phalanx*, 195–99; Rouse, *The Bugle Blast*, 158; De Forest, *A Volunteer's Adventures*, 42.

48 Dabney, *One Hundred Great Years*, 161; *Official Records*, XV, 621–22; Parton, *General Butler in New Orleans*, 522–24, 625; Lufkin, *History of the Thirteenth Maine Regiment*, 42; Chase, *Diary*, 330.

49 *Official Records*, XV, 590.

50 Porter, "Private Journal," 373–74.

51 Butler, *Butler's Book*, 530–31; New Orleans *Daily Picayune*, December 17, 1862.

52 Welles, *Diary*, I, 209.

53 George S. Denison Papers, Vol. II.

54 *Official Records*, XV, 191, 613, 615–20; Dept. of the Gulf, Letters Sent, Major General Book 4, War Records Division, National Archives; Simon G. Jerrard Papers (B), 4–5; Lewis, *Our First Admiral*, 153–54; Stanyan, *History of the Eighth Regiment, New Hampshire*, 119; Warmoth, *War, Politics and Reconstruction*, 34; New Orleans *Daily Picayune*, December 29, 1862.

55 Butler, *Butler's Book*, 532; *Official Records*, XVIII, Pt. 1, p. 557; New Orleans *Daily Picayune*, December 25, 1862; Parton, *General Butler in New Orleans*, 602, 611–12.

CHAPTER XI

Skirmishes, Secessia, and Expeditions

1 *Official Records*, LIII, 806, 812–15, VI, 888, XV, 735, 739–40, 747–54, 756, 759–61; War Department Collection of Confederate Records, Chap. VIII, Vol. CXXXVIII, Scrap Book, Louisiana Troops, 1862, War

Records Division, National Archives; Moore Papers, C, June 18, 1862.

2   Hudson Tabor and Family Papers; *Official Records,* XV, 450–57.

3   Richard L. Pugh Papers, July 3, 1862.

4   *Official Records,* XV, 766, 768, 773–74, 779, LIII, 325–26; Moore Papers, C.

5   *Official Records,* XV, 779, 790, LIII, 819; War Dept. Collection of Confederate Records, Chap. VIII, Vol. CXXXVIII, Scrap Book, Louisiana Troops, 1862, War Records Division, National Archives; Harris and Hulse (comps.), *History of Claiborne Parish,* 238; Hardin, *Northwestern Louisiana,* II, 152.

6   *Official Records,* XV, 789, 791; Jackson Beauregard Davis, "The Life of Richard Taylor," *Louisiana Historical Quarterly,* XXIV (January, 1941), 67.

7   Dupuy Diary.

8   Sidney A. Marchand, *The Story of Ascension Parish, Louisiana* (Baton Rouge, 1931), 63–66; Marchand, *The Flight of a Century,* 154–55.

9   Moore Papers.

10   *Official Records,* XV, 798, 803–804; War Dept. Collection of Confederate Records, Chap. VIII, Vol. CXXXVIII, Scrap Book, Louisiana Troops, 1862, War Records Division, National Archives; Odom, "The Political Career of Thomas Overton Moore," *loc. cit.,* 1025.

11   Anderson (ed.), *Brokenburn,* 138–39; *Official Records,* XV, 919–20; Hall, *The Story of the 26th Louisiana,* 59; Harris and Hulse (comps.), *The History of Claiborne Parish,* 220–21, 228; Prudhomme Family Papers.

12   *Official Records,* XV, 805; Harris and Hulse (comps.), *The History of Claiborne Parish,* 221, 238–39.

13   *Official Records,* XV, 132.

14   Butler Family Papers.

15   *Ibid.; Official Records,* XV, 133–38.

16   Lester and Bromwell, *Military and Naval Laws of the Confederate States,* 58, 62; Opelousas *Courier,* September 6, 1862; *Official Records,* LIII, 900–901.

17   *Official Records,* XV, 820.

18   Arthur W. Hyatt Papers, Diary No. 1.

19   *Ibid.;* Irwin, *History of the Nineteenth Army Corps,* 46; *Official Records,* XV, 166, 176; Smith, *Leaves From a Soldier's Diary,* 31; Alexander F. Pugh and Family Collection, Diary, 1862.

20   Parton, *General Butler in New Orleans,* 580–81; De Forest, *A Volunteer's Adventures,* 56; *Official Records,* XV, 162, 170.

21   Tabor Papers.

22   Marchand, *The Story of Ascension Parish,* 68.

23   *Official Records,* XV, 168–78; De Forest, *A Volunteer's Adventures,* 53, 58–69; Sprague, *History of the 13th Connecticut,* 81–87; Stanyan,

History of the Eighth Regiment of New Hampshire Volunteers, 143–45; Butler, *Butler's Book,* 495.

24 Hyatt Papers, Diary No. 1; *Official Records,* XV, 169–70, 177–79, 183–87, 587, 859–60.

25 Stanyan, *History of the Eighth Regiment of New Hampshire Volunteers,* 156.

26 Alexander F. Pugh and Family Collection, Diary.

27 Stanyan, *History of the Eighth Regiment of New Hampshire Volunteers,* 153.

28 Alexander F. Pugh and Family Collection, Diary.

29 Shreveport *Semi-Weekly News,* December 9, 1862; Bragg, *Louisiana In the Confederacy,* 139–40; *Official Records,* XV, 873–74, 877.

30 Hyatt Papers, Diary No. 1; Powhatan Clarke Diary, 1862–63; *Official Records,* XV, 874, 887, 903, 910, 914, LIII, 836–37, Ser. IV, Vol. II, 162, 286–87, 553, 690–91; Shreveport *Semi-Weekly News,* December 5, 1862; Moore Papers.

31 Lonn, *Foreigners In the Confederacy,* 396; *Louisiana Acts,* 1862–63, pp. 5–6.

32 *Official Records,* XV, 768, 777.

33 *Ibid.,* 804.

34 *Ibid.,* 138–41.

35 *Ibid.,* 808, 886, 913; Dawson, *A Confederate Girl's Diary,* 234; Alcée Fortier (ed.), *Louisiana* (Atlanta, 1909), I, 489–90.

36 *A Memorial of Lt. Daniel Perkins Dewey, of the Twenty-Fifth Regiment Connecticut Volunteers (His Letters)* (Hartford, 1864), 46, 48, 57; Jerrard Papers, (B), 1862–63.

37 J. F. Moors, *History of the Fifty-second Regiment Massachusetts Volunteers* (Boston, 1893), 53.

38 *Ibid.,* 33–34; *Official Records,* XV, 630–33.

39 *Official Records,* XV, 627; William B. Stevens, *History of the Fiftieth Regiment of Infantry Massachusetts Volunteer Militia in the Late War of the Rebellion* (Boston, 1907), 54–55; Lewis, *Our First Admiral,* 152–53.

Chapter XII

Canals and Stalemates

1 Welles, *Diary,* I, 157–58, 167, 273.

2 *Ibid.,* 272; *Official Records,* XV, 827; John C. Pemberton, *Pemberton Defender of Vicksburg* (Chapel Hill, 1942), 60–62; U. S. Grant, *Personal Memoirs of U. S. Grant* (Cleveland, 1952), 222–23; T. Harry Williams, *Lincoln and His Generals* (New York, 1952), 217–18; Bruce

Catton, *Grant Moves South* (Boston, 1960), 332–43; Crandall and Newell, *History of the Ram Fleet,* 249–52; West, *Second Admiral,* 180.

3   J. F. C. Fuller, *The Generalship of Ulysses S. Grant* (London, 1929), 127–29, 131; West, *Second Admiral,* 182; Adam Badeau, *Military History of Ulysses S. Grant, From April, 1861 to April, 1865* (New York, 1868–81), I, 136; Greene, *The Mississippi,* 73; Florison D. Pitts, Diary; T. B. Marshall, *History of the Eighty-Third Ohio Volunteer Infantry, The Greyhound Regiment* (Cincinnati, 1912), 49–50; *Official Records,* XV, 952–53, 962, 983–84, XXIV, Part III, 1056–57; Shreveport *Semi-Weekly News,* December 30, 1862, January 20, 1863.

4   W. H. Bentley, *History of the 77th Illinois Volunteer Infantry, Sept. 2, 1862–July 10, 1865* (Peoria, Ill., 1883), 108–109; Pemberton, *Pemberton Defender of Vicksburg,* 67–68; Fuller, *The Generalship of Ulysses S. Grant,* 131; T. Harry Williams, *Lincoln and His Generals,* 220; *The Story of the Fifty-Fifth Regiment Illinois Volunteer Infantry in the Civil War 1861–1865* (Clinton, Mass., 1887), 187–205; Catton, *Grant Moves South,* 343; Kenneth P. Williams, *Lincoln Finds a General,* IV, 210–18; Badeau, *Military History of Ulysses S. Grant,* I, 148–49; Porter, *Naval History of the Civil War,* 289–93.

5   Pemberton, *Pemberton, Defender of Vicksburg,* 62–64; Badeau, *Military History of Ulysses S. Grant,* I, 138–43; Fuller, *The Generalship of Ulysses S. Grant,* 129–31; T. Harry Williams, *Lincoln and His Generals,* 220; Kenneth P. Williams, *Lincoln Finds a General,* IV, 196–203, 310–11; *Official Records,* XXIV, Pt. 1, pp. 8, 11, 13; West, *The Second Admiral,* 202; Earl S. Miers, *The Web of Victory* (New York, 1955), 62–63; Grant, *Memoirs,* 230–32; Thomas H. Barton, *Autobiography of Dr. Thomas H. Barton* (Charleston, W. Va., 1890), 95–96; Mildred Throne (ed.), *The Civil War Diary of Cyrus F. Boyd, Fifteenth Iowa Infantry 1861–1863* (Iowa City, 1953), 114–16; William T. Sherman, *Memoirs of General William T. Sherman* (New York, 1875), I, 305; Catton, *Grant Moves South,* 376–78.

6   The Papers of William T. Sherman, XI, 1862–63, p. 1525, Manuscript Division, Library of Congress.

7   Howe (ed.), *Home Letters of General Sherman,* 237.

8   Throne (ed.), *The Civil War Diary of Cyrus F. Boyd,* 115–16.

9   *Official Records,* XXIV, Pt. 3, pp. 4–7, 9–10; Barton, *Autobiography,* 96; Records of the War Dept., Dept. of Tennessee, Letters Sent, I, 264, 267–68, War Records Division, National Archives.

10   Throne (ed.), *The Civil War Diary of Cyrus F. Boyd,* 118.

11   *Official Records,* XXIV, Pt. 1, p. 14, Pt. 3, p. 17; Grant, *Memoirs,* 232–33; Barton, *Autobiography,* 97–98; Catton, *Grant Moves South,* 378–79.

12   *D.A.B.,* XVIII, 93–97; Clarence Edward Macartney, *Grant and His Generals* (New York, 1953), 267–70; *The Story of the Fifty-Fifth*

Regiment Illinois, 39; Gamaliel Bradford, *Union Portraits* (Boston, 1916), 134, 157; Porter, "Private Journal," 437; Benjamin P. Thomas (ed.), *Three Years with Grant as Recalled by War Correspondent Sylvanus Cadwallader* (New York, 1956), 341; Charles A. Dana, *Recollections of the Civil War* (New York, 1902), 57; William F. G. Shanks, *Personal Recollections of Distinguished Generals* (New York, 1866), 17–19, 24–26, 35, 37, 53–54, 56–57.

13 Greene, *The Mississippi*, 107; Margaret Leech, *Reveille in Washington 1860–1865* (New York, 1941), 127, 168, 311–12; Macartney, *Grant and His Generals*, 277–79; T. Harry Williams, *Lincoln and His Generals*, 225–26; Earl S. Miers, *The General Who Marched to Hell* (New York, 1951), 26, 29.

14 James H. Wilson, *Under the Old Flag* (New York, 1912), 139.

15 Dana, *Recollections of the Civil War*, 25, 61–62.

16 James H. Wilson, *The Life of John A. Rawlins* (New York, 1916), 67, 74, 77–78, 96; John G. Nicolay and John Hay, *Abraham Lincoln, A History* (New York, 1914), VII, 153–54; Badeau, *Military History of Ulysses S. Grant*, I, 179–81; Rachel S. Thorndike (ed.), *The Sherman Letters, Correspondence Between General and Senator Sherman from 1837 to 1891* (New York, 1894), 186–88, 197; Thomas (ed.), *Three Years With Grant*, 11–12, 23, 44–46; Walter G. Smith, *Life and Letters of Thomas Kilby Smith* (New York, 1898), 268–69; Franc B. Wilkie, *Pen and Powder* (Boston, 1888), 225, 227–28.

17 Thomas (ed.), *Three Years With Grant*, 49, 54; Wilkie, *Pen and Powder*, 283; Chambers Diary; Walter G. Smith, *Life and Letters of Thomas Kilby Smith*, 269; Pitts Diary; B. F. Stevenson, *Letters from the Army* (Cincinnati, 1884), 181; Barton, *Autobiography*, 143; Badeau, *Military History of Ulysses S. Grant*, I, 160–61; Alonzo L. Brown, *History of the Fourth Regiment of Minnesota Infantry Volunteers During the Great Rebellion 1861–1865* (St. Paul, 1892), 183; Robert J. Burdette, *The Drums of the 47th* (Indianapolis, 1914), 139; War Dept. Records, Book 15, pp. 180–335, Special Orders and Special Field Orders, October, 1862 to August, 1863, War Records Division, National Archives.

18 *Official Records*, XXIV, Pt. 1, pp. 121–22, Pt. 3, p. 38; Thorndike (ed.), *The Sherman Letters*, 183–84; *Navy Records*, XXIV, 240; Samuel R. Reed, *The Vicksburg Campaign, and the Battles About Chattanooga Under the Command of General U. S. Grant, In 1862–1863* (Cincinnati, 1882), 20–21; Records of the War Dept., Dept. of Tennessee, Letters Sent, I, War Records Division, National Archives; Badeau, *Military History of Ulysses S. Grant*, I, 164–66; F. H. Mason, *The Forty-Second Ohio Infantry: A History of the Organization and Services of That Regiment in the War of the Rebellion* (Cleveland, 1876), 182; William F. Vilas, *A View of the Vicksburg Campaign* (Madison, Wis., 1908), 24; B. F. Stevenson, *Letters From the Army*, 195, 199; John A. Bering

and Thomas Montgomery, *History of the Forty-Eighth Ohio Vet. Vol. Inf.* (Hillsboro, Ohio, 1880), 74.

19 Sherman, *Memoirs,* I, 305–307; Alexander R. Miller Diary; *Official Records,* XXIV, Pt. 1, p. 23; Vilas, *A View of the Vicksburg Campaign,* 24.

20 *Official Records,* XXIV, Pt. 1, p. 18, Pt. 3, pp. 32–33, 96; Wales W. Wood, *A History of the Ninety-Fifth Regiment Illinois Infantry Volunteers* . . . (Chicago, 1865), 56–58; Greene, *The Mississippi,* 96; R. L. Howard, *History of the 124th Regiment Illinois Infantry Volunteers* (Springfield, Ill., 1880), 59, 61–62; Leo M. Kaiser, "In Sight of Vicksburg," *The Historical Bulletin,* XXXIV (May, 1956), 212, 215–16, 218; Throne (ed.), *The Civil War Diary of Cyrus F. Boyd,* 119–21, 122–24; *Experience In the War of the Great Rebellion By a Soldier of the Eighty-First Regiment Illinois Volunteer Infantry* (Carbondale, Ill., 1880), 32–33; Thomas M. Stevenson, *History of the 78th Regiment O.V.V.I.* . . . (Zanesville, Ohio, 1865), 24, 225.

21 Throne (ed.), *The Civil War Diary of Cyrus F. Boyd,* 128–29, 133–34; Thomas M. Stevenson, *History of the 78th Regiment O.V.V.I.,* 230–31.

22 Throne (ed.), *The Civil War Diary of Cyrus F. Boyd,* 122, 124–25, 132; Kaiser, "In Sight of Vicksburg," *loc. cit.,* 213; *History of the Fifteenth Regiment, Iowa Veteran Volunteer Infantry* (Keokuk, Iowa, 1887), 244–45; Records of the War Dept., Dept. of Tennessee, Letters Sent, I, 330, War Records Division, National Archives; *Official Records,* XXIV, Pt. 3, p. 85.

23 *Official Records,* XXIV, Pt. 1, p. 20, Pt. 3, pp. 76, 78, 79, 85, 98, 120, 159; Grant, *Memoirs,* 233–34; Vilas, *A View of the Vicksburg Campaign,* 25; Brown, *History of the Fourth Regiment of Minnesota,* 166–67; Newsome, *Experience in the War,* 19–21; Kaiser, "In Sight of Vicksburg," *loc. cit.,* 213–14; Thomas M. Stevenson, *History of the 78th Regiment, O.V.V.I.,* 225–27; Wood, *A History of the Ninety-Fifth Regiment, Illinois Infantry Volunteers,* 59; *Experience in the War, Eighty-First Illinois Regiment,* 35–36; Butler Family Papers (C) Part 3; Greene, *The Mississippi,* 97.

24 *Official Records,* XXIV, Pt. 3, p. 126, XV, 300; Grant, *Memoirs,* 234–36; Catton, *Grant Moves South,* 379–81; *Navy Records,* XXIV, 249, 475–501; Barton, *Autobiography,* 97–98; Vilas, *A View of the Vicksburg Campaign,* 20; Wilson, *Under the Old Flag,* 151–52; Charles A. Dana and J. H. Wilson, *The Life of Ulysses S. Grant, General of the Armies of the United States* (Springfield, Mass., 1868), 107; Badeau, *Military History of Ulysses S. Grant,* I, 170–72; Pemberton, *Pemberton, Defender of Vicksburg,* 77; Porter, "Private Journal," 533–40; Brown, *History of the Fourth Regiment of Minnesota,* 168–72; S. C. Jones, *Reminiscences of the Twenty-Second Iowa Volunteer Infantry* (Iowa City, Iowa, 1907), 40–45; Sherman, *Memoirs,* I, 307–13; Porter, *In-*

cidents and Anecdotes, 145–72; Howe (ed.), *Home Letters of General Sherman,* 244–46.

25 Records of the War Dept., Dept. of Tennessee, Letters Sent, I, 340, 362–65, War Records Division, National Archives; *Official Records,* XXIV, Pt. 1, pp. 26, 44–45, 70–71, 76, 125, Pt. 2, pp. 234–35, Pt. 3, pp. 33–34, 151, 234–35, 736; Cloyd Bryner, *Bugle Echoes, The Story of Illinois 47th* (Springfield, Ill., 1905), 77; George W. Driggs, *Opening of the Mississippi* (Madison, Wis., 1864), 24; *Story of the Fifty-Fifth Regiment Illinois,* 223; Albert O. Marshall, *Army Life* (Joliet, Ill., 1884), 194; Barton, *Autobiography,* 107; Howe (ed.), *Home Letters of General Sherman,* 250; Reed, *The Vicksburg Campaign,* 113–14; Dana, *Recollections of the Civil War,* 30, 35; Grant, *Memoirs,* 237–38.

CHAPTER XIII

Vicksburg, Act Two

1 *Navy Records,* XXIV, 217, 219–24, 379–81, 383–86, 402–407, 410–11; Scharf, *History of the Confederate States Navy,* 351–64; Crandall and Newell, *History of the Ram Fleet,* 161–85, 192–93, 196–219; *Official Records,* XXIV, Pt. 1, pp. 341–44, 362–64, 370, Pt. 3, p. 143, XV, 302; Gosnell, *Guns On the Western Waters,* 178–92; Dorsey, *Recollections of Henry Watkins Allen,* 153–57; Shreveport *Semi-Weekly News,* March 3, 1863; Butler Family Papers (C), Part III, March 12, 1863; Porter, *Incidents and Anecdotes,* 134–35; Lewis E. Ellis, "Reminiscences of New Orleans, Jackson and Vicksburg," *Confederate Annals,* I (August, 1883), 54; Nicolay and Hay, *Abraham Lincoln,* VII, 158.

2 Grant, *Memoirs,* 242; *Official Records,* XXIV, Pt. 1, pp. 141, 489–92, Pt. 3, pp. 170–71, 173; Dorsey, *Recollections of Henry Watkins Allen,* 162–63.

3 Howard, *History of the 124th Illinois,* 65; *Experience in the War, Eighty-First Illinois Regiment,* 37–38; Newsome, *Experience in the War,* 22; *History of the Fifteenth Regiment, Iowa,* 251; Wilkie, *Pen and Powder,* 323; Brown, *History of the Fourth Regiment of Minnesota,* 179.

4 *Official Records,* XXIV, Pt. 1, pp. 30–31, Pt. 3, p. 220.

5 Wilson, *Life of John A. Rawlins,* 109, 114–15; Vilas, *A View of the Vicksburg Campaign,* 27–32; Grant, *Memoirs,* 239–41; Wilbur F. Crummer, *With Grant at Fort Donelson, Shiloh and Vicksburg* (Oak Park, Ill., 1915), 93–94; Brown, *History of the Fourth Regiment of Minnesota,* 175–79, Dana, *Recollections of the Civil War,* 36–38; *Official Records,* XXIV, Pt. 1, pp. 30, 47, Pt. 3, p. 745; Wilkie, *Pen and Powder,* 315; Sherman, *Memoirs,* I, 317–18; Porter, *Incidents and Anecdotes,*

175–76; Hall, *The Story of the 26th Louisiana,* 61; Pemberton, *Pemberton, Defender of Vicksburg,* 96; Wilson, *Under the Old Flag,* 163–64; *Navy Records,* XXIV, 552–65; B. F. Booth, *Dark Days of the Rebellion* (Indianola, Iowa, 1897), 20–22; Lewis, *Our First Admiral,* 193; Nicolay and Hay, *Abraham Lincoln,* VII, 158–60.

6 Bering and Montgomery, *History of the Forty-Eighth Ohio,* 75, 78; Bentley, *History of the 77th Illinois,* 132–33; Jones, *Reminiscences of the Twenty-Second Iowa,* 27; George Crooke (comp.), *The Twenty-First Regiment of Iowa Volunteer Infantry* (Milwaukee, Wis., 1891), 49–50; Charles B. Johnson, *Muskets and Medicine or Army Life in the Sixties* (Philadelphia, 1917), 70–71; *Official Records,* XXIV, Pt. 1, pp. 77, 494, 496, Pt. 3, pp. 195, 197, 205, 754; Dorsey, *Recollections of Henry Watkins Allen,* 165; Dana, *Recollections of the Civil War,* 38; Grant, *Memoirs,* 242, 245–47.

7 *Official Records,* XXIV, Pt. 1, pp. 31, 47, 126, 139, 141–42, 494, 571–72, 601, 615, 633–34; Grant, *Memoirs,* 245, 248–52; Dana, *Recollections of the Civil War,* 38–39; Greene, *The Mississippi,* 115; Sherman, *Memoirs,* I, 318–20; Howe (ed.), *Home Letters of General Sherman,* 253–54, 258–60; Stevenson, *History of the 78th Regiment O.V.V.I.,* 233; Barton, *Autobiography,* 109; Howard, *History of the 124th Illinois,* 67, 69, 72–74; Crooke (comp.), *The Twenty-First Regiment of Iowa,* 50, 58; General Orders No. 32, War Dept. Records, General Orders, Dept. and Army of the Tennessee, 1863, Printed Orders, Book 924, War Records Division, National Archives; Dorsey, *Recollections of Henry Watkins Allen,* 165–67, 171; *Experience in the War, Eighty-First Illinois Regiment,* 40; Newsome, *Experience in the War,* 23–24; Johnson, *Muskets and Medicine,* 71–75; Marshall, *Army Life,* 194–95; Bentley, *History of the 77th Illinois,* 133; Bering and Montgomery, *History of the Forty-Eighth Ohio,* 78–79; Ephraim McD. Anderson, *Memoirs: Historical and Personal* (St. Louis, 1868), 281–88; Calhoun, "A History of Concordia Parish" *loc. cit.* (Part V), 117–19; Driggs, *Opening of the Mississippi,* 130–31; *Story of the Fifty-Fifth Regiment Illinois,* 231; J. J. Kellogg, *War Experiences and the Story of the Vicksburg Campaign From "Milliken's Bend" to July 4, 1863* (n.p., 1913), 21.

8 Porter, "Private Journal," 581–89; *Official Records,* XXIV, Pt. 1, pp. 32, 47, 48, 142, 574–75, 615, 634, 642, 663, Pt. 3, pp. 237, 246; Wilson, *The Life of John A. Rawlins,* 105; Dana, *Recollections of the Civil War,* 39–44; Miers, *The Web of Victory,* 147; Albert O. Marshall, *Army Life,* 197; Grant, *Personal Memoirs,* 248–52; Jones, *Reminiscences of the Twenty-Second Iowa Volunteer Infantry,* 28–29; Anderson, *Memoirs,* 288; Crooke (comp.), *The Twenty-First Regiment of Iowa,* 54–55; Lewis, *Our First Admiral,* 195; Vilas, *A View of the Vicksburg Campaign,* 32; Howard, *History of The 124th Illinois,* 74–75; Warmoth, *War, Politics and Reconstruction,* 16.

9   Nicolay and Hay, *Abraham Lincoln*, VII, 162–63: Kenneth P. Williams, *Lincoln Finds a General*, IV, 338–39; Catton, *Grant Moves South*, 422; D. Alexander Brown in his book *Grierson's Raid* (Urbana, Ill., 1954) gives an excellent, detailed account of this famous raid.

10 Sherman, *Memoirs*, I, 319; Nicolay and Hay, *Abraham Lincoln*, VII, 162; Grant, *Personal Memoirs*, 251–52; *Navy Records*, XXIV, 588–600; West, *Second Admiral*, 227; *The Story of the Fifty-Fifth Regiment Illinois*, 227–28; Howe (ed.), *Home Letters of General Sherman*, 258; *Official Records*, XXIV, Pt. 1, pp. 726, 758, Pt. 3, pp. 242–43, 246, 268, 273, 281, 284; Thomas (ed.), *Three Years With Grant*, 53; Bruce Catton, *U. S. Grant and the American Military Tradition* (Boston, 1954), 41–42, 100.

11 Porter, "Private Journal," 629–30; Lewis, *Our First Admiral*, 196; *Official Records*, XXIV, Pt. 1, pp. 309, 684–86, 700–701; West, *The Second Admiral*, 228; Miller Diary; Porter, *Naval History of the Civil War*, 318–19; J. P. Blessington, *The Campaigns of Walker's Texas Division* (New York, 1875), 81–82.

12 West, *The Second Admiral*, 214, 229–30; Farragut, *The Life of David Glasgow Farragut*, 348.

13 *Official Records*, XXIV, Pt. 1, pp. 694–700, Pt. 3, pp. 301–303, 846; Marie Louise Benton Bankston, *Camp-Fire Stories of the Mississippi Valley Campaign* (New Orleans, 1914), 139; Napier Bartlett (ed.), *Military Record of Louisiana Including Biographical and Historical Papers Relating to the Military Organization of the State* (New Orleans, 1875), 34–35; Joseph Howard Parks, *General Edmund Kirby Smith, C. S. A.* (Baton Rouge, 1954), 268–70.

14 *Official Records*, XXIV, Pt. 2, pp. 447–72, Pt. 3, pp. 378, 425–26, 443; Blessington, *The Campaigns of Walker's Texas Division*, 86–91, 93–108; *Navy Records*, XXIV, 46–47, 59–60, XXV, 163; Porter, *Naval History of the Civil War*, 335; Dana, *Recollections of the Civil War*, 86; Williams, *A History of the Negro Troops*, 224–25; William Wells Brown, *The Negro in the American Rebellion* (Boston, 1867), 137–40; Quarles, *The Negro In the Civil War*, 220–24; Wilson, *The Black Phalanx*, 203–207; Walter G. Smith, *Life and Letters of Thomas Kilby Smith*, 69–70.

15 *Official Records*, XXIV, Pt. 1, p. 102, Pt. 2, pp. 448–54, 460–62, Pt. 3, p. 390; Bartlett (ed.), *Military Record of Louisiana*, 35–36; Bankston, *Camp-Fire Stories of the Mississippi Valley Campaign*, 140; Records of the War Dept., Dept. of Tennessee, Letters Sent, I, 438, War Records Division, National Archives.

16 *Navy Records*, XXV, 175–76, 215–16; Crandall and Newell, *History of the Ram Fleet*, 300; Blessington, *The Campaigns of Walker's Texas Division*, 110–14; Driggs, *Opening of the Mississippi*, 26.

17 *Official Records,* XXIV, Pt. 2, p. 466; Blessington, *The Campaigns of Walker's Texas Division,* 115–18, 127.

18 Porter, "Private Journal," 651–68; *Official Records,* XXIV, Pt. 3, pp. 333, 337, 342; *Navy Records,* XXV, 17, 21–23, 30–31, 38, 60–61, 77, 83, 104, 111–12; Warmoth, *War, Politics and Reconstruction,* 17; Dana, *Recollections of the Civil War,* 87; Thomas H. Parker, *History of the 51st Regiment of P.V. and V.V.* (Philadelphia, 1869), 319; Driggs, *Opening of the Mississippi,* 26–27; Miers, *The General who Marched to Hell,* 265; Alonzo Brown, *History of the Fourth Regiment of Minnesota,* 189; West, *The Second Admiral,* 232–34.

19 *Official Records,* XXIV, Pt. 3, pp. 982–83.

20 Welles, *Diary,* I, 364–65; Greene, *The Mississippi,* 205–206.

CHAPTER XIV

Time of Indecision

1 *Official Records,* XV, 639, 643–44, 654, 1115–16; Stanyan, *History of the Eighth Regiment of New Hampshire Volunteers,* 119; Porter, *Incidents and Anecdotes,* 80; Chase, *Diary,* 346, 359, 362.

2 Reed, *Life of A. P. Dostie,* 50–55.

3 Bragg, *Louisiana in the Confederacy,* 277; War Dept. Records, Book 28, Special Orders, Order 39, War Records Division, National Archives.

4 George S. Denison Papers, II, Manuscript Division, Library of Congress; *Official Records,* XXV, 640, 644, 1109; Chase, *Diary,* 349, 402–403.

5 Charles P. Bosson, *History of the Forty-Second Regiment Infantry, Massachusetts Volunteers, 1862, 1863, 1864* (Boston, 1886), 335–37, 344; Chase, *Diary,* 351–52, 361, 366, 373, 378–79; *Official Records* XV, 666–67, XXVI, Pt. 1, pp. 688–89; Jerrard Papers; Charles Kassel, "The Labor System of General Banks," Reprint from *The Open Court* (January, 1928), 43–49; George H. Hepworth, *The Whip, Hoe, and Sword* (Boston, 1864), 25–31; Orton S. Clark, *The One Hundred and Sixteenth Regiment of New York State Volunteers* (Buffalo, 1868), 117–18; George W. Williams, *A History of the Negro Troops in the War of the Rebellion,* 140.

6 *Acts Passed by the Twenty-Seventh Legislature of the State of Louisiana in Extra Session at Opelousas, December, 1862 & January, 1863* (Natchitoches, La., 1864), 18–20, 35–36; Bragg, *Louisiana in the Confederacy,* 144.

7 *Louisiana Acts, Opelousas, 1862–63,* 10–11, 29–30; Shreveport *Semi-Weekly News,* January 16, 1863.

8 *Acts Passed by the Sixth Legislature of the State of Louisiana at Its
Extra Session, Held in the City of Shreveport, on the 4th of May, 1863*
(New Orleans, 1897), 36, 42–48; Bragg, *Louisiana in the Confederacy,*
144–45; Shugg, *Origins of Class Struggle in Louisiana,* 178; Williamson and Goodman (eds.), *Eastern Louisiana,* I, 143; Lester and Bromwell, *Military and Naval Laws of the Confederate States,* 177–79, 181,
196.

9 *Louisiana Acts, Shreveport,* 1863, pp. 18–30; *Louisiana Acts, Opelousas,*
1862–63, pp. 35–36; Frances Fearn (ed.), *Diary of a Refugee* (New
York, 1910), 29–34; Anderson (ed.), *Brokenburn,* 186–91; McLure
and Howe (eds.), *History of Shreveport and Shreveport Builders,* I,
33; Bragg, *Louisiana in the Confederacy,* 216; Shreveport *Semi-Weekly
News,* January 2, 1863.

10 Shreveport *Semi-Weekly News,* January 27, March 31, April 24, 1863.

11 *Official Records,* XXVI, Pt. 1, pp. 3–7.

12 *Ibid.,* 5–8, XV, 233–37, 1089; Stanyan, *History of the Eighth Regiment
of New Hampshire Volunteers,* 162–64; Greene, *The Mississippi,* 213;
William T. Palfrey Papers, Plantation Diary, 1860–1865; Scharf, *History of the Confederate States Navy,* 503; Hyatt Papers, Diary, 1862–
1863, No. 1.

13 De Forest, *A Volunteer's Adventures,* 86.

14 Palfrey Papers; Stanyan, *History of the Eighth Regiment of New
Hampshire Volunteers,* 164, 165, 172.

15 *Official Records,* XV, 252–54, 692, XXVI, Pt. 1, pp. 8–9; Greene, *The
Mississippi,* 214; Stevens, *History of the Fiftieth Regiment of Infantry,
Massachusetts,* 66–70, 80; *A Memorial of Lt. Daniel Perkins Dewey,*
74–75.

16 Frank M. Flinn, *Campaigning with Banks in Louisiana, '63 and '64*
(Lynn, Mass., 1887), 19–21.

17 Jerrard Papers; James K. Hosmer, *The Color-Guard: Being a Corporal's
Notes of Military Service in the Nineteenth Army Corps* (Boston, 1864),
89, 92–97, 100; Orton S. Clark, *The One Hundred and Sixteenth Regi-
ment of New York,* 55–56; Francis W. Palfrey, *Memoir of William
Francis Bartlett* (Boston, 1878), 59, 62, 74; Stanyan, *History of the
Eighth Regiment of New Hampshire Volunteers,* 190; Flinn, *Cam-
paigning with Banks in Louisiana,* 21; Lea Papers; *Official Records,*
XV, 252–53, 692, XXVI, Pt. 1, p. 9; Stevens, *History of the Fiftieth
Regiment of Infantry, Massachusetts,* 72, 79–80; Luther T. Town-
send, *History of the Sixteenth Regiment, New Hampshire Volunteers*
(Washington, 1897), 61, 89; Goodloe, *Some Rebel Relics,* 201.

18 Lewis, *Our First Admiral,* 169–72, 181–84; *Official Records,* XV, 251,
262, 271, 274–75, 278, XXVI, Pt. 1, p. 8; Stevens, *History of the Fiftieth
Regiment of Infantry, Massachusetts,* 79; Dewey, *Autobiography,* 86–
103; Kendall, "Recollections of a Confederate Officer," *loc. cit.,* 1109;
M. J. Smith and James Freret, "Fortification and Siege of Port Hudson,"

Southern Historical Society Papers, XIV (1886), 308–10; Edward Y. McMorries, *History of the First Regiment Alabama Volunteer Infantry C.S.A.* (Montgomery, Ala., 1904), 53–56; Watson, *Life in the Confederate Army,* 442–44; Flinn, *Campaigning with Banks in Louisiana,* 24; Orton S. Clark, *The One Hundred and Sixteenth Regiment of New York,* 57.

19 Townsend, *History of the Sixteenth Regiment, New Hampshire Volunteers,* 90, 97–98; Rodney W. Torrey, *War Diary of Rodney W. Torrey, 1862–1863* (n.p., n.d.), 35–36; Goodloe, *Some Rebel Relics,* 205; Francis Palfrey, *Memoir of William Francis Bartlett,* 73, 76–77; Orton S. Clark, *The One Hundred and Sixteenth Regiment of New York,* 57–58; Hosmer, *The Color-Guard,* 99–108; Stevens, *History of the Fiftieth Regiment of Infantry, Massachusetts,* 67, 70; Moors, *History of the Fifty-Second Regiment Massachusetts Volunteers,* 81, 91–92; *A Memorial of Lt. Daniel Perkins Dewey,* 71–72; Croffut and Morris, *The Military and Civil History of Connecticut,* 402–403; *Official Records,* XV, 255–56; Dept. of the Gulf, Book No. 4, Letters Sent, p. 408, War Records Division, National Archives; Stanyan, *History of the Eighth Regiment of New Hampshire Volunteers,* 190.

20 Stevens, *History of the Fiftieth Regiment of Infantry, Massachusetts,* 70–71.

21 McMorries, *History of the First Regiment Alabama Volunteer Infantry, C.S.A.,* 51–52; Taylor (ed.), *Reluctant Rebel,* 48–60, 64–70, 74–107.

22 *Official Records,* XV, 259, 280–85, 287–89, 1023, 1038–39, XXVI, Pt. 1, p. 9; Edward Bacon, *Among the Cotton Thieves,* 53–86, 114–18; Flinn, *Campaigning with Banks in Louisiana,* 25–26; Irwin, *History of the Nineteenth Army Corps,* 182, 187, 188, 199, 200.

CHAPTER XV

By the Back Door

1 *Official Records,* XV, 972, 1005; Parks, *General Edmund Kirby Smith,* 251; Albert N. Garland, "E. Kirby Smith and the Trans-Mississippi Confederacy" (Master's thesis, Louisiana State University, 1947), iv, 37; William R. Boggs, *Military Reminiscences of Gen. Wm. R. Boggs, C.S.A.* (Durham, N.C., 1913), 54; Arthur H. Noll, *General Kirby-Smith* (Sewanee, Tenn., 1907), 226.

2 *Official Records,* XV, 290; Palfrey Papers; A. J. H. Duganne, *Camps and Prisons: Twenty Months In the Department of the Gulf* (New York, 1865), 195–201; Flinn, *Campaigning With Banks,* 30–31; Scharf, *History of the Confederate States Navy,* 503.

3 *Official Records,* XV, 257–58, 294, 296, 320, 322–24, 330–89, 397, 1089–90, XXVI, Pt. 1, p. 10; Irwin, *History of the Nineteenth Army Corps,*

90–93; Harris H. Beecher, *Record of the 114th Regiment, N.Y.S.V.* (n.p., n.d.), 135–42; De Forest, *A Volunteer's Adventures,* 87–88; Elias P. Pellet, *History of the 114th Regiment, New York State Volunteers* (Norwich, N.Y., 1866), 65–67.

4 *Official Records,* XV, 296, 319–24, 330–31, 388–91, 396–98, 1090–95; Irwin, *History of the Nineteenth Army Corps,* 94–100; Scharf, *History of the Confederate States Navy,* 504; Beecher, *Record of the 114th Regiment N.Y.S.V.,* 143–45; Pellet, *History of the 114th Regiment,* 68; Carpenter, *History of the Eighth Regiment Vermont,* 102–104; De Forest, *A Volunteer's Adventures,* 88–91; George W. Powers, *The Story of the Thirty-Eighth Regiment of Massachusetts Volunteers* (Cambridge, Mass., 1866), 66–70; Henry A. Willis, *Fitchburg in the War of the Rebellion* (Fitchburg, Mass., 1866), 80; William Fowler, *Memorials of William Fowler* (New York, 1875), 35–39.

5 De Forest, *A Volunteer's Adventures,* 90–91; *Official Records,* XV, 296–97, 324, 330–31, 389–98, 1092; Irwin, *History of the Nineteenth Army Corps,* 99–101, 104–109; Pellet, *History of the 114th Regiment,* 69–70; Powers, *The Story of the Thirty-Eighth Regiment of Massachusetts Volunteers,* 71; Willis, *Fitchburg in the War of the Rebellion,* 80; Carpenter, *History of the Eighth Regiment Vermont,* 104–105; Fowler, *Memorials of William Fowler,* 39.

6 *Official Records,* XV, 297, 391–92, 398; Irwin, *History of the Nineteenth Army Corps,* 109–14; Theophilus Noel, *Autobiography and Reminiscences of Theophilus Noel* (Chicago, 1904), 91–93; Hyatt Papers; Edward Duffy, *History of the 159th Regiment N.Y.S.V.* (New York, 1890), 9–12; Sprague, *History of the 13th Connecticut,* 108–120; James K. Ewer, *The Third Massachusetts Cavalry in the War for the Union* (Maplewood, Mass., 1903), 71–74; Gouverneur Morris, *The History of a Volunteer Regiment* (New York, 1891), 99–102.

7 *Official Records,* XV, 319, 324, 331, 392–93, 398, 1092, 1093–94; Irwin, *History of the Nineteenth Army Corps,* 115–20; Beecher, *Record of the 114th Regiment, N.Y.S.V.,* 146, 151–53; Sprague, *History of the 13th Connecticut,* 108–20; Morris, *The History of a Volunteer Regiment,* 94, 98, 121; Ewer, *The Third Massachusetts Cavalry,* 74–76.

8 Irwin, *History of the Nineteenth Army Corps,* 116, 121–22; Scharf, *History of the Confederate States Navy,* 363.

9 *Official Records,* XV, 393, 399, 1094; Hyatt Papers.

10 Hyatt Papers.

11 *Official Records,* XV, 393, 1092.

12 *Ibid.,* 393–94, 1049.

13 *Ibid.,* 297, 324, 361, 373, 382, 399; Morris, *The History of a Volunteer Regiment,* 104; Ewer, *The Third Massachusetts Cavalry,* 76; Irwin, *History of the Nineteenth Army Corps,* 123–24; Ella Lonn, *Salt As a Factor in the Confederacy* (New York, 1933), 32–33, 192–93, 208;

William H. Perrin (ed.), *Southwest Louisiana, Biographical and Historical* (New Orleans, 1891), 97–98.

14 *Official Records*, XV, 298, 324, 394, 399, 1092; Hyatt Papers; Irwin, *History of the Nineteenth Army Corps*, 122–23, 124–25; De Forest, *A Volunteer's Adventures*, 92, 99; Beecher, *Record of the 114th Regiment, N.Y.S.V.*, 95, 153–56; Willis, *Fitchburg in the War of the Rebellion*, 81; Willoughby M. Babcock, *Selections from the Letters and Diaries of Brevet-Brigadier General Willoughby Babcock of the Seventy-Fifth New York Volunteers* (n.p., 1922), 59; Henry T. Johns, *Life with the Forty-Ninth Massachusetts Volunteers* (Washington, 1890), 199.

15 *Official Records*, XV, 298, 393–94; Hyatt Papers; Babcock, *Selections from the Letters and Diaries*, 59–60; Irwin, *History of the Nineteenth Army Corps*, 126–30; Beecher, *Record of the 114th Regiment, N.Y.S.V.*, 172.

16 *Official Records*, XV, 299, 300, 386, 394, 1054; Irwin, *History of the Nineteenth Army Corps*, 126–27; Townsend, *History of the Sixteenth Regiment, New Hampshire*, 189, 196; Willis, *Fitchburg in the War of the Rebellion*, 81.

17 Fleming, *Louisiana State University*, 113–18.

18 *Official Records*, XV, 311–12; Irwin, *History of the Nineteenth Army Corps*, 144, 146–47; Powers, *The Story of the Thirty-Eighth Regiment of Massachusetts Volunteers*, 83–84; Babcock, *Selections from the Letters and Diaries*, 60; Hyatt Papers; Porter, "Private Journal," 638–39.

19 Babcock, *Selections from the Letters and Diaries*, 60–61.

20 Powers, *The Story of the Thirty-Eighth Regiment of Massachusetts Volunteers*, 84; Porter, "Private Journal," 640–44; Walke, *Naval Scenes and Reminiscences*, 396.

21 Hyatt Papers.

22 De Forest, *A Volunteer's Adventures*, 104; *Official Records*, XV, 306, 333, 701.

23 Beecher, *Record of the 114th Regiment, N.Y.S.V.*, 148–49, 171.

24 Powers, *The Story of the Thirty-Eighth Regiment of Massachusetts Volunteers*, 75; Hepworth, *The Whip, Hoe, and Sword*, 283.

25 Hepworth, *The Whip, Hoe, and Sword*, 284.

26 L. Carroll Root, "Private Journal of William H. Root, Second Lieutenant, Seventy-Fifth New York Volunteers, April 1–June 14, 1863," *Louisiana Historical Quarterly*, XIX (April, 1936), 644, 646.

27 Hepworth, *The Whip, Hoe, and Sword*, 272.

28 Powers, *The Story of the Thirty-Eighth Regiment of Massachusetts Volunteers*, 75–76; Pellet, *History of the 114th Regiment*, 78; Moore Papers; Jerrard Papers; Hepworth, *The Whip, Hoe, and Sword*, 279; Hosmer, *The Color-Guard*, 139.

29 *Official Records*, XV, 305–306, 309, 311, 333–34, 368–70, 373, 706, 716,

727–28, 1117–19; Irwin, *History of the Nineteenth Army Corps*, 145–46; Morris, *The History of a Volunteer Regiment*, 108–109, 122; Records of the War Dept., Dept. of the Gulf, Vol. V, Letters Sent, 87, 93, War Records Division, National Archives; Jerrard Papers; Moore Papers; Moors, *History of the Fifty-Second Regiment, Massachusetts*, 134–35; Powers, *The Story of the Thirty-Eighth Regiment of Massachusetts Volunteers*, 81; Pellet, *History of the 114th Regiment*, 78–82; Ewer, *The Third Massachusetts Cavalry*, 78; Townsend, *History of the Sixteenth Regiment, New Hampshire Volunteers*, 146; Flinn, *Campaigning with Banks in Louisiana*, 65; Hosmer, *The Color-Guard*, 154; Beecher, *Record of the 114th Regiment, N.Y.S.V.*, 158, 161; Bartlett (ed.), *Military Record of Louisiana*, 10.

30   Smith, *Leaves From a Soldier's Diary*, 51.

31   Babcock, *Selections from the Letters and Diaries*, 63; Quarles, *The Negro in the Civil War*, 55–56.

32   Moore Papers.

33   Jerrard Papers.

34   Moore Papers.

35   Records of the War Department, Dept. of the Gulf, V, Letters Sent, pp. 132–33, War Records Division, National Archives; *Official Records*, XV, 716–17.

36   *Official Records*, XV, 314–16, 720, 727–29, 732, XXVI, Pt. 1, p. 500; Irwin, *History of the Nineteenth Army Corps*, 149–51; Greene, *The Mississippi*, 220–25.

37   *Official Records*, XV, 314.

38   *Ibid.*, 314–16, 720, 727–29, 731–32, XXVI, Pt. 1, p. 500, Pt. 3, pp. 288, 298, 303–304; Irwin, *History of the Nineteenth Army Corps*, 149–51, 157–58; Greene, *The Mississippi*, 223–25.

39   Babcock, *Selections from the Letters and Diaries*, 61–63; Irwin, *History of the Nineteenth Army Corps*, 152–55, 159, 160; *Official Records*, XXVI, Pt. 1, p. 43.

40   William H. Whitney Letters; Powers, *The Story of the Thirty-Eighth Regiment of Massachusetts Volunteers*, 88; Smith, *Leaves from a Soldier's Diary*, 56.

CHAPTER XVI

Port Hudson, May 27

1   Johns, *Life With the Forty-Ninth Massachusetts Volunteers*, 162, 167, 202–207, 213.

2   Stevens, *History of the Fiftieth Regiment of Infantry, Massachusetts*, 98.

3 *Official Records,* XXIV, Pt. 1, pp. 528, 540, 542–43, 550, XV, 1075; Orton S. Clark, *The One Hundred and Sixteenth Regiment of New York,* 70–71; Stevens, *History of the Fiftieth Regiment of Infantry, Massachusetts,* 98.

4 *Official Records,* XXIV, Pt. 3, pp. 828, 835, 842, 845, XV, 1071, 1074, 1076, 1080–81, XXVI, Pt. 1, p. 180; Smith and Freret, "Fortification and Siege of Port Hudson," *loc. cit.,* 311–13; Irwin, *History of the Nineteenth Army Corps,* 164–65.

5 Orton S. Clark, *The One Hundred and Sixteenth Regiment of New York,* 74–81; Irwin, *History of the Nineteenth Army Corps,* 159–61, 162; *Official Records,* XXVI, Pt. 1, pp. 67, 120–21, 167–68; Johns, *Life with the Forty-Ninth Massachusetts Volunteers,* 230–35; Smith and Freret, "Fortification and Siege of Port Hudson," *loc. cit.,* 313–14; Kendall, "Recollections of a Confederate Officer," *loc. cit.,* 110–12; Francis W. Palfrey, *Memoir of William Francis Bartlett,* 65; W. H. Pascoe, "Confederate Cavalry Around Port Hudson," *Southern Historical Society Papers,* XXXIII (1905), 86–87.

6 *Official Records,* XXVI, Pt. 1, p. 43; Irwin, *History of the Nineteenth Army Corps,* 159–60.

7 *Official Records,* XXVI, Pt. 1, pp. 138, 167–69, 506, Pt. 2, p. 10; Smith and Freret, "Fortification and Siege of Port Hudson," *loc. cit.,* 304–307, 314–19; McMorries, *History of the First Regiment Alabama Volunteer Infantry, C.S.A.,* 48, 57–62; Smith, *Leaves from a Soldier's Diary,* 55–57; Stanyan, *History of the Eighth Regiment of New Hampshire Volunteers,* 220; Francis W. Preston, *Port Hudson: A History of the Investment, Siege and Capture* (Brooklyn, N.Y., 1892), 11–12, 20; Powers, *The Story of the Thirty-Eighth Regiment of Massachusetts Volunteers,* 90–91; Irwin, *History of the Nineteenth Army Corps,* 163–68; Hosmer, *The Color-Guard,* 223, 227; Greene, *The Mississippi,* 225–27; De Forest, *A Volunteer's Adventures,* 105; Ewer, *The Third Massachusetts Cavalry,* 89; Stevens, *History of the Fiftieth Regiment of Infantry Massachusetts,* 152–56; Greene, *The Mississippi,* 228.

8 *Official Records,* XXVI, Pt. 1, p. 507; Irwin, *History of the Nineteenth Army Corps,* 165–68; Lewis, *Our First Admiral,* 199; Johns, *Life with the Forty-Ninth Massachusetts Volunteers,* 243–45; Orton S. Clark, *The One Hundred and Sixteenth Regiment of New York,* 84–85; Albert Plummer, *History of the Forty-Eighth Regiment M.V.M. During the Civil War* (Boston, 1907), 36–37; Dow, *Reminiscences,* 691–92; Edward Bacon, *Among the Cotton Thieves,* 135–36.

9 *Official Records,* XXVI, Pt. 1, pp. 13, 43–45, 123–25, 132–33, 163, 169–70, 510–11, 515; McMorries, *History of the First Regiment Alabama Volunteer Infantry, C.S.A.,* 18, 62–64; Flinn, *Campaigning with Banks,* 73–78; Stevens, *History of the Fiftieth Regiment of Infantry Massachusetts,* 83, 141–46; Irwin, *History of the Nineteenth Army Corps,*

166–81; De Forest, *A Volunteer's Adventures,* 105–14; Carpenter, *History of the Eighth Regiment Vermont Volunteers,* 112–15; Powers, *The Story of the Thirty-Eighth Regiment of Massachusetts Volunteers,* 92–94; Smith, *Leaves from a Soldier's Diary,* 58–64; Willis, *Fitchburg in the War of the Rebellion,* 82–83; Torrey, *War Diary of Rodney W. Torrey,* 52, 65–66; Croffut and Morris, *The Military and Civil History of Connecticut,* 410–11; Otis F. R. Waite, *New Hampshire in the Great Rebellion* (Claremont, N.H., 1870), 380–81, 520–25; Charles McGregor, *History of the Fifteenth Regiment New Hampshire Volunteers 1862–1863* (Concord, N.H., 1900), 328, 337–50, 372–78, 382–96, 398–400; Smith and Freret, "Fortification and Siege of Port Hudson," *loc. cit.,* 319–25; Babcock, *Selections from the Letters and Diaries,* 30–31; Root, "Private Journal of William H. Root," *loc. cit.,* 658–60; Hepworth, *The Whip, Hoe, and Sword,* 187–89; Edward Bacon, *Among the Cotton Thieves,* 135–44, 158–60; Johns, *Life with the Forty-Ninth Massachusetts Volunteers,* 140–41, 245–46, 249–82; Stanyan, *History of the Eighth Regiment of New Hampshire Volunteers,* 229; Noel, *Autobiography,* 116; Wilson, *The Black Phalanx,* 525–26; George W. Williams, *A History of the Negro Troops,* 215–21; Brown, *The Negro in the American Rebellion,* 168–73; Quarles, *The Negro in the Civil War,* 215–20; John C. Palfrey, "Port Hudson," in *The Mississippi Valley, Tennessee, Georgia, Alabama, 1861–1864; Papers of the Military Historical Society of Massachusetts,* VIII (Boston, 1910), 39–41; Kendall, "Recollections of a Confederate Officer," *loc. cit.,* 1113–16; Dow, *The Reminiscences of Neal Dow,* 691–97; Hoffman, *Camp, Court and Siege,* 70–71; Lawrence Van Alstyne, *Diary of an Enlisted Man* (New Haven, Conn., 1910), 112–19; Preston, *Port Hudson,* 14–18; Plummer, *History of the Forty-Eighth Regiment M.V.M.,* 36–38; Orton S. Clark, *The One Hundred and Sixteenth Regiment of New York,* 87–93; Francis W. Palfrey, *Memoir of William Francis Bartlett,* 83; McMorries, *History of the First Regiment Alabama Volunteer Infantry, C.S.A.,* 64.

10 Johns, *Life with the Forty-Ninth Massachusetts Volunteers,* 268.

11 *Official Records,* XXVI, Pt. 1, pp. 13, 169, 511–17; Johns, *Life with the Forty-Ninth Massachusetts Volunteers,* 280–81; McMorries, *History of the First Regiment Alabama Volunteer Infantry, C.S.A.,* 64; Van Alstyne, *Diary of an Enlisted Man,* 118–19; John C. Palfrey, "Port Hudson," *loc. cit.,* 41; Smith and Freret, "Fortification and Siege of Port Hudson," *loc. cit.,* 325; Smith, *Leaves from a Soldier's Diary,* 66; Powers, *The Story of the Thirty-Eighth Regiment of Massachusetts Volunteers,* 94–98; Townsend, *History of the Sixteenth Regiment, New Hampshire Volunteers,* 233; Irwin, *The Nineteenth Army Corps,* 181–82; Fowler, *Memorials of William Fowler,* 44–45; Thomas L. Livermore, *Numbers and Losses in the Civil War in America, 1861–65,* 101, 140.

12 *Official Records,* XXVI, Pt. 1, pp. 44, 511, 520; Irwin, *The Nineteenth Army Corps,* 185–86; Records of the War Department, Dept. of the Gulf, V, Letters Sent, War Records Division, National Archives, pp. 249, 266, 271.

13 *Official Records,* XXVI, Pt. 1, p. 44; Beecher, *Record of the 114th Regiment, N.Y.S.V.,* 198–99; McGregor, *History of the Fifteenth Regiment New Hampshire Volunteers,* 416, 429, 434, 446, 450; Croffut and Morris, *The Military and Civil History of Connecticut,* 411; De Forest, *A Volunteer's Adventures,* 116, 118–19; Smith and Freret, "Fortification and Siege of Port Hudson," *loc. cit.,* 326; Pellet, *History of the 114th Regiment,* 102–103; Powers, *The Story of the Thirty-Eighth Regiment of Massachusetts Volunteers,* 104–105; Van Alstyne, *Diary of an Enlisted Man,* 121–22, 126; Carpenter, *History of the Eighth Regiment Vermont Volunteers,* 117–21; Babcock, *Selections from the Letters and Diaries,* 25; Johns, *Life with the Forty-Ninth Massachusetts Volunteers,* 289–91, 296, 311, 314, 316–18, 342; Fowler, *Memorials of William Fowler,* 45; Orton S. Clark, *The One Hundred and Sixteenth Regiment of New York,* 94.

14 Pascoe, "Confederate Cavalry Around Port Hudson," *loc. cit.,* 87–89, 91–93; *Official Records,* XXVI, Pt. 1, pp. 134–36, 172, 181; Preston, *Port Hudson,* 25–27; Willis, *Fitchburg in the War of the Rebellion,* 83–84; Powers, *The Story of the Thirty-Eighth Regiment of Massachusetts Volunteers,* 102–103.

15 *Official Records,* XXVI, Pt. 1, pp. 14, 131–32, 157–58; Preston, *Port Hudson,* 28; Pellet, *History of the 114th Regiment,* 106–107; Smith, *Leaves from a Soldier's Diary,* 68; Smith and Freret, "Fortification and Seige of Port Hudson," *loc. cit.,* 326; De Forest, *A Volunteer's Adventures,* 124–27.

16 McMorries, *History of the First Regiment Alabama Volunteer Infantry, C.S.A.,* 67.

17 *Official Records,* XXVI, Pt. 1, pp. 131–32, 157–59; Pellet, *History of the 114th Regiment,* 108–109; Smith, *Leaves from a Soldier's Diary,* 68; Irwin, *The Nineteenth Army Corps,* 192; De Forest, *A Volunteer's Adventures,* 127–31.

18 *Official Records,* XXVI, Pt. 1, pp. 536–37, 546–55; Edward Bacon, *Among the Cotton Thieves,* 128; Orton S. Clark, *The One Hundred and Sixteenth Regiment of New York,* 94; Van Alstyne, *Diary of an Enlisted Man,* 122; Smith and Freret, "Fortification and Siege of Port Hudson," *loc. cit.,* 329–30; Lewis, *Our First Admiral,* 201–202; Preston, *Port Hudson,* 31; Johns, *Life with the Forty-Ninth Massachusetts Volunteers,* 314–15.

Goodloe, *Some Rebel Relics,* 209–10; McMorries, *History of the First Regiment Alabama Volunteer Infantry, C.S.A.,* 67–68; Smith and Freret, "Fortification and Siege of Port Hudson," *loc. cit.,* 339.

14 Babcock, *Selections From the Letters and Diaries,* 95.

15 Preston, *Port Hudson,* 3–5; *Official Records,* XXVI, Pt. 1, pp. 14, 17, 48, 52–55, 144, 146; Smith and Freret, "Fortification and Siege of Port Hudson," *loc. cit.,* 338–44; Hosmer, *The Color-Guard,* 228; Edward Bacon, *Among the Cotton Thieves,* 274, 281, 282; McGregor, *History of the Fifteenth Regiment New Hampshire Volunteers,* 531–33; Croffut and Morris, *The Military and Civil History of Connecticut,* 419; Irwin, *The Nineteenth Army Corps,* 224–32; McMorries, *History of the First Regiment Alabama Volunteer Infantry, C.S.A.,* 68–70; De Forest, *A Volunteer's Adventures,* 145–46; Orton S. Clark, *The One Hundred and Sixteenth Regiment of New York,* 104–106; Hoffman, *Camp, Court and Siege,* 72–73; Preston, *Port Hudson,* 6–12; Plummer, *History of the Forty-Eight Regiment, M.V.M.,* 47; Johns, *Life with the Forty-Ninth Massachusetts Volunteers,* 363–65; Powers, *The Story of the Thirty-Eighth Regiment of Massachusetts Volunteers,* 115; Lewis, *Our First Admiral,* 207–208.

16 *Official Records,* XXVI, Pt. 1, pp. 17, 55, 144, 642; Irwin, *The Nineteenth Army Corps,* 233–34.

CHAPTER XVIII

The Teche, the Mississippi, and Texas

1 *Official Records,* XV, 1054–55, XXVI, Pt. 1, pp. 14, 46, 53, 185–86, 188, 191–92, 216–18, Pt. 2, p. 71; John C. Palfrey, "Port Hudson," *loc. cit.,* 154; Irwin, *History of the Nineteenth Army Corps,* 214, 235–38; Flinn, *Campaigning With Banks in Louisiana,* 88; Parks, *General Edmund Kirby Smith,* 273–74; Duganne, *Camps and Prisons,* 108–19, 140; Gustave Lauve Letter, 1863; Farragut, *The Life of David Glasgow Farragut,* 371; Bosson, *History of the Forty-Second Massachusetts,* 254–61; Andrew M. Sherman, *In the Lowlands of Louisiana in 1863* (Morristown, N.J., 1908), 22; Croffut and Morris, *The Military and Civil History of Connecticut,* 429.

2 *Official Records,* XXVI, Pt. 1, pp. 15, 46, 187–88, 192–97, 199, 218–19; Lauve Letter, 1863; Bosson, *History of the Forty-Second Massachusetts,* 261–68, 286–300; Duganne, *Camps and Prisons,* 116, 119–29; Irwin, *The Nineteenth Army Corps,* 238–39; Andrew M. Sherman, *In the Lowlands of Louisiana in 1863,* 24–25; Croffut and Morris, *The Military and Civil History of Connecticut,* 429.

3 *Official Records,* XXVI, Pt. 1, pp. 15, 189, 209, 215–19, 223–26; Alex-

ander F. Pugh Family Collection, Diary; Palfrey Papers, Plantation Diary; Irwin, *The Nineteenth Army Corps*, 238, 340–41; Andrew M. Sherman, *In the Lowlands of Louisiana in 1863*, 27–32; Duganne, *Camps and Prisons*, 118, 143–53; Bosson, *History of the Forty-Second Massachusetts*, 268–83; Charles C. Nott, *Sketches in Prison Camps* (New York, 1865), 41, 47–55; Flinn, *Campaigning With Banks in Louisiana*, 89.

4   *Official Records*, XXVI, Pt. 1, pp. 189, 199–200, 210–15, 219–20; Duganne, *Camps and Prisons*, 131, 137–38, 155–80; Irwin, *The Nineteenth Army Corps*, 241–42; Bosson, *History of the Forty-Second Massachusetts*, 272–74.

5   *Official Records*, XXVI, Pt. 1, pp. 15, 46–47, 190, 202–203, 212, 227–30; Smith, *Leaves From a Soldier's Diary*, 37–38, 80–83; Irwin, *The Nineteenth Army Corps*, 242–49; Whitman and True, *Maine in the War for the Union*, 544–46; Davis, *The Rise and Fall of the Confederate Government*, II, 419–20; Farragut, *The Life of David Glasgow Farragut*, 371–72.

6   *Official Records*, XXVI, Pt. 1, pp. 15, 204–208, 214, 230–32; Dupuy Diary; Orton S. Clark, *The One Hundred and Sixteenth Regiment of New York*, 107, 109–13; Irwin, *The Nineteenth Army Corps*, 251–53; Torrey, *War Diary of Rodney W. Torrey*, 62–64; Beecher, *Record of the 114th Regiment N.Y.S.V.*, 232.

7   *Official Records*, XXVI, Pt. 1, pp. 204–208.

8   *Ibid.*, 232, 661; Palfrey Papers; Irwin, *The Nineteenth Army Corps*, 254–55; Sprague, *History of the 13th Connecticut*, 175–80; Beecher, *Record of the 114th Regiment, N.Y.S.V.*, 234–41; Flinn, *Campaigning With Banks in Louisiana*, 91; De Forest, *A Volunteer's Adventures*, 149–51; Orton S. Clark, *The One Hundred and Sixteenth Regiment of New York*, 114–15.

9   Irwin, *The Nineteenth Army Corps*, 258–63.

10 *Official Records*, XXVI, Pt. 1, pp. 18–19, 286–87, 673, 692–93, 695–98.

11 James S. Clark, *Life in the Middle West* (Chicago, 1915), 101; Walter G. Smith, *Life and Letters of Thomas Kilby Smith*, 334–35; Wilson, *Under the Old Flag*, 244; Badeau, *Military History of Ulysses S. Grant*, I, 416–17; Catton, *U. S. Grant and the American Military Tradition*, 113, 117; Macartney, *Grant and His Generals*, 91.

12 *Official Records*, XXVI, Pt. 1, pp. 19, 288–90, 306; New Orleans *Times*, October 5, 1863; Irwin, *The Nineteenth Army Corps*, 267–72; Duganne, *Camps and Prisons*, 258–67; Beecher, *Record of the 114th Regiment, N.Y.S.V.*, 247–52; Van Alstyne, *Diary of an Enlisted Man*, 179–83; Scharf, *History of the Confederate States Navy*, 521–26; Orton S. Clark, *The One Hundred and Sixteenth Regiment of New York*, 124–28; Pellet, *History of the 114th Regiment*, 147–53; Hoffman, *Camp, Court and Siege*, 74–76.

13 Irwin, *The Nineteenth Army Corps,* 272–75; *Official Records,* XXVI,
    Pt. 1, pp. 19, 320–32, 338–39, 369, 377, 386, 388–90, 758, 761–63; *Navy
    Records,* XXV, 439–40; Hyatt Diary; Bartlett (ed.), *Military Record of
    Louisiana,* 11; Duganne, *Camps and Prisons,* 331–33; Palfrey Papers;
    James Earl Bradley Family Papers; De Forest, *A Volunteer's Adven-
    tures,* 154–56; Bentley, *History of the 77th Illinois,* 205–207; Orton S.
    Clark, *The One Hundred and Sixteenth Regiment of New York,* 129–
    33; Crooke (comp.), *The Twenty-First Regiment of Iowa Volunteers,*
    116–17.

14 *Official Records,* XXVI, Pt. 1, pp. 19–21, 286, 729, 776, 778, 785, 788,
    793, 800, 810, 811–13, 837, 862, 867, 879; Irwin, *The Nineteenth Army
    Corps,* 274–76; Jones, *Reminiscences of the Twenty-Second Iowa Volun-
    teer Infantry,* 53–60; Bentley, *History of the 77th Illinois,* 234–43; Bering
    and Montgomery, *History of the Forty-Eighth Ohio,* 112–19; Albert O.
    Marshall, *Army Life,* 293.

15 *D.A.B.,* VI, 601–602; Pellet, *History of the 114th Regiment,* 156–57,
    169–70; *Official Records,* XXVI, Pt. 1, pp. 291, 332–33, 342–49, 355–
    378, 391–95, 477, 811; Irwin, *The Nineteenth Army Corps,* 277–78;
    Blessington, *The Campaigns of Walker's Texas Division,* 136–49, 157–
    60; Bentley, *History of the 77th Illinois,* 213–17; Bering and Mont-
    gomery, *History of the Forty-Eighth Ohio,* 109–11; T. B. Marshall,
    History of the Eighty-Third Ohio, 112–16; Orton S. Clark, *The One
    Hundred and Sixteenth Regiment of New York,* 133–34; Hyatt Diary.

16 Beecher, *Record of the 114th Regiment, N.Y.S.V.,* 277.

CHAPTER XIX

Minor Engagements and Reorganization

1 Wood, *A History of the Ninety-Fifth Regiment Illinois,* 82–83; Calhoun, "A History of Concordia Parish," *loc. cit.,* 120–22; Crandall and
   Newell, *History of the Ram Fleet,* 309–11; Porter, *The Naval History
   of the Civil War,* 337; *Official Records,* XXVI, Pt. 1, p. 248; *Experience
   in the War of the Eighty-First Illinois Regiment,* 88; *History of the
   Fifteenth Regiment, Iowa,* 279.

2 *Official Records,* XXVI, Pt. 1, pp. 248, 249, 273–83, 314–15.

3 *Navy Records,* XXV, 572–74; Crandall and Newell, *History of the
   Ram Fleet,* 334, 341–42; John N. Edwards, *Noted Guerrillas, Or the
   Warfare of the Border* (St. Louis, 1880), 221–25, 270–73; Murphy,
   Notes From the History of Madison Parish, 13.

4 *Official Records,* XXVI, Pt. 1, pp. 238–40, Pt. 2, pp. 56, 85–86, 580,
   XXII, Pt. 2, pp. 855, 990.

5 *Official Records,* XXII, Pt. 2, pp. 799, 854, 872, 969, 1134, 1139, XXVI, Pt. 2, pp. 20, 136, 227, 304, 365, 545, 579, LVIII, 777; Noll, *General Kirby-Smith,* 226–30; Boggs, *Military Reminiscences,* 61–62.

6 Lester and Bromwell, *Military and Naval Laws of the Confederate States,* 62; *Official Records,* XXVI, Pt. 2, pp. 194, 232, 241, 381, 996, XXXIV, Pt. 4, p. 700, LIII, 900–901; J. D. Garland Collection; Shreveport *Semi-Weekly News,* July 19, August 7, September 18, 1863, January 19, 1864; Opelousas *Courier,* September 5, 12, 1863; Shugg, *Origins of Class Struggle in Louisiana,* 179; Hyatt Diary; Bragg, *Louisiana in the Confederacy,* 256–57.

7 Bradley Papers.

8 *Official Records,* XXVI, Pt. 2, pp. 541–43.

9 Bradley Papers.

10 Shreveport *Semi-Weekly News,* May 19, 1863; Merrick, *Old Times in Dixie Land,* 72–73; Anderson (ed.), *Brokenburn,* 219–23, 248.

11 Weeks Papers.

12 Shreveport *Semi-Weekly News,* May 12, 26, June 30, July 14, 24, 1863; Anderson (ed.), *Brokenburn,* 267; Moore Papers; Hyatt Diary.

13 Flanders Papers.

14 West, *Second Admiral,* 240; Chase, *Diary and Correspondence,* 412, 415; *Official Records,* XXVI, Pt. 2, pp. 434–35, 558.

15 Shreveport *Semi-Weekly News,* March 13, 1863; Lonn, *Salt As a Factor in the Confederacy,* 22–24, 48, 68–71, 75, 84–85, 91–93, 130, 147, 207, 235, 264, 272–73; Hardin, *Northwestern Louisiana,* II, 155.

16 Shreveport *Semi-Weekly News,* March 24, 25, May 1, August 4, 28, Sept. 29, 1863.

17 Walke, *Naval Scenes and Reminiscences,* 414; West, *Second Admiral,* 241; Knox, *Camp-Fire and Cotton-Field,* 311–46; Badeau, *Military History of Ulysses S. Grant,* I, 664; *Official Records,* XXIV, Pt. 3, p. 128, XXVI, Pt. 1, pp. 667–68, 764; Williamson and Goodman (eds.), *Eastern Louisiana,* I, 149–50; Bragg, *Louisiana in the Confederacy,* 213–15.

18 *Official Records,* XXVI, Pt. 1, p. 737.

19 *Ibid.,* 741.

20 Irwin, *History of the Nineteenth Army Corps,* 261–62; Van Alstyne, *Diary of an Enlisted Man,* 194; New Orleans *Times,* December 24, 1863; Dudley T. Cornish, "The Union Army As a Training School For Negroes," *Journal of Negro History,* XXXVII (October, 1952), 373; Records of the War Department, Dept. of the Gulf, Letters Sent, Vol. CXCI, 1–3, War Records Division, National Archives.

21 Murray, *History of the Ninth Connecticut,* 166.

22 Irwin, *History of the Nineteenth Army Corps,* 260–62.

23 *Official Records,* XXVI, Pt. 1, pp. 456–78.

24 Williamson and Goodman (eds.), *Eastern Louisiana,* I, 152.

CHAPTER XX

The Campaign Opens

1 Dorsey, *Recollections of Henry Watkins Allen,* 235–36, 377–78; Shreveport *Semi-Weekly News,* January 29, February 12, 16, 1864; "Historical Militia Data on Louisiana Militia," 398–99; Bragg, *Louisiana in the Confederacy,* 162–63, 238–41, 260–62; Laura B. W. Jones, "Official Announcements State, Military and Confederate States of America from Shreveport *News,* January, 1862–July, 1865" (Baton Rouge, 1940), 21.

2 War Department Collection of Confederate Records, Chap. VIII, Vol. CXXXIV, Account Book, 1864, pp. 21–22, 25, 26, War Records Division, National Archives.

3 Dorsey, *Recollections of Henry Watkins Allen,* 238–59.

4 *Official Records,* XXXIV, Pt. 1, p. 483.

5 *Ibid.,* 902–903, 964; Bragg, *Louisiana in the Confederacy,* 165; Parks, *General Edmund Kirby Smith,* 350–51, 365; Garland, "E. Kirby Smith and the Trans-Mississippi Confederacy," 56–58.

6 Garland Collection; War Department Collection of Confederate Records, Chap. II, Vol. LXXV, Letters Sent, Dist. of W. La., 1864, pp. 163, 175, 225–28, LXXVI, 27–28, War Records Division, National Archives; *Official Records,* XXXIV, Pt. 2, pp. 977–78, Pt. 1, pp. 495, 633, LIII, 971–74.

7 *Official Records,* XXXIV, Pt. 1, pp. 965–66, Pt. 2, p. 1025.

8 War Department Collection of Confederate Records, Chap. II, Vol. LXXVI, Letters Sent, Dist. of W. La., 1864, p. 68, War Records Division, National Archives.

9 *Official Records,* XXXIV, Pt. 2, p. 944.

10 *Ibid.,* 967; War Department Collection of Confederate Records, Chap. II, Vol. LXXVI, Letters Sent, Dist. of W. La., 1864, p. 64, War Records Division, National Archives; Crandall and Newell, *History of the Ram Fleet,* 362, 364.

11 *Official Records,* XXXIV, Pt. 1, pp. 129–30, Pt. 2, pp. 952, 977; Calhoun, "A History of Concordia Parish," *loc. cit.,* 119–21; Garland Collection; *Navy Records,* XXV, 748–51; Porter, *Naval History of the Civil War,* 555.

12 War Department Collection of Confederate Records, Chap. II, Vol. LXXVI, Letters Sent, Dist. of W. La., 1864, pp. 112–13, 142–44, War Records Division, National Archives; *Official Records,* XXXIV, Pt. 2, pp. 971, 977–78.

13 War Department Collection of Confederate Records, Chap. II, Vol. LXXV, Letters Sent, Dist. of W. La., 55–56, 167–70, 224–25, 244–45, Vol.

LXXVI, 2–3, War Records Division, National Archives; *Official Records,* XXXIV, Pt. 1, pp. 483, 560, Pt. 2, pp. 952–53, 1024, XLI, Pt. 1, p. 114.

14 *Official Records,* XXXIV, Pt. 2, pp. 15, 55–56; U.S. Congress. Joint Committee on the Conduct of the War, *Report of the Joint Committee on the Conduct of the War At the Second Session Thirty-Eighth Congress* (Washington, 1865), II, xxiv–xxv. Cited hereafter as *Report of the Joint Committee on the Conduct of the War.*

15 *Report of the Joint Committee on the Conduct of the War,* II, xxv–xxvi, xxxi; Ludwell H. Johnson, *Red River Campaign, Politics and Cotton In the Civil War* (Baltimore, 1958), 5–49; *Official Records,* XXXIV, Pt. 1, p. 195, Pt. 2, pp. 134, 494, 496, 512, 535, 544–45, 562, 598; Porter, "Private Journal," 718–19; Irwin, *History of the Nineteenth Army Corps,* 279–81, 288–89; Bering and Montgomery, *History of the Forty-Eighth Ohio,* 121–27.

16 New Orleans *Times,* February 18, 21, 23, March 5, 1864; Chase, *Diary,* 431; Bragg, *Louisiana in the Confederacy,* 287–89; *Official Records,* XXXIV, Pt. 2, pp. 512–13; Emily Reed, *Life of A. P. Dostie,* 95–98.

17 *Official Records,* XXXIV, Pt. 1, pp. 304–305, 362, 492, 560–61, 573–74, 598, 600–601, Pt. 2, pp. 534, 611, 1024, 1027, 1029–30, 1044, 1046, 1052, XLI, Pt. 1, p. 114; Crandall and Newell, *History of the Ram Fleet,* 376; Walter G. Smith, *Life and Letters of Thomas Kilby Smith,* 89–92; *Experience in the War, Eighty-First Illinois Regiment,* 110–15; Porter, *Naval History of the Civil War,* 495–96; Bryner, *Bugle Echoes,* 99–100; Blessington, *The Campaigns of Walker's Texas Division,* 173–76.

18 *Official Records,* XXXIV, Pt. 1, pp. 484, 494, 633, XLI, Pt. 1, p. 114.

19 *Ibid.,* XXXIV, Pt. 1, pp. 305–306, Pt. 2, p. 611; Porter, *Incidents and Anecdotes,* 214–16; Walter G. Smith, *Life and Letters of Thomas Kilby Smith,* 92; *Experience in the War, Eighty-First Illinois Regiment,* 115–16; Wood, *A History of the Ninety-Fifth Regiment, Illinois,* 99–100.

20 Hyatt Diary; Scharf, *History of the Confederate States Navy,* 520; *Official Records,* XXXIV, Pt. 1, p. 561, Pt. 2, p. 1046.

21 *Official Records,* XXXIV, Pt. 1, pp. 177, 181, 195, 197, 306, 307, 323, 326, 334, 335, 340, 501, 561–62, Pt. 2, p. 562; Porter, *Incidents and Anecdotes,* 216; Porter, *Naval History of the Civil War,* 498; Van Alstyne, *Diary of An Enlisted Man,* 292; Bryner, *Bugle Echoes,* 100; Ewer, *The Third Massachusetts Cavalry,* 137–39; *Experience in the War, Eighty-First Illinois Regiment,* 117–18; Irwin, *History of the Nineteenth Army Corps,* 289–90; Blessington, *The Campaigns of Walker's Texas Division,* 177–78; David W. Reed, *Campaigns and Battles of the Twelfth Regiment Iowa Veteran Volunteer Infantry* (n.p., 1903), 148–49; Pellet, *History of the 114th Regiment,* 172–78; *Official Report Relative to the Conduct of Federal Troops,* 11–13; Palfrey Papers; Bradley Papers; Beecher, *Record of the 114th Regiment N.Y.S.V.,* 300.

22 *Official Records,* XXXIV, Pt. 1, pp. 197, 212–14, 307, 510, Pt. 2, pp. 654, 715, 722–23, 735; *Experience in the War, Eighty-First Illinois Regiment,* 121; Crandall and Newell, *History of the Ram Fleet,* 378; *Navy Records,* XXVI, 35–36; *Report of the Joint Committee on the Conduct of the War,* II, x–xv, xlvii, xlviii, 54, 66, 72–74, 80–81, 87, 176–77, 197–98, 208–209, 216, 223–25, 271, 273, 283–85, 289, 290, 291, 297, 302, 335; Miller Diary; John Homans, "The Red River Expedition," in *The Mississippi Valley, Tennessee, Georgia, Alabama, 1861–1864, Papers of the Military Historical Society of Massachusetts,* VIII (Boston, 1910), 69–70; West, *Second Admiral,* 247–48; Porter, *Incidents and Anecdotes,* 226; Newsome, *Experience in the War of the Great Rebellion,* 69; Pellet, *History of the 114th Regiment,* 183–86; Van Alstyne, *Diary of An Enlisted Man,* 294, 304; Flinn, *Campaigning With Banks in Louisiana,* 96.

23 *Report of the Joint Committee on the Conduct of the War,* II, ix, xv, xlix, 280, 285, 335.

24 *Ibid.,* xlix; Emily Reed, *Life of A. P. Dostie,* 101; Chase, *Diary,* 435; Bragg, *Louisiana in the Confederacy,* 289.

25 *Official Records,* XXXIV, Pt. 1, pp. 181, 197, 214, 307; *Report of the Joint Committee on the Conduct of the War,* II, xxxv–xxxvi, xliii, 270; Smith, *Leaves from a Soldier's Diary,* 93; Irwin, *History of the Nineteenth Army Corps,* 290–91; *Experience in the War, Eighty-First Illinois Regiment,* 120–23.

26 *Official Records,* XXXIV, Pt. 1, p. 197.

27 *Ibid.,* 162, 216, Pt. 2, pp. 513–16, 616; Smith, *Leaves from a Soldier's Diary,* 93; Irwin, *History of the Nineteenth Army Corps,* 292.

28 *Official Records,* XXXIV, Pt. 2, pp. 610–11.

29 *Ibid.,* 180, 197; Irwin, *History of the Nineteenth Army Corps,* 294–95.

30 Bering and Montgomery, *History of the Forty-Eighth Ohio,* 128–29; Beecher, *Record of the 114th Regiment, N.Y.S.V.,* 302–306; Pellet, *History of the 114th Regiment,* 186–92; Marshall, *History of the Eighty-Third Ohio,* 123–24; John M. Gould, *History of the First-Tenth-Twenty-Ninth Maine Regiment* (Portland, Maine, 1871), 408; Orton S. Clark, *The One Hundred and Sixteenth Regiment of New York,* 149–51.

31 Orton S. Clark, *The One Hundred and Sixteenth Regiment of New York,* 151; Beecher, *Record of the 114th Regiment, N.Y.S.V.,* 306; *Official Records,* XXXIV, Pt. 1, pp. 511–15, 518, 561–62.

32 *Official Records,* XXXIV, Pt. 1, pp. 484, 513–19, 521–22.

33 *Ibid.,* 179–81, 197–98, 214, 307, 633; Newsome, *Experience in the War of the Great Rebellion,* 71; Irwin, *History of the Ninteenth Army Corps,* 295–96; Gould, *History,* 411; Hoffman, *Camp, Court and Siege,* 87; Ewer, *The Third Massachusetts Cavalry,* 142; Homans, "The Red River Expedition," *loc. cit.,* 76–77; L. H. Johnson, *Red River Cam-*

paign, 113–16; Beecher, *Record of the 114th Regiment, N.Y.S.V.,* 307–308; Bryner, *Bugle Echoes,* 101–102; Orton S. Clark, *The One Hundred and Sixteenth Regiment of New York,* 152–53; Pellet, *The 114th Regiment,* 193.

34 *Official Records,* XXXIV, Pt. 1, pp. 114, 181, 198–99, 237, 256–57, 450, 472, 478–80, 485, 519–20, 523, 526, 528, 563, 606, 616; Bringier Papers; Beecher, *Record of the 114th Regiment, N.Y.S.V.,* 308; Blessington, *The Campaigns of Walker's Texas Division,* 179–82; Ewer, *The Third Massachusetts Cavalry,* 143; X. B. Debray, "A Sketch of Debray's Twenty-Sixth Regiment of Texas Cavalry," *Southern Historical Society Papers,* XIII (January–December, 1885), 154–57; L. H. Johnson, *Red River Campaign,* 124–25.

35 *Official Records,* XXXIV, Pt. 1, pp. 526, 563; L. H. Johnson, *Red River Campaign,* 131.

CHAPTER XXI

Mansfield and Pleasant Hill

1 *Official Records,* XXXIV, Pt. 1, pp. 563–64; John C. Moncure Papers; Davis, *The Rise and Fall of the Confederate Government,* II, 542–43; Marshall, *History of the Eighty-Third Ohio,* 127–28; Blessington, *The Campaigns of Walker's Texas Division,* 184–86.

2 Hyatt Diary.

3 *Official Records,* XXXIV, Pt. 1, pp. 127, 169–70, 181–82, 199–200, 238, 257, 264–66, 282, 285, 290–92, 389, 398, 416, 420, 450, 455–57, 472–73, 527, 606, 616; Irwin, *History of the Nineteenth Army Corps,* 296–303; Marshall, *History of the Eighty-Third Ohio,* 129–31; Pellet, *History of the 114th Regiment,* 195; *Report of the Joint Committee on the Conduct of the War,* II, vi, xxxvii–xxxviii, xlvii–xlviii; Homans, "The Red River Expedition," *loc. cit.,* 79; Bentley, *History of the 77th Illinois,* 249–50; Hoffman, *Camp, Court and Siege,* 87; Orton S. Clark, *The One Hundred and Sixteenth Regiment of New York,* 152–54; Stanyan, *A History of the Eighth Regiment of New Hampshire Volunteers,* 400–401; Flinn, *Campaigning With Banks,* 104–105; L. H. Johnson, *Red River Campaign,* 125–34.

4 *Official Records,* XXXIV, Pt. 1, pp. 282, 450–52, 527, 564; John Dimitry, "Louisiana," *Confederate Military History* (Atlanta, 1899), X, 137–41.

5 *Official Records,* XXXIV, Pt. 1, p. 564.

6 *Ibid.,* 200, 266, 282, 527, 564–65, 606, 617; Dimitry, "Louisiana," *loc. cit.,* 138–41; Bartlett (ed.), *Military Record of Louisiana,* 13; L. H. Johnson, *Red River Campaign,* 134–36.

7 *Official Records,* XXXIV, Pt. 1, pp. 182, 200, 257, 266–68, 282–94,

452–53, 473, 527, 564–65, 606, 617; Dimitry, "Louisiana," *loc. cit.*, 141–42; Bentley, *History of the 77th Illinois*, 250–53; Orton S. Clark, *The One Hundred and Sixteenth Regiment of New York*, 154–56; Bryner, *Bugle Echoes*, 103; Blessington, *The Campaigns of Walker's Texas Division*, 187–88; Stanyan, *History of the Eighth Regiment of New Hampshire Volunteers*, 401; Irwin, *History of the Nineteenth Army Corps*, 303–308; Pellet, *History of the 114th Regiment*, 196; Beecher, *Record of the 114th Regiment, N.Y.S.V.*, 310–11; Flinn, *Campaigning with Banks in Louisiana*, 108–109; Homans, "The Red River Expedition," *loc. cit.*, 80; Marshall, *History of the Eighty-Third Ohio*, 131–35; Bering and Montgomery, *History of the Forty-Eighth Ohio*, 131–41; Ewer, *The Third Massachusetts Cavalry*, 147–55.

8   *Official Records*, XXXIV, Pt. 1, pp. 127, 182, 200–201, 238, 257–58, 263–64, 296–303, 307–308, 389–92, 416–17, 420–22, 458–60, 464–65, 473, 527, 553, 564–65, 607; Dimitry, "Louisiana," *loc. cit.*, 143; Blessington, *The Campaigns of Walker's Texas Division*, 188–90; Irwin, *History of the Nineteenth Army Corps*, 307–11; Pellet, *History of the 114th Regiment*, 196–200; Beecher, *Record of the 114th Regiment, N.Y.S.V.*, 311–14; Lufkin, *History of the Thirteenth Maine*, 78–80; Gould, *History*, 412–17; Ewer, *The Third Massachusetts Cavalry*, 150–51; Orton S. Clark, *The One Hundred and Sixteenth Regiment of New York*, 156–57; *Report of the Joint Committee on the Conduct of the War*, II, 180, 185, 187; Homans, "The Red River Expedition," *loc. cit.*, 77–79.

9   Orton S. Clark, *The One Hundred and Sixteenth Regiment of New York*, 157–59; *Official Records*, XXXIV, Pt. 1, pp. 128, 183; Bentley, *History of the 77th Illinois*, 258, 307–308; Ewer, *The Third Massachusetts Cavalry*, 157–58; Gould, *History*, 417, 420; Lufkin, *History of the Thirteenth Maine*, 83; Beecher, *Record of the 114th Regiment, N.Y.S.V.*, 319–20; Marshall, *History of the Eighty-Third Ohio*, 136.

10 *Official Records*, XXXIV, Pt. 1, pp. 183, 201, 238, 308, 319, 340, 345–46, 362, 373, 423, 528, 565–66, 607, 617, LIII, 477; Moncure Papers; Blessington, *The Campaigns of Walker's Texas Division*, 193; Davis, *The Rise and Fall of the Confederate Government*, II, 544; Gould, *History*, 420–21; Debray, "A Sketch of Debray's Twenty-Sixth Regiment of Texas Cavalry," *loc. cit.*, 158; Lufkin, *History of the Thirteenth Maine*, 84; Bentley, *History of the 77th Illinois*, 308; Beecher, *Record of the 114th Regiment, N.Y.S.V.*, 320–21; Irwin, *History of the Nineteenth Army Corps*, 313–16.

11 *Official Records*, XXXIV, Pt. 1, pp. 183–84, 201–202, 238–39, 258, 308–309, 312, 317–19, 321–22, 324, 328–29, 333, 335–37, 340–42, 345–47, 349–50, 354–57, 361–63, 365–69, 371, 373–76, 391–94, 409–14, 418, 423–26, 430–33, 437–38, 452, 459, 472–73, 476–77, 480, 485, 553–54, 565–70, 596, 602–605, 607–609, 617–18, Pt. 3, p. 128, LIII, 477; Irwin,

History of the Nineteenth Army Corps, 317–22; Blessington, *The Campaigns of Walker's Texas Division,* 194–200; Noel, *Autobiography,* 138–41; Bryner, *Bugle Echoes,* 104–105; Orton S. Clark, *The One Hundred and Sixteenth Regiment of New York,* 160–63; Beecher, *Records of the 114th Regiment, N.Y.S.V.,* 321–25; Lufkin, *History of the Thirteenth Maine,* 84–86; Gould, *History,* 421–25; Pellet, *History of the 114th Regiment,* 208–10; L. H. Johnson, *Red River Campaign,* 168–69.

CHAPTER XXII

"Skedaddle"

1 *Official Records,* XXXIV, Pt. 1, pp. 184–86, 202–204, 485, Pt. 2, p. 171, Pt. 3, pp. 24, 100, XLI, Pt. 1, p. 115; *Report of the Joint Committee on the Conduct of the War,* II, xxxviii, 13, 35, 95, 179, 190–91; Ewer, *The Third Massachusetts Cavalry,* 161–62; Gould, *History,* 426.
2 Bryner, *Bugle Echoes,* 106–107; Johnson, *Red River Campaign,* 164.
3 *Official Records,* XXXIV, Pt. 1, pp. 184, 205, 250, 569, 609; Pellet, *History of the 114th Regiment,* 211, 215–19; Gould, *History,* 426–27; Lufkin, *History of the Thirteenth Maine,* 87; Irwin, *History of the Nineteenth Army Corps,* 323; Bentley, *History of the 77th Illinois,* 310; Beecher, *Record of the 114th Regiment, N.Y.S.V.,* 326–27; Marshall, *History of the Eighty-Third Ohio,* 137–38; Orton S. Clark, *The One Hundred and Sixteenth Regiment of New York,* 163–65; Powers, *The Story of the Thirty-Eighth Massachusetts,* 135–36; Hoffman, *Camp, Court and Siege,* 96–97; H. P. Bee, "Battle of Pleasant Hill—An Error Corrected," *Southern Historical Society Papers,* VIII (April, 1880), 185.
4 Miss Sidney Harding Diaries.
5 *Official Records,* XXXIV, Pt. 1, pp. 480, 569, 609–610; Debray, "A Sketch of Debray's Twenty-Sixth Regiment of Texas Cavalry," *loc. cit.,* 161.
6 *Official Records,* XXXIV, Pt. 1, pp. 172–204, 215, 380–81, 571, 633; Wood, *A History of the Ninety-Fifth Regiment, Illinois,* 101–103; *Experience in the War, Eighty-First Illinois Regiment,* 125–27; Porter, *Incidents and Anecdotes,* 231–33; Porter, *Naval History of the Civil War,* 502, 510; Mahan, *The Gulf and Inland Waters,* 196–97; West, *Second Admiral,* 251–52; Gosnell, *Guns On the Western Waters,* 249; *Navy Records,* XXVI, 49–50.
7 Noel, *Autobiography,* 100, 143.
8 Porter, "Private Journal," 763.
9 *Official Records,* XXXIV, Pt. 1, pp. 204, 310, 381–82, 530, 533, 571, 610,

633, Pt. 2, pp. 173–74; Wood, *A History of the Ninety-Fifth Regiment Illinois,* 103; Pellet, *History of the 114th Regiment,* 222; *Experience in the War, Eighty-First Illinois Regiment,* 123–33.

10 *Official Records,* XXXIV, Pt. 1, pp. 186–87, 203–205, 216–17, Pt. 2, p. 161, Pt. 3, pp. 24, 128, 275; Powers, *The Story of the Thirty-Eighth Regiment of Massachusetts Volunteers,* 130–33; Smith, *Leaves From a Soldier's Diary,* 99; Irwin, *History of the Nineteenth Army Corps,* 326–27.

11 *Official Records,* XXXIV, Pt. 1, pp. 531–34, 571–72.

12 L. H. Johnson, *Red River Campaign,* 170–205.

13 *Official Records,* XXXIV, Pt. 1, pp. 205–207, 262–63, 310, 572; Powers, *The Story of the Thirty-Eighth Regiment of Massachusetts Volunteers,* 136–37; Beecher, *Record of the 114th Regiment, N.Y.S.V.,* 330–32; Orton S. Clark, *The One Hundred and Sixteenth Regiment of New York,* 166–68; Lufkin, *History of the Thirteenth Maine,* 87; Irwin, *History of the Nineteenth Army Corps,* 328–30; Wood, *A History of the Ninety-Fifth Regiment, Illinois,* 103; Pellet, *History of the 114th Regiment,* 324–25; Smith, *Leaves from a Soldier's Diary,* 100; *Experience in the War, Eighty-First Illinois Regiment,* 134–35.

14 *Official Records,* XXXIV, Pt. 1, pp. 190, 207–208, 262–63, 275, 394–96, 402, 406–407, 418–19, 432–35, 439–40, 580, 610–14, 618–20; Bentley, *History of the 77th Illinois,* 310–11; Ewer, *The Third Massachusetts Cavalry,* 165–66; Gould, *History,* 434–35; Lufkin, *History of the Thirteenth Maine,* 88; Beecher, *Record of the 114th Regiment, N.Y.S.V.,* 332–34; Pellet, *History of the 114th Regiment,* 225–26; Smith, *Leaves from a Soldier's Diary,* 101–102; Powers, *The Story of the Thirty-Eighth Regiment of Massachusetts Volunteers,* 137–40; Irwin, *History of the Nineteenth Army Corps,* 330–33; Debray, "A Sketch of Debray's Twenty-Sixth Regiment of Texas Cavalry," *loc. cit.,* 161; Sprague, *History of the 13th Connecticut,* 194–201; L. H. Johnson, *Red River Campaign,* 232–33.

15 *Official Records,* XXXIV, Pt. 1, pp. 191, 250, 263, 580–81, 583, 610–15, 620; Beecher, *Record of the 114th Regiment, N.Y.S.V.,* 336–38; Smith, *Leaves from a Soldier's Diary,* 103–105; *Experience in the War, Eighty-First Illinois Regiment,* 138–39.

16 Ewer, *The Third Massachusetts Cavalry,* 166, 168.

17 Pellet, *History of the 114th Regiment,* 229.

18 *Official Records,* XXXIV, Pt. 1, p. 581.

19 *Official Report Relative to the Conduct of Federal Troops,* 13–14, 22–69.

20 *Official Records,* XXXIV, Pt. 3, p. 307.

21 Smith, *Leaves from a Soldier's Diary,* 104.

22 Powers, *The Story of the Thirty-Eighth Regiment of Massachusetts Volunteers,* 142.

23 *Official Records,* XXXIV, Pt. 1, pp. 191–92, 210, Pt. 2, pp. 293–96;

Pellet, *History of the 114th Regiment,* 229; *Experience in the War, Eighty-First Illinois Regiment,* 140; Beecher, *Record of the 114th Regiment N.Y.S.V.,* 338–39; Orton S. Clark, *The One Hundred and Sixteenth Regiment of New York,* 173; Irwin, *History of the Nineteenth Army Corps,* 334.

24 *Official Records,* XXXIV, Pt. 1, pp. 583–85, 635–36; Flournoy Papers; Mahan, *The Gulf and Inland Waters,* 198–203.

25 *Official Records,* XXXIV, Pt. 1, pp. 219–21.

26 *Ibid.,* 162, 193, 209–11, 219–21, 250–51, 253–56, 310–11, 324, 331–32, 343, 359, 384, 403–404, 461, 474–75, 584–91, 612, 621–23, 626, 627, 635, 637, Pt. 2, p. 53; Gould, *History,* 439–46; Irwin, *History of the Nineteenth Army Corps,* 337–43; Beecher, *Record of the 114th Regiment, N.Y.S.V.,* 341–46; Orton S. Clark, *The One Hundred and Sixteenth Regiment of New York,* 174–78; Van Alstyne, *Diary of an Enlisted Man,* 317–18; Hoffman, *Camp, Court and Siege,* 100–101; Powers, *The Story of the Thirty-Eighth Regiment of Massachusetts Volunteers,* 143–44; Porter, *Incidents and Anecdotes,* 245–51; Mahan, *The Gulf and Inland Waters,* 203–209; *Navy Records,* XXVI, 123–24.

27 *Official Records,* XXXIV, Pt. 1, pp. 590–91.

28 *Ibid.,* Pt. 2, pp. 209, 269, 277–78, 534, Pt. 3, p. 101; *Report of the Joint Committee on the Conduct of the War,* II, xiii, 81–83, 209, 277.

29 *Official Records,* XXXIV, Pt. 2, pp. 515, 532.

30 *Ibid.,* Pt. 1, p. 213, Pt. 2, p. 558; Porter, *Incidents and Anecdotes,* 258; Sprague, *History of the 13th Connecticut,* 206–207.

31 Noel, *Autobiography,* 143.

32 Bringier Papers.

33 *Official Records,* XXXIV, Pt. 1, p. 212; *Report of the Joint Committee on the Conduct of the War,* II, 23.

34 *Official Report Relative to the Conduct of Federal Troops,* 71.

35 *Official Records,* XXXIV, Pt. 2, p. 521.

36 Orton S. Clark, *The One Hundred and Sixteenth Regiment of New York,* 178–79; Irwin, *History of the Nineteenth Army Corps,* 334; Ewer, *The Third Massachusetts Cavalry,* 180.

37 Ewer, *The Third Massachusetts Cavalry,* 180.

38 *Official Report Relative to the Conduct of Federal Troops,* 70–75.

39 *Report of the Joint Committee on the Conduct of the War,* II, 23.

40 Van Alstyne, *Diary of an Enlisted Man,* 320–21; *Official Records,* XXXIV, Pt. 1, p. 212.

41 Porter, *Incidents and Anecdotes,* 258–59.

42 *Official Records,* XXXIV, Pt. 1, pp. 162, 193, 211, 310–11, 591–94, 623–24, Pt. 2, p. 823; Smith, *Leaves from a Soldier's Diary,* 113–17; Lufkin, *History of the Thirteenth Maine,* 91–92; Irwin, *The Nineteenth Army Corps,* 344–46; Powers, *The Story of the Thirty-Eighth Regiment of Massachusetts Volunteers,* 147; Beecher, *Record of the*

114th Regiment, N.Y.S.V., 349–53; Orton S. Clark, *The One Hundred and Sixteenth Regiment of New York*, 179–80; Bryner, *Bugle Echoes*, 114–15; *Official Records*, XXXIV, Pt. 1, pp. 312, 320–21, 347–49, 595, 625; Ewer, *The Third Massachusetts Cavalry*, 183–85.

43 *Official Records*, XXXIV, Pt. 1, pp. 594–95.

44 *Ibid.*, 212, 312, Pt. 2, pp. 644, 680, 694; Hoffman, *Camp, Court and Siege*, 102; Beecher, *Record of the 114th Regiment, N.Y.S.V.*, 353–58; Mason, *The Forty-Second Ohio Infantry*, 249–50; Marshall, *History of the Eighty-Third Ohio*, 144–45; Irwin, *History of the Nineteenth Army Corps*, 346–47; Gould, *History*, 453–54; Jones, *Reminiscences of the Twenty-Second Iowa*, 69–70; *Experience in the War, Eighty-First Illinois Infantry*, 151–53; *Official Report Relative to the Conduct of Federal Troops*, 76, 78.

45 *Official Records*, XXXIV, Pt. 1, pp. 193, 212, Pt. 3, pp. 409, 490–91, 583, 644; Irwin, *History of the Nineteenth Army Corps*, 347–48; Parks, *General Edmund Kirby Smith*, 403.

Chapter XXIII

The Quiet Period

1 *Official Records*, XXXIV, Pt. 1, pp. 480, 534–48, 557, Pt. 2, p. 810, Pt. 4, p. 664, XLI, Pt. 1, pp. 115–16.

2 *Ibid.*, XLVIII, Pt. 1, p. 548, XLI, Pt. 1, pp. 90–104, 109–12, 117, Pt. 2, pp. 1035–38, 1066.

3 Blessington, *The Campaigns of Walker's Texas Division*, 272–74; W. W. Heartsill, *Fourteen Hundred and 91 Days in the Confederate Army* (Jackson, Tenn., 1954), 211–16.

4 *Official Records*, XLI, Pt. 1, p. 117.

5 Richard Taylor, "A Chapter of History," *Southern Historical Society Papers*, XXXI (1903), 48.

6 *Official Records*, XLI, Pt. 1, pp. 118, 120–22, Pt. 2, pp. 1039–41; Parks, *General Edmund Kirby Smith*, 433.

7 Blessington, *The Campaigns of Walker's Texas Division*, 275–77; Heartsill, *Fourteen Hundred and 91 Days in the Confederate Army*, 216–17; *Official Records*, XLI, Pt. 1, p. 123, Pt. 2, pp. 765–67, Pt. 4, pp. 1082–83, XLVIII, Pt. 1, pp. 1411, 1418; Parks, *General Edmund Kirby Smith*, 442–44.

8 *Official Records*, XXXIV, Pt. 4, p. 28.

9 Bringier Papers.

10 *Official Records*, XLI, Pt. 3, p. 774.

11 Shreveport *Semi-Weekly News*, May 12, July 26, 1864.

12 *Official Records*, XXXIV, Pt. 4, p. 688.

13 War Department Collection of Confederate Records, Chapter II, Vol. LXXXI, 66, War Records Division, National Archives; Tunnard, *A Southern Record*, 319, 326; *Official Records*, XLI, Pt. 3, p. 854.

14 *Official Records*, XLI, Pt. 2, p. 1005, Pt. 3, pp. 1071–73, XLVIII, Pt. 2, pp. 398–403, XXXIV, Pt. 3, pp. 814–15, Pt. 4, p. 639, LIII, 1009; Shreveport *Weekly News*, June 28, 1864; Hyatt Papers.

15 Flanders Papers.

16 *Official Records*, LIII, 1032; Dorsey, *Recollections of Henry Watkins Allen*, 280–83.

17 Flanders Papers.

18 *Official Records*, XXXIV, Pt. 4, p. 659, XLI, Pt. 4, pp. 1109, 1129–30; Shreveport *Weekly News*, December 6, 1864; Ellis Family Collection; Bringier Papers.

19 Harding Diaries; Tunnard, *A Southern Record*, 327; Gras-Lauzin Papers.

20 Civil War Letters of Colonel George W. Guess.

21 Gras-Lauzin Papers.

22 Bradley Papers.

23 *Official Records*, XXXIV, Pt. 1, p. 636; Edwards, *Noted Guerrillas*, 270–75.

24 Bradley Papers.

25 Gras-Lauzin Papers.

26 Shreveport *Weekly News*, October 18, December 13, 1864; Hyatt Papers.

27 *Official Records*, XLI, Pt. 3, pp. 574–75.

28 George S. Denison Papers.

29 Chase, *Diary*, 438–39, 444.

30 Emily Reed, *Life of A. P. Dostie*, 101; Bragg, *Louisiana in the Confederacy*, 289.

31 Chase, *Diary*, 439; Bragg, *Louisiana in the Confederacy*, 290.

32 Bragg, *Louisiana in the Confederacy*, 290.

33 Chase, *Diary*, 444; Emily Reed, *Life of A. P. Dostie*, 125, 133–34; Warmoth, *War, Politics and Reconstruction*, 36; Bragg, *Louisiana in the Confederacy*, 290–93.

34 J. Chandler Gregg, *Life in the Army, in the Departments of Virginia, and the Gulf, Including Observations in New Orleans* (Philadelphia, 1866), 138–68.

35 George H. Gordon, *A War Diary of Events In the War of the Great Rebellion, 1863–1865* (Boston, 1882), 306–307.

36 George S. Denison Papers.

37 Whitney Letters.

38 *Ibid.;* Beecher, *Record of the 114th Regiment, N.Y.S.V.*, 361–65; Orton S. Clark, *The One Hundred and Sixteenth Regiment of New York*, 185–87; Van Alstyne, *Diary of an Enlisted Man*, 333; *Complete History of the 46th Illinois Veteran Volunteer Infantry* (Freeport, Ill., 1866), 68;

Irwin, *History of the Nineteenth Army Corps,* 348–49, 351–54; *Official Records,* XXXIV, Pt. 4, p. 528, XLI, Pt. 2, pp. 17–18, LIII, 605; Ewer, *The Third Massachusetts Cavalry,* 188–90; Smith, *Leaves from a Soldier's Diary,* 125.

39 *Official Records,* XLI, Pt. 2, pp. 228, 229, XXXIV, Pt. 1, p. 33, LIII, 605; George S. Denison Papers, III.
40 George S. Denison Papers, III.
41 New Orleans *Tribune,* August 2, 1864.
42 *Official Records,* XLI, Pt. 3, p. 880.
43 New Orleans *Times,* October 29, 1864.
44 Edwards, *Noted Guerrillas,* 270–80; Crandall and Newell, *History of the Ram Fleet,* 385; *Official Records,* XXXIV, Pt. 4, p. 636, XLI, Pt. 1, pp. 294–95.
45 *Official Records,* XXXIV, Pt. 4, p. 688.
46 Knox, *Camp-Fire and Cotton-Field,* 449.
47 *Official Records,* XLI, Pt. 1, pp. 122, 215–17, 274–75, 803, 881, Pt. 2, pp. 567, 582, 599, 780–81, Pt. 3, p. 402, XLVIII, Pt. 1, pp. 442–43, 703–704, 707–709.
48 Ellis Family Collection, 1863–1865; *Official Records,* XLI, Pt. 1, p. 981; Smith, *Leaves from a Soldier's Diary,* 129–31; Marchand, *Flight of a Century,* 162–63.
49 Knox, *Camp-Fire and Cotton-Field,* 365; William H. Chenery, *The Fourteenth Regiment Rhode Island Heavy Artillery (Colored,) In the War to Preserve the Union, 1861–1865* (Providence, R.I., 1898), 114; Gregg, *Life in the Army,* 206.
50 Williamson and Goodman (eds.), *Eastern Louisiana,* I, 272–74.
51 New Orleans *Times,* September 21, 1864.
52 *Ibid.,* September 7, 28, October 20, 24, December 7, 1864.
53 New Orleans *Tribune,* October, November, 1864.
54 New Orleans *Times,* October 29, 1864.

CHAPTER XXIV

Eventide

1 Hyatt Papers.
2 Blessington, *The Campaigns of Walker's Texas Division,* 288–89.
3 Pitts Diary.
4 New Orleans *Times,* January 30, 1865; Gregg, *Life in the Army,* 226; New Orleans *Tribune,* March 14, May 25, 1865.
5 Emily Reed, *Life of A. P. Dostie,* 156–59, 161; David W. Reed, *Campaigns and Battles of the Twelfth Regiment Iowa,* 225–26; New Orleans *Tribune,* March 15, May 21, 1865.

6   Chase, *Diary*, 456–57; Emily Reed, *Life of A. P. Dostie*, 181–83.
7   *Official Records*, XLVIII, Pt. 1, pp. 1174–76.
8   Emily Reed, *Life of A. P. Dostie*, 184–93.
9   *Official Records*, XLVIII, Pt. 1, pp. 400–401, 530, 553, 727, 1360, 1364–65, LIII, 1043.
10 Shreveport *Semi-Weekly News*, March 18, April 1, 1865; *Official Records*, XLVIII, Pt. 1, p. 1443.
11 *Official Records*, XLVIII, Pt. 1, pp. 1056, 1311, 1381, 1409–10, 1414–15, 1423, 1436, 1445.
12 Shreveport *Semi-Weekly News*, April 1, 1865.
13 *Official Records*, XLVIII, Pt. 1, p. 720; Opelousas *Courier*, March 11, 1865; Bragg, *Louisiana In the Confederacy*, 227–35.
14 Shreveport *Semi-Weekly News*, April 1, 1865.
15 *Official Records*, XLVIII, Pt. 1, pp. 774–75, 1146–48; New Orleans *Times*, February 10, 1865; New Orleans *Tribune*, March 18, 1865.
16 Good Hope Plantation Collection.
17 Alexander F. Pugh Family Papers.
18 *Official Records*, XLVIII, Pt. 1, pp. 831, 1445.
19 *Ibid.*, 38–39, 54–62, 65–68, 76–77, 80–84, 106–107, 112–15, 146, 168–69, 175–77, 238–39, 241–48, 626–27, 690–91, 710, 740, 831, 869, 927, Pt. 2, p. 63.
20 *Official Records*, XLVIII, Pt. 1, pp. 100–102, 787, 984–85, 1190.
21 *Ibid.*, 68–72, 108, 471–72, 665–66, 805–806, 1085–86, 1099, 1129, 1206–1207.
22 *Ibid.*, 721, 1321, 1337–38; Hall, *The Story of the 26th Louisiana*, 125; Blessington, *The Campaigns of Walker's Texas Division*, 291–99; Bragg, *Louisiana in the Confederacy*, 298.
23 *Official Records*, XLVIII, Pt. 1, pp. 1406, 1411–12.
24 John A. Cawthon (ed.), "Letters of a North Louisiana Private To His Wife, 1862–1865," *Mississippi Valley Historical Review*, XXX (March, 1944), 544–45.
25 *Official Records*, XLVIII, Pt. 1, pp. 625, 721.
26 Gras-Lauzin Papers.
27 *Official Records*, XLVIII, Pt. 1, pp. 1197, 1409, 1422, 1430–31; Hyatt Papers.
28 *Official Records*, XLVIII, Pt. 1, pp. 455, 1062–63, 1359, 1385–86, 1450.
29 *Official Records*, LIII, 605–609; George S. Denison Papers; David W. Reed, *Campaigns and Battles*, 225–33; Wood, *A History of the Ninety-Fifth Regiment Illinois*, 156–61; Crooke (comp.), *The Twenty-First Regiment of Iowa Volunteer Infantry*, 135–36.

CHAPTER XXV

Surrender

1 Renwick Papers.
2 *Official Records,* XLVIII, Pt. 1, p. 186; Shreveport *Semi-Weekly News,* April 22, 27, 1865; New Orleans *Tribune,* April 20, 1865.
3 Emily Reed, *Life of A. P. Dostie,* 169–70.
4 Gregg, *Life in the Army,* 233; Dawson, *A Confederate Girl's Diary,* 437.
5 Baton Rouge *Gazette and Comet,* April 22, 1865.
6 *Official Records,* XLVIII, Pt. 2, pp. 400, 1284.
7 Noll, *General Kirby-Smith,* 258.
8 Mrs. Thomas H. Morris and Mrs. Mary W. Sibley Papers.
9 Shreveport *Semi-Weekly News,* May 4, 1865; Tunnard, *A Southern Record,* 335.
10 *Navy Records,* XXII, 141–70; *Official Records,* XLVIII, Pt. 1, pp. 203–206, Pt. 2, pp. 169, 171–72, 204; Scharf, *History of the Confederate States Navy,* 364–67; Shreveport *Semi-Weekly News,* May 6, 1865; New Orleans *Tribune,* April 25, 1865.
11 *Official Records,* XLVIII, Pt. 1, pp. 186–93.
12 Moore Papers.
13 Dorsey, *Recollections of Henry Watkins Allen,* 290, 294–95.
14 Tunnard, *A Southern Record,* 335–37.
15 *Ibid.,* 337–38; Dorsey, *Recollections of Henry Watkins Allen,* 295.
16 Small, *Memories of the Civil War,* 10–11.
17 *Official Records,* XLVIII, Pt. 1, pp. 193–94, Pt. 2, pp. 1294–95, 1300, 1310; Hall, *The Story of the 26th Louisiana,* 127–37; Blessington, *The Campaigns of Walker's Texas Division,* 306–307; Dorsey, *Recollections of Henry Watkins Allen,* 301; Noll, *General Kirby-Smith,* 260–62.
18 *Official Records,* XLVIII, Pt. 1, pp. 193–94.
19 Dorsey, *Recollections of Henry Watkins Allen,* 301–302.
20 *Official Records,* XLVIII, Pt. 2, pp. 562–63, 591, 600–601, 604.
21 *Ibid.,* 976; Dorsey, *Recollections of Henry Watkins Allen,* 296–300, 302, 307; Noll, *General Kirby-Smith,* 262, 264, 266; Shreveport *Semi-Weekly News,* June 6, 1865; Wallace P. Reed, "Last Forlorn Hope of the Confederacy," *Southern Historical Society Papers,* XXX (1902), 119.
22 *Official Records,* XLVIII, Pt. 2, pp. 475–76, 726, 746; Shreveport *Semi-Weekly News,* June 3, June 6, 1865; *Complete History of the 46th Illinois,* 74–75.
23 Shreveport *Semi-Weekly News,* June 17, 20, 24, 1865.
24 Scharf, *History of the Confederate States Navy,* 529–30; Porter, *The Naval History of the Civil War,* 806.

25 Andrew B. Booth (comp.), *Records of Louisiana Confederate Soldiers and Louisiana Confederate Commands* (New Orleans, 1920), I, 6; A. B. Booth, "Louisiana Confederate Military Records," *Louisiana Historical Quarterly,* IV (July, 1921), 369–418; Shugg, *Origins of Class Struggle in Louisiana,* 191–95.
26 Weeks Papers.

BIBLIOGRAPHY

PRIMARY SOURCES

MANUSCRIPT COLLECTIONS

A. *Department of Archives, Louisiana State University*
  Boyd (David F.) Papers D, Part I, 1854–1924
  Bradley (James Earl, and Family) Papers and Diary, 1862–1865
  Bringier (Louis A., and Family) Papers, 1860 to December 31, 1864
  Butler (Family) Papers, Part III
  Capell (Eli J., and Family) Papers, 1840–1886
  Chadbourne (D. S.) Letters, 1862–1863
  Chambers (Roland) Diary, 1858–1863
  Chickering (Thomas E.) Diary of Forty-First Infantry, Massachusetts Volunteers
  Clarke (Powhatan) Diary, 1862–1863
  Confederate States Army Papers (D), 1863
  Dupuy (Helene) Diary, April 12, 1861—April 13, 1865
  Durnin (John, and James) Papers, 1861–1862
  Ellis (E. John, Thomas C. W., and Family) Collection, 1860–1865
  Flanders (Benjamin F.) Papers, 1827–1865
  Flournoy (Alfred) Papers, 1824–1935
  Garland (J. D.) Collection, 1863–1870
  Gay (Edward, and Family) Papers, 1834–1892
  Good Hope Plantation Collection, 1846–1866
  Gras-Lauzin (Family) Papers, 1860–1865
  Guess (George W.) Letters to Mrs. Sarah Horton Cockrell
  Guion (Lewis) Diary, 1862–1863
  Gurley (John W.) Papers, 1858–1866
  Hardin (J. Fair) Collection
  Harding (Miss Sidney) Diaries, 1863–1864, 2 vols.

Hawkes (John) Letters, 1863
Hinckley (Orramel, and Family) Papers, 1861–1865
Hyatt (Arthur W.) Papers and Diaries, 1861–1865
Jerrard (Simon G.) Papers
Johnson (Charles James) Papers, 1860–1862
Knox (J. P., and Family) Papers, 1851–1867
Koch (Christian D., and Family) Collection, 1850–1864
Lauve (Gustave) Letter, 1863
Lea (Lemanda E.) Papers, 1861–1864
Leblanc (Family) Papers (Record Book) 1859–1866
Liddell (Moses, St. John R., and Family) Papers, 1861–1865
Lowry (K. B.) Notice, 1862
Markham (Thomas R.) Papers, 1847–1940
Marston (Henry, and Family) Papers, two diaries, 1864
Mathews (Charles L., and Family) Papers, 1860–1865
Mercer (William N.) Papers
Miangolarra (Juan) Papers
Miller (Alexander R.) Diary, 1861–1864
Minor (William J., and Family) Papers
Moncure (John C.) Papers, 1861–1877
Moore (Thomas O.) Papers, 1832–1877
Morris (Mrs. Thomas H., and Sibley, Mrs. Mary W.) Papers
Newell (Robert A.) Papers, 1861–1864
Nicholson (William) Papers, 1861
Palfrey (William T.) Papers, Plantation Diary, 1860–1865
Pitts (Florison D.) Diary, microfilm
Prudhomme (Family) Papers, 1836–1868
Pugh (Alexander F., and Family) Collection, 1861–1865
Pugh (Richard L.) Papers, 1844–1896
Randolph (John H.) Papers, 1860–1865
Renwick (W. P., and Joseph) Papers, 1864–1865
Reynes (Joseph, and Family) Collection, 1862–1864
Robinson (Harai) Papers, 1861–1889
Roy (John) Diary, 1860–1862
Russell (Will) Letter, 1864
Sanders (Jared Y., and Family) Papers, 1860–1865
Shute (Mrs. James D.) Record Book, 1863
Sibley (Mrs. Mary W., and Morris, Mrs. Thomas H.) Papers
Solomon (Clara E.) Diary, 1861–1862 (Typed copy, Louisiana Room,
    Louisiana State University Library)
Spears (Ann E.) Papers, 1861–1864
Taber (Frederick R.) Papers, 1861–1862
Tabor (Hudson, and Family) Papers, 1862
Thomason (Mathew D.) Diary, 1861–1863

United States Army Collection (C), 1863–1896
Vidal (Joseph) Papers
Vinet (John B.) Papers, 1861–1900
Weeks (David, and Family) Papers, 1861–1865
West Feliciana Parish Military Board Minute Book, 1862–1863
White (Silas T.) Papers, 1861–1862
Whitney (William H.) Letters, 1863–1864

B. *Manuscript Division, Library of Congress*
Butler (Benjamin F.) Papers
Denison (George S.) Papers
Porter (David Dixon) Papers, 1842–1864
Porter (David Dixon), "Private Journal of Occurrences During the Great
War of the Rebellion, 1860–1865"
Sherman (William T.) Papers, 1837–1867

C. *War Records Division, National Archives (U.S. Records)*
Department of the Gulf, General Benjamin F. Butler, Book No. 1.
Department of the Gulf, Major General N. P. Banks, Book No. 4, Letters
Sent.
Department of the Gulf, Records of the War Department, Vols. V, VII,
CXCI, Letters Sent.
Department of the Gulf, Butler, Banks, Hurlbut, Banks, Canby, March,
1862—July, 1865, Letters Received.
Department of the Gulf, Special and General Orders.
Department of the Gulf, Civil Affairs.
Department of the Gulf, Board of Prison Inspectors, Proceedings of
Board, January, 1863 to May, 1863.
Department of the Gulf, General Recruiting Service, Letters Sent, Septem-
ber, 1864 to February, 1865.
Department of the Gulf, Sequestration Commission, Letters Sent, Novem-
ber, 1862 to June, 1865.
Department of the Gulf, Prisoners Commission, Proceedings and Docket,
Letters Sent, June, 1864 to October, 1864.
Department of the Gulf, Records of the Inspector General, Inspection
Reports, Books Nos. 40, 43, Letters Sent, November, 1862 to July, 1865.
Department of the Gulf, Cavalry Camp Instructions, Greenville and
Kenner, Louisiana, Letters Sent, 1865–1866.
Department of the Gulf, Chief Signal Officer, Letters Sent, Letters
Received.
Department of the Gulf, Records of the Provost Marshal General, State
of Louisiana, Letters Sent, Letters Received, Property Confiscated,
Seizures, January, 1863 to December, 1865.

Department of the Gulf, Provost Court, Docket, June, 1863 to November, 1863.

Department of the Gulf, Provost Sheriff, Prisoners Received, Prison Affairs, Letters Sent, January, 1864—May, 1865.

Department of the Gulf, Defenses of New Orleans, Letters Sent, January 10, 1863 to February 11, 1865.

Department of the Gulf, U.S. Colored Troops and Forces, Morganza, Special and General Orders, Circulars, Letters, and Telegrams Sent, 1864.

Department of the Gulf, 1st Division, U.S. Colored Troops, Letters Sent, November, 1863 to May, 1864.

Department of the Gulf, Parish of Orleans, Provost Marshal, Letters Sent, Letters Received, February, 1863 to July, 1865.

Department of the Gulf, Chief of Police, New Orleans, Letters Sent, October, 1863 to June, 1865.

Department of the Gulf, Parish of Orleans, Board of Enrollment, Recruiting Depot, Letters Sent.

Department of the Gulf, U.S. Forces, New Orleans and Algiers, Letters Sent, Letters Received, September, 1862—July, 1864.

District of Baton Rouge and Port Hudson, Records, August, 1864—February, 1865.

District of Northeastern Louisiana, Letters Sent, August, 1863—September, 1865.

Military Division of West Mississippi, Records of the Provost Marshal General, Letters Sent, Letters Received, July, 1864—June, 1865, Statements August, 1864—April, 1865.

Military Division of West Mississippi, Records of the Inspector General.

Military Division of West Mississippi, Agent of Exchange, Letters Sent, March, 1865—June, 1865, Letters Received, April, 1865—May, 1865.

Military Division of West Mississippi, Commissary of Prisoners, Letters Received, August, 1864—June, 1865, Letters Sent, March, 1865—June, 1865.

Northern Division of Louisiana, Letters Sent, Letters Received, February, 1865—June, 1865.

Post of U.S. Forces, Port Hudson, Louisiana, Corps D'Afrique & U.S. Colored Troops, July, 1863—December, 1864.

Records of the War Department, Department of Tennessee, Letters Sent, Vol. I.

Right Wing Before Port Hudson, C. Grover, June 18th to July 10th, 1863.

Southern Division of Louisiana, Letters Sent, Letters Received, February, 1865—July, 1865.

U.S. Forces, Baton Rouge, 1st Division, D.G., 19th Army Corps, C. C. Augur, Inspection Records, Letters Sent, Letters Received, January, 1865—February, 1865.

War Department Records, Department of the Gulf, Book No. 15, Special Field Orders, October, 1862 to August, 1863.

War Department Records, Department of the Gulf, Book No. 26, General and Special Orders, February 26, 1862 to June 18, 1862.

War Department Records, Department of the Gulf, Books No. 27–28, Special Orders.

War Department Records, Department and Army of the Tennessee, General Orders, 1863, Book No. 924, Printed Orders.

War Department Collection of Confederate Records

Chapter I, Vol. CXIII, Partisan Rangers (Confederate Cavalry), Louisiana.

Chapter II, Vol. VIII, Military Departments, Letters Sent, Port Hudson, Louisiana, 1862–1863.

Chapter II, Vol. LXX, Military Departments, Letters Sent, Department of the Trans-Mississippi, March, 1863—January, 1864.

Chapter II, Vols. LXXV, LXXVI, Letters Sent, R. Taylor, District of Western Louisiana, January 13 to February 13, 1864.

Chapter II, Vols. LXXX–LXXXI, Military Departments, General and Special Orders, Department of the Trans-Mississippi, January, 1864—May, 1865.

Chapter II, Vol. CXCVIII, Gardner, General, Port Hudson, Louisiana, General and Special Orders, January, 1862 to July, 1863.

Chapter VIII, Vol. CXXXII, Executive Journal, February, 1860 to May 20, 1865.

Chapter VIII, Vol. CXXXIV, Account Book, 1864, Contracts Between the Governor of Louisiana and Others to Furnish Provisions, Cotton Cards &c

Chapter VIII, Vol. CXXXVIII, Scrap Book, Louisiana Troops, 1862, Military Orders of the Governor of Louisiana.

Chapter VIII, Vol. CXL, CXLI, Executive Communications, Louisiana, Letters Sent by the Major-General of Militia, 1854–1864.

Chapter VIII, Vol. CXLII, Executive Communications, Letters Received, 1st Division, Louisiana State Troops, 1861.

Chapter VIII, Vols. CXLIII–CXLIV, Executive Communications, Louisiana State Troops, November, 1861 to April, 1862, Letters Received.

Chapter VIII, Vol. CLI (C), Special Orders, 1st Division, Louisiana State Troops, January—December, 1861.

Chapter VIII, Vols. CLII–CLIV, Special Orders, Louisiana State Troops, December, 1862.

Chapter VIII, Vol. CLXVI, Returns of Troops, Louisiana State Troops.

Gardner, Frank G., General, Letter Book.

NEWSPAPERS

Alexandria *Constitutional*
Baton Rouge *Daily Advocate*
Baton Rouge *Gazette and Comet*
Baton Rouge *Weekly Advocate*
Baton Rouge *Weekly Gazette and Comet*
Bayou Sara *Ledger*
False River *Pointe Coupee Democrat*
Natchitoches *Union*
New Orleans *Bee*
New Orleans *Commercial Bulletin*
New Orleans *Daily Crescent*
New Orleans *Daily Delta*
New Orleans *Daily Picayune*
New Orleans *Daily True Delta*
New Orleans *Price Current*
New Orleans *Sunday Delta*
New Orleans *Times*
New Orleans *Tribune*
New Orleans *Weekly Crescent*
New Orleans *Weekly Delta*
Opelousas *Courier (Le Courrier des Opelousas)*
Opelousas *Patriot*
Plaquemine *Gazette and Sentinel*
Shreveport *Daily News*
Shreveport *News*
Shreveport *Semi-Weekly News*
Shreveport *Weekly News*
West Baton Rouge *Sugar Planter*

PUBLISHED PUBLIC RECORDS, UNITED STATES, CONFEDERATE, LOUISIANA

Acts Passed by the Fifth Legislature of the State of Louisiana, Second Session, 1861. Baton Rouge: 1861.

Acts Passed by the Sixth Legislature of the State of Louisiana, First Session, 1861–1862. Baton Rouge: 1862.

Acts Passed by the Sixth Legislature of the State of Louisiana, Extra Session, Shreveport, May 4, 1863. New Orleans: 1897. (Reprint.)

Acts Passed by the Twenty-Seventh Legislature of the State of Louisiana, Extra Session, Opelousas, December, 1862, January, 1863. Natchitoches, La.: 1864. (Reprint.)

Correspondence Between the War Department and General Lovell Relating to the Defences of New Orleans Submitted in Response to a Resolution of the House of Representatives Passed Third February, 1863. Richmond: 1863.

Documents of the First Session of the Fifth Legislature of the State of Louisiana, 1860. Baton Rouge: 1861.

Documents of the Second Session of the Fifth Legislature of the State of Louisiana, 1861. Baton Rouge: 1861.

Documents of the First Session of the Sixth Legislature of the State of Louisiana, 1862. Baton Rouge: 1862.

General Orders from Headquarters, Department of the Gulf, Issued by Major-General B. F. Butler from May 1st, 1862 to the Present Time. New Orleans: 1862.

Official Journal of the Proceedings of the Convention of the State of Louisiana, 1861. New Orleans: 1861.

Official Records of the Union and Confederate Navies in the War of the Rebellion. 31 vols. Washington: 1894–1922.

Official Report Relative to the Conduct of Federal Troops in Western Louisiana, During the Invasions of 1863 and 1864, Compiled from Sworn Testimony, Under Direction of Governor Henry W. Allen. Shreveport: 1865.

Official Reports of Battles (Confederate). Richmond: 1862.

Proceedings of the Louisiana State Convention, Together With the Ordinances Passed by Said Convention and the Constitution of the State as Amended. New Orleans: 1861.

U.S. Census Office. 8th. Census, 1860. *Agriculture of the United States in 1860*. Under the Direction of the Secretary of the Interior by Joseph C. G. Kennedy, Superintendent of Census. Washington: 1864.

U.S. Census Office. 8th. Census, 1860. *Manufactures of the United States in 1860*. Under the Direction of the Secretary of the Interior. Washington: 1865.

U.S. Census Office. 8th. Census, 1860. *Population of the United States in 1860*. Under the Direction of the Secretary of the Interior by Joseph C. G. Kennedy, Superintendent of Census. Washington: 1864.

U.S. Census Office. 8th. Census, 1860. *Statistics of the United States, (Including Mortality, Property, &c.,) in 1860*. Under the Direction of the Secretary of the Interior. Washington: 1866.

U.S. Congress. Joint Committee on the Conduct of the War. *Report of the Joint Committee on the Conduct of the War at the Second Session Thirty-Eighth Congress*. 3 vols. Washington: 1865.

The War of the Rebellion: A Compilation of the Official Records of the Union and Confederate Armies. 128 vols. Washington: 1880–1901.

DIARIES, MEMOIRS, LETTERS, REGIMENTAL HISTORIES,
AND OTHER PRIMARY SOURCES

PRIMARY BOOKS

The American Annual Cyclopaedia and Register of Important Events of the Year 1861. New York: 1862.

Anderson, Ephraim McD. *Memoirs: Historical and Personal; Including the Campaigns of the First Missouri Confederate Brigade.* St. Louis: 1868.

Anderson, John Q. (ed.). *Brokenburn, the Journal of Kate Stone, 1861–1868.* Baton Rouge: 1955.

Babcock, Willoughby M. *Selections from the Letters and Diaries of Brevet-Brigadier General Willoughby Babcock of the Seventy-Fifth New York Volunteers: A Study of Camp Life in the Union Armies During the Civil War.* n.p.: 1922.

Bacon, Edward. *Among the Cotton Thieves.* Detroit: 1867.

Barber, Lucius W. *Army Memoirs of Lucius W. Barber, Company "D," 15th Illinois Volunteer Infantry.* Chicago: 1894.

Barney, C. *Recollections of Field Service With the Twentieth Iowa Infantry Volunteers.* Davenport, Iowa: 1865.

Bartlett, Napier. *A Soldier's Story of the War; Including the Marches and Battles of the Washington Artillery and of Other Louisiana Troops.* New Orleans: 1874.

———— (ed.). *Military Record of Louisiana Including Biographical and Historical Papers Relating to the Military Organizations of the State.* New Orleans: 1875.

Barton, Thomas H. *Autobiography of Dr. Thomas H. Barton, the Self-Made Physician of Syracuse, Ohio, Including a History of the Fourth Regt. West Va. Vol. Inf'y, With an Account of Col. Lightburn's Retreat Down the Kanawha Valley, Gen. Grant's Vicksburg and Chattanooga Campaigns, Together With the Several Battles in Which the Fourth Regiment was Engaged, and Its Losses by Disease, Desertion and in Battle.* Charleston, W. Va.: 1890.

Battle-Fields of the South, from Bull Run to Fredericksburgh; With Sketches of Confederate Commanders, and Gossip of the Camps. New York: 1864.

Battles and Leaders of the Civil War, ed. R. U. Johnson and C. C. Buel. 4 vols. New York: 1887–88.

Beecher, Harris H. *Record of the 114th Regiment, N.Y.S.V. Where it Went, What it Saw, and What it Did.* n.p.: n.d.

Beers, Fannie A. *Memories. A Record of Personal Experience and Adventure During Four Years of War.* Philadelphia: 1888.

Belknap, George E. (ed.). *Letters of Capt. Geo. Hamilton Perkins.* Concord, N.H.: 1886.

Bentley, W. H. *History of the 77th Illinois Volunteer Infantry, Sept. 2, 1862—July 10, 1865.* Peoria, Ill.: 1883.

Bering, John A., and Montgomery, Thomas. *History of the Forty-Eighth Ohio Vet. Vol. Inf.* Hillsboro, Ohio: 1880.

Blessington, J. P. *The Campaigns of Walker's Texas Division.* New York: 1875.

Boggs, Wm. R. *Military Reminiscences of Gen. Wm. R. Boggs, C.S.A.* Durham, N.C.: 1913.

Booth, Andrew B. (comp.). *Records of Louisiana Confederate Soldiers and Louisiana Confederate Commands.* 3 vols. New Orleans: 1920.

Booth, B. F. *Dark Days of the Rebellion, or, Life in Southern Military Prisons Giving a Correct and Thrilling History of Unparalleled Suffering, Narrow Escapes, Heroic Encounters, Bold Achievements, Cold Blooded Murders, Severe Tests of Loyalty, and Patriotism.* Indianola, Iowa: 1897.

Bosson, Charles P. *History of the Forty-Second Regiment Infantry, Massachusetts Volunteers, 1862, 1863, 1864.* Boston: 1886.

Brown, Alonzo L. *History of the Fourth Regiment of Minnesota Infantry Volunteers During the Great Rebellion 1861–1865.* St. Paul: 1892.

Browne, Junius Henri. *Four Years in Secessia: Adventures Within and Beyond the Union Lines: Embracing a Great Variety of Facts, Incidents, and Romance of the War,* Hartford, Conn.: 1865.

Bryner, Cloyd. *Bugle Echoes: The Story of Illinois 47th.* Springfield, Ill.: 1905.

Burdette, Robert J. *The Drums of the 47th.* Indianapolis: 1914.

Butler, Benjamin F. *Autobiography and Personal Reminiscences of Major-General Benj. F. Butler; Butler's Book.* Boston: 1892.

———. *Private and Official Correspondence of Gen. Benjamin F. Butler During the Period of the Civil War.* 5 vols. Norwood, Mass.: 1917.

Byers, S. H. M. *Iowa in War Times.* Des Moines: 1888.

Calvert, Henry Murray. *Reminiscences of a Boy in Blue, 1862–1865.* New York: 1920.

Carpenter, George N. *History of the Eighth Regiment Vermont Volunteers, 1861–1865.* Boston: 1886.

Carter, Howell. *A Cavalryman's Reminiscences of the Civil War.* New Orleans: 1900.

Chase, Salmon Portland. *Diary and Correspondence of Salmon P. Chase,* in *American Historical Association Annual Report . . . for the Year 1902.* Vol. II, 11–527. Washington: 1903.

Chenery, William H. *The Fourteenth Regiment Rhode Island Heavy Artillery (Colored,) in the War to Preserve the Union, 1861–1865.* Providence: 1898.

Clare, Mrs. Josephine. *Narrative of the Adventures and Experiences of Mrs. Josephine Clare, a Resident of the South at the Breaking Out of the Rebellion, Her Final Escape from Natchitoches, La., and Safe Arrival at Home, in Marietta, Pa.* Lancaster, Pa.: 1865.

Clark, James S. *Life in the Middle West*. Chicago: 1915.

Clark, Orton S. *The One Hundred and Sixteenth Regiment of New York State Volunteers: Being a Complete History of its Organization and of its Nearly Three Years Active Service in the Great Rebellion*. Buffalo: 1868.

Clarke, H. C. (comp.). *The Confederate States Almanac and Repository of Useful Knowledge for 1862*. Vicksburg: 1862.

Cogley, Thomas S. *History of the Seventh Indiana Cavalry Volunteers*. Laporte, Ind.: 1876.

Complete History of the 46th Illinois Veteran Volunteer Infantry, from the Date of Its Organization in 1861, to Its Final Discharge, February 1st, 1866 Containing a Full and Authentic Account of the Participation of the Regiment in the Battles, Sieges, Skirmishes and Expeditions in Which it Has Been Engaged, Together with a Complete Roster of the Regiment, Showing the Promotions, Commissioned and Non-Commissioned, Deaths, Discharges and Desertions. Freeport, Ill.: 1866.

Corsan, W. C. *Two Months in the Confederate States, Including a Visit to New Orleans Under the Domination of General Butler*. London: 1863.

Crandall, Warren D., and Newell, Isaac D. *History of the Ram Fleet and the Mississippi Marine Brigade in the War for the Union on the Mississippi and its Tributaries. The Story of the Ellets and Their Men*. St. Louis: 1907.

Crooke, George (comp.), *The Twenty-First Regiment of Iowa Volunteer Infantry. A Narrative of its Experience in Active Service, Including a Military Record of Each Officer, Non-Commissioned Officer, and Private Soldier of the Organization*. Milwaukee: 1891.

Crummer, Wilbur Fisk. *With Grant at Fort Donelson, Shiloh and Vicksburg, and an Appreciation of General U. S. Grant*. Oak Park, Ill.: 1915.

Dana, Charles A. *Recollections of the Civil War*. New York: 1902.

Davis, Jefferson. *The Rise and Fall of the Confederate Government*. 2 vols. New York: 1881.

Dawson, Sarah Morgan. *A Confederate Girl's Diary*. Boston: 1913.

De Forest, John William. *A Volunteer's Adventures*. New Haven: 1946.

DeLeon, T. C. *Four Years in Rebel Capitals*. Mobile: 1892.

Dewey, George. *Autobiography of George Dewey, Admiral of the Navy*. New York: 1913.

Dorsey, Sarah A. *Recollections of Henry Watkins Allen, Brigadier-General Confederate States Army, Ex-Governor of Louisiana*. New Orleans: 1866.

Dow, Neal. *The Reminiscences of Neal Dow*. Portland, Maine: 1898.

Driggs, George W. *Opening of the Mississippi*. Madison: 1864.

Duffy, Edward. *History of the 159th Regiment, N.Y.S.V.* New York: 1890.

Duganne, A. J. H. *Camps and Prisons; Twenty Months in the Department of the Gulf.* New York: 1865.

Ewer, James K. *The Third Massachusetts Cavalry in the War for the Union.* Maplewood, Mass.: 1903.

Experience in the War of the Great Rebellion, by a Soldier of the Eighty-First Regiment Illinois Volunteer Infantry. Carbondale, Ill.: 1880.

Fearn, Frances (ed.). *Diary of a Refugee.* New York: 1910.

Flinn, Frank M. *Campaigning With Banks in Louisiana, '63 and '64, and With Sheridan in the Shenandoah Valley in '64 and '65.* Lynn, Mass.: 1887.

Fowler, William. *Memorials of William Fowler.* New York: 1875.

Fremantle, Arthur J. L. *Three Months in the Southern States: April—June, 1863.* New York: 1864.

Gardner, Charles (ed.). *Gardner's New Orleans Directory for 1861 Including Jefferson City, Gretna, Carrollton, Algiers and McDonogh.* New Orleans: 1861.

Goodloe, Albert Theodore. *Some Rebel Relics from the Seat of War.* Nashville, Tenn.: 1893.

Gordon, George H. *A War Diary of Events in the War of the Great Rebellion, 1863–1865.* Boston: 1882.

Gould, John M. *History of the First-Tenth-Twenty-ninth Maine Regiment.* Portland, Maine: 1871.

Grant, U. S. *Personal Memoirs of U. S. Grant.* Cleveland: 1952.

Greene, John W. *Camp Ford Prison; and How I Escaped.* Toledo: 1893.

Gregg, J. Chandler. *Life in the Army, in the Departments of Virginia, and the Gulf, Including Observations in New Orleans, With an Account of the Author's Life and Experience in the Ministry.* Philadelphia: 1866.

Hall, Winchester. *The Story of the 26th Louisiana Infantry, in the Service of the Confederate States.* n.p., n.d.

Harris, D. W. and Hulse, B. M. (comps.). *The History of Claiborne Parish, Louisiana.* New Orleans: 1886.

Heartsill, W. W. *Fourteen Hundred and 91 Days in the Confederate Army.* Jackson, Tenn.: 1954.

Hepworth, George H. *The Whip, Hoe, and Sword; or, the Gulf-Department in '63.* Boston: 1864.

Hills, Alfred C. *Macpherson, the Confederate Philosopher.* New York: 1864.

History of the Fifteenth Regiment, Iowa Veteran Volunteer Infantry, from October, 1861, to August, 1865, when Disbanded at End of the War. Keokuk: 1887.

Hoffman, Wickham. *Camp, Court and Siege.* New York: 1877.

Holbrook, Wm. C. *A Narrative of the Services of the Officers and Enlisted Men of the 7th Regiment of Vermont Volunteers (Veterans), From 1862 to 1866.* New York: 1882.

Homans, John. "The Red River Expedition," in *The Mississippi Valley, Tennessee, Georgia, Alabama, 1861–1864. Papers of The Military Historical Society of Massachusetts*. Vol. VIII. Boston: 1910.

Hosmer, James K. *The Color-Guard: Being a Corporal's Notes of Military Service in the Nineteenth Army Corps*. Boston: 1864.

Howard, R. L. *History of the 124th Regiment Illinois Infantry Volunteers, Otherwise Known as the "Hundred And Two Dozen," From August, 1862, to August, 1865*. Springfield, Ill.: 1880.

Howe, M. A. DeWolfe (ed.). *Home Letters of General Sherman*. New York: 1909.

Irwin, Richard B. *History of the Nineteenth Army Corps*. New York: 1892.

Jackson, Oscar L. *The Colonel's Diary, Journals Kept Before and During the Civil War by the Late Colonel Oscar L. Jackson of New Castle, Pennsylvania, Sometime Commander of the 63rd Regiment O.V.I.*, ed. David P. Jackson. n.p.: 1922.

Johns, Henry T. *Life With the Forty-Ninth Massachusetts Volunteers*. Washington: 1890.

Johnson, Charles B. *Muskets and Medicine or Army Life in the Sixties*. Philadelphia: 1917.

Jones, Jenkin Lloyd. *An Artilleryman's Diary*. Madison: 1914.

Jones, S. C. *Reminiscences of the Twenty-Second Iowa Volunteer Infantry, Giving its Organization, Marches, Skirmishes, Battles, and Sieges, as Taken from the Diary of Lieutenant S. C. Jones of Company A*. Iowa City, Iowa: 1907.

Kellogg, J. J. *War Experiences and the Story of the Vicksburg Campaign from "Milliken's Bend" to July 4, 1863, Being an Accurate and Graphic Account of Campaign Events Taken from the Diary of Capt J.J. Kellogg of Co. B., 113th Illinois Volunteer Infantry*. n.p.: 1913.

Kirwan, A. D. (ed.). *Johnny Green of the Orphan Brigade, The Journal of a Confederate Soldier*. Lexington, Ky.: 1956.

Knox, Thomas W. *Camp-Fire and Cotton-Field: Southern Adventure in Time of War*. New York: 1865.

Lester, W. W., and Bromwell, William J. *A Digest of the Military and Naval Laws of the Confederate States, from the Commencement of the Provisional Congress to the End of the First Congress Under the Permanent Constitution*. Columbia, S.C.: 1864.

Lufkin, Edwin B. *History of the Thirteenth Maine Regiment from Its Organization in 1861 to Its Muster-Out in 1865*. Bridgton, Maine: 1898.

McGregor, Charles. *History of the Fifteenth Regiment New Hampshire Volunteers 1862–1863*. Concord, N.H.: 1900.

McHatton-Ripley, Eliza. *From Flag to Flag; A Woman's Adventures and Experiences in the South During the War, in Mexico, and in Cuba*. New York: 1889.

————. *Social Life in Old New Orleans, Being Recollections of My Girlhood.* New York: 1912.

McMorries, Edward Y. *History of the First Regiment Alabama Volunteer Infantry C.S.A.* Montgomery, Ala.: 1904.

Marshall, Albert O. *Army Life; From a Soldier's Journal.* Joliet, Ill.: 1884.

Marshall, T. B. *History of the Eighty-Third Ohio Volunteer Infantry, The Greyhound Regiment.* Cincinnati: 1912.

Mason, F. H. *The Forty-Second Ohio Infantry: A History of the Organization and Services of that Regiment in the War of the Rebellion.* Cleveland: 1876.

A Memorial of Lt. Daniel Perkins Dewey, of the Twenty-Fifth Regiment Connecticut Volunteers. (His Letters.) Hartford, Conn.: 1864.

Merrick, Caroline E. *Old Times in Dixie Land, A Southern Matron's Memories.* New York: 1901.

Moore, Frank (ed.). *The Rebellion Record: A Diary of American Events With Documents, Narratives, Illustrative Incidents, Poetry, etc.* 10 Vols. New York: 1864–1868.

Moors, J. F. *History of the Fifty-Second Regiment Massachusetts Volunteers.* Boston: 1893.

Morgan, James Morris. *Recollections of a Rebel Reefer.* Boston: 1917.

Morris, Gouverneur. *The History of a Volunteer Regiment.* New York: 1891.

Murray, Thomas Hamilton. *History of the Ninth Regiment, Connecticut Volunteer Infantry, "The Irish Regiment" In the War of the Rebellion, 1861–65.* New Haven: 1903.

Nevins, Allan, and Thomas, Milton Halsey. *The Diary of George Templeton Strong.* 4 vols. New York: 1952.

Newsome, Edmund. *Experience in the War of the Great Rebellion.* Carbondale, Ill.: 1879.

Noel, Theophilus. *Autobiography and Reminiscences of Theophilus Noel.* Chicago: 1904.

Nott, Charles C. *Sketches in Prison Camps: A Continuation of Sketches of the War.* New York: 1865.

Oldroyd, Osborn H. *A Soldier's Story of the Siege of Vicksburg.* Springfield, Ill.: 1885.

Owen, William Miller. *In Camp and Battle With the Washington Artillery of New Orleans.* Boston: 1885.

Palfrey, Francis Winthrop. *Memoir of William Francis Bartlett.* Boston: 1878.

Palfrey, John C. "Port Hudson," in *The Mississippi Valley, Tennessee, Georgia, Alabama, 1861–1864. Papers of the Military Historical Society of Massachusetts.* Vol. VIII. Boston: 1910.

Parker, Thomas H. *History of the 51st Regiment of P.V. and V.V. from Its Organization, at Camp Curtin, Harrisburg, Pa., in 1861, to Its Be-*

ing Mustered Out of the United States Service at Alexandria, Va., July 27th, 1865. Philadelphia: 1869.

Pellet, Elias P. *History of the 114th Regiment, New York State Volunteers.* Norwich, N.Y.: 1866.

Plummer, Albert. *History of the Forty-Eight Regiment M.V.M. During the Civil War.* Boston: 1907.

Porter, David D. *Incidents and Anecdotes of the Civil War.* New York: 1885.
————. *The Naval History of the Civil War.* New York: 1886.

Porter, Horace. *Campaigning With Grant.* New York: 1897.

Powers, George W. *The Story of the Thirty-Eighth Regiment of Massachusetts Volunteers.* Cambridge, Mass.: 1866.

Preston, Francis W. *Port Hudson: A History of the Investment, Siege and Capture.* Brooklyn: 1892.

The Rebellion: Its Consequences and the Congressional Committee With Their Action. New Orleans: 1866.

Reed, David W. *Campaigns and Battles of the Twelfth Regiment Iowa Veteran Volunteer Infantry from Organization, September, 1861, to Muster-Out, January 20, 1866.* n.p.: 1903.

Reed, Samuel Rockwell. *The Vicksburg Campaign, and the Battles About Chattanooga under the Command of General U.S. Grant, in 1862–1863.* Cincinnati: 1882.

Richardson, Albert D. *The Secret Service, the Field, the Dungeon, and the Escape.* Hartford, Conn.: 1865.

Rouse, E. S. S. *The Bugle Blast; or, Spirit of the Conflict.* Philadelphia: 1864.

Rowland, Kate M. and Croxall, Mrs. Morris L. (eds.). *The Journal of Julia LeGrand, New Orleans 1862–1863.* Richmond, Va.: 1911.

Russell, William H. *My Diary North and South.* Boston: 1863.

Schwartz, Stephan. *Twenty-Two Months a Prisoner of War.* St. Louis: 1892.

Scott, Wm. Forse. *The Story of a Cavalry Regiment: The Career of the Fourth Iowa Veteran Volunteers From Kansas to Georgia, 1861–1865.* New York: 1893.

Shanks, William F. G. *Personal Recollections of Distinguished Generals.* New York: 1866.

Sherman, Andrew M. *In the Lowlands of Louisiana in 1863.* Morristown, N.J.: 1908.

Sherman, William T. *Memoirs of General William T. Sherman.* 2 Vols. New York: 1875.

Small, J. A. *Memories of the Civil War as Experienced by an Old Veteran.* n.p.: n.d.

Smith, George G. *Leaves from a Soldier's Diary.* Putnam, Conn.: 1906.

Smith, Gustavus W. *Confederate War Papers.* New York: 1864.

Southwood, Marion. *"Beauty and Booty," The Watchword of New Orleans.* New York: 1867.

Sprague, Homer B. *History of the 13th Infantry Regiment of Connecticut Volunteers, During the Great Rebellion.* Hartford, Conn.: 1867.

Stanyan, John M. *A History of the Eighth Regiment of New Hampshire Volunteers.* Concord, N.H.: 1892.

Stevens, William B. *History of the Fiftieth Regiment of Infantry Massachusetts Volunteer Militia in the Late War of the Rebellion.* Boston: 1907.

Stevenson, B. F. *Letters from the Army.* Cincinnati: 1884.

Stevenson, Thomas M. *History of the 78th Regiment O.V.V.I., from Its "Muster-In" to Its "Muster-Out."* Zanesville, Ohio: 1865.

The Story of the Fifty-Fifth Regiment Illinois Volunteer Infantry in the Civil War 1861–1865. Clinton, Mass.: 1887.

Taylor, F. Jay (ed.). *Reluctant Rebel; The Secret Diary of Robert Patrick 1861–1865.* Baton Rouge: 1959.

Taylor, Gorham C. *Notes of Conversations With a Volunteer Officer in the United States Navy, on the Passage of the Forts Below New Orleans April 24th, 1862 and other Points of Service on the Mississippi River During that Year.* New York: 1868.

Taylor, Richard. *Destruction and Reconstruction: Personal Experiences of the Late War.* New York: 1879.

Tenney, W. J. *The Military and Naval History of the Rebellion in the United States.* New York: 1866.

Thomas, Benjamin P. (ed.). *Three Years With Grant As Recalled by War Correspondent Sylvanus Cadwallader.* New York: 1955.

Thorndike, Rachel S. (ed.). *The Sherman Letters, Correspondence Between General and Senator Sherman from 1837 to 1891.* New York: 1894.

Throne, Mildred (ed.). *The Civil War Diary of Cyrus F. Boyd, Fifteenth Iowa Infantry 1861–1863.* Iowa City: 1953.

Torrey, Rodney W. *War Diary of Rodney W. Torrey, 1862–1863.* n.p.: n.d.

Townsend, Luther Tracy. *History of the Sixteenth Regiment, New Hampshire Volunteers.* Washington: 1897.

Truesdale, John. *The Blue Coats and How They Lived, Fought and Died for the Union.* Philadelphia: 1867.

Tunnard, W. H. *A Southern Record.* Baton Rouge: 1866.

Van Alstyne, Lawrence. *Diary of an Enlisted Man.* New Haven: 1910.

Velazquez, Loreta Janeta. *The Woman In Battle: A Narrative of the Exploits, Adventures, and Travels of Mudame Loreta Janeta Velazquez, Otherwise Known as Lieutenant Harry T. Buford, Confederate States Army.* Hartford: 1876.

Vilas, William Freeman. *A View of the Vicksburg Campaign.* Madison: 1908.

Warmoth, Henry Clay. *War, Politics and Reconstruction; Stormy Days in Louisiana.* New York: 1930.

Watson, William. *Life in the Confederate Army, Being the Observations and Experiences of an Alien in the South During the American Civil War.* New York: 1888.

Welles, Gideon. *Diary of Gideon Welles, Secretary of the Navy Under Lincoln and Johnson.* 3 Vols. Boston: 1911.

Wiley, Bell Irvin. *"This Infernal War," The Confederate Letters of Sgt. Edwin H. Fay.* Austin, Tex.: 1959.

Wilkie, Franc B. *Pen and Powder.* Boston: 1888.

Willis, Henry A. *Fitchburg in the War of the Rebellion.* Fitchburg, Mass.: 1866.

Wilson, James H. *Under the Old Flag.* New York: 1912.

Wood, Wales W. *A History of the Ninety-Fifth Regiment Illinois Infantry Volunteers, from Its Organization in the Fall of 1862, Until Its Final Discharge from the United States Service, in 1865.* Chicago: 1865.

SECONDARY BOOKS

Anderson, John Q. *A Texas Surgeon in the C.S.A.* Tuscaloosa, Ala.: 1957.

Andrews, J. Cutler. *The North Reports the Civil War.* Pittsburgh: 1955.

Arthur, Stanley C. *Old New Orleans; A History of the Vieux Carré, Its Ancient and Historical Buildings.* New Orleans: 1936.

Asbury, Herbert. *The French Quarter, An Informal History of the New Orleans Underworld.* New York: 1936.

Badeau, Adam. *Military History of Ulysses S. Grant, From April, 1861 to April, 1865.* 3 vols. New York: 1868–1881.

Bankston, Marie Louise Benton. *Camp-Fire Stories of the Mississippi Valley Campaign.* New Orleans: 1914.

Belisle, John G. *History of Sabine Parish, Louisiana.* Many, La.: 1912.

Bland, T. A. *Life of Benjamin F. Butler.* Boston: 1879.

Bonham, Milledge L., Jr. *The British Consuls in the Confederacy.* New York: 1911.

———. "The French Consuls in the Confederate States" in *Studies in Southern History and Politics; Inscribed to William Archibald Dunning. . . .* New York: 1914.

Bradford, Gamaliel. *Union Portraits.* Boston: 1916.

Bragg, Jefferson Davis. *Louisiana in the Confederacy.* Baton Rouge: 1941.

Brawley, Benjamin. *A Short History of the American Negro.* New York: 1919.

Brown, D. Alexander. *Grierson's Raid.* Urbana, Ill.: 1954.

Brown, William Wells, *The Negro in the American Rebellion, His Heroism and His Fidelity.* Boston: 1867.

Caldwell, Stephen A. *A Banking History of Louisiana.* Baton Rouge: 1935.

Caskey, Willie M. *Secession and Restoration of Louisiana.* Baton Rouge: 1938.

Catton, Bruce. *Grant Moves South.* Boston: 1960.

————. *U. S. Grant and the American Military Tradition.* Boston: 1954.

Chambers, Henry E. *A History of Louisiana.* 3 vols. Chicago: 1925.

The City of New Orleans. The Book of the Chamber of Commerce and Industry of Louisiana and Other Public Bodies of the "Crescent City." New Orleans: 1894.

Coulter, E. Merton. *The Confederate States of America, 1861–1865.* Baton Rouge: 1950.

————. *Travels in the Confederate States, A Bibliography.* Norman, Okla.: 1948.

Croffut, W. A., and Morris, John M. *The Military and Civil History of Connecticut During the War of 1861–1865.* New York: 1868.

Curtis, Nathaniel C. *New Orleans: Its Old Houses, Shops, and Public Buildings.* Philadelphia: 1933.

Dabney, Thomas Ewing. *One Hundred Great Years, The Story of the Times-Picayune from Its Founding to 1940.* Baton Rouge: 1944.

Dana, Charles A., and Wilson, J. H. *The Life of Ulysses S. Grant, General of the Armies of the United States.* Springfield, Mass.: 1868.

Dawson, George Francis. *Life and Services of Gen. John A. Logan As Soldier and Statesman.* Chicago and New York: 1887.

Dictionary of American Biography, ed. Dumas Malone. 20 vols. New York: 1928–1936.

Dimitry, John. "Louisiana," *Confederate Military History,* ed. Clement A. Evans. Vol. X. Atlanta: 1899.

Dufour, Charles L. *Gentle Tiger; the Gallant Life of Roberdeau Wheat.* Baton Rouge: 1957.

————. *The Night the War Was Lost.* New York: 1960.

Edwards, John N. *Noted Guerrillas, Or The Warfare of the Border.* . . . St. Louis: 1880.

Eliot, Ellsworth. *West Point in the Confederacy.* New York: 1941.

Farragut, Loyall. *The Life of David Glasgow Farragut, First Admiral of the United States Navy, Embodying His Journal and Letters.* New York: 1879.

Fay, Edwin W. *The History of Education in Louisiana.* Washington: 1898.

Ficklen, John Rose. *History of Reconstruction in Louisiana (Through 1868).* Baltimore: 1910.

Fiske, John. *The Mississippi Valley in the Civil War.* Boston: 1900.

Fleming, Walter Lynwood. *Louisiana State University, 1860–1896.* Baton Rouge: 1898.

Fortier, Alcée. *A History of Louisiana.* 4 vols. New York: 1904.

———— (ed.). *Louisiana.* 2 vols. Atlanta: 1909.

Fuller, J. F. C. *The Generalship of Ulysses S. Grant.* London: 1929.

Gayarré, Charles. *History of Louisiana.* 4 vols. New York: 1854–1866.

Gosnell, H. Allen. *Guns on the Western Waters, The Story of River Gunboats in the Civil War.* Baton Rouge: 1949.

Greene, Francis Vinton. *The Mississippi*. New York: 1882.

Hardin, J. Fair. *Northwestern Louisiana, A History of the Watershed of the Red River 1714–1937*. 3 vols. Louisville: [1939].

Harrington, Fred H. *Fighting Politician: Major General N. P. Banks*. Philadelphia: 1948.

Heyman, Max L., Jr. *Prudent Soldier, A Biography of Major General E. R. S. Canby*. Glendale, Calif.: 1959.

Historical Sketch Book and Guide to New Orleans and Environs. New York: 1885.

Holzman, Robert S. *Stormy Ben Butler*. New York: 1954.

Howe, J. Ed. "Progressive History of Bossier Parish, 1843 to 1950," bound with McLure and Howe (eds.), *History of Shreveport and Shreveport Builders,* II [*infra*].

Johnson, Ludwell H. *Red River Campaign, Politics and Cotton in the Civil War*. Baltimore: 1958.

Kendall, John S. *History of New Orleans*. 3 vols. Chicago: 1922.

King, Grace E. *New Orleans, The Place and the People*. New York: 1902.

Landry, Stuart O. *History of the Boston Club Organized in 1841*. New Orleans: 1938.

Learsi, Rufus. *The Jews in America: A History*. Cleveland: 1954.

Leech, Margaret. *Reveille in Washington 1860–1865*. New York: 1941.

Lewis, Charles Lee. *David Glasgow Farragut: Our First Admiral*. Annapolis: 1943.

Liddell Hart, B. H. *Sherman; Soldier, Realist, American*. New York: 1930.

Livermore, Thomas L. *Numbers and Losses in the Civil War in America, 1861–65*. Boston and New York: 1901.

Lonn, Ella. *Foreigners in the Confederacy*. Chapel Hill: 1940.

———. *Salt as a Factor in the Confederacy*. New York: 1933.

Macartney, Clarence Edward. *Grant and His Generals*. New York: 1953.

McGinty, Garnie William. *A History of Louisiana*. New York: 1949.

McLure, Lilla and Howe, J. Ed (eds.). *History of Shreveport and Shreveport Builders*. 2 vols. Shreveport, La.: 1937, 1951.

Mahan, A. T. *The Gulf and Inland Waters*. New York: 1883.

Marchand, Sidney A. *The Flight of a Century (1800–1900) in Ascension Parish, Louisiana*. Baton Rouge: 1936.

———. *The Story of Ascension Parish, Louisiana*. Baton Rouge: 1931.

Massey, Mary Elizabeth. *Ersatz in the Confederacy*. Columbia, S.C.: 1952.

Miers, Earl S. *The General Who Marched to Hell; William Tecumseh Sherman and His March to Fame and Infamy*. New York: 1951.

———. *The Web of Victory; Grant at Vicksburg*. New York: 1955.

Moore, Albert B. *Conscription and Conflict in the Confederacy*. New York: 1924.

Murphy, William M. *Notes from the History of Madison Parish, Louisiana*. Ruston, La.: 1927.

Nicolay, John G. and Hay, John. *Abraham Lincoln, A History.* 10 vols. New York: 1914.

Noll, Arthur Howard. *General Kirby-Smith.* Sewanee, Tenn.: 1907.

O'Connor, Thomas. *History of the Fire Department of New Orleans from the Earliest Days to the Present Time.* New Orleans: 1895.

Owsley, Frank Lawrence. *King Cotton Diplomacy; Foreign Relations of the Confederate States of America.* Chicago: 1931.

Parks, Joseph Howard. *General Edmund Kirby Smith, C.S.A.* Baton Rouge: 1954.

Parton, James. *General Butler in New Orleans.* Boston: 1864.

Pemberton, John C. *Pemberton, Defender of Vicksburg.* Chapel Hill: 1942.

Perrin, William Henry (ed.). *Southwest Louisiana, Biographical and Historical.* New Orleans: 1891.

Pratt, Fletcher. *Civil War on Western Waters.* New York: 1956.

Quarles, Benjamin. *The Negro in the Civil War.* Boston: 1953.

Reed, Emily Hazen. *Life of A. P. Dostie; Or, The Conflict of New Orleans.* New York: 1868.

Rightor, Henry (ed.). *Standard History of New Orleans, Louisiana.* Chicago: 1900.

Roberts, W. Adolphe. *Lake Pontchartrain.* New York: 1946.

Roman, Alfred. *The Military Operations of General Beauregard in the War Between the States 1861 to 1865 Including a Brief Personal Sketch and a Narrative of His Services in the War With Mexico 1846–8.* 2 vols. New York: 1884.

Saucier, Corinne L. *History of Avoyelles Parish, Louisiana.* New Orleans: 1943.

Saxon, Lyle. *Fabulous New Orleans.* New York: 1928.

Scharf, J. Thomas. *History of the Confederate States Navy from its Organization to the Surrender of its Last Vessel.* San Francisco and New York: 1887.

Schwab, John C. *The Confederate States of America 1861–1865: A Financial and Industrial History of the South During the Civil War.* New York: 1901.

Scroggs, William O. *The Story of Louisiana.* Indianapolis: 1924.

Shugg, Roger W. *Origins of Class Struggle in Louisiana, A Social History of White Farmers and Laborers During Slavery and After, 1840–1875.* Baton Rouge: 1939.

Sinclair, Harold. *The Port of New Orleans.* Garden City, N.Y.: 1942.

Smith, Walter G. *Life and Letters of Thomas Kilby Smith, Brevet Major-General United States Volunteers 1820–1887.* New York: 1898.

Soley, James Russell. *The Blockade and the Cruisers.* New York: 1883.

The South in the Building of the Nation; A History of the Southern States Designed to Record the South's Part in the Making of the American Nation. 13 vols. Richmond: 1909–1913.

Spears, John R. *David G. Farragut*. Philadelphia: 1905.

Steiner, Bernard C. *Life of Reverdy Johnson*. Baltimore: 1914.

Stillwell, Lucille. *John Cabell Breckinridge*. Caldwell, Idaho: 1936.

Tatum, Georgia L. *Disloyalty in the Confederacy*. Chapel Hill: 1934.

Waite, Otis F. R. *New Hampshire in the Great Rebellion Containing Histories of the Several New Hampshire Regiments, and Biographical Notices of the Prominent Actors in the Civil War of 1861–65*. Claremont, N.H.: 1870.

Walke, H. *Naval Scenes and Reminiscences of the Civil War in the United States, on the Southern and Western Waters During the Years, 1861, 1862, and 1863*. New York: 1877.

West, Richard S., Jr. *The Second Admiral, A Life of David Dixon Porter 1813–1891*. New York: 1937.

Whitman, William E. S. and True, Charles H. *Maine in the War for the Union: A History of the Part Borne by Maine Troops in the Suppression of the American Rebellion*. Lewiston, Maine: 1865.

Williams, George W. *A History of the Negro Troops in the War of the Rebellion 1861–1865 Preceded by a Review of the Military Services of Negroes in Ancient and Modern Times*. New York: 1888.

Williams, Kenneth P. *Lincoln Finds a General*. 5 vols. New York: 1949–1959.

Williams, T. Harry. *Lincoln and His Generals*. New York: 1952.

———. *P. G. T. Beauregard, Napoleon in Gray*. Baton Rouge: 1954.

Williamson, Frederick William and Goodman, George T. (eds.). *Eastern Louisiana, A History of the Watershed of the Ouachita River and the Florida Parishes*. 3 vols. Louisville, Ky., Monroe, La., Shreveport, La.: [1940].

Wilson, James Harrison. *The Life of John A. Rawlins Lawyer, Assistant Adjutant-General, Chief of Staff, Major General of Volunteers, and Secretary of War*. New York: 1916.

Wilson, Joseph T. *The Black Phalanx; A History of the Negro Soldiers of the United States in the Wars of 1775–1812, 1861–'65*. Hartford: 1888.

Young, Perry. *The Mistick Krewe; Chronicles of Comus and His Kin*. New Orleans: 1931.

PERIODICALS, PRIMARY AND SECONDARY

Bacon, George B. "One Night's Work, April 20, 1862. Breaking the Chain for Farragut's Fleet at the Forts Below New Orleans," *Magazine of American History*, XV (March, 1886), 305–307

Bee, H. P. "Battle of Pleasant Hill—An Error Corrected," *Southern Historical Society Papers*, VIII (April, 1880), 184–86.

Binder, Frederick M. "Pennsylvania Negro Regiments in the Civil War," *Journal of Negro History*, XXXVII (October, 1952), 384–417.

Booth, A. B. "Louisiana Confederate Military Records," *Louisiana Historical Quarterly,* IV (July, 1921), 369–418.

Calhoun, Robert Dabney. "A History of Concordia Parish," *Louisiana Historical Quarterly,* XV, XVI, XVII (January, 1932—October, 1935). Used XVI (January, 1933), 92–124, for this study.

Cawthon, John A. (ed.). "Letters of a North Louisiana Private to His Wife, 1862–1865," *Mississippi Valley Historical Review,* XXX (March, 1944), 533–50.

Clark, Robert T. "The New Orleans German Colony in the Civil War," *Louisiana Historical Quarterly,* XX (October, 1937), 990–1015.

Cornish, Dudley T. "The Union Army as a Training School for Negroes," *Journal of Negro History,* XXXVII (October, 1952), 368–82.

Dabney, Thomas Ewing. "The Butler Regime in Louisiana," *Louisiana Historical Quarterly,* XXVII (April, 1944), 487–526.

Davis, Jackson Beauregard. "The Life of Richard Taylor," *Louisiana Historical Quarterly,* XXIV (January, 1941), 49–126.

Debray, Xavier B. "A Sketch of Debray's Twenty-Sixth Regiment of Texas Cavalry," *Southern Historical Society Papers,* XII (October through December, 1884), 547–54, XIII (January–December, 1885), 153–65.

deVerges, Mrs. Edwin X. "Honorable John T. Monroe—The Confederate Mayor of New Orleans," *Louisiana Historical Quarterly,* XXXIV (January, 1951), 25–34.

Dyer, Brainerd. "The Treatment of Colored Union Troops by Confederates, 1861–1865," *Journal of Negro History,* XX (January, 1935), 273–86.

Ellis, Lewis E. "Reminiscences of New Orleans, Jackson and Vicksburg," *Confederate Annals,* I (August, 1883). (Reprint.)

Gift, George W. "The Story of the Arkansas," *Southern Historical Society Papers,* XII (January and February, 1884), 48–54 (March, 1884), 115–19 (April, 1884), 163–70 (May, 1884), 205–12.

Greer, J. K. "Louisiana Politics, 1845–1861," *Louisiana Historical Quarterly,* XII (July, 1929), 381–402 (October, 1929), 555–610, XIII, (January, 1930), 67–116 (April, 1930), 257–303 (July, 1930), 444–83 (October, 1930), 617–54.

"History Set Right. Attack on New Orleans and Its Defenses, by the Fleet Under Admiral Farragut, April 24, 1862," from the *Army and Navy Journal* (July 17, 1869). (Reprint.)

Johnson, Howard Palmer. "New Orleans Under General Butler," *Louisiana Historical Quarterly,* XXIV (April, 1941), 434–536.

Johnson, John. "Story of the Confederate Armored Ram Arkansas," *Southern Historical Society Papers,* XXXIII (January–December, 1905), 1–15.

Kaiser, Leo M. "In Sight of Vicksburg," *The Historical Bulletin,* XXXIV (May, 1956), 202–21.

Kassel, Charles. "The Labor System of General Banks—A Lost Episode of Civil War History," reprinted from *The Open Court* (January, 1928).

Kendall, John Smith. "Recollections of a Confederate Officer," *Louisiana Historical Quarterly,* XXIX (October, 1946), 1041–1240.

Kendall, Lane Carter. "The Interregnum in Louisiana in 1861," *Louisiana Historical Quarterly,* XVI (April, 1933), 175–208 (July, 1933), 374–408, (October, 1933), 639–69, XVII (January, 1934), 124–38 (April, 1934), 339–48 (July, 1934), 524–36.

Landers, H. L. "Wet Sand and Cotton—Banks' Red River Campaign," *Louisiana Historical Quarterly,* XIX (January, 1936), 150–95.

McGrath, John. "In a Louisiana Regiment," *Southern Historical Society Papers,* XXXI (January–December, 1903), 103–20.

Odom, Van D. "The Political Career of Thomas Overton Moore, Secession Governor of Louisiana," *Louisiana Historical Quarterly,* XXVI (October, 1943), 975–1054.

Pascoe, W. H. "Confederate Cavalry Around Port Hudson," *Southern Historical Society Papers,* XXXIII (January, 1905), 83–96.

Pirtle, John B. "Defence of Vicksburg in 1862—The Battle of Baton Rouge," *Southern Historical Society Papers,* VIII (June and July, 1880), 324–32.

Prichard, Walter (ed.). "A Tourist's Description of Louisiana in 1860," *Louisiana Historical Quarterly,* XXI (October, 1938), 1110–1214.

Reed, Wallace P. "Last Forlorn Hope of the Confederacy," *Southern Historical Society Papers,* XXX (January–December, 1902), 117–21.

Richardson, Frank L. "War As I Saw It," *Louisiana Historical Quarterly,* VI (January, 1923), 86–106 (April, 1923), 223–54.

Root, L. Carroll. "Private Journal of William H. Root, Second Lieutenant, Seventy-Fifth New York Volunteers, April 1–June 14, 1863," *Louisiana Historical Quarterly,* XIX (April, 1936), 637–67.

Smith, M. J. and Freret, James. "Fortification and Siege of Port Hudson," *Southern Historical Society Papers,* XIV (January to December, 1886), 305–48.

Stephenson, Wendell Holmes and Davis, Edwin Adams (eds.). "The Civil War Diary of Willie Micajah Barrow, Sept. 23, 1861—July 13, 1862," *Louisiana Historical Quarterly,* XVII (July, 1934), 436–51.

Taylor, Richard. "A Chapter of History," *Southern Historical Society Papers,* XXXI (January to December, 1903), 48–52.

Vandiver, Frank E. (ed.). "A Collection of Louisiana Confederate Letters," *Louisiana Historical Quarterly,* XXVI (October, 1943), 937–74.

Wesley, Charles H. "The Employment of Negroes As Soldiers in the Confederate Army," *Journal of Negro History,* IV (July, 1919), 239–53.

Whittington, G. P. "Thomas O. Moore, Governor of Louisiana," *Louisiana Historical Quarterly,* XIII (January, 1930), 5–31.

Williams, G. Mott. "Letters of General Thomas Williams," *American Historical Review,* XIV (January, 1909), 304–28.

Williams, Richard Hobson. "General Banks' Red River Campaign," *Louisiana Historical Quarterly,* XXXII (January, 1949), 103–44.

Wooster, Ralph. "The Louisiana Secession Convention," *Louisiana Historical Quarterly,* XXXIV (April, 1951), 103–33.

UNPUBLISHED WORKS

Aertker, Robert. "A Social History of Baton Rouge, 1860–1865." M.A. Thesis, Louisiana State University, 1947.

"Annual Report of the Adjutant General to the Governor of Louisiana, Nov. 1861." Baton Rouge: 1861. (Typed copy, Louisiana Room, Louisiana State University Library, W.P.A., 1939, Jackson Barracks, New Orleans).

Brown, Harry Bates, Jr. "Port Hudson: A Study in Historical Geography." M.A. Thesis, Louisiana State University, 1936.

Chandler, Luther Edward. "The Career of Henry Watkins Allen." Ph.D. Dissertation, Louisiana State University, 1940.

Cook, Curtis Taylor. "The Siege of Port Hudson." M.A. Thesis, Louisiana State University, 1934.

Garland, Albert N. "E. Kirby Smith and the Trans-Mississippi Confederacy." M.A. Thesis, Louisiana State University, 1947.

Highsmith, William Edward. "Louisiana During Reconstruction." Ph.D. Dissertation, Louisiana State University, 1953.

"Historical Militia Data on Louisiana Militia," W.P.A., Jackson Barracks, New Orleans, 1938. (Typed copy, Louisiana Room, Louisiana State University Library).

Jones, Laura B. W. "Official Announcements State, Military and Confederate States of America from Shreveport *News* January, 1862–July, 1865." Louisiana State University Library School, 1940.

"Legislative Acts of Louisiana Militia 1857 to 1865." (Typed copy, Louisiana Room, Louisiana State University Library).

Leland, Edwin Albert. "Organization and Administration of the Louisiana Army During the Civil War." M.A. Thesis, Louisiana State University, 1938.

Roland, Charles P. "The Louisiana Sugar Plantations During the Civil War." Ph.D. Dissertation, Louisiana State University, 1951. This work has recently been published: Roland, Charles P. *Louisiana Sugar Plantations During the American Civil War.* Leiden, Netherlands: 1957.

Solomon, Clara E. "Diary of a New Orleans Girl, 1861–1862" (Typed copy, Louisiana Room, Louisiana State University Library).

Winters, John D. "Confederate New Orleans, 1861–1862." M.A. Thesis, Louisiana State University, 1947.

INDEX